INVESTMENTS

Principles of Portfolio and Equity Analysis

CFA Institute is the premier association for investment professionals around the world, with over 101,000 members in 134 countries. Since 1963, the organization has developed and administered the renowned Chartered Financial Analyst® Program. With a rich history of leading the investment profession, CFA Institute has set the highest standards in ethics, education, and professional excellence within the global investment community, and is the foremost authority on investment profession conduct and practice.

Each book in the CFA Institute Investment Series is geared toward industry practitioners along with graduate-level finance students and covers the most important topics in the industry. The authors of these cutting-edge books are themselves industry professionals and academics and bring their wealth of knowledge and expertise to this series.

INVESTMENTS

Principles of Portfolio and Equity Analysis

Michael G. McMillan, CFA

Jerald E. Pinto, CFA

Wendy L. Pirie, CFA

Gerhard Van de Venter, CFA

WILEY

John Wiley & Sons, Inc.

Published by John Wiley & Sons, Inc., Hoboken, New Jersey
Published simultaneously in Canada

Library of Congress Cataloging-in-Publication Data:

Investments : principles of portfolio and equity analysis / Michael G. McMillan.
p. cm. — (CFA institute investment series)
Includes bibliographical references and index.
ISBN 978-0-470-91580-6 (cloth); ISBN 978-1-118-00114-1 (ebk);
ISBN 978-1-118-00115-8 (ebk); ISBN 978-1-118-00116-5 (ebk)
1. Portfolio management. 2. Investment analysis. I. McMillan, Michael G.
HG4529.5.I59 2011
332.6—dc22

2010032749

Printed in the United States of America

10 9 8 7 6

CONTENTS

FOREWORD

As I read *Investments: Principles of Portfolio and Equity Analysis*, I was struck by how much the investment profession has evolved over the past 40 years. Although the changes have been mostly for the better, the market events of the past decade suggest that we still have more to learn in order to avoid repeating some of our recent mistakes. We witnessed the bursting of two bubbles—technology and housing/credit—which resulted in a lost decade for equities: The S&P 500 generated negative returns for the 10 years ended December 2009.

I remember learning modern portfolio theory as a student when it was indeed relatively modern. Although analytical techniques for managing portfolios have improved since the 1970s, the investment landscape has become much more complex. The number of markets, institutions, and securities has exploded alongside improvements in security selection/analysis, portfolio construction, and risk management. Aided by ever-increasing information and computing power, institutional investors have become bigger, more numerous, more global, and seemingly more sophisticated. They have attracted the best and brightest from the world's leading universities. These growing armies of professional investors all compete to be the next Warren Buffett or top hedge fund manager.

New investment texts that keep up with the changing markets and analytical techniques are needed. *Investments: Principles of Portfolio and Equity Analysis* is a valuable addition to the bookshelves of all investment professionals and students of finance. It has kept pace with the changes in the institutional aspects of investing, as well as the advances in asset pricing and portfolio theory and the practical applications of such tools.

As chief investment officer of Georgetown University, I am responsible for investing its endowment. I also teach investment courses in the MBA program at Georgetown. I am a consumer of this book for both parts of my professional life. As an endowment manager, I know that our investment process involves asset allocation, investment manager selection, portfolio construction, and risk management. The governance for this process is set forth in our investment policy statement. Thoroughly covering all these topics, *Investments: Principles of Portfolio and Equity Analysis* discusses the theory and application of how endowments, pensions, and other institutions invest their sizable pools of capital. Although we are not directly involved with security selection at our endowment, it is important that we understand the best practices followed by investment managers (e.g., mutual funds, hedge funds, and other investment advisers) to help us in our selection of such managers. We must also be able to recognize opportunities for managers to add value relative to a passive index. Although many investors scoff at the notion of market efficiency, most managers fail to beat passive benchmarks. This book does a wonderful job of addressing not only market efficiency and whether and when active management can add value, but also the institutional details of investing—the mechanics of trading and custody; the array of institutions (e.g., endowments, pensions, and sovereign wealth funds); and the growing number of investment vehicles available to institutions (e.g., exchange-traded funds [ETFs] for passive implementation and hedge funds for active management).

As someone who spans both the academic and the real world of investing, I understand the challenge and importance of writing a book that is able to cover and meld both investment theory and implementation. I believe readers will find that *Investments: Principles of Portfolio and Equity Analysis* succeeds on both fronts. The book will help professional investors understand a broad body of investment theory. More importantly, it will help them apply this knowledge to the actual practice of investing.

Lawrence E. Kochard, CFA
Chief Investment Officer
Georgetown University
September 2010

ACKNOWLEDGMENTS

We would like to thank the many individuals who played important roles in producing this book.

Robert R. Johnson, CFA, Senior Managing Director of CFA Institute, originally saw the need for specialized curriculum materials and initiated their development. We appreciate his support. Robert E. Lamy, CFA, Head of CFA Program Content, initiated the project and oversaw its final development. The Education Advisory Committee, through the global practice analysis, provides valuable input in the development and review of the CFA Program curriculum.

We would especially like to thank James Bronson, CFA; Yves Courtois, CFA; Benoit Descourtieux, CFA; Doug Manz, CFA; George Troughton, CFA; and Philip Young, CFA, for their advice on the curriculum relevancy of each chapter.

Manuscript reviewers and authors of practice problems were as follows: William Akmentins, CFA; Christopher Anderson, CFA; Evan Ashcraft, CFA; Mark Bhasin, CFA; Michael J. Carr; David Cox, CFA; Lee Dunham, CFA; Philip Fanara Jr., CFA; Jane Farris, CFA; Thomas Franckowiak, CFA; Martha Freitag, CFA; Jacques Gagne, CFA; Bryan Gardiner, CFA; Gregory Gocek, CFA; Usman Hayat, CFA; Bradley Herndon, CFA; Glen Holden, CFA; C. Thomas Howard, PhD; Stephen Huffman, CFA; Muhammad Jawaid Iqbal, CFA; Frank Laatsch, CFA; David Landis, CFA; Dan Larocco, CFA; Sanford Leeds, CFA; Barbara MacLeod, CFA; Frank Magiera, CFA; John Maginn, CFA; Ronald Moy, CFA; Gregory Noronha, CFA; Edgar Norton, CFA; Michael Pompian, CFA; Murli Rajan, CFA; Raymond Rath, CFA; Victoria Rati, CFA; Joel Ray, CFA; Knut Reinertz, CFA; Karen O'Connor Rubsam, CFA; Sanjiv Sabherwal; Frank Smudde, CFA; Lavone Whitmer, CFA; and Pamela Yang, CFA.

Samuel Lum, CFA, Director of Private Wealth and Capital Markets in the Hong Kong office of CFA Institute, helpfully shared his expertise. Wanda Lauziere, Project Manager in Curriculum Development, expertly guided the reading manuscripts from planning through production. Tabitha Gore, Administrative Assistant in Curriculum Development, provided valuable assistance at various stages.

Thanks are due to the Editorial Services group at CFA Institute for their extraordinary support of the book's copyediting needs.

INTRODUCTION

CFA Institute is pleased to provide you with this Investment Series covering major areas in the field of investments. These texts are thoroughly grounded in the highly regarded CFA Program Candidate Body of Knowledge that serves as the anchor for the three levels of the CFA Program. Currently, nearly 200,000 aspiring investment professionals from over 150 countries are devoting hundreds of hours each year to master this material, as well as other elements of the Candidate Body of Knowledge, to obtain the coveted CFA designation. We provide these materials for the same reason we have been chartering investment professionals for over 45 years: to lead the investment profession globally by setting the highest standards of ethics, education, and professional excellence.

HISTORY

This book series draws on the rich history and origins of CFA Institute. In the 1940s, several local societies for investment professionals developed around common interests in the evolving investment industry. At that time, the idea of purchasing common stock as an investment—as opposed to pure speculation—was still a relatively new concept for the general public. Just 10 years before, the U.S. Securities and Exchange Commission had been formed to help referee a playing field marked by robber barons and stock market panics.

In January 1945, a fundamental analysis–driven professor and practitioner from Columbia University and Graham-Newman Corporation wrote an article in the precursor of today's CFA Institute *Financial Analysts Journal*, making the case that people who research and manage portfolios should have some sort of credential to demonstrate competence and ethical behavior. This person was none other than Benjamin Graham, the father of security analysis and future mentor to well-known modern investor Warren Buffett.

Creating such a credential took 16 years. By 1963, 284 brave souls—all over the age of 45—took an exam and successfully launched the CFA credential. What many do not fully understand is that this effort was driven by a desire to create professional standards for practitioners dedicated to serving individual investors. In so doing, a fairer and more productive capital market would result.

Most professions—including medicine, law, and accounting—have certain hallmark characteristics that help to attract serious individuals and motivate them to devote energy to their life's work. First, there must be a body of knowledge. Second, entry requirements must exist, such as those required to achieve the CFA credential. Third, there must be a commitment to continuing education. Finally, a profession must serve a purpose beyond one's individual interests. By properly conducting one's affairs and putting client interests first, the investment professional encourages general participation in the incredibly productive global capital markets. This encourages the investing public to part with their hard-earned savings for redeployment in the fair and productive pursuit of appropriate returns.

As C. Stewart Sheppard, founding executive director of the Institute of Chartered Financial Analysts, said:

> *Society demands more from a profession and its members than it does from a professional craftsman in trade, arts, or business. In return for status, prestige, and autonomy, a profession extends a public warranty that it has established and maintains conditions of entry, standards of fair practice, disciplinary procedures, and continuing education for its particular constituency. Much is expected from members of a profession, but over time, more is given.*

For more than 40 years, hundreds upon hundreds of practitioners and academics have served on CFA Institute curriculum committees, sifting through and winnowing out all the many investment concepts and ideas to create a body of investment knowledge and the CFA curriculum. One of the hallmarks of curriculum development at CFA Institute is its extensive use of practitioners in all phases of the process. CFA Institute has followed a formal practice analysis process since 1995. Most recently, the effort involves special practice analysis forums held at 20 locations around the world and surveys of 70,000 practicing CFA charterholders for verification and confirmation. In 2007, CFA Institute moved to implement an ongoing practice analysis to update the body of knowledge continuously, making use of a collaborative web-based site and wiki technology. In addition, CFA Institute has moved in recent years from using traditional academic textbooks in its curriculum to commissioning prominent practitioners and academics to create custom material based on this practice analysis. The result is practical, globally relevant material that is provided to CFA candidates in the CFA Program curriculum and published in this series for investment professionals and others.

What this means for the reader is that the concepts highlighted in these texts were selected by practitioners who fully understand the skills and knowledge necessary for success. We are pleased to put this extensive effort to work for the benefit of the readers of the Investment Series.

BENEFITS

This series will prove useful to those contemplating entry into the extremely competitive field of investment management, as well as those seeking a means of keeping one's knowledge fresh and up to date. Regardless of its use, this series was designed to be both user friendly and highly relevant. Each chapter within the series includes extensive references for those who would like to further probe a given concept. I believe that the general public seriously underestimates the disciplined processes needed for the best investment firms and individuals to prosper. This material will help you better understand the investment field. For those new to the industry, the essential concepts that any investment professional needs to master are presented in a time-tested fashion. These volumes lay the basic groundwork for many of the processes that successful firms use on a day-to-day basis. Without this base level of understanding and an appreciation for how the capital markets operate, it becomes challenging to find competitive success. Furthermore, the concepts presented herein provide a true sense of the kind of work that is to be found managing portfolios, doing research, or pursuing related endeavors.

The investment profession, despite its relatively lucrative compensation, is not for everyone. It takes a special kind of individual to fundamentally understand and absorb the teachings from this body of work and then successfully apply them in practice. In fact, most individuals who enter the field do not survive in the long run. The aspiring professional should think long and hard about whether this is the right field. There is no better way to make such a critical decision than by reading and evaluating the classic works of the profession.

The more experienced professional understands that the nature of the capital markets requires a commitment to continuous learning. Markets evolve as quickly as smart minds can find new ways to create exposure, attract capital, or manage risk. A number of the concepts in these books did not exist a decade or two ago, when many were starting out in the business. In fact, as we talk to major employers about their training needs, we are often told that one of the biggest challenges they face is how to help the experienced professional keep up with the recent graduates. This series can be part of that answer.

As markets invent and reinvent themselves, a best-in-class foundation investment series is of great value. Investment professionals must continuously hone their skills and knowledge if they are to compete with the young talent that constantly emerges. Further, the best investment management firms are run by those who carefully form investment hypotheses and test them rigorously in the marketplace, whether it be in a quant strategy, comparative shopping for stocks within an industry, or hedge fund strategies. Their goal is to create investment processes that can be replicated with some statistical reliability. I believe those who embraced the so-called academic side of the learning equation have been much more successful as real-world investment managers.

THE TEXTS

One of the most prominent texts over the years in the investment management industry has been Maginn and Tuttle's *Managing Investment Portfolios: A Dynamic Process.* The third edition updates key concepts from the 1990 second edition. Some of the more experienced members of our community own the prior two editions and will add the third edition to their libraries. Not only does this seminal work take the concepts from the other readings and put them in a portfolio context, but it also updates the concepts of alternative investments, performance presentation standards, portfolio execution, and, very importantly, managing individual investor portfolios. Focusing attention away from institutional portfolios and toward the individual investor makes this edition an important and timely work.

Quantitative Investment Analysis focuses on some key tools that are needed for today's professional investor. In addition to classic time value of money, discounted cash flow applications, and probability material, there are two aspects that can be of value over traditional thinking.

The first involves the chapters dealing with correlation and regression that ultimately figure into the formation of hypotheses for purposes of testing. This gets to a critical skill that challenges many professionals: the ability to distinguish useful information from the overwhelming quantity of available data. For most investment researchers and managers, their analysis is not solely the result of newly created data and tests that they perform. Rather, they synthesize and analyze primary research done by others. Without a rigorous manner by which to understand quality research, you cannot understand good research, nor do you have a basis on which to evaluate less rigorous research.

Second, the last chapter of *Quantitative Investment Analysis* covers portfolio concepts and takes the reader beyond the traditional capital asset pricing model (CAPM) type of tools and into the more practical world of multifactor models and arbitrage pricing theory.

Equity Asset Valuation is a particularly cogent and important resource for anyone involved in estimating the value of securities and understanding security pricing. A well-informed professional knows that the common forms of equity valuation—dividend discount modeling, free cash flow modeling, price/earnings models, and residual income models—can all be reconciled with one another under certain assumptions. With a deep understanding of the underlying assumptions, the professional investor can better understand what other investors assume when calculating their valuation estimates. This volume has a global orientation, including emerging markets. The second edition provides new coverage of private company valuation and expanded coverage on required rate of return estimation.

Fixed Income Analysis has been at the forefront of new concepts in recent years, and this particular book offers some of the most recent material for the seasoned professional who is not a fixed income specialist. The application of option and derivative technology to the once-staid province of fixed income has helped contribute to an explosion of thought in this area. Not only have professionals been challenged to stay up to speed with credit derivatives, swaptions, collateralized mortgage securities, mortgage-backed securities, and other vehicles, but this explosion of products strained the world's financial markets and challenged central banks to provide sufficient oversight. Armed with a thorough grasp of the new exposures, the professional investor is much better able to anticipate and understand the challenges our central bankers and markets face.

Corporate Finance: A Practical Approach is a solid foundation for those looking to achieve lasting business growth. In today's competitive business environment, companies must find innovative ways to enable rapid and sustainable growth. This volume equips readers with the foundational knowledge and tools for making smart business decisions and formulating strategies to maximize company value. It covers everything from managing relationships between stakeholders to evaluating mergers and acquisitions bids, as well as the companies behind them.

Through extensive use of real-world examples, readers will gain critical perspective into interpreting corporate financial data, evaluating projects, and allocating funds in ways that increase corporate value. Readers will gain insights into the tools and strategies used in modern corporate financial management.

International Financial Statement Analysis is designed to address the ever-increasing need for investment professionals and students to think about financial statement analysis from a global perspective. The work is a practically oriented introduction to financial statement analysis that is distinguished by its combination of a true international orientation, a structured presentation style, and abundant illustrations and tools covering concepts as they are introduced in the text. The authors cover this discipline comprehensively and with an eye to ensuring the reader's success at all levels in the complex world of financial statement analysis.

Investments: Principles of Portfolio and Equity Analysis provides an accessible yet rigorous introduction to portfolio and equity analysis. Portfolio planning and portfolio management are presented within a context of up-to-date, global coverage of security markets, trading, and market-related concepts and products. The essentials of equity analysis and valuation are explained in detail and profusely illustrated. The book includes coverage of practitioner-important but often neglected topics such as industry analysis. Throughout, the focus is on the practical application of key concepts with examples drawn from both emerging and developed markets. Each chapter affords the reader many opportunities to self-check his or her understanding of topics. In contrast to other texts, the chapters are collaborations of respected senior investment practitioners and leading business school teachers from around the globe. By virtue of its well-rounded, expert, and global perspectives, the book should be of interest to anyone who is looking for an introduction to portfolio and equity analysis.

I hope you find this new series helpful in your efforts to grow your investment knowledge, whether you are a relatively new entrant or an experienced veteran ethically bound to keep up to date in the ever-changing market environment. CFA Institute, as a long-term, committed participant in the investment profession and a not-for-profit global membership association, is pleased to provide you with this opportunity.

Robert R. Johnson, PhD, CFA
Senior Managing Director
CFA Institute
September 2010

INVESTMENTS

Principles of Portfolio and Equity Analysis

CHAPTER 1

MARKET ORGANIZATION AND STRUCTURE

Larry Harris
Los Angeles, CA, U.S.A.

LEARNING OUTCOMES

After completing this chapter, you will be able to do the following:

- Explain and illustrate the main functions of the financial system.
- Describe classifications of assets and markets.
- Describe the major types of securities, currencies, contracts, commodities, and real assets that trade in organized markets, including their distinguishing characteristics and major subtypes.
- Describe the types of financial intermediaries and the services that they provide.
- Compare and contrast the positions an investor can take in an asset.
- Calculate and interpret the leverage ratio, the rate of return on a margin transaction, and the security price at which the investor would receive a margin call.
- Compare and contrast execution, validity, and clearing instructions.
- Compare and contrast market orders with limit orders.
- Describe the primary and secondary markets and explain how secondary markets support primary markets.
- Describe how securities, contracts, and currencies are traded in quote-driven markets, order-driven markets, and brokered markets.
- Describe the characteristics of a well-functioning financial system.
- Describe the objectives of market regulation.

1. INTRODUCTION

Financial analysts gather and process information to make investment decisions, including those related to buying and selling assets. Generally, the decisions involve trading securities, currencies, contracts, commodities, and real assets such as real estate. Consider several examples:

- Fixed-income analysts evaluate issuer creditworthiness and macroeconomic prospects to determine which bonds and notes to buy or sell to preserve capital while obtaining a fair rate of return.
- Stock analysts study corporate values to determine which stocks to buy or sell to maximize the value of their stock portfolios.
- Corporate treasurers analyze exchange rates, interest rates, and credit conditions to determine which currencies to trade and which notes to buy or sell to have funds available in a needed currency.
- Risk managers work for producers or users of commodities to calculate how many commodity futures contracts to buy or sell to manage inventory risks.

Financial analysts must understand the characteristics of the markets in which their decisions will be executed. This chapter, by examining those markets from the analyst's perspective, provides that understanding.

This chapter is organized as follows. Section 2 examines the functions of the financial system. Section 3 introduces assets that investors, information-motivated traders, and risk managers use to advance their financial objectives and presents ways practitioners classify these assets into markets. These assets include such financial instruments as securities, currencies, and some contracts; certain commodities; and real assets. Financial analysts must know the distinctive characteristics of these trading assets.

Section 4 is an overview of financial intermediaries (entities that facilitate the functioning of the financial system). Section 5 discusses the positions that can be obtained while trading assets. You will learn about the benefits and risks of long and short positions, how these positions can be financed, and how the financing affects their risks. Section 6 discusses how market participants order trades and how markets process those orders. These processes must be understood to achieve trading objectives while controlling transaction costs.

Section 7 focuses on describing primary markets. Section 8 describes the structures of secondary markets in securities. Sections 9 and 10 close the chapter with discussions of the characteristics of a well-functioning financial system and of how regulation helps make financial markets function better. A conclusions and summary section reviews the chapter's major ideas and points, and practice problems conclude.

2. THE FUNCTIONS OF THE FINANCIAL SYSTEM

The financial system includes markets and various financial intermediaries that help transfer financial assets, real assets, and financial risks in various forms from one entity to another, from one place to another, and from one point in time to another. These transfers take place whenever someone exchanges one asset or financial contract for another. The assets and contracts that people (people act on behalf of themselves, companies, charities, governments, etc., so the term "people" has a broad definition in this chapter) trade include notes, bonds, stocks, exchange-traded funds, currencies, forward contracts, futures contracts, option contracts, swap contracts, and certain commodities. When the buyer and seller voluntarily arrange their trades, as is usually the case, the buyer and the seller both expect to be better off.

People use the financial system for six main purposes:

1. To save money for the future.
2. To borrow money for current use.

3. To raise equity capital.
4. To manage risks.
5. To exchange assets for immediate and future deliveries.
6. To trade on information.

The main functions of the financial system are to facilitate:

1. The achievement of the purposes for which people use the financial system.
2. The discovery of the rates of return that equate aggregate savings with aggregate borrowings.
3. The allocation of capital to the best uses.

These functions are extremely important to economic welfare. In a well-functioning financial system, transaction costs are low, analysts can value savings and investments, and scarce capital resources are used well.

Sections 2.1 through 2.3 expand on these three functions. The subsections of Section 2.1 cover the six main purposes for which people use the financial system and how the financial system facilitates the achievement of those purposes. Sections 2.2 and 2.3 discuss determining rates of return and capital allocation efficiency, respectively.

2.1. Helping People Achieve Their Purposes in Using the Financial System

People often arrange transactions to achieve more than one purpose when using the financial system. For example, an investor who buys the stock of an oil producer may do so to move her wealth from the present to the future, to hedge the risk that she will have to pay more for energy in the future, and to exploit insightful research that she conducted that suggests the company's stock is undervalued in the marketplace. If the investment proves to be successful, she will have saved money for the future, managed her energy risk exposure, and obtained a return on her research.

The separate discussions of each of the six main uses of the financial system by people will help you better identify the reasons why people trade. Your ability to identify the various uses of the financial system will help you avoid confusion that often leads to poor financial decisions. The financial intermediaries that are mentioned in these discussions are explained further in Section 4.

2.1.1. Saving

People often have money that they choose not to spend now and that they want available in the future. For example, workers who save for their retirements need to move some of their current earnings into the future. When they retire, they will use their savings to replace the wages that they will no longer be earning. Similarly, companies save money from their sales revenue so that they can pay vendors when their bills come due, repay debt, or acquire assets (for example, other companies or machinery) in the future.

To move money from the present to the future, savers buy notes, certificates of deposit, bonds, stocks, mutual funds, or real assets such as real estate. These alternatives generally provide a better expected rate of return than simply storing money. Savers then sell these assets in the future to fund their future expenditures. When savers commit money to earn a financial return, they commonly are called investors. They *invest* when they purchase assets, and they *divest* when they sell them.

Investors require a fair rate of return while their money is invested. The required fair rate of return compensates them for the use of their money and for the risk that they may lose money if the investment fails or if inflation reduces the real value of their investments.

The financial system facilitates savings when institutions create investment vehicles, such as bank deposits, notes, stocks, and mutual funds, that investors can acquire and sell without paying substantial transaction costs. When these instruments are fairly priced and easy to trade, investors will use them to save more.

2.1.2. Borrowing

People, companies, and governments often want to spend money now that they do not have. They can obtain money to fund projects that they wish to undertake now by borrowing it. Companies can also obtain funds by selling ownership or equity interests (covered in Section 2.1.3). Banks and other investors provide those requiring funds with money because they expect to be repaid with interest or because they expect to be compensated with future disbursements, such as dividends and capital gains, as the ownership interest appreciates in value.

People may borrow to pay for such items as vacations, homes, cars, or education. They generally borrow through mortgages and personal loans, or by using credit cards. People typically repay these loans with money they earn later.

Companies often require money to fund current operations or to engage in new capital projects. They may borrow the needed funds in a variety of ways, such as arranging a loan or a line of credit with a bank, or selling fixed-income securities to investors. Companies typically repay their borrowing with income generated in the future. In addition to borrowing, companies may raise funds by selling ownership interests.

Governments may borrow money to pay salaries and other expenses, to fund projects, to provide welfare benefits to their citizens and residents, and to subsidize various activities. Governments borrow by selling bills, notes, or bonds. Governments repay their debt using future revenues from taxes and in some instances from the projects funded by these debts.

Borrowers can borrow from lenders only if the lenders believe that they will be repaid. If the lenders believe, however, that repayment in full with interest may not occur, they will demand higher rates of interest to cover their expected losses and to compensate them for the discomfit they experience wondering whether they will lose their money. To lower the costs of borrowing, borrowers often pledge assets as collateral for their loans. The assets pledged as collateral often include those that will be purchased by the proceeds of the loan. If the borrowers do not repay their loans, the lenders can sell the collateral and use the proceeds to settle the loans.

Lenders often will not loan to borrowers who intend to invest in risky projects, especially if the borrowers cannot pledge other collateral. Investors may still be willing to supply capital for these risky projects if they believe that the projects will likely produce valuable future cash flows. Rather than lending money, however, they will contribute capital in exchange for equity in the projects.

The financial system facilitates borrowing. Lenders aggregate from savers the funds that borrowers require. Borrowers must convince lenders that they can repay their loans, and that, in the event they cannot, lenders can recover most of the funds lent. Credit bureaus, credit rating agencies, and governments promote borrowing; credit bureaus and credit rating agencies do so by collecting and disseminating information that lenders need to analyze credit prospects and governments do so by establishing bankruptcy codes and courts that define and enforce the rights of borrowers and lenders. When the transaction costs of loans (i.e., the costs of arranging, monitoring, and collecting them) are low, borrowers can borrow more to fund current expenditures with credible promises to return the money in the future.

2.1.3. Raising Equity Capital

Companies often raise money for projects by selling (issuing) ownership interests (e.g., corporate common stock or partnership interests). Although these equity instruments legally represent ownership in companies rather than loans to the companies, selling equity to raise capital is simply another mechanism for moving money from the future to the present. When shareholders or partners contribute capital to a company, the company obtains money in the present in exchange for equity instruments that will be entitled to distributions in the future. Although the repayment of the money is not scheduled as it would be for loans, equity instruments also represent potential claims on money in the future.

The financial system facilitates raising equity capital. Investment banks help companies issue equities, analysts value the securities that companies sell, and regulatory reporting requirements and accounting standards attempt to ensure the production of meaningful financial disclosures. The financial system helps promote capital formation by producing the financial information needed to determine fair prices for equity. Liquid markets help companies raise capital. In these markets, shareholders can easily divest their equities as desired. When investors can easily value and trade equities, they are more willing to fund reasonable projects that companies wish to undertake.

EXAMPLE 1-1 Financing Capital Projects

As a chief financial officer (CFO) of a large industrial firm, you need to raise cash within a few months to pay for a project to expand existing and acquire new manufacturing facilities. What are the primary options available to you?

Solution: Your primary options are to borrow the funds or to raise the funds by selling ownership interests. If the company borrows the funds, you may have the company pledge some or all of the project as collateral to reduce the cost of borrowing.

2.1.4. Managing Risks

Many people, companies, and governments face financial risks that concern them. These risks include default risk and the risk of changes in interest rates, exchange rates, raw material prices, and sale prices, among many other risks. These risks are often managed by trading contracts that serve as hedges for the risks.

For example, a farmer and a food processor both face risks related to the price of grain. The farmer fears that prices will be lower than expected when his grain is ready for sale whereas the food processor fears that prices will be higher than expected when she has to buy grain in the future. They both can eliminate their exposures to these risks if they enter into a binding forward contract for the farmer to sell a specified quantity of grain to the food processor at a future date at a mutually agreed upon price. By entering into a forward contract that sets the future trade price, they both eliminate their exposure to changing grain prices.

In general, hedgers trade to offset or insure against risks that concern them. In addition to forward contracts, they may use futures contracts, option contracts, or insurance contracts to transfer risk to other entities more willing to bear the risks (these contracts will be covered in Section 3.4). Often the hedger and the other entity face exactly the opposite risks, so the transfer makes both more secure, as in the grain example.

The financial system facilitates risk management when liquid markets exist in which risk managers can trade instruments that are correlated (or inversely correlated) with the risks that concern them without incurring substantial transaction costs. Investment banks, exchanges, and insurance companies devote substantial resources to designing such contracts and to ensuring that they will trade in liquid markets. When such markets exist, people are better able to manage the risks that they face and often are more willing to undertake risky activities that they expect will be profitable.

2.1.5. Exchanging Assets for Immediate Delivery (Spot Market Trading)

People and companies often trade one asset for another that they rate more highly or, equivalently, that is more useful to them. They may trade one currency for another currency, or money for a needed commodity or right. Following are some examples that illustrate these trades:

- Volkswagen pays its German workers in euros, but the company receives dollars when it sells cars in the United States. To convert money from dollars to euros, Volkswagen trades in the foreign exchange markets.
- A Mexican investor who is worried about the prospects for peso inflation or a potential devaluation of the peso may buy gold in the spot gold market. (This transaction may hedge against the risk of devaluation of the peso because the value of gold may increase with inflation.)
- A plastic producer must buy carbon credits to emit carbon dioxide when burning fuel to comply with environmental regulations. The carbon credit is a legal right that the producer must have to engage in activities that emit carbon dioxide.

In each of these cases, the trades are considered spot market trades because the instruments trade for immediate delivery. The financial system facilitates these exchanges when liquid spot markets exist in which people can arrange and settle trades without substantial transaction costs.

2.1.6. Information-Motivated Trading

Information-motivated traders trade to profit from information that they believe allows them to predict future prices. Like all other traders, they hope to buy at low prices and sell at higher prices. Unlike pure investors, however, they expect to earn a return on their information in addition to the normal return expected for bearing risk through time.

Active investment managers are information-motivated traders who collect and analyze information to identify securities, contracts, and other assets that their analyses indicate are under- or overvalued. They then buy those that they consider undervalued and sell those that they consider overvalued. If successful, they obtain a greater return than the unconditional return that would be expected for bearing the risk in their positions. The return that they expect to obtain is a conditional return earned on the basis of the information in their analyses. Practitioners often call this process active portfolio management.

Note that the distinction between pure investors and information-motivated traders depends on their motives for trading and not on the risks that they take or their expected holding periods. Investors trade to move wealth from the present to the future whereas information-motivated traders trade to profit from superior information about future values. When trading to move wealth forward, the time period may be short or long. For example, a bank treasurer may only need to move money overnight and might use money market instruments trading in an interbank funds market to accomplish that. A pension fund, however, may need to move money 30 years forward and might do that by using shares trading in a stock market. Both are investors although their expected holding periods and the risks in the instruments that they trade are vastly different.

In contrast, information-motivated traders trade because their information-based analyses suggest to them that prices of various instruments will increase or decrease in the future at a rate faster than others without their information or analytical models would expect. After establishing their positions, they hope that prices will change quickly in their favor so that they can close their positions, realize their profits, and redeploy their capital. These price changes may occur almost instantaneously, or they may take years to occur if information about the mispricing is difficult to obtain or understand.

The two categories of traders are not mutually exclusive. Investors also are often information-motivated traders. Many investors who want to move wealth forward through time collect and analyze information to select securities that will allow them to obtain conditional returns that are greater than the unconditional returns expected for securities in their assets classes. If they have rational reasons to expect that their efforts will indeed produce superior returns, they are information-motivated traders. If they consistently fail to produce such returns, their efforts will be futile, and they would have been better off simply buying and holding well-diversified portfolios.

EXAMPLE 1-2 Investing versus Information-Motivated Trading

The head of a large labor union with a pension fund asks you, a pension consultant, to distinguish between investing and information-motivated trading. You are expected to provide an explanation that addresses the financial problems that she faces. How would you respond?

Solution: The object of investing for the pension fund is to move the union's pension assets from the present to the future when they will be needed to pay the union's retired pensioners. The pension fund managers will typically do this by buying stocks, bonds, and perhaps other assets. The pension fund managers expect to receive a fair rate of return on the pension fund's assets without paying excessive transaction costs and management fees. The return should compensate the fund for the risks that it bears and for the time that other people are using the fund's money.

The object of information-motivated trading is to earn a return in excess of the fair rate of return. Information-motivated traders analyze information that they collect with the hope that their analyses will allow them to predict better than others where prices will be in the future. They then buy assets that they think will produce excess returns and sell those that they think will underperform. Active investment managers are information-motivated traders.

The characteristic that most distinguishes investors from information-motivated traders is the return that they expect. Although both types of traders hope to obtain extraordinary returns, investors rationally expect to receive only fair returns during the periods of their investments. In contrast, information-motivated traders expect to make returns in excess of required fair rates of return. Of course, not all investing or information-motivated trading is successful (in other words, the actual returns may not equal or exceed the expected returns).

The financial system facilitates information-motivated trading when liquid markets allow active managers to trade without significant transaction costs. Accounting standards and reporting requirements that produce meaningful financial disclosures reduce the costs of being well informed, but do not necessarily help informed traders profit because they often compete with each other. The most profitable well-informed traders are often those who have the most unique insights into future values.

2.1.7. Summary

People use the financial system for many purposes, the most important of which are saving, borrowing, raising equity capital, managing risk, exchanging assets in spot markets, and information-motivated trading. The financial system best facilitates these uses when people can trade instruments that interest them in liquid markets, when institutions provide financial services at low cost, when information about assets and about credit risks is readily available, and when regulation helps ensure that everyone faithfully honors their contracts.

2.2. Determining Rates of Return

Saving, borrowing, and selling equity are all means of moving money through time. Savers move money from the present to the future whereas borrowers and equity issuers move money from the future to the present.

Because time machines do not exist, money can travel forward in time only if an equal amount of money is travelling in the other direction. This equality always occurs because borrowers and equity sellers create the securities in which savers invest. For example, the bond sold by a company that needs to move money from the future to the present is the same bond bought by a saver who needs to move money from the present to the future.

The aggregate amount of money that savers will move from the present to the future is related to the expected rate of return on their investments. If the expected return is high, they will forgo current consumption and move more money to the future. Similarly, the aggregate amount of money that borrowers and equity sellers will move from the future to the present depends on the costs of borrowing funds or of giving up ownership. These costs can be expressed as the rate of return that borrowers and equity sellers are expected to deliver in exchange for obtaining current funds. It is the same rate that savers expect to receive when delivering current funds. If this rate is low, borrowers and equity sellers will want to move more money to the present from the future. In other words, they will want to raise more funds.

Because the total money saved must equal the total money borrowed and received in exchange for equity, the expected rate of return depends on the aggregate supply of funds through savings and the aggregate demand for funds. If the rate is too high, savers will want to move more money to the future than borrowers, and equity issuers will want to move to the present. The expected rate will have to be lower to discourage the savers and to encourage the borrowers and equity issuers. Conversely, if the rate is too low, savers will want to move less money forward than borrowers and equity issuers will want to move to the present. The expected rate will have to be higher to encourage the savers and to discourage the borrowers and equity issuers. Between rates too high and too low, an expected rate of return exists, in theory, in which the aggregate supply of funds for investing (supply of funds saved) and the aggregate demand for funds through borrowing and equity issuing are equal.

Economists call this rate the equilibrium interest rate. It is the price for moving money through time. Determining this rate is one of the most important functions of the financial system. The equilibrium interest rate is the only interest rate that would exist if all securities were equally risky, had equal terms, and were equally liquid. In fact, the required rates of return for securities vary by their risk characteristics, terms, and liquidity. For a given issuer, investors generally require higher rates of return for equity than for debt, for long-term securities than for short-term securities, and for illiquid securities than for liquid ones. Financial analysts recognize that all required rates of return depend on a common equilibrium interest rate plus adjustments for risk.

EXAMPLE 1-3 Interest Rates

For a presentation to private wealth clients by your firm's chief economist, you are asked to prepare the audience by explaining the most fundamental facts concerning the role of interest rates in the economy. You agree. What main points should you try to convey?

Solution: Savers have money now that they will want to use in the future. Borrowers want to use money now that they do not have, but they expect that they will have money in the future. Borrowers are loaned money by savers and promise to repay it in the future.

The interest rate is the return that lenders, the savers, expect to receive from borrowers for allowing borrowers to use the savers' money. The interest rate is the price of using money.

Interest rates depend on the total amount of money that people want to borrow and the total amount of money that people are willing to lend. Interest rates are high when, in aggregate, people value having money now substantially more than they value having money in the future. In contrast, if many people with money want to use it in the future and few people presently need more money than they have, interest rates will be low.

2.3. Capital Allocation Efficiency

Primary capital markets (primary markets) are the markets in which companies and governments raise capital (funds). Companies may raise funds by borrowing money or by issuing equity. Governments may raise funds by borrowing money.

Economies are said to be allocationally efficient when their financial systems allocate capital (funds) to those uses that are most productive. Although companies may be interested in getting funding for many potential projects, not all projects are worth funding. One of the most important functions of the financial system is to ensure that only the best projects obtain scarce capital funds; the funds available from savers should be allocated to the most productive uses.

In market-based economies, savers determine, directly or indirectly, which projects obtain capital. Savers determine capital allocations directly by choosing which securities they will invest in. Savers determine capital allocations indirectly by giving funds to financial intermediaries that then invest the funds. Because investors fear the loss of their money, they will lend at lower interest rates to borrowers with the best credit prospects or the best collateral, and they will lend at higher rates to other borrowers with less secure prospects. Similarly, they will buy only those equities that they believe have the best prospects relative to their prices and risks.

To avoid losses, investors carefully study the prospects of the various investment opportunities available to them. The decisions that they make tend to be well informed, which helps ensure that capital is allocated efficiently. The fear of losses by investors and by those raising funds to invest in projects ensures that only the best projects tend to be funded. The process works best when investors are well informed about the prospects of the various projects.

In general, investors will fund an equity project if they expect that the value of the project is greater than its cost, and they will not fund projects otherwise. If the investor expectations are accurate, only projects that should be undertaken will be funded and all such projects will be funded. Accurate market information thus leads to efficient capital allocation.

EXAMPLE 1-4 Primary Market Capital Allocation

How can poor information about the value of a project result in poor capital allocation decisions?

Solution: Projects should be undertaken only if their value is greater than their cost. If investors have poor information and overestimate the value of a project in which its true value is less than its cost, a wealth-diminishing project may be undertaken. Alternatively, if investors have poor information and underestimate the value of a project in which its true value is greater than its cost, a wealth-enhancing project may not be undertaken.

3. ASSETS AND CONTRACTS

People, companies, and governments use many different assets and contracts to further their financial goals and to manage their risks. The most common assets include financial assets (such as bank deposits, certificates of deposit, loans, mortgages, corporate and government bonds and notes, common and preferred stocks, real estate investment trusts, master limited partnership interests, pooled investment products, and exchange-traded funds), currencies, certain commodities (such as gold and oil), and real assets (such as real estate). The most common contracts are option, futures, forward, swap, and insurance contracts. People, companies, and governments use these assets and contracts to raise funds, to invest, to profit from information-motivated trading, to hedge risks, and/or to transfer money from one form to another.

3.1. Classifications of Assets and Markets

Practitioners often classify assets and the markets in which they trade by various common characteristics to facilitate communications with their clients, with each other, and with regulators.

The most actively traded assets are securities, currencies, contracts, and commodities. In addition, real assets are traded. Securities generally include debt instruments, equities, and shares in pooled investment vehicles. Currencies are monies issued by national monetary authorities. Contracts are agreements to exchange securities, currencies, commodities, or other contracts in the future. Commodities include precious metals, energy products, industrial metals, and agricultural products. Real assets are tangible properties such as real estate, airplanes, or machinery. Securities, currencies, and contracts are classified as financial assets whereas commodities and real assets are classified as physical assets.

Securities are further classified as debt or equity. Debt instruments (also called fixed-income instruments) are promises to repay borrowed money. Equities represent ownership in companies. Pooled investment vehicle shares represent ownership of an undivided interest in an investment portfolio. The portfolio may include securities, currencies, contracts, commodities, or real assets. Pooled investment vehicles, such as exchange-traded funds, which exclusively own shares in other companies generally are also considered equities.

Securities are also classified by whether they are public or private securities. Public securities are those registered to trade in public markets, such as on exchanges or through dealers. In most jurisdictions, issuers must meet stringent minimum regulatory standards, including reporting and corporate governance standards, to issue publicly traded securities.

Private securities are all other securities. Often, only specially qualified investors can purchase private equities and private debt instruments. Investors may purchase them directly from the issuer or indirectly through an investment vehicle specifically formed to hold such securities. Issuers often issue private securities when they find public reporting standards too burdensome or when they do not want to conform to the regulatory standards associated with public equity. **Venture capital** is private equity that investors supply to companies when or shortly after they are founded. Private securities generally are illiquid. In contrast, many public securities trade in liquid markets in which sellers can easily find buyers for their securities.

Contracts are derivative contracts if their values depend on the prices of other underlying assets. Derivative contracts may be classified as physical or financial depending on whether the underlying instruments are physical products or financial securities. Equity derivatives are contracts whose values depend on equities or indices of equities. Fixed-income derivatives are contracts whose values depend on debt securities or indices of debt securities.

Practitioners classify markets by whether the markets trade instruments for immediate delivery or for future delivery. Markets that trade contracts that call for delivery in the future are forward or futures markets. Those that trade for immediate delivery are called spot markets to distinguish them from forward markets that trade contracts on the same underlying instruments. Options markets trade contracts that deliver in the future, but delivery takes place only if the holders of the options choose to exercise them.

When issuers sell securities to investors, practitioners say that they trade in the **primary market**. When investors sell those securities to others, they trade in the **secondary market**. In the primary market, funds flow to the issuer of the security from the purchaser. In the secondary market, funds flow between traders.

Practitioners classify financial markets as money markets or capital markets. Money markets trade debt instruments maturing in one year or less. The most common such instruments are repurchase agreements (defined in Section 3.2.1), negotiable certificates of deposit, government bills, and commercial paper. In contrast, capital markets trade instruments of longer duration, such as bonds and equities, whose values depend on the creditworthiness of the issuers and on payments of interest or dividends that will be made in the future and may be uncertain. Corporations generally finance their operations in the capital markets, but some also finance a portion of their operations by issuing short-term securities, such as commercial paper.

Finally, practitioners distinguish between traditional investment markets and alternative investment markets. Traditional investments include all publicly traded debts and equities and shares in pooled investment vehicles that hold publicly traded debts and/or equities. Alternative investments include hedge funds, private equities (including venture capital), commodities, real estate securities and real estate properties, securitized debts, operating leases, machinery, collectibles, and precious gems. Because these investments are often hard to trade and hard to value, they may sometimes trade at substantial deviations from their intrinsic values. The discounts compensate investors for the research that they must do to value these assets and for their inability to easily sell the assets if they need to liquidate a portion of their portfolios.

The remainder of this section describes the most common assets and contracts that people, companies, and governments trade.

EXAMPLE 1-5 Asset and Market Classification

The investment policy of a mutual fund permits the fund to invest only in public equities traded in secondary markets. Would the fund be able to purchase:

1. Common stock of a company that trades on a large stock exchange?
2. Common stock of a public company that trades only through dealers?
3. A government bond?
4. A single stock futures contract?
5. Common stock sold for the first time by a properly registered public company?
6. Shares in a privately held bank with €10 billion of capital?

Solutions:

1. Yes. Common stock is equity. Those common stocks that trade on large exchanges invariably are public equities that trade in secondary markets.
2. Yes. Dealer markets are secondary markets and the security is a public equity.
3. No. Although government bonds are public securities, they are not equities. They are debt securities.

4. No. Although the underlying instruments for single stock futures are invariably public equities, single stock futures are derivative contracts not equities.
5. No. The fund would not be able to buy these shares because a purchase from the issuer would be in the primary market. The fund would have to wait until it could buy the shares from someone other than the issuer.
6. No. These shares are private equities, not public equities. The public prominence of the company does not make its securities public securities unless they have been properly registered as public securities.

3.2. Securities

People, companies, and governments sell securities to raise money. Securities include bonds, notes, commercial paper, mortgages, common stocks, preferred stocks, warrants, mutual fund shares, unit trusts, and depository receipts. These can be classified broadly as fixed-income instruments, equities, and shares in pooled investment vehicles. Note that the legal definition of a security varies by country and may or may not coincide with the usage here. Securities that are sold to the public or that can be resold to the public are called issues. Companies and governments are the most common issuers.

3.2.1. Fixed Income

Fixed-income instruments contractually include predetermined payment schedules that usually include interest and principal payments. Fixed-income instruments generally are promises to repay borrowed money but may include other instruments with payment schedules, such as settlements of legal cases or prizes from lotteries. The payment amounts may be prespecified or they may vary according to a fixed formula that depends on the future values of an interest rate or a commodity price. Bonds, notes, bills, certificates of deposit, commercial paper, repurchase agreements, loan agreements, and mortgages are examples of promises to repay money in the future. People, companies, and governments create fixed-income instruments when they borrow money.

Corporations and governments issue bonds and notes. Fixed-income securities with shorter maturities are called "notes," those with longer maturities are called "bonds." The cutoff is usually at 10 years. In practice, however, the terms are generally used interchangeably. Both become short-term instruments when the remaining time until maturity is short, usually taken to be one year or less.

Some corporations issue convertible bonds, which are typically convertible into stock, usually at the option of the holder after some period. If stock prices are high so that conversion is likely, convertibles are valued like stock. Conversely, if stock prices are low so that conversion is unlikely, convertibles are valued like bonds.

Bills, certificates of deposit, and commercial paper are respectively issued by governments, banks, and corporations. They usually mature within a year of being issued; certificates of deposit sometimes have longer initial maturities.

Repurchase agreements (repos) are short-term lending instruments. The term can be as short as overnight. A borrower seeking funds will sell an instrument—typically a high-quality bond—to a lender with an agreement to repurchase it later at a slightly higher price based on an agreed-upon interest rate.

Practitioners distinguish between short-term, intermediate-term, and long-term fixed-income securities. No general consensus exists about the definition of short-term, intermediate-term, and long-term. Instruments that mature in less than one to two years are considered short-term instruments whereas those that mature in more than five to ten years are considered long-term instruments. In the middle are intermediate-term instruments.

Instruments trading in money markets are called money market instruments. Such instruments are traded debt instruments maturing in one year or less. Money market funds and corporations seeking a return on their short-term cash balances typically hold money market instruments.

3.2.2. Equities

Equities represent ownership rights in companies. These include common and preferred shares. Common shareholders own residual rights to the assets of the company. They have the right to receive any dividends declared by the boards of directors, and in the event of liquidation, any assets remaining after all other claims are paid. Acting through the boards of directors that they elect, common shareholders usually can select the managers who run the corporations.

Preferred shares are equities that have preferred rights (relative to common shares) to the cash flows and assets of the company. Preferred shareholders generally have the right to receive a specific dividend on a regular basis. If the preferred share is a cumulative preferred equity, the company must pay the preferred shareholders any previously omitted dividends before it can pay dividends to the common shareholders. Preferred shareholders also have higher claims to assets relative to common shareholders in the event of corporate liquidation. For valuation purposes, financial analysts generally treat preferred stocks as fixed-income securities when the issuers will clearly be able to pay their promised dividends in the foreseeable future.

Warrants are securities issued by a corporation that allow the warrant holders to buy a security issued by that corporation, if they so desire, usually at any time before the warrants expire or, if not, upon expiration. The security that warrant holders can buy usually is the issuer's common stock, in which case the warrants are considered equities because the warrant holders can obtain equity in the company by exercising their warrants. The warrant exercise price is the price that the warrant holder must pay to buy the security.

EXAMPLE 1-6 Securities

What factors distinguish fixed-income securities from equities?

Solution: Fixed-income securities generate income on a regular schedule. They derive their value from the promise to pay a scheduled cash flow. The most common fixed-income securities are promises made by people, companies, and governments to repay loans.

Equities represent residual ownership in companies after all other claims—including any fixed-income liabilities of the company—have been satisfied. For corporations, the claims of preferred equities typically have priority over the claims of common equities. Common equities have the residual ownership in corporations.

3.2.3. Pooled Investments

Pooled investment vehicles are mutual funds, trusts, depositories, and hedge funds that issue securities that represent shared ownership in the assets that these entities hold. The securities created by mutual funds, trusts, depositories, and hedge funds are respectively called *shares*, *units*, *depository receipts*, and *limited partnership interests* but practitioners often use these terms interchangeably. People invest in pooled investment vehicles to benefit from the investment management services of their managers and from diversification opportunities that are not readily available to them on an individual basis.

Mutual funds are investment vehicles that pool money from many investors for investment in a portfolio of securities. They are often legally organized as investment trusts or as corporate investment companies. Pooled investment vehicles may be open-ended or closed-ended. Open-ended funds issue new shares and redeem existing shares on demand, usually on a daily basis. The price at which a fund redeems and sells the fund's shares is based on the net asset value of the fund's portfolio, which is the difference between the fund's assets and liabilities, expressed on a per share basis. Investors generally buy and sell open-ended mutual funds by trading with the mutual fund.

In contrast, closed-end funds issue shares in primary market offerings that the fund or its investment bankers arrange. Once issued, investors cannot sell their shares of the fund back to the fund by demanding redemption. Instead, investors in closed-end funds must sell their shares to other investors in the secondary market. The secondary market prices of closed-end funds may differ—sometimes quite significantly—from their net asset values. Closed-end funds generally trade at a discount to their net asset values. The discount reflects the expenses of running the fund and sometimes investor concerns about the quality of the management. Closed-end funds may also trade at a discount or a premium to net asset value when investors believe that the portfolio securities are overvalued or undervalued. Many financial analysts thus believe that discounts and premiums on closed-end funds measure market sentiment.

Exchange-traded funds (ETFs) and exchange-traded notes (ETNs) are open-ended funds that investors can trade among themselves in secondary markets. The prices at which ETFs trade rarely differ much from net asset values because a class of investors, known as authorized participants (APs), has the option of trading directly with the ETF. If the market price of an equity ETF is sufficiently below its net asset value, APs will buy shares in the secondary market at market price and redeem shares at net asset value with the fund. Conversely, if the price of an ETF is sufficiently above its net asset value, APs will buy shares from the fund at net asset value and sell shares in the secondary market at market price. As a result, the market price and net asset values of ETFs tend to converge.

Many ETFs permit only in-kind deposits and redemptions. Buyers who buy directly from such a fund pay for their shares with a portfolio of securities rather than with cash. Similarly, sellers receive a portfolio of securities. The transaction portfolio generally is very similar—often essentially identical—to the portfolio held by the fund. Practitioners sometimes call such funds "depositories" because they issue depository receipts for the portfolios that traders deposit with them. The traders then trade the receipts in the secondary market. Some warehouses holding industrial materials and precious metals also issue tradable warehouse receipts.

Asset-backed securities are securities whose values and income payments are derived from a pool of assets, such as mortgage bonds, credit card debt, or car loans. These securities typically pass interest and principal payments received from the pool of assets through to their holders on a monthly basis. These payments may depend on formulas that give some classes of securities—called tranches—backed by the pool more value than other classes.

Hedge funds are investment funds that generally organize as limited partnerships. The hedge fund managers are the general partners. The limited partners are qualified investors who are wealthy enough and well informed enough to tolerate and accept substantial losses, should they occur. The regulatory requirements to participate in a hedge fund and the regulatory restrictions on hedge funds vary by jurisdiction. Most hedge funds follow only one investment strategy, but no single investment strategy characterizes hedge funds as a group. Hedge funds exist that follow almost every imaginable strategy ranging from long–short arbitrage in the stock markets to direct investments in exotic alternative assets.

The primary distinguishing characteristic of hedge funds is their management compensation scheme. Almost all funds pay their managers with an annual fee that is proportional to their assets and with an additional performance fee that depends on the wealth that the funds generate for their shareholders. A secondary distinguishing characteristic of many hedge funds is the use of leverage to increase risk exposure and to hopefully increase returns.

3.3. Currencies

Currencies are monies issued by national monetary authorities. Approximately 175 currencies are currently in use throughout the world. Some of these currencies are regarded as reserve currencies. Reserve currencies are currencies that national central banks and other monetary authorities hold in significant quantities. The primary reserve currencies are the U.S. dollar and the euro. Secondary reserve currencies include the British pound, the Japanese yen, and the Swiss franc.

Currencies trade in foreign exchange markets. In spot currency transactions, one currency is immediately or almost immediately exchanged for another. The rate of exchange is called the spot exchange rate. Traders typically negotiate institutional trades in multiples of large quantities, such as US$1 million or ¥100 million. Institutional trades generally settle in two business days.

Retail currency trades most commonly take place through commercial banks when their customers exchange currencies at a location of the bank, use ATM machines when traveling to withdraw a different currency than the currency in which their bank accounts are denominated, or use credit cards to buy items priced in different currencies. Retail currency trades also take place at airport kiosks, at storefront currency exchanges, or on the street.

3.4. Contracts

A contract is an agreement among traders to do something in the future. Contracts include forward, futures, swap, option, and insurance contracts. The values of most contracts depend on the value of an underlying asset. The underlying asset may be a commodity, a security, an index representing the values of other instruments, a currency pair or basket, or other contracts.

Contracts provide for some physical or cash settlement in the future. In a physically settled contract, settlement occurs when the parties to the contract physically exchange some item, such as tomatoes, pork bellies, or gold bars. Physical settlement also includes the delivery of such financial instruments as bonds, equities, or futures contracts even though the delivery is electronic. In contrast, cash settled contracts settle through cash payments. The amount of the payment depends on formulas specified in the contracts.

Financial analysts classify contracts by whether they are physical or financial based on the nature of the underlying asset. If the underlying asset is a physical product, the contract is a physical; otherwise, the contract is a financial. Examples of assets classified as physical include contracts for the delivery of petroleum, lumber, and gold. Examples of assets classified as financial include option contracts and contracts on interest rates, stock indices, currencies, and credit default swaps.

Contracts that call for immediate delivery are called spot contracts, and they trade in spot markets. Immediate delivery generally is three days or less, but depends on each market. All other contracts involve what practitioners call futurity. They derive their values from events that will take place in the future.

EXAMPLE 1-7 Contracts for Difference

Contracts for difference (CFD) allow people to speculate on price changes for an underlying asset, such as a common stock or an index. Dealers generally sell CFDs to their clients. When the clients sell the CFDs back to their dealer, they receive any appreciation in the underlying asset's price between the time of purchase and sale (open and close) of the contract. If the underlying asset's price drops over this interval, the client pays the dealer the difference.

1. Are contracts for difference derivative contracts?
2. Are contracts for difference based on copper prices cash settled or physically settled?

Solution to 1: Contracts for difference are derivative contracts because their values are derived from changes in the prices of the underlying asset on which they are based.

Solution to 2: All contracts for difference are cash-settled contracts regardless of the underlying asset on which they are based because they settle in cash and not in the underlying asset.

3.4.1. Forward Contracts

A **forward contract** is an agreement to trade the underlying asset in the future at a price agreed upon today. For example, a contract for the sale of wheat after the harvest is a forward contract. People often use forward contracts to reduce risk. Before planting wheat, farmers like to know the price at which they will sell their crop. Similarly, before committing to sell flour to bakers in the future, millers like to know the prices that they will pay for wheat. The farmer and the miller both reduce their operating risks by agreeing to trade wheat forward.

Practitioners call such traders hedgers because they use their contractual commitments to hedge their risks. If the price of wheat falls, the wheat farmer's crop will drop in value on the spot market but he has a contract to sell wheat in the future at a higher fixed price. The forward contract has become more valuable to the farmer. Conversely, if the price of wheat rises, the miller's future obligation to sell flour will become more burdensome because of the high price he would have to pay for wheat on the spot market, but the miller has a contract to buy wheat at a lower fixed price. The forward contract has become more valuable to the miller. In both cases, fluctuations in the spot price are hedged by the forward contract. The forward contract offsets the operating risks that the hedgers face.

Consider a simple example of hedging. A tomato farmer in southern Ontario, Canada, grows tomatoes for processing into tomato sauce. The farmer expects to harvest 250,000 bushels and that the price per bushel at harvest will be \$1.03. That price, however, could fluctuate significantly before the harvest. If the price of tomatoes drops to \$0.75, the farmer would lose \$0.28 per bushel (\$1.03 – \$0.75) relative to his expectations, or a total of \$70,000. Now, suppose that the farmer can sell tomatoes forward to Heinz at \$1.01 for delivery at the harvest. If the farmer sells 250,000 bushels forward, and the price of tomatoes drops to \$0.75, the farmer would still be able to sell his tomatoes for \$1.01, and thus would not suffer from the drop in price of tomatoes.

EXAMPLE 1-8 Hedging Gold Production

An Indonesian gold producer invests in a mine expansion project on the expectation that gold prices will remain at or above 35,000 rupiah per gram when the new project starts producing ore.

1. What risks does the gold producer face with respect to the price of gold?
2. How might the gold producer hedge its gold price risk?

Solution to 1: The gold producer faces the risk that the price of gold could fall below 35,000 rupiah before it can sell its new production. If so, the investment in the expansion project will be less profitable than expected, and may even generate losses for the mine.

Solution to 2: The gold producer could hedge the gold price risk by selling gold forward, hopefully at a price near 35,000 rupiah. Even if the price of gold falls, the gold producer would get paid the contract price.

Forward contracts are very common, but two problems limit their usefulness for many market participants. The first problem is counterparty risk. **Counterparty risk** is the risk that the other party to a contract will fail to honor the terms of the contract. Concerns about counterparty risk ensure that generally only parties who have long-standing relationships with each other execute forward contracts. Trustworthiness is critical when prices are volatile because, after a large price change, one side or the other may prefer not to settle the contract.

The second problem is liquidity. Trading out of a forward contract is very difficult because it can only be done with the consent of the other party. The liquidity problem ensures that forward contracts tend to be executed only among participants for whom delivery is economically efficient and quite certain at the time of contracting so that both parties will want to arrange for delivery.

The counterparty risk problem and the liquidity problem often make it difficult for market participants to obtain the hedging benefits associated with forward contracting. Fortunately, futures contracts have been developed to mitigate these problems.

3.4.2. Futures Contracts

A **futures contract** is a standardized forward contract for which a clearinghouse guarantees the performance of all traders. The buyer of a futures contract is the side that will take physical delivery or its cash equivalent. The seller of a futures contract is the side that is liable for the delivery or its cash equivalent. A **clearinghouse** is an organization that ensures that no trader is harmed if another trader fails to honor the contract. In effect, the clearinghouse acts as the buyer for every seller and as the seller for every buyer. Buyers and sellers, therefore, can trade futures without worrying whether their counterparties are creditworthy. Because futures contracts are standardized, a buyer can eliminate his obligation to buy by selling his contract to anyone. A seller similarly can eliminate her obligation to deliver by buying a contact from anyone. In either case, the clearinghouse will release the trader from all future obligations if his or her long and short positions exactly offset each other.

To protect against defaults, futures clearinghouses require that all participants post with the clearinghouse an amount of money known as **initial margin** when they enter a contract. The clearinghouse then settles the margin accounts on a daily basis. All participants who have lost on their contracts that day will have the amount of their losses deducted from their margin by the clearinghouse. The clearinghouse similarly increases margins for all participants who gained on that day. Participants whose margins drop below the required **maintenance margin** must replenish their accounts. If a participant does not provide sufficient additional margin when required, the participant's broker will immediately trade to offset the participant's position. These **variation margin payments** ensure that the liabilities associated with futures contracts do not grow large.

EXAMPLE 1-9 Futures Margin

NYMEX's Light Sweet Crude Oil futures contract specifies the delivery of 1,000 barrels of West Texas Intermediate (WTI) Crude Oil when the contract finally settles. A broker requires that its clients post an initial overnight margin of \$7,763 per contract and an overnight maintenance margin of \$5,750 per contract. A client buys 10 contracts at \$75 per barrel through this broker. On the next day, the contract settles for \$72 per barrel. How much additional margin will the client have to provide to his broker?

Solution: The client lost three dollars per barrel (he is the side committed to take delivery or its cash equivalent at \$75 per barrel). This results in a \$3,000 loss on each of his 10 contracts, and a total loss of \$30,000. His initial margin of \$77,630 is reduced by \$30,000 leaving \$47,630 in his margin account. Because his account has dropped below the maintenance margin requirement of \$57,500, the client will get a margin call. The client must provide an additional \$30,000 = \$77,630 – \$47,630 to replenish his margin account; the account is replenished to the amount of the initial margin. The client will only receive another margin call if his account drops to below \$57,500 again.

Futures contracts have vastly improved the efficiency of forward contracting markets. Traders can trade standardized futures contracts with anyone without worrying about counterparty risk, and they can close their positions by arranging offsetting trades. Hedgers for whom the terms of the standard contract are not ideal generally still use the futures markets because the contracts embody most of the price risk that concerns them. They simply offset (close out) their futures positions at the same time they enter spot contracts on which they make or take ultimate delivery.

EXAMPLE 1-10 Forward and Futures Contracts

What feature most distinguishes futures contracts from forward contracts?

Solution: A futures contract is a standardized forward contract for which a clearinghouse guarantees the performance of all buyers and sellers. The clearinghouse reduces the counterparty risk problem. The clearinghouse allows a buyer who has bought a contract from one person and sold the same contract to another person to net out the two obligations so that she is no longer liable for either side of the contract; the positions are closed. The ability to trade futures contracts provides liquidity in futures contracts compared with forward contracts.

3.4.3. Swap Contracts

A **swap contract** is an agreement to exchange payments of periodic cash flows that depend on future asset prices or interest rates. For example, in a typical **interest rate swap**, at periodic intervals, one party makes fixed cash payments to the counterparty in exchange for variable cash payments from the counterparty. The variable payments are based on a prespecified variable interest rate such as the London Interbank Offered Rate (LIBOR). This swap effectively exchanges fixed interest payments for variable interest payments. Because the variable rate is set in the future, the cash flows for this contract are uncertain when the parties enter the contract.

Investment managers often enter interest rate swaps when they own a fixed long-term income stream that they want to convert to a cash flow that varies with current short-term interest rates, or vice versa. The conversion may allow them to substantially reduce the total interest rate risk to which they are exposed. Hedgers often use swap contracts to manage risks.

In a **commodity swap**, one party typically makes fixed payments in exchange for payments that depend on future prices of a commodity such as oil. In a **currency swap**, the parties exchange payments denominated in different currencies. The payments may be fixed, or they may vary depending on future interest rates in the two countries. In an **equity swap**, the parties exchange fixed cash payments for payments that depend on the returns to a stock or a stock index.

EXAMPLE 1-11 Swap and Forward Contracts

What feature most distinguishes a swap contract from a cash-settled forward contract?

Solution: Both contracts provide for the exchange of cash payments in the future. A forward contract only has a single cash payment at the end that depends on an underlying price or index at the end. In contrast, a swap contract has several scheduled periodic payments, each of which depends on an underlying price or index at the time of the payment.

3.4.4. Option Contracts

An **option contract** allows the holder (the purchaser) of the option to buy or sell, depending on the type of option, an underlying instrument at a specified price at or before a specified date in the future. Those who do buy or sell are said to **exercise** their contracts. An option to buy is a **call option**, and an option to sell is a **put option**. The specified price is called the strike price (exercise price). If the holders can exercise their contracts only when they mature, they are **European-style contracts**. If they can exercise the contracts earlier, they are **American-style contracts**. Many exchanges list standardized option contracts on individual stocks, stock indices, futures contracts, currencies, swaps, and precious metals. Institutions also trade many customized option contracts with dealers in the over-the-counter derivative market.

Option holders generally will exercise call options if the strike price is below the market price of the underlying instrument, in which case, they will be able to buy at a lower price than the market price. Similarly, they will exercise put options if the strike price is above the underlying instrument price so that they sell at a higher price than the market price. Otherwise, option holders allow their options to expire as worthless.

The price that traders pay for an option is the option premium. Options can be quite expensive because, unlike forward and futures contracts, they do not impose any liability on the holder. The premium compensates the sellers of options—called option writers—for giving the call option holders the right to potentially buy below market prices and put option holders the right to potentially sell above market prices. Because the writers must trade if the holders exercise their options, option contracts may impose substantial liabilities on the writers.

EXAMPLE 1-12 Option and Forward Contracts

What feature most distinguishes option contracts from forward contracts?

Solution: The holder of an option contract has the right, but not the obligation, to buy (for a call option) or sell (for a put option) the underlying instrument at some time in the future. The writer of an option contract must trade the underlying instrument if the holder exercises the option.

In contrast, the two parties to a forward contract must trade the underlying instrument (or its equivalent value for a cash-settled contract) at some time in the future if either party wants to settle the contract.

3.4.5. Other Contracts

Insurance contracts pay their beneficiaries a cash benefit if some event occurs. Life, liability, and automobile insurance are examples of insurance contracts sold to retail clients. People generally use insurance contracts to compensate for losses that they will experience if bad things happen unexpectedly. Insurance contracts allow them to hedge risks that they face.

Credit default swaps (CDS) are insurance contracts that promise payment of principal in the event that a company defaults on its bonds. Bondholders use credit default swaps to convert risky bonds into more secure investments. Other creditors of the company may also buy them to hedge against the risk they will not be paid if the company goes bankrupt.

Well-informed traders who believe that a corporation will default on its bonds may buy credit default swaps written on the corporation's bonds if the swap prices are sufficiently low. If they are correct, the traders will profit if the payoff to the swap is more than the cost of buying and maintaining the swap position.

People sometimes also buy insurance contracts as investments, especially in jurisdictions where payouts from insurance contracts are not subject to as much taxation as are payouts to other investment vehicles. They may buy these contracts directly from insurance companies, or they may buy already issued contracts from their owners. For example, the life settlements market trades life insurance contracts that people sell to investors when they need cash.

3.5. Commodities

Commodities include precious metals, energy products, industrial metals, agricultural products, and carbon credits. Spot commodity markets trade commodities for immediate delivery whereas the forward and futures markets trade commodities for future delivery. Managers seeking positions in commodities can acquire them directly by trading in the spot markets or indirectly by trading forward and futures contracts.

The producers and processors of industrial metals and agricultural products are the primary users of the spot commodity markets because they generally are best able to take and make delivery and to store physical products. They undertake these activities in the normal course of operating their businesses. Their ability to handle physical products and the information that they gather while operating businesses also gives them substantial advantages as information-motivated traders in these markets. Many producers employ financial analysts to help them analyze commodity market conditions so that they can best manage their inventories to hedge their operational risks and to speculate on future price changes.

Commodities also interest information-motivated traders and investment managers because they can use them as hedges against risks that they hold in their portfolios or as vehicles to speculate on future price changes. Most such traders take positions in the futures markets because they usually do not have facilities to handle most physical products nor can they easily obtain them. They also cannot easily cope with the normal variation in qualities that characterizes many commodities. Information-motivated traders and investment managers also prefer to trade in futures markets because most futures markets are more liquid than their associated spot markets and forward markets. The liquidity allows them to easily close their positions before delivery so that they can avoid handling physical products.

Some information-motivated traders and investment managers, however, trade in the spot commodity markets, especially when they can easily contract for low-cost storage. Commodities for which delivery and storage costs are lowest are nonperishable products for which the ratio of value to weight is high and variation in quality is low. These generally include precious metals, industrial diamonds, such high-value industrial metals as copper, aluminum, and mercury, and carbon credits.

3.6. Real Assets

Real assets include such tangible properties as real estate, airplanes, machinery, or lumber stands. These assets normally are held by operating companies, such as real estate developers, airplane leasing companies, manufacturers, or loggers. Many institutional investment managers, however, have been adding real assets to their portfolios as direct investments (involving direct ownership of the real assets) and indirect investments (involving indirect ownership, for example, purchase of securities of companies that invest in real assets or real estate investment trusts). Investments in real assets are attractive to them because of the income and tax benefits that they often generate, and because changes in their values may have a low correlation with other investments that the managers hold.

Direct investments in real assets generally require substantial management to ensure that the assets are maintained and used efficiently. Investment managers investing in such assets must either hire personnel to manage them or hire outside management companies. Either way, management of real assets is quite costly.

Real assets are unique properties in the sense that no two assets are alike. An example of a unique property is a real estate parcel. No two parcels are the same because, if nothing else, they are located in different places. Real assets generally differ in their conditions, remaining useful lives, locations, and suitability for various purposes. These differences are very important to the people who use them, so the market for a given real asset may be very limited. Thus, real assets tend to trade in very illiquid markets.

The heterogeneity of real assets, their illiquidity, and the substantial costs of managing them are all factors that complicate the valuation of real assets and generally make them unsuitable for most investment portfolios. These same problems, however, often cause real assets to be misvalued in the market, so astute information-motivated traders may occasionally identify significantly undervalued assets. The benefits from purchasing such assets, however, are often offset by the substantial costs of searching for them and by the substantial costs of managing them.

Many financial intermediaries create entities, such as real estate investment trusts (REITs) and master limited partnerships (MLPs), to securitize real assets and to facilitate indirect investment in real assets. The financial intermediaries manage the assets and pass through the net benefits after management costs to the investors who hold these securities. Because these securities are much more homogenous and divisible than the real assets that they represent, they tend to trade in much more liquid markets. Thus, they are much more suitable as investments than the real assets themselves.

Of course, investors seeking exposure to real assets can also buy shares in corporations that hold and operate real assets. Although almost all corporations hold and operate real assets, many specialize in assets that particularly interest investors seeking exposure to specific real asset classes. For example, investors interested in owning aircraft can buy an aircraft leasing company such as Waha Capital (Abu Dhabi Securities Exchange) and Aircastle Limited (NYSE).

EXAMPLE 1-13 Assets and Contracts

Consider the following assets and contracts:

Bank deposits	Hedge funds
Certificates of deposit	Master limited partnership interests

Common stocks	Mortgages
Corporate bonds	Mutual funds
Currencies	Stock option contracts
Exchange-traded funds	Preferred stocks
Lumber forward contracts	Real estate parcels
Crude oil futures contracts	Interest rate swaps
Gold	Treasury notes

1. Which of these represent ownership in corporations?
2. Which of these are debt instruments?
3. Which of these are created by traders rather than by issuers?
4. Which of these are pooled investment vehicles?
5. Which of these are real assets?
6. Which of these would a home builder most likely use to hedge construction costs?
7. Which of these would a corporation trade when moving cash balances among various countries?

Solutions:

1. Common and preferred stocks represent ownership in corporations.
2. Bank deposits, certificates of deposit, corporate bonds, mortgages, and Treasury notes are all debt instruments. They respectively represent loans made to banks, corporations, mortgagees (typically real estate owners), and the Treasury.
3. Lumber forward contracts, crude oil futures contracts, stock option contracts, and interest rate swaps are created when the seller sells them to a buyer.
4. Exchange-traded funds, hedge funds, and mutual funds are pooled investment vehicles. They represent shared ownership in a portfolio of other assets.
5. Real estate parcels are real assets.
6. A builder would buy lumber forward contracts to lock in the price of lumber needed to build homes.
7. Corporations often trade currencies when moving cash from one country to another.

4. FINANCIAL INTERMEDIARIES

Financial intermediaries help entities achieve their financial goals. These intermediaries include commercial, mortgage, and investment banks; credit unions, credit card companies, and various other finance corporations; brokers and exchanges; dealers and arbitrageurs; clearinghouses and depositories; mutual funds and hedge funds; and insurance companies. The services and products that financial intermediaries provide allow their clients to solve the financial problems that they face more efficiently than they could do so by themselves. Financial intermediaries are essential to well-functioning financial systems.

Financial intermediaries are called intermediaries because the services and products that they provide help connect buyers to sellers in various ways. Whether the connections are easy to identify or involve complex financial structures, financial intermediaries stand between one or more buyers and one or more sellers and help them transfer capital and risk between them. Financial intermediaries' activities allow buyers and sellers to benefit from trading, often without any knowledge of the other.

This section introduces the main financial intermediaries that provide services and products in well-developed financial markets. The discussion starts with those intermediaries whose services most obviously connect buyers to sellers and then proceeds to those intermediaries whose services create more subtle connections. Because many financial intermediaries provide many different types of services, some are mentioned more than once. The section concludes with a general characterization of the various ways in which financial intermediaries add value to the financial system.

4.1. Brokers, Exchanges, and Alternative Trading Systems

Brokers are agents who fill orders for their clients. They do not trade with their clients. Instead, they search for traders who are willing to take the other side of their clients' orders. Individual brokers may work for large brokerage firms, the brokerage arm of banks, or at exchanges. Some brokers match clients to clients personally. Others use specialized computer systems to identify potential trades and help their clients fill their orders. Brokers help their clients trade by reducing the costs of finding counterparties for their trades.

Block brokers provide brokerage service to large traders. Large orders are hard to fill because finding a counterparty willing to do a large trade is often quite difficult. A large buy order generally will trade at a premium to the current market price, and a large sell order generally will trade at a discount to the current market price. These price concessions encourage other traders to trade with the large traders. They also make large traders reluctant, however, to expose their orders to the public before their trades are arranged because they do not want to move the market. Block brokers, therefore, carefully manage the exposure of the orders entrusted to them, which makes filling them difficult.

Investment banks provide advice to their mostly corporate clients and help them arrange transactions such as initial and seasoned securities offerings. Their corporate finance divisions help corporations finance their business by issuing securities, such as common and preferred shares, notes, and bonds. Another function of corporate finance divisions is to help companies identify and acquire other companies (i.e., in mergers and acquisitions).

Exchanges provide places where traders can meet to arrange their trades. Historically, brokers and dealers met on an exchange floor to negotiate trades. Increasingly, exchanges arrange trades for traders based on orders that brokers and dealers submit to them. Such exchanges essentially act as brokers. The distinction between exchanges and brokers has become quite blurred. Exchanges and brokers that use electronic order matching systems to arrange trades among their clients are functionally indistinguishable in this respect. Examples of exchanges include the NYSE-Euronext, Eurex, Deutsche Börse, the Chicago Mercantile Exchange, the Tokyo Stock Exchange, and the Singapore Exchange.

Exchanges are easily distinguished from brokers by their regulatory operations. Most exchanges regulate their members' behavior when trading on the exchange, and sometimes away from the exchange.

Many securities exchanges regulate the issuers that list their securities on the exchange. These regulations generally require timely financial disclosure. Financial analysts use this information to value the securities traded at the exchange. Without such disclosure, valuing securities could be very difficult and market prices might not reflect the fundamental values of the securities. In such situations, well-informed participants may profit from less-informed participants. To avoid such losses, the less-informed participants may withdraw from the market, which can greatly increase corporate costs of capital.

Some exchanges also prohibit issuers from creating capital structures that would concentrate voting rights in the hands of a few owners who do not own a commensurate share of the equity. These regulations attempt to ensure that corporations are run for the benefit of all shareholders and not to promote the interests of controlling shareholders who do not have significant economic stakes in the company.

Exchanges derive their regulatory authority from their national or regional governments, or through the voluntary agreements of their members and issuers to subject themselves to the exchange regulations. In most countries, government regulators oversee the exchange rules and the regulatory operations. Most countries also impose financial disclosure standards on public issuers. Examples of government regulatory bodies include the Japanese Financial Services Agency, the Hong Kong Securities and Futures Commission, the British Financial Services Authority, the German Bundesanstalt für Finanzdienstleistungsaufsicht, the U.S. Securities and Exchange Commission, the Ontario Securities Commission, and the Mexican Comisión Nacional Bancaria y de Valores.

Alternative trading systems (ATSs), also known as electronic communications networks (ECNs) or multilateral trading facilities (MTFs) are trading venues that function like exchanges but that do not exercise regulatory authority over their subscribers except with respect to the conduct of their trading in their trading systems. Some ATSs operate electronic trading systems that are otherwise indistinguishable from the trading systems operated by exchanges. Others operate innovative trading systems that suggest trades to their customers based on information that their customers share with them or that they obtain through research into their customers' preferences. Many ATSs are known as **dark pools** because they do not display the orders that their clients send to them. Large investment managers especially like these systems because market prices often move to their disadvantage when other traders know about their large orders. ATSs may be owned and operated by broker–dealers, exchanges, banks, or by companies organized solely for this purpose, many of which may be owned by a consortia of brokers–dealers and banks. Examples of ATSs include PureTrading (Canada), the Order Machine (Netherlands), Chi-X Europe, BATS (U.S.), POSIT (U.S.), Liquidnet (U.S.), Baxter-FX (Ireland), and Turquoise (Europe). Many of these ATSs provide services in many markets besides the ones in which they are domiciled.

4.2. Dealers

Dealers fill their clients' orders by trading with them. When their clients want to sell securities or contracts, dealers buy the instruments for their own accounts. If their clients want to buy securities, dealers sell securities that they own or have borrowed. After completing a transaction, dealers hope to reverse the transaction by trading with another client on the other side of the market. When they are successful, they effectively connect a buyer who arrived at one point in time with a seller who arrived at another point in time.

The service that dealers provide is liquidity. **Liquidity** is the ability to buy or sell with low transactions costs when you want to trade. By allowing their clients to trade when they want to trade, dealers provide liquidity to them. In over-the-counter markets, dealers offer liquidity when their clients ask them to trade with them. In exchange markets, dealers offer liquidity to anyone who is willing to trade at the prices that the dealers offer at the exchange. Dealers profit when they can buy at prices that on average are lower than the prices at which they sell.

Dealers may organize their operations within proprietary trading houses, investment banks, and hedge funds, or as sole proprietorships. Some dealers are traditional dealers in the sense that individuals make trading decisions. Others use computerized trading to make all trading decisions. Examples of companies with large dealing operations include Deutsche Securities (Germany), RBC Capital Markets (Canada), Nomura (Japan), Timber Hill (U.S.), Knight Securities (U.S.), Goldman Sachs (U.S.), and IG Group plc (U.K.). Almost all investment banks have large dealing operations.

Most dealers also broker orders, and many brokers deal to their customers. Accordingly, practitioners often use the term **broker–dealer** to refer to dealers and brokers. Broker–dealers have a conflict of interest with respect to how they fill their customers' orders. When acting as a broker, they must seek the best price for their customers' orders. When acting as dealers, however, they profit most when they sell to their customers at high prices or buy from their customers at low prices. The problem is most serious when the customer allows the broker–dealer to decide whether to trade the order with another trader or to fill it as a dealer. Consequently, when trading with a broker–dealer, some customers specify how they want their orders filled. They may also trade only with pure agency brokers who do not also deal.

Primary dealers are dealers with whom central banks trade when conducting monetary policy. They buy bills, notes, and bonds when the central banks sell them to decrease the money supply. The dealers then sell these instruments to their clients. Similarly, when the central banks want to increase the money supply, the primary dealers buy these instruments from their clients and sell them to the central banks.

EXAMPLE 1-14 Brokers and Dealers

What characteristic *most likely* distinguishes brokers from dealers?

Solution: Brokers are agents who arrange trades on behalf of their clients. They do not trade with their clients. In contrast, dealers are proprietary traders who trade with their clients.

4.3. Securitizers

Banks and investment companies create new financial products when they buy and repackage securities or other assets. For example, mortgage banks commonly originate hundreds or thousands of residential mortgages by lending money to homeowners. They then place the mortgages in a pool and sell shares of the pool to investors as mortgage pass-through securities, which are also known as mortgage-backed securities. All payments of principal and interest are passed through to the investors each month, after deducting the costs of servicing the mortgages. Investors who purchase these pass-through securities obtain securities that in aggregate have the same net cash flows and associated risks as the pool of mortgages.

The process of buying assets, placing them in a pool, and then selling securities that represent ownership of the pool is called securitization.

Mortgage-backed securities have the advantage that default losses and early repayments are much more predictable for a diversified portfolio of mortgages than they are for individual mortgages. They are also attractive to investors who cannot efficiently service mortgages but wish to invest in mortgages. By securitizing mortgage pools, the mortgage banks allow investors who are not large enough to buy hundreds of mortgages to obtain the benefits of diversification and economies of scale in loan servicing.

Securitization greatly improves liquidity in the mortgage markets because it allows investors in the pass-through securities to buy mortgages indirectly that they otherwise would not buy. Because the financial risks associated with mortgage-backed securities (debt securities with specified claims on the cash flows of a portfolio of mortgages) are much more predictable than those of individual mortgages, mortgage-backed securities are easier to price and thus easier to sell when investors need to raise cash. These characteristics make the market for mortgage-backed securities much more liquid than the market for individual mortgages. Because investors value liquidity—the ability to sell when they want to—they will pay more for securitized mortgages than for individual mortgages. The homeowners benefit because higher mortgage prices imply lower interest rates.

The mortgage bank is a financial intermediary because it connects investors who want to buy mortgages to homeowners who want to borrow money. The homeowners sell mortgages to the bank when the bank lends them money.

Some mortgage banks form mortgage pools from mortgages that they buy from other banks that originate the loans. These mortgage banks are also financial intermediaries because they connect sellers of mortgages to buyers of mortgage-backed securities. Although the sellers of the mortgages are the originating lenders and not the borrowers, the benefits of creating liquid mortgage-backed securities ultimately flow back to the borrowers.

The creation of the pass-through securities generally takes place on the accounts of the mortgage bank. The bank buys mortgages and sells pass-through securities whose values depend on the mortgage pool. The mortgages appear on the bank's accounts as assets and the mortgage-backed securities appear as liabilities.

In many securitizations, the financial intermediary avoids placing the assets and liabilities on its balance sheet by setting up a special corporation or trust that buys the assets and issues the securities. Those corporations and trusts are called **special purpose vehicles** (SPVs) or alternatively **special purpose entities** (SPEs). Conducting a securitization through a special purpose vehicle is advantageous to investors because their interests in the asset pool are better protected in an SPV than they would be on the balance sheet of the financial intermediary if the financial intermediary were to go bankrupt.

Financial intermediaries securitize many assets. Besides mortgages, banks securitize car loans, credit card receivables, bank loans, and airplane leases, to name just a few assets. As a class, these securities are called asset-backed securities.

When financial intermediaries securitize assets, they often create several classes of securities, called tranches, that have different rights to the cash flows from the asset pool. The tranches are structured so that some produce more predictable cash flows than do others. The senior tranches have first rights to the cash flow from the asset pool. Because the overall risk of a given asset pool cannot be changed, the more junior tranches bear a disproportionate share of the risk of the pool. Practitioners often call the most junior tranche toxic waste because it is so risky. The complexity associated with slicing asset pools into tranches can make the resulting securities difficult to value. Mistakes in valuing these securities contributed to the financial crisis that started in 2007.

Investment companies also create pass-through securities based on investment pools. For example, an exchange-traded fund is an asset-backed security that represents ownership in the securities and contracts held by the fund. The shareholders benefit from the securitization because they can buy or sell an entire portfolio in a single transaction. Because the transaction cost savings are quite substantial, exchange-traded funds often trade in very liquid markets. The investment companies (and sometimes the arbitrageurs) that create exchange-traded funds are financial intermediaries because they connect the buyers of the funds to the sellers of the assets that make up the fund portfolios.

More generally, the creators of all pooled investment vehicles are financial intermediaries that transform portfolios of securities and contracts into securities that represent undivided ownership of the portfolios. The investors in these funds thus indirectly invest in the securities held by the fund. They benefit from the expertise of the investment manager and from obtaining a portfolio that may be more diversified than one they might otherwise be able to hold.

4.4. Depository Institutions and Other Financial Corporations

Depository institutions include commercial banks, savings and loan banks, credit unions, and similar institutions that raise funds from depositors and other investors and lend it to borrowers. The banks give their depositors interest and transaction services, such as check writing and check cashing, in exchange for using their money. They may also raise funds by selling bonds or equity in the bank.

These banks are financial intermediaries because they transfer funds from their depositors and investors to their borrowers. The depositors and investors benefit because they obtain a return (in interest, transaction services, dividends, or capital appreciation) on their funds without having to contract with the borrowers and manage their loans. The borrowers benefit because they obtain the funds that they need without having to search for investors who will trust them to repay their loans.

Many other financial corporations provide credit services. For example, acceptance corporations, discount corporations, payday advance corporations, and factors provide credit to borrowers by lending them money secured by such assets as consumer loans, machinery, future paychecks, or accounts receivables. They finance these loans by selling commercial paper, bonds, and shares to investors. These corporations are intermediaries because they connect investors to borrowers. The investors obtain investments secured by a diversified portfolio of loans while the borrowers obtain funds without having to search for investors.

Brokers also act as financial intermediaries when they lend funds to clients who want to buy securities on margin. They generally obtain the funds from other clients who deposit them in their accounts. Brokers who provide these services to hedge funds and other similar institutions are called prime brokers.

Banks, financial corporations, and brokers can only raise money from depositors and other lenders because their equity owners retain residual interests in the performance of the loans that they make. If the borrowers default, the depositors and other lenders have priority claims over the equity owners. If insufficient money is collected from the borrowers, shareholders' equity is used to pay their depositors and other lenders. The risk of losing capital focuses the equity owners' and management's attention so that credit is not offered foolishly.

Because the ability of these companies to cover their credit losses is limited by the capital that their owners invest in them, the depositors and other investors who lend them money pay close attention to how much money the owners have at risk. For example, if a finance corporation is poorly capitalized, its shareholders will lose little if its clients default on the loans that the finance corporation makes to them. In that case, the finance corporation will have little incentive to lend only to creditworthy borrowers and to effectively manage collection on those loans once they have been made. Worse, it may even choose to lend to borrowers with poor credit because the interest rates that they can charge such borrowers are higher. Until those loans default, the higher income will make the corporation appear to be more profitable than it actually is. Depositors and other investors are aware of these problems and generally pay close attention to them. Accordingly, poorly capitalized financial institutions cannot easily borrow money to finance their operations at favorable rates.

Depository banks and financial corporations are similar to securitized asset pools that issue pass-through securities. Their depositors and investors own securities that ultimately are backed by an asset pool consisting of their loan portfolios. The depositors generally hold the most senior tranche, followed by the other creditors. The shareholders hold the most junior tranche. In the event of bankruptcy, they are paid only if everyone else is paid.

EXAMPLE 1-15 Commercial Banks

What services do commercial banks provide that make them financial intermediaries?

Solution: Commercial banks collect deposits from investors and lend them to borrowers. They are intermediaries because they connect lenders to borrowers. Commercial banks also provide transaction services that make it easier for the banks' depository customers to pay bills and collect funds from their own customers.

4.5. Insurance Companies

Insurance companies help people and companies offset risks that concern them. They do this by creating insurance contracts (policies) that provide a payment in the event that some loss occurs. The insured buy these contracts to hedge against potential losses. Common examples of insurance contracts include auto, fire, life, liability, medical, theft, and disaster insurance contracts.

Credit default swaps are also insurance contracts, but historically they have not been subject to the same reserve requirements that most governments apply to more traditional insurance contracts. They may be sold by insurance companies or by other financial entities, such as investment banks or hedge funds.

Insurance contracts transfer risk from those who buy the contracts to those who sell them. Although insurance companies occasionally broker trades between the insured and the insurer, they more commonly provide the insurance themselves. In that case, the insurance company's owners and creditors become the indirect insurers of the risks that the insurance company assumes. Insurance companies also often transfer risks that they do not wish to bear by buying reinsurance policies from reinsurers.

Insurers are financial intermediaries because they connect the buyers of their insurance contracts with investors, creditors, and reinsurers who are willing to bear the insured risks. The buyers benefit because they can easily obtain the risk transfers that they seek without searching for entities that would be willing to assume those risks.

The owners, creditors, and reinsurers of the insurance company benefit because the company allows them to sell their tolerance for risk easily without having to manage the insurance contracts. Instead, the company manages the relationships with the insured—primarily collections and claims—and hopefully controls the various problems—fraud, moral hazard, and adverse selection—that often plague insurance markets. Fraud occurs when people deliberately cause or falsely report losses to collect on insurance. Moral hazard occurs when people are less careful about avoiding insured losses than they would be if they were not insured so that losses occur more often than they would otherwise. Adverse selection occurs when only those who are most at risk buy insurance so that insured losses tend to be greater than average.

Everyone benefits because insurance companies hold large diversified portfolios of policies. Loss rates for well-diversified portfolios of insurance contracts are much more predictable than for single contracts. For such contracts as auto insurance in which losses are almost uncorrelated across policies, diversification ensures that the financial performance of a large portfolio of contracts will be quite predictable and so holding the portfolio will not be very risky. The insured benefit because they do not have to pay the insurers much to compensate them for bearing risk (the expected loss is quite predictable so the risk is relatively low). Instead, their insurance premiums primarily reflect the expected loss rate in the portfolio plus the costs of running and financing the company.

4.6. Arbitrageurs

Arbitrageurs trade when they can identify opportunities to buy and sell identical or essentially similar instruments at different prices in different markets. They profit when they can buy in one market for less than they sell in another market. Arbitrageurs are financial intermediaries because they connect buyers in one market to sellers in another market.

The purest form of arbitrage involves buying and selling the same instrument in two different markets. Arbitrageurs who do such trades sell to buyers in one market and buy from sellers in the other market. They provide liquidity to the markets because they make it easier for buyers and sellers to trade when and where they want to trade.

Because dealers and arbitrageurs both provide liquidity to other traders, they compete with each other. The dealers connect buyers and sellers who arrive in the same market at different times whereas the arbitrageurs connect buyers and sellers who arrive at the same time in different markets. In practice, traders who profit from offering liquidity rarely are purely dealers or purely arbitrageurs. Instead, most traders attempt to identify and exploit every opportunity they can to manage their inventories profitably.

If information about prices is readily available to market participants, pure arbitrages involving the same instrument will be quite rare. Traders who are well informed about market conditions usually route their orders to the market offering the best price so that arbitrageurs will have few opportunities to match traders across markets when they want to trade the exact same instrument.

Arbitrageurs often trade securities or contracts whose values depend on the same underlying factors. For example, dealers in equity option contracts often sell call options in the contract market and buy the underlying shares in the stock market. Because the values of the call options and of the underlying shares are closely correlated (the value of the call increases with the value of the shares), the long stock position hedges the risk in the short call position so that the dealer's net position is not too risky.

Similar to the pure arbitrage that involves the same instrument in different markets, these arbitrage trades connect buyers in one market to sellers in another market. In this case, however, the buyers and sellers are interested in different instruments whose values are closely related. In the example, the buyer is interested in buying a call options contract, the value of which is a nonlinear function of the value of the underlying stock; the seller is interested in selling the underlying stock.

Options dealers buy stock and sell calls when calls are overpriced relative to the underlying stocks. They use complicated financial models to value options in relation to underlying stock values, and they use financial engineering techniques to control the risk of their portfolios. Successful arbitrageurs must know valuation relations well and they must manage the risk in their portfolios well to trade profitably. They profit by buying the relatively undervalued instrument and selling the relatively overvalued instrument.

Buying a risk in one form and selling it another form involves a process called replication. Arbitrageurs use various trading strategies to replicate the returns to securities and contracts. If they can substantially replicate those returns, they can use the replication trading strategy to offset the risk of buying or selling the actual securities and contracts. The combined effect of their trading is to transform risk from one form to another. This process allows them to create or eliminate contracts in response to the excess demand for, and supply of, contracts.

For example, when traders want to buy more call contracts than are presently available, they push the call contract prices up so that calls become overvalued relative to the underlying stock. The arbitrageurs replicate calls by using a particular financial engineering strategy to buy the underlying stock, and then create the desired call option contracts by selling them short. In contrast, if more calls have been created than traders want to hold, call prices will fall so that calls become undervalued relative to the underlying stock. The arbitrageurs will trade stocks and contracts to absorb the excess contracts. Arbitrageurs who use these strategies are financial intermediaries because they connect buyers and sellers who want to trade the same underlying risks but in different forms.

EXAMPLE 1-16 Dealers and Arbitrageurs

With respect to providing liquidity to market participants, what characteristics most clearly distinguish dealers from arbitrageurs?

Solution: Dealers provide liquidity to buyers and sellers who arrive at the same market at different times. They move liquidity through time. Arbitrageurs provide liquidity to buyers and sellers who arrive at different markets at the same time. They move liquidity across markets.

4.7. Settlement and Custodial Services

In addition to connecting buyers to sellers through a variety of direct and indirect means, financial intermediaries also help their customers settle their trades and ensure that the resulting positions are not stolen or pledged more than once as collateral.

Clearinghouses arrange for final settlement of trades. In futures markets, they guarantee contract performance. In other markets, they may act only as escrow agents, transferring money from the buyer to the seller while transferring securities from the seller to the buyer.

The members of a clearinghouse are the only traders for whom the clearinghouse will settle trades. To ensure that their members settle the trades that they present to the clearinghouse, clearinghouses require that their members have adequate capital and post-performance bonds (margins). Clearinghouses also limit the aggregate net (buy minus sell) quantities that their members can settle.

Brokers and dealers who are not members of the clearinghouse must arrange to have a clearinghouse member settle their trades. To ensure that the nonmember brokers and dealers can settle their trades, clearinghouse members require that their customers (the nonmember brokers and dealers) have adequate capital and postmargins. They also limit the aggregate net quantities that their customers can settle and they monitor their customers' trading to ensure that they do not arrange trades that they cannot settle.

Brokers and dealers similarly monitor the trades made by their retail and institutional customers, and regulate their customers to ensure that they do not arrange trades that they cannot settle.

This hierarchical system of responsibility generally ensures that traders settle their trades. The brokers and dealers guarantee settlement of the trades they arrange for their retail and institutional customers. The clearinghouse members guarantee settlement of the trades that their customers present to them, and clearinghouses guarantee settlement of all trades presented to them by their members. If a clearinghouse member fails to settle a trade, the clearinghouse settles the trade using its own capital or capital drafted from the other members.

Reliable settlement of all trades is extremely important to a well-functioning financial system because it allows strangers to confidently contract with each other without worrying too much about counterparty risk, the risk that their counterparties will not settle their trades. A secure clearinghouse system thus greatly increases liquidity because it greatly increases the number of counterparties with whom a trader can safely arrange a trade.

In many national markets, clearinghouses clear all securities trades so that traders can trade securities through any exchange, broker, alternative trading system, or dealer. These clearinghouse systems promote competition among these exchange service providers.

In contrast, most futures exchanges have their own clearinghouses. These clearinghouses usually will not accept trades arranged away from their exchanges so that a competing exchange cannot trade another exchange's contracts. Competing exchanges may create similar contracts, but moving traders from one established market to a new market is extraordinarily difficult because traders prefer to trade where other traders trade.

Depositories or custodians hold securities on behalf of their clients. These services, which are often offered by banks, help prevent the loss of securities through fraud, oversight, or natural disaster. Broker–dealers also often hold securities on behalf of their customers so that the customers do not have to hold the securities in certificate form. To avoid problems with lost certificates, securities increasingly are issued only in electronic form.

EXAMPLE 1-17 Financial Intermediaries

As a relatively new member of the business community, you decide it would be advantageous to join the local lunch club to network with businesspeople. Upon learning that you are a financial analyst, club members soon enlist you to give a lunch speech. During the question and answer session afterward, a member of the audience asks, "I keep reading in the newspaper about the need to regulate 'financial intermediaries,' but really don't understand exactly what they are. Can you tell me?" How do you answer?

Solution: Financial intermediaries are companies that help their clients achieve their financial goals. They are called intermediaries because, in some way or another, they stand between two or more people who would like to trade with each other, but for various reasons find it difficult to do so directly. The intermediary arranges the trade for them, or more often, trades with both sides.

For example, a commercial bank is an intermediary that connects investors with money to borrowers who need money. The investors buy certificates of deposit from the bank, buy bonds or stock issued by the bank, or simply are depositors in the bank. The borrowers borrow this money from the bank when they arrange loans. Without the bank's intermediation, the investors would have to find trustworthy borrowers themselves, which would be difficult, and the borrowers would have to find trusting lenders, which would also be difficult.

Similarly, an insurance company is an intermediary because it connects customers who want to insure risks with investors who are willing to bear those risks. The investors own shares or bonds issued by the insurance company, or they have sold reinsurance contracts to the insurance company. The insured benefit because they can more easily buy a policy from an insurance company than they can find counterparties who would be willing to bear their risks. The investors benefit because the insurance company creates a diversified portfolio of risks by selling insurance to thousands or millions of customers. Diversification ensures that the net risk borne by the insurance company and its investors will be predictable and thus financially manageable.

In both cases, the financial intermediary also manages the relationships with its customers and investors so that neither side has to worry about the creditworthiness or trustworthiness of its counterparties. For example, the bank manages credit quality and collections on its loans and the insurance company manages risk exposure and collections on its policies. These services benefit both sides by reducing the costs of connecting investors to borrowers or of insured to insurers.

These are only two examples of financial intermediation. Many others involve firms engaged in brokerage, dealing, arbitrage, securitization, investment management, and the clearing and settlement of trades. In all cases, the financial intermediary stands between a buyer and a seller, offering them services that allow them to better achieve their financial goals in a cost effective and efficient manner.

4.8. Summary

By facilitating transactions among buyers and sellers, financial intermediaries provide services essential to a well-functioning financial system. They facilitate transactions in the following ways:

1. Brokers, exchanges, and various alternative trading systems match buyers and sellers interested in trading the same instrument at the same place and time. These financial intermediaries specialize in discovering and organizing information about who wants to trade.
2. Dealers and arbitrageurs connect buyers to sellers interested in trading the same instrument but who are not present at the same place and time. Dealers connect buyers to sellers who are present at the same place but at different times whereas arbitrageurs connect buyers to sellers who are present at the same time but in different places. These financial intermediaries trade for their own accounts when providing these services. Dealers buy or sell with one client and hope to do the offsetting transaction later with another client. Arbitrageurs buy from a seller in one market while simultaneously selling to a buyer in another market.
3. Many financial intermediaries create new instruments that depend on the cash flows and associated financial risks of other instruments. The intermediaries provide these services when they securitize assets, manage investment funds, operate banks and other finance corporations that offer investments to investors and loans to borrowers, and operate insurance companies that pool risks. The instruments that they create generally are more attractive to their clients than the instruments on which they are based. The new instruments also may be differentiated to appeal to diverse clienteles. Their efforts connect buyers of one or more instruments to sellers of other instruments, all of which in aggregate provide the same cash flows and risk exposures. Financial intermediaries thus effectively arrange trades among traders who otherwise would not trade with each other.
4. Arbitrageurs who conduct arbitrage among securities and contracts whose values depend on common factors convert risk from one form to another. Their trading connects buyers and sellers who want to trade similar risks expressed in different forms.
5. Banks, clearinghouses, and depositories provide services that ensure traders settle their trades and that the resulting positions are not stolen or pledged more than once as collateral.

5. POSITIONS

People generally solve their financial and risk management problems by taking positions in various assets or contracts. A **position** in an asset is the quantity of the instrument that an entity owns or owes. A portfolio consists of a set of positions. (See Exhibit 1-1.)

People have **long positions** when they own assets or contracts. Examples of long positions include ownership of stocks, bonds, currencies, contracts, commodities, or real assets. Long positions benefit from an appreciation in the prices of the assets or contracts owned.

People have **short positions** when they have sold assets that they do not own, or when they write and sell contracts. Short positions benefit from a decrease in the prices of the assets or contracts sold. Short sellers profit by selling at high prices and repurchasing at lower prices. Information-motivated traders sell assets and contract short positions when they believe that prices will fall.

Hedgers also often sell instruments short. They short securities and contracts when the financial risks inherent in the instruments are positively correlated with the risks to which they are exposed. For example, to hedge the risk associated with holding copper inventories, a wire manufacturer would sell short copper futures. If the price of copper falls, the manufacturer will lose on his copper inventories but gain on his short futures position. (If the risk in an instrument is inversely correlated with a risk to which hedgers are exposed, the hedgers will hedge with long positions.)

Contracts have long sides and short sides. The long side of a forward or futures contract is the side that will take physical delivery or its cash equivalent. The short side of such contracts is the side that is liable for the delivery. The long side of a futures contract increases in value when the value of the underlying asset increases in value.

The identification of the two sides can be confusing for option contracts. The long side of an option contract is the side that holds the right to exercise the option. The short side is the side that must satisfy the obligation. Practitioners say that the long side *holds* the option and the short side *writes* the option, so the long side is the holder and the short side is the writer. The put contracts are the source of the potential confusion. The put contract holder has the right to sell the underlying to the writer. The holder will benefit if the price of the underlying falls, in which case the price of the put contract will rise. The holder is long the put contract and has an indirect short position in the underlying instrument. Analysts call the indirect short position short exposure to the underlying. The put contract holders have long exposure to their option contract and short exposure to the underlying instrument.

EXHIBIT 1-1 Option Positions and Their Associated Underlying Risk Exposures

Type of Option	Option Position	Exposure to Underlying Risk
Call	Long	Long
Call	Short	Short
Put	Long	Short
Put	Short	Long

The identification of the long side in a swap contract is often arbitrary because swap contracts call for the exchange of contractually determined cash flows rather than for the purchase (or the cash equivalent) of some underlying instrument. In general, the side that benefits from an increase in the quoted price is the long side.

The identification of the long side in currency contracts also may be confusing. In this case, the confusion stems from symmetry in the contracts. The buyer of one currency is the seller of the other currency, and vice versa for the seller. Thus, a long forward position in one currency is a short forward position in the other currency. When practitioners describe a position, they generally will say, "I'm long the dollar against the yen," which means they have bought dollars and sold yen.

5.1. Short Positions

Short sellers create short positions in contracts by selling contracts that they do not own. In a sense, they become the issuers of the contract when they create the liabilities associated with their contracts. This analogy will also help you better understand risk when you study corporate finance: Corporations create short positions in their bonds when they issue bonds in exchange for cash. Although bonds are generally considered to be securities, they are also contracts between the issuer and the bondholder.

Short sellers create short positions in securities by borrowing securities from security lenders who are long holders. The short sellers then sell the borrowed securities to other traders. Short sellers close their positions by repurchasing the securities and returning them to the security lenders. If the securities drop in value, the short sellers profit because they repurchase the securities at lower prices than the prices at which they sold the securities. If the securities rise in value, they will lose. Short sellers who buy to close their positions are said to cover their positions.

The potential gains in a long position generally are unbounded. For example, the stock prices of such highly successful companies as Yahoo! have increased more than 50-fold since they were first publicly traded. The potential losses on long positions, however, are limited to no more than 100 percent—a complete loss—for long positions without any associated liabilities.

In contrast, the potential gains on a short position are limited to no more than 100 percent whereas the potential losses are unbounded. The unbounded potential losses on short positions make short positions very risky in volatile instruments. For example, if you shorted 100 shares of Yahoo! in July 1996 at $20 and you kept your position open for four years, you would have lost $148,000 on your $2,000 initial short position. During this period, Yahoo! rose 75-fold to $1,500 on a split-adjusted equivalent basis.

Although security lenders generally believe that they are long the securities that they lend, in fact, they do not actually own the securities during the periods of their loans. Instead, they own promises made by the short sellers to return the securities. These promises are memorialized in security lending agreements. These agreements specify that the short sellers will pay the long sellers all dividends or interest that they otherwise would have received had they not lent their securities. These payments are called payments-in-lieu of dividends (or of interest), and they may have different tax treatments than actual dividends and interest. The security lending agreements also protect the lenders in the event of a stock split.

To secure the security loans, lenders require that the short seller leave the proceeds of the short sale on deposit with them as collateral for the stock loan. They invest the collateral in short-term securities, and they rebate the interest to the short sellers at rates called short rebate rates. The short rebate rates are determined in the market and generally are available only to institutional short-sellers and some large retail traders. If a security is hard to borrow, the rebate rate may be very small or even negative. Such securities are said to be "on special." Otherwise, the rebate rate is usually 10 basis points less than the overnight rate in the interbank funds market. Most security lending agreements require various margin payments to keep the credit risk among the parties from growing when prices change.

Securities lenders lend their securities because the short rebate rates they pay on the collateral are lower than the interest rates they receive from investing the collateral. The difference is because of the implicit loan fees that they receive from the borrowers for borrowing the stock. The difference also compensates lenders for risks that the lenders take when investing the collateral and for the risk that the borrowers will default if prices rise significantly.

EXAMPLE 1-18 Short Positions in Securities and Contracts

How is the process of short selling shares of Siemens different from that of short selling a Siemens equity call option contract?

Solution: To short sell shares of Siemens, the seller (or his broker) must borrow the shares from a long holder so that he can deliver them to the buyer. To short sell a Siemens equity call option contract, the seller simply creates the contract when he sells it to the buyer.

5.2. Levered Positions

In many markets, traders can buy securities by borrowing some of the purchase price. They usually borrow the money from their brokers. The borrowed money is called the **margin loan**, and they are said to buy on margin. The interest rate that the buyers pay for their margin loan is called the **call money rate**. The call money rate is above the government bill rate and is negotiable. Large buyers generally obtain more favorable rates than do retail buyers. For institutional-size buyers, the call money rate is quite low because the loans are generally well secured by securities held as collateral by the lender.

Trader's equity is that portion of the security price that the buyer must supply. Traders who buy securities on margin are subject to minimum margin requirements. The **initial margin requirement** is the minimum fraction of the purchase price that must be trader's equity. This requirement may be set by the government, the exchange, or the exchange clearinghouse. For example, in the United States, the Federal Reserve Board sets the initial margin requirement through Regulation T. In Hong Kong, the Securities and Futures Commission sets the margin requirements. In all markets, brokers often require more equity than the government-required minimum from their clients when lending to them.

Many markets allow brokers to lend their clients more money if the brokers use risk models to measure and control the overall risk of their clients' portfolios. This system is called portfolio margining.

Buying securities on margin can greatly increase the potential gains or losses for a given amount of equity in a position because the trader can buy more securities on margin than he could otherwise. The buyer thus earns greater profits when prices rise and suffers greater losses when prices fall. The relation between risk and borrowing is called **financial leverage** (often simply called leverage). Traders leverage their positions when they borrow to buy more securities. A highly leveraged position is large relative to the equity that supports it.

The leverage ratio is the ratio of the value of the position to the value of the equity investment in it. The leverage ratio indicates how many times larger a position is than the equity that supports it. The maximum leverage ratio associated with a position financed by the minimum margin requirement is one divided by the minimum margin requirement. If the requirement is 40 percent, then the maximum leverage ratio is $2.5 = 100\%$ position $\div$ 40% equity.

The leverage ratio indicates how much more risky a leveraged position is relative to an unleveraged position. For example, if a stock bought on 40 percent margin rises 10 percent, the buyer will experience a 25 percent (2.5 × 10%) return on the equity investment in her leveraged position. But if the stock falls by 10 percent, the return on the equity investment will be −25 percent (before the interest on the margin loan and before payment of commissions).

Financial analysts must be able to compute the total return to the equity investment in a leveraged position. The total return depends on the price change of the purchased security, the dividends or interest paid by the security, the interest paid on the margin loan, and the commissions paid to buy and sell the security. The following example illustrates the computation of the total return to a leveraged purchase of stock that pays a dividend.

EXAMPLE 1-19 Computing Total Return to a Leveraged Stock Purchase

A buyer buys stock on margin and holds the position for exactly one year, during which time the stock pays a dividend. For simplicity, assume that the interest on the loan and the dividend are both paid at the end of the year.

Purchase price	$20/share
Sale price	$15/share
Shares purchased	1,000
Leverage ratio	2.5
Call money rate	5%
Dividend	$0.10/share
Commission	$0.01/share

1. What is the total return on this investment?
2. Why is the loss greater than the 25 percent decrease in the market price?

Solution to 1: To find the return on this investment, first determine the initial equity and then determine the equity remaining after the sale. The total purchase price is $20,000. The leverage ratio of 2.5 indicates that the buyer's equity financed 40 percent = (1 ÷ 2.5) of the purchase price. Thus, the equity investment is $8,000 = 40% of $20,000. The $12,000 remainder is borrowed. The actual investment is slightly higher because the buyer must pay a commission of $10 = $0.01/share × 1,000 shares to buy the stock. The total initial investment is $8,010.

At the end of the year, the stock price has declined by $5/share. The buyer lost $5,000 = $5/share × 1,000 shares as a result of the price change. In addition, the buyer has to pay interest at 5 percent on the $12,000 loan, or $600. The buyer also receives a dividend of $0.10/share, or $100. The trader's equity remaining after the sale is computed from the initial equity investment as follows:

Initial investment	$8,010
Purchase commission	−10
Trading gains/losses	−5,000
Margin interest paid	−600
Dividends received	100
Sales commission paid	−10
Remaining equity	$2,490

or

Proceeds on sale	$15,000
Payoff loan	−12,000
Margin interest paid	−600
Dividends received	100
Sales commission paid	−10
Remaining equity	$2,490

so that the return on the initial investment of $8,010 is (2,490 − 8,010)/8,010 = −68.9%.

Solution to 2: The realized loss is substantially greater than the stock price return of ($15 − $20)/$20 = −25%. Most of the difference is because of the leverage, with the remainder primarily the result of the interest paid on the loan. Based on the leverage alone and ignoring the other cash flows, we would expect that the return on the equity would be −62.5% = 2.5 leverage times the –25% stock price return.

In the preceding example, if the stock dropped more than the buyer's original 40 percent margin (ignoring commissions, interest, and dividends), the trader's equity would have become negative. In that case, the investor would owe his broker more than the stock is worth. Brokers often lose money in such situations if the buyer does not repay the loan out of other funds.

To prevent such losses, brokers require that margin buyers always have a minimum amount of equity in their positions. This minimum is called the **maintenance margin requirement**. It is usually 25 percent of the current value of the position, but it may be higher or lower depending on the volatility of the instrument and the policies of the broker.

If the value of the equity falls below the maintenance margin requirement, the buyer will receive a **margin call**, or request for additional equity. If the buyer does not deposit additional equity with the broker in a timely manner, the broker will close the position to prevent further losses and thereby secure repayment of the margin loan.

When you buy securities on margin, you must know the price at which you will receive a margin call if prices drop. The answer to this question depends on your initial equity and on the maintenance margin requirement.

EXAMPLE 1-20 Margin Call Price

A trader buys stock on margin posting 40 percent of the initial stock price of $20 as equity. The maintenance margin requirement for the position is 25 percent. At what price will a margin call occur?

Solution: The trader's initial equity is 40 percent of the initial stock price of $20, or $8 per share. Subsequent changes in equity per share are equal to the share price change so that equity per share is equal to $8+(P – 20) where P is the current share price. The margin call takes place when equity drops below the 25 percent maintenance margin requirement. The price at which a margin call will take place is the solution to the following equation:

$$\frac{\text{Equity/share}}{\text{Price/share}} = \frac{\$8 + P - 20}{P} = 25\%$$

which occurs at $P = 16$. When the price drops to $16, the equity will be worth $4/share, which will be exactly 25 percent of the price.

Traders who sell securities short are also subject to margin requirements because they have borrowed securities. Initially, the trader's equity supporting the short position must be at least equal to the margin requirement times the initial value of the short position. If prices rise, equity will be lost. At some point, the short seller will have to contribute additional equity to meet the maintenance margin requirement. Otherwise, the broker will buy the security back to cover the short position to prevent further losses and thereby secure repayment of the stock loan.

6. ORDERS

Buyers and sellers communicate with the brokers, exchanges, and dealers that arrange their trades by issuing **orders**. All orders specify what instrument to trade, how much to trade, and whether to buy or sell. Most orders also have other instructions attached to them. These additional instructions may include execution instructions, validity instructions, and clearing instructions. **Execution instructions** indicate how to fill the order, **validity instructions** indicate when the order may be filled, and **clearing instructions** indicate how to arrange the final settlement of the trade.

In this section, we introduce various order instructions and explain how traders use them to achieve their objectives. We discuss execution mechanisms—how exchanges, brokers, and dealers fill orders—in the next section. To understand the concepts in this section, however, you need to know a little about order execution mechanisms.

In most markets, dealers and various other proprietary traders often are willing to buy from, or sell to, other traders seeking to sell or buy. The prices at which they are willing to buy are called **bid** prices and those at which they are willing to sell are called **ask** prices, or sometimes offer prices. The ask prices are invariably higher than the bid prices.

The traders who are willing to trade at various prices may also indicate the quantities that they will trade at those prices. These quantities are called **bid sizes** and **ask sizes**, depending on whether they are attached to bids or offers.

Practitioners say that the traders who offer to trade *make a market*. Those who trade with them *take the market*.

The highest bid in the market is the **best bid**, and the lowest ask in the market is the **best offer**. The difference between the best bid and the best offer is the **market bid–ask spread**. When traders ask, "What's the market?" they want to know the best bid and ask prices and their associated sizes. Bid–ask spreads are an implicit cost of trading. Markets with small bid–ask spreads are markets in which the costs of trading are small, at least for the sizes quoted. Dealers often quote both bid and ask prices, and in that case, practitioners say that they quote a two-sided market. The market spread is never more than any dealer spread.

6.1. Execution Instructions

Market and limit orders convey the most common execution instructions. A **market order** instructs the broker or exchange to obtain the best price immediately available when filling the order. A **limit order** conveys almost the same instruction: Obtain the best price immediately available, but in no event accept a price higher than a specified limit price when buying or accept a price lower than a specified limit price when selling.

Many people mistakenly believe that limit orders specify the prices at which the orders will trade. Although limit orders do often trade at their limit prices, remember that the first instruction is to obtain the best price available. If better prices are available than the limit price, brokers and exchanges should obtain those prices for their clients.

Market orders generally execute immediately if other traders are willing to take the other side of the trade. The main drawback with market orders is that they can be expensive to execute, especially when the order is placed in a market for a thinly traded security, or more generally, when the order is large relative to the normal trading activity in the market. In that case, a market buy order may fill at a high price, or a market sell order may fill at a low price if no traders are willing to trade at better prices. High purchase prices and low sale prices represent price concessions given to other traders to encourage them to take the other side of the trade. Because the sizes of price concessions can be difficult to predict, and because prices often change between when a trader submits an order and when the order finally fills, the execution prices for market orders are often uncertain.

Buyers and sellers who are concerned about the possibility of trading at unacceptable prices add limit price instructions to their orders. The main problem with limit orders is that they may not execute. Limit orders do not execute if the limit price on a buy order is too low, or if the limit price on a sell order is too high. For example, if an investment manager submits a limit order to buy at the limit price of 20 (buy limit 20) and nobody is willing to sell at or below 20, the order will not trade. If prices never drop to 20, the manager will never buy. If the price subsequently rises, the manager will have lost the opportunity to profit from the price rise.

Whether traders use market orders or limit orders when trying to arrange trades depends on their concerns about price, trading quickly, and failing to trade. On average, limit orders trade at better prices than do market orders, but they often do not trade. Traders generally regret when their limit orders fail to trade because they usually would have profited if they had traded. Limit buy orders do not fill when prices are rising, and limit sell orders do not fill when prices are falling. In both cases, traders would be better off if their orders had filled.

The probability that a limit order will execute depends on where the order is placed relative to market prices. An aggressively priced order is more likely to trade than is a less aggressively priced order. A limit buy order is aggressively priced when the limit price is high relative to the market bid and ask prices. If the limit price is placed above the best offer, the buy order generally will partially or completely fill at the best offer price, depending on the size available at the best offer. Such limit orders are called **marketable limit orders** because at least part of the order can trade immediately. A limit buy order with a very high price relative to the market is essentially a market order.

If the buy order is placed above the best bid but below the best offer, traders say the order makes a new market because it becomes the new best bid. Such orders generally will not immediately trade, but they may attract sellers who are interested in trading. A buy order placed at the best bid is said to make market. It may have to wait until all other buy orders at that price trade first. Finally, a buy order placed below the best bid is **behind the market**. It will not execute unless market prices drop. Traders call limit orders that are waiting to trade **standing limit orders**.

Sell limit orders are aggressively priced if the limit price is low relative to market prices. The limit price of a marketable sell limit order is below the best bid. A limit sell order placed between the best bid and the best offer makes a new market on the sell side, one placed at the best offer makes market, and one placed above the best offer is behind the market.

Exhibit 1-2 presents a simplified **limit order book** in which orders are presented ranked by their limit prices for a hypothetical market. The market is "26 bid, offered at 28" because the best bid is 26 and the best offer (ask) is 28.

EXHIBIT 1-2 Terms Traders Use to Describe Standing Limit Orders

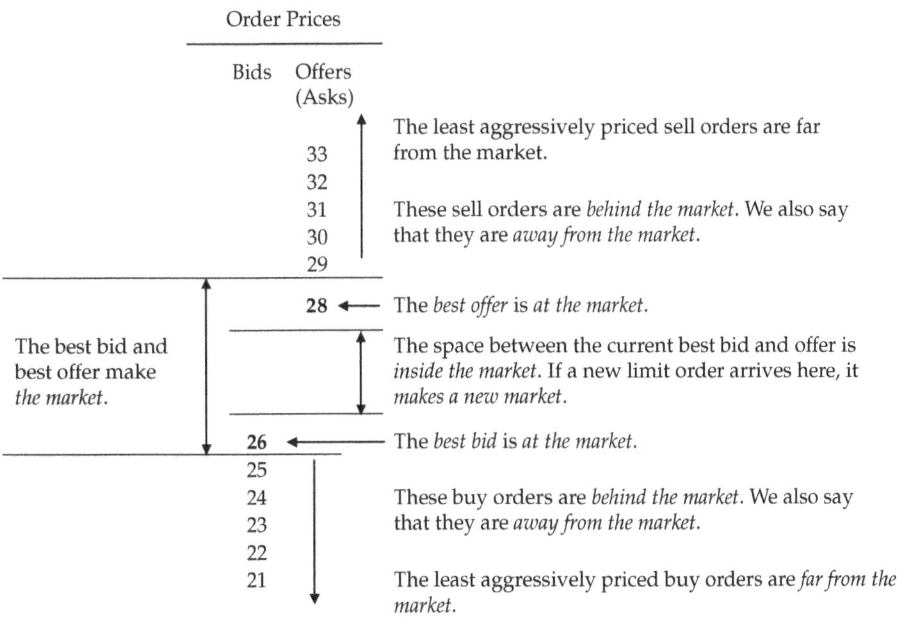

Source: Harris, 2003.

EXAMPLE 1-21 Making and Taking

1. What is the difference between making a market and taking a market?
2. What order types are most likely associated with making a market and taking a market?

Solution to 1: A trader makes a market when the trader offers to trade. A trader takes a market when the trader accepts an offer to trade.

Solution to 2: Traders place standing limit orders to give other traders opportunities to trade. Standing limit orders thus make markets. In contrast, traders use market orders or marketable limit orders to take offers to trade. These marketable orders take the market.

A trade-off exists between how aggressively priced an order is and the ultimate trade price. Although aggressively priced orders fill faster and with more certainty than do less aggressively priced limit orders, the prices at which they execute are inferior. Buyers seeking to trade quickly must pay higher prices to increase the probability of trading quickly. Similarly, sellers seeking to trade quickly must accept lower prices to increase the probability of trading quickly.

Some order execution instructions specify conditions on size. For example, **all-or-nothing orders** (AON) can only trade if their entire sizes can be traded. Traders can similarly specify minimum fill sizes. This specification is common when settlement costs depend on the number of trades made to fill an order and not on the aggregate size of the order.

Exposure instructions indicate whether, how, and perhaps to whom orders should be exposed. **Hidden orders** are exposed only to the brokers or exchanges that receive them. These agencies cannot disclose hidden orders to other traders until they can fill them. Traders use hidden orders when they are afraid that other traders might behave strategically if they knew that a large order was in the market. Traders can discover hidden size only by submitting orders that will trade with that size. Thus, traders can only learn about hidden size after they have committed to trading with it.

Traders also often indicate a specific **display size** for their orders. Brokers and exchanges then expose only the display size for these orders. Any additional size is hidden from the public but can be filled if a suitably large order arrives. Traders sometimes call such orders **iceberg orders** because most of the order is hidden. Traders specify display sizes when they do not want to display their full sizes, but still want other traders to know that someone is willing to trade at the displayed price. Traders on the opposite side who wish to trade additional size at that price can discover the hidden size only if they trade the displayed size, at which point the broker or exchange will display any remaining size up to the display size. They also can discover the hidden size by submitting large orders that will trade with that size.

EXAMPLE 1-22 Market versus Limit and Hidden versus Displayed Orders

You are the buy-side trader for a very clever investment manager. The manager has hired a commercial satellite firm to take regular pictures of the parking lots in which new car dealers store their inventories. It has also hired some part-time workers to count the cars on the lots. With this information and some econometric analyses, the manager can predict weekly new car sale announcements more accurately than can most analysts. The manager typically makes a quarter percent each week on this strategy. Once a week, a day before the announcements are made, the manager gives you large orders to buy or sell car manufacturers based on his insights into their dealers' sales. What primary issues should you consider when deciding whether to:

1. Use market or limit orders to fill his orders?
2. Display the orders or hide them?

Solution to 1: The manager's information is quite perishable. If his orders are not filled before the weekly sales are reported to the public, the manager will lose the opportunity to profit from the information as prices immediately adjust to the news. The manager, therefore, needs to get the orders filled quickly. This consideration suggests that the orders should be submitted as market orders. If submitted as limit orders, the orders might not execute and the firm would lose the opportunity to profit.

Large market orders, however, can be very expensive to execute, especially if few people are willing to trade significant size on the other side of the market. Because transaction costs can easily exceed the expected quarter percent return, you should submit limit orders to limit the execution prices that you are willing to accept. It is better to fail to trade than to trade at losing prices.

Solution to 2: Your large orders could easily move the market if many people were aware of them, and even more so if others were aware that you are trading on behalf of a successful information-motivated trader. You thus should consider submitting hidden orders. The disadvantage of hidden orders is that they do not let people know that they can trade the other side if they want to.

6.2. Validity Instructions

Validity instructions indicate when an order may be filled. The most common validity instruction is the **day order**. A day order is good for the day on which it is submitted. If it has not been filled by the close of business, the order expires unfilled.

Good-till-cancelled orders (GTC) are just that. In practice, most brokers limit how long they will manage an order to ensure that they do not fill orders that their clients have forgotten. Such brokers may limit their GTC orders to a few months.

Immediate or cancel orders (IOC) are good only upon receipt by the broker or exchange. If they cannot be filled in part or in whole, they cancel immediately. In some markets these orders are also known as **fill or kill** orders. When searching for hidden liquidity, electronic algorithmic trading systems often submit thousands of these IOC orders for every order that they fill.

Good-on-close orders can only be filled at the close of trading. These orders often are market orders, so traders call them market-on-close orders. Traders often use on-close orders when they want to trade at the same prices that will be published as the closing prices of the day. Mutual funds often like to trade at such prices because they value their portfolios at closing prices. Many traders also use **good-on-open** orders.

6.2.1. Stop Orders

A **stop order** is an order in which a trader has specified a stop price condition. The stop order may not be filled until the stop price condition has been satisfied. For a sell order, the stop price condition suspends execution of the order until a trade occurs at or below the stop price. After that trade, the stop condition is satisfied and the order becomes valid for execution, subject to all other execution instructions attached to it. If the market price subsequently rises above the sell order's stop price before the order trades, the order remains valid. Similarly, a buy order with a stop condition becomes valid only after a price rises above the specified stop price.

Traders often call stop orders *stop-loss orders* because many traders use them with the hope of stopping losses on positions that they have established. For example, a trader who has bought stock at 40 may want to sell the stock if the price falls below 30. In that case, the trader might submit a "GTC, stop 30, market sell" order. If the price falls to or below 30, the market order becomes valid and it should immediately execute at the best price then available in the market. That price may be substantially lower than 30 if the market is falling quickly. The stop-loss order thus does not guarantee a stop to losses at the stop price. If potential sellers are worried about trading at too low of a price, they can attach stop instructions to limit orders instead of market orders. In this example, if the trader is unwilling to sell below 25, the trader would submit a "GTC, stop 30, limit 25 sell" order.

If a trader wants to guarantee that he can sell at 30, the trader would buy a put option contract struck at 30. The purchase price of the option would include a premium for the insurance that the trader is buying. Option contracts can be viewed as limit orders for which execution is guaranteed at the strike price. A trader similarly might use a stop-buy order or a call option to limit losses on a short position.

A portfolio manager might use a stop-buy order when the manager believes that a security is undervalued but is unwilling to trade without market confirmation. For example, suppose that a stock currently trades for 50 RMB and a manager believes that it should be worth 100 RMB. Further, the manager believes that the stock will much more likely be worth 100 RMB if other traders are willing to buy it above 65 RMB. To best take advantage of this information, the manager would consider issuing a "GTC, stop 65 RMB, limit 100 RMB buy" order. Note that if the manager relies too much on the market when making this trading decision, however, he may violate CFA Standard of Professional Conduct V.A.2, which requires that all investment actions have a reasonable and adequate basis supported by appropriate research and investigation.

Because stop-sell orders become valid when prices are falling and stop-buy orders become valid when prices are rising, traders using stop orders contribute to market momentum as their sell orders push prices down further and their buy orders push prices up. Execution prices for stop orders thus are often quite poor.

EXAMPLE 1-23 Limit and Stop Instructions

In what ways do limit and stop instructions differ?

Solution: Although both limit and stop instructions specify prices, the role that these prices play in the arrangement of a trade are completely different. A limit price places a limit on what trade prices will be acceptable to the trader. A buyer will accept prices only at or lower than the limit price whereas a seller will accept prices only at or above the limit price.

In contrast, a stop price indicates when an order can be filled. A buy order can only be filled once the market has traded at a price at or above the stop price. A sell order can only be filled once the market has traded at a price at or below the stop price.

Both order instructions may delay or prevent the execution of an order. A buy limit order will not execute until someone is willing to sell at or below the limit price. Similarly, a sell limit order will not execute until someone is willing to buy at or above the limit sell price. In contrast, a stop-buy order will not execute if the market price never rises to the stop price. Similarly, a stop-sell order will not execute if the market price never falls to the stop price.

6.3. Clearing Instructions

Clearing instructions tell brokers and exchanges how to arrange final settlement of trades. Traders generally do not attach these instructions to each order—instead they provide them as standing instructions. These instructions indicate what entity is responsible for clearing and settling the trade. For retail trades, that entity is the customer's broker. For institutional trades, that entity may be a custodian or another broker. When a client uses one broker to arrange trades and another broker to settle trades, traders say that the first broker gives up the trade to the other broker, who is often known as the prime broker. Institutional traders provide these instructions so they can obtain specialized execution services from different brokers while maintaining a single account for custodial services and other prime brokerage services, such as margin loans.

An important clearing instruction that must appear on security sale orders is an indication of whether the sale is a long sale or a short sale. In either case, the broker representing the sell order must ensure that the trader can deliver securities for settlement. For a long sale, the broker must confirm that the securities held are available for delivery. For a short sale, the broker must either borrow the security on behalf of the client or confirm that the client can borrow the security.

7. PRIMARY SECURITY MARKETS

When issuers first sell their securities to investors, practitioners say that the trades take place in the primary markets. An issuer makes an **initial public offering** (IPO)—sometimes called a placing—of a security issue when it sells the security to the public for the first time.

A **seasoned security** is a security that an issuer has already issued. If the issuer wants to sell additional units of a previously issued security, it makes a **seasoned offering** (sometimes called a secondary offering). Both types of offerings occur in the primary market where issuers sell their securities to investors. Later, if investors trade these securities among themselves, they trade in secondary markets. This section discusses primary markets and the procedures that issuers use to offer their securities to the public.

7.1. Public Offerings

Corporations generally contract with an investment bank to help them sell their securities to the public. The investment bank then lines up subscribers who will buy the security. Investment bankers call this process **book building**. In London, the book builder is called the book runner. The bank tries to build a book of orders to which they can sell the offering. Investment banks often support their book building by providing investment information and opinion about the issuer to their clients and to the public. Before the offering, the issuer generally makes a very detailed disclosure of its business, of the risks inherent in it, and of the uses to which the new funds will be placed.

When time is of the essence, issuers in Europe may issue securities through an **accelerated book build**, in which the investment bank arranges the offering in only one or two days. Such sales often occur at discounted prices.

The first public offering of common stock in a company consists of newly issued shares to be sold by the company. It may also include shares that the founders and other early investors in the company seek to sell. The initial public offering provides these investors with a means of liquidating their investments.

In an **underwritten offering**—the most common type of offering—the investment bank guarantees the sale of the issue at an offering price that it negotiates with the issuer. If the issue is undersubscribed, the bank will buy whatever securities it cannot sell at the offering price. In the case of an IPO, the underwriter usually also promises to make a market in the security for about a month to ensure that the secondary market will be liquid and to provide price support, if necessary. For large issues, a syndicate of investment banks and broker–dealers helps the lead underwriter build the book. The issuer usually pays an underwriting fee of about 7 percent for these various services. The underwriting fee is a placement cost of the offering.

In a **best efforts offering**, the investment bank acts only as broker. If the offering is undersubscribed, the issuer will not sell as much as it hoped to sell.

For both types of offerings, the issuer and the bank usually jointly set the offering price following a negotiation. If they set a price that buyers consider too high, the offering will be undersubscribed, and they will fail to sell the entire issue. If they set the price too low, the offering will be oversubscribed, in which case the securities are often allocated to preferred clients or on a pro-rata basis.

(Note that CFA Standard of Professional Conduct III.B—fair dealing—requires that the allocation be based on a written policy disclosed to clients and suggests that the securities be offered on a pro-rata basis among all clients who have comparable relationships with their broker–dealers.)

Investment banks have a conflict of interest with respect to the offering price in underwritten offerings. As agents for the issuers, they generally are supposed to select the offering price that will raise the most money. But as underwriters, they have strong incentives to choose a low price. If the price is low, the banks can allocate valuable shares to benefit their clients and thereby indirectly benefit the banks. If the price is too high, the underwriters will have to buy overvalued shares in the offering and perhaps also during the following month if they must support the price in the secondary market, which directly costs the banks. These considerations tend to lower initial offering prices so that prices in the secondary market often rise immediately following an IPO. They are less important in a seasoned offering because trading in the secondary market helps identify the proper price for the offering.

First time issuers generally accept lower offering prices because they and many others believe that an undersubscribed IPO conveys very unfavorable information to the market about the company's prospects at a time when it is most vulnerable to public opinion about its prospects. They fear that an undersubscribed initial public offering will make it substantially harder to raise additional capital in subsequent seasoned offerings.

EXAMPLE 1-24 The Playtech Initial Public Offering

Playtech is a designer, developer, and licensor of software for the gambling industry. On 28 March 2006, Playtech raised approximately £265 million gross through an initial public offering of 103,142,466 ordinary shares at £2.57 per ordinary share. After the initial public offering, Playtech had 213,333,333 ordinary shares issued and outstanding.

Playtech received gross proceeds of approximately £34.3 million and net proceeds of £31.8 million. The ordinary shares that were sold to the public represented approximately 48 percent of Playtech's total issued ordinary shares.

The shares commenced trading at 8:00 A.M. on the AIM market of the London Stock Exchange where Playtech opened at £2.74, traded 37 million shares between £2.68 and £2.74, and closed at £2.73.

1. Approximately how many new shares were issued by the company and how many shares were sold by the company's founders? What fraction of their holdings in the company did the founders sell?
2. Approximately what return did the subscribers who participated in the IPO make on the first day it traded?
3. Approximately how much did Playtech pay in placement costs as a percentage of the new funds raised?

Solution to 1: Playtech received gross proceeds of £34.3 million at £2.57 per share so the company issued and sold 13,346,304 shares (= £34.3 million/£2.57 per share). The total placement was for 103,142,466 shares, so the founders sold 89,796,162 shares (= 103,142,466 shares − 13,346,304 shares). Because approximately 200 million = 213.3 million − 13.3 million shares were outstanding before the placement, the founders sold approximately 45 percent (= 90 million/200 million) of the company.

Solution to 2: The subscribers bought the stock for £2.57 per share and it closed at £2.73. The first day return thus was $6.2\% = \frac{2.73 - 2.57}{2.57} \times 100$.

Solution to 3: Playtech obtained gross proceeds of £34.3 million, but only raised net proceeds of £31.8 million. The £2.5 million difference was the total cost of the placement to the firm, which is 7.9 percent of £31.8 million net proceeds.

7.2. Private Placements and Other Primary Market Transactions

Corporations sometimes issue their securities in private placements. In a **private placement**, corporations sell securities directly to a small group of qualified investors, usually with the assistance of an investment bank. Qualified investors have sufficient knowledge and experience to recognize the risks that they assume, and sufficient wealth to assume those risks responsibly. Most countries allow corporations to do private placements without nearly as much public disclosure as is required for public offerings. Private placements, therefore, may be cheaper than public offerings, but the buyers generally require higher returns (lower purchase prices) because they cannot subsequently trade the securities in an organized secondary market.

Corporations sometimes sell new issues of seasoned securities directly to the public on a piecemeal basis via a shelf registration. In a **shelf registration**, the corporation makes all public disclosures that it would for a regular offering, but it does not sell the shares in a single transaction. Instead, it sells the shares directly into the secondary market over time, generally when it needs additional capital. Shelf registrations provide corporations with flexibility in the timing of their capital transactions, and they can alleviate the downward price pressures often associated with large secondary offerings.

Many corporations may also issue shares via dividend reinvestment plans (DRPs or DRIPs, for short) that allow their shareholders to reinvest their dividends in newly issued shares of the corporation (in particular, DRPs specify that the corporation issue new shares for the plan rather than purchase them on the open market). These plans sometimes also allow existing shareholders and other investors to buy additional stock at a slight discount to current prices.

Finally, corporations can issue new stock via a rights offering. In a rights offering, the corporation distributes rights to buy stock at a fixed price to existing shareholders in proportion to their holdings. Because the rights need not be exercised, they are options. The exercise price, however, is set below the current market price of the stock so that buying stock with the rights is immediately profitable. Consequently, shareholders will experience dilution in the value of their existing shares. They can offset the dilution loss by exercising their rights or by selling the rights to others who will exercise them. Shareholders generally do not like rights offerings because they must provide additional capital (or sell their rights) to avoid losses through dilution. Financial analysts recognize that these securities, although called rights, are actually short-term stock warrants and value them accordingly.

The national governments of financially strong countries generally issue their bonds, notes, and bills in public auctions organized by a government agency (usually associated with the finance ministry). They may also sell them directly to dealers.

Smaller and less financially secure national governments and most regional governments often contract with investment banks to help them sell and distribute their securities. The laws of many governments, however, require that they auction their securities.

EXAMPLE 1-25 Private and Public Placements

In what ways do private placements differ from public placements?

Solution: Issuers make private placements to a limited number of investors who generally are financially sophisticated and well informed about risk. The investors generally have some relationship to the issuer. Issuers make public placements when they sell securities to the general public. Public placements generally require substantially more financial disclosure than do private placements.

7.3. Importance of Secondary Markets to Primary Markets

Corporations and governments can raise money in the primary markets at lower cost when their securities will trade in liquid secondary markets. In a **liquid market**, traders can buy or sell with low transaction costs and small price concessions when they want to trade. Buyers value liquidity because they may need to sell their securities to meet liquidity needs. Investors thus will pay more for securities that they can easily sell than for those that they cannot easily sell. Higher prices translate into lower costs of capital for the issuers.

8. SECONDARY SECURITY MARKET AND CONTRACT MARKET STRUCTURES

Trading is the successful outcome to a bilateral search in which buyers look for sellers and sellers look for buyers. Many market structures have developed to reduce the costs of this search. Markets are liquid when the costs of finding a suitable counterparty to a trade are low.

Trading in securities and contracts takes place in a variety of market structures. The structures differ by when trades can be arranged, who arranges the trades, how they do so, and how traders learn about possible trading opportunities and executed trades. This section introduces the various market structures used to trade securities and contracts. We first consider trading sessions, then execution mechanisms, and finally market information systems.

8.1. Trading Sessions

Markets are organized as call markets or as continuous trading markets. In a **call market**, trades can be arranged only when the market is called at a particular time and place. In contrast in a **continuous trading market**, trades can be arranged and executed any time the market is open.

Buyers can easily find sellers and vice versa in call markets because all traders interested in trading (or orders representing their interests) are present at the same time and place. Call markets thus have the potential to be very liquid when they are called. But they are completely illiquid between trading sessions. In contrast, traders can arrange and execute their trades at any time in continuous trading markets, but doing so can be difficult if the buyers and sellers (or their orders) are not both present at the same time.

Most call markets use single price auctions to match buyers to sellers. In these auctions, the market constructs order books representing all buy orders and all seller orders. The market then chooses a single trade price that will maximize the total volume of trade. The order books are supply and demand schedules, and the point at which they cross determines the trade price.

Call markets usually are organized just once a day, but some markets organize calls at more frequent intervals.

Many continuous trading markets start their trading with a call market auction. During a preopening period, traders submit their orders for the market call. At the opening, any possible trades are arranged and then trading continues in the continuous trading session. Some continuous trading markets also close their trading with a call. In these markets, traders who are only interested in trading in the closing call submit market- or limit-on-close orders.

EXAMPLE 1-26 Call Markets and Continuous Trading Markets

1. What is the main advantage of a call market compared with a continuous trading market?
2. What is the main advantage of a continuous trading market compared with a call market?

Solution to 1: By gathering all traders to the same place at the same time, a call market makes it easier for buyers to find sellers and vice versa. In contrast, if buyers and sellers (or their orders) are not present at the same time in a continuous market, they cannot trade.

Solution to 2: In a continuous trading market, a willing buyer and seller can trade any time the market is open. In contrast, in a call market trading can take place only when the market is called.

8.2. Execution Mechanisms

The three main types of market structures are quote-driven markets (sometimes called price-driven or dealer markets), order-driven markets, and brokered markets. In **quote-driven markets**, customers trade with dealers. In **order-driven markets**, an order matching system run by an exchange, a broker, or an alternative trading system uses rules to arrange trades based on the orders that traders submit. Most exchanges and ECNs organize order-driven markets. In **brokered markets**, brokers arrange trades between their customers. Brokered markets are common for transactions of unique instruments, such as real estate properties, intellectual properties, or large blocks of securities. Many trading systems use more than one type of market structure.

8.2.1. Quote-Driven Markets

Worldwide, most trading, other than in stocks, takes place in quote-driven markets. Almost all bonds and currencies and most spot commodities trade in quote-driven markets. Traders call them quote-driven (or price-driven or dealer) because customers trade at the prices quoted by dealers. Depending on the instrument traded, the dealers work for commercial banks, for investment banks, for broker–dealers, or for proprietary trading houses.

Quote-driven markets also often are called over-the-counter (OTC) markets because securities used to be literally traded over the dealer's counter in the dealer's office. Now, most trades in OTC markets are conducted over proprietary computer communications networks, by telephone, or sometimes over instant messaging systems.

8.2.2. Order-Driven Markets

Order-driven markets arrange trades using rules to match buy orders to sell orders. The orders may be submitted by customers or by dealers. Almost all exchanges use order-driven trading systems, and every automated trading system is an order-driven system.

Because rules match buyers to sellers, traders often trade with complete strangers. Order-driven markets thus must have procedures to ensure that buyers and sellers perform on their trade contracts. Otherwise, dishonest traders would enter contracts that they would not settle if a change in market conditions made settlement unprofitable.

Two sets of rules characterize order-driven market mechanisms: Order matching rules and trade pricing rules. The order matching rules match buy orders to sell orders. The trade pricing rules determine the prices at which the matched trades take place.

8.2.2.1. Order Matching Rules

Order-driven trading systems match buyers to sellers using rules that rank the buy orders and the sell orders based on price, and often along with other secondary criteria. The systems then match the highest-ranking buy order with the highest-ranking sell order. If the buyer is willing to pay at least as much as the seller is willing to receive, the system will arrange a trade for the minimum of the buy and sell quantities. The remaining size, if any, is then matched with the next order on the other side and the process continues until no further trades can be arranged.

The **order precedence hierarchy** determines which orders go first. The first rule is **price priority**: The highest priced buy orders and the lowest prices sell orders go first. They are the most aggressively priced orders. **Secondary precedence rules** determine how to rank orders at the same price. Most trading systems use time precedence to rank orders at the same price. The first order to arrive has precedence over other orders. In trading systems that permit hidden and partially hidden orders, displayed quantities at a given price generally have precedence over the undisplayed quantities. So the complete precedence hierarchy is given by price priority, display precedence at a given price, and finally time precedence among all orders with the same display status at a given price. These rules give traders incentives to improve price, display their orders, and arrive early if they want to trade quickly. These incentives increase market liquidity.

8.2.2.2. Trade Pricing Rules

After the orders are matched, the trading system then uses its trade pricing rule to determine the trade price. The three rules that various order-driven markets use to price their trades are the uniform pricing rule, the discriminatory pricing rule, and the derivative pricing rule.

Call markets commonly use the uniform pricing rule. Under this rule, all trades execute at the same price. The market chooses the price that maximizes the total quantity traded.

Continuous trading markets use the **discriminatory pricing rule**. Under this rule, the limit price of the order or quote that first arrived—the standing order—determines the trade price. This rule allows a large arriving trader to discriminate among standing limit orders by filling the most aggressively priced orders first at their limit prices and then filling less aggressively priced orders at their less favorable (from the point of view of the arriving trader) limit prices. If trading systems did not use this pricing rule, large traders would break their orders into pieces to price discriminate on their own.

EXAMPLE 1-27 Filling a Large Order in a Continuous Trading Market

Before the arrival of a large order, a market has the following limit orders standing on its book:

Buyer	Bid Size	Limit Price	Offer Size	Seller
Takumi	15	¥100.1		
Hiroto	8	¥100.2		
Shou	10	¥100.3		
		¥100.4	4	Hina
		¥100.5	6	Sakur
		¥100.6	12	Miku

Buyer Tsubasa submits a day order to buy 15 contracts, limit ¥100.5. With whom does he trade, what is his average trade price, and what does the limit order book look like afterward?

Solution: Tsubasa's buy order first fills with the most aggressively priced sell order, which is Hina's order for four contracts. A trade takes place at ¥100.4 for four contracts, Hina's order fills completely, and Tsubasa still has 11 more contracts remaining.

The next most aggressively priced sell order is Sakur's order for six contracts. A second trade takes place at ¥100.5 for six contracts, Sakur's order fills completely, and Tsubasa still has five more contracts remaining.

The next most aggressively priced sell order is Miku's order at ¥100.6. No further trade is possible, however, because her limit sell price is above Tsubasa's limit buy price.

$$\text{Tsubasa's average trade price is ¥}100.46 = \frac{4 \times \text{¥}100.4 + 6 \times \text{¥}100.5}{4 + 6}$$

Because Tsubasa issued a day order, the remainder of his order is placed on the book on the buy side at ¥100.5. The following orders are then on the book:

Buyer	Bid Size	Limit Price	Offer Size	Seller
Takumi	15	¥100.1		
Hiroto	8	¥100.2		
Shou	10	¥100.3		
		¥100.4		
Tsubasa	5	¥100.5		
		¥100.6	12	Miku

If Tsubasa had issued an immediate-or-cancel order, the remaining five contracts would have been cancelled.

Crossing networks use the derivative pricing rule. **Crossing networks** are trading systems that match buyers and sellers who are willing to trade at prices obtained from other markets. Most systems cross their trades at the midpoint of the best bid and ask quotes published by the exchange at which the security primarily trades. This pricing rule is called a **derivative pricing rule** because the price is derived from another market. In particular, the price does not depend on the orders submitted to the crossing network. Some crossing networks are organized as call markets and others as continuously trading markets. The most important crossing market is the equity trading system POSIT.

8.2.3. Brokered Markets

The third execution mechanism is the brokered market, in which brokers arrange trades among their clients. Brokers organize markets for instruments for which finding a buyer or a seller willing to trade is difficult because the instruments are unique and thus of interest only to a limited number of people or institutions. These instruments generally are also infrequently traded and expensive to carry in inventory. Examples of such instruments include very large blocks of stock, real estate properties, fine art masterpieces, intellectual properties, operating companies, liquor licenses, and taxi medallions. Because dealers generally are unable or unwilling to hold these assets in their inventories, they will not make markets in them. Organizing order-driven markets for these instruments is not sensible because too few traders would submit orders to them.

Successful brokers in these markets try to know everyone who might now or in the future be willing to trade. They spend most of their time on the telephone and in meetings building their networks.

EXAMPLE 1-28 Quote-Driven, Order-Driven, and Brokered Markets

What are the primary advantages of quote-driven, order-driven, and brokered markets?

Solution: In a quote-driven market, dealers generally are available to supply liquidity. In an order-driven market, traders can supply liquidity to each other. In a brokered market, brokers help find traders who are willing to trade when dealers would not be willing to make markets and when traders would not be willing to post orders.

8.3. Market Information Systems

Markets vary in the type and quantity of data that they disseminate to the public. Traders say that a market is pretrade transparent if the market publishes real-time data about quotes and orders. Markets are posttrade transparent if the market publishes trade prices and sizes soon after trades occur.

Buy-side traders value transparency because it allows them to better manage their trading, understand market values, and estimate their prospective and actual transaction costs. In contrast, dealers prefer to trade in opaque markets because, as frequent traders, they have an information advantage over those who know less than they do. Bid–ask spreads tend to be wider and transaction costs tend to be higher in opaque markets because finding the best available price is harder for traders in such markets.

9. WELL-FUNCTIONING FINANCIAL SYSTEMS

The financial system allows traders to solve financing and risk management problems. In a well-functioning financial system:

- Investors can easily move money from the present to the future while obtaining a fair rate of return for the risks that they bear.
- Borrowers can easily obtain funds that they need to undertake current projects if they can credibly promise to repay the funds in the future.
- Hedgers can easily trade away or offset the risks that concern them.
- Traders can easily trade currencies for other currencies or commodities that they need.

If the assets or contracts needed to solve these problems are available to trade, the financial system has **complete markets**. If the costs of arranging these trades are low, the financial system is **operationally efficient**. If the prices of the assets and contracts reflect all available information related to fundamental values, the financial system is **informationally efficient**.

Well-functioning financial systems are characterized by:

- The existence of well-developed markets that trade instruments that help people solve their financial problems (complete markets).
- Liquid markets in which the costs of trading—commissions, bid–ask spreads, and order price impacts—are low (operationally efficient markets).
- Timely financial disclosures by corporations and governments that allow market participants to estimate the fundamental values of securities (support informationally efficient markets).
- Prices that reflect fundamental values so that prices vary primarily in response to changes in fundamental values and not to demands for liquidity made by uninformed traders (informationally efficient markets).

Such complete and operationally efficient markets are produced by financial intermediaries who:

- Organize exchanges, brokerages, and alternative trading systems that match buyers to sellers.
- Provide liquidity on demand to traders.
- Securitize assets to produce investment instruments that are attractive to investors and thereby lower the costs of funds for borrowers.
- Run banks that match investors to borrowers by taking deposits and making loans.
- Run insurance companies that pool uncorrelated risks.
- Provide investment advisory services that help investors manage and grow their assets at low cost.
- Organize clearinghouses that ensure everyone settles their trades and contracts.
- Organize depositories that ensure nobody loses their assets.

The benefits of a well-functioning financial system are huge. In such systems, investors who need to move money to the future can easily connect with entrepreneurs who need money now to develop new products and services. Similarly, producers who would otherwise avoid valuable projects because they are too risky can easily transfer those risks to others who can better bear them. Most importantly, these transactions generally can take place among strangers so that the benefits from trading can be derived from an enormous number of potential matches.

In contrast, economies that have poorly functioning financial systems have great difficulties allocating capital among the many companies who could use it. Financial transactions tend to be limited to arrangements within families when people cannot easily find trustworthy counterparties who will honor their contracts. In such economies, capital is allocated inefficiently, risks are not easily shared, and production is inefficient.

An extraordinarily important by-product of an operationally efficient financial system is the production of informationally efficient prices. Prices are informationally efficient when they reflect all available information about fundamental values. Informative prices are crucially important to the welfare of an economy because they help ensure that resources go where they are most valuable. Economies that use resources where they are most valuable are **allocationally efficient**. Economies that do not use resources where they are most valuable waste their resources and consequently often are quite poor.

Well-informed traders make prices informationally efficient. When they buy assets and contracts that they think are undervalued, they tend to push the assets' prices up. Similarly, when they sell assets and contracts that they think are overvalued, they tend to push the assets' prices down. The effect of their trading thus causes prices to reflect their information about values.

How accurately prices reflect fundamental information depends on the costs of obtaining fundamental information and on the liquidity available to well-informed traders. Accounting standards and reporting requirements that produce meaningful and timely financial disclosures reduce the costs of obtaining fundamental information and thereby allow analysts to form more accurate estimates of fundamental values. Liquid markets allow well-informed traders to fill their orders at low cost. If filling orders is very costly, informed trading may not be profitable. In that case, information-motivated traders will not commit resources to collect and analyze data and they will not trade. Without their research and their associated trading, prices would be less informative.

EXAMPLE 1-29 Well-Functioning Financial Systems

As a financial analyst specializing in emerging market equities, you understand that a well-functioning financial system contributes to the economic prosperity of a country. You are asked to start covering a new small market country. What factors will you consider when characterizing the quality of its financial markets?

Solution: In general, you will consider whether:

- The country has markets that allow its companies and residents to finance projects, save for the future, and exchange risk.
- The costs of trading in those markets is low.
- Prices reflect fundamental values.

You may specifically check to see whether:

- Fixed income and stock markets allow borrowers to easily obtain capital from investors.
- Corporations disclose financial and operating data on a timely basis in conformity to widely respected reporting standards, such as IFRS.
- Forward, futures, and options markets trade instruments that companies need to hedge their risks.
- Dealers and arbitrageurs allow traders to trade when they want to.
- Bid–ask spreads are small.
- Trades and contracts invariably settle as expected.
- Investment managers provide high-quality management services for reasonable fees.
- Banks and other financing companies are well capitalized and thus able to help investors provide capital to borrowers.
- Securitized assets are available and represent reasonable credit risks.
- Insurance companies are well capitalized and thus able to help those exposed to risks insure against them.
- Price volatility appears consistent with changes in fundamental values.

10. MARKET REGULATION

Government agencies and practitioner organizations regulate many markets and the financial intermediaries that participate in them. The regulators generally seek to promote fair and orderly markets in which traders can trade at prices that accurately reflect fundamental values without incurring excessive transaction costs. This section identifies the problems that financial regulators hope to solve and the objectives of their regulations.

Regrettably, some people will steal from each other if given a chance, especially if the probability of detection is low or if the penalty for being caught is low. The number of ways that people can steal or misappropriate wealth generally increases with the complexity of their relationships and with asymmetries in their knowledge. Because financial markets tend to be complex, and because customers are often much less sophisticated than the professionals that serve them, the potential for losses through various frauds can be unacceptably high in unregulated markets.

Regulators thus ensure that systems are in place to protect customers from fraud. In principle, the customers themselves would demand such systems as a condition of doing business. When customers are unsophisticated or poorly informed, however, they may not know how to protect themselves. When the costs of learning are large—as they often are in complex financial markets—having regulators look out for the public interest can be economically efficient.

More customer money is probably lost in financial markets through negligence than through outright fraud. Most customers in financial markets use various agents to help them solve problems that they do not understand well. These agents include securities brokers, financial advisers, investment managers, and insurance agents. Because customers generally do not have much information about market conditions, they find it extremely difficult to measure the added value they obtain from their agents. This problem is especially challenging when performance has a strong random component. In that case, determining whether agents are skilled or lucky is very difficult. Moreover, if the agent is a good salesman, the customer may not critically evaluate their agent's performance. These conditions, which characterize most financial markets, ensure that customers cannot easily determine whether their agents are working faithfully for them. They tend to lose if their agents are unqualified or lazy, or if they unconsciously favor themselves and their friends over their clients, as is natural for even the most honest people.

Regulators help solve these agency problems by setting minimum standards of competence for agents and by defining and enforcing minimum standards of practice. CFA Institute provides significant standard-setting leadership in the areas of investment management and investment performance reporting through its Chartered Financial Analyst program and its Global Investment Performance Standards. In principle, regulation would not be necessary if customers could identify competent agents and effectively measure their performance. In the financial markets, doing so is very difficult.

Regulators often act to level the playing field for market participants. For example, in many jurisdictions, insider trading in securities is illegal. The rule prevents corporate insiders and others with access to corporate information from trading on material information that has not been released to the public. The purpose of the rule is to reduce the profits that insiders could extract from the markets. These profits would come from other traders who would lose when they trade with well-informed insiders. Because traders tend to withdraw from markets when they lose, rules against insider trading help keep markets liquid. They also keep corporate insiders from hoarding information.

Many situations arise in financial markets in which common standards benefit everyone involved. For example, having all companies report financial results on a common basis allows financial analysts to easily compare companies. Accordingly, the International Accounting Standards Board (IASB) and the U.S.-based Financial Accounting Standards Board, among many others, promulgate common financial standards to which all companies must report. The benefits of having common reporting standards have led to a very successful and continuing effort to converge all accounting standards to a single worldwide standard. Without such regulations, investors might eventually refuse to invest in companies that do not report to a common standard, but such market-based discipline is a very slow regulator of behavior, and it would have little effect on companies that do not need to raise new capital.

Regulators generally require that financial firms maintain minimum levels of capital. These capital requirements serve two purposes. First, they ensure that the companies will be able to honor their contractual commitments when unexpected market movements or poor decisions cause them to lose money. Second, they ensure that the owners of financial firms have substantial interest in the decisions that they make. Without a substantial financial interest in the decisions that they make, companies often take too many risks and exercise poor judgment about extending credit to others. When such companies fail, they impose significant costs on others. Minimum capital requirements reduce the probability that financial firms will fail and they reduce the disruptions associated with those failures that do occur. In principle, a firm's customers and counterparties could require minimum capital levels as a condition of doing business with the firm, but they have more difficulty enforcing their contracts than do governments who can imprison people.

Regulators similarly regulate insurance companies and pension funds that make long-term promises to their clients. Such entities need to maintain adequate reserves to ensure that they can fund their liabilities. Unfortunately, their managers have a tendency to underestimate these reserves if they will not be around when the liabilities come due. Again, in principle, policyholders and employees could regulate the behavior of their insurance funds and their employers by refusing to contract with them if they do not promise to adequately fund their liabilities. In practice, however, the sophistication, information, and time necessary to write and enforce contracts that control these problems are beyond the reach of most people. The government thus is a sensible regulator of such problems.

Many regulators are self-regulating organizations (SROs) that regulate their members. Exchanges, clearinghouses, and dealer trade organizations are examples of self-regulating organizations. In some cases, the members of these organizations voluntarily subject themselves to the SRO's regulations to promote the common good. In other cases, governments delegate regulatory and enforcement authorities to SROs, usually subject to the supervision of a government agency, such as a national securities and exchange authority. Exchanges, dealer associations, and clearing agencies often regulate their members with these delegated powers.

By setting high standards of behavior, SROs help their members obtain the confidence of their customers. They also reduce the chance that members of the SRO will incur losses when dealing with other members of the SRO.

When regulators fail to solve the problems discussed here, the financial system does not function well. People who lose money stop saving and borrowers with good ideas cannot fund their projects. Similarly, hedgers withdraw from markets when the costs of hedging are high. Without the ability to hedge, producers become reluctant to specialize because specialization generally increases risk. Because specialization also decreases costs, however, production becomes less efficient as producers chose safer technologies. Economies that cannot solve the regulatory problems described in this section tend to operate less efficiently than do better regulated economies, and they tend to be less wealthy.

To summarize, the objectives of market regulation are to:

1. Control fraud.
2. Control agency problems.
3. Promote fairness.
4. Set mutually beneficial standards.
5. Prevent undercapitalized financial firms from exploiting their investors by making excessively risky investments.
6. Ensure that long-term liabilities are funded.

Regulation is necessary because regulating certain behaviors through market-based mechanisms is too costly for people who are unsophisticated and uninformed. Effectively regulated markets allow people to better achieve their financial goals.

EXAMPLE 1-30 Bankrupt Traders

You are the chief executive officer of a brokerage that is a member of a clearinghouse. A trader who clears through your firm is bankrupt at midday, but you do not yet know it even though your clearing agreement with him explicitly requires that he immediately report significant losses. The trader knows that if he takes a large position, prices might move in his favor so that he will no longer be bankrupt. The trader attempts to do so and succeeds. You find out about this later in the evening.

1. Why does the clearinghouse regulate its members?
2. What should you do about the trader?
3. Why would the clearinghouse allow you to keep his trading profits?

Solution to 1: The clearinghouse regulates its members to ensure that no member imposes costs on another member by failing to settle a trade.

Solution to 2: You should immediately end your clearing relationship with the trader and confiscate his trading profits. The trader was trading with your firm's capital after he became bankrupt. Had he lost, your firm would have borne the loss.

Solution to 3: If the clearinghouse did not permit you to keep his trading profits, other traders similarly situated might attempt the same strategy.

11. SUMMARY

This chapter introduces how the financial system operates and explains how well-functioning financial systems lead to wealthy economies. Financial analysts need to understand how the financial system works because their analyses often lead to trading decisions.

The financial system consists of markets and the financial intermediaries that operate in them. These institutions allow buyers to connect with sellers. They may trade directly with each other when they trade the same instrument or they only may trade indirectly when a financial intermediary connects the buyer to the seller through transactions with each that appear on the intermediary's balance sheet. The buyer and seller may exchange instruments, cash flows, or risks.

The following points, among others, were made in this chapter:

- The financial system consists of mechanisms that allow strangers to contract with each other to move money through time, to hedge risks, and to exchange assets that they value less for those that they value more.

- Investors move money from the present to the future when they save. They expect a normal rate of return for bearing risk through time. Borrowers move money from the future to the present to fund current projects and expenditures. Hedgers trade to reduce their exposure to risks they prefer not to take. Information-motivated traders are active investment managers who try to identify under- and overvalued instruments.
- Securities are first sold in primary markets by their issuers. They then trade in secondary markets.
- People invest in pooled investment vehicles to benefit from the investment management services of their managers.
- Forward contracts allow buyers and sellers to arrange for future sales at predetermined prices. Futures contracts are forward contracts guaranteed by clearinghouses. The guarantee ensures that strangers are willing to trade with each other and that traders can offset their positions by trading with anybody. These features of futures contract markets make them highly attractive to hedgers and information-motivated traders.
- Many financial intermediaries connect buyers to sellers in a given instrument, acting directly as brokers and exchanges or indirectly as dealers and arbitrageurs.
- Financial intermediaries create instruments when they conduct arbitrage, securitize assets, borrow to lend, manage investment funds, or pool insurance contracts. These activities all transform cash flows and risks from one form to another. Their services allow buyers and sellers to connect with each other through instruments that meet their specific needs.
- Financial markets work best when strangers can contract with each other without worrying about whether their counterparts are able and willing to honor their contract. Clearinghouses, variation margins, maintenance margins, and settlement guarantees made by creditworthy brokers on behalf of their clients help manage credit risk and ultimately allow strangers to contract with each other.
- Information-motivated traders short sell when they expect that prices will fall. Hedgers short sell to reduce the risks of a long position in a related contract or commodity.
- Margin loans allow people to buy more securities than their equity would otherwise permit them to buy. The larger positions expose them to more risk so that gains and losses for a given amount of equity will be larger. The leverage ratio is the value of a position divided by the value of the equity supporting it. The returns to the equity in a position are equal to the leverage ratio times the returns to the unleveraged position.
- To protect against credit losses, brokers demand maintenance margin payments from their customers who have borrowed cash or securities when adverse price changes cause their customer's equity to drop below the maintenance margin ratio. Brokers close positions for customers who do not satisfy these margin calls.
- Orders are instructions to trade. They always specify instrument, side (buy or sell), and quantity. They usually also provide several other instructions.
- Market orders tend to fill quickly but often at inferior prices. Limit orders generally fill at better prices if they fill, but they may not fill. Traders choose order submission strategies on the basis of how quickly they want to trade, the prices they are willing to accept, and the consequences of failing to trade.
- Stop instructions are attached to other orders to delay efforts to fill them until the stop condition is satisfied. Although stop orders are often used to stop losses, they are not always effective.
- Issuers sell their securities using underwritten public offerings, best efforts public offerings, private placements, shelf registrations, dividend reinvestment programs, and rights offerings. Investment banks have a conflict of interest when setting the initial offering price in an IPO.

- Well-functioning secondary markets are essential to raising capital in the primary markets because investors value the ability to sell their securities if they no longer want to hold them or if they need to disinvest to raise cash. If they cannot trade their securities in a liquid market, they will not pay as much for them.
- Matching buyers and sellers in call markets is easy because the traders (or their orders) come together at the same time and place.
- Dealers provide liquidity in quote-driven markets. Public traders as well as dealers provide liquidity in order-driven markets.
- Order-driven markets arrange trades by ranking orders using precedence rules. The rules generally ensure that traders who provide the best prices, display the most size, and arrive early trade first. Continuous order-driven markets price orders using the discriminatory pricing rule. Under this rule, standing limit orders determine trade prices.
- Brokers help people trade unique instruments or positions for which finding a buyer or a seller is difficult.
- Transaction costs are lower in transparent markets than in opaque markets because traders can more easily determine market value and more easily manage their trading in transparent markets.
- A well-functioning financial system allows people to trade instruments that best solve their wealth and risk management problems with low transaction costs. Complete and liquid markets characterize a well-functioning financial system. Complete markets are markets in which the instruments needed to solve investment and risk management problems are available to trade. Liquid markets are markets in which traders can trade when they want to trade at low cost.
- The financial system is operationally efficient when its markets are liquid. Liquid markets lower the costs of raising capital.
- A well-functioning financial system promotes wealth by ensuring that capital allocation decisions are well made. A well-functioning financial system also promotes wealth by allowing people to share the risks associated with valuable products that would otherwise not be undertaken.
- Prices are informationally efficient when they reflect all available information about fundamental values. Information-motivated traders make prices informationally efficient. Prices will be most informative in liquid markets because information-motivated traders will not invest in information and research if establishing positions based on their analyses is too costly.
- Regulators generally seek to promote fair and orderly markets in which traders can trade at prices that accurately reflect fundamental values without incurring excessive transaction costs. Governmental agencies and self-regulating organizations of practitioners provide regulatory services that attempt to make markets safer and more efficient.
- Mandated financial disclosure programs for the issuers of publicly traded securities ensure that information necessary to estimate security values is available to financial analysts on a consistent basis.

PROBLEMS

1. Akihiko Takabe has designed a sophisticated forecasting model, which predicts the movements in the overall stock market, in the hope of earning a return in excess of a fair return for the risk involved. He uses the predictions of the model to decide whether to

buy, hold, or sell the shares of an index fund that aims to replicate the movements of the stock market. Takabe would *best* be characterized as a(n):

A. Hedger.
B. Investor.
C. Information-motivated trader.

2. James Beach is young and has substantial wealth. A significant proportion of his stock portfolio consists of emerging market stocks that offer relatively high expected returns at the cost of relatively high risk. Beach believes that investment in emerging market stocks is appropriate for him given his ability and willingness to take risk. Which of the following labels *most appropriately* describes Beach?

   A. Hedger.
   B. Investor.
   C. Information-motivated trader.

3. Lisa Smith owns a manufacturing company in the United States. Her company has sold goods to a customer in Brazil and will be paid in Brazilian real (BRL) in three months. Smith is concerned about the possibility of the BRL depreciating more than expected against the U.S. dollar (USD). Therefore, she is planning to sell three-month futures contracts on the BRL. The seller of such contracts generally gains when the BRL depreciates against the USD. If Smith were to sell these futures contracts, she would *most appropriately* be described as a(n):

   A. Hedger.
   B. Investor.
   C. Information-motivated trader.

4. Which of the following is *not* a function of the financial system?

   A. To regulate arbitrageurs' profits (excess returns).
   B. To help the economy achieve allocational efficiency.
   C. To facilitate borrowing by businesses to fund current operations.

5. An investor primarily invests in stocks of publicly traded companies. The investor wants to increase the diversification of his portfolio. A friend has recommended investing in real estate properties. The purchase of real estate would *best* be characterized as a transaction in the:

   A. Derivative investment market.
   B. Traditional investment market.
   C. Alternative investment market.

6. A hedge fund holds its excess cash in 90-day commercial paper and negotiable certificates of deposit. The cash management policy of the hedge fund is *best described* as using:

   A. Capital market instruments.
   B. Money market instruments.
   C. Intermediate-term debt instruments.

7. An oil and gas exploration and production company announces that it is offering 30 million shares to the public at $45.50 each. This transaction is *most likely* a sale in the:

   A. Futures market.
   B. Primary market.
   C. Secondary market.

8. Consider a mutual fund that invests primarily in fixed-income securities that have been determined to be appropriate given the fund's investment goal. Which of the following is *least likely* to be a part of this fund?

   A. Warrants.
   B. Commercial paper.
   C. Repurchase agreements.

9. A friend has asked you to explain the differences between open-end and closed-end funds. Which of the following will you *most likely* include in your explanation?

   A. Closed-end funds are unavailable to new investors.
   B. When investors sell the shares of an open-end fund, they can receive a discount or a premium to the fund's net asset value.
   C. When selling shares, investors in an open-end fund sell the shares back to the fund whereas investors in a closed-end fund sell the shares to others in the secondary market.

10. The usefulness of a forward contract is limited by some problems. Which of the following is *most likely* one of those problems?

    A. Once you have entered into a forward contract, it is difficult to exit from the contract.
    B. Entering into a forward contract requires the long party to deposit an initial amount with the short party.
    C. If the price of the underlying asset moves adversely from the perspective of the long party, periodic payments must be made to the short party.

11. Tony Harris is planning to start trading in commodities. He has heard about the use of futures contracts on commodities and is learning more about them. Which of the following is Harris *least likely* to find associated with a futures contract?

    A. Existence of counterparty risk.
    B. Standardized contractual terms.
    C. Payment of an initial margin to enter into a contract.

12. A German company that exports machinery is expecting to receive $10 million in three months. The firm converts all its foreign currency receipts into euros. The chief financial officer of the company wishes to lock in a minimum fixed rate for converting the $10 million to euro but also wants to keep the flexibility to use the future spot rate if it is favorable. What hedging transaction is *most likely* to achieve this objective?

    A. Selling dollars forward.
    B. Buying put options on the dollar.
    C. Selling futures contracts on dollars.

13. A book publisher requires substantial quantities of paper. The publisher and a paper producer have entered into an agreement for the publisher to buy and the producer to supply a given quantity of paper four months later at a price agreed upon today. This agreement is a:

    A. Futures contract.
    B. Forward contract.
    C. Commodity swap.

14. The Standard & Poor's Depositary Receipts (SPDRs) is an investment that tracks the S&P 500 stock market index. Purchases and sales of SPDRs during an average trading day are *best* described as:

    A. Primary market transactions in a pooled investment.
    B. Secondary market transactions in a pooled investment.
    C. Secondary market transactions in an actively managed investment.

15. The Standard & Poor's Depositary Receipts (SPDRs) is an exchange-traded fund in the United States that is designed to track the S&P 500 stock market index. The current price of a share of SPDRs is $113. A trader has just bought call options on shares of SPDRs for a premium of $3 per share. The call options expire in five months and have an exercise price of $120 per share. On the expiration date, the trader will exercise the call options (ignore any transaction costs) if and only if the shares of SPDRs are trading:

    A. Below $120 per share.
    B. Above $120 per share.
    C. Above $123 per share.

16. Which of the following statements about exchange-traded funds is *most correct*?

    A. Exchange-traded funds are not backed by any assets.
    B. The investment companies that create exchange-traded funds are financial intermediaries.
    C. The transaction costs of trading shares of exchange-traded funds are substantially greater than the combined costs of trading the underlying assets of the fund.

17. Jason Schmidt works for a hedge fund and he specializes in finding profit opportunities that are the result of inefficiencies in the market for convertible bonds—bonds that can be converted into a predetermined amount of a company's common stock. Schmidt tries to find convertibles that are priced inefficiently relative to the underlying stock. The trading strategy involves the simultaneous purchase of the convertible bond and the short sale of the underlying common stock. The above process could best be described as:

    A. Hedging.
    B. Arbitrage.
    C. Securitization.

18. Pierre-Louis Robert just purchased a call option on shares of the Michelin Group. A few days ago he wrote a put option on Michelin shares. The call and put options have the same exercise price, expiration date, and number of shares underlying. Considering both positions, Robert's exposure to the risk of the stock of the Michelin Group is:

    A. Long.
    B. Short.
    C. Neutral.

19. An online brokerage firm has set the minimum margin requirement at 55 percent. What is the maximum leverage ratio associated with a position financed by this minimum margin requirement?

    A. 1.55.
    B. 1.82.
    C. 2.22.

20. A trader has purchased 200 shares of a non-dividend-paying firm on margin at a price of $50 per share. The leverage ratio is 2.5. Six months later, the trader sells these shares at $60 per share. Ignoring the interest paid on the borrowed amount and the transaction costs, what was the return to the trader during the six-month period?

    A. 20 percent.
    B. 33.33 percent.
    C. 50 percent.

21. Jason Williams purchased 500 shares of a company at $32 per share. The stock was bought on 75 percent margin. One month later, Williams had to pay interest on the amount borrowed at a rate of 2 percent per month. At that time, Williams received a dividend of $0.50 per share. Immediately after that he sold the shares at $28 per share. He paid commissions of $10 on the purchase and $10 on the sale of the stock. What was the rate of return on this investment for the one-month period?

    A. −12.5 percent.
    B. −15.4 percent.
    C. −50.1 percent.

22. Caroline Rogers believes the price of Gamma Corp. stock will go down in the near future. She has decided to sell short 200 shares of Gamma Corp. at the current market price of €47. The initial margin requirement is 40 percent. Which of the following is an appropriate statement regarding the margin requirement that Rogers is subject to on this short sale?

    A. She will need to contribute €3,760 as margin.
    B. She will need to contribute €5,640 as margin.
    C. She will only need to leave the proceeds from the short sale as deposit and does not need to contribute any additional funds.

23. The current price of a stock is $25 per share. You have $10,000 to invest. You borrow an additional $10,000 from your broker and invest $20,000 in the stock. If the maintenance margin is 30 percent, at what price will a margin call first occur?

    A. $9.62.
    B. $17.86.
    C. $19.71.

24. You have placed a sell market-on-open order—a market order that would automatically be submitted at the market's open tomorrow and would fill at the market price. Your instruction, to sell the shares at the market open, is a(n):

    A. Execution instruction.
    B. Validity instruction.
    C. Clearing instruction.

25. A market has the following limit orders standing on its book for a particular stock. The bid and ask sizes are number of shares in hundreds.

Bid Size	Limit Price	Offer Size
5	€9.73	
12	€9.81	
4	€9.84	
6	€9.95	
	€10.02	5
	€10.10	12
	€10.14	8

What is the market?

A. 9.73 bid, offered at 10.14.
B. 9.81 bid, offered at 10.10.
C. 9.95 bid, offered at 10.02.

26. Consider the following limit order book for a stock. The bid and ask sizes are number of shares in hundreds.

Bid Size	Limit Price	Offer Size
3	¥122.80	
8	¥123.00	
4	¥123.35	
	¥123.80	7
	¥124.10	6
	¥124.50	7

A new buy limit order is placed for 300 shares at ¥123.40. This limit order is said to:

A. Take the market.
B. Make the market.
C. Make a new market.

27. Currently, the market in a stock is "$54.62 bid, offered at $54.71." A new sell limit order is placed at $54.62. This limit order is said to:

A. Take the market.
B. Make the market.
C. Make a new market.

28. Jim White has sold short 100 shares of Super Stores at a price of $42 per share. He has also simultaneously placed a "good-till-cancelled, stop 50, limit 55 buy" order. Assume

that if the stop condition specified by White is satisfied and the order becomes valid, it will get executed. Excluding transaction costs, what is the maximum possible loss that White can have?

A. $800.
B. $1,300.
C. Unlimited.

29. You own shares of a company that are currently trading at $30 a share. Your technical analysis of the shares indicates a support level of $27.50. That is, if the price of the shares is going down, it is more likely to stay above this level rather than fall below it. If the price does fall below this level, however, you believe that the price may continue to decline. You have no immediate intent to sell the shares but are concerned about the possibility of a huge loss if the share price declines below the support level. Which of the following types of orders could you place to most appropriately address your concern?

A. Short sell order.
B. Good-till-cancelled stop sell order.
C. Good-till-cancelled stop buy order.

30. In an underwritten offering, the risk that the entire issue may not be sold to the public at the stipulated offering price is borne by the:

A. Issuer.
B. Investment bank.
C. Buyers of the part of the issue that is sold.

31. A British company listed on the Alternative Investment Market of the London Stock Exchange, announced the sale of 6,686,665 shares to a small group of qualified investors at £0.025 per share. Which of the following *best describes* this sale?

A. Shelf registration.
B. Private placement.
C. Initial public offering.

32. A German publicly traded company, to raise new capital, gave its existing shareholders the opportunity to subscribe for new shares. The existing shareholders could purchase two new shares at a subscription price of €4.58 per share for every 15 shares held. This is an example of a(n):

A. Rights offering.
B. Private placement.
C. Initial public offering.

33. Consider an order-driven system that allows hidden orders. The following four sell orders on a particular stock are currently in the system's limit order book. Based on the commonly used order precedence hierarchy, which of these orders will have precedence over others?

Order Number	Time of Arrival (HH:MM:SS)	Limit Price	Special Instruction (If any)
I	9:52:01	€20.33	
II	9:52:08	€20.29	Hidden order

Order Number	Time of Arrival (HH:MM:SS)	Limit Price	Special Instruction (If any)
III	9:53:04	€20.29	
IV	9:53:49	€20.29	

A. Order I (time of arrival of 9:52:01).
B. Order II (time of arrival of 9:52:08).
C. Order III (time of arrival of 9:53:04).

34. Zhenhu Li has submitted an immediate-or-cancel buy order for 500 shares of a company at a limit price of CNY 74.25. There are two sell limit orders standing in that stock's order book at that time. One is for 300 shares at a limit price of CNY 74.30 and the other is for 400 shares at a limit price of CNY 74.35. How many shares in Li's order would get cancelled?

A. None (the order would remain open but unfilled).
B. 200 (300 shares would get filled).
C. 500 (there would be no fill).

35. A market has the following limit orders standing on its book for a particular stock:

Buyer	Bid Size (number of shares)	Limit Price	Offer Size (number of shares)	Seller
Keith	1,000	£19.70		
Paul	200	£19.84		
Ann	400	£19.89		
Mary	300	£20.02		
		£20.03	800	Jack
		£20.11	1,100	Margaret
		£20.16	400	Jeff

Ian submits a day order to sell 1,000 shares, limit £19.83. Assuming that no more buy orders are submitted on that day after Ian submits his order, what would be Ian's average trade price?

A. £19.70.
B. £19.92.
C. £20.05.

36. A financial analyst is examining whether a country's financial market is well functioning. She finds that the transaction costs in this market are low and trading volumes are high. She concludes that the market is quite liquid. In such a market:

A. Traders will find it hard to make use of their information.
B. Traders will find it easy to trade and their trading will make the market less informationally efficient.
C. Traders will find it easy to trade and their trading will make the market more informationally efficient.

37. The government of a country whose financial markets are in an early stage of development has hired you as a consultant on financial market regulation. Your first task is to prepare a list of the objectives of market regulation. Which of the following is *least likely* to be included in this list of objectives?

    A. Minimize agency problems in the financial markets.
    B. Ensure that financial markets are fair and orderly.
    C. Ensure that investors in the stock market achieve a rate of return that is at least equal to the risk-free rate of return.

CHAPTER 2

SECURITY MARKET INDICES

Paul D. Kaplan, CFA
London, U.K.

Dorothy C. Kelly, CFA
Charlottesville, VA, U.S.A.

LEARNING OUTCOMES

After completing this chapter, you will be able to do the following:

- Describe a security market index.
- Calculate and interpret the value, price return, and total return of an index.
- Discuss the choices and issues in index construction and management.
- Compare and contrast the different weighting methods used in index construction.
- Calculate and interpret the value and return of an index on the basis of its weighting method.
- Discuss rebalancing and reconstitution.
- Discuss uses of security market indices.
- Discuss types of equity indices.
- Discuss types of fixed-income indices.
- Discuss indices representing alternative investments.
- Compare and contrast the types of security market indices.

1. INTRODUCTION

Investors gather and analyze vast amounts of information about security markets on a continual basis. Because this work can be both time consuming and data intensive, investors often use a single measure that consolidates this information and reflects the performance of an entire security market.

in dex, *noun* (*pl.* in dex es *or* in di ces)

Latin *indic-, index,* from *indicare* to indicate: an indicator, sign, or measure of something.

Security market indices were first introduced as a simple measure to reflect the performance of the U.S. stock market. Since then, security market indices have evolved into important multipurpose tools that help investors track the performance of various security markets, estimate risk, and evaluate the performance of investment managers. They also form the basis for new investment products.

Origin of Market Indices

Investors had access to regularly published data on individual security prices in London as early as 1698, but nearly 200 years passed before they had access to a simple indicator to reflect security market information.[1] To give readers a sense of how the U.S. stock market in general performed on a given day, publishers Charles H. Dow and Edward D. Jones introduced the Dow Jones Average, the world's first security market index, in 1884.[2] The index, which appeared in *The Customers' Afternoon Letter*, consisted of the stocks of nine railroads and two industrial companies. It eventually became the Dow Jones Transportation Average.[3] Convinced that industrial companies, rather than railroads, would be "the great speculative market" of the future, Dow and Jones introduced a second index in May 1896—the Dow Jones Industrial Average (DJIA). It had an initial value of 40.94 and consisted of 12 stocks from major U.S. industries.[4] Today, investors can choose from among thousands of indices to measure and monitor different security markets and asset classes.

This chapter is organized as follows. Section 2 defines a security market index and explains how to calculate the price return and total return of an index for a single period and over multiple periods. Section 3 describes how indices are constructed and managed. Section 4 discusses the use of market indices. Sections 5, 6, and 7 discuss various types of indices, and Section 8 concludes and summarizes the chapter. Practice problems follow the conclusions and summary.

[1]London Stock Exchange, "Our History" (2009): www.londonstockexchange.com.

[2]Dow Jones & Company, "Dow Jones Industrial Average Historical Components," (2008):2.

[3]Dow Jones & Company, "Dow Jones History" (2009): www.dowjones.com/TheCompany/History/History.htm.

[4]Dow Jones & Company, *The Market's Measure*, edited by John A. Presbo (1999):11.

2. INDEX DEFINITION AND CALCULATIONS OF VALUE AND RETURNS

A **security market index** represents a given security market, market segment, or asset class. Most indices are constructed as portfolios of marketable securities.

The value of an index is calculated on a regular basis using either the actual or estimated market prices of the individual securities, known as **constituent securities**, within the index. For each security market index, investors may encounter two versions of the same index (i.e., an index with identical constituent securities and weights): one version based on price return and one version based on total return. As the name suggests, a **price return index**, also known as a **price index**, reflects *only* the prices of the constituent securities within the index. A **total return index**, in contrast, reflects not only the prices of the constituent securities but also the reinvestment of all income received since inception.

At inception, the values of the price and total return versions of an index are equal. As time passes, however, the value of the total return index, which includes the reinvestment of all dividends and/or interest received, will exceed the value of the price return index by an increasing amount. A look at how the values of each version are calculated over multiple periods illustrates why.

The value of a price return index is calculated as:

$$V_{PRI} = \frac{\sum_{i=1}^{N} n_i P_i}{D} \tag{2.1}$$

where

V_{PRI} = the value of the price return index
n_i = the number of units of constituent security i held in the index portfolio
N = the number of constituent securities in the index
P_i = the unit price of constituent security i
D = the value of the divisor

The **divisor** is a number initially chosen at inception. It is frequently chosen so that the price index has a convenient initial value, such as 1,000. The index provider then adjusts the value of the divisor as necessary to avoid changes in the index value that are unrelated to changes in the prices of its constituent securities. For example, when changing index constituents, the index provider may adjust the divisor so that the value of the index with the new constituents equals the value of the index prior to the changes.

Index return calculations, like calculations of investment portfolio returns, may measure price return or total return. **Price return** measures only price appreciation or percentage change in price. **Total return** measures price appreciation plus interest, dividends, and other distributions.

2.1. Calculation of Single-Period Returns

For a security market index, price return can be calculated in two ways: either the percentage change in value of the price return index, or the weighted average of price returns of the constituent securities. The price return of an index can be expressed as:

$$\mathrm{PR}_I = \frac{V_{PRI1} - V_{PRI0}}{V_{PRI0}} \tag{2.2}$$

where

PR_I = the price return of the index portfolio (as a decimal number, i.e., 12 percent is 0.12)
V_{PRI1} = the value of the price return index at the end of the period
V_{PRI0} = the value of the price return index at the beginning of the period

Similarly, the price return of each constituent security can be expressed as:

$$\mathrm{PR}_i = \frac{P_{i1} - P_{i0}}{P_{i0}} \tag{2.3}$$

where

PR_i = the price return of constituent security i (as a decimal number)
P_{i1} = the price of constituent security i at the end of the period
P_{i0} = the price of constituent security i at the beginning of the period

Because the price return of the index equals the weighted average of price returns of the individual securities, we can write:

$$\mathrm{PR}_I = \sum_{i=1}^{N} \mathrm{w}_i \mathrm{PR}_i = \sum_{i=1}^{N} \mathrm{w}_i \left(\frac{P_{i1} - P_{i0}}{P_{i0}} \right) \tag{2.4}$$

where

PR_I = the price return of index portfolio (as a decimal number)
PR_i = the price return of constituent security i (as a decimal number)
N = the number of individual securities in the index
w_i = the weight of security i (the fraction of the index portfolio allocated to security i)
P_{i1} = the price of constituent security i at the end of the period
P_{i0} = the price of constituent security i at the beginning of the period

Equation 2.4 can be rewritten simply as

$$\mathrm{PR}_I = \mathrm{w}_I \mathrm{PR}_I + \mathrm{w}_2 \mathrm{PR}_2 + \ldots + \mathrm{w}_N \mathrm{PR}_N \tag{2.5}$$

where

PR_I = the price return of index portfolio (as a decimal number)
PR_i = the price return of constituent security i (as a decimal number)
w_i = the weight of security i (the fraction of the index portfolio allocated to security i)
N = the number of securities in the index

Total return measures price appreciation plus interest, dividends, and other distributions. Thus, the total return of an index is the price appreciation, or change in the value of the price return index, plus income (dividends and/or interest) over the period, expressed as a percentage of the beginning value of the price return index. The total return of an index can be expressed as:

$$\mathrm{TR}_I = \frac{V_{PRI1} - V_{PRI0} + \mathrm{Inc}_I}{V_{PRI0}} \quad (2.6)$$

where

TR_I = the total return of the index portfolio (as a decimal number)
V_{PRI1} = the value of the price return index at the end of the period
V_{PRI0} = the value of the price return index at the beginning of the period
Inc_I = the total income (dividends and/or interest) from all securities in the index held over the period

The total return of an index can also be calculated as the weighted average of total returns of the constituent securities. The total return of each constituent security in the index is calculated as:

$$\mathrm{TR}_i = \frac{P_{1i} - P_{0i} + \mathrm{Inc}_i}{P_{0i}} \quad (2.7)$$

where

TR_i = the total return of constituent security i (as a decimal number)
P_{1i} = the price of constituent security i at the end of the period
P_{0i} = the price of constituent security i at the beginning of the period
Inc_i = the total income (dividends and/or interest) from security i over the period

Because the total return of an index can be calculated as the weighted average of total returns of the constituent securities, we can express total return as:

$$\mathrm{TR}_I = \sum_{i=1}^{N} \mathrm{w}_i \mathrm{TR}_i = \sum_{i=1}^{N} \mathrm{w}_i \left(\frac{P_{1i} - P_{0i} + \mathrm{Inc}_i}{P_{0i}} \right) \quad (2.8)$$

Equation 2.8 can be rewritten simply as

$$\mathrm{TR}_I = \mathrm{w}_1 \mathrm{TR}_1 + \mathrm{w}_2 \mathrm{TR}_2 + \ldots + \mathrm{w}_N \mathrm{TR}_N \quad (2.9)$$

where

TR_I = the total return of the index portfolio (as a decimal number)
TR_i = the total return of constituent security i (as a decimal number)
w_i = the weight of security i (the fraction of the index portfolio allocated to security i)
N = the number of securities in the index

2.2. Calculation of Index Values over Multiple Time Periods

The calculation of index values over multiple time periods requires geometrically linking the series of index returns. With a series of price returns for an index, we can calculate the value of the price return index with the following equation:

$$\mathrm{V}_{\mathrm{PR}IT} = \mathrm{V}_{\mathrm{PR}I0}(1 + \mathrm{PR}_{I1})(1 + \mathrm{PR}_{I2}) \ldots (1 + \mathrm{PR}_{IT}) \quad (2.10)$$

where

$V_{PR/0}$ = the value of the price return index at inception
$V_{PR/T}$ = the value of the price return index at time t
$PR_{/T}$ = the price return (as a decimal number) on the index over period t, $t = 1, 2, \ldots, T$

For an index with an inception value set to 1,000 and price returns of 5 percent and 3 percent for Periods 1 and 2 respectively, the values of the price return index would be calculated as follows:

Period	Return (%)	Calculation	Ending Value
0		1,000(1.00)	1,000.00
1	5.00	1,000(1.05)	1,050.00
2	3.00	1,000(1.05)(1.03)	1,081.50

Similarly, the series of total returns for an index is used to calculate the value of the total return index with the following equation:

$$V_{TR/T} = V_{TR/0}(1 + TR_{/1})(1 + TR_{/2}) \ldots (1 + TR_{/T}) \quad (2.11)$$

where

$V_{TR/0}$ = the value of the index at inception
$V_{TR/T}$ = the value of the total return index at time t
$TR_{/T}$ = the total return (as a decimal number) on the index over period t, $t = 1, 2, \ldots, T$

Suppose that the same index yields an additional 1.5 percent return from income in Period 1 and an additional 2.0 percent return from income in Period 2, bringing the total returns for Periods 1 and 2, respectively, to 6.5 percent and 5 percent. The values of the total return index would be calculated as follows:

Period	Return (%)	Calculation	Ending Value
0		1,000(1.00)	1,000.00
1	6.50	1,000(1.065)	1,065.00
2	5.00	1,000(1.065)(1.05)	1,118.25

As illustrated here, as time passes, the value of the total return index, which includes the reinvestment of all dividends and/or interest received, exceeds the value of the price return index by an increasing amount.

3. INDEX CONSTRUCTION AND MANAGEMENT

Constructing and managing a security market index is similar to constructing and managing a portfolio of securities. Index providers must decide the following:

1. Which target market should the index represent?
2. Which securities should be selected from that target market?

3. How much weight should be allocated to each security in the index?
4. When should the index be rebalanced?
5. When should the security selection and weighting decision be reexamined?

3.1. Target Market and Security Selection

The first decision in index construction is identifying the target market, market segment, or asset class that the index is intended to represent. The target market may be defined very broadly or narrowly. It may be based on asset class (e.g., equities, fixed income, real estate, commodities, hedge funds); geographic region (e.g., Japan, South Africa, Latin America, Europe); the exchange on which the securities are traded (e.g., Shanghai, Toronto, Tokyo), and/or other characteristics (e.g., economic sector, company size, investment style, duration, or credit quality).

The target market determines the investment universe and the securities available for inclusion in the index. Once the investment universe is identified, the number of securities and the specific securities to include in the index must be determined. The constituent securities could be nearly all those in the target market or a representative sample of the target market. Some equity indices, such as the S&P 500 Index and the FTSE 100, fix the number of securities included in the index and indicate this number in the name of the index. Other indices allow the number of securities to vary to reflect changes in the target market or to maintain a certain percentage of the target market. For example, the Tokyo Stock Price Index (TOPIX) represents and includes all of the largest stocks, known as the First Section, listed on the Tokyo Stock Exchange. To be included in the First Section—and thus the TOPIX—stocks must meet certain criteria, such as the number of shares outstanding, the number of shareholders, and market capitalization. Stocks that no longer meet the criteria are removed from the First Section and also the TOPIX. Objective or mechanical rules determine the constituent securities of most, but not all, indices. The Sensex of Bombay and the S&P 500, for example, use a selection committee and more subjective decision-making rules to determine constituent securities.

3.2. Index Weighting

The weighting decision determines how much of each security to include in the index and has a substantial impact on an index's value. Index providers use a number of methods to weight the constituent securities in an index. Indices can be price weighted, equal weighted, market-capitalization weighted, or fundamentally weighted. Each weighting method has its advantages and disadvantages.

3.2.1. Price Weighting

The simplest method to weight an index and the one used by Charles Dow to construct the Dow Jones Industrial Average is **price weighting**. In price weighting, the weight on each constituent security is determined by dividing its price by the sum of all the prices of the constituent securities. The weight is calculated using the following formula:

$$w_i^P = \frac{P_i}{\sum_{i=1}^{N} P_i} \tag{2.12}$$

EXHIBIT 2-1 Example of a Price-Weighted Equity Index

Security	Shares in Index	BOP Price	Value (Shares × BOP Price)	BOP Weight %	EOP Price	Dividends Per Share	Value (Shares × EOP Price)	Total Dividends	Price Return %	Total Return %	BOP Weight × Price Return %	BOP Weight × Total Return %	EOP Weight %
A	1	50.00	50.00	49.26	55.00	0.75	55.00	0.75	10.00	11.50	4.93	5.66	52.38
B	1	25.00	25.00	24.63	22.00	0.10	22.00	0.10	−12.00	−11.60	−2.96	−2.86	20.95
C	1	12.50	12.50	12.32	8.00	0.00	8.00	0.00	−36.00	−36.00	−4.43	−4.43	7.62
D	1	10.00	10.00	9.85	14.00	0.05	14.00	0.05	40.00	40.50	3.94	3.99	13.33
E	1	4.00	4.00	3.94	6.00	0.00	6.00	0.00	50.00	50.00	1.97	1.97	5.72
Total			**101.50**	**100.00**			**105.00**	**0.90**			**3.45**	**4.33**	**100.00**
Index Value			**20.30**				**21.00**	**0.18**	**3.45**	**4.33**			

Divisor = 5
BOP = Beginning of period
EOP = End of period

Type of Index	BOP Value	Return %	EOP Value
Price Return	20.30	3.45	21.00
Total Return	20.30	4.33	21.18

Exhibit 2-1 illustrates the values, weights, and single-period returns following inception of a price-weighted equity index with five constituent securities. The value of the price-weighted index is determined by dividing the sum of the security values (101.50) by the divisor, which is typically set at inception to equal the initial number of securities in the index. Thus, in our example, the divisor is 5 and the initial value of the index is calculated as $101.50 \div 5 = 20.30$.

As illustrated in this exhibit, Security A, which has the highest price, also has the highest weighting and thus will have the greatest impact on the return of the index. Note how both the price return and the total return of the index are calculated on the basis of the corresponding returns on the constituent securities.

A property unique to price-weighted indices is that a stock split on one constituent security changes the weights on all the securities in the index.[5] To prevent the stock split and the resulting new weights from changing the value of the index, the index provider must adjust the value of the divisor as illustrated in Exhibit 2-2. Given a 2-for-1 split in Security A, the divisor is adjusted by dividing the sum of the constituent prices *after* the split (77.50) by the value of the index *before* the split (21.00). This adjustment results in changing the divisor from 5 to 3.69 so that the index value is maintained at 21.00.

EXHIBIT 2-2 Impact of 2-for-1 Split in Security A

Security	Price before Split	Weight before Split (%)	Price after Split	Weight after Split (%)
A	55.00	52.38	27.50	35.48
B	22.00	20.95	22.00	28.39
C	8.00	7.62	8.00	10.32
D	14.00	13.33	14.00	18.07
E	6.00	5.72	6.00	7.74
Total	**105.00**	**100.00**	**77.50**	**100.00**
Divisor	**5.00**		**3.69**	
Index Value	**21.00**		**21.00**	

The primary advantage of price weighting is its simplicity. The main disadvantage of price weighting is that it results in arbitrary weights for each security. In particular, a stock split in any one security causes arbitrary changes in the weights of all the constituents' securities.

3.2.2. Equal Weighting

Another simple index weighting method is **equal weighting**. This method assigns an equal weight to each constituent security at inception. The weights are calculated as:

$$w_i^E = \frac{1}{N} \tag{2.13}$$

[5]A stock split is an increase in the number of shares outstanding and a proportionate decrease in the price per share such that the total market value of equity, as well as investors' proportionate ownership in the company, does not change.

where

w_i = fraction of the portfolio that is allocated to security i or weight of security i
N = number of securities in the index

To construct an equal-weighted index from the five securities in Exhibit 2-1, the index provider allocates one-fifth (20 percent) of the value of the index (at the beginning of the period) to each security. Dividing the value allocated to each security by each security's individual share price determines the number of shares of each security to include in the index. Unlike a price-weighted index, where the weights are arbitrarily determined by the market prices, the weights in an equal-weighted index are arbitrarily assigned by the index provider.

Exhibit 2-3 illustrates the values, weights, and single-period returns following inception of an equal-weighted index with the same constituent securities as those in Exhibit 2-1. This example assumes a beginning index portfolio value of 10,000 (i.e., an investment of 2,000 in each security). To set the initial value of the index to 1,000, the divisor is set to 10 (10,000 ÷ 10 = 1,000).

Exhibits 2-1 and 2-3 demonstrate how different weighting methods result in different returns. The 10.4 percent price return of the equal-weighted index shown in Exhibit 2-3 differs significantly from the 3.45 percent price return of the price-weighted index in Exhibit 2-1.

Like price weighting, the primary advantage of equal weighting is its simplicity. Equal weighting, however, has a number of disadvantages. First, securities that constitute the largest fraction of the target market value are underrepresented, and securities that constitute a small fraction of the target market value are overrepresented. Second, after the index is constructed and the prices of constituent securities change, the index is no longer equally weighted. Therefore, maintaining equal weights requires frequent adjustments (rebalancing) to the index.

3.2.3. Market-Capitalization Weighting

In **market-capitalization weighting**, or value weighting, the weight on each constituent security is determined by dividing its market capitalization by the total market capitalization (the sum of the market capitalization) of all the securities in the index. Market capitalization or value is calculated by multiplying the number of shares outstanding by the market price per share.

The market-capitalization weight of security i is:

$$w_i^M = \frac{Q_i P_i}{\sum_{j=1}^{N} Q_j P_j} \tag{2.14}$$

where

w_i = fraction of the portfolio that is allocated to security i or weight of security i
Q_i = number of shares outstanding of security i
P_i = share price of security i
N = number of securities in the index

Exhibit 2-4 illustrates the values, weights, and single-period returns following inception of a market-capitalization-weighted index for the same five-security market. Security A, with 3,000 shares outstanding and a price of 50 per share, has a market capitalization of 150,000 or 26.29 percent (150,000/570,500) of the entire index portfolio. The resulting index

EXHIBIT 2-3 Example of an Equal-Weighted Equity Index

Security	Shares in Index	BOP Price	Value (Shares × BOP Price)	Weight %	EOP Price	Dividends Per Share	Value (Shares × EOP Price)	Total Dividends	Price Return %	Total Return %	Weight × Price Return %	Weight × Total Return %	EOP Weight %
A	40	50.00	2,000	20.00	55.00	0.75	2,200	30	10.00	11.50	2.00	2.30	19.93
B	80	25.00	2,000	20.00	22.00	0.10	1,760	8	−12.00	−11.60	−2.40	−2.32	15.94
C	160	12.50	2,000	20.00	8.00	0.00	1,280	0	−36.00	−36.00	−7.20	−7.20	11.60
D	200	10.00	2,000	20.00	14.00	0.05	2,800	10	40.00	40.50	8.00	8.10	25.36
E	500	4.00	2,000	20.00	6.00	0.00	3,000	0	50.00	50.00	10.00	10.00	27.17
Total			**10,000**	**100.00**			**11,040**	**48**			**10.40**	**10.88**	**100.00**
Index Value			**1,000**				**1,104**	**4.80**	**10.40**	**10.88**			

Divisor = 10
BOP = Beginning of period
EOP = End of period

Type of Index	BOP Value	Return %	EOP Value
Price Return	1,000.00	10.40	1,104.00
Total Return	1,000.00	10.88	1,108.80

EXHIBIT 2-4 Example of a Market-Capitalization-Weighted Equity Index

Stock	Shares Outstanding	BOP Price	BOP Market Cap	BOP Weight %	EOP Price	Dividends Per Share	EOP Market Cap	Total Dividends	Price Return %	Total Return %	BOP Weight × Price Return %	BOP Weight × Total Return %	EOP Weight %
A	3,000	50.00	150,000	26.29	55.00	0.75	165,000	2,250	10.00	11.50	2.63	3.02	28.50
B	10,000	25.00	250,000	43.82	22.00	0.10	220,000	1,000	− 12.00	− 11.60	− 5.26	− 5.08	38.00
C	5,000	12.50	62,500	10.96	8.00	0.00	40,000	0	− 36.00	− 36.00	− 3.95	− 3.95	6.91
D	8,000	10.00	80,000	14.02	14.00	0.05	112,000	400	40.00	40.50	5.61	5.68	19.34
E	7,000	4.00	28,000	4.91	6.00	0.00	42,000	0	50.00	50.00	2.46	2.46	7.25
Total			**570,500**	**100.00**			**579,000**	**3,650**			**1.49**	**2.13**	**100.00**
Index Value			**1,000**				**1,014.90**	**6.40**	**1.49**	**2.13**			

Divisor = 570.50
BOP = Beginning of period
EOP = End of period

Type of Index	BOP Value	Return %	EOP Value
Price Return	1,000.00	1.49	1,014.90
Total Return	1,000.00	2.13	1,021.30

weights in the exhibit reflect the relative value of each security as measured by its market capitalization.

As shown in Exhibits 2-1, 2-3, and 2-4, the weighting method affects the index's returns. The price and total returns of the market-capitalization index in Exhibit 2-4 (1.49 percent and 2.13 percent, respectively) differ significantly from those of the price-weighted (3.45 percent and 4.33 percent, respectively) and equal-weighted (10.40 percent and 10.88 percent, respectively) indices. To understand the source and magnitude of the difference, compare the weights and returns of each security under each of the weighting methods. The weight of Security A, for example, ranges from 49.26 percent in the price-weighted index to 20 percent in the equal-weighted index. With a price return of 10 percent, Security A contributes 4.93 percent to the price return of the price-weighted index, 2.00 percent to the price return of the equal-weighted index, and 2.63 percent to the price return of the market-capitalization-weighted index. With a total return of 11.50 percent, Security A contributes 5.66 percent to the total return of the price-weighted index, 2.30 percent to the total return of the equal-weighted index, and 3.02 percent to the total return of the market-capitalization-weighted index.

3.2.3.1. Float-Adjusted Market-Capitalization Weighting

In **float-adjusted market-capitalization weighting**, the weight on each constituent security is determined by adjusting its market capitalization for its **market float**. Typically, market float is the number of shares of the constituent security that are available to the investing public. For companies that are closely held, only a portion of the shares outstanding are available to the investing public (the rest are held by a small group of controlling investors). In addition to excluding shares held by controlling shareholders, most float-adjusted market-capitalization-weighted indices also exclude shares held by other corporations and governments. Some providers of indices that are designed to represent the investment opportunities of global investors further reduce the number of shares included in the index by excluding shares that are not available to foreigner investors. The index providers may refer to these indices as "free-float-adjusted market-capitalization-weighted indices."

Float-adjusted market-capitalization-weighted indices reflect the shares available for public trading by multiplying the market price per share by the number of shares available to the investing public (i.e., the float-adjusted market capitalization) rather than the total number of shares outstanding (total market capitalization). Currently, most market-capitalization-weighted indices are float adjusted. Therefore, unless otherwise indicated, for the remainder of this chapter, "market-capitalization" weighting refers to float-adjusted market-capitalization weighting.

The float-adjusted market-capitalization weight of security i is calculated as:

$$w_i^M = \frac{f_i Q_i P_i}{\sum_{j=1}^{N} f_j Q_j P_j} \quad (2.15)$$

where

f_i = fraction of shares outstanding in the market float
w_i = fraction of the portfolio that is allocated to security i or weight of security i
Q_i = number of shares outstanding of security i
P_i = share price of security i
N = number of securities in the index

EXHIBIT 2-5 Example of Float-Adjusted Market-Capitalization-Weighted Equity Index

Stock	Shares Outstanding	% Shares in Market Float	Shares in Index	BOP Price	BOP Float Adjusted Market Cap	BOP Weight %	EOP Price	Dividends Per Share	Ending Float Adjusted Market Cap	Total Dividends	Price Return %	Total Return %	BOP Weight × Price Return %	BOP Weight × Total Return %	EOP Weight %
A	3,000	100	3,000	50.00	150,000	35.40	55.00	0.75	165,000	2,250	10.00	11.50	3.54	4.07	39.61
B	10,000	70	7,000	25.00	175,000	41.31	22.00	0.10	154,000	700	− 12.00	− 11.60	− 4.96	− 4.79	36.97
C	5,000	90	4,500	12.50	56,250	13.28	8.00	0.00	36,000	0	− 36.00	− 36.00	− 4.78	− 4.78	8.64
D	8,000	25	2,000	10.00	20,000	4.72	14.00	0.05	28,000	100	40.00	40.50	1.89	1.91	6.72
E	7,000	80	5,600	4.00	22,400	5.29	6.00	0.00	33,600	0	50.00	50.00	2.65	2.65	8.06
Total					**423,650**	**100.00**			**416,600**	**3,050**			**−1.66**	**−0.94**	**100.00**
Index Value					**1,000**				**983.36**	**7.20**	**−1.66**	**−0.94**			

Divisor = 423.65
BOP = Beginning of period
EOP = End of period

Type of Index	Initial Value	Return %	Ending Value
Price Return	1,000.00	− 1.66	983.36
Total Return	1,000.00	− 0.94	990.56

Exhibit 2-5 illustrates the values, weights, and single-period returns following inception of a float-adjusted market-capitalization-weighted equity index using the same five securities as before. The low percentage of shares of Security D in the market float compared with the number of shares outstanding indicates that the security is closely held.

The primary advantage of market-capitalization weighting (including float adjusted) is that constituent securities are held in proportion to their value in the target market. The primary disadvantage is that constituent securities whose prices have risen the most (or fallen the most) have a greater (or lower) weight in the index (i.e., as a security's price rises relative to other securities in the index, its weight increases; and as its price decreases in value relative to other securities in the index, its weight decreases). This weighting method leads to over-weighting stocks that have risen in price (and may be overvalued) and underweighting stocks that have declined in price (and may be undervalued). The effect of this weighting method is similar to a momentum investment strategy in that over time, the securities that have risen in price the most will have the largest weights in the index.

3.2.4. Fundamental Weighting

Fundamental weighting attempts to address the disadvantages of market-capitalization weighting by using measures of a company's size that are independent of its security price to determine the weight on each constituent security. These measures include book value, cash flow, revenues, earnings, dividends, and number of employees.

Some fundamental indices use a single measure, such as total dividends, to weight the constituent securities, whereas others combine the weights from several measures to form a composite value that is used for weighting.

Letting F_i denote a given fundamental size measure of company i, the fundamental weight on security i is

$$w_i^F = \frac{F_i}{\sum_{j=1}^{N} F_j} \tag{2.16}$$

Relative to a market-capitalization-weighted index, a fundamental index with weights based on such an item as earnings will result in greater weights on constituent securities with earnings yields (earnings divided by price) that are higher than the earnings yield of the overall market-weighted portfolio. Similarly, stocks with earnings yields less than the yield on the overall market-weighted portfolio will have lower weights. For example, suppose there are two stocks in an index. Stock A has a market capitalization of €200 million, Stock B has a market capitalization of €800 million, and their aggregate market capitalization is €1 billion (€1,000 million). Both companies have earnings of €20 million and aggregate earnings of €40 million. Thus, Stock A has an earnings yield of 10 percent (20/200) and Stock B has an earnings yield of 2.5 percent (20/800). The earnings weight of Stock A is 50 percent (20/40) which is higher than its market-capitalization weight of 20 percent (200/1,000). The earnings weight of Stock B is 50 percent (20/40), which is less than its market-capitalization weight of 80 percent (800/1,000). Relative to the market-cap-weighted index, the earnings-weighted index overweights the high-yield Stock A and underweights the low-yield Stock B.

The most important property of fundamental weighting is that it leads to indices that have a "value" tilt. That is, a fundamentally weighted index has ratios of book value, earnings, dividends, and so forth to market value that are higher than its market-capitalization-weighted counterpart. Also, in contrast to the momentum "effect" of market-capitalization-weighted indices, fundamentally weighted indices generally will have a contrarian "effect" in that the portfolio weights will shift away from securities that have increased in relative value and toward securities that have fallen in relative value whenever the portfolio is rebalanced.

3.3. Index Management: Rebalancing and Reconstitution

So far, we have discussed index construction. Index management entails the two remaining questions:

- When should the index be rebalanced?
- When should the security selection and weighting decisions be reexamined?

3.3.1. Rebalancing

Rebalancing refers to adjusting the weights of the constituent securities in the index. To maintain the weight of each security consistent with the index's weighting method, the index provider rebalances the index by adjusting the weights of the constituent securities on a regularly scheduled basis (rebalancing dates)—usually quarterly. Rebalancing is necessary because the weights of the constituent securities change as their market prices change. Note, for example, that the weights of the securities in the equal-weighted index (Exhibit 2-3) at the end of the period are no longer equal (i.e., 20 percent):

Security A	19.93%
Security B	15.94
Security C	11.60
Security D	25.36
Security E	27.17

In rebalancing the index, the weights of Securities D and E (which had the highest returns) would be decreased and the weights of Securities A, B, and C (which had the lowest returns) would be increased. Thus, rebalancing creates turnover within an index.

Price-weighted indices are not rebalanced because the weight of each constituent security is determined by its price. For market-capitalization-weighted indices, rebalancing is less of a concern because the indices largely rebalance themselves. In our market-capitalization index, for example, the weight of Security C automatically declined from 10.96 percent to 6.91 percent, reflecting the 36 percent decline in its market price. Market-capitalization weights are only adjusted to reflect mergers, acquisitions, liquidations, and other corporate actions between rebalancing dates.

3.3.2. Reconstitution

Reconstitution is the process of changing the constituent securities in an index. It is similar to a portfolio manager deciding to change the securities in his or her portfolio. Reconstitution is part of the rebalancing cycle. The reconstitution date is the date on which index providers review the constituent securities, reapply the initial criteria for inclusion in the index, and select which securities to retain, remove, or add. Constituent securities that no longer meet the criteria are replaced with securities that do meet the criteria. Once the revised list of constituent securities is determined, the weighting method is reapplied. Indices are

EXHIBIT 2-6 Three-Month Performance of Uranium Energy Corporation and NASDAQ April through June 2009

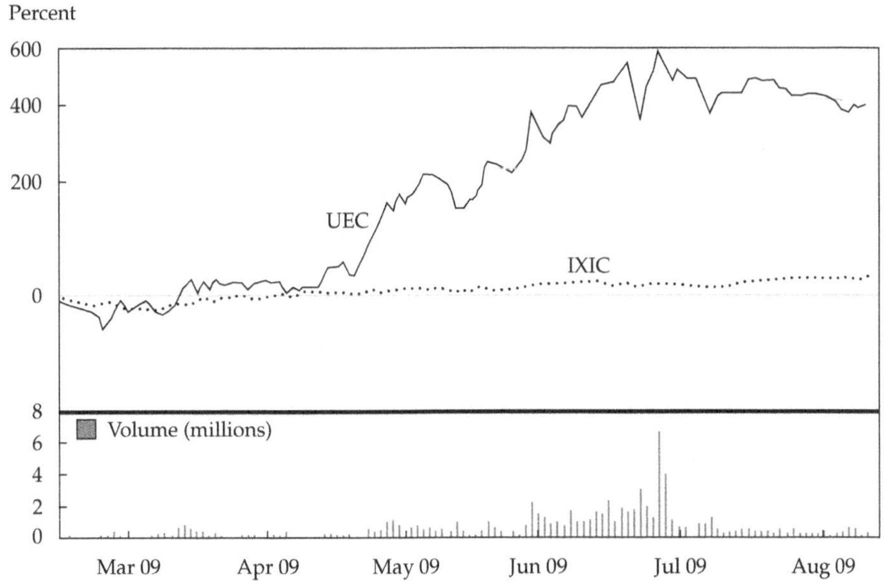

Note: Data as of 12 August 2009.
Source: Yahoo! Finance.

reconstituted to reflect changes in the target market (bankruptcies, de-listings, mergers, acquisitions, etc.) and/or to reflect the judgment of the selection committee.

Reconstitution creates turnover in a number of different ways, particularly for market-capitalization-weighted indices. When one security is removed and another is added, the index provider has to change the weights of the other securities in order to maintain the market-capitalization weighting of the index.

The frequency of reconstitution is a major issue for widely used indices and their constituent securities. The Russell 2000 Index, for example, reconstitutes annually. It is used as a benchmark by numerous investment funds, and each year, prior to the index's reconstitution, the managers of these funds buy stocks they think will be added to the index—driving those stocks' prices up—and sell stocks they think will be deleted from the index—driving those stocks' prices down. Exhibit 2-6 illustrates the potential impact of these decisions. Beginning in late April 2009, some managers began acquiring and bidding up the price of Uranium Energy Corporation (UEC) because they believed that it would be included in the reconstituted Russell 2000 Index. On 12 June, Russell listed UEC as a preliminary addition to the Russell 2000 Index and the Russell 3000 Index.[6] By that time, the stock value had increased by more than 300 percent. Investors continued to bid up the stock price in the weeks following the announcement, and the stock closed on the reconstitution date of 30 June at USD2.90, up nearly 400 percent for the quarter.

[6]According to the press release, final membership in the index would be published after market close on Friday, 26 June.

4. USES OF MARKET INDICES

Indices were initially created to give a sense of how a particular security market performed on a given day. With the development of modern financial theory, their uses in investment management have expanded significantly. Some of the major uses of indices include:

- Gauges of market sentiment.
- Proxies for measuring and modeling returns, systematic risk, and risk-adjusted performance.
- Proxies for asset classes in asset allocation models.
- Benchmarks for actively managed portfolios.
- Model portfolios for such investment products as index funds and exchange-traded funds (ETFs).

Investors using security market indices must be familiar with how various indices are constructed in order to select the index or indices most appropriate for their needs.

4.1. Gauges of Market Sentiment

The original purpose of stock market indices was to provide a gauge of investor confidence or market sentiment. As indicators of the collective opinion of market participants, indices reflect investor attitudes and behavior. The Dow Jones Industrial Average has a long history, is frequently quoted in the media, and remains a popular gauge of market sentiment. It may not accurately reflect the overall attitude of investors or the "market," however, because the index consists of only 30 of the thousands of U.S. stocks traded each day.

4.2. Proxies for Measuring and Modeling Returns, Systematic Risk, and Risk-Adjusted Performance

The capital asset pricing model (CAPM) defines beta as the systematic risk of a security with respect to the entire market. The market portfolio in the CAPM consists of all risky securities. To represent the performance of the market portfolio, investors use a broad index. For example, the Tokyo Stock Price Index (TOPIX) and the S&P 500 often serve as proxies for the market portfolio in Japan and the United States, respectively, and are used for measuring and modeling systematic risk and market returns.

Security market indices also serve as market proxies when measuring risk-adjusted performance. The beta of an actively managed portfolio allows investors to form a passive alternative with the same level of systematic risk. For example, if the beta of an actively managed portfolio of global stocks is 0.95 with respect to the MSCI World Index, investors can create a passive portfolio with the same systematic risk by investing 95 percent of their portfolio in a MSCI World Index fund and holding the remaining 5 percent in cash. Alpha, the difference between the return of the actively managed portfolio and the return of the passive portfolio, is a measure of risk-adjusted return or investment performance. Alpha can be the result of manager skill (or lack thereof), transaction costs, and fees.

4.3. Proxies for Asset Classes in Asset Allocation Models

Because indices exhibit the risk and return profiles of select groups of securities, they play a critical role as proxies for asset classes in asset allocation models. They provide the historical data used to model the risks and returns of different asset classes.

4.4. Benchmarks for Actively Managed Portfolios

Investors often use indices as benchmarks to evaluate the performance of active portfolio managers. The index selected as the benchmark should reflect the investment strategy used by the manager. For example, an active manager investing in global small-capitalization stocks should be evaluated using a benchmark index, such as the FTSE Global Small Cap Index, which includes 4,600 small-capitalization stocks across 48 countries.

The choice of an index to use as a benchmark is important because an inappropriate index could lead to incorrect conclusions regarding an active manager's investment performance. Suppose that the small-cap manager underperformed the small-cap index but outperformed a broad equity market index. If investors use the broad market index as a benchmark, they might conclude that the small-cap manager is earning his or her fees and should be retained or given additional assets to invest. Using the small-cap index as a benchmark might lead to a very different conclusion.

4.5. Model Portfolios for Investment Products

Indices also serve as the basis for the development of new investment products. Using indices as benchmarks for actively managed portfolios has led some investors to conclude that they should invest in the benchmarks instead. Based on the CAPM's conclusion that investors should hold the market portfolio, broad market index funds have been developed to function as proxies for the market portfolio.

Investment management firms initially developed and managed index portfolios for institutional investors. Eventually, mutual fund companies introduced index funds for individual investors. Subsequently, investment management firms introduced exchange-traded funds, which are managed the same way as index mutual funds but trade like stocks.

The first ETFs were based on existing indices. As the popularity of ETFs increased, index providers created new indices for the specific purpose of forming ETFs, leading to the creation of numerous narrowly defined indices with corresponding ETFs. The Market Vectors Vietnam ETF, for example, allows investors to invest in the equity market of Vietnam.

The choice of indices to meet the needs of investors is extensive. Index providers are constantly looking for opportunities to develop indices to meet the needs of investors.

5. EQUITY INDICES

A wide variety of equity indices exist, including broad market, multimarket, sector, and style indices.

5.1. Broad Market Indices

A broad equity market index, as its name suggests, represents an entire given equity market and typically includes securities representing more than 90 percent of the selected market. For example, the Shanghai Stock Exchange Composite Index (SSE) is a market-capitalization-weighted index of all shares that trade on the Shanghai Stock Exchange. In the United States, the Wilshire 5000 Total Market Index is a market-capitalization-weighted index that includes more than 6,000 equity securities and is designed to represent the entire U.S. equity market.[7] The Russell 3000, consisting of the largest 3,000 stocks by market capitalization, represents 99 percent of the U.S. equity market.

5.2. Multimarket Indices

Multimarket indices usually comprise indices from different countries and are designed to represent multiple security markets. Multimarket indices may represent multiple national markets, geographic regions, economic development groups, and, in some cases, the entire world. World indices are of importance to investors who take a global approach to equity investing without any particular bias toward a particular country or region. A number of index providers publish families of multimarket equity indices.

MSCI Barra offers a number of multimarket indices. As shown in Exhibit 2-7, MSCI Barra classifies countries along two dimensions: level of economic development and geographic region. Developmental groups, which MSCI Barra refers to as market classifications, include developed markets, emerging markets, and frontier markets. The geographic regions are largely divided by longitudinal lines of the globe: the Americas, Europe with Africa, and Asia with the Pacific. MSCI Barra provides country-specific indices for each of the developed and emerging market countries within its multimarket indices. MSCI Barra periodically reviews the market classifications of countries in its indices for movement from frontier markets to emerging markets and from emerging markets to developed markets and reconstitutes the indices accordingly.

5.2.1. Fundamental Weighting in Multimarket Indices

Some index providers weight the securities within each country by market capitalization and then weight each country in the overall index in proportion to its relative GDP, effectively creating fundamental weighting in multimarket indices. GDP-weighted indices were some of the first fundamentally weighted indices created. Introduced in 1987 by MSCI to address the 60 percent weight of Japanese equities in the market-capitalization-weighted MSCI EAFE Index at the time, GDP-weighted indices reduced the allocation to Japanese equities by half.[8]

5.3. Sector Indices

Sector indices represent and track different economic sectors—such as consumer goods, energy, finance, health care, and technology—on either a national, regional, or global basis. Because different sectors of the economy behave differently over the course of the business cycle, some investors may seek to overweight or underweight their exposure to particular sectors.

Sector indices are organized as families; each index within the family represents an economic sector. Typically, the aggregation of a sector index family is equivalent to a broad market index. Economic sector classification can be applied on a global, regional, or country-specific basis, but no universally agreed upon sector classification method exists.

Sector indices play an important role in performance analysis because they provide a means to determine whether a portfolio manager is more successful at stock selection or sector allocation. Sector indices also serve as model portfolios for sector-specific ETFs and other investment products.

[7]Despite its name, the Wilshire 5000 has no constraint on the number of securities that can be included. It included approximately 5,000 securities at inception.

[8]Schoenfeld (2004), p. 220.

EXHIBIT 2-7 MSCI International Equity Indices—Country and Market Coverage (as of June 2009)

Developed Markets		
Americas	Europe	Pacific
Canada, United States	Austria, Belgium, Denmark, Finland, France, Germany, Greece, Ireland, Italy, Netherlands, Norway, Portugal, Spain, Sweden, Switzerland, United Kingdom	Australia, Hong Kong, Japan, New Zealand, Singapore

Emerging Markets		
Americas	Europe, Middle East, Africa	Asia
Argentina,[a] Brazil, Chile, Colombia, Mexico, Peru	Czech Republic, Egypt, Hungary, Israel, Jordan, Morocco, Poland, Russia, South Africa, Turkey	China, India, Indonesia, South Korea, Malaysia, Pakistan,[b] Philippines, Taiwan, Thailand

Frontier Markets				
Americas	Central & Eastern Europe & CIS	Africa	Middle East	Asia
Jamaica,[c] Trinidad & Tobago[c]	Bulgaria, Croatia, Estonia, Lithuania, Kazakhstan, Romania, Serbia, Slovenia, Ukraine	Botswana,[d] Ghana,[d] Kenya, Mauritius, Nigeria, Tunisia	Lebanon, Bahrain, Kuwait, Oman, Qatar, United Arab Emirates, Saudi Arabia[e]	Sri Lanka, Vietnam

[a]The MSCI Argentina Index was reclassified from the MSCI Emerging Markets Index to the MSCI Frontier Markets Index at the end of May 2009 to coincide with the May 2009 Semi-Annual Index Review.

[b]The MSCI Pakistan Index was removed from the MSCI Emerging Markets Index as of the close of December 31, 2008 to reflect the deterioration of investability conditions in the Pakistani equity market. In May 2009, the MSCI Pakistan Index was added to the MSCI Frontier Markets Index to coincide with the May 2009 Semi-Annual Index Review.

[c]In May 2009, the MSCI Trinidad & Tobago Index was added to the MSCI Frontier Markets Index. However, the MSCI Jamaica Index continues to be maintained as a stand-alone country index because it does not meet the liquidity requirements of the Frontiers Market Index.

[d]Botswana and Ghana currently stand alone and are not included in the MSCI Frontier Markets Index. The addition of these two countries to the MSCI Frontier Market Index is under consideration.

[e]Saudi Arabia is currently not included in the MSCI Frontier Markets Index but is part of the MSCI GCC Countries Index.

Source: MSCI Barra (www.mscibarra.com/products/indices/equity/index.jsp), June 2009.

5.4. Style Indices

Style indices represent groups of securities classified according to market capitalization, value, growth, or a combination of these characteristics. They are intended to reflect the investing styles of certain investors, such as the growth investor, value investor, and small-cap investor.

5.4.1. Market Capitalization

Market-capitalization indices represent securities categorized according to the major capitalization categories: large cap, midcap, and small cap. With no universal definition of these categories, the indices differ on the distinctions between large cap and midcap and between midcap and small cap, as well as the minimum market-capitalization size required to be included in a small-cap index. Classification into categories can be based on absolute market capitalization (e.g., below €100 million) or relative market capitalization (e.g., the smallest 2,500 stocks).

5.4.2. Value/Growth Classification

Some indices represent categories of stocks based on their classifications as either value or growth stocks. Different index providers use different factors and valuation ratios (low price-to-book ratios, low price-to-earnings ratios, high dividend yields, etc.) to distinguish between value and growth equities.

5.4.3. Market Capitalization and Value/Growth Classification

Combining the three market-capitalization groups with value and growth classifications results in six basic style index categories:

Large-Cap Value	Large-Cap Growth
Mid-Cap Value	Mid-Cap Growth
Small-Cap Value	Small-Cap Growth

Because indices use different size and valuation classifications, the constituents of indices designed to represent a given style, such as small-cap value, may differ—sometimes substantially.

Because valuation ratios and market capitalizations change over time, stocks frequently migrate from one style index category to another on reconstitution dates. As a result, style indices generally have much higher turnover than do broad market indices.

6. FIXED-INCOME INDICES

A wide variety of fixed-income indices exists, but the nature of the fixed-income markets and fixed-income securities leads to some very important challenges to fixed-income index construction and replication. These challenges are the number of securities in the fixed-income universe, the availability of pricing data, and the liquidity of the securities.

6.1. Construction

The fixed-income universe includes securities issued by governments, government agencies, and corporations. Each of these entities may issue a variety of fixed-income securities with different characteristics. As a result, the number of fixed-income securities is many times larger than the number of equity securities. To represent a specific fixed-income market or segment, indices may include thousands of different securities. Over time, these fixed-income securities mature, and issuers offer new securities to meet their financing needs, leading to turnover in fixed-income indices.

Another challenge in index construction is that fixed-income markets are predominantly dealer markets. This means that firms (dealers) are assigned to specific securities and are responsible for creating liquid markets for those securities by purchasing and selling them from their inventory. In addition, many securities do not trade frequently and, as a result, are relatively illiquid. As a result, index providers must contact dealers to obtain current prices on constituent securities to update the index or they must estimate the prices of constituent securities using the prices of traded fixed-income securities with similar characteristics.

These challenges can result in indices with dissimilar numbers of bonds representing the same markets. As seen in Exhibit 2-8, the differences can be large. The large number of fixed-income securities—combined with the lack of liquidity of some securities—has made it more costly and difficult, compared with equity indices, for investors to replicate fixed-income indices and duplicate their performance.

EXHIBIT 2-8 Comparison of Minimum Issue Size and Bond Holdings by Index

	Barclays Capital		Markit iBoxx		Morningstar	
Index	Minimum (thousands)	Number of Bonds	Minimum (thousands)	Number of Bonds	Minimum (thousands)	Number of Bonds
U.S. agency	250,000	988	500,000	435	1,000,000	193
U.S. corporate	250,000	3,134	500,000	1,694	500,000	1,862
U.K. corporate	250,000	916	100,000	713	225,000	303
Euro corporate	300,000	1,285	500,000	1,167	325,000	829

Source: Morningstar.

6.2. Types of Fixed-Income Indices

The wide variety of fixed-income securities, ranging from zero-coupon bonds to bonds with embedded options (i.e., callable or putable bonds), results in a number of different types of fixed-income indices. Similar to equities, fixed-income securities can be categorized according to the issuer's economic sector, the issuer's geographic region, or the economic development of the issuer's geographic region. Fixed-income securities can also be classified along the following dimensions:

- Type of issuer (government, government agency, corporation).
- Type of financing (general obligation, collateralized).
- Currency of payments.
- Maturity.
- Credit quality (investment grade, high yield, credit agency ratings).
- Absence or presence of inflation protection.

Fixed-income indices are based on these various dimensions and can be categorized as follows:

- Aggregate or broad market indices.
- Market sector indices.
- Style indices.
- Economic sector indices.
- Specialized indices such as high-yield, inflation-linked, and emerging market indices.

The first fixed-income index created, the Barclays Capital U.S. Aggregate Bond Index (formerly the Lehman Brothers Aggregate Bond Index), is an example of a single-country aggregate index. Designed to represent the broad market of U.S. fixed-income securities, it comprises more than 9,200 securities, including U.S. Treasury, government-related, corporate, mortgage-backed, asset-backed, and commercial mortgage-backed securities.

Aggregate indices can be subdivided by market sector (government, government agency, collateralized, corporate); style (maturity, credit quality); economic sector, or some other characteristic to create more narrowly defined indices. A common distinction reflected in indices is between investment grade (e.g., those with a Standard & Poor's credit rating of BBB– or better) and high-yield securities. Investment-grade indices are typically further subdivided by maturity (i.e., short, intermediate, or long) and by credit rating (e.g., AAA, BBB, etc.).[9] The wide variety of fixed-income indices reflects the partitioning of fixed-income securities on the basis of a variety of dimensions.

Exhibit 2-9 illustrates how the major types of fixed-income indices can be organized on the basis of various dimensions.

EXHIBIT 2-9 Dimensions of Fixed-Income Indices

Market	Global			
	Regional			
	Country or currency zone			
Type	Corporate	Collateralized *Securitized* *Mortgage-backed*	Government agency	Government
Maturity	For example, 1–3, 3–5, 5–7, 7–10, 10 + years; short-term, medium-term, or long-term			
Credit quality	For example, AAA, AA, A, BBB, etc.; Aaa, Aa, A, Baa, etc.; investment grade, high yield			

All aggregate indices include a variety of market sectors and credit ratings. The breakdown of the Barclays Capital Global Aggregate Bond Index by market sectors and by credit rating is shown in Exhibit 2-10 and Exhibit 2-11, respectively.

7. INDICES FOR ALTERNATIVE INVESTMENTS

Many investors seek to lower the risk or enhance the performance of their portfolios by investing in asset classes other than equities and fixed income. Interest in alternative assets and investment strategies has led to the creation of indices designed to represent broad classes of alternative investments. Three of the most widely followed alternative investment classes are commodities, real estate, and hedge funds.

[9]The credit rating categories vary based on the credit rating agency used by the index provider.

EXHIBIT 2-10 Market Sector Breakdown of the Barclays Capital Global Aggregate Bond Index

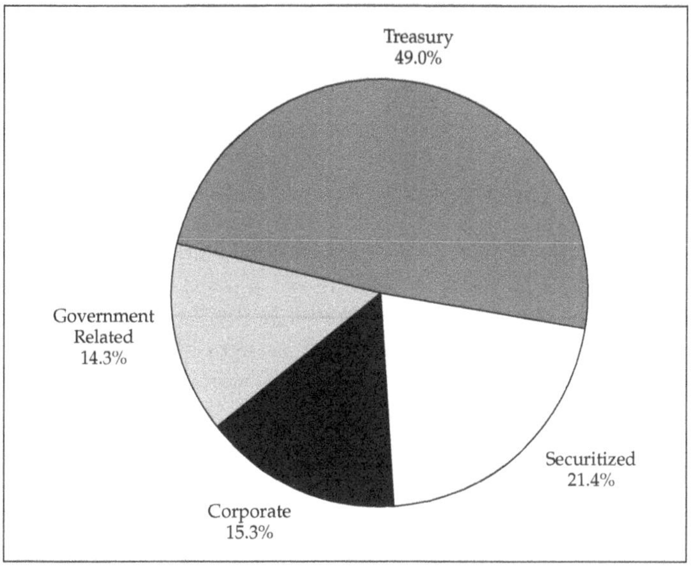

Note: Sector breakdown as of 31 October 2008.
Source: Barclays Capital, "The Benchmark in Fixed Income: Barclays Capital Indices" (December 2008).

EXHIBIT 2-11 Credit Breakdown of the Barclays Capital Global Aggregate Bond Index

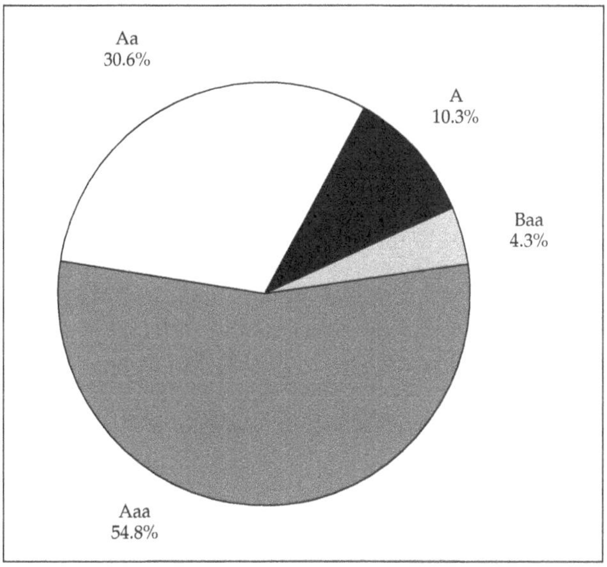

Note: Quality breakdown as of 31 October 2008.
Source: Barclays Capital, "The Benchmark in Fixed Income: Barclays Capital Indices" (December 2008).

7.1. Commodity Indices

Commodity indices consist of futures contracts on one or more commodities, such as agricultural products (rice, wheat, sugar), livestock (cattle, hogs), precious and common metals (gold, silver, copper), and energy commodities (crude oil, natural gas).

Although some commodity indices may include the same commodities, the returns of these indices may differ because each index may use a different weighting method. Because commodity indices do not have an obvious weighting mechanism, such as market capitalization, commodity index providers create their own weighting methods. Some indices, such as the Commodity Research Bureau (CRB) Index, contain a fixed number of commodities that are weighted equally. The S&P GSCI uses a combination of liquidity measures and world production values in its weighting scheme and allocates more weight to commodities that have risen in price. Other indices have fixed weights that are determined by a committee.

The different weighting methods can also lead to large differences in exposure to specific commodities. The S&P GSCI, for example, has approximately double the energy-sector weighting and one-third the agriculture sector weighting of the CRB Index. These differences result in indices with very different risk and return profiles. Unlike commodity indices, broad equity and fixed-income indices that target the same markets share similar risk and return profiles.

The performance of commodity indices can also be quite different from their underlying commodities because the indices consist of futures contracts on the commodities rather than the actual commodities. Index returns are affected by factors other than changes in the prices of the underlying commodities because futures contracts must be continually "rolled over" (i.e., replacing a contract nearing expiration with a new contract). Commodity index returns reflect the risk-free interest rate, the changes in future prices, and the roll yield. Therefore, a commodity index return can be quite different from the return based on changes in the prices of the underlying commodities.

7.2. Real Estate Investment Trust Indices

Real estate indices represent not only the market for real estate securities but also the market for real estate—a highly illiquid market and asset class with infrequent transactions and pricing information. Real estate indices can be categorized as appraisal indices, repeat sales indices, and real estate investment trust (REIT) indices.

REIT indices consist of shares of publicly traded REITs. REITs are public or private corporations organized specifically to invest in real estate, either through ownership of properties or investment in mortgages. Shares of public REITs are traded on the world's various stock exchanges and are a popular choice for investing in commercial real estate properties. Because REIT indices are based on publicly traded REITs with continuous market pricing, the value of REIT indices is calculated continuously.

The FTSE EPRA/NAREIT global family of REIT indices shown in Exhibit 2-12 seeks to represent trends in real estate stocks worldwide and includes representation from the European Real Estate Association (EPRA) and the National Association of Real Estate Investment Trusts (NAREIT).

7.3. Hedge Fund Indices

Hedge fund indices reflect the returns on hedge funds. **Hedge funds** are private investment vehicles that typically use leverage and long and short investment strategies.

A number of research organizations maintain databases of hedge fund returns and summarize these returns into indices. These database indices are designed to represent the

EXHIBIT 2-12 The FTSE EPRA/NAREIT Global REIT Index Family

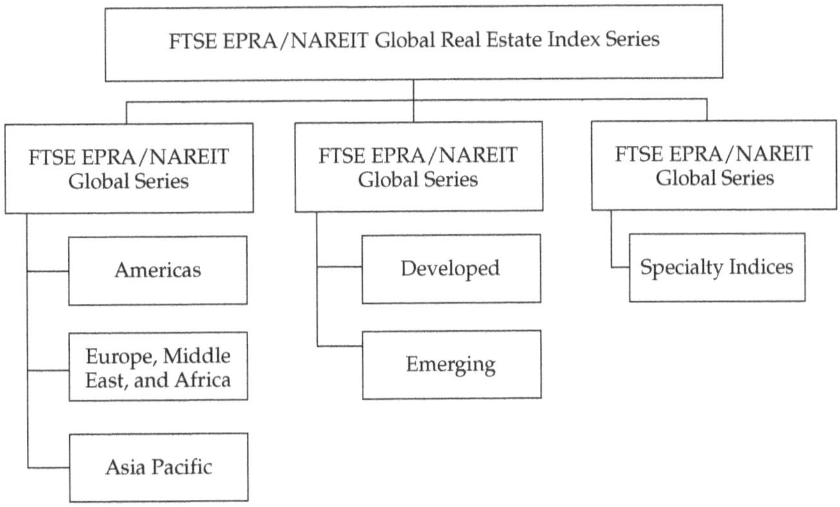

Source: FTSE International, "FTSE EPRA/NAREIT Global & Global Ex US Indices" (Factsheet 2009).

performance of the hedge funds on a very broad global level (hedge funds in general) or the strategy level. Most of these indices are equal weighted and represent the performance of the hedge funds within a particular database.

Most research organizations rely on the voluntary cooperation of hedge funds to compile performance data. As unregulated entities, however, hedge funds are not required to report their performance to any party other than their investors. Therefore, each hedge fund decides to which database(s) it will report its performance. As a result, rather than index providers determining the constituents, the constituents determine the index.

Frequently, a hedge fund reports its performance to only one database. The result is little overlap of funds covered by the different indices. With little overlap between their constituents, different global hedge fund indices may reflect very different performance for the hedge fund industry over the same period of time.

Another consequence of the voluntary performance reporting is the potential for survivorship bias and, therefore, inaccurate performance representation. This means that hedge funds with poor performance may be less likely to report their performance to the database or may stop reporting to the database, so their returns may be excluded when measuring the return of the index. As a result, the index may not accurately reflect actual hedge fund performance so much as the performance of hedge funds that are performing well.

Representative Indices Worldwide

As indicated in this chapter, the choice of indices to meet the needs of investors is extensive. Investors using security market indices must be careful in their selection of the index or indices most appropriate for their needs. The following table illustrates the variety of indices reflecting different asset classes, markets, and weighting methods.

Index	Representing	Number of Securities	Weighting Method	Comments
Dow Jones Industrial Average	U.S. blue-chip companies	30	Price	The oldest and most widely known U.S. equity index. *Wall Street Journal* editors choose 30 stocks from among large, mature blue-chip companies.
Nikkei Stock Average	Japanese blue-chip companies	225	Modified price	Known as the Nikkei 225 and originally formulated by Dow Jones & Company. Because of extreme variation in price levels of component securities, some high-priced shares are weighted as a fraction of share price. Index contains some illiquid stocks.
TOPIX	All companies listed on the Tokyo Stock Exchange First Section	Varies	Float-adjusted market cap	Represents about 93 percent of the market value of all Japanese equities. Contains a large number of very small, illiquid stocks, making exact replication difficult.
MSCI All Country World Index	Stocks of 23 developed and 22 emerging markets	Varies	Free-float-adjusted market cap	Composed of companies representative of the market structure of developed and emerging market countries in the Americas, Europe/Middle East, and Asia/Pacific regions. Price return and total return versions available in both USD and local currencies.
S&P Developed Ex-U.S. BMI Energy Sector Index	Energy sector of developed global markets outside the United States	Varies	Float-adjusted market cap	Serves as a model portfolio for the SPDR® S&P Energy Sector Exchange-Traded Fund (ETF).
Barclays Capital Global Aggregate Bond Index	Investment-grade bonds in the North American, European, and Asian markets	Varies	Market cap	Formerly known as Lehman Brothers Global Aggregate Bond Index.
Markit iBoxx Euro High-Yield Bond Indices	Sub-investment-grade, euro-denominated corporate bonds	Varies	Market cap and variations	Rebalanced monthly. Represents tradable part of market. Price and total return versions available with

Index	Representing	Number of Securities	Weighting Method	Comments
				such analytical values as yield, duration, modified duration, and convexity. Provides platform for research and structured products.
FTSE EPRA/NAREIT Global Real Estate Index	Real estate securities in the North American, European, and Asian markets	335	Float-adjusted market cap	The stocks of REITs that constitute the index trade on public stock exchanges and may be constituents of equity market indices.
HFRX Global Hedge Fund Index	Overall composition of the HFR database	Varies	Asset weighted	Comprises all eligible hedge fund strategies. Examples include convertible arbitrage, distressed securities, market neutral, event driven, macro, and relative value arbitrage. Constituent strategies are asset weighted on the basis of asset distribution within the hedge fund industry.
HFRX Equal Weighted Strategies EUR Index	Overall composition of the HFR database	Varies	Equal weighted	Denominated in euros and is constructed from the same strategies as the HFRX Global Hedge Fund Index.
Morningstar Style Indices	U.S. stocks classified by market cap and value/growth orientation	Varies	Float-adjusted market cap	The nine indices defined by combinations of market cap (large, mid, and small) and value/growth orientation (value, core, growth) have mutually exclusive constituents and are exhaustive with respect to the Morningstar U.S. Market Index. Each is a model portfolio for one of the iShares Morningstar ETFs.

8. SUMMARY

This chapter explains and illustrates the construction, management, and uses of security market indices. It also discusses various types of indices. Security market indices are invaluable tools for investors, who can select from among thousands of indices representing a variety of security markets, market segments, and asset classes. These indices range from those representing the global market for major asset classes to those representing alternative investments in specific geographic markets. To benefit from the use of security market indices, investors must understand their construction and determine whether the selected index is appropriate for their purposes. Frequently, an index that is well suited for one purpose may not be well suited for other purposes. Users of indices must be familiar with how various indices are constructed in order to select the index or indices most appropriate for their needs.

Among the key points made in this chapter are the following:

- Security market indices are intended to measure the values of different target markets (security markets, market segments, or asset classes).
- The constituent securities selected for inclusion in the security market index are intended to represent the target market.
- A price return index reflects only the prices of the constituent securities.
- A total return index reflects not only the prices of the constituent securities but also the reinvestment of all income received since the inception of the index.
- Methods used to weight the constituents of an index range from the very simple, such as price and equal weightings, to the more complex, such as market-capitalization and fundamental weightings.
- Choices in index construction—in particular, the choice of weighting method—affect index valuation and returns.
- Index management includes (1) periodic rebalancing to ensure that the index maintains appropriate weightings and (2) reconstitution to ensure the index represents the desired target market.
- Rebalancing and reconstitution create turnover in an index. Reconstitution can dramatically affect prices of current and prospective constituents.
- Indices serve a variety of purposes. They gauge market sentiment and serve as benchmarks for actively managed portfolios. They act as proxies for measuring systematic risk and risk-adjusted performance. They also serve as proxies for asset classes in asset allocation models and as model portfolios for investment products.
- Investors can choose from security market indices representing various asset classes, including equity, fixed-income, commodity, real estate, and hedge fund indices.
- Within most asset classes, index providers offer a wide variety of indices, ranging from broad market indices to highly specialized indices based on the issuer's geographic region, economic development group, or economic sector or other factors.
- Proper use of security market indices depends on understanding their construction and management.

PROBLEMS

1. A security market index represents the:

   A. Risk of a security market.
   B. Security market as a whole.
   C. Security market, market segment, or asset class.

2. Security market indices are:

   A. Constructed and managed like a portfolio of securities.
   B. Simple interchangeable tools for measuring the returns of different asset classes.
   C. Valued on a regular basis using the actual market prices of the constituent securities.

3. When creating a security market index, an index provider must first determine the:

   A. Target market.
   B. Appropriate weighting method.
   C. Number of constituent securities.

4. One month after inception, the price return version and total return version of a single index (consisting of identical securities and weights) will be equal if:

   A. Market prices have not changed.
   B. Capital gains are offset by capital losses.
   C. The securities do not pay dividends or interest.

5. The values of a price return index and a total return index consisting of identical equal-weighted dividend-paying equities will be equal:

   A. Only at inception.
   B. At inception and on rebalancing dates.
   C. At inception and on reconstitution dates.

6. An analyst gathers the following information for an equal-weighted index comprised of assets Able, Baker, and Charlie:

Security	Beginning of Period Price (€)	End of Period Price (€)	Total Dividends (€)
Able	10.00	12.00	0.75
Baker	20.00	19.00	1.00
Charlie	30.00	30.00	2.00

   The price return of the index is:

   A. 1.7%.
   B. 5.0%.
   C. 11.4%.

7. An analyst gathers the following information for an equal-weighted index comprised of assets Able, Baker, and Charlie:

Security	Beginning of Period Price (€)	End of Period Price (€)	Total Dividends (€)
Able	10.00	12.00	0.75
Baker	20.00	19.00	1.00
Charlie	30.00	30.00	2.00

The total return of the index is:

A. 5.0%.
B. 7.9%.
C. 11.4%.

8. An analyst gathers the following information for a price-weighted index comprised of securities ABC, DEF, and GHI:

Security	Beginning of Period Price (£)	End of Period Price (£)	Total Dividends (£)
ABC	25.00	27.00	1.00
DEF	35.00	25.00	1.50
GHI	15.00	16.00	1.00

The price return of the index is:

A. –4.6%.
B. –9.3%.
C. –13.9%.

9. An analyst gathers the following information for a market-capitalization-weighted index comprised of securities MNO, QRS, and XYZ:

Security	Beginning of Period Price (¥)	End of Period Price (¥)	Dividends Per Share (¥)	Shares Outstanding
MNO	2,500	2,700	100	5,000
QRS	3,500	2,500	150	7,500
XYZ	1,500	1,600	100	10,000

The price return of the index is:

A. –9.33%.
B. –10.23%.
C. –13.90%.

10. An analyst gathers the following information for a market-capitalization-weighted index comprised of securities MNO, QRS, and XYZ:

Security	Beginning of Period Price (¥)	End of Period Price (¥)	Dividends Per Share (¥)	Shares Outstanding
MNO	2,500	2,700	100	5,000
QRS	3,500	2,500	150	7,500
XYZ	1,500	1,600	100	10,000

The total return of the index is:

A. 1.04%.
B. –5.35%.
C. –10.23%.

11. When creating a security market index, the target market:

A. Determines the investment universe.
B. Is usually a broadly defined asset class.
C. Determines the number of securities to be included in the index.

12. An analyst gathers the following data for a price-weighted index:

	Beginning of Period		End of Period	
Security	Price (€)	Shares	Price (€)	Shares
A	20.00	300	22.00	300
B	50.00	300	48.00	300
C	26.00	2,000	30.00	2,000

The price return of the index over the period is:

A. 4.2%.
B. 7.1%.
C. 21.4%.

13. An analyst gathers the following data for a value-weighted index:

	Beginning of Period		End of Period	
Security	Price (£)	Shares	Price (£)	Shares
A	20.00	300	22.00	300
B	50.00	300	48.00	300
C	26.00	2,000	30.00	2,000

The return on the value-weighted index over the period is:

A. 7.1%.
B. 11.0%.
C. 21.4%.

14. An analyst gathers the following data for an equal-weighted index:

	Beginning of Period		End of Period	
Security	Price (¥)	Shares	Price (¥)	Shares
A	20.00	300	22.00	300
B	50.00	300	48.00	300
C	26.00	2,000	30.00	2,000

The return on the index over the period is:

A. 4.2%.
B. 6.8%.
C. 7.1%.

15. Which of the following index weighting methods requires an adjustment to the divisor after a stock split?

A. Price weighting.
B. Fundamental weighting.
C. Market-capitalization weighting.

16. If the price return of an equal-weighted index exceeds that of a market-capitalization-weighted index comprised of the same securities, the *most likely* explanation is:

A. Stock splits.
B. Dividend distributions.
C. Outperformance of small-market-capitalization stocks.

17. A float-adjusted market-capitalization-weighted index weights each of its constituent securities by its price and:

A. Its trading volume.
B. The number of its shares outstanding.
C. The number of its shares available to the investing public.

18. Which of the following index weighting methods is most likely subject to a value tilt?

A. Equal weighting.
B. Fundamental weighting.
C. Market-capitalization weighting.

19. Rebalancing an index is the process of periodically adjusting the constituent:

A. Securities' weights to optimize investment performance.
B. Securities to maintain consistency with the target market.
C. Securities' weights to maintain consistency with the index's weighting method.

20. Which of the following index weighting methods requires the most frequent rebalancing?

A. Price weighting.
B. Equal weighting.
C. Market-capitalization weighting.

21. Reconstitution of a security market index reduces:

A. Portfolio turnover.
B. The need for rebalancing.
C. The likelihood that the index includes securities that are not representative of the target market.

22. Security market indices are used as:

A. Measures of investment returns.
B. Proxies to measure unsystematic risk.
C. Proxies for specific asset classes in asset allocation models.

23. Uses of market indices do not include serving as a:
    A. Measure of systematic risk.
    B. Basis for new investment products.
    C. Benchmark for evaluating portfolio performance.

24. Which of the following statements regarding sector indices is *most* accurate? Sector indices:
    A. Track different economic sectors and cannot be aggregated to represent the equivalent of a broad market index.
    B. Provide a means to determine whether an active investment manager is more successful at stock selection or sector allocation.
    C. Apply a universally agreed-upon sector classification system to identify the constituent securities of specific economic sectors, such as consumer goods, energy, finance, health care.

25. Which of the following is an example of a style index? An index based on:
    A. Geography.
    B. Economic sector.
    C. Market capitalization.

26. Which of the following statements regarding fixed-income indices is *most* accurate?
    A. Liquidity issues make it difficult for investors to easily replicate fixed-income indices.
    B. Rebalancing and reconstitution are the only sources of turnover in fixed-income indices.
    C. Fixed-income indices representing the same target market hold similar numbers of bonds.

27. An aggregate fixed-income index:
    A. Is comprised of corporate and asset-backed securities.
    B. Represents the market of government-issued securities.
    C. Can be subdivided by market or economic sector to create more narrowly defined indices.

28. Fixed-income indices are *least likely* constructed on the basis of:
    A. Maturity.
    B. Type of issuer.
    C. Coupon frequency.

29. Commodity index values are based on:
    A. Futures contract prices.
    B. The market price of the specific commodity.
    C. The average market price of a basket of similar commodities.

30. Which of the following statements is *most* accurate?
    A. Commodity indices all share similar weighting methods.
    B. Commodity indices containing the same underlying commodities offer similar returns.
    C. The performance of commodity indices can be quite different from that of the underlying commodities.

31. Which of the following is *not* a real estate index category?

    A. Appraisal index.
    B. Initial sales index.
    C. Repeat sales index.

32. A unique feature of hedge fund indices is that they:

    A. Are frequently equal weighted.
    B. Are determined by the constituents of the index.
    C. Reflect the value of private rather than public investments.

33. The returns of hedge fund indices are *most likely*:

    A. Biased upward.
    B. Biased downward.
    C. Similar across different index providers.

34. In comparison to equity indices, the constituent securities of fixed-income indices are:

    A. More liquid.
    B. Easier to price.
    C. Drawn from a larger investment universe.

CHAPTER 3

MARKET EFFICIENCY

W. Sean Cleary, CFA
Kingston, Canada

Howard J. Atkinson, CFA
Toronto, Canada

Pamela Peterson Drake, CFA
Harrisonburg, VA, U.S.A.

LEARNING OUTCOMES

After completing this chapter, you will be able to do the following:

- Discuss market efficiency and related concepts, including their importance to investment practitioners.
- Explain the factors affecting a market's efficiency.
- Distinguish between market value and intrinsic value.
- Compare and contrast the weak-form, semistrong-form, and strong-form market efficiency.
- Explain the implications of each form of market efficiency for fundamental analysis, technical analysis, and the choice between active and passive portfolio management.
- Discuss identified market pricing anomalies and explain possible inconsistencies with market efficiency.
- Compare and contrast the behavioral finance view of investor behavior with that of traditional finance in regards to market efficiency.

1. INTRODUCTION

Market efficiency concerns the extent to which market prices incorporate available information. If market prices do not fully incorporate information, then opportunities may exist to make a profit from the gathering and processing of information. The subject of market efficiency is, therefore, of great interest to investment managers, as illustrated in Example 3-1.

EXAMPLE 3-1 Market Efficiency and Active Manager Selection

The chief investment officer (CIO) of a major university endowment fund has listed eight steps in the active manager selection process that can be applied both to traditional investments (e.g., common equity and fixed-income securities) and to alternative investments (e.g., private equity, hedge funds, and real assets). The first step specified is the evaluation of market opportunity:

> *What is the opportunity and why is it there? To answer this question we start by studying capital markets and the types of managers operating within those markets. We identify market inefficiencies and try to understand their causes, such as regulatory structures or behavioral biases. We can rule out many broad groups of managers and strategies by simply determining that the degree of market inefficiency necessary to support a strategy is implausible. Importantly, we consider the past history of active returns meaningless unless we understand why markets will allow those active returns to continue into the future.*[1]

The CIO's description underscores the importance of not assuming that past active returns that might be found in a historical dataset will repeat themselves in the future. **Active returns** refer to returns earned by strategies that do *not* assume that all information is fully reflected in market prices.

Governments and market regulators also care about the extent to which market prices incorporate information. Efficient markets imply informative prices—prices that accurately reflect available information about fundamental values. In market-based economies, market prices help determine which companies (and which projects) obtain capital. If these prices do not efficiently incorporate information about a company's prospects, then it is possible that funds will be misdirected. By contrast, prices that are informative help direct scarce resources and funds available for investment to their highest-valued uses.[2] Informative prices thus promote economic growth. The efficiency of a country's capital markets (in which businesses raise financing) is an important characteristic of a well-functioning financial system.

The remainder of this chapter is organized as follows. Section 2 provides specifics on how the efficiency of an asset market is described and discusses the factors affecting (i.e., contributing to and impeding) market efficiency. Section 3 presents an influential three-way classification of the efficiency of security markets and discusses its implications for fundamental analysis, technical analysis, and portfolio management. Section 4 presents several market anomalies (apparent market inefficiencies that have received enough attention to be individually identified and named) and describes how these anomalies relate to investment strategies. Section 5 introduces behavioral finance and how that field of study relates to market efficiency. Section 6 concludes and provides a summary.

[1]The CIO is Christopher J. Brightman, CFA, of the University of Virginia Investment Management Company, as reported in Yau, Schneeweis, Robinson, and Weiss (2007, pp. 481–482).
[2]This concept is known as *allocative efficiency.*

2. THE CONCEPT OF MARKET EFFICIENCY

2.1. The Description of Efficient Markets

An **informationally efficient market** (an **efficient market**) is a market in which asset prices reflect new information quickly and rationally. An efficient market is thus a market in which asset prices reflect all past and present information.[3]

In this section we expand on this definition by clarifying the time frame required for an asset's price to incorporate information as well as describing the elements of information releases assumed under market efficiency. We discuss the difference between market value and intrinsic value and illustrate how inefficiencies or discrepancies between these values can provide profitable opportunities for active investment. As financial markets are generally not considered being either completely efficient or inefficient, but rather falling within a range between the two extremes, we describe a number of factors that contribute to and impede the degree of efficiency of a financial market. Finally, we conclude our overview of market efficiency by illustrating how the costs incurred by traders in identifying and exploiting possible market inefficiencies affect how we interpret market efficiency.

Investment managers and analysts, as noted, are interested in market efficiency because the extent to which a market is efficient affects how many profitable trading opportunities (market inefficiencies) exist. Consistent, superior, risk-adjusted returns (net of all expenses) are not achievable in an efficient market.[4] In a highly efficient market, a **passive investment** strategy (i.e., buying and holding a broad market portfolio) that does not seek superior risk-adjusted returns is preferred to an **active investment** strategy because of lower costs (for example, transaction and information-seeking costs). By contrast, in a very inefficient market, opportunities may exist for an active investment strategy to achieve superior risk-adjusted returns (net of all expenses in executing the strategy) as compared with a passive investment strategy. In inefficient markets, an active investment strategy may outperform a passive investment strategy on a risk-adjusted basis. Understanding the characteristics of an efficient market and being able to evaluate the efficiency of a particular market are important topics for investment analysts and portfolio managers.

An efficient market is a market in which asset prices reflect information quickly. But what is the time frame of "quickly"? Trades are the mechanism by which information can be incorporated into asset transaction prices. The time needed to execute trades to exploit an inefficiency may provide a baseline for judging speed of adjustment.[5] The time frame for an asset's price to incorporate information must be at least as long as the shortest time a trader needs to execute a transaction in the asset. In certain markets, such as foreign exchange and developed equity markets, market efficiency relative to certain types of information has been studied using time frames as short as one minute or less. If the time frame of price adjustment

---

[3]This definition is convenient for making several instructional points. The definition that most simply explains the sense of the word *efficient* in this context can be found in Fama (1976): "An efficient capital market is a market that is efficient in processing information" (p. 134).

[4]The technical term for *superior* in this context is *positive abnormal* in the sense of higher than expected given the asset's risk (as measured, according to capital market theory, by the asset's contribution to the risk of a well-diversified portfolio).

[5]Although the original theory of market efficiency does not quantify this speed, the basic idea is that it is sufficiently swift to make it impossible to consistently earn abnormal profits. Chordia, Roll, and Subrahmanyam (2005) suggest that the adjustment to information on the New York Stock Exchange (NYSE) is between 5 and 60 minutes.

allows many traders to earn profits with little risk, then the market is relatively inefficient. These considerations lead to the observation that market efficiency can be viewed as falling on a continuum.

Finally, an important point is that in an efficient market, prices should be expected to react only to the elements of information releases that are not anticipated fully by investors—that is, to the "unexpected" or "surprise" element of such releases. Investors process the unexpected information and revise expectations (for example, about an asset's future cash flows, risk, or required rate of return) accordingly. The revised expectations enter or get incorporated in the asset price through trades in the asset. Market participants who process the news and believe that at the current market price an asset does not offer sufficient compensation for its perceived risk will tend to sell it or even sell it short. Market participants with opposite views should be buyers. In this way the market establishes the price that balances the various opinions after expectations are revised.

EXAMPLE 3-2 Price Reaction to the Default on a Bond Issue

Suppose that a speculative-grade bond issuer announces, just before bond markets open, that it will default on an upcoming interest payment. In the announcement, the issuer confirms various reports made in the financial media in the period leading up to the announcement. Prior to the issuer's announcement, the financial news media reported the following: (1) suppliers of the company were making deliveries only for cash payment, reducing the company's liquidity; (2) the issuer's financial condition had probably deteriorated to the point that it lacked the cash to meet an upcoming interest payment; and (3) although public capital markets were closed to the company, it was negotiating with a bank for a private loan that would permit it to meet its interest payment and continue operations for at least nine months. If the issuer defaults on the bond, the consensus opinion of analysts is that bondholders will recover approximately \$0.36 to \$0.38 per dollar face value.

1. If the market for the bond is highly efficient, the bond's market price is *most likely* to fully reflect the bond's value after default:
   A. In the period leading up to the announcement.
   B. In the first trade prices after the market opens on the announcement day.
   C. When the issuer actually misses the payment on the interest payment date.
2. If the market for the bond is highly efficient, the piece of information that bond investors *most likely* focused on in the issuer's announcement was that the issuer:
   A. Had failed in its negotiations for a bank loan.
   B. Lacked the cash to meet the upcoming interest payment.
   C. Had been required to make cash payments for supplier deliveries.

Solution to 1: B is correct. The announcement removed any uncertainty about default. In the period leading up to the announcement, the bond's market price incorporated a probability of default but the price would not have fully reflected the bond's value after default. The possibility that a bank loan might permit the company to avoid default was not eliminated until the announcement.

Solution to 2: A is correct. The failure of the loan negotiations first becomes known in this announcement. The failure implies default.

2.2. Market Value versus Intrinsic Value

Market value is the price at which an asset can currently be bought or sold. **Intrinsic value** (sometimes called **fundamental value**) is, broadly speaking, the value that would be placed on it by investors if they had a complete understanding of the asset's investment characteristics.[6] For a bond, for example, such information would include its interest (coupon) rate, principal value, the timing of its interest and principal payments, the other terms of the bond contract (indenture), a precise understanding of its default risk, the liquidity of its market, and other issue-specific items. In addition, market variables such as the term structure of interest rates and the size of various market premiums applying to the issue (for default risk, etc.) would enter into a discounted cash flow estimate of the bond's intrinsic value (discounted cash flow models are often used for such estimates). The word *estimate* is used because in practice, intrinsic value can be estimated but is not known for certain.

If investors believe a market is highly *efficient*, they will usually accept market prices as accurately reflecting intrinsic values. Discrepancies between market price and intrinsic value are the basis for profitable active investment. Active investors seek to own assets selling below perceived intrinsic value in the marketplace and to sell or sell short assets selling above perceived intrinsic value.

If investors believe an asset market is relatively *inefficient*, they may try to develop an independent estimate of intrinsic value. The challenge for investors and analysts is estimating an asset's intrinsic value. Numerous theories and models, including the dividend discount model, can be used to estimate an asset's intrinsic value, but they all require some form of judgment regarding the size, timing, and riskiness of the future cash flows associated with the asset. The more complex an asset's future cash flows, the more difficult it is to estimate its intrinsic value. These complexities and the estimates of an asset's market value are reflected in the market through the buying and selling of assets. The market value of an asset represents the intersection of supply and demand—the point that is low enough to induce at least one investor to buy while being high enough to induce at least one investor to sell. Because information relevant to valuation flows continually to investors, estimates of intrinsic value change, and hence, market values change.

EXAMPLE 3-3 Intrinsic Value

1. An analyst estimates that a security's intrinsic value is lower than its market value. The security appears to be:

[6] Intrinsic value is often defined as the present value of all expected future cash flows of the asset.

A. Undervalued.
B. Fairly valued.
C. Overvalued.

2. A market in which assets' market values are, on average, equal to or nearly equal to intrinsic values is *best described* as a market that is attractive for:
   A. Active investment.
   B. Passive investment.
   C. Both active and passive investment.
3. Suppose that the future cash flows of an asset are accurately estimated. The asset trades in a market that you believe is highly efficient based on most evidence. But your intrinsic value estimate exceeds market value by a moderate amount. The most likely conclusion is that you have:
   A. Overestimated the asset's risk.
   B. Underestimated the asset's risk.
   C. Identified a market inefficiency.

Solution to 1: C is correct. The market is valuing the asset at more than its true worth.

Solution to 2: B is correct because an active investment is not expected to earn superior risk-adjusted returns. The additional costs of active investment are not justified in such a market.

Solution to 3: B is correct. If risk is underestimated, the discount rate being applied to find the present value of the expected cash flows (estimated intrinsic value) will be too low and the intrinsic value estimate will be too high.

2.3. Factors Contributing to and Impeding a Market's Efficiency

For markets to be efficient, prices should adjust quickly and rationally to the release of new information. In other words, prices of assets in an efficient market should "fully reflect" all information. Financial markets, however, are generally not classified at the two extremes as either completely inefficient or completely efficient but, rather, as exhibiting various degrees of efficiency. In other words, market efficiency should be viewed as falling on a continuum between extremes of completely efficient, at one end, and completely inefficient, at the other. Asset prices in a highly efficient market, by definition, reflect information more quickly and more accurately than in a less-efficient market. These degrees of efficiency also vary through time, across geographical markets, and by type of market. A number of factors contribute to and impede the degree of efficiency in a financial market.

2.3.1. Market Participants

One of the most critical factors contributing to the degree of efficiency in a market is the number of market participants. Consider the following example that illustrates the relationship between the number of market participants and market efficiency.

EXAMPLE 3-4 Illustration of Market Efficiency

Assume that the shares of a small market capitalization (cap) company trade on a public stock exchange. Because of its size, it is not considered "blue-chip" and not many professional investors follow the activities of the company.[7] A small-cap fund analyst reports that the most recent annual operating performance of the company has been surprisingly good, considering the recent slump in its industry. The company's share price, however, has been slow to react to the positive financial results because the company is not being recommended by the majority of research analysts. This mispricing implies that the market for this company's shares is less than fully efficient. The small-cap fund analyst recognizes the opportunity and immediately recommends the purchase of the company's shares. The share price gradually increases as more investors purchase the shares once the news of the mispricing spreads through the market. As a result, it takes a few days for the share price to fully reflect the information.

Six months later, the company reports another solid set of interim financial results. But because the previous mispricing and subsequent profit opportunities have become known in the market, the number of analysts following the company's shares has increased substantially. As a result, as soon as unexpected information about the positive interim results are released to the public, a large number of buy orders quickly drive up the stock price, thereby making the market for these shares more efficient than before.

A large number of investors (individual and institutional) follow the major financial markets closely on a daily basis, and if mispricings exist in these markets, as illustrated by the example, investors will act so that these mispricings disappear quickly. Besides the number of investors, the number of financial analysts who follow or analyze a security or asset should be positively related to market efficiency. The number of market participants and resulting trading activity can vary significantly through time. A lack of trading activity can cause or accentuate other market imperfections that impede market efficiency. In fact, in many of these markets, such as China, trading in many of the listed stocks is restricted for foreigners. By nature, this limitation reduces the number of market participants, restricts the potential for trading activity, and hence reduces market efficiency.

EXAMPLE 3-5 Factors Affecting Market Efficiency

The expected effect on market efficiency of opening a securities market to trading by foreigners would be to:

[7]A "blue-chip" share is one from a well-recognized company that is considered to be high quality but low risk. This term generally refers to a company that has a long history of earnings and paying dividends.

A. Decrease market efficiency.
B. Leave market efficiency unchanged.
C. Increase market efficiency.

Solution: C is correct. The opening of markets as described should increase market efficiency by increasing the number of market participants.

2.3.2. Information Availability and Financial Disclosure

Information availability (e.g., an active financial news media) and financial disclosure should promote market efficiency. Information regarding trading activity and traded companies in such markets as the New York Stock Exchange, the London Stock Exchange, and the Tokyo Stock Exchange is readily available. Many investors and analysts participate in these markets, and analyst coverage of listed companies is typically substantial. As a result, these markets are quite efficient. In contrast, trading activity and material information availability may be lacking in smaller securities markets, such as those operating in some emerging markets.

Similarly, significant differences may exist in the efficiency of different types of markets. For example, many securities trade primarily or exclusively in dealer or over-the-counter (OTC) markets, including bonds, money market instruments, currencies, mortgage-backed securities, swaps, and forward contracts. The information provided by the dealers who serve as market makers for these markets can vary significantly in quality and quantity, both through time and across different product markets.

Treating all market participants fairly is critical for the integrity of the market and explains why regulators place such an emphasis on "fair, orderly, and efficient markets."[8] A key element of this fairness is that all investors have access to the information necessary to value securities that trade in the market. Rules and regulations that promote fairness and efficiency in a market include those pertaining to the disclosure of information and illegal insider trading.

For example, U.S. Securities and Exchange Commission's (SEC's) Regulation FD (Fair Disclosure) requires that if security issuers provide nonpublic information to some market professionals or investors, they must also disclose this information to the public.[9] This requirement helps provide equal and fair opportunities, which is important in encouraging participation in the market. A related issue deals with illegal insider trading. The SEC's rules, along with court cases, define illegal insider trading as trading in securities by market participants who are considered insiders "while in possession of material, nonpublic information about the security."[10,11] Although these rules cannot guarantee that some participants will not

[8]"The Investor's Advocate: How the SEC Protects Investors, Maintains Market Integrity, and Facilitates Capital Formation," U.S. Securities and Exchange Commission (www.sec.gov/about/whatwedo.shtml).
[9]Regulation FD, "Selective Disclosure and Insider Trading," 17 CFR Parts 240, 243, and 249, effective 23 October 2000.
[10]Although not the focus of this particular chapter, it is important to note that a party is considered an insider not only when the individual is a corporate insider, such as an officer or director, but also when the individual is aware that the information is nonpublic information [Securities and Exchange Commission, Rules 10b5-1 ("Trading on the Basis of Material Nonpublic Information in Insider Trading Cases") and Rule 10b5-2 ("Duties of Trust or Confidence in Misappropriation Insider Trading Cases")].
[11]In contrast to the situation in the United States, in other developed markets, the insider trading laws are generally promulgated by the courts, although the definition of "insider trading" is generally through statutes. See, for example, the European Community's (EC's) Insider Trading Directive, *Council Directive Coordinating Regulations on Insider Dealing*, Directive 89/592, article 32, 1989 OJ (L 334) 30, 1.

have an advantage over others and that insiders will not trade on the basis of inside information, the civil and criminal penalties associated with breaking these rules are intended to discourage illegal insider trading and promote fairness.

2.3.3. Limits to Trading

Arbitrage is a set of transactions that produces riskless profits. Arbitrageurs are traders who engage in such trades to benefit from pricing discrepancies (inefficiencies) in markets. Such trading activity contributes to market efficiency. For example, if an asset is traded in two markets but at different prices, the actions of buying the asset in the market in which it is underpriced and selling the asset in the market in which it is overpriced will eventually bring these two prices together. The presence of these arbitrageurs helps pricing discrepancies disappear quickly. Obviously, market efficiency is impeded by any limitation on arbitrage resulting from operating inefficiencies, such as difficulties in executing trades in a timely manner, prohibitively high trading costs, and a lack of transparency in market prices.

Some market experts argue that restrictions on short selling limit arbitrage trading, which impedes market efficiency. **Short selling** is the transaction whereby an investor sells shares that he or she does not own by borrowing them from a broker and agreeing to replace them at a future date. Short selling allows investors to sell securities they believe to be overvalued, much in the same way they can buy those they believe to be undervalued. In theory, such activities promote more efficient pricing. Regulators and others, however, have argued that short selling may exaggerate downward market movements, leading to crashes in affected securities. In contrast, some researchers report evidence indicating that when investors are unable to borrow securities (that is, to short the security), or when costs to borrow shares are high, market prices may deviate from intrinsic values.[12] Furthermore, research suggests that short selling is helpful in price discovery (that is, it facilitates supply and demand in determining prices).[13]

2.4. Transaction Costs and Information-Acquisition Costs

The costs incurred by traders in identifying and exploiting possible market inefficiencies affect the interpretation of market efficiency. The two types of costs to consider are transaction costs and information-acquisition costs.

- *Transaction costs:* Practically, transaction costs are incurred in trading to exploit any perceived market inefficiency. Thus, "efficient" should be viewed as efficient within the bounds of transaction costs. For example, consider a violation of the principle that two identical assets should sell for the same price in different markets. Such a violation can be considered to be a rather simple possible exception to market efficiency because prices appear to be inconsistently processing information. To exploit the violation, a trader could arbitrage by simultaneously shorting the asset in the higher-price market and buying the asset in the lower-price market. If the price discrepancy between the two markets is smaller than the transaction costs involved in the arbitrage for the lowest cost traders, the arbitrage will not occur, and both prices are in effect efficient within the bounds of arbitrage. These

[12]A significant amount of research supports this view, including Jones and Lamont (2002) and Duffie, Garleanu, and Pederson (2002).

[13]See Bris, Goetzmann, and Zhu (2009).

bounds of arbitrage are relatively narrow in highly liquid markets, such as the market for U.S. Treasury bills, but could be wide in illiquid markets.
- *Information-acquisition costs:* Practically, expenses are always associated with gathering and analyzing information. New information is incorporated in transaction prices by traders placing trades based on their analysis of information. Active investors who place trades based on information they have gathered and analyzed play a key role in market prices adjusting to reflect new information. The classic view of market efficiency is that active investors incur information acquisition costs but that money is wasted because prices already reflect all relevant information. This view of efficiency is very strict in the sense of viewing a market as inefficient if active investing can recapture any part of the costs, such as research costs and active asset selection. Grossman and Stiglitz (1980) argue that prices must offer a return to information acquisition; in equilibrium, if markets are efficient, returns net of such expenses are just fair returns for the risk incurred. The modern perspective views a market as inefficient if, after deducting such costs, active investing can earn superior returns. Gross of expenses, a return should accrue to information acquisition in an efficient market.

In summary, a modern perspective calls for the investor to consider transaction costs and information-acquisition costs when evaluating the efficiency of a market. A price discrepancy must be sufficiently large to leave the investor with a profit (adjusted for risk) after taking account of the transaction costs and information-acquisition costs to reach the conclusion that the discrepancy may represent a market inefficiency. Prices may not fully reflect available information but still not provide a true market opportunity for active investors.

3. FORMS OF MARKET EFFICIENCY

Eugene Fama developed a framework for describing the degree to which markets are efficient.[14] In his efficient market hypothesis, markets are efficient when prices reflect *all* relevant information at any point in time. This means that the market prices observed for securities, for example, reflect the information available at the time.

In his framework, Fama defines three forms of efficiency: weak, semistrong, and strong. Each form is defined with respect to the available information that is reflected in prices.

	Market Prices Reflect:		
Forms of Market Efficiency	Past Market Data	Public Information	Private Information
Weak form of market efficiency	✓		
Semistrong form of market efficiency	✓	✓	
Strong form of market efficiency	✓	✓	✓

A finding that investors can consistently earn **abnormal returns** by trading on the basis of information is evidence contrary to market efficiency. In general, abnormal returns are returns in excess of those expected given a security's risk and the market's return. In other words, abnormal return equals actual return less expected return.

[14] Fama (1970).

3.1. Weak Form

In the **weak form** of the efficient market hypothesis, security prices fully reflect *all past market data*, which refers to all historical price and trading volume information. If markets are weak-form efficient, past trading data are already reflected in current prices and investors cannot predict future price changes by extrapolating prices or patterns of prices from the past.[15]

Tests of whether securities markets are weak-form efficient require looking at patterns of prices. One approach is to see whether there is any serial correlation in security returns, which would imply a predictable pattern.[16] Although there is some weak correlation in daily security returns, there is not enough correlation to make this a profitable trading rule after considering transaction costs.

An alternative approach to test weak-form efficiency is to examine specific trading rules that attempt to exploit historical trading data. If any such trading rule consistently generates abnormal risk-adjusted returns after trading costs, this evidence will contradict weak-form efficiency. This approach is commonly associated with **technical analysis**, which involves the analysis of historical trading information (primarily pricing and volume data) in an attempt to identify recurring patterns in the trading data that can be used to guide investment decisions. Many technical analysts, also referred to as "technicians," argue that many movements in stock prices are based, in large part, on psychology. Many technicians attempt to predict how market participants will behave, based on analyses of past behavior, and then trade on those predictions. Technicians often argue that simple statistical tests of trading rules are not conclusive because they are not applied to the more sophisticated trading strategies that can be used and that the research excludes the technician's subjective judgment. Thus, it is difficult to definitively refute this assertion because there are an unlimited number of possible technical trading rules.

Can technical analysts profit from trading on past trends? Overall, the evidence indicates that investors cannot consistently earn abnormal profits using past prices or other technical analysis strategies in developed markets.[17] Some evidence suggests, however, that there are opportunities to profit on technical analysis in countries with developing markets, including China, Hungary, Bangladesh, and Turkey.[18]

3.2. Semistrong Form

In a **semistrong-form efficient market**, prices reflect all publicly known and available information. Publicly available information includes financial statement data (such as earnings, dividends, corporate investments, changes in management, etc.) and financial market data (such as closing prices, shares traded, etc.). Therefore, the semistrong form of market efficiency encompasses the weak form. In other words, if a market is semistrong efficient, then it must also be weak-form efficient. A market that quickly incorporates all publicly available information into its prices is semistrong efficient.

---

[15]Market efficiency should not be confused with the **random walk hypothesis**, in which price changes over time are independent of one another. A random walk model is one of many alternative expected-return-generating models. Market efficiency does not require that returns follow a random walk.

[16]Serial correlation is a statistical measure of the degree to which the returns in one period are related to the returns in another period.

[17]Bessembinder and Chan (1998) and Fifield, Power, and Sinclair (2005).

[18]Fifield, Power, and Sinclair (2005), Chen and Li (2006), and Mobarek, Mollah, and Bhuyan (2008).

In a semistrong market, efforts to analyze publicly available information are futile. That is, analyzing earnings announcements of companies to identify underpriced or overpriced securities is pointless because the prices of these securities already reflect all publicly available information. If markets are semistrong efficient, no single investor has access to information that is not already available to other market participants, and as a consequence, no single investor can gain an advantage in predicting future security prices. In a semistrong efficient market, prices adjust quickly and accurately to new information. Suppose a company announces earnings that are higher than expected. In a semistrong efficient market, investors would not be able to act on this announcement and earn abnormal returns.

A common empirical test of investors' reaction to information releases is the event study. Suppose a researcher wants to test whether investors react to the announcement that the company is paying a special dividend. The researcher identifies a sample period and then those companies that paid a special dividend in the period and the date of the announcement. Then, for each company's stock, the researcher calculates the expected return on the share for the event date. This expected return may be based on many different models, including the capital asset pricing model, a simple market model, or a market index return. The researcher calculates the excess return as the difference between the actual return and the expected return. Once the researcher has calculated the event's excess return for each share, statistical tests are conducted to see whether the abnormal returns are statistically different from zero. The process of an event study is outlined in Exhibit 3-1.

EXHIBIT 3-1 The Event Study Process

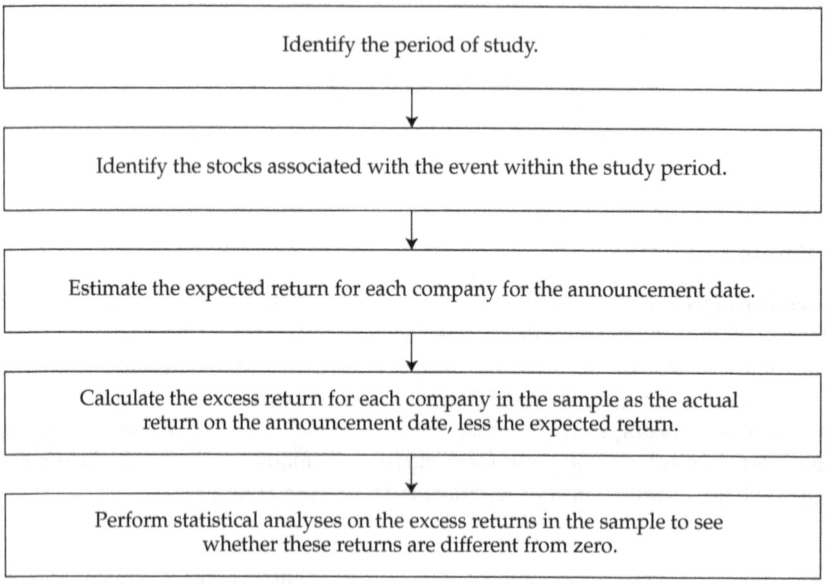

How do event studies relate to efficient markets? In a semistrong efficient market, share prices react quickly and accurately to public information. Therefore, if the information is good news, such as better-than-expected earnings, one would expect the company's shares to increase immediately at the time of the announcement; if it is bad news, one would expect a swift, negative reaction. If actual returns exceed what is expected in absence of the announcement and these returns are confined to the announcement period, then they are consistent with the idea that market prices react quickly to new information. In other words, the finding of excess returns at the time of the announcement does not necessarily indicate market inefficiency. In contrast, the finding of consistent excess returns following the announcement would suggest a trading opportunity. Trading on the basis of the announcement—that is, once the announcement is made—would not, on average, yield abnormal returns.

EXAMPLE 3-6 Information Arrival and Market Reaction

Consider an example of a news item and its effect on a share's price. In June 2008, the U.S. Federal Trade Commission (FTC) began an investigation of Intel Corporation regarding noncompetitiveness, and on 16 December 2009, the FTC announced that it was suing Intel over noncompetitive issues. This announcement was made before the market opened for trading on 16 December.

Intel stock closed at \$19.78 on 15 December 2009 but opened at \$19.50 on 16 December. The stock then traded in the range from \$19.45 to \$19.68 within the first half hour as the news of the suit and Intel's initial response were spreading among investors. Exhibit 3-2 illustrates the price of Intel for the first 90 minutes of trading on 16 December.

EXHIBIT 3-2 Price of Intel: 16 December 2009

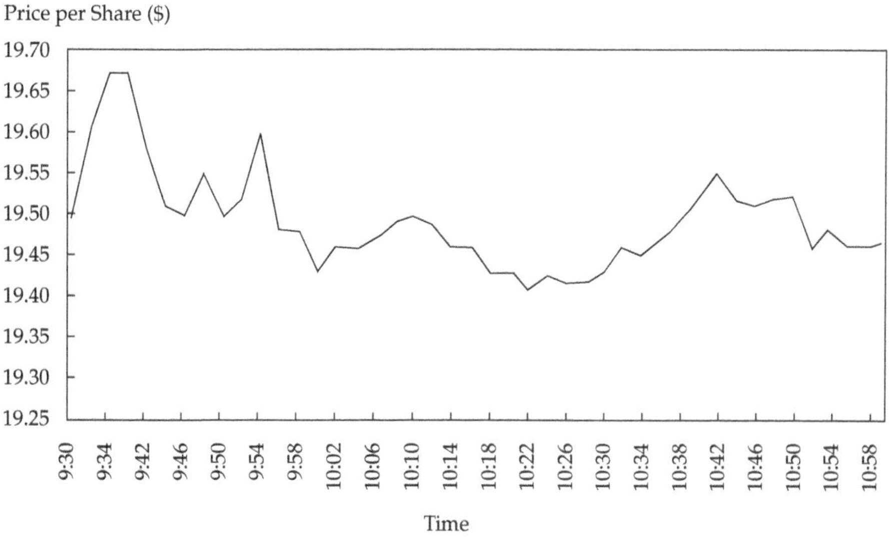

Source: Price data from Yahoo! Finance.

Is the fact that the price of Intel moves up immediately and then comes down indicative of an inefficiency regarding information? Not necessarily. Does it mean that investors overreacted? Not necessarily. During the morning, both before and after the market opened, news flowed about the lawsuit and the company's reaction to the lawsuit. The price of the shares reflects investors' reactions to this news. Why didn't Intel's shares simply move to a new level and stay there? Because (1) information continued to flow during the day on Intel and investors' estimate of the importance of this news on Intel's stock value continued to change, and (2) other news, related to other events and issues (such as the economy), affected stock prices.

Researchers have examined many different company-specific information events, including stock splits, dividend changes, and merger announcements, as well as economy-wide events, such as regulation changes and tax rate changes. The results of most research are consistent with the view that developed securities markets might be semistrong efficient. But some evidence suggests that the markets in developing countries may not be semistrong efficient.[19]

3.3. Strong Form

In the **strong form** of efficient markets, security prices fully reflect both public and private information. A market that is strong-form efficient is, by definition, also semistrong- and weak-form efficient. In the case of a strong-form efficient market, insiders would not be able to earn abnormal returns from trading on the basis of private information. A strong-form efficient market also means that prices reflect all private information, which means that prices reflect everything that the management of a company knows about the financial condition of the company that has not been publicly released. However, this is not likely because of the strong prohibitions against insider trading that are found in most countries. If a market is strong-form efficient, those with insider information cannot earn abnormal returns.

Researchers test whether a market is strong-form efficient by testing whether investors can earn abnormal profits by trading on nonpublic information. The results of these tests are consistent with the view that securities markets are not strong-form efficient; many studies have found that abnormal profits can be earned when nonpublic information is used.[20]

3.4. Implications of the Efficient Market Hypothesis

The implications of efficient markets to investment managers and analysts are important because they affect the value of securities and how these securities are managed. Several implications can be drawn from the evidence on efficient markets for developed markets:

- Securities markets are weak-form efficient, and therefore, investors cannot earn abnormal returns by trading on the basis of past trends in price.

[19]See Gan, Lee, Hwa, and Zhang (2005) and Raja, Sudhahar, and Selvam (2009).

[20]Evidence that finds that markets are not strong-form efficient include Jaffe (1974) and Rozeff and Zaman (1988).

- Securities markets are semistrong efficient, and therefore, analysts who collect and analyze information must consider whether that information is already reflected in security prices and how any new information affects a security's value.[21]
- Securities markets are not strong-form efficient because securities laws are intended to prevent exploitation of private information.

3.4.1. Fundamental Analysis

Fundamental analysis is the examination of publicly available information and the formulation of forecasts to estimate the intrinsic value of assets. Fundamental analysis involves the estimation of an asset's value using company data, such as earnings and sales forecasts, and risk estimates as well as industry and economic data, such as economic growth, inflation, and interest rates. Buy and sell decisions depend on whether the current market price is less than or greater than the estimated intrinsic value.

The semistrong form of market efficiency says that all available public information is reflected in current prices. So, what good is fundamental analysis? Fundamental analysis is necessary in a well-functioning market because this analysis helps the market participants understand the value implications of information. In other words, fundamental analysis facilitates a semistrong efficient market by disseminating value-relevant information. And, although fundamental analysis requires costly information, this analysis can be profitable in terms of generating abnormal returns if the analyst creates a comparative advantage with respect to this information.[22]

3.4.2. Technical Analysis

Investors using technical analysis attempt to profit by looking at patterns of prices and trading volume. Although some price patterns persist, exploiting these patterns may be too costly and, hence, would not produce abnormal returns.

Consider a situation in which a pattern of prices exists. With so many investors examining prices, this pattern will be detected. If profitable, exploiting this pattern will eventually affect prices such that this pattern will no longer exist; it will be arbitraged away. In other words, by detecting and exploiting patterns in prices, technical analysts assist markets in maintaining weak-form efficiency. Does this mean that technical analysts cannot earn abnormal profits? Not necessarily, because there may be a possibility of earning abnormal profits from a pricing inefficiency. But would it be possible to earn abnormal returns on a consistent basis from exploiting such a pattern? No, because the actions of market participants will arbitrage this opportunity quickly, and the inefficiency will no longer exist.

3.4.3. Portfolio Management

If securities markets are weak-form and semistrong-form efficient, the implication is that active trading, whether attempting to exploit price patterns or public information, is not likely to generate abnormal returns. In other words, portfolio managers cannot beat the market on a consistent basis, so therefore, passive portfolio management should outperform active portfolio management. Researchers have observed that mutual funds do not, on average,

---

[21]In the case of the Intel example, this implication would mean estimating how the actual filing of the lawsuit and the company's reaction to the lawsuit affect the value of Intel, while keeping in mind that the expectation of a lawsuit was already impounded in Intel's stock price.

[22]Brealey (1983).

outperform the market on a risk-adjusted basis.[23] Mutual funds perform, on average, similar to the market before considering fees and expenses and perform worse than the market, on average, once fees and expenses are considered. Even if a mutual fund is not actively managed, there are costs to managing these funds, which reduces net returns.

So, what good are portfolio managers? The role of a portfolio manager is not necessarily to beat the market but, rather, to establish and manage a portfolio consistent with the portfolio's objectives, with appropriate diversification and asset allocation, while taking into consideration the risk preferences and tax situation of the investor.

4. MARKET PRICING ANOMALIES

Although considerable evidence shows that markets are efficient, researchers have also reported a number of potential inefficiencies, or anomalies, that result in the mispricing of securities. These market anomalies, if persistent, are exceptions to the notion of market efficiency. In other words, a **market anomaly** occurs if a change in the price of an asset or security cannot directly be linked to current relevant information known in the market or to the release of new information into the market. Although the list is far from exhaustive, in this section, several well-known anomalies in financial markets are discussed.

The validity of any evidence supporting the existence of such market inefficiencies must be *consistent* over reasonably long periods. Otherwise, a detected market anomaly may largely be an artifact of the sample period chosen. In the widespread search for discovering profitable anomalies, many findings could simply be the product of a process called **data mining**, also known as **data snooping**. In generally accepted research practice, an initial hypothesis is developed which is based on economic rationale, followed by tests conducted on objectively selected data to either confirm or reject the original hypothesis. However, with data mining the process is reversed where data is often examined with the intent to develop a hypothesis, instead of developing a hypothesis first. This is done by analyzing data in various manners, and even utilizing different empirical approaches until you find support for a desired result, in this case a profitable anomaly. Can researchers look back on data and find a trading strategy that would have yielded abnormal returns? Absolutely. Will this trading strategy provide abnormal returns in the future? Perhaps not. It is always possible that enough data snooping can detect a trading strategy that would have worked in the past, and it is always possible that some trading strategy can produce abnormal returns simply by chance. But in an efficient market, such a strategy is unlikely to generate abnormal returns on a consistent basis in the future. Although identified anomalies may frequently appear to produce excess returns, it is generally difficult to profitably exploit the anomalies after accounting for risk, trading costs, and so on.

Several anomalies are listed in Exhibit 3-3. This list is by no means exhaustive, but it provides information on the breadth of the anomalies. A few of these anomalies are discussed in more detail in the following sections. The anomalies are placed into categories based on the research method that identified the anomaly. Time-series anomalies were identified using time series of data. Cross-sectional anomalies were identified based on analyzing a cross section of companies that differ on some key characteristics. Other anomalies were identified by a variety of means, including event studies.

[23]See Malkiel (1995). One of the challenges to evaluating mutual fund performance is that the researcher must control for survivorship bias.

EXHIBIT 3-3 Sampling of Observed Pricing Anomalies

Time Series	Cross-Sectional	Other
January effect	Size effect	Closed-end fund discount
Day-of-the-week effect	Value effect	Earnings surprise
Weekend effect	Book-to-market ratios	Initial public offerings
Turn-of-the-month effect	P/E ratio effect	Distressed securities effect
Holiday effect	Value Line enigma	Stock splits
Time-of-day effect		Super Bowl
Momentum		
Overreaction		

4.1. Time-Series Anomalies

Two of the major categories of time-series anomalies that have been documented are (1) calendar anomalies and (2) momentum and overreaction anomalies.

4.1.1. Calendar Anomalies

In the 1980s, a number of researchers reported that stock market returns in January were significantly higher compared to the rest of the months of the year, with most of the abnormal returns reported during the first five trading days in January. Since its first documentation in the 1980s, this pattern, known as the **January effect**, has been observed in most equity markets around the world. This anomaly is also known as the **turn-of-the-year effect**, or even often referred to as the "small firm in January effect" because it is most frequently observed for the returns of small market capitalization stocks.[24]

The January effect contradicts the efficient market hypothesis because excess returns in January are not attributed to any new and relevant information or news. A number of reasons have been suggested for this anomaly, including tax-loss selling. Researchers have speculated that, in order to reduce their tax liabilities, investors sell their "loser" securities in December for the purpose of creating capital losses, which can then be used to offset any capital gains. A related explanation is that these losers tend to be small-cap stocks with high volatility.[25] This increased supply of equities in December depresses their prices, and then these shares are bought in early January at relatively attractive prices. This demand then drives their prices up again. Overall, the evidence indicates that tax-loss selling may account for a portion of January abnormal returns, but it does not explain all of it.

Another possible explanation for the anomaly is so-called "window dressing," a practice in which portfolio managers sell their riskier securities prior to 31 December. The explanation is as follows: many portfolio managers prepare the annual reports of their portfolio holdings as of 31 December. Selling riskier securities is an attempt to make their portfolios appear less risky. After 31 December, a portfolio manager would then simply purchase riskier securities in an attempt to earn higher returns. However, similar to the tax-loss selling hypothesis, the

[24]There is also evidence of a January effect in bond returns that is more prevalent in high-yield corporate bonds, similar to the small-company effect for stocks.
[25]See Roll (1983).

research evidence in support of the window dressing hypothesis explains some, but not all, of the anomaly.

Recent evidence for both stock and bond returns suggests that the January effect is not persistent and, therefore, is not a pricing anomaly. Once an appropriate adjustment for risk is made, the January "effect" does not produce abnormal returns.[26]

Several other calendar effects, including the day-of-the-week and the weekend effects, have been found. These anomalies are summarized in Exhibit 3-4.[27] But like the size effect, which will be described later, most of these anomalies have been eliminated over time. One view is that the anomalies have been exploited such that the effect has been arbitraged away. Another view, however, is that increasingly sophisticated statistical methodologies fail to detect pricing inefficiencies.

EXHIBIT 3-4 Calendar-Based Anomalies

Anomaly	Observation
Turn-of-the-month effect	Returns tend to be higher on the last trading day of the month and the first three trading days of the next month.
Day-of-the-week effect	The average Monday return is negative and lower than the average returns for the other four days, which are all positive.
Weekend effect	Returns on weekends tend to be lower than returns on weekdays.[28]
Holiday effect	Returns on stocks in the day prior to market holidays tend to be higher than other days.

4.1.2. Momentum and Overreaction Anomalies

Momentum anomalies relate to short-term share price patterns. One of the earliest studies to identify this type of anomaly was conducted by Werner DeBondt and Richard Thaler, who argued that investors overreact to the release of unexpected public information.[29] Therefore, stock prices will be inflated (depressed) for those companies releasing good (bad) information. This anomaly has become known as the overreaction effect. Using the overreaction effect, they proposed a strategy that involved buying "loser" portfolios and selling "winner" portfolios. They defined stocks as winners or losers based on their total returns over the previous three- to five-year period. They found that in a subsequent period, the loser portfolios outperformed the market, while the winner portfolios underperformed the market. Similar patterns have been documented in many, but not all, global stock markets as well as in bond markets. One criticism is that the observed anomaly may be the result of statistical problems in the analysis.

[26]See, for example, Kim (2006).

[27]For a discussion of several of these anomalous patterns, see Jacobs and Levy (1988).

[28]The weekend effect consists of a pattern of returns around the weekend: abnormal positive returns on Fridays followed by abnormally negative returns on Mondays. This is a day-of-the-week effect that specifically links Friday and Monday returns. It is interesting to note that in 2009, the weekend effect in the United States was inverted, with 80 percent of the gains from March 2009 onward coming from the first trading day of the week.

[29]DeBondt and Thaler (1985).

A contradiction to weak-form efficiency occurs when securities that have experienced high returns in the short term tend to continue to generate higher returns in subsequent periods.[30] Empirical support for the existence of momentum in stock returns in most stock markets around the world is well documented. If investors can trade on the basis of momentum and earn abnormal profits, then this anomaly contradicts the weak form of the efficient market hypothesis because it represents a pattern in prices that can be exploited by simply using historical price information.[31]

Researchers have argued that the existence of momentum is rational and not contrary to market efficiency because it is plausible that there are shocks to the expected growth rates of cash flows to shareholders and that these shocks induce a serial correlation that is rational and short lived.[32] In other words, having stocks with some degree of momentum in their security returns may not imply irrationality but, rather, may reflect prices adjusting to a shock in growth rates.

4.2. Cross-Sectional Anomalies

Two of the most researched cross-sectional anomalies in financial markets are the size effect and the value effect.

4.2.1. Size Effect

The size effect results from the observation that equities of small-cap companies tend to outperform equities of large-cap companies on a risk-adjusted basis. Many researchers documented a small-company effect soon after the initial research was published in 1981. This effect, however, was not apparent in subsequent studies.[33] Part of the reason that the size effect was not confirmed by subsequent studies may be because of the fact that if it were truly an anomaly, investors acting on this effect would reduce any potential returns. But some of the explanation may simply be that the effect as originally observed was a chance outcome and, therefore, not actually an inefficiency.

4.2.2. Value Effect

A number of global empirical studies have shown that value stocks, which are generally referred to as stocks that have below-average price-to-earnings (P/E) and market-to-book (M/B) ratios, and above-average dividend yields, have consistently outperformed growth stocks over long periods of time.[34] If the effect persists, the value stock anomaly contradicts

[30]Notice that this pattern lies in sharp contrast to DeBondt and Thaler's reversal pattern that is displayed over longer periods of time. In theory, the two patterns could be related. In other words, it is feasible that prices are bid up extremely high, perhaps too high, in the short term for companies that are doing well. In the longer term (three to five years), the prices of these short-term winners correct themselves and they do poorly.

[31]Jegadeesh and Titman (2001).

[32]Johnson (2002).

[33]Although many studies document a small-company effect, these studies are concentrated in a period similar to that of the original research and, therefore, use a similar data set. The key to whether something is a true anomaly is persistence in out-of-sample tests. Fama and French (2008) document that the size effect is apparent only in microcap stocks but not in small- and large-cap stocks, and these microcap stocks may have a significant influence in studies that document a size effect.

[34]For example, see Capaul, Rowley, and Sharpe (1993) and Fama and French (1998).

semistrong market efficiency because all the information used to categorize stocks in this manner is publicly available.

Fama and French developed a three-factor model to predict stock returns.[35] In addition to the use of market returns as specified by the capital asset pricing model (CAPM), the Fama and French model also includes the size of the company as measured by the market value of its equity and the company's book value of equity divided by its market value of equity, which is a value measure. The Fama and French model captures risk dimensions related to stock returns that the CAPM model does not consider. Fama and French find that when they apply the three-factor model instead of the CAPM, the value stock anomaly disappears.

4.3. Other Anomalies

A number of additional anomalies have been documented in the financial markets, including the existence of closed-end investment fund discounts, price reactions to the release of earnings information, returns of initial public offerings, and the predictability of returns based on prior information.

4.3.1. Closed-End Investment Fund Discounts

A closed-end investment fund issues a fixed number of shares at inception and does not sell any additional shares after the initial offering. Therefore, the fund capitalization is fixed unless a secondary public offering is made. The shares of closed-end funds trade on stock markets like any other shares in the equity market (i.e., their prices are determined by supply and demand).

Theoretically, these shares should trade at a price approximately equal to their net asset value (NAV) per share, which is simply the total market value of the fund's security holdings less any liabilities divided by the number of shares outstanding. An abundance of research, however, has documented that, on average, closed-end funds trade at a discount from NAV. Most studies have documented average discounts in the 4–10 percent range, although individual funds have traded at discounts exceeding 50 percent and others have traded at large premiums.[36]

The closed-end fund discount presents a puzzle because conceptually, an investor could purchase all the shares in the fund, liquidate the fund, and end up making a profit. Some researchers have suggested that these discounts are attributed to management fees or expectations of the managers' performance, but these explanations are not supported by the evidence.[37] An alternative explanation for the discount is that tax liabilities are associated with unrealized capital gains and losses that exist prior to when the investor bought the shares, and hence, the investor does not have complete control over the timing of the realization of gains and losses.[38] Although the evidence supports this hypothesis to a certain extent, the tax effect is not large enough to explain the entire discount. Finally, it has often been argued that the discounts exist because of liquidity problems and errors in calculating NAV. The illiquidity

[35]Fama and French (1995).

[36]See Dimson and Minio-Kozerski (1999) for a review of this literature.

[37]See Lee, Sheifer, and Thaler (1990).

[38]The return to owners of closed-end fund shares has three parts: (1) the price appreciation or depreciation of the shares themselves, (2) the dividends earned and distributed to owners by the fund, and (3) the capital gains and losses earned by the fund that are distributed by the fund. The explanation of the anomalous pricing has to do with the timing of the distribution of capital gains.

explanation is plausible if shares are recorded at the same price as more liquid, publicly traded stocks; some evidence supports this assertion. But as with tax reasons, liquidity issues explain only a portion of the discount effect.

Can these discounts be exploited to earn abnormal returns if transaction costs are taken into account? No. First, the transaction costs involved in exploiting the discount—buying all the shares and liquidating the fund—would eliminate any profit.[39] Second, these discounts tend to revert to zero over time. Hence, a strategy to trade on the basis of these discounts would not likely be profitable.[40]

4.3.2. Earnings Surprise

Although most event studies have supported semistrong market efficiency, some researchers have provided evidence that questions semistrong market efficiency. One of these studies relates to the extensively examined adjustment of stock prices to earnings announcements.[41] The unexpected part of the earnings announcement, or **earnings surprise**, is the portion of earnings that is unanticipated by investors and, according to the efficient market hypothesis, merits a price adjustment. Positive (negative) surprises should cause appropriate and rapid price increases (decreases). Several studies have been conducted using data from numerous markets around the world. Most of the results indicate that earnings surprises are reflected quickly in stock prices, but the adjustment process is not always efficient. In particular, although a substantial adjustment occurs prior to and at the announcement date, an adjustment also occurs after the announcement.[42]

As a result of these slow price adjustments, companies that display the largest positive earnings surprises subsequently display superior stock return performance, whereas poor subsequent performance is displayed by companies with low or negative earnings surprises.[43] This finding implies that investors could earn abnormal returns using publicly available information by buying stocks of companies that had positive earnings surprises and selling those with negative surprises.

Although there is support for abnormal returns associated with earnings surprises, and some support for such returns beyond the announcement period, there is also evidence indicating that these observed abnormal returns are an artifact of studies that do not sufficiently control for transaction costs and risk.[44]

4.3.3. Initial Public Offerings (IPOs)

When a company offers shares of its stock to the public for the first time, it does so through an initial public offering (or IPO). This offering involves working with an investment bank

[39]See, for example, the study by Pontiff (1996), which shows how the cost of arbitraging these discounts eliminates the profit.

[40]See Pontiff (1995).

[41]See Jones, Rendleman, and Latané (1984).

[42]Not surprisingly, it is often argued that this slow reaction contributes to a momentum pattern.

[43]A similar pattern has been documented in the corporate bond market, where bond prices react too slowly to new company earnings announcements as well as to changes in company debt ratings.

[44]See Brown (1997) for a summary of evidence supporting the existence of this anomaly. See Zarowin (1989) for evidence regarding the role of size in explaining abnormal returns to surprises; Alexander, Goff, and Peterson (1989) for evidence regarding transaction costs and unexpected earnings strategies; and Kim and Kim (2003) for evidence indicating that the anomalous returns can be explained by risk factors.

that helps price and market the newly issued shares. After the offering is complete, the new shares trade on a stock market for the first time. Given the risk that investment bankers face in trying to sell a new issue for which the true price is unknown, it is perhaps not surprising to find that, on average, the initial selling price is set too low and that the price increases dramatically on the first trading day. The percentage difference between the issue price and the closing price at the end of the first day of trading is often referred to as the degree of underpricing.

The evidence suggests that, on average, investors who are able to buy the shares of an IPO at their offering price may be able to earn abnormal profits. For example, during the Internet bubble of 1995–2000, many IPOs ended their first day of trading up by more than 100 percent. Such performance, however, is not always the case. Sometimes the issues are priced too high, which means that share prices drop on their first day of trading. In addition, the evidence also suggests that investors buying after the initial offering are not able to earn abnormal profits because prices adjust quickly to the "true" values, which supports semistrong market efficiency. In fact, the subsequent long-term performance of IPOs is generally found to be below average. Taken together, the IPO underpricing and the subsequent poor performance suggests that the markets are overly optimistic initially (i.e., investors overreact).

Some researchers have examined closely why IPOs may appear to have anomalous returns. Because of the small size of the IPO companies and the method of equally weighting the samples, what appears to be an anomaly may simply be an artifact of the methodology.[45]

4.3.4. Predictability of Returns Based on Prior Information

A number of researchers have documented that equity returns are related to prior information on such factors as interest rates, inflation rates, stock volatility, and dividend yields.[46] But finding that equity returns are affected by changes in economic fundamentals is not evidence of market inefficiency and would not result in abnormal trading returns.[47]

Furthermore, the relationship between stock returns and the prior information is not consistent over time. For example, in one study, the relationship between stock prices and dividend yields changed from positive to negative in different periods.[48] Hence, a trading strategy based on dividend yields would not yield consistent abnormal returns.

4.4. Implications for Investment Strategies

Although it is interesting to consider the anomalies just described, attempting to benefit from them in practice is not easy. In fact, most researchers conclude that observed anomalies are not violations of market efficiency but, rather, are the result of statistical methodologies used to detect the anomalies. As a result, if the methodologies are corrected, most of these anomalies disappear.[49] Another point to consider is that in an efficient market, overreactions may occur, but then so do underreactions.[50] Therefore, on average, the markets are efficient. In other words, investors face challenges when they attempt to translate statistical anomalies

[45]See Brav and Gompers (1997) and Brav, Geczy, and Gompers (1995).

[46]See, for example, Fama and Schwert (1977) and Fama and French (1988).

[47]See Fama and French (2008).

[48]Schwert (2003, Chapter 15).

[49]Fama (1998).

[50]This point is made by Fama (1998).

into economic profits. Consider the following quote regarding anomalies from the *Economist* ("Frontiers of Finance Survey," 9 October 1993):

> *Many can be explained away. When transactions costs are taken into account, the fact that stock prices tend to over-react to news, falling back the day after good news and bouncing up the day after bad news, proves unexploitable: price reversals are always within the bid-ask spread. Others such as the small-firm effect, work for a few years and then fail for a few years. Others prove to be merely proxies for the reward for risk taking. Many have disappeared since (and because) attention has been drawn to them.*

It is difficult to envision entrusting your retirement savings to a manager whose strategy is based on buying securities on Mondays, which tends to have negative returns on average, and selling them on Fridays. For one thing, the negative Monday returns are merely an average, so on any given week, they could be positive. In addition, such a strategy would generate large trading costs. Even more importantly, investors would likely be uncomfortable investing their funds in a strategy that has no compelling underlying economic rationale.

5. BEHAVIORAL FINANCE

Behavioral finance is a field of financial thought that examines investor behavior and how this behavior affects what is observed in the financial markets. The behavior of individuals, in particular their cognitive biases, has been offered as a possible explanation for a number of pricing anomalies. In a broader sense, behavioral finance attempts to explain why individuals make the decisions that they do, whether these decisions are rational or irrational. The focus of much of the work in this area is on the cognitive biases that affect investment decisions.

Most asset-pricing models assume that markets are rational and that the intrinsic value of a security reflects this rationality. But market efficiency and asset-pricing models do not require that each individual is rational—rather, only that the market is rational. This leaves a lot of room for individual behavior to deviate from rationality. Even if individuals deviate from rationality, however, there may still be no room for profitable arbitrage for any observed mispricing in the financial markets.

5.1. Loss Aversion

In most financial models, the assumption is that investors are risk averse. **Risk aversion** implies that, although investors dislike risk, they are willing to assume risk if adequately compensated in the form of higher expected returns. In the most general models, researchers assume that investors do not like risk, whether the risk is that the returns are higher than expected or lower than expected. Behavioralists, however, allow for the possibility that this dislike for risk is not symmetrical. For example, some argue that behavioral theories of loss aversion can explain observed overreaction in markets, such that investors dislike losses more than they like comparable gains.[51] If loss aversion is more important than risk aversion, researchers should observe that investors overreact.[52] Although this can explain the

[51]See DeBondt and Thaler (1985) and Tversky and Kahneman (1981).

[52]See Fama (1998).

overreaction anomaly, evidence also suggests that underreaction is just as prevalent as overreaction, which counters these arguments.

5.2. Overconfidence

One of the behavioral biases offered to explain pricing anomalies is overconfidence. If investors are overconfident, they place too much emphasis on their ability to process and interpret information about a security. Overconfident investors do not process information appropriately, and if there is a sufficient number of these investors, stocks will be mispriced.[53] But most researchers argue that this mispricing is temporary, with prices correcting eventually. The issues, however, are how long it takes prices to become correctly priced, whether this mispricing is predictable, and whether investors can consistently earn abnormal profits.

Evidence has suggested that overconfidence results in mispricing for U.S., U.K., German, French, and Japanese markets.[54] This overconfidence, however, is predominantly in higher-growth companies, whose prices react slowly to new information.[55]

5.3. Other Behavioral Biases

Other behavioral theories that have been put forth as explaining investor behavior include the following:

- **Representativeness**, with investors assessing probabilities of outcomes depending on how similar they are to the current state.
- **Gambler's fallacy**, in which recent outcomes affect investors' estimates of future probabilities.
- **Mental accounting**, in which investors keep track of the gains and losses for different investments in separate mental accounts.
- **Conservatism**, where investors tend to be slow to react to changes.
- **Disposition effect**, in which investors tend to avoid realizing losses but, rather, seek to realize gains.
- **Narrow framing**, in which investors focus on issues in isolation.[56]

The basic idea of these theories is that investors are humans and, therefore, imperfect and that the beliefs they have about a given asset's value may not be homogeneous. These behaviors help explain observed pricing anomalies. But the issue, which is controversial, is whether these insights help exploit any mispricing. In other words, researchers can use investor behavior to explain pricing, but can investors use it to predict how asset prices will be affected?

---

[53]Another aspect to overconfidence is that investors who are overconfident in their ability to select investments and manage a portfolio tend to use less diversification, investing in what is most familiar. Therefore, investor behavior may affect investment results—returns and risk—without implications for the efficiency of markets.

[54]Scott, Stumpp, and Xu (2003) and Boujelbene Abbes, Boujelbene, and Bouri (2009).

[55]Scott, Stumpp, and Xu (2003).

[56]For a review of these behavioral issues, see Hirshleifer (2001).

5.4. Information Cascades

One application of behavioral theories to markets and pricing focuses on the role of personal learning in markets, where personal learning is what investors learn by observing trading outcomes and what they learn from "conversations"—ideas shared among investors about specific assets and the markets.[57] This approach argues that social interaction and the resultant contagion is important in pricing and can explain such phenomena as price changes without accompanying news and mistakes in valuation.

Biases that investors possess, such as framing or mental accounting, can lead to herding behavior or information cascades. Herding and information cascades are related but not identical concepts. **Herding** is clustered trading that may or may not be based on information.[58] An **information cascade**, in contrast, is the transmission of information from those participants who act first and whose decisions influence the decisions of others. Those who are acting on the choices of others may be ignoring their own preferences in favor of imitating the choices of others. In particular, information cascades may occur with respect to the release of accounting information because accounting information is noisy. For example, the release of earnings is noisy because it is uncertain what the current earnings imply about future earnings.

Information cascades may result in serial correlation of stock returns, which is consistent with overreaction anomalies. Do information cascades result in correct pricing? Some argue that if a cascade is leading toward an incorrect value, this cascade is "fragile" and will be corrected because investors will ultimately give more weight to public information or the trading of a recognized informed trader.[59] Information cascades, although documented in markets, do not necessarily mean that investors can exploit them as profitable trading opportunities.

Are information cascades rational? If the informed traders act first and uninformed traders imitate the informed traders, this behavior is consistent with rationality. The imitation trading by the uninformed traders helps the market incorporate relevant information and improves market efficiency.[60] The empirical evidence is consistent with the idea that information cascades are greater for a stock when the information quality regarding the company is poor.[61] Hence, information cascades are enhancing the information available to traders.

5.5. Behavioral Finance and Efficient Markets

The use of behavioral theories to explain observed pricing is an important part of the understanding of how markets function and how prices are determined. Whether there is a behavioral explanation for market anomalies remains a debate. Pricing anomalies are continually being uncovered, and then statistical and behavioral explanations are offered to explain these anomalies.

On the one hand, if investors must be rational for efficient markets to exist, then all the foibles of human investors suggest that markets cannot be efficient. On the other hand, if all that is required for markets to be efficient is that investors cannot consistently beat the market on a risk-adjusted basis, then the evidence does support market efficiency.

---

[57]Hirshleifer and Teoh (2009).

[58]The term used when there is herding without information is "spurious herding."

[59]Avery and Zemsky (1999).

[60]Another alternative is that the uninformed traders are the majority of the market participants and the imitators are imitating not because they agree with the actions of the majority but because they are looking to act on the actions of the uninformed traders.

[61]Avery and Zemsky (1999) and Bikhchandani, Hirshleifer, and Welch (1992).

6. SUMMARY

This chapter has provided an overview of the theory and evidence regarding market efficiency and has discussed the different forms of market efficiency as well as the implications for fundamental analysis, technical analysis, and portfolio management. The general conclusion drawn from the efficient market hypothesis is that it is not possible to beat the market on a consistent basis by generating returns in excess of those expected for the level of risk of the investment.

Additional key points include the following:

- The efficiency of a market is affected by the number of market participants and depth of analyst coverage, information availability, and limits to trading.
- There are three forms of efficient markets, each based on what is considered to be the information used in determining asset prices. In the weak form, asset prices fully reflect all market data, which refers to all past price and trading volume information. In the semistrong form, asset prices reflect all publicly known and available information. In the strong form, asset prices fully reflect all information, which includes both public and private information.
- Intrinsic value refers to the true value of an asset, whereas market value refers to the price at which an asset can be bought or sold. When markets are efficient, the two should be the same or very close. But when markets are not efficient, the two can diverge significantly.
- Most empirical evidence supports the idea that securities markets in developed countries are semistrong-form efficient; however, empirical evidence does not support the strong form of the efficient market hypothesis.
- A number of anomalies have been documented that contradict the notion of market efficiency, including the size anomaly, the January anomaly, and the winners–losers anomalies. In most cases, however, contradictory evidence both supports and refutes the anomaly.
- Behavioral finance uses human psychology, such as cognitive biases, in an attempt to explain investment decisions. Whereas behavioral finance is helpful in understanding observed decisions, a market can still be considered efficient even if market participants exhibit seemingly irrational behaviors, such as herding.

PROBLEMS

1. In an efficient market, the change in a company's share price is *most likely* the result of:

   A. Insiders' private information.
   B. The previous day's change in stock price.
   C. New information coming into the market.

2. Regulation that restricts some investors from participating in a market will *most likely*:

   A. Impede market efficiency.
   B. Not affect market efficiency.
   C. Contribute to market efficiency.

3. With respect to efficient market theory, when a market allows short selling, the efficiency of the market is *most likely* to:

   A. Increase.
   B. Decrease.
   C. Remain the same.

4. Which of the following regulations will *most likely* contribute to market efficiency? Regulatory restrictions on:

   A. Short selling.
   B. Foreign traders.
   C. Insiders trading with nonpublic information.

5. Which of the following market regulations will *most likely* impede market efficiency?

   A. Restricting traders' ability to short sell.
   B. Allowing unrestricted foreign investor trading.
   C. Penalizing investors who trade with nonpublic information.

6. If markets are efficient, the difference between the intrinsic value and market value of a company's security is:

   A. Negative.
   B. Zero.
   C. Positive.

7. The intrinsic value of an undervalued asset is:

   A. Less than the asset's market value.
   B. Greater than the asset's market value.
   C. The value at which the asset can currently be bought or sold.

8. The market value of an undervalued asset is:

   A. Greater than the asset's intrinsic value.
   B. The value at which the asset can currently be bought or sold.
   C. Equal to the present value of all the asset's expected cash flows.

9. With respect to the efficient market hypothesis, if security prices reflect *only* past prices and trading volume information, then the market is:

   A. Weak-form efficient.
   B. Strong-form efficient.
   C. Semistrong-form efficient.

10. Which one of the following statements *best* describes the semistrong form of market efficiency?

    A. Empirical tests examine the historical patterns in security prices.
    B. Security prices reflect all publicly known and available information.
    C. Semistrong-form efficient markets are not necessarily weak-form efficient.

11. If markets are semistrong efficient, standard fundamental analysis will yield abnormal trading profits that are:

    A. Negative.
    B. Equal to zero.
    C. Positive.

12. If prices reflect all public and private information, the market is *best* described as:

    A. Weak-form efficient.
    B. Strong-form efficient.
    C. Semistrong-form efficient.

13. If markets are semistrong-form efficient, then passive portfolio management strategies are *most likely* to:
    A. Earn abnormal returns.
    B. Outperform active trading strategies.
    C. Underperform active trading strategies.
14. If a market is semistrong-form efficient, the risk-adjusted returns of a passively managed portfolio relative to an actively managed portfolio are *most likely*:
    A. Lower.
    B. Higher.
    C. The same.
15. Technical analysts assume that markets are:
    A. Weak-form efficient.
    B. Weak-form inefficient.
    C. Semistrong-form efficient.
16. Fundamental analysts assume that markets are:
    A. Weak-form inefficient.
    B. Semistrong-form efficient.
    C. Semistrong-form inefficient.
17. If a market is weak-form efficient but semistrong-form inefficient, then which of the following types of portfolio management is *most likely* to produce abnormal returns?
    A. Passive portfolio management.
    B. Active portfolio management based on technical analysis.
    C. Active portfolio management based on fundamental analysis.
18. An increase in the time between when an order to trade a security is placed and when the order is executed *most likely* indicates that market efficiency has:
    A. Decreased.
    B. Remained the same.
    C. Increased.
19. With respect to efficient markets, a company whose share price reacts gradually to the public release of its annual report *most likely* indicates that the market where the company trades is:
    A. Semistrong-form efficient.
    B. Subject to behavioral biases.
    C. Receiving additional information about the company.
20. Which of the following is *least likely* to explain the January effect anomaly?
    A. Tax-loss selling.
    B. Release of new information in January.
    C. Window dressing of portfolio holdings.
21. If a researcher conducting empirical tests of a trading strategy using time series of returns finds statistically significant abnormal returns, then the researcher has *most likely* found:
    A. A market anomaly.
    B. Evidence of market inefficiency.
    C. A strategy to produce future abnormal returns.

22. Which of the following market anomalies is inconsistent with weak-form market efficiency?
    A. Earnings surprise.
    B. Momentum pattern.
    C. Closed-end fund discount.

23. Researchers have found that value stocks have consistently outperformed growth stocks. An investor wishing to exploit the value effect should purchase the stock of companies with above-average:
    A. Dividend yields.
    B. Market-to-book ratios.
    C. Price-to-earnings ratios.

24. With respect to rational and irrational investment decisions, the efficient market hypothesis requires:
    A. Only that the market is rational.
    B. That all investors make rational decisions.
    C. That some investors make irrational decisions.

25. Observed overreactions in markets can be explained by an investor's degree of:
    A. Risk aversion.
    B. Loss aversion.
    C. Confidence in the market.

26. Like traditional finance models, the behavioral theory of loss aversion assumes that investors dislike risk; however, the dislike of risk in behavioral theory is assumed to be:
    A. Leptokurtic.
    B. Symmetrical.
    C. Asymmetrical.

CHAPTER 4

PORTFOLIO MANAGEMENT: AN OVERVIEW

Robert M. Conroy, CFA
Charlottesville, VA, U.S.A.

Alistair Byrne, CFA
Edinburgh, U.K.

LEARNING OUTCOMES

After completing this chapter, you will be able to do the following:

- Explain the importance of the portfolio perspective.
- Discuss the types of investment management clients and the distinctive characteristics and needs of each.
- Describe the steps in the portfolio management process.
- Describe, compare, and contrast mutual funds and other forms of pooled investments.

1. INTRODUCTION

In this chapter we explain why the portfolio approach is important to all types of investors in achieving their financial goals. We compare the financial needs of different types of individual and institutional investors. After we outline the steps in the portfolio management process, we compare and contrast the types of investment management products that are available to investors and how they apply to the portfolio approach.

2. A PORTFOLIO PERSPECTIVE ON INVESTING

One of the biggest challenges faced by individuals and institutions is to decide how to invest for future needs. For individuals, the goal might be to fund retirement needs. For such institutions as insurance companies, the goal is to fund future liabilities in the form of insurance claims, whereas endowments seek to provide income to meet the ongoing needs of such institutions as universities. Regardless of the ultimate goal, all face the same set of challenges that extend beyond just the choice of what asset classes to invest in. They ultimately center on formulating basic principles that determine how to think about investing. One important question is: Should we invest in individual securities, evaluating each in isolation, or should we take a portfolio approach? By "portfolio approach," we mean evaluating individual securities in relation to their contribution to the investment characteristics of the whole portfolio. In the following section, we illustrate a number of reasons why a diversified portfolio perspective is important.

2.1. Portfolio Diversification: Avoiding Disaster

Portfolio diversification helps investors avoid disastrous investment outcomes. This benefit is most convincingly illustrated by examining what may happen when individuals have *not* diversified.

We are usually not able to observe how individuals manage their personal investments. However, in the case of U.S. 401(k) individual retirement portfolios,[1] it is possible to see the results of individuals' investment decisions. When we examine their retirement portfolios, we find that some individual participants make suboptimal investment decisions.

During the 1990s, Enron Corporation was one of the most admired corporations in the United States. A position in Enron shares returned over 27 percent per year from 1990 to September 2000, compared to 13 percent for the S&P 500 Index for the same time period (see Exhibit 4-1).

During this time period, thousands of Enron employees participated in the company's 401(k) retirement plan. The plan allowed employees to set aside some of their earnings in a tax-deferred account. Enron participated by matching the employees' contributions. Enron made the match by depositing required amounts in the form of Enron shares. Enron restricted the sale of its contributed shares until an employee turned 50 years old. In January 2001, the employees' 401(k) retirement accounts were valued at over US$2 billion, of which US$1.3 billion (or 62 percent) was in Enron shares. Although Enron restricted the sale of shares it contributed, less than US$150 million of the total of US$1.3 billion in shares had this restriction. The implication was that Enron employees continued to hold large amounts of Enron shares even though they were free to sell them and invest the proceeds in other assets.

A typical individual was Roger Bruce,[2] a 67-year-old Enron retiree who held all of his US$2 million in retirement funds in Enron shares. Unlike most stories, this one does not have a happy ending. Between January 2001 and January 2002, Enron's share price fell from about US$90 per share to zero (see Exhibit 4-2).

[1]In the United States, 401(k) plans are employer-sponsored individual retirement savings plans. They allow individuals to save a portion of their current income and defer taxation until the time when the savings and earnings are withdrawn. In some cases, the sponsoring firm will also make matching contributions in the form of cash or shares. Individuals within certain limits have control of the invested funds and consequently can express their preferences as to which assets to invest in.

[2]Singletary (2001).

EXHIBIT 4-1 Value of US$1 Invested from January 1990 to September 2000, Enron versus S&P 500 Composite Index

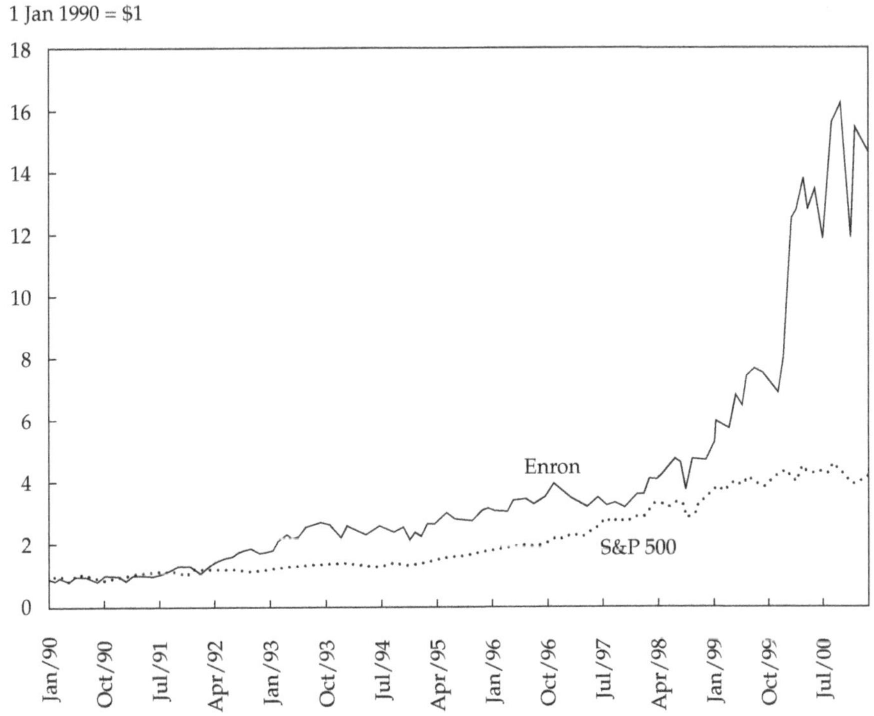

Source for data: Datastream.

Employees and retirees who had invested all or most of their retirement savings in Enron shares, just like Mr. Bruce, experienced financial ruin. The hard lesson that the Enron employees learned from this experience was to "not put all your eggs in one basket."[3] Unfortunately, the typical Enron employee did have most of his or her eggs in one basket. Most employees' wages and financial assets were dependent on Enron's continued viability; hence, any financial distress on Enron would have a material impact on an employee's financial health. The bankruptcy of Enron resulted in the closing of its operations, the dismissal of thousands of employees, and its shares becoming worthless. Hence, the failure of Enron was disastrous to the typical Enron employee.

Enron employees were not the only ones to be victims of overinvestment in a single company's shares. Another form of pension arrangement in many corporations is the defined contribution plan, in which the employer makes periodic cash contributions to a retirement fund managed by the employees themselves instead of guaranteeing a certain pension at retirement. In the defined contribution retirement plans at Owens Corning, Northern Telecom, Corning, and ADC Telecommunications, employees all held more than 25 percent of their assets in the company's shares during a time (March 2000 to December 2001) in which the share prices in these companies fell by almost 90 percent. The good news in this

[3]This expression, which most likely originated in England in the 1700s, has a timeless sense of wisdom.

EXHIBIT 4-2 Value of US$1 Invested from January 1990 to January 2002, Enron versus S&P 500 Composite Index

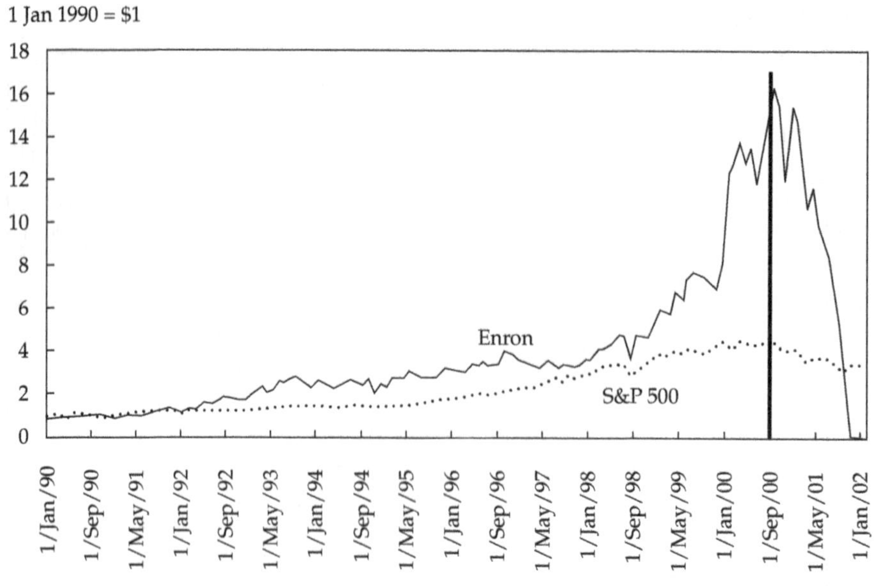

Source for data: Datastream.

story is that the employees participating in employer-matched 401(k) plans since 2001 have significantly reduced their holdings of their employers' shares.

Thus, by taking a diversified portfolio approach, investors can spread away some of the risk. All rational investors are concerned about the risk–return trade off of their investments. The portfolio approach provides investors with a way to reduce the risk associated with their wealth without necessarily decreasing their expected rate of return.

2.2. Portfolios: Reduce Risk

In addition to avoiding a potential disaster associated with overinvesting in a single security, portfolios also generally offer equivalent expected returns with lower overall **volatility** of returns—as represented by a measure such as standard deviation. Consider this simple example: Suppose you wish to make an investment in companies listed on the Hong Kong Stock Exchange (HKSE) and you start with a sample of five companies.[4] The cumulative returns for the five companies from Q2 2004 through Q2 2008 are shown in Exhibit 4-3.

The individual quarterly returns for each of the five shares are shown in Exhibit 4-4. The annualized means and annualized standard deviations for each are also shown.[5]

[4]A sample of five companies from a similar industry group was arbitrarily selected for illustration purposes.

[5]Mean quarterly returns are annualized by multiplying the quarterly mean by 4. Quarterly standard deviations are annualized by taking the quarterly standard deviation and multiplying it by 2.

EXHIBIT 4-3 Cumulative Wealth Index of Sample of Shares Listed on HKSE

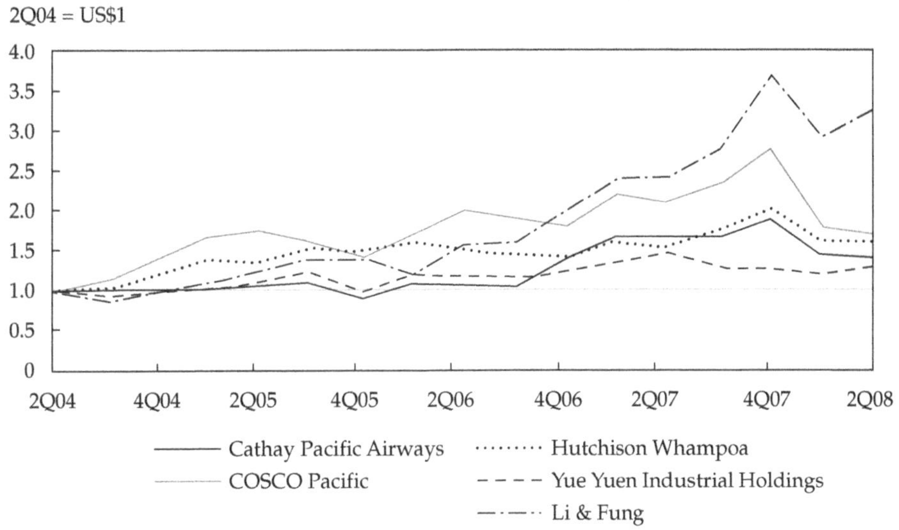

Source for data: Datastream.

Suppose you want to invest in one of these five securities next year. There is a wide variety of risk–return trade-offs for the five shares selected. If you believe that the future will replicate the past, then choosing Li & Fung would be a good choice. For the prior four years, Li & Fung provided the best trade-off between return and risk. In other words, it provided the most return per unit of risk. However, if there is no reason to believe that the future will replicate the past, it is more likely that the risk and return on the one security selected will be more like selecting one randomly. When we randomly selected one security each quarter, we found an average annualized return of 15.1 percent and an average annualized standard deviation of 24.9 percent, which would now become your expected return and standard deviation, respectively.

Alternatively, you could invest in an equally weighted portfolio of the five shares, which means that you would invest the same dollar amount in each security for each quarter. The quarterly returns on the equally weighted portfolio are just the average of the returns of the individual shares. As reported in Exhibit 4-4, the equally weighted portfolio has an average return of 15.1 percent and a standard deviation of 17.9 percent. As expected, the equally weighted portfolio's return is the same as the return on the randomly selected security. However, the same does not hold true for the portfolio standard deviation. That is, the standard deviation of an equally weighted portfolio is not simply the average of the standard deviations of the individual shares. In a later chapter we will demonstrate in greater mathematical detail how such a portfolio offers a lower standard deviation of return than the average of its individual components due to the correlations or interactions between the individual securities.

Because the mean return is the same, a simple measure of the value of diversification is calculated as the ratio of the standard deviation of the equally weighted portfolio to

EXHIBIT 4-4 Quarterly Returns (in percent) for Sample of HKSE Listed Shares, End of Q2 2004–End of Q2 2008

	Yue Yuen Industrial	Cathay Pacific Airways	Hutchison Whampoa	Li & Fung	COSCO Pacific	Equally Weighted Portfolio
Q3 2004	−11.1%	−2.3%	0.6%	−13.2%	−1.1%	−5.4%
Q4 2004	−0.5	−5.4	10.8	1.7	21.0	5.5
Q1 2005	5.7	6.8	19.1	13.8	15.5	12.2
Q2 2005	5.3	4.6	−2.1	16.9	12.4	7.4
Q3 2005	17.2	2.4	12.6	14.5	−7.9	7.8
Q4 2005	−17.6	−10.4	−0.9	4.4	−16.7	−8.2
Q1 2006	12.6	7.4	4.2	−10.9	15.4	5.7
Q2 2006	7.5	−0.4	−3.6	29.2	21.9	10.9
Q3 2006	−7.9	1.3	−5.1	−2.0	−1.6	−3.1
Q4 2006	8.2	27.5	0.1	26.0	−10.1	10.3
Q1 2007	18.3	24.3	16.5	22.8	25.7	21.5
Q2 2007	0.1	−2.6	−6.7	−0.4	0.3	−1.8
Q3 2007	−6.2	−4.2	16.7	11.9	11.1	5.8
Q4 2007	−8.0	17.9	−1.8	12.4	8.4	5.8
Q1 2008	3.5	−20.1	−8.5	−20.3	−31.5	−15.4
Q2 2008	2.1	−11.8	−2.6	24.2	−6.1	1.2
Mean annual return	7.3%	8.7%	12.3%	32.8%	14.2%	15.1%
Annual standard deviation	20.2%	25.4%	18.1%	29.5%	31.3%	17.9%
Diversification ratio						71.0%

Source for data: Datastream.

the standard deviation of the randomly selected security. This ratio may be referred to as the **diversification ratio**. In this case, the equally weighted portfolio's standard deviation is approximately 71 percent of that of a security selected at random. The diversification ratio of the portfolio's standard deviation to the individual asset's standard deviation measures the risk reduction benefits of a simple portfolio construction method, equal weighting. Even though the companies were chosen from a similar industry grouping, we see significant risk reduction. An even greater portfolio effect (i.e., lower diversification ratio) could have been realized if we had chosen companies from completely different industries.

This example illustrates one of the critical ideas about portfolios: Portfolios affect risk more than returns. In the prior section portfolios helped avoid the effects of downside risk associated with investing in a single company's shares. In this section we extended the notion of risk reduction through portfolios to illustrate why individuals and institutions should hold portfolios.

2.3. Portfolios: Composition Matters for the Risk–Return Tradeoff

In the previous section we compared an equally weighted portfolio to the selection of a single security. In this section we examine additional combinations of the same set of shares and observe the trade-offs between portfolio volatility of returns and expected return (for short, their risk–return trade-offs). If we select the portfolios with the best combination of risk and return (taking historical statistics as our expectations for the future), we produce the set of portfolios shown in Exhibit 4-5.

EXHIBIT 4-5 Optimal Portfolios for Sample of HKSE Listed Shares

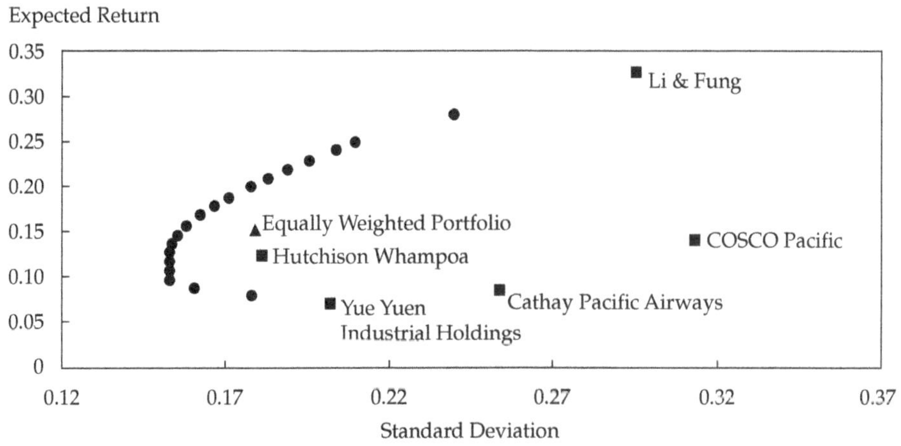

Source for data: Datastream.

In addition to illustrating that the diversified portfolio approach reduces risk, Exhibit 4-5 also shows that the composition of the portfolio matters. For example, an equally weighted portfolio (20 percent of the portfolio in each security) of the five shares has an expected return of 15.1 percent and a standard deviation of 17.9 percent. Alternatively, a portfolio with 25 percent in Yue Yuen Industrial (Holdings), 3 percent in Cathay Pacific, 52 percent in Hutchison Whampoa, 20 percent in Li & Fung, and 0 percent in COSCO Pacific produces a portfolio with an expected return of 15.1 percent and a standard deviation of 15.6 percent. Compared to a simple equally weighted portfolio, this provides an improved tradeoff between risk and return because a lower level of risk was achieved for the same level of return.

2.4. Portfolios: Not Necessarily Downside Protection

A major reason that portfolios can effectively reduce risk is that combining securities whose returns do not move together provides diversification. Sometimes a subset of assets will go up in value at the same time that another will go down in value. The fact that these may offset each other creates the potential diversification benefit we attribute to portfolios. However, an important issue is that the co-movement or correlation pattern of the securities' returns in the portfolio can change in a manner unfavorable to the investor. We use historical return data from a set of global indices to show the impact of changing co-movement patterns.

When we examine the returns of a set of global equity indices over the past 15 years, we observe a reduction in the diversification benefit due to a change in the pattern of co-movements of returns. Exhibits 4-6 and 4-7 show the cumulative returns for a set of five global indices[6] for two different time periods. Comparing the first time period, from Q4 1993 through Q3 2000 (as shown in Exhibit 4-6), with the last time period, from Q1 2006 through Q1 2009 (as shown in Exhibit 4-7), we show that the degree to which these global equity indices move together has increased over time.

EXHIBIT 4-6 Returns to Global Equity Indices, Q4 1993–Q3 2000

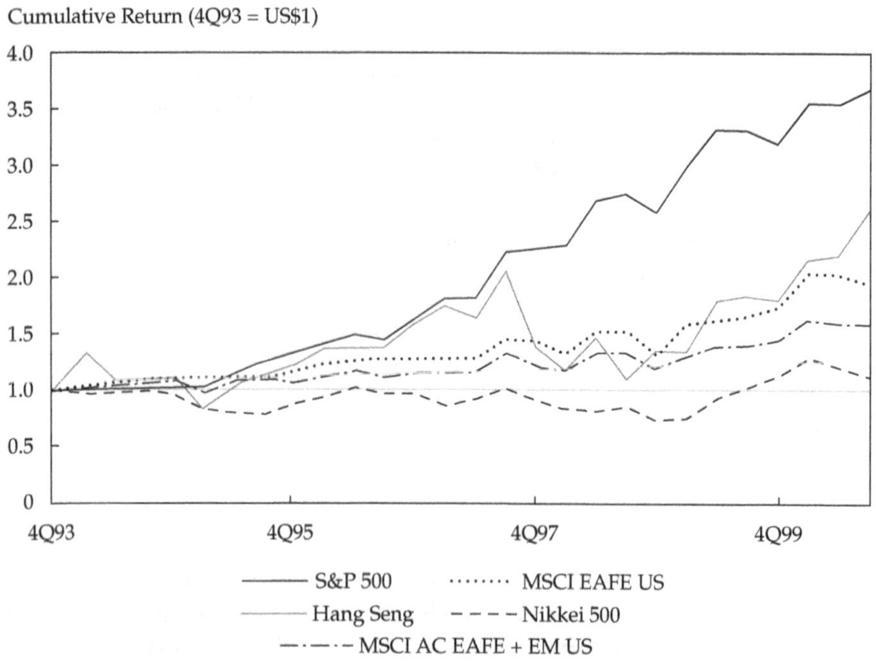

Source for data: Datastream.

The latter part of the second time period, from Q4 2007 to Q1 2009, was a period of dramatic declines in global share prices. Exhibit 4-8 shows the mean annual returns and standard deviation of returns for this time period.

During the period Q4 2007 through Q1 2009, the average return for the equally weighted portfolio, including dividends, was –48.5 percent. Other than reducing the risk of earning the return of the worst performing market, the diversification benefits were small. Exhibit 4-9 shows the cumulative quarterly returns of each of the five indices over this time period. All of the indices declined in unison. The lesson is that although portfolio diversification generally does reduce risk, it does not necessarily provide the same level of risk

[6]The S&P 500, Hang Seng, and Nikkei 500 are broad-based composite equity indices designed to measure the performance of equities in the United States, Hong Kong, and Japan. MSCI stands for Morgan Stanley Capital International. EAFE refers to developed markets in Europe, Australasia, and the Far East. AC indicates all countries, and EM is emerging markets. All index returns are in U.S. dollars.

EXHIBIT 4-7 Returns to Global Equity Indices, Q1 2006–Q1 2009

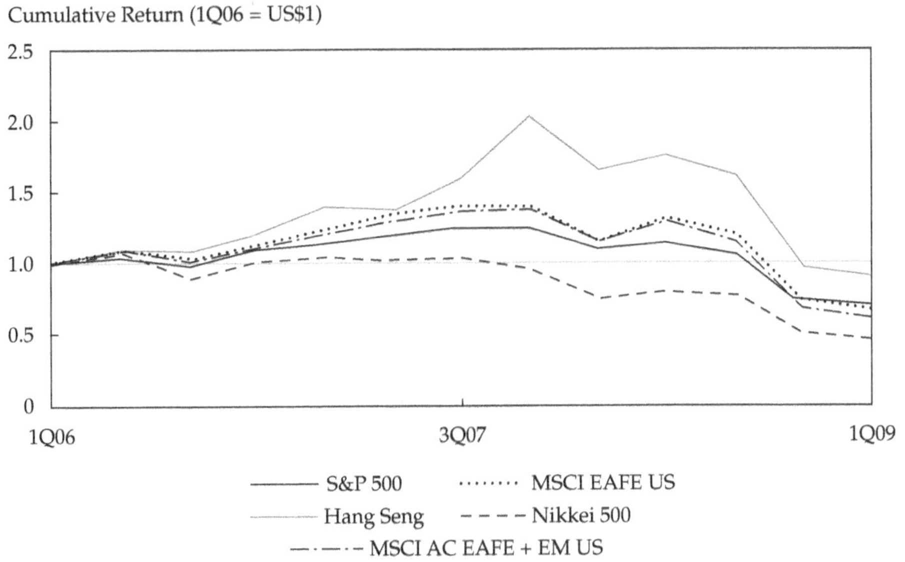

Source for data: Datastream.

EXHIBIT 4-8 Returns to Global Equity Indices

	Q4 1993–Q3 2000		Q1 2006–Q1 2009		Q4 2007–Q1 2009	
Global Index	Mean	Standard Deviation	Mean	Standard Deviation	Mean	Standard Deviation
S&P 500	20.5%	13.9%	−6.3%	21.1%	−40.6%	23.6%
MSCI EAFE US$	10.9	14.2	−3.5	29.4	−48.0	35.9
Hang Seng	20.4	35.0	5.1	34.2	−53.8	34.0
Nikkei 500	3.3	18.0	−13.8	27.6	−48.0	30.0
MSCI AC EAFE+EM US$	7.6	13.2	−4.9	30.9	−52.0	37.5
Randomly selected index	12.6%	18.9%	−4.7%	28.6%	−48.5%	32.2%
Equally weighted portfolio	12.6%	14.2%	−4.7%	27.4%	−48.5%	32.0%
Diversification ratio		75.1%		95.8%		99.4%

Source for data: Datastream.

reduction during times of severe market turmoil as it does when the economy and markets are operating "normally." In fact, if the economy or markets fail totally (which has happened numerous times around the world), then diversification is a false promise. In the face of a worldwide contagion, diversification was ineffective, as illustrated at the end of 2008.

EXHIBIT 4-9 Return to Global Equity Indices, Q4 2007–Q1 2009

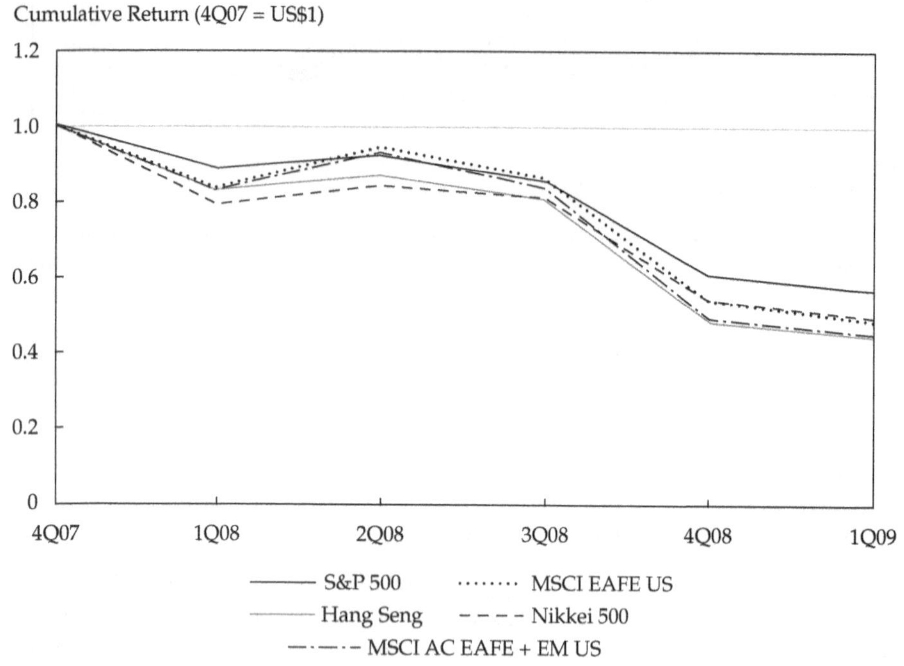

Source for data: Datastream.

Portfolios are *most likely* to provide:

A. Risk reduction.
B. Risk elimination.
C. Downside protection.

Solution: A is correct. Combining assets into a portfolio should reduce the portfolio's volatility. However, the portfolio approach does not necessarily provide downside protection or eliminate all risk.

2.5. Portfolios: The Emergence of Modern Portfolio Theory

The concept of diversification has been around for a long time and has a great deal of intuitive appeal. However, the actual theory underlying this basic concept and its application to investments only emerged in 1952 with the publication of Harry Markowitz's classic article on portfolio selection.[7] The article provided the foundation for what is now known as **modern portfolio theory** (MPT). The main conclusion of MPT is that investors should not only hold portfolios but should also focus on how individual securities in the portfolios are related to one another. In addition to the diversification benefits of portfolios to investors, the work of William Sharpe (1964), John Lintner (1965), and Jack Treynor (1961) demonstrated the role that portfolios play in determining the appropriate individual asset risk premium (i.e., the return in excess of the risk-free return expected by investors as compensation for the asset's risk). According to capital market theory, the priced risk of an individual security is affected by holding it in a well-diversified portfolio. The early research provided the insight that an asset's risk should be measured in relation to the remaining systematic or nondiversifiable risk, which should be the only risk that affects the asset's price. This view of risk is the basis of the capital asset pricing model, or CAPM. Although MPT has limitations, the concepts and intuitions illustrated in the theory continue to be the foundation of knowledge for portfolio managers.

3. INVESTMENT CLIENTS

Portfolio managers are employed or contracted by a wide variety of investment clients. We can group the clients into categories based on their distinctive characteristics and needs. Our initial distinction is between management of the private wealth of individual investors and investment management for institutional investors.

3.1. Individual Investors

Individual investors have a variety of motives for investing and constructing portfolios. Short-term goals can include providing for children's education, saving for a major purchase (such as a vehicle or a house), or starting a business. The retirement goal—investing to provide for an income in retirement—is a major part of the investment planning of most individuals. Many employees of public and private companies invest for retirement through a **defined contribution** (DC) pension plan. A DC plan is a pension plan in which contributions rather than benefits are specified, such as 401(k) plans in the United States, group personal pension schemes in the United Kingdom, and superannuation plans in Australia. Individuals will invest part of their wages while working, expecting to draw on the accumulated funds to provide income during retirement or to transfer some of their wealth to their heirs. The key to a DC plan is that the employee accepts the investment risk and is responsible for ensuring that there are enough funds in the plan to meet their needs upon retirement.

Some individuals will be investing for growth and will therefore seek assets that have the potential for capital gains. Others, such as retirees, may need to draw an income from their assets and may therefore choose to invest in fixed-income and dividend-paying shares. The investment needs of individuals will depend in part on their broader financial circumstances, such as their employment prospects and whether or not they own their own residence. They may also need to consider such issues as building up a cash reserve and the purchase of appropriate insurance policies before undertaking longer-term investments.

[7]Markowitz (1952).

3.2. Institutional Investors

There are many different types of institutional investors. Examples include defined benefit pensions plans, university endowments, charitable foundations, banks, insurance companies, investment companies, and sovereign wealth funds (SWFs). Institutional investors are major participants in the investment markets. Exhibit 4-10 shows the relative size and growth rates of the key categories across the Organisation for Economic Co-operation and Development (OECD) countries. Investment funds are the largest category, with insurance companies and pension funds not far behind. The relative importance of these categories does vary significantly across the individual OECD countries.

EXHIBIT 4-10 Institutional Assets (in US$ billions) 1995 to 2005

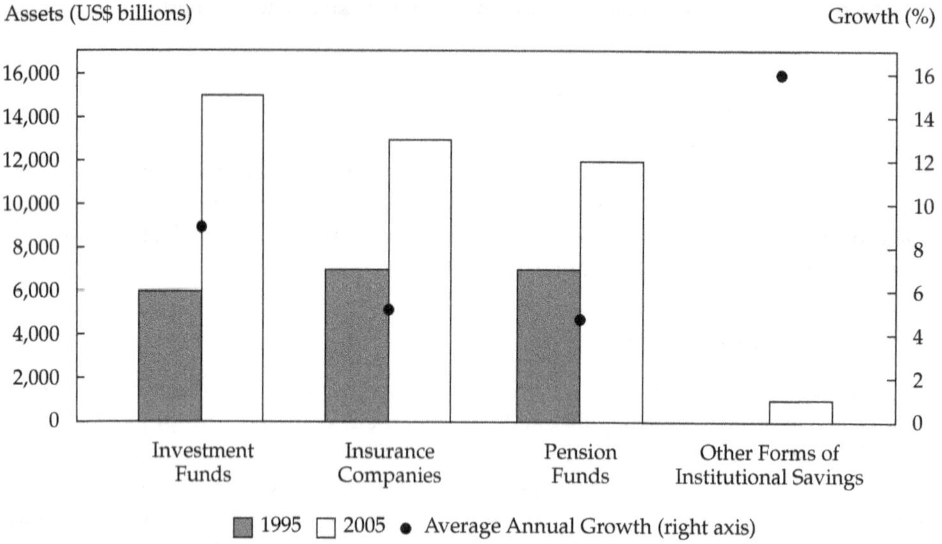

Source: OECD, "Recent Trends in Institutional Investors Statistics" (2008): www.oecd.org/dataoecd/53/49/42143444.pdf.

3.2.1. Defined Benefit Pension Plans

In a **defined benefit** (DB) pension plan, an employer has an obligation to pay a certain annual amount to its employees when they retire. In other words, the future benefit is defined because the DB plan requires the plan sponsor to specify the obligation stated in terms of the retirement income benefits owed to participants. DB plans need to invest the assets that will provide cash flows that match the timing of the future pension payments (i.e., liabilities). Plans are committed to paying pensions to members, and the assets of these plans are there to fund those payments. Plan managers need to ensure that sufficient assets will be available to pay pension benefits as they come due. The plan may have an indefinitely long time horizon if new plan members are being admitted or a finite time horizon if the plan has been closed to new members. Even a plan closed to new members may still have a time horizon of 70 or 80 years. For example, a plan member aged 25 may not retire for another 40 years and may live 30 years in retirement. Hence, pension plans can be considered long-term investors. In some cases, the plan managers attempt to match the fund's assets to its liabilities by, for example, investing in bonds that will produce cash flows corresponding to expected future pension payments. There may be many different investment philosophies for pension plans, depending on funded status and other variables.

3.2.2. Endowments and Foundations

University endowments are established to provide continuing financial support to a university and its students (e.g., scholarships). Endowments vary in size (assets under management), but many are major investors. It is common for U.S. universities to have large endowments, but it is somewhat less common elsewhere in the world. Exhibit 4-11 shows the top ten U.S. university endowments by assets as of the end of 2008. In terms of non-U.S. examples, the University of Oxford, United Kingdom, and its various colleges were estimated to have a total endowment of £4.8 billion as of 2004 and the University of Cambridge, United Kingdom, and its colleges, £5.3 billion. These were by far the largest endowments in the United Kingdom. The third largest, University of Edinburgh, was £156 million.[8] The French business school INSEAD's endowment was valued at €105 million as of 2008.[9]

EXHIBIT 4-11 Top Ten U.S. University Endowments by Asset Value

Rank	Institution	State	Endowment Funds 2008 (US$000)
1	Harvard University	MA	$36,556,284
2	Yale University	CT	22,869,700
3	Stanford University	CA	17,200,000
4	Princeton University	NJ	16,349,329
5	University of Texas System	TX	16,111,184
6	Massachusetts Institute of Technology	MA	10,068,800
7	University of Michigan	MI	7,571,904
8	Northwestern University	IL	7,243,948
9	Columbia University	NY	7,146,806
10	Texas A&M University System and foundations	TX	6,659,352

Source: NACUBO, "2008 NACUBO Endowment Study" (January 2009): www.nacubo.org/Research/NACUBO_Endowment_Study.html.

Charitable foundations invest donations made to them for the purpose of funding grants that are consistent with the charitable foundation's objectives. Similar to university endowments, many charitable foundations are substantial investors. Exhibit 4-12 lists U.S. grant-making foundations ranked by the market value of their assets based on the most current audited financial data in the Foundation Center's database as of 5 February 2009. Again, large foundations are most common in the United States, but they also exist elsewhere. For example, the Wellcome Trust is a U.K.-based medical charity that had approximately £13 billion of

[8]Acharya and Dimson (2007).
[9]See www.insead.com/campaign/endowment/index.cfm.

assets as of 2008.[10] The Li Ka Shing Foundation is a Hong Kong–based education and medical charity with grants, sponsorships, and commitments amounting to HK$10.7 billion.

EXHIBIT 4-12 Top Ten U.S. Foundation Endowments by Asset Value

Rank	Foundation	Assets (US$000)	As of Fiscal Year-End Date
1	Bill & Melinda Gates Foundation	$38,921,022	12/31/07
2	J. Paul Getty Trust	11,187,007	06/30/07
3	Ford Foundation	11,045,128	09/30/08
4	Robert Wood Johnson Foundation	10,722,296	12/31/07
5	William and Flora Hewlett Foundation	9,284,917	12/31/07
6	W.K. Kellogg Foundation	8,402,996	08/31/07
7	Lilly Endowment	7,734,860	12/31/07
8	John D. and Catherine T. MacArthur Foundation	7,052,165	12/31/07
9	David and Lucile Packard Foundation	6,594,540	12/31/07
10	Andrew W. Mellon Foundation	6,539,865	12/31/07

Source: Foundation Center (2009): http://foundationcenter.org.

A typical investment objective of an endowment or a foundation is to maintain the real (inflation-adjusted) capital value of the fund while generating income to fund the objectives of the institution. Most foundations and endowments are established with the intent of having perpetual lives. Example 4-1 describes the US$22 billion Yale University endowment's approach to balancing short-term spending needs with ensuring that future generations also benefit from the endowment, and it also shows the £13 billion Wellcome Trust's approach. The investment approach undertaken considers the objectives and constraints of the institution (for example, no tobacco investments for a medical endowment).

EXAMPLE 4-1 Spending Rules

The following examples of spending rules are from the Yale University endowment (in the United States) and from the Wellcome Trust (in the United Kingdom).

Yale University Endowment

The spending rule is at the heart of fiscal discipline for an endowed institution. Spending policies define an institution's compromise between the conflicting goals

[10]See www.wellcome.ac.uk/Investments/History-and-objectives/index.htm.

of providing substantial support for current operations and preserving purchasing power of Endowment assets. The spending rule must be clearly defined and consistently applied for the concept of budget balance to have meaning.

Yale's policy is designed to meet two competing objectives. The first goal is to release substantial current income to the operating budget in a stable stream, since large fluctuations in revenues are difficult to accommodate through changes in University activities or programs. The second goal is to protect the value of Endowment assets against inflation, allowing programs to be supported at today's level far into the future.

Yale's spending rule attempts to achieve these two objectives by using a long-term spending rate of 5.25 percent combined with a smoothing rule that adjusts spending gradually to changes in Endowment market value. The amount released under the spending rule is based on a weighted average of prior spending adjusted for inflation (80 percent weight) and an amount determined by applying the target rate to the current Endowment market value (20 percent weight) with an adjustment factor based on inflation and the expected growth of the Endowment net of spending.

(*"2007 Yale Endowment Annual Report," p. 15* [*www.yale.edu/investments/Yale_Endowment_07.pdf*])

Wellcome Trust

Our overall investment objective is to generate 6 per cent real return over the long term. This is to provide for real increases in annual expenditure while preserving at least the Trust's capital base in real terms in order to balance the needs of both current and future beneficiaries. We use this absolute return strategy because it aligns asset allocation with funding requirements and it provides a competitive framework in which to judge individual investments.

(*Wellcome Trust, "History and Objectives: Investment Goals"* [*www.wellcome.ac.uk/Investments/History-and-objectives/index.htm*])

3.2.3. Banks

Banks typically accept deposits and extend loans. In some cases, banks need to invest their excess reserves (i.e., when deposits have not been used to make loans). The investments of excess reserves need to be conservative, emphasizing fixed-income and money market instruments rather than equities and other riskier assets. In some countries, including the United States, there are legal restrictions on banks owning equity investments.[11] In addition to low risk, the investments also need to be relatively liquid so that they can be sold quickly if depositors wish to withdraw their funds. The bank's objective is to earn a return on its reserves that exceeds the rate of interest it pays on its deposits.

[11]See, for example, www.minneapolisfed.org/publications_papers/pub_display.cfm?id=3518.

3.2.4. Insurance Companies

Insurance companies receive premiums for the policies they write, and they need to invest these premiums in a manner that will allow them to pay claims. Similar to banks, such investments need to be relatively conservative given the necessity of paying claims when due. Life insurance companies and non-life insurance companies (for example, auto and home insurance) differ in their purpose and objectives and hence in their investment time horizons. Life insurance companies have longer time horizons than non-life insurance companies as a result of different expectations of when payments will be required under policies.

3.2.5. Investment Companies

Investment companies that manage mutual funds are also institutional investors. The mutual fund is a collective financial institution in which investors pool their capital to have it invested by a professional manager. The investors own shares or units in the fund. For many investment managers, the mutual fund is, in effect, their client. However, mutual funds are slightly different in that they can also be considered a financial product. For many individual investors, the mutual fund is an efficient means to benefit from portfolio diversification and the skill of a professional manager. The mutual fund is likely to invest in a particular category of investments, such as U.S. small capitalization equities. Mutual funds may also have certain limits and restrictions that apply to their investments, either as set by regulation and law or as decided by the board of directors of the investment company. We will revisit these investment vehicles in greater detail when we discuss pooled investments in Section 5.

3.2.6. Sovereign Wealth Funds

Sovereign wealth funds (SWFs) are government-owned investment funds, of which many are very sizable. For example, the largest SWF, managed by Abu Dhabi Investment Authority, is funded with oil revenues that amounted to US$627 billion[12] as of March 2009. Exhibit 4-13 provides a listing of the top 10 sovereign wealth funds as of March 2009.

EXHIBIT 4-13 Sovereign Wealth Funds by Asset Value

Fund	Assets as of March 2009 (US$ bns)	Inception Date	Country
Abu Dhabi Investment Authority	$627	1976	Abu Dhabi, UAE
SAMA Foreign Holdings	431	n/a	Saudi Arabia
SAFE Investment Company	347	n/a	People's Republic of China
Norwegian Government Pension Fund-Global	326	1990	Norway
Government of Singapore Investment Corporation	248	1981	Singapore

[12]SWF Institute (www.Swfinstitute.org/funds.php).

EXHIBIT 4-13 (*Continued*)

Fund	Assets as of March 2009 (US$ bns)	Inception Date	Country
National Welfare Fund	220	2008	Russia
Kuwait Investment Authority	203	1953	Kuwait
China Investment Corporation	190	2007	People's Republic of China
Hong Kong Monetary Authority Investment Portfolio	173	1998	People's Republic of China
Temasek Holdings	85	1974	Singapore
Total of top 10 SWFs	$2,850		
Total of all SWFs	$3,582		

Source: SWF Institute (www.swfinstitute.org).

Some funds have been established to invest revenues from finite natural resources (e.g., oil) for the benefit of future generations of citizens. Others manage foreign exchange reserves or other assets of the state. Some funds are quite transparent in nature—disclosing their investment returns and their investment holdings—whereas relatively little is known about the investment operations of others.

Exhibit 4-14 summarizes how investment needs vary across client groups. In some cases, generalizations are possible. In others, needs vary by client.

EXHIBIT 4-14 Summary of Investment Needs by Client Type

Client	Time Horizon	Risk Tolerance	Income Needs	Liquidity Needs
Individual investors	Varies by individual	Varies by individual	Varies by individual	Varies by individual
Defined benefit pension plans	Typically long-term	Typically quite high	High for mature funds; low for growing funds	Typically quite low
Endowments and foundations	Very long-term	Typically high	To meet spending commitments	Typically quite low
Banks	Short-term	Quite low	To pay interest on deposits and operational expenses	High to meet repayment of deposits
Insurance companies	Short-term for property and casualty; long-term for life insurance companies	Typically quite low	Typically low	High to meet claims
Investment companies	Varies by fund	Varies by fund	Varies by fund	High to meet redemptions

4. STEPS IN THE PORTFOLIO MANAGEMENT PROCESS

In the previous section we discussed the different types of investment management clients and the distinctive characteristics and needs of each. The following steps in the investment process are critical in the establishment and management of a client's investment portfolio.

- The Planning Step
  - Understanding the client's needs.
  - Preparation of an investment policy statement (IPS).
- The Execution Step
  - Asset allocation.
  - Security analysis.
  - Portfolio construction.
- The Feedback Step
  - Portfolio monitoring and rebalancing.
  - Performance measurement and reporting.

4.1. Step One: The Planning Step

The first step in the investment process is to understand the client's needs (objectives and constraints) and develop an **investment policy statement** (IPS). A portfolio manager is unlikely to achieve appropriate results for a client without a prior understanding of the client's needs. The IPS is a written planning document that describes the client's investment objectives and the constraints that apply to the client's portfolio. The IPS may state a benchmark—such as a particular rate of return or the performance of a particular market index—that can be used in the feedback stage to assess the performance of the investments and whether objectives have been met. The IPS should be reviewed and updated regularly (for example, either every three years or when a major change in a client's objectives, constraints, or circumstances occurs).

4.2. Step Two: The Execution Step

The next step is for the portfolio manager to construct a suitable portfolio based on the IPS of the client. The portfolio execution step consists of first deciding on a target asset allocation, which determines the weighting of asset classes to be included in the portfolio. This step is followed by the analysis, selection, and purchase of individual investment securities.

4.2.1. Asset Allocation

The next step in the process is to assess the risk and return characteristics of the available investments. The analyst forms economic and capital market expectations that can be used to form a proposed allocation of asset classes suitable for the client. Decisions that need to be made in the **asset allocation** of the portfolio include the distribution between equities, fixed-income securities, and cash; subasset classes, such as corporate and government bonds; and geographical weightings within asset classes. Alternative assets—such as real estate, commodities, hedge funds, and private equity—may also be included.

Economists and market strategists may set the top down view on economic conditions and broad market trends. The returns on various asset classes are likely to be affected by economic conditions; for example, equities may do well when economic growth has been unexpectedly strong whereas bonds may do poorly if inflation increases. The economists and strategists will attempt to forecast these conditions.

Top down—A top down analysis begins with consideration of macroeconomic conditions. Based on the current and forecasted economic environment, analysts evaluate markets and industries with the purpose of investing in those that are expected to perform well. Finally, specific companies within these industries are considered for investment.
Bottom up—Rather than emphasizing economic cycles or industry analysis, a bottom up analysis focuses on company-specific circumstances, such as management quality and business prospects. It is less concerned with broad economic trends than is the case for top down analysis, but instead focuses on company specifics.

4.2.2. Security Analysis

The top down view can be combined with the bottom up insights of security analysts who are responsible for identifying attractive investments in particular market sectors. They will use their detailed knowledge of the companies and industries they cover to assess the expected level and risk of the cash flows that each security will produce. This knowledge allows the analysts to assign a valuation to the security and identify preferred investments.

4.2.3. Portfolio Construction

The portfolio manager will then construct the portfolio, taking account of the target asset allocation, security analysis, and the client's requirements as set out in the IPS. A key objective will be to achieve the benefits of diversification (i.e., to avoid putting all the eggs in one basket). Decisions need to be taken on asset class weightings, sector weightings within an asset class, and the selection and weighting of individual securities or assets. The relative importance of these decisions on portfolio performance depends at least in part on the investment strategy selected; for example, consider an investor that actively adjusts asset sector weights in relation to forecasts of sector performance and one who does not. Although all decisions have an effect on portfolio performance, the asset allocation decision is commonly viewed as having the greatest impact.

Exhibit 4-15 shows the broad portfolio weights of the endowment funds of Yale University and the University of Virginia as of June 2008. As you can see, the portfolios have a heavy emphasis on such alternative assets as hedge funds, private equity, and real estate—Yale University particularly so.

Risk management is an important part of the portfolio construction process. The client's risk tolerance will be set out in the IPS, and the portfolio manager must make sure the portfolio is consistent with it. As noted previously, the manager will take a diversified portfolio perspective: What is important is not the risk of any single investment, but rather how all the investments perform as a portfolio.

EXHIBIT 4-15 Endowment Portfolio Weights, June 2008

Asset Class	Yale University Endowment	University of Virginia Endowment
Public equity	25.3%	53.6%
Fixed income	4.0	15.0
Private equity	20.2	19.6
Real assets (e.g., real estate)	29.3	10.1
Absolute return (e.g., hedge funds)	25.1	8.1
Cash	−3.9	−6.5
Portfolio value	US$22.9bn	US$5.1bn

Note: The negative cash positions indicate that at the point the figures were taken, the funds had net borrowing rather than net cash.
Sources: "2008 Yale Endowment Annual Report" (p. 2): www.yale.edu/investments/Yale_Endowment_08.pdf, "University of Virginia Investment Management Company Annual Report 2008" (p. 16): http://uvm-web.eservices.virginia.edu/public/reports/FinancialStatements_2008.pdf.

EXHIBIT 4-16 Insurance Company Portfolios, December 2008[13]

Asset Classes	MassMutual Portfolio	MetLife Portfolio
Bonds	56.4%	58.7%
Preferred and common shares	2.2	1.0
Mortgages	15.1	15.9
Real estate	1.3	2.4
Policy loans	10.6	3.0
Partnerships	6.4	1.9
Other assets	4.5	5.3
Cash	3.5	11.8

Note: MetLife is the Metropolitan Life Insurance Company.
Sources: "MassMutual Financial Group 2008 Annual Report" (p. 26): www.massmutual.com/mmfg/docs/annual_report/index.html, "MetLife 2008 Annual Report" (p. 83): http://investor.metlife.com/phoenix.zhtml?c=121171&p=irol-reportsannual.

[13]Asset class definitions: Bonds—Debt instruments of corporations and governments as well as various types of mortgage- and asset-backed securities; Preferred and Common Shares—Investments in preferred and common equities; Mortgages—Mortgage loans secured by various types of commercial property as well as residential mortgage whole loan pools; Real Estate—Investments in real estate; Policy Loans—Loans by policyholders that are secured by insurance and annuity contracts; Partnerships—Investments in partnerships and limited liability companies; Cash—Cash, short-term investments, receivables for securities, and derivatives. Cash equivalents have short maturities (less than one year) or are highly liquid and able to be readily sold.

The endowments just shown are relatively risk tolerant investors. Contrast the asset allocation of the endowment funds with the portfolio mix of the insurance companies shown in Exhibit 4-16. You will notice that the majority of the insurance assets are invested in fixed-income investments, typically of high quality. Note that the Yale University portfolio has only 4 percent invested in fixed income, with the remainder invested in such growth assets as equity, real estate, and hedge funds. This allocation is in sharp contrast to the Massachusetts Mutual Life Insurance Company (MassMutual) portfolio, which is over 80 percent invested in bonds, mortgages, loans, and cash—reflecting the differing risk tolerance and constraints (life insurers face regulatory constraints on their investments).

The portfolio construction phase also involves trading. Once the portfolio manager has decided which securities to buy and in what amounts, the securities must be purchased. In many investment firms, the portfolio manager will pass the trades to a buy side trader—a colleague who specializes in securities trading—who will contact a stockbroker or dealer to have the trades executed.

Sell side firm—A broker or dealer that sells securities to and provides independent investment research and recommendations to investment management companies.
Buy side firm—Investment management companies and other investors that use the services of brokers or dealers (i.e., the clients of the sell side firms).

4.3. Step Three: The Feedback Step

Finally, the feedback step assists the portfolio manager in rebalancing the portfolio due to a change in, for example, market conditions or the circumstances of the client.

4.3.1. Portfolio Monitoring and Rebalancing

Once the portfolio has been constructed, it needs to be monitored and reviewed and the composition revised as the security analysis changes because of changes in security prices and changes in fundamental factors. When security and asset weightings have drifted from the intended levels as a result of market movements, some rebalancing may be required. The portfolio may also need to be revised if it becomes apparent that the client's needs or circumstances have changed.

4.3.2. Performance Measurement and Reporting

Finally, the performance of the portfolio must be measured, which will include assessing whether the client's objectives have been met. For example, the investor will wish to know whether the return requirement has been achieved and how the portfolio has performed relative to any benchmark that has been set. Analysis of performance may suggest that the client's objectives need to be reviewed and perhaps changes made to the IPS. As we will discuss in the next section, there are numerous investment products that clients can use to meet their investment needs. Many of these products are diversified portfolios that an investor can purchase.

5. POOLED INVESTMENTS

The challenge faced by all investors is finding the right set of investment products to meet their needs. Just as there are many different types of investment management clients, there is a diverse set of investment products available to investors. These vary from a simple brokerage account in which the individual creates her own portfolio by assembling individual securities, to large institutions that hire individual portfolio managers for all or part of their investment management needs. Although the array of products is staggering, there are some general categories of pooled investment products that represent the full range of what is available. At one end are mutual funds and exchange-traded funds in which investors can participate with a small initial investment. At the other end are hedge funds and private equity funds, which might require a minimum investment of US$1 million or more. In this context, the amount of funds that an individual or institution can commit to a particular product has a significant impact on which products are available. Exhibit 4-17 provides a general breakdown of what investment products are available to investors based on investable funds.

EXHIBIT 4-17 Investment Products by Minimum Investment

• Mutual funds • Exchange-traded funds	• Mutual funds • Exchange-traded funds • Separately managed accounts	• Mutual funds • Exchange-traded funds • Separately managed accounts • Hedge funds • Private equity funds
As little as US$50 Minimum Investment	US$100,000	US$1,000,000+

5.1. Mutual Funds

Rather than assemble a portfolio on their own, individual investors and institutions can turn over the selection and management of their investment portfolio to a third party. One alternative is a **mutual fund**. This type of fund is a comingled investment pool in which investors in the fund each have a pro-rata claim on the income and value of the fund. The value of a mutual fund is referred to as the "net asset value." It is computed daily based on the closing price of the securities in the portfolio. At the end of the third quarter of 2008,[14] the Investment Company Institute reported over 48,000 mutual funds in over 23 countries with a total net asset value of approximately US$20 trillion. Exhibit 4-18 shows the breakdown of mutual fund assets across the major regions of the world as of the end of 2007.

Mutual funds are one of the most important investment vehicles for individuals and institutions. The best way to understand how a mutual fund works is to consider a simple example. Suppose that an investment firm wishes to start a mutual fund with a target amount

[14]Investment Company Institute (2009b).

of US$10 million. It is able to reach this goal through investments from five individuals and two institutions. The investment of each is as follows:

Investor	Amount Invested (US$)	Percent of Total	Number of Shares
Individuals			
A	$1.0 million	10%	10,000
B	1.0 million	10%	10,000
C	0.5 million	5%	5,000
D	2.0 million	20%	20,000
E	0.5 million	5%	5,000
Institutions			
X	2.0 million	20%	20,000
Y	3.0 million	30%	30,000
Totals	**$10.0 million**	**100%**	**100,000**

EXHIBIT 4-18 Global Allocation of Mutual Fund Assets: 2007

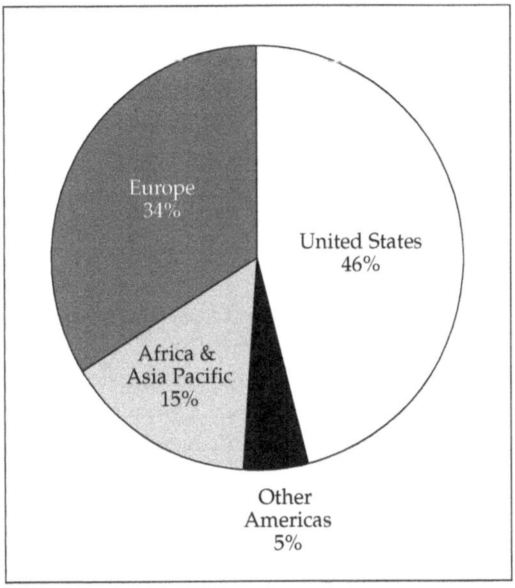

Source for data: 2008 Investment Company Fact Book, 48th ed., p. 20 (www.ici.org/pdf/2008_factbook.pdf).

Based on the US$10 million value (net asset value), the investment firm sets a total of 100,000 shares at an initial value of US$100 per share (US$10 million/100,000 = US$100). The investment firm will appoint a portfolio manager to be responsible for the investment of the US$10 million. Going forward, the total value of the fund or net asset value will depend on the value of the assets in the portfolio.

The fund can be set up as an open-end fund or a closed-end fund. If it is an **open-end fund**, it will accept new investment money and issue additional shares at a value equal to the net asset value of the fund at the time of investment. For example, assume that at a later date the net asset value of the fund increases to US$12.0 million and the new net asset value per share is US$120. A new investor, F, wishes to invest US$0.96 million in the fund. If the total value of the assets in the fund is now US$12 million or US$120 per share, in order to accommodate the new investment the fund would create 8,000 (US$0.96 million/US$120) new shares. After this investment, the net asset value of the fund would be US$12.96 million and there would be a total of 108,000 shares.

Funds can also be withdrawn at the net asset value per share. Suppose on the same day Investor E wishes to withdraw all her shares in the mutual fund. To accommodate this withdrawal, the fund will have to liquidate US$0.6 million in assets to retire 5,000 shares at a net asset value of US$120 per share (US$0.6 million/US$120). The combination of the inflow and outflow on the same day would be as follows:

Type	Investment (US$)	Shares
Inflow (Investor F buys)	+$960,000	+8,000
Outflow (Investor E sells)	−$600,000	−5,000
Net	+$360,000	+3,000

The net of the inflows and outflows on that day would be US$360,000 of new funds to be invested and 3,000 new shares created. However, the number of shares held and the value of the shares of all remaining investors, except Investor E, would remain the same.

An alternative to setting the fund up as an open-end fund would be to create a **closed-end fund** in which no new investment money is accepted into the fund. New investors invest by buying existing shares, and investors in the fund liquidate by selling their shares to other investors. Hence, the number of outstanding shares does not change. One consequence of this fixed share base is that, unlike open-end funds in which new shares are created and sold at the current net asset value per share, closed-end funds can sell for a premium or discount to net asset value depending on the demand for the shares.

There are advantages and disadvantages to each type of fund. The open-end fund structure makes it easy to grow in size but creates pressure on the portfolio manager to manage the cash inflows and outflows. One consequence of this structure is the need to liquidate assets that the portfolio manager might not want to sell at the time to meet redemptions. Conversely, the inflows require finding new assets in which to invest. As such, open-end funds tend not to be fully invested but rather keep some cash for redemptions not covered by new investments. Closed-end funds do not have these problems, but they do have a limited ability to grow. Of the total net asset value of all U.S. mutual funds at the end of 2008 (US$9.6 trillion), only approximately 2 percent were in the form of closed-end funds.

In addition to open-end or closed-end funds, mutual funds can be classified as load or no-load funds. The primary difference between the two is how the fund's management is compensated. In the case of the **no-load fund**, there is no fee for investing in the fund or for redemption but there is an annual fee based on a percentage of the fund's net asset value. **Load funds** are funds in which, in addition to the annual fee, a percentage fee is charged to invest in the fund and/or for redemptions from the fund. In addition, load funds are usually sold through retail brokers who receive part of the up-front fee. Overall, the number and importance of load funds has declined over time.

Mutual funds also differ in terms of the type of assets that they invest in. Broadly speaking, there are four different types of funds that are differentiated by broad asset type: stock funds (domestic and international), bond funds (taxable and nontaxable), hybrid or balanced funds (combination of stocks and bonds), and money market funds (taxable and nontaxable). The approximately US$9.6 trillion in U.S. mutual fund net asset value by asset type as of the end of 2008 is shown in Exhibit 4-19. A breakdown for the European mutual fund market is shown in Exhibit 4-20.

EXHIBIT 4-19 Mutual Funds Net Asset Value by Asset Type, End of 2007 and 2008

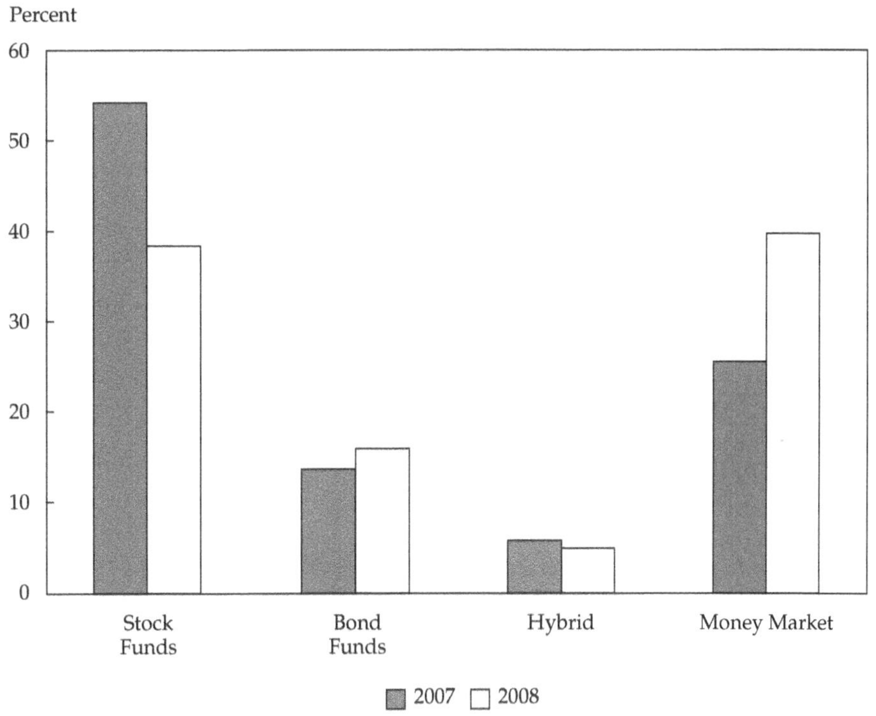

Source for data: Investment Company Institute (2009a).

Stock and money market funds make up the largest segments of the U.S. mutual fund industry. Between 2007 and 2008, however, there was a dramatic shift in the relative proportion of net asset value in stock funds and money market funds. Although there was a significant increase in the total value of assets in money market funds (24 percent, or approximately US$700 billion), the biggest change was in the value of total assets of stock funds, which fell by 43 percent or approximately US$2.8 trillion. Close to 10 percent of this drop, or US$280 billion, was the result of redemptions exceeding new investments, with the

EXHIBIT 4-20 European Mutual Fund (UCITS) Assets

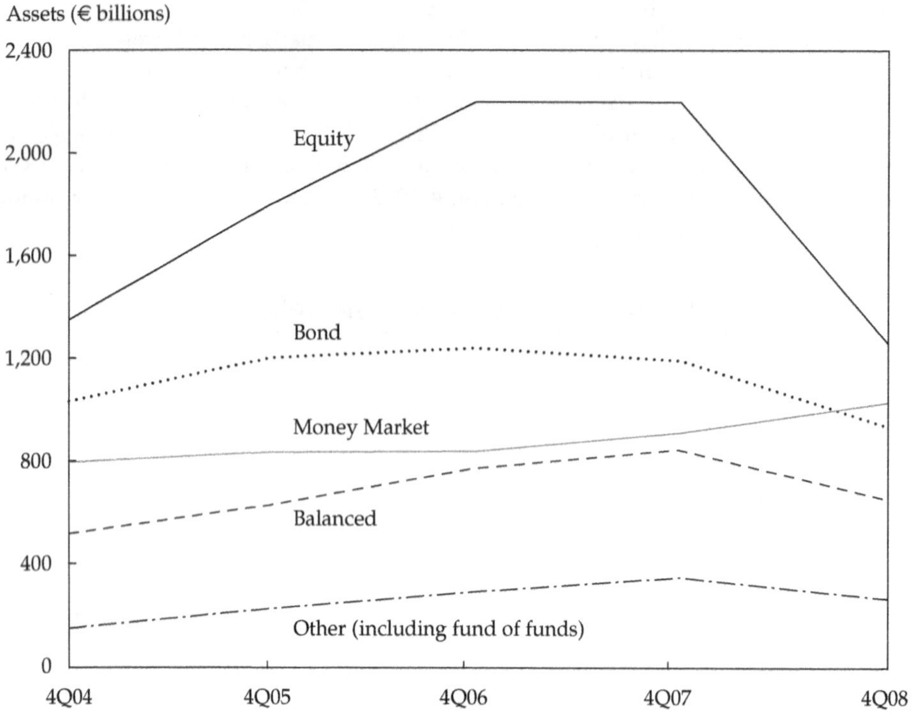

Note: UCITS (Undertakings for Collective Investments in Transferable Securities) are a set of regulations designed to help the European Union achieve a single funds market across Europe.
Source: EFAMA Quarterly Statistical Release No. 36 (Fourth Quarter of 2008). EFAMA is the European Fund and Asset Management Association.

remaining of the decline attributed to the dramatic fall in share prices during 2008.[15] A similar drop in equity assets is evident in the European data.

5.2. Types of Mutual Funds

The following section introduces the major types of mutual funds differentiated by the asset type that they invest in: money market funds, bond mutual funds, stock mutual funds, and hybrid or balanced funds.

5.2.1. Money Market Funds

Although money market funds have been a substitute for bank savings accounts since the early 1980s, they are not insured in the same way as bank deposits. At the end of 2008, the total net asset value of U.S. money market funds was in excess of US$3.8 trillion, with a further €1 trillion in European money market funds. In the United States, there are two basic types of money market funds: taxable and tax-free. Taxable money market funds invest in high

[15]These figures were extracted from data in Investment Company Institute (2009a).

quality, short-term corporate debt and federal government debt. Tax-free money market funds invest in short-term state and local government debt. At the end of 2008 in the United States, there were approximately 540 taxable funds with about US$3.3 trillion in net asset value and approximately 250 tax-free money market funds with a total net asset value of about US$490 million. From an investor's point of view, these funds are essentially cash holdings. As such, the presumption of investors is that the net asset value of a money market fund is always US$1.00 per share.

In September 2008 two large money market funds "broke the buck"; that is, the net asset value of the shares fell below US$1.00 per share. This drop in value caused investors to question the safety of money market funds and resulted in a massive outflow of funds from money market funds. This outflow continued until the U.S. Federal Reserve intervened to provide short-term insurance for some money market funds. This insurance, although similar to bank deposits, was limited in scope and time.

5.2.2. Bond Mutual Funds

A bond mutual fund is an investment fund consisting of a portfolio of individual bonds and, occasionally, preferred shares. The net asset value of the fund is the sum of the value of each bond in the portfolio divided by the number of shares. Investors in the mutual fund hold shares, which account for their pro-rata share or interest in the portfolio. The advantage is that an investor can invest in a bond fund for as little as US$100, which provides a stake in a diversified bond portfolio in which each individual bond may cost between US$10,000 and US$100,000. The major difference between a bond mutual fund and a money market fund is the maturity of the underlying assets. In a money market fund the maturity is as short as overnight and rarely longer than 90 days. A bond mutual fund, however, holds bonds with maturities as short as one year and as long as 30 years. Exhibit 4-21 illustrates the general categories of bond mutual funds.

EXHIBIT 4-21 Bond Mutual Funds

Type of Bond Mutual Fund	Securities Held
Global	Domestic and nondomestic government, corporate, and securitized debt
Government	Government bonds and other government-affiliated bonds
Corporate	Corporate debt
High yield	Below investment-grade corporate debt
Inflation protected	Inflation-protected government debt
National tax-free bonds	National tax-free bonds[16] (e.g., U.S. municipal bonds)

An example of a typical bond mutual fund is the T. Rowe Price Corporate Income Fund. Exhibit 4-22 shows the asset composition, credit quality, and maturity diversification for this bond mutual fund.

[16]In the United States, judicial rulings on federal powers of taxation have created a distinction between (federally) taxable and (federally) tax-exempt bonds and a parallel distinction for U.S. bond mutual funds.

EXHIBIT 4-22 Asset Composition of T. Rowe Price Corporate Income Fund As of 31 March 2009

Asset Composition		Credit Quality Diversification		Maturity Diversification	
Assets	% of Total	Bond Rating[17]	% of Total	Maturity (years)	% of Total
U.S. corporate	78.7%	AAA	7.1%	0–1 year	3.7%
Foreign bonds	18.4	AA	7.4	1–5 years	31.3
Cash	2.4	A	28.1	5–10 years	46.2
Other	0.5	BBB	48.8	10+ years	18.7
		BB	5.8		
		Other and not rated	0.3		
		Cash	2.4		

Source: T. Rowe Price (www.troweprice.com).

5.2.3. Stock Mutual Funds

Historically, the largest types of mutual funds based on market value of assets under management are stock or equity funds. At the end of the third quarter of 2008, the worldwide investment in stock mutual funds totaled around US$8.6 trillion, with approximately US$4 trillion of that in U.S. stock mutual funds.

There are two types of stock mutual funds. The first is an actively managed fund in which the portfolio manager seeks outstanding performance through the selection of the appropriate stocks to be included in the portfolio. Passive management is followed by index funds that are very different from actively managed funds. Their goal is to match or track the performance of different indices. The first index fund was introduced in 1976 by the Vanguard Group. At the end of 2008, index funds held approximately 13 percent of the total net asset value of stock mutual funds.[18]

There are several major differences between actively managed funds and index funds. First, management fees for actively managed funds are higher than for index funds. The higher fees for actively managed funds reflect its goal to outperform an index, whereas the index fund simply aims to match the return on the index. Higher fees are required to pay for the research conducted to actively select securities. A second difference is that the level of trading in an actively managed fund is much higher than in an index fund, which has obvious tax implications. Mutual funds are required to distribute all income and capital gains realized in the portfolio, so the actively managed fund tends to have more opportunity to realize capital gains. This results in higher taxes relative to an index fund, which uses a buy-and-hold strategy. Consequently, there is less buying and selling in an index fund and less likelihood of realizing capital gains distributions.

[17]Bond rating is from Standard & Poor's. AAA represents the highest credit quality. Bonds rated BBB and above are considered to be investment-grade bonds. Bonds rated below BBB are non-investment-grade bonds and are also known as high-yield or junk bonds.

[18]Mamudi (2009).

5.2.4. Hybrid/Balanced Funds

Hybrid or balanced funds are mutual funds that invest in both bonds and shares. These types of funds represent a small fraction of the total investment in U.S. mutual funds but are more common in Europe. (See Exhibits 4-19 and 4-20.) These types of funds, however, are gaining popularity with the growth of life-cycle funds. These are funds that manage the asset mix based on a desired retirement date. For example, if an investor is 40 years old in 2008 and planned to retire at the age of 67, he could invest in a mutual fund with a target date of 2035 and the fund would manage the appropriate asset mix over the next 27 years. In 2008 it might be 90 percent invested in shares and 10 percent in bonds. As time passes, however, the fund would gradually change the mix of shares and bonds to reflect the appropriate mix given the time to retirement.

5.3. Other Investment Products

In addition to mutual funds, a number of pooled investment products are increasingly popular in meeting the individual needs of clients. The following section introduces these products: exchange-traded funds, separately managed accounts, hedge funds, and buyout and venture capital funds.

5.3.1. Exchange-Traded Funds[19]

Exchange-traded funds (ETFs) combine features of closed-end and open-end mutual funds. ETFs trade like closed-end mutual funds; however, like open-end funds, ETFs' prices track net asset value due to an innovative redemption procedure. ETFs are created by fund sponsors who determine which securities will be included in the basket of securities. To obtain the basket, the fund sponsors contact an institutional investor who deposits the securities with the fund sponsor. In return, the institutional investor receives creation units that typically represent between 50,000 and 100,000 ETF shares. These shares can then be sold to the public by the institutional investor. The institutional investor can redeem the securities held in the ETF by returning the number of shares in the original creation unit. This process prevents meaningful premiums or discounts from net asset value. Closed-end mutual funds are predominantly actively managed stock or bond funds whereas ETFs are typically index funds. The first ETF was created in the United States in 1993 and in Europe in 1999. At the end of 2008, there were over 700 ETFs available in the United States with a total net asset value of over US$500 billion. A breakdown of the types of ETFs is shown in Exhibit 4-23.

The major difference between an index mutual fund and an ETF is that an investor investing in an index mutual fund buys the fund shares directly from the fund and all investments are settled at the net asset value. In the case of an ETF, however, investors buy the shares from other investors just as if they were buying or selling shares of stock. This setup includes the opportunity to short the shares or even purchase the shares on margin. The price an investor pays is based on the prevailing price at the time the transaction was made. This price may or may not be equal to the net asset value at the time, but it represents the price at that time for a willing buyer and seller. In practice, the market price of the ETF is likely to be close to the net asset value of the underlying investments.

---

[19]For more-detailed information on ETFs, see Investment Company Institute (2007) or Gastineau (2002). An additional resource for information on ETFs can be found in the American Association of Individual Investors' *AAII Journal*, which publishes an annual guide to ETFs in its October issue (see www.aaii.com/journal/index.cfm).

EXHIBIT 4-23 Types of Exchange-Traded Funds (ETFs) January 2009

Type of ETF	End of 2008	Totals (in US$ millions)	Asset Class by Type of ETF as a Percentage of Assets under Management							
Broad-based equity			Total Market	Large Cap	Mid Cap	Broad-Based, Other				
	50.6%	$266,161	7.4%	69.4%	9.4%	3.4%				
Sector			Commodities	Consumer	Financial	Natural Resources	Real Estate	Technology	Utilities	Other Sectors
	17.9%	94,101	38.0%	5.0%	16.6%	7.0%	12.8%	7.9%	4.8%	4.6%
Global/ international			Global	International	Regional	Single Country	Emerging Markets			
	19.7%	103,713	8.8%	41.4%	5.6%	11.5%	42.3%			
Hybrid			Hybrid							
	0.0%	125	100%							
Bond			Government Bond	Municipal Bond	Corporate Bond	International Bond				
	11.8%	62,185	44.7%	3.5%	41.4%	2.4%				
Totals	100.0%	$526,285								

Source: Investment Company Institute, "Exchange-Traded Fund Assets, January 2009" (25 February 2009): http://ici.org/research/stats/etf/ci.etfs_01_09.print.

Other main differences between an index mutual fund and an index ETF are transaction costs, transaction price, treatment of dividends, and the minimum investment amount. Expenses are lower for ETFs but, unlike mutual funds, investors do incur brokerage costs. Also as noted previously, all purchases and redemptions in a mutual fund take place at the same price at the close of business. ETFs are constantly traded throughout the business day, and as such each purchase or sale takes place at the prevailing market price at that time. In the case of the ETF, dividends are paid out to the shareholders whereas index mutual funds usually reinvest the dividends. Hence, there is a direct cash flow from the ETF that is not there with the index mutual fund. Depending on the investor, this cash flow may or may not be desirable. Note that the tax implications are the same with either fund type. Finally, the minimum required investment in an ETF is usually smaller. Investors can purchase as little as one share in an ETF, which is usually not the case with an index mutual fund.

ETFs are often cited as having tax advantages over index mutual funds. The advantage is not related to the dividends but rather to capital gains. As long as there is no sale of assets in either fund, no taxable capital gains would be realized by investors. It is possible, however, that because of the flow of funds into and out of index mutual funds, these funds would have a greater likelihood of generating taxable capital gains for investors. Overall, it is not clear how much of an advantage there is or if there is any advantage at all.

5.3.2. Separately Managed Accounts

A fund management service for institutions or individual investors with substantial assets is the **separately managed account** (SMA), which is also commonly referred to as a "managed account," "wrap account," or "individually managed account." An SMA is an investment portfolio managed exclusively for the benefit of an individual or institution. The account is managed by an individual investment professional to meet the specific needs of the client in relation to investment objectives, risk tolerance, and tax situation. In an SMA, the individual shares are held directly by the investor; and in return for annual fees, an individual can receive personalized investment advice.

The key difference between an SMA and a mutual fund is that the assets are owned directly by the individual. Therefore, unlike a mutual fund, the investor has control over which assets are bought and sold and the timing of the transactions. Moreover, in a mutual fund, there is no consideration given to the tax position of the individual asset. In an SMA, the transactions can take into account the specific tax needs of the investor. The main disadvantage of an SMA is that the required minimum investment is usually much higher than is the case with a mutual fund. Usually, the minimum investment is between US$100,000 and US$500,000.

Large institutions often use segregated accounts, which means their investments are held in an account on their behalf and managed by a portfolio manager or team. They can also use mutual funds. The decision on which approach to take often depends on the value of assets involved. Larger amounts of assets are more likely to be managed on a segregated basis.

5.3.3. Hedge Funds

The origin of **hedge funds**[20] can be traced back as far as 1949 to a fund managed by A.W. Jones & Co. It offered a strategy of a noncorrelated offset to the "long-only" position typical of most portfolios. From this start emerged a whole new industry of hedge funds. Hedge fund

[20]For a more comprehensive discussion of hedge funds, refer to Sihler (2004). Most of the discussion here is drawn from that document.

strategies generally involve a significant amount of risk, driven in large measure by the liberal use of leverage and complexity. More recently, it has also involved the extensive use of derivatives.

A key difference between hedge funds and mutual funds is that the vast majority of hedge funds are exempt from many of the reporting requirements for the typical public investment company. In the United States, investment companies do not have to register with the U.S. Securities and Exchange Commission (SEC) if they have 100 or fewer investors [Section 3(c)1 of the Investment Company Act of 1940] or if the investor base is greater than 100 but less than 500 "qualified purchasers"[21] [Section 3(c)7 of the Investment Company Act of 1940]. In order to qualify for the exemption, hedge funds cannot be offered for sale to the general public; they can only be sold via private placement. In addition, Regulation D of the Securities Act of 1933 requires that hedge funds be offered solely to "accredited investors."[22] The net effect of these regulations is that the hedge fund investor base is generally very different from that of the typical mutual fund.

From its start in 1955 to the end of 2008, the hedge fund industry has grown to over 9,200 hedge funds with approximately US$1.4 trillion in assets.[23] Not all hedge funds are the same, however. Many different strategies are employed. A few examples[24] include:

- **Convertible arbitrage**—Buying such securities as convertible bonds that can be converted into shares at a fixed price and simultaneously selling the stock short.
- **Dedicated short bias**—Taking more short positions than long positions.
- **Emerging markets**—Investing in companies in emerging markets by purchasing corporate or sovereign securities.
- **Equity market neutral**—Attempting to eliminate the overall market movement by going short overvalued securities and going long a nearly equal value of undervalued securities.
- **Event driven**—Attempting to take advantage of specific company events. Event-driven strategies take advantage of transaction announcements and other one-time events.
- **Fixed-income arbitrage**—Attempting to profit from arbitrage opportunities in interest-rate securities. When using a fixed-income arbitrage strategy, the investor assumes opposing positions in the market to take advantage of small price discrepancies while limiting interest rate risk.
- **Global macro**—Trying to capture shifts between global economies, usually using derivatives on currencies or interest rates.
- **Long/short**—Buying long equities that are expected to increase in value and selling short equities that are expected to decrease in value. Unlike the equity market neutral strategy,

[21]A "qualified purchaser" is an individual with over US$5 million in investment assets.

[22]An "accredited individual" investor must have a minimum net worth of US$1 million or a minimum individual income of US$200,000 in each of the two most recent years with the expectation of having the same income in the current year. An accredited institution must have a minimum of US$5 million in invested assets.

[23]Both the number of hedge funds and the value of assets under management fell dramatically in the second half of 2008. According to Hedge Fund Research, Inc., during 2008 the total number of funds fell by 8 percent and the value of assets under management fell from approximately US$1.9 trillion to US$1.4 trillion at the end of 2008.

[24]In the examples, "long" refers to owning the security and "selling short" refers to a strategy of borrowing shares and converting them to cash with the intention of repaying the shares at a later date by buying them back at a lower price. Long positions have a positive return when the price of the security increases, and short positions have a positive return when the price of the security falls.

this strategy attempts to profit from market movements, not just from identifying overvalued and undervalued equities.

The preceding list is not all-inclusive; there are many other strategies. Hedge funds are not readily available to all investors. They require a minimum investment that is typically US$250,000 for new funds and US$1 million or more for well-established funds. In addition, they usually have restricted liquidity that could be in the form of allowing only quarterly withdrawals or having a fixed-term commitment of up to five years. Management fees are not only a fixed percentage of the funds under management; managers also collect fees based on performance. A typical arrangement would include a 1 percent to 2 percent fee on assets under management and 20 percent of the outperformance as compared to a stated benchmark.

5.3.4. Buyout and Venture Capital Funds

Two areas that have grown considerably over the past 15 years have been buyout and venture capital funds. Both take equity positions but in different types of companies. An essential feature of both is that they are not passive investors, and as such, they play a very active role in the management of the company. Furthermore, the equity they hold is private rather than traded on public markets. In addition, neither intends to hold the equity for the long term; from the beginning, both plan for an exit strategy that will allow them to liquidate their positions. Both venture capital funds and private equity funds operate in a manner similar to hedge funds. A minimum investment is required, there is limited liquidity during some fixed time period, and management fees are based not only on funds under management but also on the performance of the fund.

Buyout funds. The essence of a buyout fund is that it buys all the shares of a public company and, by holding all the shares, the company becomes private. The early **leveraged buyouts** (LBOs) of the mid-1960s through the early 1990s created the modern private equity firm. These were highly levered transactions that used the company's cash flow to pay down the debt and build the equity position. In its current form, private equity firms raise money specifically for the purpose of buying public companies, converting them to private companies, and simultaneously restructuring the company. The purchase is usually financed through a significant increase in the amount of debt issued by the company. A typical financing would include 25 percent equity and 75 percent debt in one form or another. The high level of debt is also accompanied by a restructuring of the operations of the company. The key is to increase the cash flow. Most private equity funds do not intend to hold the company for the long run because their goal is to exit the investment in three to five years either through an initial public offering (IPO) or a sale to another company. Generally, a private equity firm makes a few very large investments.

Venture capital funds. Venture capital differs from a buyout fund in that a venture capital firm does not buy established companies but rather provides financing for companies in their start-up phase. Venture capital funds play a very active role in the management of the companies in which they invest; beyond just providing money, they provide close oversight and advice. Similar to buyout funds, venture capital funds typically have a finite investment horizon and, depending on the type of business, make the investment with the intent to exit in three to five years. These funds make a large number of small investments with the expectation that only a small number will pay off. The assumption is that the one that does pay off will pay off big enough to compensate for the ones that do not pay off.

6. SUMMARY

- In this chapter we have discussed how a portfolio approach to investing could be preferable to simply investing in individual securities.
- The problem with focusing on individual securities is that this approach may lead to the investor "putting all her eggs in one basket."
- Portfolios provide important diversification benefits, allowing risk to be reduced without necessarily affecting or compromising return.
- We have outlined the differing investment needs of various types of individual and institutional investors. Institutional clients include defined benefit pension plans, endowments and foundations, banks, insurance companies, investment companies, and sovereign wealth funds.
- Understanding the needs of your client and creating an investment policy statement represent the first steps of the portfolio management process. Those steps are followed by security analysis, portfolio construction, monitoring, and performance measurement stages.
- We also discussed the different types of investment products that investors can use to create their portfolio. These range from mutual funds, to exchange-traded funds, to hedge funds, to private equity funds.

PROBLEMS[25]

1. Investors should use a portfolio approach to:

   A. Reduce risk.
   B. Monitor risk.
   C. Eliminate risk.

2. Which of the following is the *best* reason for an investor to be concerned with the composition of a portfolio?

   A. Risk reduction.
   B. Downside risk protection.
   C. Avoidance of investment disasters.

3. With respect to the formation of portfolios, which of the following statements is most *accurate*?

   A. Portfolios affect risk less than returns.
   B. Portfolios affect risk more than returns.
   C. Portfolios affect risk and returns equally.

4. Which of the following institutions will *on average* have the greatest need for liquidity?

   A. Banks.
   B. Investment companies.
   C. Non-life insurance companies.

[25]These practice questions were developed by Stephen P. Huffman, CFA (University of Wisconsin, Oshkosh).

5. Which of the following institutional investors will *most likely* have the longest time horizon?
   A. Defined benefit plan.
   B. University endowment.
   C. Life insurance company.
6. A defined benefit plan with a large number of retirees is *likely* to have a high need for:
   A. Income.
   B. Liquidity.
   C. Insurance.
7. Which of the following institutional investors is *most likely* to manage investments in mutual funds?
   A. Insurance companies.
   B. Investment companies.
   C. University endowments.
8. With respect to the portfolio management process, the asset allocation is determined in the:
   A. Planning step.
   B. Feedback step.
   C. Execution step.
9. The planning step of the portfolio management process is *least likely* to include an assessment of the client's:
   A. Securities.
   B. Constraints.
   C. Risk tolerance.
10. With respect to the portfolio management process, the rebalancing of a portfolio's composition is *most likely* to occur in the:
    A. Planning step.
    B. Feedback step.
    C. Execution step.
11. An analyst gathers the following information for the asset allocations of three portfolios:

Portfolio	Fixed Income	Equity	Alternative Assets
1	25%	60%	15%
2	60%	25%	15%
3	15%	60%	25%

Which of the portfolios is *most likely* appropriate for a client who has a high degree of risk tolerance?
    A. Portfolio 1.
    B. Portfolio 2.
    C. Portfolio 3.

12. Which of the following investment products is *most likely* to trade at their net asset value per share?
    A. Exchange-traded funds.
    B. Open-end mutual funds.
    C. Closed-end mutual funds.
13. Which of the following financial products is *least likely* to have a capital gain distribution?
    A. Exchange-traded funds.
    B. Open-end mutual funds.
    C. Closed-end mutual funds.
14. Which of the following forms of pooled investments is subject to the least amount of regulation?
    A. Hedge funds.
    B. Exchange-traded funds.
    C. Closed-end mutual funds.
15. Which of the following pooled investments is *most likely* characterized by a few large investments?
    A. Hedge funds.
    B. Buyout funds.
    C. Venture capital funds.

CHAPTER 5

PORTFOLIO RISK AND RETURN: PART I

Vijay Singal, CFA
Blacksburg, VA, U.S.A.

LEARNING OUTCOMES

After completing this chapter, you will be able to do the following:

- Calculate and interpret major return measures and describe their applicability.
- Describe the characteristics of the major asset classes that investors would consider in forming portfolios according to mean–variance portfolio theory.
- Calculate and interpret the mean, variance, and covariance (or correlation) of asset returns based on historical data.
- Explain risk aversion and its implications for portfolio selection.
- Calculate and interpret portfolio standard deviation.
- Describe the effect on a portfolio's risk of investing in assets that are less than perfectly correlated.
- Describe and interpret the minimum-variance and efficient frontiers of risky assets and the global minimum-variance portfolio.
- Discuss the selection of an optimal portfolio, given an investor's utility (or risk aversion) and the capital allocation line.

1. INTRODUCTION

Construction of an optimal portfolio is an important objective for an investor. In this chapter, we will explore the process of examining the risk and return characteristics of individual assets, creating all possible portfolios, selecting the most efficient portfolios, and ultimately choosing the optimal portfolio tailored to the individual in question.

During the process of constructing the optimal portfolio, several factors and investment characteristics are considered. The most important of those factors are risk and return of the individual assets under consideration. Correlations among individual assets along with risk and return are important determinants of portfolio risk. Creating a portfolio for an investor requires an understanding of the risk profile of the investor. Although we will not discuss the process of determining risk aversion for individuals or institutional investors, it is necessary to obtain such information for making an informed decision. In this chapter, we will explain the broad types of investors and how their risk–return preferences can be formalized to select the optimal portfolio from among the infinite portfolios contained in the investment opportunity set.

The chapter is organized as follows: Section 2 discusses the investment characteristics of assets. In particular, we show the various types of returns and risks, their computation and their applicability to the selection of appropriate assets for inclusion in a portfolio. Section 3 discusses risk aversion and how indifference curves, which incorporate individual preferences, can be constructed. The indifference curves are then applied to the selection of an optimal portfolio using two risky assets. Section 4 provides an understanding and computation of portfolio risk. The role of correlation and diversification of portfolio risk are examined in detail. Section 5 begins with the risky assets available to investors and constructs a large number of risky portfolios. It illustrates the process of narrowing the choices to an efficient set of risky portfolios before identifying the optimal risky portfolio. The risky portfolio is combined with investor risk preferences to generate the optimal risky portfolio. Section 6 summarizes the concepts discussed in this chapter.

2. INVESTMENT CHARACTERISTICS OF ASSETS

Financial assets are generally defined by their risk and return characteristics. Comparison along these two dimensions simplifies the process of selecting from millions of assets and makes financial assets substitutable. These characteristics distinguish financial assets from physical assets, which can be defined along multiple dimensions. For example, wine is characterized by its grapes, aroma, sweetness, alcohol content, and age, among other factors. The price of a television depends on picture quality, manufacturer, screen size, number and quality of speakers, and so on, none of which are similar to the characteristics for wine. Therein lies one of the biggest differences between financial and physical assets. Although financial assets are generally claims on real assets, their commonality across two dimensions (risk and return) simplifies the issue and makes them easier to value than real assets. In this section, we will compute, evaluate, and compare various measures of return and risk.

2.1. Return

Financial assets normally generate two types of return for investors. First, they may provide periodic income through cash dividends or interest payments. Second, the price of a financial asset can increase or decrease, leading to a capital gain or loss.

Certain financial assets, through design or choice, provide return through only one of these mechanisms. For example, investors in non-dividend-paying stocks, such as Google or Baidu, obtain their return from capital appreciation only. Similarly, you could also own or have a claim to assets that only generate periodic income. For example, defined benefit pension plans, retirement annuities, and reverse mortgages[1] make income payments as long as you live.

[1]A reverse mortgage is a type of loan that allows individuals to convert part of their home equity into cash. The loan is usually disbursed in a stream of payments made to the homeowner by the lender. As long as the homeowner lives in the home, they need not be repaid during the lifetime of the homeowner. The loan, however, can be paid off at any time by the borrower not necessarily by selling the home.

You should be aware that returns reported for stock indices are sometimes misleading because most index levels only capture price appreciation and do not adjust for cash dividends unless the stock index is labeled "total return" or "net dividends reinvested." For example, as reported by Yahoo! Finance, the S&P 500 Index of U.S. stocks was at 903.25 on 31 December 2008. Similarly, Yahoo! Finance reported that the index closed on 30 July 2002 at 902.78 implying a return of close to 0 percent over the approximately six-and-a-half-year period. The results are very different, however, if the total return S&P 500 Index is considered. The index was at 1283.62 on 30 July 2002 and had risen 13.2 percent to 1452.98 on 31 December 2008, giving an annual return of 1.9 percent. The difference in the two calculations arises from the fact that index levels reported by Yahoo! Finance and other reporting agencies do not include cash dividends, which are an important part of the total return. Thus, it is important to recognize and account for income from investments.

In the following subsection, we consider various types of returns, their computation, and their application.

2.1.1. Holding Period Return

Returns can be measured over a single period or over multiple periods. Single period returns are straightforward because there is only one way to calculate them. Multiple period returns, however, can be calculated in various ways and it is important to be aware of these differences to avoid confusion.

A **holding period return** is the return earned from holding an asset for a single specified period of time. The period may be 1 day, 1 week, 1 month, 5 years, or any specified period. If the asset (bond, stock, etc.) is bought now, time ($t-1$), at a price of 100 and sold later, say at time t, at a price of 105 with no dividends or other income, then the holding period return is 5 percent [105 – (100/100)]. If the asset also pays an income of 2 units at time t, then the total return is 7 percent. This return can be generalized and shown as a mathematical expression:

$$R = \frac{P_t - P_{t-1} + D_t}{P_{t-1}} = \frac{P_t - P_{t-1}}{P_{t-1}} + \frac{D_t}{P_{t-1}} = \text{Capital gain} + \text{Dividend yield}$$
$$= \frac{P_T + D_T}{P_0} - 1$$

In the preceding expression, P is the price and D is the dividend. The subscript indicates the time of that price or dividend: $t-1$ is the beginning of the period and t is the end of the period. The following two observations are important.

- We computed a capital gain of 5 percent and a dividend yield of 2 percent in the previous example. For ease of illustration, we assumed that the dividend is paid at time t. If the dividend was received any time before t, our holding period return would have been higher because we would have earned a return by putting the dividend in the bank for the remainder of the period.
- Return can be expressed in decimals (0.07), fractions (7/100), or as a percent (7%). They are all equivalent.

The holding period return can be computed for a period longer than one year. For example, you may need to compute a three-year holding period return from three annual returns. In that case, the holding period return is computed by compounding the three annual returns: $R = [(1 + R_1) \times (1 + R_2) \times (1 + R_3)] - 1$, where R_1, R_2, and R_3 are the three annual returns.

In this and succeeding parts of Section 2.1, we consider the aggregation of several single period returns.

2.1.2. Arithmetic or Mean Return

When assets have returns for multiple holding periods, it is necessary to aggregate those returns into one overall return for ease of comparison and understanding. It is also possible to compute the return for a long or an unusual holding period. Such returns, however, may be difficult to interpret. For example, a return of 455 percent earned by AstraZeneca PLC over the last 16 years (1993 to 2008) may not be meaningful unless all other returns are computed for the same period. Therefore, most holding period returns are reported as daily, monthly, or annual returns.

Aggregating returns across several holding periods becomes a challenge and can lead to different conclusions depending on the method of aggregation. The remainder of this section is designed to present various ways of computing average returns as well as discussing their applicability.

The simplest way to compute the return is to take the simple average of all holding period returns. Thus, three annual returns of –50 percent, 35 percent, and 27 percent will give us an average of 4 percent per year $= \left(\frac{-50\% + 35\% + 27\%}{3}\right)$. The arithmetic return is easy to compute and has known statistical properties, such as standard deviation. We can calculate the arithmetic return and its standard deviation to determine how dispersed the observations are around the mean or if the mean return is statistically different from zero.

In general, the **arithmetic** or **mean return** is denoted by $\bar{R}_i$ and given by the following equation for asset i, where R_{it} is the return in period t and T is the total number of periods.

$$\bar{R}_i = \frac{R_{i1} + R_{i2} + \cdots + R_{i,T-1} + R_{iT}}{T} = \frac{1}{T}\sum_{t=1}^{T} R_{it}$$

2.1.3. Geometric Mean Return

The arithmetic mean return is the average of the returns earned on a unit of investment at the beginning of each holding period. It assumes that the amount invested at the beginning of each period is the same, similar to the concept of calculating simple interest. However, because the base amount changes each year (the previous year's earnings needs to be added to or "compounded" to the beginning value of the investment), a holding or geometric period return may be quite different from the return implied by the arithmetic return. The geometric mean return assumes that the investment amount is not reset at the beginning of each year and, in effect, accounts for the compounding of returns. Basically, the geometric mean reflects a "buy-and-hold" strategy whereas arithmetic reflects a constant dollar investment at the beginning of each time period.[2]

[2]A buy-and-hold strategy assumes that the money invested initially grows or declines with time depending on whether a particular period's return is positive or negative. On the one hand, a geometric return compounds the returns and captures changes in values of the initial amount invested. On the other hand, arithmetic return assumes that we start with the same amount of money every period without compounding the return earned in a prior period.

A geometric mean return provides a more accurate representation of the return that an investor will earn than an arithmetic mean return assuming that the investor holds the investment for the entire time. In general, the **geometric mean return** is denoted by $\bar{R}_{Gi}$ and given by the following equation for asset *i*,

$$\bar{R}_{Gi} = \sqrt[T]{(1 + R_{i1}) \times (1 + R_{i2}) \times \cdots \times (1 + R_{i,T-1}) \times (1 + R_{iT})} - 1 = \sqrt[T]{\prod_{t=1}^{T} (1 + R_{it})} - 1$$

where R_{it} is the return in period *t* and *T* is the total number of periods.

In the example in Section 2.1.2, we calculated the arithmetic mean to be 4 percent. Exhibit 5-1 shows the actual return for each year and the actual amount at the end of each year using actual returns. Beginning with an initial investment of €1.0000, we will have €0.8573 at the end of the three-year period as shown in the third column. Note that we compounded the returns because, unless otherwise stated, we receive return on the amount at the end of the prior year. That is, we will receive a return of 35 percent in the second year on the amount at the end of the first year, which is only €0.5000, not the initial amount of €1.0000. Let us compare the actual amount at the end of the three-year period, €0.8573, with the amount we get using an annual arithmetic mean return of 4 percent calculated previously. The year-end amounts are shown in the fourth column using the arithmetic return of 4 percent. At the end of the three-year period, €1 will be worth €1.1249 ($= 1.0000 \times 1.04^3$). This ending amount of €1.1249 is much larger than the actual amount of €0.8573. Clearly, the calculated arithmetic return is greater than the actual return. In general, the arithmetic return is biased upward unless the actual holding period returns are equal. The bias in arithmetic mean returns is particularly severe if holding period returns are a mix of both positive and negative returns, as in the example.

EXHIBIT 5-1

	Actual Return for the Year	Year-End Actual Amount	Year-End Amount Using Arithmetic Return of 4%	Year-End Amount Using Geometric Return of –5%
Year 0		€1.0000	€1.0000	€1.0000
Year 1	–50%	€0.5000	€1.0400	€0.9500
Year 2	35%	€0.6750	€1.0816	€0.9025
Year 3	27%	€0.8573	€1.1249	€0.8574

For our example and using the previous formula, the geometric mean return per year is −5.0 percent, compared with an arithmetic mean return of 4.0 percent. The last column of Exhibit 5-1 shows that using the geometric return of –5.0 percent generates a value of €0.8574 at the end of the three-year period, which is very close to the actual value of €0.8573. The small difference in ending values is the result of a slight approximation used in computing the geometric return of –5.0 percent. Because of the effect of compounding, the geometric mean return is always less than or equal to the arithmetic mean return, $\bar{R}_{Gi} \leq \bar{R}_i$, unless there is no variation in returns, in which case they are equal.

2.1.4. Money-Weighted Return or Internal Rate of Return

The preceding return computations do not account for the amount of money invested in different periods. It matters to an investor how much money was invested in each of the three years. If she had invested €10,000 in the first year, €1,000 in the second year, and €1,000 in the third year, then the return of –50 percent in the first year significantly hurts her. On the other hand, if she had invested only €100 in the first year, the effect of the –50 percent return is drastically reduced.

The **money-weighted return** accounts for the money invested and provides the investor with information on the return she earns on her actual investment. The money-weighted return and its calculation are similar to the **internal rate of return** and the yield to maturity. Just like the internal rate of return, amounts invested are cash outflows from the investor's perspective and amounts returned or withdrawn by the investor, or the money that remains at the end of an investment cycle, is a cash inflow for the investor.

The money-weighted return can be illustrated most effectively with an example. In this example, we use the actual returns from the previous example. Assume that the investor invests €100 in a mutual fund at the beginning of the first year, adds another €950 at the beginning of the second year, and withdraws €350 at the end of the second year. The cash flows are shown in Exhibit 5-2.

EXHIBIT 5-2

Year	1	2	3
Balance from previous year	€0	€50	€1,000
New investment by the investor (cash inflow for the mutual fund) at the start of the year	100	950	0
Net balance at the beginning of year	100	1,000	1,000
Investment return for the year	–50%	35%	27%
Investment gain (loss)	–50	350	270
Withdrawal by the investor (cash outflow for the mutual fund) at the end of the year	0	–350	0
Balance at the end of year	€50	€1,000	€1,270

The internal rate of return is the discount rate at which the sum of present values of these cash flows will equal zero. In general, the equation may be expressed as follows, where T is the number of periods, CF_t is the cash flow at time t, and IRR is the internal rate of return or the money-weighted rate of return:

$$\sum_{t=0}^{T} \frac{CF_t}{(1+IRR)^t} = 0$$

A cash flow can be positive or negative; a positive cash flow is an inflow where money flows to the investor whereas a negative cash flow is an outflow where money flows away from the investor. We can compute the internal rate of return by using the preceding equation. The flows are expressed as follows, where each cash inflow or outflow occurs at the end of each year. Thus, CF_0 refers to the cash flow at the end of year 0 or beginning of year 1, and CF_3

refers to the cash flow at end of year 3 or beginning of year 4. Because cash flows are being discounted to the present—that is, end of year 0 or beginning of year 1—the period of discounting CF_0 is zero.

$$CF_0 = -100$$
$$CF_1 = -950$$
$$CF_2 = +350$$
$$CF_3 = +1,270$$

$$\frac{CF_0}{(1+IRR)^0} + \frac{CF_1}{(1+IRR)^1} + \frac{CF_2}{(1+IRR)^2} + \frac{CF_3}{(1+IRR)^3}$$
$$= \frac{-100}{1} + \frac{-950}{(1+IRR)^1} + \frac{+350}{(1+IRR)^2} + \frac{+1270}{(1+IRR)^3} = 0$$
$$IRR = 26.11\%$$

IRR = 26.11% is the internal rate of return, or the money-weighted rate of return, which tells the investor what she earned on the actual euros invested for the entire period. This return is much greater than the arithmetic and geometric mean returns because only a small amount was invested when the mutual fund's return was –50 percent.

Although the money-weighted return is an accurate measure of what the investor actually earned on the money invested, it is limited in its applicability to other situations. For example, it does not allow for return comparison between different individuals or different investment opportunities. Two investors in the *same* mutual fund may have different money-weighted returns because they invested different amounts in different years.

2.1.5. Comparison of Returns

The previous subsections have introduced a number of return measures. The following example illustrates the computation, comparison, and applicability of each measure.

EXAMPLE 5-1 Computation of Returns

Ulli Lohrmann and his wife, Suzanne Lohrmann, are planning for retirement and want to compare the past performance of a few mutual funds they are considering for investment. They believe that a comparison over a five-year period would be appropriate. They are given the following information about the Rhein Valley Superior Fund that they are considering.

Year	Assets Under Management at the Beginning of Year	Net Return
1	€30 million	15%
2	€45 million	–5%
3	€20 million	10%
4	€25 million	15%
5	€35 million	3%

The Lohrmanns are interested in aggregating this information for ease of comparison with other funds.

1. Compute the holding period return for the five-year period.
2. Compute the arithmetic mean annual return.
3. Compute the geometric mean annual return. How does it compare with the arithmetic mean annual return?
4. The Lohrmanns want to earn a minimum annual return of 5 percent. Is the money-weighted annual return greater than 5 percent?

Solution to 1: The holding period return is $R = (1 + R_1)(1 + R_2)(1 + R_3)(1 + R_4)(1 + R_5) - 1 = (1.15)(0.95)(1.10)(1.15)(1.03) - 1 = 0.4235 = 42.35\%$ for the five-year period.

Solution to 2: The arithmetic mean annual return can be computed as an arithmetic mean of the returns given by this equation: $\bar{R}_i = \dfrac{15\% - 5\% + 10\% + 15\% + 3\%}{5} = 7.60\%$.

Solution to 3: The geometric mean annual return can be computed using this equation:

$$\bar{R}_{Gi} = \sqrt[T]{(1 + R_{i1}) \times (1 + R_{i2}) \times \cdots \times (1 + R_{i,T-1}) \times (1 + R_{iT})} - 1$$

$$= \sqrt[5]{1.15 \times 0.95 \times 1.10 \times 1.15 \times 1.03} - 1 = \sqrt[5]{1.4235} - 1 = 0.0732 = 7.32\%$$

Thus, the geometric mean annual return is 7.32 percent, slightly less than the arithmetic mean return.

Solution to 4: To calculate the money-weighted rate of return, tabulate the annual returns and investment amounts to determine the cash flows, as shown in Exhibit 5-3. All amounts are in millions of euros.

EXHIBIT 5-3

Year	1	2	3	4	5
Balance from previous year	0	34.50	42.75	22.00	28.75
New investment by the investor (cash inflow for the Rhein fund)	30.00	10.50	0	3.00	6.25
Withdrawal by the investor (cash outflow for the Rhein fund)	0	0	–22.75	0	0
Net balance at the beginning of year	30.00	45.00	20.00	25.00	35.00
Investment return for the year	15%	–5%	10%	15%	3%
Investment gain (loss)	4.50	–2.25	2.00	3.75	1.05
Balance at the end of year	34.50	42.75	22.00	28.75	36.05

$$CF_0 = -30.00, CF_1 = -10.50, CF_2 = +22.75$$
$$CF_3 = -3.00, CF_4 = -6.25, CF_5 = +36.05$$

For clarification, it may be appropriate to explain the notation for cash flows. Each cash inflow or outflow occurs at the end of each year. Thus, CF_0 refers to the cash flow at the end of year 0 or beginning of year 1, and CF_5 refers to the cash flow at end of year 5 or beginning of year 6. Because cash flows are being discounted to the present—that is, end of year 0 or beginning of year 1—the period of discounting CF_0 is zero whereas the period of discounting for CF_5 is 5 years.

To get the exact money-weighted rate of return (IRR), the following equation would be equal to zero. Instead of calculating, however, use the 5 percent return to see whether the value of the expression is positive or not. If it is positive, then the money-weighted rate of return is greater than 5 percent, because a 5 percent discount rate could not reduce the value to zero.

$$\frac{-30.00}{(1.05)^0} + \frac{-10.50}{(1.05)^1} + \frac{22.75}{(1.05)^2} + \frac{-3.00}{(1.05)^3} + \frac{-6.25}{(1.05)^4} + \frac{36.05}{(1.05)^5} = 1.1471$$

Because the value is positive, the money-weighted rate of return is greater than 5 percent. Using a financial calculator, the exact money-weighted rate of return is 5.86 percent.

2.1.6. Annualized Return

The period during which a return is earned or computed can vary and often we have to annualize a return that was calculated for a period that is shorter (or longer) than one year. You might buy a short-term treasury bill with a maturity of 3 months, or you might take a position in a futures contract that expires at the end of the next quarter. How can we compare these returns? In many cases, it is most convenient to annualize all available returns. Thus, daily, weekly, monthly, and quarterly returns are converted to an annual return. In addition, many formulas used for calculating certain values or prices may require all returns and periods to be expressed as annualized rates of return. For example, the most common version of the Black–Scholes option-pricing model requires annualized returns and periods to be in years.

To annualize any return for a period shorter than one year, the return for the period must be compounded by the number of periods in a year. A monthly return is compounded 12 times, a weekly return is compounded 52 times, and a quarterly return is compounded 4 times. Daily returns are normally compounded 365 times. For an uncommon number of days, we compound by the ratio of 365 to the number of days.

If the weekly return is 0.2 percent, then the compound annual return is computed as shown because there are 52 weeks in a year:

$$\begin{aligned} r_{annual} &= (1 + r_{weekly})^{52} - 1 = (1 + 0.2\%)^{52} - 1 \\ &= (1.002)^{52} - 1 = 0.1095 = 10.95\% \end{aligned}$$

If the return for 15 days is 0.4 percent, the annualized return is computed assuming 365 days in a year. Thus,

$$r_{annual} = (1 + r_{15})^{365/15} - 1 = (1 + 0.4\%)^{365/15} - 1$$
$$= (1.004)^{365/15} - 1 = 0.1020 = 10.20\%$$

A general equation to annualize returns is given, where c is the number of periods in a year. For a quarter, $c = 4$ and for a month, $c = 12$:

$$r_{annual} = (1 + r_{period})^{c} - 1$$

How can we annualize a return when the holding period return is more than one year? For example, how do we annualize an 18-month holding period return? Because one year contains two-thirds of 18-month periods, $c = 2/3$ in the preceding equation. An 18-month return of 20 percent can be annualized, as shown:

$$r_{annual} = (1 + r_{18month})^{2/3} - 1 = (1 + 0.20)^{2/3} - 1 = 0.1292 = 12.92\%$$

Similar expressions can be constructed when quarterly or weekly returns are needed for comparison instead of annual returns. In such cases, c is equal to the number of holding periods in a quarter or in a week. For example, assume that you want to convert daily returns to weekly returns or annual returns to weekly returns for comparison between weekly returns. For converting daily returns to weekly returns, $c = 5$, assuming that there are five trading days in a week. For converting annual returns to weekly returns, $c = 1/52$. The expressions for annual returns can then be rewritten as expressions for weekly returns, as shown:

$$r_{weekly} = (1 + r_{daily})^{5} - 1; \quad r_{weekly} = (1 + r_{annual})^{1/52} - 1$$

One major limitation of annualizing returns is the implicit assumption that returns can be repeated precisely; that is, money can be reinvested repeatedly while earning a similar return. This type of return is not always possible. An investor may earn a return of 5 percent during a week because the market went up that week or he got lucky with his stock, but it is highly unlikely that he will earn a return of 5 percent every week for the next 51 weeks, resulting in an annualized return of 1,164.3 percent ($= 1.05^{52} - 1$). Therefore, it is important to annualize short-term returns with this limitation in mind. Annualizing returns, however, allows for comparison among different assets and over different time periods.

EXAMPLE 5-2 Annualized Returns

London Arbitrageurs, PLC, employs many analysts who devise and implement trading strategies. Mr. Brown is trying to evaluate three trading strategies that have been used for different periods of time.

- Keith believes that he can predict share price movements based on earnings announcements. In the last 100 days he has earned a return of 6.2 percent.
- Thomas has been very successful in predicting daily movements of the Australian dollar and the Japanese yen based on the carry trade. In the last four weeks, he has earned 2 percent after accounting for all transactions costs.

- Lisa follows the fashion industry and luxury retailers. She has been investing in these companies for the last three months. Her return is 5 percent.

Mr. Brown wants to give a prize to the best performer but is somewhat confused by the returns earned over different periods. Annualize returns in all three cases and advise Mr. Brown.

Solution:

Annualized return for Keith: $R_{Keith} = (1 + 0.062)^{365/100} - 1 = 0.2455 = 24.55\%$
Annualized return for Thomas: $R_{Thomas} = (1 + 0.02)^{52/4} - 1 = 0.2936 = 29.36\%$
Annualized return for Lisa: $R_{Lisa} = (1 + 0.05)^4 - 1 = 0.2155 = 21.55\%$

Thomas earned the highest return and deserves the reward, assuming the performance of all traders is representative of what they can achieve over the year.

2.1.7. Portfolio Return

When several individual assets are combined into a portfolio, we can compute the portfolio return as a weighted average of the returns in the portfolio. The portfolio return is simply a weighted average of the returns of the individual investments, or assets. If asset 1 has a return of 20 percent and constitutes 25 percent of the portfolio's investment, then the contribution to the portfolio return is 5 percent (= 25% of 20%). In general, if asset i has a return of R_i and has a weight of w_i in the portfolio, then the portfolio return, R_P, is given as:

$$R_P = \sum_{i=1}^{N} w_i R_i, \quad \sum_{i=1}^{N} w_i = 1$$

Note that the weights must add up to 1 because the assets in a portfolio, including cash, must account for 100 percent of the investment. Also, note that these are single period returns, so there are no cash flows during the period and the weights remain constant.

A two-asset portfolio is easier to work with, so we will use only two assets to illustrate most concepts. Extending the analysis to multiple assets, however, is easily achieved and covered in later sections. With only two assets in the portfolio, the portfolio return can be written as shown, where w_1 and w_2 are weights in assets 1 and 2.

$$R_P = w_1 R_1 + w_2 R_2$$

Because the portfolio consists of only two assets, the sum of the two weights should equal 100 percent. Therefore, $w_1 + w_2 = 1$ or $w_2 = (1 - w_1)$. By substituting, we can rewrite the preceding equation as follows:

$$R_P = w_1 R_1 + (1 - w_1) R_2$$

2.2. Other Major Return Measures and Their Applications

The statistical measures of return discussed in the previous section are generally applicable across a wide range of assets and time periods. Special assets, however, such as mutual funds, and other considerations, such as taxes or inflation, may require return measures that are specific to a particular application.

Although it is not possible to consider all types of special applications, we will discuss the effect of fees (gross versus net returns), taxes (pre-tax and after-tax returns), inflation (nominal and real returns), and leverage. Many investors use mutual funds or other external entities (i.e., investment vehicles) for investment. In those cases, funds charge management fees and expenses to the investors. Consequently, gross and net-of-fund-expense returns should also be considered. Of course, an investor may be interested in the net-of-expenses after-tax real return, which is in fact what an investor truly receives. We consider these additional return measures in the following sections.

2.2.1. Gross and Net Return

A **gross return** is the return earned by an asset manager prior to deductions for management expenses, custodial fees, taxes, or any other expenses that are not directly related to the generation of returns but rather related to the management and administration of an investment. These expenses are not deducted from the gross return because they may vary with the amount of assets under management or may vary because of the tax status of the investor. Trading expenses, however, such as commissions, are accounted for in (i.e., deducted from) the computation of gross return because trading expenses contribute directly to the return earned by the manager. Thus, gross return is an appropriate measure for evaluating and comparing the investment skill of asset managers because it does not include any fees related to the management and administration of an investment.

Net return is a measure of what the investment vehicle (mutual fund, etc.) has earned for the investor. Net return accounts for (i.e., deducts) all managerial and administrative expenses that reduce an investor's return. Because individual investors are most concerned about the net return (i.e., what they actually receive), small mutual funds with a limited amount of assets under management are at a disadvantage compared with the larger funds that can spread their largely fixed administrative expenses over a larger asset base. As a result, many small-sized mutual funds waive part of the expenses to keep the funds competitive.

2.2.2. Pre-Tax and After-Tax Nominal Return

All return measures discussed previously are pre-tax nominal returns—that is, no adjustment has been made for taxes or inflation. In general, all returns are pre-tax nominal returns unless they are otherwise designated.

Investors are concerned about the tax liability of their returns because taxes reduce the actual return that they receive. The two types of returns, capital gains (change in price) and income (such as dividends or interest), are usually taxed differently. Capital gains come in two forms: short-term capital gains and long-term capital gains. Long-term capital gains typically receive preferential tax treatment in a number of countries. Interest income is taxed as ordinary income in most countries. Dividend income may be taxed as ordinary income, may have a lower tax rate, or may be exempt from taxes depending on the country and the type of investor. The after-tax nominal return is computed as the total return minus any allowance for taxes on realized gains.[3]

[3]Bonds issued at a discount to the par value may be taxed based on accrued gains instead of realized gains.

Because taxes are paid on realized capital gains and income, the investı can minimize the tax liability by selecting appropriate securities (e.g., those more favorable taxation, all other investment considerations equal) and reducing turnover. Therefore, many investors evaluate investment managers based on the after-tax nominal return.

2.2.3. Real Returns

A nominal return (r) consists of three components: a real risk-free return as compensation for postponing consumption (r_{rF}), inflation as compensation for loss of purchasing power (π), and a risk premium for assuming risk (RP). Thus, nominal return and real return can be expressed as:

$$(1 + r) = (1 + r_{rF}) \times (1 + \pi) \times (1 + RP)$$

$$(1 + r_{real}) = (1 + r_{rF}) \times (1 + RP) \quad \text{or}$$

$$(1 + r_{real}) = (1 + r) \div (1 + \pi)$$

Often the real risk-free return and the risk premium are combined to arrive at the real "risky" rate as given in the second equation above, simply referred to as the *real return.* Real returns are particularly useful in comparing returns across time periods because inflation rates may vary over time. Real returns are also useful in comparing returns among countries when returns are expressed in local currencies instead of a constant investor currency in which inflation rates vary between countries (which are usually the case). Finally, the after-tax real return is what the investor receives as compensation for postponing consumption and assuming risk after paying taxes on investment returns. As a result, the after-tax real return becomes a reliable benchmark for making investment decisions. Although it is a measure of an investor's benchmark return, it is not commonly calculated by asset managers because it is difficult to estimate a general tax component applicable to all investors. For example, the tax component depends on an investor's specific taxation rate (marginal tax rate), how long the investor holds an investment (long-term versus short-term), and the type of account the asset is held in (tax-exempt, tax-deferred, or normal).

2.2.4. Leveraged Return

In the previous calculations, we have assumed that the investor's position in an asset is equal to the total investment made by an investor using his or her own money. This section differs in that the investor creates a **leveraged** position. There are two ways of creating a claim on asset returns that are greater than the investment of one's own money. First, an investor may trade futures contracts in which the money required to take a position may be as little as 10 percent of the notional value of the asset. In this case, the leveraged return, the return on the investor's own money, is 10 times the actual return of the underlying security. Note that both the gains and losses are amplified by a factor of 10.

Investors can also invest more than their own money by borrowing money to purchase the asset. This approach is easily done in stocks and bonds, and very common when investing in real estate. If half (50 percent) of the money invested is borrowed, then the asset return to the investor is doubled but the investor must account for interest to be paid on borrowed money.

EXAMPLE 5-3 Computation of Special Returns

Let's return to Example 5-1. After reading this section, Mr. Lohrmann decided that he was not being fair to the fund manager by including the asset management fee and other expenses because the small size of the fund would put it at a competitive disadvantage. He learns that the fund spends a fixed amount of €500,000 every year on expenses that are unrelated to the manager's performance.

Mr. Lohrmann has become concerned that both taxes and inflation may reduce his return. Based on the current tax code, he expects to pay 20 percent tax on the return he earns from his investment. Historically, inflation has been around 2 percent and he expects the same rate of inflation to be maintained.

1. Estimate the annual gross return for the first year by adding back the fixed expenses.
2. What is the net return that investors in the Rhein Valley Superior Fund earned during the five-year period?
3. What is the after-tax net return for the first year that investors earned from the Rhein Valley Superior Fund? Assume that all gains are realized at the end of the year and the taxes are paid immediately at that time.
4. What is the anticipated after-tax real return that investors would have earned in the fifth year?

Solution to 1: The gross return for the first year is higher by 1.67 percent (= €500,000/€30,000,000) than the investor return reported by the fund. Thus, the gross return is 16.67 percent (= 15% + 1.67%).

Solution to 2: The investor return reported by the mutual fund is the net return of the fund after accounting for all direct and indirect expenses. The net return is also the pre-tax nominal return because it has not been adjusted for taxes or inflation. The net return for the five-year holding period was 42.35 percent.

Solution to 3: The net return earned by investors during the first year was 15 percent. Applying a 20 percent tax rate, the after-tax return that accrues to the investors is 12 percent [= 15% – (0.20 × 15%)].

Solution to 4: As in Part 3, the after-tax return earned by investors in the fifth year is 2.4 percent [= 3% – (0.20 × 3%)]. Inflation reduces the return by 2 percent so the after-tax real return earned by investors in the fifth year is 0.39 percent, as shown:

$$= \frac{(1 + 2.40\%)}{(1 + 2.00\%)} - 1 = \frac{(1 + 0.0240)}{(1 + 0.0200)} - 1 = 1.0039 - 1 = 0.0039 = 0.39\%$$

Note that taxes are paid before adjusting for inflation.

2.3. Variance and Covariance of Returns

Having discussed the various kinds of returns in considerable detail, we now turn to measures of riskiness of those returns. Just like return, there are various kinds of risk. For now, we will consider the total risk of an asset or a portfolio of assets as measured by its standard deviation, which is the square root of variance.

2.3.1. Variance of a Single Asset

Variance, or risk, is a measure of the volatility or the dispersion of returns. Variance is measured as the average squared deviation from the mean. Higher variance suggests less predictable returns and therefore a more risky investment. The variance (σ^2) of asset returns is given by the following equation,

$$\sigma^2 = \frac{\sum_{t=1}^{T}(R_t - \mu)^2}{T}$$

where R_t is the return for period t, T is the total number of periods, and μ is the mean of T returns, assuming T is the population of returns.

If only a sample of returns is available instead of the population of returns (as is usually the case in the investment world), then the previous expression underestimates the variance. The correction for *sample* variance is made by replacing the denominator with $(T - 1)$, as shown next, where $\bar{R}$ is the mean return of the sample observations and s^2 is the sample variance:

$$s^2 = \frac{\sum_{t=1}^{T}(R_t - \bar{R})^2}{T - 1}$$

2.3.2. Standard Deviation of an Asset

The **standard deviation** of returns of an asset is the square root of the variance of returns. The *population* standard deviation (σ) and the *sample* standard deviation (s) are given next.

$$\sigma = \sqrt{\frac{\sum_{t=1}^{T}(R_t - \mu)^2}{T}}, \quad s = \sqrt{\frac{\sum_{t=1}^{T}(R_t - \bar{R})^2}{T - 1}}$$

Standard deviation is another measure of the risk of an asset, which may also be referred to as its volatility. In a later section, we will decompose this risk measure into its separate components.

2.3.3. Variance of a Portfolio of Assets

Like a portfolio's return, we can calculate a portfolio's variance. When computing the variance of portfolio returns, standard statistical methodology can be used by finding the variance of the full expression of portfolio return. Although the return of a portfolio is simply a weighted average of the returns of each security, this is not the case with the standard deviation of a portfolio (unless all securities are perfectly correlated—that is, correlation equals one). Variance can be expressed more generally for N securities in a portfolio using the notation from Section 2.1.7 of this chapter:

$$\sum_{i=1}^{N} w_i = 1$$

$$\sigma_P^2 = Var(R_P) = Var\left(\sum_{i=1}^{N} w_i R_i\right)$$

The right side of the equation is the variance of the weighted average returns of individual securities. Weight is a constant, but the returns are variables whose variance is shown by $Var(R_i)$. We can rewrite the equation as shown next. Because the covariance of an asset with itself is the variance of the asset, we can separate the variances from the covariances in the second equation:

$$\sigma_P^2 = \sum_{i,j=1}^{N} w_i w_j Cov(R_i, R_j)$$

$$\sigma_P^2 = \sum_{i=1}^{N} w_i^2 Var(R_i) + \sum_{i,j=1, i \neq j}^{N} w_i w_j Cov(R_i, R_j)$$

$Cov(R_i, R_j)$ is the covariance of returns, R_i and R_j, and can be expressed as the product of the correlation between the two returns ($\rho_{1,2}$) and the standard deviations of the two assets. Thus, $Cov(R_i, R_j) = \rho_{ij}\sigma_i\sigma_j$.

For a two-asset portfolio, the expression for portfolio variance simplifies to the following using covariance and then using correlation:

$$\sigma_P^2 = w_1^2\sigma_1^2 + w_2^2\sigma_2^2 + 2w_1w_2Cov(R_1, R_2)$$

$$\sigma_P^2 = w_1^2\sigma_1^2 + w_2^2\sigma_2^2 + 2w_1w_2\rho_{12}\sigma_1\sigma_2$$

The standard deviation of a two-asset portfolio is given by the square root of the portfolio's variance:

$$\sigma_P = \sqrt{w_1^2\sigma_1^2 + w_2^2\sigma_2^2 + 2w_1w_2Cov(R_1, R_2)} \text{ or,}$$

$$\sigma_P = \sqrt{w_1^2\sigma_1^2 + w_2^2\sigma_2^2 + 2w_1w_2\rho_{12}\sigma_1\sigma_2}$$

EXAMPLE 5-4 Return and Risk of a Two-Asset Portfolio

Assume that as a U.S. investor, you decide to hold a portfolio with 80 percent invested in the S&P 500 U.S. stock index and the remaining 20 percent in the MSCI Emerging Markets index. The expected return is 9.93 percent for the S&P 500 and 18.20 percent for the Emerging Markets index. The risk (standard deviation) is 16.21 percent for the S&P 500 and 33.11 percent for the Emerging Markets index. What will be the portfolio's expected return and risk given that the covariance between the S&P 500 and the Emerging Markets index is 0.5 percent or 0.0050? Note that units for covariance and variance are written as $\%^2$ when not expressed as a fraction. These are units of measure like squared feet and the numbers themselves are not actually squared.

Solution:

$$\text{Portfolio return, } R_P = w_1R_1 + (1 - w_1)R_2 = (0.80 \times 0.0993) + (0.20 \times 0.1820)$$
$$= 0.1158 = 11.58\%.$$

$$\text{Portfolio risk} = \sigma_P = \sqrt{w_1^2\sigma_1^2 + w_2^2\sigma_2^2 + 2w_1w_2Cov(R_1, R_2)}$$

$$\sigma_p^2 = w_{US}^2\sigma_{US}^2 + w_{EM}^2\sigma_{EM}^2 + 2w_{US}w_{EM}Cov_{US,EM}$$
$$\sigma_p^2 = (0.80^2 \times 0.1621^2) + (0.20^2 \times 0.3311^2) + (2 \times 0.80 \times 0.20 \times 0.0050)$$
$$\sigma_p^2 = 0.01682 + 0.00439 + 0.00160 = 0.02281$$
$$\sigma_p = 0.15103 = 15.10\%$$

The portfolio's expected return is 11.58 percent and the portfolio's risk is 15.10 percent. Look at this example closely. It shows that we can take the portfolio of a U.S. investor invested only in the S&P 500, combine it with a *riskier* portfolio consisting of emerging markets securities, and the return of the U.S. investor increases from 9.93 percent to 11.58 percent while the risk of the portfolio actually falls from 16.21 percent to 15.10 percent. Exhibit 5-4 depicts how the combination of the two assets results in a superior risk–return trade-off. Not only does the investor get a higher return, but he also gets it at a lower risk. That is the power of diversification as you will see later in this chapter.

EXHIBIT 5-4 Combination of Two Assets

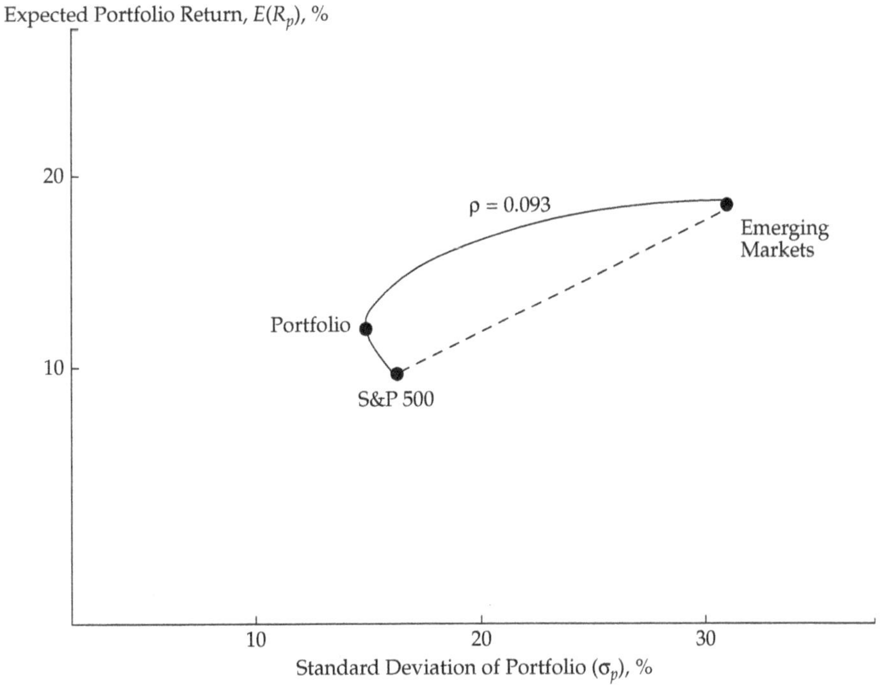

2.4. Historical Return and Risk

At this time, it is beneficial to look at historical risk and returns for the three main asset categories: stocks, bonds, and Treasury bills. Stocks refer to corporate ownership, bonds refer to long-term fixed-income securities, and Treasury bills refer to short-term government debt securities. Although there is generally no expectation of default on government securities, long-term government bond prices are volatile (risky) because of possible future changes in interest rates. In addition, bondholders also face the risk that inflation will reduce the purchasing power of their cash flows.

2.4.1. Historical Mean Return and Expected Return

Before examining historical data, it is useful to distinguish between the historical mean return and expected return, which are very different concepts but easy to confuse. **Historical return** is what was actually earned in the *past*, whereas **expected return** is what an investor anticipates to earn in the *future*.

Expected return is the nominal return that would cause the marginal investor to invest in an asset based on the real risk-free interest rate (r_{rF}), expected inflation [$E(\pi)$], and expected risk premium for the risk of the asset [$E(RP)$]. The real risk-free interest rate is expected to be positive as compensation for postponing consumption. Similarly, the risk premium is expected to be positive in most cases.[4] The expected inflation rate is generally positive, except when the economy is in a deflationary state and prices are falling. Thus, expected return is generally positive. The relationship between the expected return and the real risk-free interest rate, inflation rate, and risk premium can be expressed by the following equation:

$$1 + E(R) = (1 + r_{rF}) \times [1 + E(\pi)] \times [1 + E(RP)]$$

The historical mean return for investment in a particular asset, however, is obtained from the actual return that was earned by an investor. Because the investment is risky, there is no guarantee that the actual return will be equal to the expected return. In fact, it is very unlikely that the two returns are equal for a specific time period being considered. Given a long enough period of time, we can *expect* that the future (expected) return will equal the average historical return. Unfortunately, we do not know how long that period is—10 years, 50 years, or 100 years. As a practical matter, we often assume that the historical mean return is an adequate representation of the expected return, although this assumption may not be accurate. For example, Exhibit 5-5 shows that the historical equity returns in the past nine years (2000–2008) for large U.S. company stocks were negative whereas the expected return was nearly always positive. Nonetheless, longer-term returns (1926–2008) were positive and could be consistent with expected return. Though it is unknown if the historical mean returns accurately represent expected returns, it is an assumption that is commonly made.

Going forward, be sure to distinguish between expected return and historical mean return. We will alert the reader whenever historical returns are used to estimate expected returns.

---

[4]There are exceptions when an asset reduces overall risk of a portfolio. We will consider those exceptions in Section 4.3.

EXHIBIT 5-5 Risk and Return for U.S. Asset Classes by Decade (%)

		1930s	1940s	1950s	1960s	1970s	1980s	1990s	2000s*	1926–2008
Large company stocks	Return	–0.1	9.2	19.4	7.8	5.9	17.6	18.2	–3.6	9.6
	Risk	41.6	17.5	14.1	13.1	17.2	19.4	15.9	15.0	20.6
Small company stocks	Return	1.4	20.7	16.9	15.5	11.5	15.8	15.1	4.1	11.7
	Risk	78.6	34.5	14.4	21.5	30.8	22.5	20.2	24.5	33.0
Long-term corporate bonds	Return	6.9	2.7	1.0	1.7	6.2	13.0	8.4	8.2	5.9
	Risk	5.3	1.8	4.4	4.9	8.7	14.1	6.9	11.3	8.4
Long-term government bonds	Return	4.9	3.2	–0.1	1.4	5.5	12.6	8.8	10.5	5.7
	Risk	5.3	2.8	4.6	6.0	8.7	16.0	8.9	11.7	9.4
Treasury bills	Return	0.6	0.4	1.9	3.9	6.3	8.9	4.9	3.1	3.7
	Risk	0.2	0.1	0.2	0.4	0.6	0.9	0.4	0.5	3.1
Inflation	Return	–2.0	5.4	2.2	2.5	7.4	5.1	2.9	2.5	3.0
	Risk	2.5	3.1	1.2	0.7	1.2	1.3	0.7	1.6	4.2

*Through 31 December 2008.
Returns are measured as annualized geometric mean returns.
Risk is measured by annualizing monthly standard deviations.
Source: 2009 Ibbotson SBBI Classic Yearbook (Tables 2-1, 6-1, C-1 to C-7).

2.4.2. Nominal Returns of Major U.S. Asset Classes

We focus on three major asset categories in Exhibit 5-5: stocks, bonds, and T-bills. The mean nominal returns for U.S. asset classes are reported decade by decade since the 1930s. The total for the 1926–2008 period is in the last column. All returns are annual geometric mean returns. Large company stocks had an overall annual return of 9.6 percent during the 83-year period. The return was negative in the 1930s and 2000s, and positive in all remaining decades. The 1950s and 1990s were the best decades for large company stocks. Small company stocks fared even better. The nominal return was never negative for any decade, and had double-digit growth in all decades except two, leading to an overall 83-year annual return of 11.7 percent.

Long-term corporate bonds and long-term government bonds earned overall returns of 5.9 percent and 5.7 percent respectively. The corporate bonds did not have a single negative decade, although government bonds recorded a negative return in the 1950s when stocks were doing extremely well. Bonds also had some excellent decades, earning double-digit returns in the 1980s and 2000s.

Treasury bills (short-term government securities) did not earn a negative return in any decade. In fact, Treasury bills earned a negative return only in 1938 (–0.02 percent) when the inflation rate was –2.78 percent. Consistently positive returns for Treasury bills are not surprising because nominal interest rates are almost never negative and the Treasury bills suffer from little interest rate or inflation risk. Since the Great Depression, there has been no deflation in any decade, although inflation rates were highly negative in 1930 (–6.03 percent), 1931 (–9.52 percent), and 1932 (–10.30 percent). Conversely, inflation rates were very high in the late 1970s and early 1980s, reaching 13.31 percent in 1979. Inflation rates have fallen since then to a negligible level of 0.09 percent in 2008. Overall, the inflation rate was 3.0 percent for the 83-year period.

2.4.3. Real Returns of Major U.S. Asset Classes

Because inflation rates can vary greatly, from −10.30 percent to +13.31 percent in the past 83 years, comparisons across various time periods is difficult and misleading using nominal returns. Therefore, it is more effective to rely on real returns. Real returns on stocks, bonds, and T-bills are reported from 1900 in Exhibits 5-6 (page 195) and 5-7 (page 196).

Exhibit 5-6 shows that $1 would have grown to $582 if invested in stocks, to only $9.90 if invested in bonds, and to $2.90 if invested in T-bills. The difference in growth among the three asset categories is huge, although the difference in real returns does not seem that large: 6.0 percent per year for equities compared with 2.2 percent per year for bonds. This difference represents the effect of compounding over a 109-year period. The graph tracks the growth of money through major economic and political events, such as the world wars, the Great Depression, oil shocks, and other economic crashes and booms. Another interesting statistic to note is that most of the total return in stocks came from dividends, not from capital gains. If an investor relied only on capital gains, his investment would have grown to only $6 instead of $582 over the 109-year period.

Exhibit 5-7 reports both the nominal and real rates of return. As we discussed earlier and as shown in the table, geometric mean is never greater than the arithmetic mean. Our analysis of returns focuses on the geometric mean because it is a more accurate representation of returns for multiple holding periods than the arithmetic mean. We observe that the real returns for U.S. stocks are higher than the real returns for U.S. bonds, and that the real returns for bonds are higher than the real returns for U.S. T-bills.

2.4.4. Nominal and Real Returns of Asset Classes in Major Countries

Along with U.S. returns, returns of major asset classes for a 17-country world and the world excluding the United States are also presented in Exhibit 5-7. Equity returns are weighted by each country's GDP before 1968 because of a lack of reliable market capitalization data. Returns are weighted by a country's market capitalization beginning with 1968. Similarly, bond returns are defined by a 17-country bond index except GDP is used to create the weights because equity market capitalization weighting is inappropriate for a bond index and bond market capitalizations were not readily available.

The nominal mean return for the world stock index over the past 109 years was 8.4 percent, and bonds had a nominal geometric mean return of 4.8 percent. The nominal geometric mean returns for the world excluding the United States are 7.9 percent for stocks and 4.2 percent for bonds. For both stocks and bonds, the United States has earned higher returns than the world excluding the U.S. Similarly, real returns for stocks and bonds in the United States are higher than the real returns for rest of the world. No separate information is available for Treasury bills for non-U.S. countries.

2.4.5. Risk of Major Asset Classes

Risk for major asset classes in the United States is reported for 1926–2008 in Exhibit 5-5, and the risk for major asset classes for the United States, the world, and the world excluding the United States are reported for 1900–2008 in Exhibit 5-7. Exhibit 5-5 shows that U.S. small company stocks had the highest risk, 33.0 percent, followed by U.S. large company stocks, 20.6 percent. Long-term government bonds and long-term corporate bonds had lower risk at 9.4 percent and 8.4 percent, with Treasury bills having the lowest risk at about 3.1 percent.

EXHIBIT 5-6 Cumulative Returns on U.S. Asset Classes in Real Terms, 1900–2008

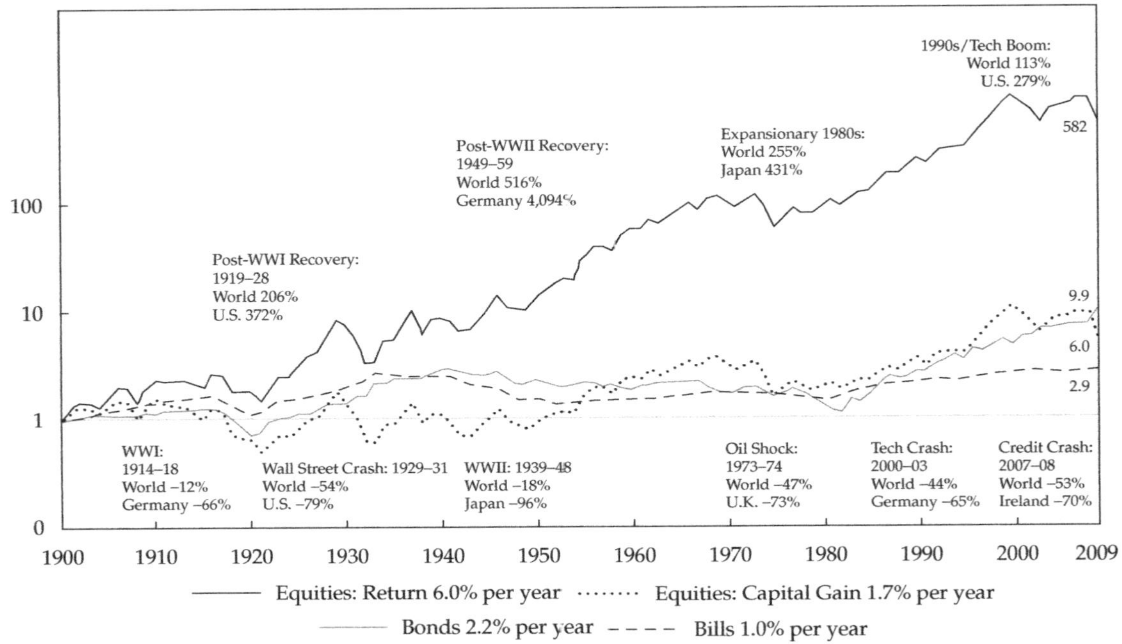

Source: E. Dimson, P. Marsh, and M. Staunton, *Credit Suisse Global Investment Returns Yearbook 2009*, Credit Suisse Research Institute (February 2009).

EXHIBIT 5-7 Nominal Returns, Real Returns, and Risk Premiums for Asset Classes (1900–2008)

		United States			World			World Excluding United States		
	Asset	*GM*	*AM*	*SD*	*GM*	*AM*	*SD*	*GM*	*AM*	*SD*
Nominal Returns	Equities	9.2%	11.1%	20.2%	8.4%	9.8%	17.3%	7.9%	9.7%	20.1%
	Bonds	5.2%	5.5%	8.3%	4.8%	5.2%	8.6%	4.2%	5.0%	13.0%
	Bills	4.0%	4.0%	2.8%	–	–	–	–	–	–
	Inflation	3.0%	3.1%	4.9%	–	–	–	–	–	–
Real Returns	Equities	6.0%	8.0%	20.4%	5.2%	6.7%	17.6%	4.8%	6.7%	20.2%
	Bonds	2.2%	2.6%	10.0%	1.8%	2.3%	10.3%	1.2%	2.2%	14.1%
	Bills	1.0%	1.1%	4.7%	–	–	–	–	–	–
Premiums	Equities vs. bills	5.0%	7.0%	19.9%	–	–	–	–	–	–
	Equities vs. bonds	3.8%	5.9%	20.6%	3.4%	4.6%	15.6%	3.5%	4.7%	15.9%
	Bonds vs. bills	1.1%	1.4%	7.9%	–	–	–	–	–	–

T-bills and inflation rates are not available for the world and world excluding the United States.
All returns are in percent per annum measured in US$.
GM = geometric mean, AM = arithmetic mean, SD = standard deviation.
"World" consists of 17 developed countries: Australia, Belgium, Canada, Denmark, France, Germany, Ireland, Italy, Japan, the Netherlands, Norway, South Africa, Spain, Sweden, Switzerland, United Kingdom, and the United States. Weighting is by each country's relative market capitalization size.
Source: Credit Suisse Global Investment Returns Yearbook, 2009. Compiled from tables 62, 65, and 68.

Exhibit 5-7 shows that the risk for world stocks is 17.3 percent and for world bonds is 8.6 percent. The world excluding the United States has risks of 20.1 percent for stocks and 13.0 percent for bonds. The effect of diversification is apparent when world risk is compared with U.S. risk and world excluding U.S. risk. Although the risk of U.S. stocks is 20.2 percent and the risk of world excluding U.S. stocks is 20.1 percent, the combination gives a risk of only 17.3 percent for world stocks. We can see a similar impact for world bonds when compared with U.S. bonds and world bonds excluding U.S. bonds. We observe a similar pattern in the risk levels of real returns.

2.4.6. Risk–Return Trade-Off

The expression "risk–return trade-off" refers to the positive relationship between expected risk and return. In other words, a higher return is not possible to attain in efficient markets and over long periods of time without accepting higher risk. Expected returns should be greater for assets with greater risk.

The historical data presented previously show the risk–return trade-off. Exhibit 5-5 shows for the United States that small company stocks had higher risk and higher return than large company stocks. Large company stocks had higher returns and higher risk than both long-term corporate bonds and government bonds. Bonds had higher returns and higher risk than Treasury bills. Uncharacteristically, however, long-term government bonds had higher total risk than long-term corporate bonds, although the returns of corporate bonds were slightly higher. These factors do not mean that long-term government bonds had greater default risk, just that they were more variable than corporate bonds during this historic period.

Turning to real returns, we find the same pattern: Higher returns were earned by assets with higher risk. Exhibit 5-7 reveals that the risk and return for stocks were the highest of the asset classes, and the risk and return for bonds were lower than stocks for the United States, the world, and the world excluding the United States. U.S. Treasury bills had the lowest return and lowest risk among T-bills, bonds, and stocks.

Another way of looking at the risk–return trade-off is to focus on the **risk premium**, which is the extra return investors can expect for assuming additional risk, after accounting for the nominal risk-free interest rate (includes both compensation for expected inflation and the real risk-free interest rate). Worldwide equity risk premiums reported at the bottom of Exhibit 5-7 show that equities outperformed bonds and bonds outperformed T-bills. Investors in equities earned a higher return than investors in T-bills because of the higher risk in stocks. Conversely, investors in T-bills cannot expect to earn as high a return as equity investors because the risk of their holdings is much lower.

A more dramatic representation of the risk–return trade-off was shown in Exhibit 5-6, which shows the cumulative returns of U.S. asset classes in real terms. The dashed line representing T-bills is much less volatile than the other lines. Adjusted for inflation, the average real return on T-bills was 1.0 percent per year. The grey line representing bonds is more volatile than the line for T-bills but less volatile than the lines representing stocks. The total return for equities including dividends and capital gains is represented by the dark line where $1 invested at the beginning of 1900 grows to $582, generating an annualized return of 6.0 percent in real terms.

Over long periods of time, we observe that higher risk does result in higher mean returns. Thus, it is reasonable to claim that, over the long term, market prices reward higher risk with higher returns, which is a characteristic of a risk-averse investor, a topic that we discuss in Section 3.

2.5. Other Investment Characteristics

In evaluating investments using mean (expected return) and variance (risk), we make two important assumptions. First, we assume that the returns are normally distributed because a normal distribution can be fully characterized by its mean and variance. Second, we assume that markets are not only informationally efficient but that they are also operationally efficient. To the extent that these assumptions are violated, we need to consider additional investment characteristics. These are discussed next.

2.5.1. Distributional Characteristics

A **normal distribution** has three main characteristics: its mean and median are equal; it is completely defined by two parameters, mean and variance; and it is symmetric around its mean with:

- 68 percent of the observations within $\pm 1\sigma$ of the mean.
- 95 percent of the observations within $\pm 2\sigma$ of the mean.
- 99 percent of the observations within $\pm 3\sigma$ of the mean.

Using only mean and variance would be appropriate to evaluate investments if returns were distributed normally. Returns, however, are not normally distributed; deviations from normality occur both because the returns are skewed, which means they are not symmetric around the mean, and because the probability of extreme events is significantly greater than what a normal distribution would suggest. The latter deviation is referred to as kurtosis or fat tails in a return distribution. The next sections discuss these deviations more in-depth.

2.5.1.1. Skewness

Skewness refers to asymmetry of the return distribution, that is, returns are not symmetric around the mean. A distribution is said to be left skewed or negatively skewed if most of the distribution is concentrated to the right, and right skewed or positively skewed if most is concentrated to the left. Exhibit 5-8 shows a typical representation of negative and positive skewness, whereas Exhibit 5-9 demonstrates the negative skewness of stock returns by plotting a histogram of U.S. large company stock returns for 1926–2008. Stock returns are usually negatively skewed because there is a higher frequency of negative deviations from the mean, which also has the effect of overestimating standard deviation.

EXHIBIT 5-8 Skewness

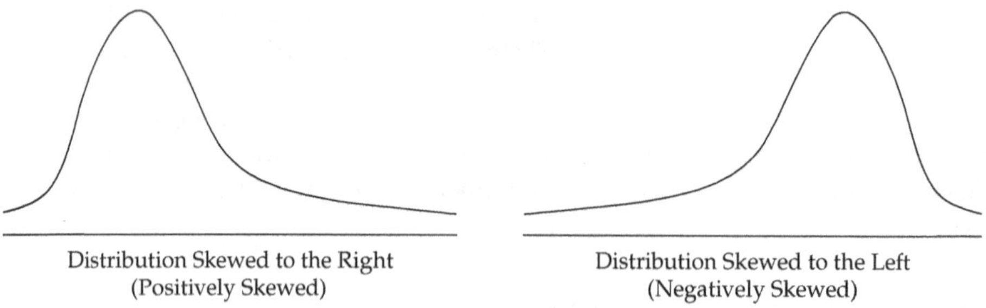

Source: Reprinted from *Fixed Income Readings for the Chartered Financial Analyst® Program.* Copyright CFA Institute.

2.5.1.2. Kurtosis

Kurtosis refers to fat tails or higher than normal probabilities for extreme returns and has the effect of increasing an asset's risk that is not captured in a mean–variance framework, as illustrated in Exhibit 5-10. Investors try to evaluate the effect of kurtosis by using such statistical techniques as value at risk (VAR) and conditional tail expectations.[5] Several market participants note that the probability and the magnitude of extreme events is underappreciated and was a primary contributing factor to the financial crisis of 2008.[6] The higher probability of extreme negative outcomes among stock returns can also be observed in Exhibit 5-9.

[5]Value at risk (VAR) is a money measure of the minimum losses expected on a portfolio during a specified time period at a given level of probability. It is commonly used to measure the losses a portfolio can suffer under normal market conditions. For example, if a portfolio's one-day 10 percent VAR is £200,000, it implies that there is a 10 percent probability that the value of the portfolio will decrease by more than £200,000 over a single one-day period (under normal market conditions). This probability implies that the portfolio will experience a loss of at least £200,000 on one out of every ten days.

[6]For example, see Bogle (2008) and Taleb (2007).

EXHIBIT 5-9 Histogram of U.S. Large Company Stock Returns, 1926–2008 (percent)

						2006				
						2004				
				2000	2007	1988	2003	1997		
				1990	2005	1986	1999	1995		
				1981	1994	1979	1998	1991		
				1977	1993	1972	1996	1989		
				1969	1992	1971	1983	1985		
				1962	1987	1968	1982	1980		
				1953	1984	1965	1976	1975		
				1946	1978	1964	1967	1955		
			2001	1940	1970	1959	1963	1950		
			1973	1939	1960	1952	1961	1945		
		2002	1966	1934	1956	1949	1951	1938	1958	
	2008	1974	1957	1932	1948	1944	1943	1936	1935	1954
1931	1937	1939	1941	1929	1947	1926	1942	1927	1928	1933

–60 –50 –40 –30 –20 –10 0 10 20 30 40 50 60 70

Source: 2009 Ibbotson SBBI Classic Yearbook (Table 2.2).

EXHIBIT 5-10 Kurtosis

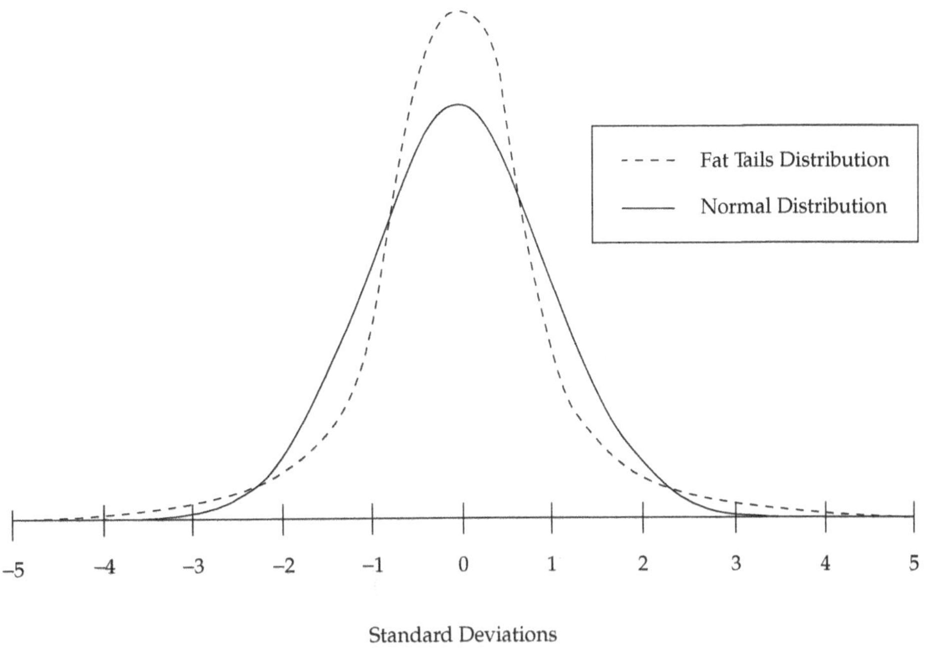

Source: Reprinted from *Fixed Income Readings for the Chartered Financial Analyst® Program*. Copyright CFA Institute.

2.5.2. Market Characteristics

In the previous analysis, we implicitly assumed that markets are both informationally and operationally efficient. Although informational efficiency of markets is a topic beyond the purview of this chapter, we should highlight certain operational limitations of the market that affect the choice of investments. One such limitation is **liquidity**.

The cost of trading has three main components—brokerage commission, bid–ask spread, and price impact—of which liquidity affects the latter two. Brokerage commission is usually negotiable and does not constitute a large fraction of the total cost of trading except in small-sized trades. Stocks with low liquidity can have wide bid–ask spreads. The bid–ask spread, which is the difference between the buying price and the selling price, is incurred as a cost of trading a security. The larger the bid–ask spread, the higher is the cost of trading. If a $100 stock has a spread of 10 cents, the bid–ask spread is only 0.1 percent ($0.10/$100). On the other hand, if a $10 stock has a spread of 10 cents, the bid–ask spread is 1 percent. Clearly, the $10 stock is more expensive to trade and an investor will need to earn 0.9 percent extra to make up the higher cost of trading relative to the $100 stock.

Liquidity also has implications for the price impact of trade. Price impact refers to how the price moves in response to an order in the market. Small orders usually have little impact, especially for liquid stocks. For example, an order to buy 100 shares of a $100 stock with a spread of 1 cent may have no effect on the price. On the other hand, an order to buy 100,000 shares may have a significant impact on the price as the buyer has to induce more and more stockholders to tender their shares. The extent of the price impact depends on the liquidity of the stock. A stock that trades millions of shares a day may be less affected than a stock that trades only a few hundred thousand shares a day. Investors, especially institutional investors managing large sums of money, must keep the liquidity of a stock in mind when making investment decisions.

Liquidity is a bigger concern in emerging markets than in developed markets because of the smaller volume of trading in those markets. Similarly, liquidity is a more important concern in corporate bond markets and especially for bonds of lower credit quality than in equity markets because an individual corporate bond issue may not trade for several days or weeks. This certainly became apparent during the global financial crisis.

There are other market-related characteristics that affect investment decisions because they might instill greater confidence in the security or might affect the costs of doing business. These include analyst coverage, availability of information, firm size, and so on. These characteristics about companies and financial markets are essential components of investment decision making.

3. RISK AVERSION AND PORTFOLIO SELECTION

As we have seen, stocks, bonds, and T-bills provide different levels of returns and have different levels of risk. Although investment in equities may be appropriate for one investor, another investor may not be inclined to accept the risk that accompanies a share of stock and may prefer to hold more cash. In the last section, we considered investment characteristics of assets in understanding their risk and return. In this section, we consider the characteristics of investors, both individual and institutional, in an attempt to pair the right kind of investors with the right kind of investments.

First, we discuss risk aversion and utility theory. Later we discuss their implications for portfolio selection.

3.1. The Concept of Risk Aversion

The concept of **risk aversion** is related to the behavior of individuals under uncertainty. Assume that an individual is offered two alternatives: one where he will get £50 for sure and the other is a gamble with a 50 percent chance that he gets £100 and 50 percent chance that he gets nothing. The expected value in both cases is £50, one with certainty and the other with uncertainty. What will an investor choose? There are three possibilities: an investor chooses the gamble, the investor chooses £50 with certainty, or the investor is indifferent. Let us consider each in turn. However, please understand that this is only a representative example, and a single choice does not determine the risk aversion of an investor.

3.1.1. Risk Seeking

If an investor chooses the gamble, then the investor is said to be risk loving or risk seeking. The gamble has an uncertain outcome, but with the same expected value as the guaranteed outcome. Thus, an investor choosing the gamble means that the investor gets extra "utility" from the uncertainty associated with the gamble. How much is that extra utility worth? Would the investor be willing to accept a smaller expected value because he gets extra utility from risk? Indeed, risk seekers will accept less return because of the risk that accompanies the gamble. For example, a risk seeker may choose a gamble with an expected value of £45 in preference to a guaranteed outcome of £50.

There is a little bit of gambling instinct in many of us. People buy lottery tickets although the expected value is less than the money they pay to buy it. Or people gamble at casinos in Macau or Las Vegas with the full knowledge that the expected return is negative, a characteristic of risk seekers. These or any other isolated actions, however, cannot be taken at face value except for compulsive gamblers.

3.1.2. Risk Neutral

If an investor is indifferent about the gamble or the guaranteed outcome, then the investor may be **risk neutral**. Risk neutrality means that the investor cares only about return and not about risk, so higher return investments are more desirable even if they come with higher risk. Many investors may exhibit characteristics of risk neutrality when the investment at stake is an insignificant part of their wealth. For example, a billionaire may be indifferent about choosing the gamble or a £50 guaranteed outcome.

3.1.3. Risk Averse

If an investor chooses the guaranteed outcome, he/she is said to be **risk averse** because the investor does not want to take the chance of not getting anything at all. Depending on the level of aversion to risk, an investor may be willing to accept a guaranteed outcome of £45 instead of a gamble with an expected value of £50.

In general, investors are likely to shy away from risky investments for a lower, but guaranteed return. That is why they want to minimize their risk for the same amount of return, and maximize their return for the same amount of risk. The risk–return trade-off discussed earlier is an indicator of risk aversion. A risk-neutral investor would maximize return irrespective of risk and a risk-seeking investor would maximize both risk and return.

Data presented in the last section illustrate the historically positive relationship between risk and return, which demonstrates that market prices were based on transactions and investments by risk-averse investors and reflect risk aversion. Therefore, for all practical purposes and for our future discussion, we will assume that the representative investor is a risk-averse investor. This assumption is the standard approach taken in the investment industry globally.

3.1.4. Risk Tolerance

Risk tolerance refers to the amount of risk an investor is willing to tolerate to achieve an investment goal. The higher the risk tolerance, the greater is the willingness to take risk. Thus, risk tolerance is negatively related to risk aversion.

3.2. Utility Theory and Indifference Curves

Continuing with our previous example, a risk-averse investor would rank the guaranteed outcome of £50 higher than the uncertain outcome with an expected value of £50. We can say that the utility that an investor or an individual derives from the guaranteed outcome of £50 is greater than the utility or satisfaction or happiness he/she derives from the alternative. In general terms, utility is a measure of relative satisfaction from consumption of various goods and services or, in the case of investments, the satisfaction that an investor derives from different portfolios.

Because individuals are different in their preferences, all risk-averse individuals may not rank investment alternatives in the same manner. Consider the £50 gamble again. All risk-averse individuals will rank the guaranteed outcome of £50 higher than the gamble. What if the guaranteed outcome is only £40? Some risk-averse investors might consider £40 inadequate, others might accept it, and still others may now be indifferent about the uncertain £50 and the certain £40.

A simple implementation of utility theory allows us to quantify the rankings of investment choices using risk and return. There are several assumptions about individual behavior that we make in the definition of utility given in the following equation. We assume that investors are risk averse. They always prefer more to less (greater return to lesser return). They are able to rank different portfolios in the order of their preference and that the rankings are internally consistent. If an individual prefers X to Y and Y to Z, then he/she must prefer X to Z. This property implies that the indifference curves (see Exhibit 5-11) for the same individual can never touch or intersect. The following is an example of a utility function:

$$U = E(r) - \frac{1}{2}A\sigma^2$$

where, U is the utility of an investment, $E(r)$ is the expected return, and σ^2 is the variance of the investment.

In the preceding equation, A is a measure of risk aversion, which is measured as the marginal reward that an investor requires to accept additional risk. More risk-averse investors require greater compensation for accepting additional risk. Thus, A is higher for more risk-averse individuals. As was mentioned previously, a risk-neutral investor would maximize return irrespective of risk and a risk-seeking investor would maximize both risk and return.

We can draw several conclusions from the utility function. First, utility is unbounded on both sides. It can be highly positive or highly negative. Second, higher return contributes to higher utility. Third, higher variance reduces the utility but the reduction in utility gets amplified by the risk aversion coefficient, A. Utility can always be increased, albeit marginally, by getting higher return or lower risk. Fourth, utility does not indicate or measure satisfaction. It can be useful only in ranking various investments. For example, a portfolio with a utility of 4 is not necessarily two times better than a portfolio with a utility of 2. The portfolio with a utility of 4 could increase our happiness 10 times or just marginally. But we do prefer a portfolio with a utility of 4 to a portfolio with a utility of 2. Utility cannot be compared among individuals or investors because it is a very personal concept. From a societal point of view, by the same argument, utility cannot be summed among individuals.

Let us explore the utility function further. The risk aversion coefficient, A, is greater than zero for a risk-averse investor. So any increase in risk reduces his/her utility. The risk aversion coefficient for a risk-neutral investor is 0, and changes in risk do not affect his/her utility. For a risk lover, the risk aversion coefficient is negative, creating an inverse situation so that additional risk contributes to an increase in his/her utility. Note that a risk-free asset ($\sigma^2 = 0$) generates the same utility for all individuals.

3.2.1. Indifference Curves

An **indifference curve** plots the combinations of risk–return pairs that an investor would accept to maintain a given level of utility (i.e., the investor is indifferent about the combinations on any one curve because they would provide the same level of overall utility). Indifference curves are thus defined in terms of a trade-off between expected rate of return and variance of the rate of return. Because an infinite number of combinations of risk and return can generate the same utility for the same investor, indifference curves are continuous at all points.

EXHIBIT 5-11 Indifference Curves for Risk-Averse Investors

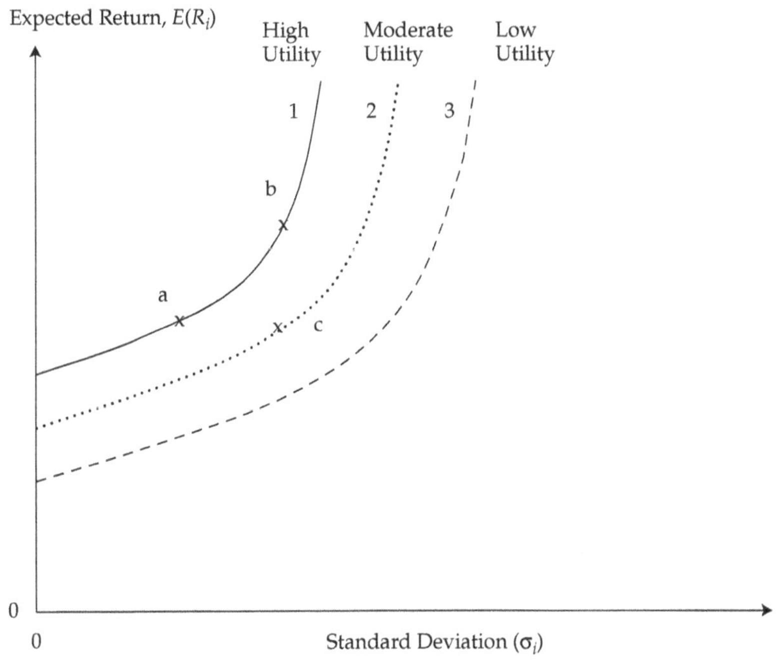

A set of indifference curves is plotted in Exhibit 5-11. By definition, all points on any one of the three curves have the same utility. An investor does not care whether he/she is at point **a** or point **b** on indifference curve 1. Point **a** has lower risk and lower return than point **b**, but the utility of both points is the same because the higher return at point **b** is offset by the higher risk.

Like curve 1, all points on curve 2 have the same utility and an investor is indifferent about where he/she is on curve 2. Now compare point **c** with point **b**. Point **c** has the same risk but significantly lower return than point **b**, which means that the utility at point **c** is less than the utility at point **b**. Given that all points on curve 1 have the same utility and all points on curve 2 have the same utility and point **b** has higher utility than point **c**, curve 1 has higher utility than curve 2. Therefore, risk-averse investors with indifference curves 1 and 2 will prefer curve 1 to curve 2. The utility of risk-averse investors always increases as you move northwest—higher return with lower risk. Because all investors prefer more utility to less, investors want to move northwest to the indifference curve with the highest utility.

The indifference curve for risk-averse investors runs from the southwest to the northeast because of the risk–return trade-off. If risk increases (going east) then it must be compensated by higher return (going north) to generate the same utility. The indifference curves are convex because of diminishing marginal utility of return (or wealth). As risk increases, an investor needs greater return to compensate for higher risk at an increasing rate (i.e., the curve gets steeper). The upward-sloping convex indifference curve has a slope coefficient closely related to the risk-aversion coefficient. The greater the slope, the higher is the risk aversion of the investor as a greater increment in return is required to accept a given increase in risk.

Indifference curves for investors with different levels of risk aversion are plotted in Exhibit 5-12. The most risk-averse investor has an indifference curve with the greatest slope. As volatility increases, this investor demands increasingly higher returns to compensate for risk. The least risk-averse investor has an indifference curve with the least slope and so the demand for higher return as risk increases is not as acute as for the more risk-averse investor. The risk-loving investor's indifference curve, however, exhibits a negative slope, implying that the risk-lover is happy to substitute risk for return. For a risk lover, the utility increases both with higher risk and higher return. Finally, the indifference curves of risk-neutral investors are horizontal because the utility is invariant with risk.

In the remaining parts of this chapter, all investors are assumed to be risk averse unless stated otherwise.

EXHIBIT 5-12 Indifference Curves for Various Types of Investors

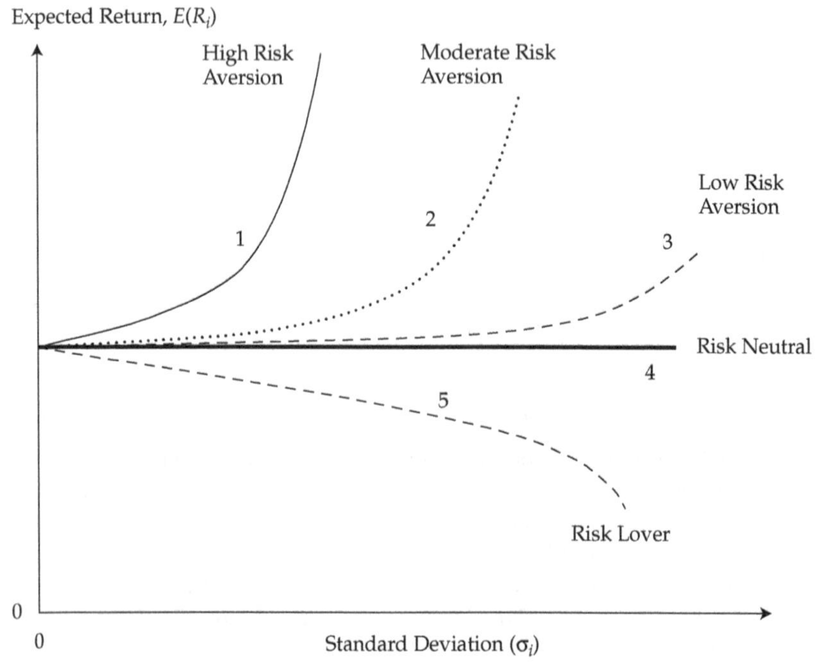

EXAMPLE 5-5 Comparing a Gamble with a Guaranteed Outcome

Assume that you are given an investment with an expected return of 10 percent and a risk (standard deviation) of 20 percent, and your risk aversion coefficient is 3.

1. What is your utility of this investment?
2. What must be the minimum risk-free return you should earn to get the same utility?

Solution to 1: $U = 0.10 - 0.5 \times 3 \times 0.20^2 = 0.04$.

Solution to 2: A risk-free return's σ is zero, so the second term disappears. To get the same utility (0.04), the risk-free return must be at least 4 percent. Thus, in your mind, a risky return of 10 percent is equivalent to a risk-free return or a guaranteed outcome of 4 percent.

EXAMPLE 5-6 Computation of Utility

Based on investment information given next and the utility formula $U = E(r) - 0.5A\sigma^2$, answer the following questions. Returns and standard deviations are both expressed as percent per year. When using the utility formula, however, returns and standard deviations must be expressed in decimals.

Investment	Expected Return $E(r)$	Standard Deviation σ
1	12%	30%
2	15	35
3	21	40
4	24	45

1. Which investment will a risk-averse investor with a risk aversion coefficient of 4 choose?
2. Which investment will a risk-averse investor with a risk aversion coefficient of 2 choose?
3. Which investment will a risk-neutral investor choose?
4. Which investment will a risk-loving investor choose?

Solutions to 1 and 2: The utility for risk-averse investors with $A = 4$ and $A = 2$ for each of the four investments are shown next in the table. Complete calculations for Investment 1 with $A = 4$ are as follows: $U = 0.12 - 0.5 \times 4 \times 0.30^2 = -0.06$.

Investment	Expected Return $E(r)$	Standard Deviation σ	Utility $A = 4$	Utility $A = 2$
1	12%	30%	–0.0600	0.0300
2	15	35	–0.0950	0.0275
3	21	40	–0.1100	0.0500
4	24	45	–0.1650	0.0375

The risk-averse investor with a risk aversion coefficient of 4 should choose Investment 1. The risk-averse investor with a risk aversion coefficient of 2 should choose Investment 3.

Solution to 3: A risk-neutral investor cares only about return. In other words, his risk aversion coefficient is 0. Therefore, a risk-neutral investor will choose Investment 4 because it has the highest return.

Solution to 4: A risk-loving investor likes both higher risk and higher return. In other words, his risk aversion coefficient is negative. Therefore, a risk-loving investor will choose Investment 4 because it has the highest return and highest risk, among the four investments.

3.3. Application of Utility Theory to Portfolio Selection

The simplest application of utility theory and risk aversion is to a portfolio of two assets, a risk-free asset and a risky asset. The risk-free asset has zero risk and a return of R_f. The risky asset has a risk of σ_i (> 0) and an expected return of $E(R_i)$. Because the risky asset has risk that is greater than that of the risk-free asset, the expected return from the risky asset will be greater than the return from the risk-free asset, that is, $E(R_i) > R_f$.

We can construct a portfolio of these two assets with a portfolio expected return, $E(R_p)$, and portfolio risk, σ_p, based on sections 2.1.7 and 2.3.3. In the following equations, w_1 is the weight in the risk-free asset and $(1 - w_1)$ is the weight in the risky asset. Because $\sigma_f = 0$ for the risk-free asset, the first and third terms in the formula for variance are zero leaving only the second term. We arrive at the last equation by taking the square root of both sides, which shows the expression for standard deviation for a portfolio of two assets when one asset is the risk-free asset:

$$E(R_p) = w_1 R_f + (1 - w_1)E(R_i)$$

$$\sigma_P^2 = w_1^2\sigma_f^2 + (1 - w_1)^2\sigma_i^2 + 2w_1(1 - w_1)\rho_{12}\sigma_f\sigma_i = (1 - w_1)^2\sigma_i^2$$

$$\sigma_p = (1 - w_1)\sigma_i$$

The two-asset portfolio is drawn in Exhibit 5-13 by varying w_1 from 0 percent to 100 percent. The portfolio standard deviation is on the horizontal axis and the portfolio return is on the vertical axis. If only these two assets are available in the economy and the risky asset represents the market, the line in Exhibit 5-13 is called the **capital allocation line**. The capital allocation line represents the portfolios available to an investor. The equation for this line can be derived from the previous two equations by rewriting the second equation as:

$$w_1 = 1 - \frac{\sigma_p}{\sigma_i}$$

Substituting the value of w_1 in the equation for expected return, we get the following for the capital allocation line:

$$E(R_p) = \left(1 - \frac{\sigma_p}{\sigma_i}\right)R_f + \frac{\sigma_p}{\sigma_i}E(R_i)$$

This equation can be rewritten in a more usable form:

$$E(R_p) = R_f + \frac{(E(R_i) - R_f)}{\sigma_i}\sigma_p$$

The capital allocation line has an intercept of R_f, and a slope of

$$\frac{(E(R_i) - R_f)}{\sigma_i}$$

which is the additional required return for every increment in risk, and is sometimes referred to as the market price of risk.

EXHIBIT 5-13 Capital Allocation Line with Two Assets

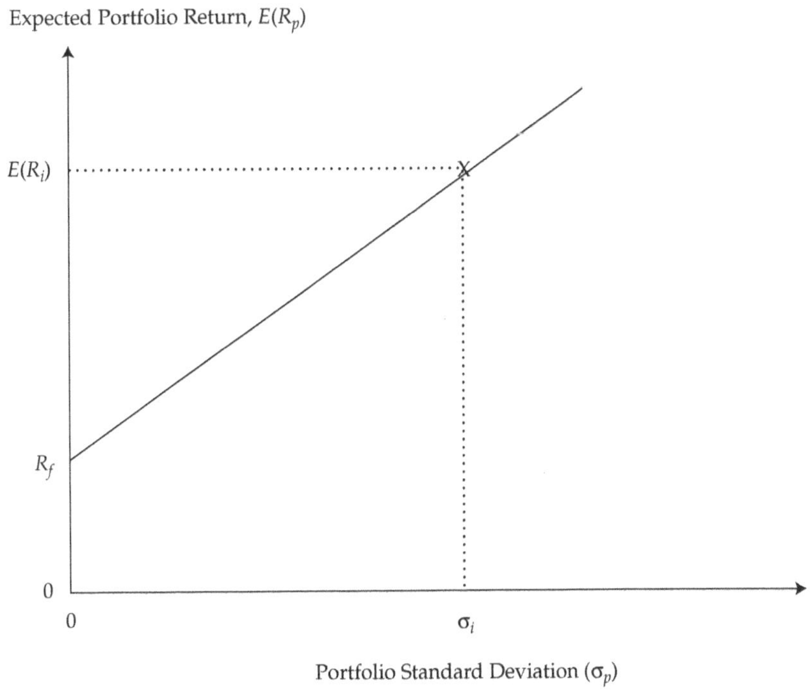

Because the equation is linear, the plot of the capital allocation line is a straight line. The line begins with the risk-free asset as the leftmost point with zero risk and a risk-free return, R_f. At that point, the portfolio consists of only the risk-free asset. If 100 percent is invested in the portfolio of all risky assets, however, we have a return of $E(R_i)$ with a risk of σ_i.

We can move further along the line in pursuit of higher returns by borrowing at the risk-free rate and investing the borrowed money in the portfolio of all risky assets. If 50 percent is borrowed at the risk-free rate, then $w_1 = -0.50$ and 150 percent is placed in the risky asset, giving a return $= 1.50E(R_i) - 0.50R_f$, which is $> E(R_i)$ because $E(R_i) > R_f$.

The line plotted in Exhibit 5-13 is composed of an unlimited number of risk–return pairs or portfolios. Which *one* of these portfolios should be chosen by an investor? The answer lies in combining indifference curves from utility theory with the capital allocation line from portfolio theory. Utility theory gives us the utility function or the indifference curves for an individual, as in Exhibit 5-11, and the capital allocation line gives us the set of feasible investments. Overlaying each individual's indifference curves on the capital allocation line will provide us with the optimal portfolio for that investor. Exhibit 5-14 illustrates this process of portfolio selection.

EXHIBIT 5-14 Portfolio Selection

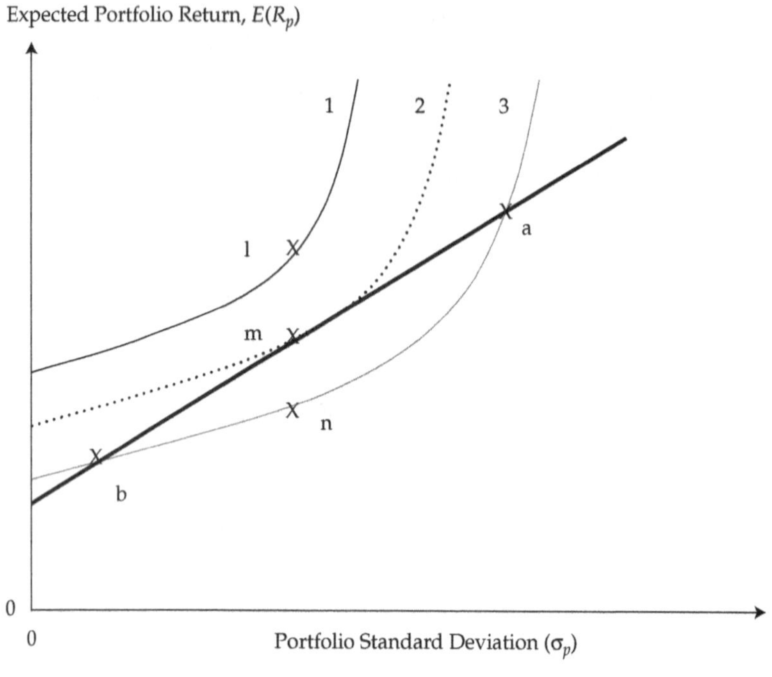

The capital allocation line consists of the set of feasible portfolios. Points under the capital allocation line may be attainable but are not preferred by any investor because the investor can get a higher return for the same risk by moving up to the capital allocation line. Points above the capital allocation line are desirable but not achievable with available assets.

Three indifference curves for the same individual are also shown in Exhibit 5-14. Curve 1 is above the capital allocation line, curve 2 is tangential to the line, and curve 3 intersects the line at two points. Curve 1 has the highest utility and curve 3 has the lowest utility. Because curve 1 lies completely above the capital allocation line, points on curve 1 are not achievable with the available assets on the capital allocation line. Curve 3 intersects the capital allocation line at two points, **a** and **b**. The investor is able to invest at either point **a** or **b** to derive the risk–return trade-off and utility associated with curve 3. Comparing points with the same risk, observe that point **n** on curve 3 has the same risk as point **m** on curve 2, yet point **m** has the higher expected return. Therefore, all investors will choose curve 2 instead of curve 3. Curve 2 is tangential to the capital allocation line at point **m**. Point **m** is on the capital allocation line and investable. Point **m** and the utility associated with curve 2 is the best that the investor can do because he/she cannot move to a higher utility indifference curve. Thus, we have been able to select the optimal portfolio for the investor with indifference curves 1, 2, and 3. Point **m**, the optimal portfolio for one investor, may not be optimal for another investor. We can follow the same process, however, for finding the optimal portfolio for other investors: the optimal portfolio is the point of tangency between the capital allocation line and the indifference curve for that investor. In other words, the optimal portfolio maximizes the return per unit of risk (as it is on the capital allocation line) and it simultaneously supplies the investor with the most satisfaction (utility).

EXHIBIT 5-15 Portfolio Selection for Two Investors with Various Levels of Risk Aversion

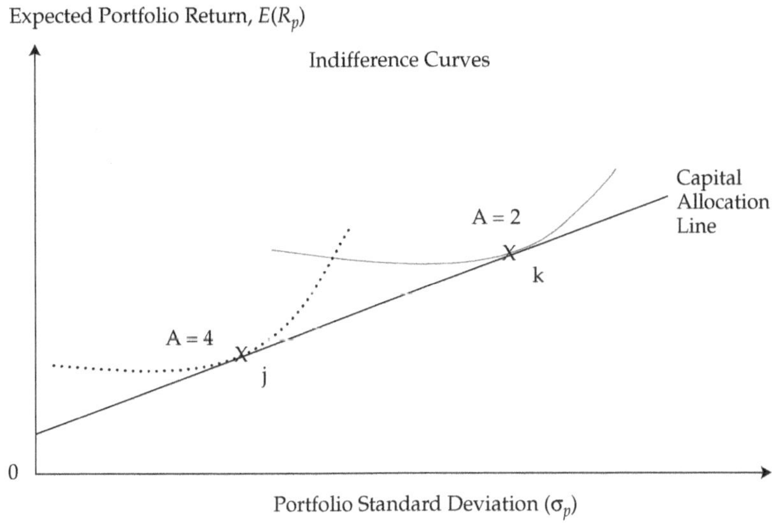

As an illustration, Exhibit 5-15 shows two indifference curves for two different investors: Kelly with a risk aversion coefficient of 2 and Jane with a risk aversion coefficient of 4. The indifference curve for Kelly is to the right of the indifference curve for Jane because Kelly is less risk averse than Jane and can accept a higher amount of risk, that is, has a higher tolerance for risk. Accordingly, their optimal portfolios are different: point **k** is the optimal portfolio for Kelly and point **j** is the optimal portfolio for Jane. In addition, for the same return, the slope of Jane's curve is higher than Kelly's suggesting that Jane needs greater incremental return as compensation for accepting an additional amount of risk compared with Kelly.

4. PORTFOLIO RISK

We have seen before that investors are risk averse and demand a higher return for a riskier investment. Therefore, ways of controlling portfolio risk without affecting return are valuable. As a precursor to managing risk, this section explains and analyzes the components of portfolio risk. In particular, it examines and describes how a portfolio consisting of assets with low correlations has the potential of reducing risk without necessarily reducing return.

4.1. Portfolio of Two Risky Assets

The return and risk of a portfolio of two assets was introduced in Section 2 of this chapter. In this section, we briefly review the computation of return and extend the concept of portfolio risk and its components.

4.1.1. Portfolio Return

When two individual assets are combined in a portfolio, we can compute the portfolio return as a weighted average of the returns of the two assets. Consider assets 1 and 2 with weights of 25 percent and 75 percent in a portfolio. If their returns are 20 percent and 5 percent, the weighted average return = (0.25 × 20%) + (0.75 × 5%) = 8.75%. More generally, the portfolio return can be written as in the following, where R_p is return of the portfolio and R_1, R_2 are returns on the two assets:

$$R_P = w_1 R_1 + (1 - w_1) R_2$$

4.1.2. Portfolio Risk

Portfolio risk or variance measures the amount of uncertainty in portfolio returns. Portfolio variance can be calculated by taking the variance of both sides of the return equation as follows, where $Cov(R_1, R_2)$ is the covariance of returns, R_1 and R_2, w_1 is the weight in asset 1, w_2 ($= 1 - w_1$) is the weight in asset 2, and σ_1^2, σ_2^2 are the variances of the two assets:

$$\begin{aligned}\sigma_P^2 &= Var(R_P) = Var(w_1 R_1 + w_2 R_2)\\ &= w_1^2 Var(R_1) + w_2^2 Var(R_2) + 2 w_1 w_2 Cov(R_1, R_2)\\ &= w_1^2 \sigma_1^2 + w_2^2 \sigma_2^2 + 2 w_1 w_2 Cov(R_1, R_2)\end{aligned}$$

The standard deviation, or risk, of a portfolio of two assets is given by the square root of the portfolio's variance:

$$\sigma_P = \sqrt{w_1^2 \sigma_1^2 + w_2^2 \sigma_2^2 + 2 w_1 w_2 Cov(R_1, R_2)}$$

4.1.3. Covariance and Correlation

The **covariance** in the formula for portfolio standard deviation can be expanded as $\text{Cov}(R_1, R_2) = \rho_{12}\sigma_1\sigma_2$ where ρ_{12} is the correlation between returns, R_1, R_2. Although covariance is important, it is difficult to interpret because it is unbounded on both sides. It is easier to understand the **correlation coefficient** (ρ_{12}), which is bounded but provides similar information.

Correlation is a measure of the consistency or tendency for two investments to act in a similar way. The correlation coefficient, ρ_{12}, can be positive or negative and ranges from −1 to +1. Consider three different values of the correlation coefficient:

- $\rho_{12} = +1$: Returns of the two assets are perfectly *positively* correlated. Assets 1 and 2 move together 100 percent of the time.
- $\rho_{12} = -1$: Returns of the two assets are perfectly *negatively* correlated. Assets 1 and 2 move in opposite directions 100 percent of the time.

- $\rho_{12} = 0$: Returns of the two assets are *uncorrelated.* Movement of asset 1 provides no prediction regarding the movement of asset 2.

The correlation coefficient between two assets determines the effect on portfolio risk when the two assets are combined. To see how this works, consider two different values of ρ_{12}. You will find that portfolio risk is unaffected when the two assets are perfectly correlated ($\rho_{12} = +1$). In other words, the portfolio's standard deviation is simply a weighted average of the standard deviations of the two assets and as such a portfolio's risk is unchanged with the addition of assets with the same risk parameters. Portfolio risk falls, however, when the two assets are not perfectly correlated ($\rho_{12} < +1$). Sufficiently low values of the correlation coefficient can make the portfolio riskless under certain conditions.

First, let $\rho_{12} = +1$

$$\sigma_p^2 = w_1^2\sigma_1^2 + w_2^2\sigma_2^2 + 2w_1w_2\rho_{12}\sigma_1\sigma_2 = w_1^2\sigma_1^2 + w_2^2\sigma_2^2 + 2w_1w_2\sigma_1\sigma_2 = (w_1\sigma_1 + w_2\sigma_2)^2$$

$$\sigma_p = w_1\sigma_1 + w_2\sigma_2$$

The first set of terms on the right side of the first equation contain the usual terms for portfolio variance. Because the correlation coefficient is equal to $+1$, the right side can be rewritten as a perfect square. The final row shows that portfolio risk is a weighted average of the risks of the individual assets' risks. In subsection 4.1.1., the portfolio return was shown always to be a weighted average of returns. Because both risk and return are just weighted averages of the two assets in the portfolio, there is no reduction in risk when $\rho_{12} = +1$.

Now let $\rho_{12} < +1$

The preceding analysis showed that portfolio risk is a weighted average of asset risks when $\rho_{12} = +1$. When $\rho_{12} < +1$, the portfolio risk is less than the weighted average of the individual assets' risks.

To show this, we begin by reproducing the general formula for portfolio risk, which is expressed by the terms to the left of the " < " sign in the following. The term to the right of " < " shows the portfolio risk when $\rho_{12} = +1$:

$$\sigma_p = \sqrt{w_1^2\sigma_1^2 + w_2^2\sigma_2^2 + 2w_1w_2\rho_{12}\sigma_1\sigma_2} < \sqrt{w_1^2\sigma_1^2 + w_2^2\sigma_2^2 + 2w_1w_2\sigma_1\sigma_2}$$

$$= (w_1\sigma_1 + w_2\sigma_2)$$

$$\sigma_p < (w_1\sigma_1 + w_2\sigma_2)$$

The left side is smaller than the right side because the correlation coefficient on the left side for the new portfolio is <1. Thus, the portfolio risk is less than the weighted average of risks while the portfolio return is still a weighted average of returns.

As you can see, we have achieved diversification by combining two assets that are not perfectly correlated. For an extreme case in which $\rho_{12} = -1$ (that is, the two asset returns move in opposite directions), the portfolio can be made risk free.

EXAMPLE 5-7 Effect of Correlation on Portfolio Risk

Two stocks have the same return and risk (standard deviation): 10 percent return with 20 percent risk. You form a portfolio with 50 percent each of stock 1 and stock 2 to examine the effect of correlation on risk.

1. Calculate the portfolio return and risk if the correlation is 1.0.
2. Calculate the portfolio return and risk if the correlation is 0.0.
3. Calculate the portfolio return and risk if the correlation is –1.0.
4. Compare the return and risk of portfolios with different correlations.

Solution to 1:

$R_1 = R_2 = 10\% = 0.10; \sigma_1 = \sigma_2 = 20\% = 0.20; W_1 = W_2 = 50\% = 0.50.$

Case 1: $\rho_{12} = +1$

$$R_p = w_1R_1 + w_2R_2$$

$$R_p = (0.5 \times 0.1) + (0.5 \times 0.1) = 0.10 = 10\%$$

$$\sigma_p^2 = w_1^2\sigma_1^2 + w_2^2\sigma_2^2 + 2w_1w_2\sigma_1\sigma_2\rho_{12}$$

$$\sigma_p^2 = (0.5^2 \times 0.2^2) + (0.5^2 \times 0.2^2) + (2 \times 0.5 \times 0.5 \times 0.2 \times 0.2 \times 1) = 0.04$$

$$\sigma_p = \sqrt{0.04} = 0.20 = 20\%$$

This equation demonstrates the earlier point that, with a correlation of 1.0, the risk of the portfolio is the same as the risk of the individual assets.

Solution to 2: $\rho_{12} = 0$

$$R_p = w_1R_1 + w_2R_2 = 0.10 = 10\%$$

$$\sigma_p^2 = w_1^2\sigma_1^2 + w_2^2\sigma_2^2 + 2w_1w_2\sigma_1\sigma_2\rho_{12}$$

$$\sigma_p^2 = (0.5^2 \times 0.2^2) + (0.5^2 \times 0.2^2) + (2 \times 0.5 \times 0.5 \times 0.2 \times 0.2 \times 0) = 0.02$$

$$\sigma_p = \sqrt{0.02} = 0.14 = 14\%$$

This equation demonstrates the earlier point that, when assets have correlations of less than 1.0, they can be combined in a portfolio that has less risk than either of the assets individually.

Solution to 3: $\rho_{12} = -1$

$$R_p = w_1R_1 + w_2R_2 = 0.10 = 10\%$$

$$\sigma_p^2 = w_1^2\sigma_1^2 + w_2^2\sigma_2^2 + 2w_1w_2\sigma_1\sigma_2\rho_{12}$$

$$\sigma_p^2 = (0.5^2 \times 0.2^2) + (0.5^2 \times 0.2^2) + (2 \times 0.5 \times 0.5 \times 0.2 \times 0.2 \times -1) = 0$$

$$\sigma_p = 0\%$$

This equation demonstrates the earlier point that, if the correlation of assets is low enough, in this case 100 percent negative correlation or –1.00 (exactly inversely related), a portfolio can be designed that eliminates risk. The individual assets retain their risk characteristics, but the portfolio is risk free.

Solution to 4: The expected return is 10 percent in all three cases; however, the returns will be more volatile in Case 1 and least volatile in Case 3. In the first case, there is no diversification of risk (same risk as before of 20 percent) and the return remains the same. In the second case, with a correlation coefficient of 0, we have achieved diversification of risk (risk is now 14 percent instead of 20 percent) again with the same return. In the third case with a correlation coefficient of –1, the portfolio is risk free although we continue to get the same return of 10 percent. This example shows the power of diversification that we expand on further in Section 4.3.

4.1.4. Relationship between Portfolio Risk and Return

The previous example illustrated the effect of correlation on portfolio risk while keeping the weights in the two assets equal and unchanged. In this section, we consider how portfolio risk and return vary with different portfolio weights and different correlations. Formulas for computation are in Subsections 4.1.1 and 4.1.2.

Asset 1 has an annual return of 7 percent and annualized risk of 12 percent, whereas asset 2 has an annual return of 15 percent and annualized risk of 25 percent. The relationship is tabulated in Exhibit 5-16 for the two assets and graphically represented in Exhibit 5-17.

EXHIBIT 5-16 Relationship between Risk and Return

Weight in Asset 1	Portfolio Return	Portfolio Risk with Correlation of			
		1.0	0.5	0.2	–1.0
0%	15.0	25.0	25.0	25.0	25.0
10%	14.2	23.7	23.1	22.8	21.3
20%	13.4	22.4	21.3	20.6	17.6
30%	12.6	21.1	19.6	18.6	13.9
40%	11.8	19.8	17.9	16.6	10.2
50%	11.0	18.5	16.3	14.9	6.5
60%	10.2	17.2	15.0	13.4	2.8
70%	9.4	15.9	13.8	12.3	0.9
80%	8.6	14.6	12.9	11.7	4.6
90%	7.8	13.3	12.2	11.6	8.3
100%	7.0	12.0	12.0	12.0	12.0

The table shows the portfolio return and risk for four correlation coefficients ranging from +1.0 to –1.0 and 11 weights ranging from 0 percent to 100 percent. The portfolio return and risk are 15 percent and 25 percent respectively when 0 percent is invested in asset 1, versus 7 percent and 12 percent when 100 percent is invested in asset 1. The portfolio return varies with weights but is unaffected by the correlation coefficient.

Portfolio risk becomes smaller with each successive decrease in the correlation coefficient, with the smallest risk when $\rho_{12} = -1$. The graph in Exhibit 5-17 shows that the risk–return relationship is a straight line when $\rho_{12} = +1$. As the correlation falls, the risk becomes smaller and smaller as in the table. The curvilinear nature of a portfolio of assets is recognizable in all investment opportunity sets (except at the extremes where $\rho_{12} = -1$ or $+1$).

EXHIBIT 5-17 Relationship between Risk and Return

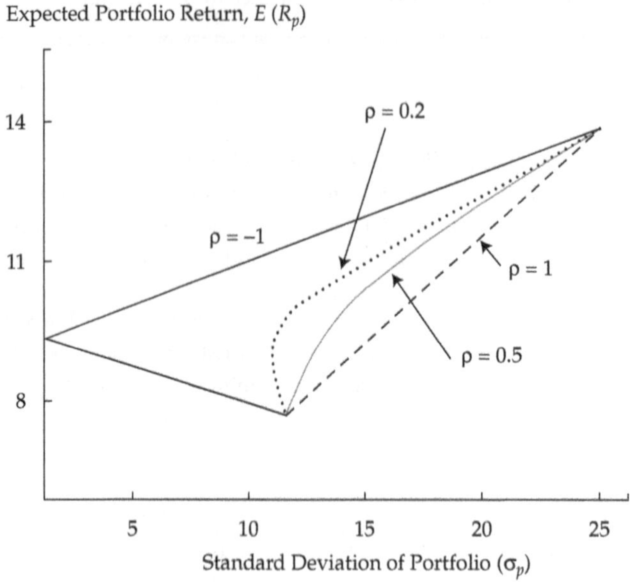

EXAMPLE 5-8 Portfolio of Two Assets

An investor is considering investing in a small-cap stock fund and a general bond fund. Their returns and standard deviations are given next and the correlation between the two fund returns is 0.10.

	Expected Annual Return	Standard Deviation of Returns
Small-cap fund, S	19%	33%
Bond fund, B	8%	13%

1. If the investor requires a portfolio return of 12 percent, what should the proportions in each fund be?
2. What is the standard deviation of the portfolio constructed in Part 1?

Solution to 1: We can calculate the weights by setting the portfolio return equal to 12 percent.

$$12\% = w_1 \times 19\% + (1 - w_1) \times 8\%;\ w_1 = 36.4\%,\ (1 - w_1) = 63.6\%.$$

Thus, 36.4 percent should be invested in the small-cap fund and 63.6 percent should be invested in the bond fund.

Solution to 2:

$$\sigma_p = \sqrt{w_1^2\sigma_1^2 + w_2^2\sigma_2^2 + 2w_1w_2\rho_{12}\sigma_1\sigma_2}$$

$$= \sqrt{(0.364^2 \times 0.33^2) + (0.636^2 \times 0.13^2) + (2 \times 0.364 \times 0.636 \times 0.10 \times 0.33 \times 0.13)}$$

$$= 15.23\%$$

The portfolio risk is 15.23 percent, which is much less than a weighted average of risks of 20.28% (63.6% × 13% + 36.4% × 33%).

4.2. Portfolio of Many Risky Assets

In the previous section, we discussed how the correlation between two assets can affect the risk of a portfolio and the smaller the correlation the lower is the risk. The previous analysis can be extended to a portfolio with many risky assets (N). Recall the following equations from Sections 2.1.7 and 2.3.3 for portfolio return and variance:

$$E(R_p) = \sum_{i=1}^{N} w_i E(R_i),\ \sigma_P^2 = \left(\sum_{i=1}^{N} w_i^2\sigma_i^2 + \sum_{i,j=1,i\neq j}^{N} w_i w_j Cov(i,j)\right),\ \sum_{i=1}^{N} w_i = 1$$

To examine how a portfolio with many risky assets works and the ways in which we can reduce the risk of a portfolio, assume that the portfolio has equal weights ($1/N$) for all N assets. In addition, assume that $\bar{\sigma}^2$ and $\overline{Cov}$ are the average variance and average covariance. Given equal weights and average variance/covariance, we can rewrite the portfolio variance as the following. Intermediate steps are omitted to focus on the main result:

$$\sigma_P^2 = \left(\sum_{i=1}^{N} w_i^2\sigma_i^2 + \sum_{i,j=1,i\neq j}^{N} w_i w_j Cov(i,j)\right);\ \sigma_P^2 = \frac{\bar{\sigma}^2}{N} + \frac{(N-1)}{N}\overline{Cov}$$

The second equation shows that as N becomes large, the first term on the right side with the denominator of N becomes smaller and smaller, implying that the contribution of one asset's variance to portfolio variance gradually becomes negligible. The second term, however, approaches the average covariance as N increases. It is reasonable to say that for portfolios with a large number of assets, covariance among the assets accounts for almost all of the portfolio's risk.

4.2.1. Importance of Correlation in a Portfolio of Many Assets

The analysis becomes more instructive and interesting if we assume that all assets in the portfolio have the same variance and the same correlation among assets. In that case, the portfolio risk can then be rewritten as:

$$\sigma_p = \sqrt{\frac{\sigma^2}{N} + \frac{(N-1)}{N}\rho\sigma^2}$$

The first term under the root sign becomes negligible as the number of assets in the portfolio increases leaving the second term (correlation) as the main determining factor for portfolio risk. If the assets are unrelated to one another, the portfolio can have close to zero risk. In the next section, we review these concepts to learn how portfolios can be diversified.

4.3. The Power of Diversification

Diversification is one of the most important and powerful concepts in investments. Because investors are risk averse, they are interested in reducing risk preferably without reducing return. In other cases, investors may accept a lower return if it will reduce the chance of catastrophic losses. In previous sections of this chapter, you learned the importance of correlation and covariance in managing risk. This section applies those concepts to explore ways for risk diversification. We begin with a simple but intuitive example.

EXAMPLE 5-9 Diversification with Rain and Shine

Assume a company, Beachwear, rents beach equipment. The annual return from the company's operations is 20 percent in years with many sunny days but falls to 0 percent in rainy years with few sunny days. The probabilities of a sunny year and a rainy year are equal at 50 percent. Thus, the average return is 10 percent, with a 50 percent chance of 20 percent return and a 50 percent chance of 0 percent return. Because Beachwear can earn a return of 20 percent or 0 percent, its average return of 10 percent is risky.

You are excited about investing in Beachwear but do not like the risk. Having heard about diversification, you decide to add another business to the portfolio to reduce your investment risk.

1. There is a snack shop on the beach that sells all the healthy food you like. You estimate that the annual return from the Snackshop is also 20 percent in years with many sunny days and 0 percent in other years. As with the Beachwear shop, the average return is 10 percent.

   You decide to invest 50 percent each in Snackshop and Beachwear. The average return is still 10 percent, with 50 percent of 10 percent from Snackshop and 50 percent of 10 percent from Beachwear. In a sunny year, you would earn 20 percent (=50% of 20% from Beachwear +50% of 20% from Snackshop). In a rainy year, you would earn 0 percent (=50% of 0% from Beachwear +50% of 0% from Snackshop). The results are tabulated in Exhibit 5-18.

EXHIBIT 5-18

Type	Company	Percent Invested	Return in Sunny Year	Return in Rainy Year	Average Return
Single stock	Beachwear	100%	20%	0%	10%
Single stock	Snackshop	100%	20%	0%	10%
Portfolio of two stocks	Beachwear	50%	20%	0%	10%
	Snackshop	50%	20%	0%	10%
	Total	100%	20%	0%	10%

These results seem counterintuitive. You thought that by adding another business you would be able to diversify and reduce your risk, but the risk is exactly the same as before. What went wrong? Note that both businesses do well when it is sunny and both businesses do poorly when it rains. The correlation between the two businesses is +1.0. No reduction in risk occurs when the correlation is +1.0.

2. To reduce risk, you must consider a business that does well in a rainy year. You find a company that rents DVDs. DVDrental company is similar to the Beachwear company, except that its annual return is 20 percent in a rainy year and 0 percent in a sunny year, with an average return of 10 percent. DVDrental's 10 percent return is also risky just like Beachwear's return.

   If you invest 50 percent each in DVDrental and Beachwear, then the average return is still 10 percent, with 50 percent of 10 percent from DVDrental and 50 percent of 10 percent from Beachwear. In a sunny year, you would earn 10 percent (=50% of 20% from Beachwear + 50% of 0% from DVDrental). In a rainy year also, you would earn 10 percent (=50% of 0% from Beachwear + 50% of 20% from DVDrental). You have no risk because you earn 10 percent in both sunny and rainy years. Thus, by adding DVDrental to Beachwear, you have reduced (eliminated) your risk without affecting your return. The results are tabulated in Exhibit 5-19.

EXHIBIT 5-19

Type	Company	Percent Invested	Return in Sunny Year	Return in Rainy Year	Average Return
Single stock	Beachwear	100%	20%	0%	10%
Single stock	DVDrental	100%	0%	20%	10%
Portfolio of two stocks	Beachwear	50%	20%	0%	10%
	DVDrental	50%	0%	20%	10%
	Total	100%	10%	10%	10%

In this case, the two businesses have a correlation of –1.0. When two businesses with a correlation of –1.0 are combined, risk can always be reduced to zero.

4.3.1. Correlation and Risk Diversification

Correlation is the key in diversification of risk. Notice that the returns from Beachwear and DVDrental always go in the opposite direction. If one of them does well, the other does not. Therefore, adding assets that do not behave like other assets in your portfolio is good and can reduce risk. The two companies in the previous example have a correlation of −1.0.

Even when we expand the portfolio to many assets, correlation among assets remains the primary determinant of portfolio risk. Lower correlations are associated with lower risk. Unfortunately, most assets have high positive correlations. The challenge in diversifying risk is to find assets that have a correlation that is much lower than +1.0.

4.3.2. Historical Risk and Correlation

When we discussed asset returns in Section 2.4.1, we were careful to distinguish between historical or past returns and expected or future returns because historical returns may not be a good indicator of future returns. Returns may be highly positive in one period and highly negative in another period depending on the risk of that asset. Exhibit 5-5 showed that returns for large U.S. company stocks were high in the 1990s but have been very low in the 2000s.

Risk for an asset class, however, does not usually change dramatically from one period to the next. Stocks have been risky even in periods of low returns. T-bills are always less risky even when they earn high returns. From Exhibit 5-5, we can see that risk has typically not varied much from one decade to the next, except that risk for bonds has been much higher in recent decades when compared with earlier decades. Therefore, it is not unreasonable to assume that historical risk can work as a good proxy for future risk.

As with risk, correlations are quite stable among assets of the same country. Intercountry correlations, however, have been on the rise in the last few decades as a result of globalization and the liberalization of many economies. A correlation above 0.90 is considered high because the assets do not provide much opportunity for diversification of risk, such as the correlations that exist among large U.S. company stocks on the NYSE, NASDAQ, S&P 500 Index, and Dow Jones Industrial Average. Correlations below 0.30 are considered attractive for portfolio diversification.

4.3.3. Historical Correlation among Asset Classes

Correlations among major U.S. asset classes and international stocks are reported in Exhibit 5-20 for 1970–2008. The highest correlation is between U.S. large company stocks and U.S. small company stocks at about 70 percent, whereas the correlation between U.S. large company stocks and international stocks is approximately 66 percent. Although these are the highest correlations, they still provide diversification benefits because the correlations are less than 100 percent. The correlation between international stocks and U.S. small company stocks is lower, at 49 percent. The lowest correlations are between stocks and bonds, with some correlations being negative, such as that between U.S. small company stocks and U.S. long-term government bonds. Similarly, the correlation between T-bills and stocks is close to zero and is marginally negative for international stocks.[7]

[7] In any short period, T-bills are riskless and uncorrelated with other asset classes. For example, a three-month U.S. Treasury bill is redeemable at its face value upon maturity irrespective of what happens to other assets. When we consider multiple periods, however, returns on T-bills may be related to other asset classes because short-term interest rates vary depending on the strength of the economy and outlook for inflation.

EXHIBIT 5-20 Correlation among U.S. Assets and International Stocks (1970–2008)

Series	International Stocks	U.S. Large Co. Stocks	U.S. Small Co. Stocks	U.S. Long-Term Corporate Bonds	U.S. Long-Term Treasury Bonds	U.S. T-Bills	U.S. Inflation
International stocks	1.00						
U.S. large co. stocks	0.66	1.00					
U.S. small co. stocks	0.49	0.71	1.00				
U.S. long-term corporate bonds	0.07	0.31	0.13	1.00			
U.S. long-term Treasury bonds	–0.04	0.13	–0.05	0.92	1.00		
U.S. T-bills	–0.02	0.15	0.07	0.02	0.90	1.00	
U.S. inflation	–0.09	–0.09	0.06	–0.40	–0.40	0.65	1.00

Source: 2009 Ibbotson SBBI Classic Yearbook (Table 13-5).

The low correlations between stocks and bonds are attractive for portfolio diversification. Similarly, including international securities in a portfolio can also control portfolio risk. It is not surprising that most diversified portfolios of investors contain domestic stocks, domestic bonds, foreign stocks, foreign bonds, real estate, cash, and other asset classes.

4.3.4. Avenues for Diversification

The reason for diversification is simple. By constructing a portfolio with assets that do not move together, you create a portfolio that reduces the ups and downs in the short-term but continues to grow steadily in the long term. Diversification thus makes a portfolio more resilient to gyrations in financial markets.

We describe a number of approaches for diversification, some of which have been discussed previously and some of which might seem too obvious. Diversification, however, is such an important part of investing that it cannot be emphasized enough, especially when we continue to meet and see many investors who are not properly diversified.

- *Diversify with asset classes.* Correlations among major asset classes[8] are not usually high, as can be observed from the few U.S. asset classes listed in Exhibit 5-20. Correlations for other asset classes and other countries are also typically low, which provides investors the opportunity to benefit from diversifying among many asset classes to achieve the biggest benefit from diversification. A partial list of asset classes includes domestic large caps, domestic small caps, growth stocks, value stocks, domestic corporate bonds, long-term domestic government bonds, domestic Treasury bills (cash), emerging market stocks, emerging market bonds, developed market stocks (i.e., developed markets excluding domestic market), developed market bonds, real estate, and gold and other commodities. In addition, industries and sectors are used to diversify portfolios. For example, energy stocks may not be well correlated with health care stocks. The exact proportions in which these assets should be included in a portfolio depend on the risk, return, and correlation characteristics of each and the home country of the investor.
- *Diversify with index funds.* Diversifying among asset classes can become costly for small portfolios because of the number of securities required. For example, creating exposure to a single category, such as a domestic large company asset class, may require a group of at least 30 stocks. Exposure to 10 asset classes may require 300 securities, which can be expensive to trade and track. Instead, it may be effective to use exchange-traded funds or mutual funds that track the respective indices, which could bring down the costs associated with building a well-diversified portfolio. Therefore, many investors should seriously consider index mutual funds as an investment vehicle as opposed to individual securities.
- *Diversification among countries.* Countries are different because of industry focus, economic policy, and political climate. The U.S. economy produces many financial and technical services and invests a significant amount in innovative research. The Chinese and Indian economies, however, are focused on manufacturing. Countries in the European Union are vibrant democracies whereas East Asian countries are experimenting with democracy. Thus, financial returns in one country over time are not likely to be highly correlated with returns in another country. Country returns may also be different because of different currencies. In other words, the return on a foreign investment may be different when translated to the home country's currency. Because currency returns are uncorrelated with stock returns,

[8]Major asset classes are distinguished from subclasses, such as U.S. value stocks and U.S. growth stocks.

they may help reduce the risk of investing in a foreign country even when that country, in isolation, is a very risky emerging market from an equity investment point of view. Investment in foreign countries is an essential part of a well-diversified portfolio.

- *Diversify by* not *owning your employer's stock.* Companies encourage their employees to invest in company stock through employee stock plans and retirement plans. You should evaluate investing in your company, however, just as you would evaluate any other investment. In addition, you should consider the nonfinancial investments that you have made, especially the human capital you have invested in your company. Because you work for your employer, you are already heavily invested in it because your earnings depend on your employer. The level of your earnings, whether your compensation improves or whether you get a promotion, depends on how well your employer performs. If a competitor drives your employer out of the market, you will be out of a job. Additional investments in your employer will concentrate your wealth in one asset even more so and make you less diversified.
- *Evaluate each asset before adding to a portfolio.* Every time you add a security or an asset class to the portfolio, recognize that there is a cost associated with diversification. There is the cost of trading an asset as well as the cost of tracking a larger portfolio. In some cases, the securities or assets may have different names but belong to an asset class in which you already have sufficient exposure. A general rule to evaluate whether a new asset should be included to an existing portfolio is based on the following risk–return trade-off relationship:

$$E(R_{new}) = R_f + \frac{\sigma_{new}\rho_{new,p}}{\sigma_p} \times [E(R_p) - R_f]$$

where $E(R)$ is the return from the asset, R_f is the return on the risk-free asset, σ is the standard deviation, ρ is the correlation coefficient, and the subscripts *new* and *p* refer to the new stock and existing portfolio. If the new asset's risk-adjusted return benefits the portfolio, then the asset should be included. The condition can be rewritten using the Sharpe ratio on both sides of the equation as:

$$\frac{E(R_{new}) - R_f}{\sigma_{new}} > \frac{E(R_p) - R_f}{\sigma_p} \times \rho_{new,p}$$

If the Sharpe ratio of the new asset is greater than the Sharpe ratio of the current portfolio times the correlation coefficient, it is beneficial to add the new asset.

- *Buy insurance for risky portfolios.* It may come as a surprise, but insurance is an investment asset—just a different kind of asset. Insurance has a negative correlation with your assets and is thus very valuable. Insurance gives you a positive return when your assets lose value, but pays nothing if your assets maintain their value. Over time, insurance generates a negative average return. Many individuals, however, are willing to accept a small negative return because insurance reduces their exposure to an extreme loss. In general, it is reasonable to add an investment with a negative return if that investment significantly reduces risk (an example of a classic case of the risk–return trade-off).

Alternatively, investments with negative correlations also exist. Historically, gold has a negative correlation with stocks; however, the expected return is usually small and sometimes even negative. Investors often include gold and other commodities in their portfolios as a way of reducing their overall portfolio risk, including currency risk and inflation risk.

Buying put options is another way of reducing risk. Because put options pay when the underlying asset falls in value (negative correlation), they can protect an investor's portfolio against catastrophic losses. Of course, put options cost money and the expected return is zero or marginally negative.

5. EFFICIENT FRONTIER AND INVESTOR'S OPTIMAL PORTFOLIO

In this section, we formalize the effect of diversification and expand the set of investments to include all available risky assets in a mean–variance framework. The addition of a risk-free asset generates an optimal risky portfolio and the capital allocation line. We can then derive an investor's optimal portfolio by overlaying the capital allocation line with the indifference curves of investors.

5.1. Investment Opportunity Set

If two assets are perfectly correlated, the risk–return opportunity set is represented by a straight line connecting those two assets. The line contains portfolios formed by changing the weight of each asset invested in the portfolio. This correlation was depicted by the straight line (with $\rho = 1$) in Exhibit 5-17. If the two assets are not perfectly correlated, the portfolio's risk is less than the weighted average risk of the components and the portfolio formed from the two assets bulges on the left as shown by curves with the correlation coefficient (ρ) less than 1.0 in Exhibit 5-17. All of the points connecting the two assets are achievable (or feasible). The addition of new assets to this portfolio creates more and more portfolios that are either a linear combination of the existing portfolio and the new asset or a curvilinear combination depending on the correlation between the existing portfolio and the new asset.

As the number of available assets increases, the number of possible combinations increases rapidly. When all investable assets are considered, and there are hundreds and thousands of them, we can construct an opportunity set of investments. The opportunity set will ordinarily span all points within a frontier because it is also possible to reach every possible point within that curve by judiciously creating a portfolio from the investable assets.

We begin with individual investable assets and gradually form portfolios that can be plotted to form a curve as shown in Exhibit 5-21. All points on the curve and points to the right of the curve are attainable by a combination of one or more of the investable assets. This set of points is called the *investment opportunity set.* Initially, the opportunity set consists of domestic assets only and is labeled as such in Exhibit 5-21.

5.1.1. Addition of Asset Classes

Exhibit 5-21 shows the effect of adding a new asset class, such as international assets. As long as the new asset class is not perfectly correlated with the existing asset class, the investment opportunity set will expand out further to the northwest providing a superior risk–return trade-off.

The investment opportunity set with international assets dominates the opportunity set that includes only domestic assets. Adding other asset classes will have the same impact on the opportunity set. Thus, we should continue to add asset classes until they do not further improve the risk–return trade-off. The benefits of diversification can be fully captured in this way in the construction of the investment opportunity set, and eventually in the selection of the optimal portfolio.

EXHIBIT 5-21 Investment Opportunity Set

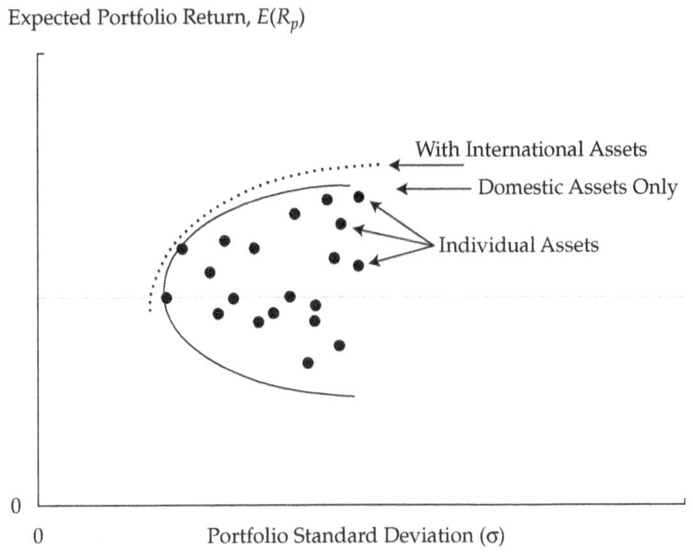

In the discussion that follows in this section, we will assume that *all* investable assets available to an investor are included in the investment opportunity set and no special attention needs to be paid to new asset classes or new investment opportunities.

5.2. Minimum-Variance Portfolios

The investment opportunity set consisting of all available investable sets is shown in Exhibit 5-22. There are a large number of portfolios available for investment, but we must choose a single optimal portfolio. In this subsection, we begin the selection process by narrowing the choice to fewer portfolios.

5.2.1. Minimum-Variance Frontier

Risk-averse investors seek to minimize risk for a given return. Consider points A, B, and X in Exhibit 5-22 and assume that they are on the same horizontal line by construction. Thus, the three points have the same expected return, $E(R_1)$, as do all other points on the imaginary line connecting A, B, and X. Given a choice, an investor will choose the point with the minimum risk, which is point X. Point X, however, is unattainable because it does not lie within the investment opportunity set. Thus, the minimum risk that we can attain for $E(R_1)$ is at point A. Point B and all points to the right of point A are feasible but they have higher risk. Therefore, a risk-averse investor will choose only point A in preference to any other portfolio with the same return.

Similarly, point C is the minimum variance point for the return earned at C. Points to the right of C have higher risk. We can extend the preceding analysis to all possible returns. In all cases, we find that the **minimum variance portfolio** is the one that lies on the solid curve drawn in Exhibit 5-22. The entire collection of these minimum-variance portfolios is referred to as the minimum-variance frontier. The minimum-variance frontier defines the smaller set of portfolios in which investors would want to invest. Note that no risk-averse investor will

EXHIBIT 5-22 Minimum-Variance Frontier

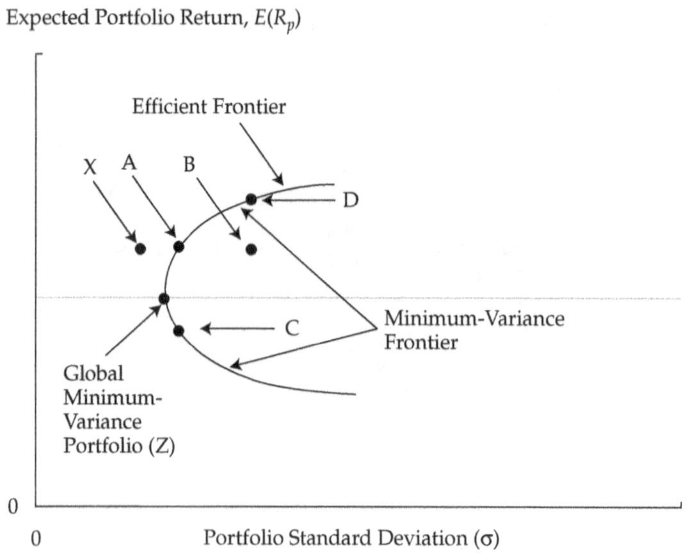

choose to invest in a portfolio to the right of the minimum-variance frontier because a portfolio on the minimum-variance frontier can give the same return but at a lower risk.

5.2.2. Global Minimum-Variance Portfolio

The left-most point on the minimum-variance frontier is the portfolio with the minimum variance among all portfolios of risky assets, and is referred to as the **global minimum-variance portfolio**. An investor cannot hold a portfolio consisting of *risky* assets that has less risk than that of the global minimum-variance portfolio. Note the emphasis on "risky" assets. Later, the introduction of a risk-free asset will allow us to relax this constraint.

5.2.3. Efficient Frontier of Risky Assets

The minimum-variance frontier gives us portfolios with the minimum variance for a given return. However, investors also want to maximize return for a given risk. Observe points A and C on the minimum-variance frontier shown in Exhibit 5-22. Both of them have the same risk. Given a choice, an investor will choose portfolio *A* because it has a higher return. No one will choose portfolio *C*. The same analysis applies to all points on the minimum-variance frontier that lie below the global minimum-variance portfolio. Thus, portfolios on the curve below the global minimum-variance portfolio and to the right of the global minimum-variance portfolio are not beneficial and are inefficient portfolios for an investor.

The curve that lies above and to the right of the global minimum-variance portfolio is referred to as the **Markowitz efficient frontier** because it contains all portfolios of risky assets that rational, risk-averse investors will choose.

An important observation that is often ignored is the slope at various points on the efficient frontier. As we move right from the global minimum-variance portfolio (point Z) in Exhibit 5-22, there is an increase in risk with a concurrent increase in return. The increase in return with every unit increase in risk, however, keeps decreasing as we move from left to the right because the slope continues to decrease. The slope at point D is less than the slope at point A, which is less than the slope at point Z. The increase in return by moving from point Z to point A is the same as the increase in return by moving from point A to point D. It can be seen that the additional risk in moving from point A to point D is three to four times more than the additional risk in moving from point Z to point A. Thus, investors obtain decreasing increases in returns as they assume more risk.

5.3. A Risk-Free Asset and Many Risky Assets

Until now, we have only considered risky assets in which the return is risky or uncertain. Most investors, however, have access to a risk-free asset, most notably from securities issued by the government. The addition of a risk-free asset makes the investment opportunity set much richer than the investment opportunity set consisting only of risky assets.

5.3.1. Capital Allocation Line and Optimal Risky Portfolio

By definition, a risk-free asset has zero risk so it must lie on the *y*-axis in a mean-variance graph. A risk-free asset with a return of R_f is plotted in Exhibit 5-23. This asset can now be combined with a portfolio of risky assets. The combination of a risk-free asset with a portfolio of risky assets is a straight line, such as in Section 3.3 (see Exhibit 5-13). Unlike in Section 3.3, however, we have many risky portfolios to choose from instead of a single risky portfolio.

All portfolios on the efficient frontier are candidates for being combined with the risk-free asset. Two combinations are shown in Exhibit 5-23: one between the risk-free asset and efficient portfolio A and the other between the risk-free asset and efficient portfolio P. Comparing capital allocation line A and capital allocation line P reveals that there is a point on CAL(P) with a higher return and same risk for each point on CAL(A). In other words, the portfolios on CAL (P) dominate the portfolios on CAL(A). Therefore, an investor will choose CAL(P) over CAL(A). We would like to move further northwest to achieve even better portfolios. None of those portfolios, however, is attainable because they are above the efficient frontier.

What about other points on the efficient frontier? For example, point X is on the efficient frontier and has the highest return of all risky portfolios for its risk. However, point Y on CAL (P), achievable by leveraging portfolio P as seen in Section 3.3, lies above point X and has the same risk but higher return. In the same way, we can observe that not only does CAL(P) dominate CAL(A) but it also dominates the Markowitz efficient frontier of risky assets.

CAL(P) is the optimal capital allocation line and portfolio *P* is the optimal risky portfolio. Thus, with the addition of the risk-free asset, we are able to narrow our selection of risky portfolios to a single optimal risky portfolio, P, which is at the tangent of CAL(P) and the efficient frontier of risky assets.

5.3.2. The Two-Fund Separation Theorem

The **two-fund separation theorem** states that all investors, regardless of taste, risk preferences, and initial wealth, will hold a combination of two portfolios or funds: a risk-free asset and an optimal portfolio of risky assets.[9]

The separation theorem allows us to divide an investor's investment problem into two distinct steps: the investment decision and the financing decision. In the first step, as in the previous analysis, the investor identifies the optimal risky portfolio. The optimal risky portfolio is selected from numerous risky portfolios without considering the investor's preferences. The

[9]In the next chapter, you will learn that the optimal portfolio of risky assets is the market portfolio.

EXHIBIT 5-23 Optimal Risky Portfolio

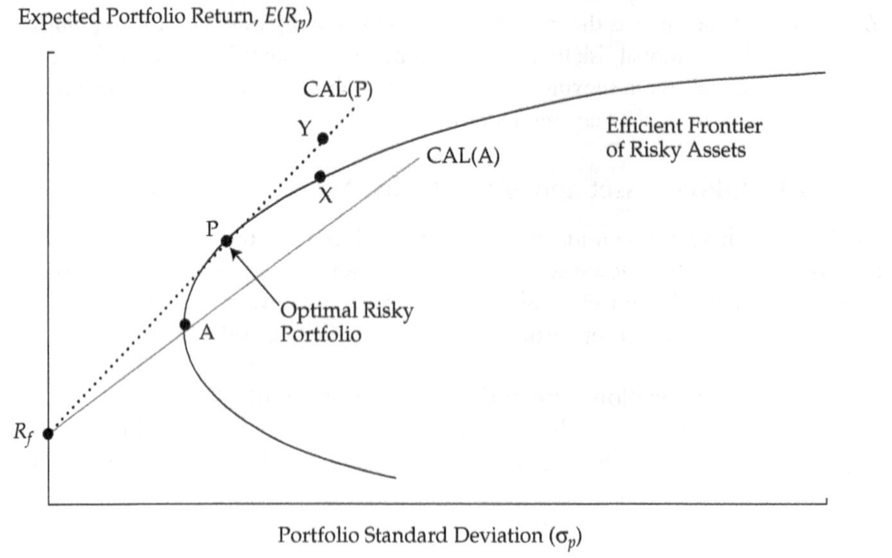

investment decision at this step is based on the optimal risky portfolio's (a single portfolio) return, risk, and correlations.

The capital allocation line connects the optimal risky portfolio and the risk-free asset. All optimal investor portfolios must be on this line. Each investor's optimal portfolio on the CAL(P) is determined in the second step. Considering each individual investor's risk preference, using indifference curves, determines the investor's allocation to the risk-free asset (lending) and to the optimal risky portfolio. Portfolios beyond the optimal risky portfolio are obtained by borrowing at the risk-free rate (i.e., buying on margin). Therefore, the individual investor's risk preference determines the amount of financing (i.e., lending to the government instead of investing in the optimal risky portfolio or borrowing to purchase additional amounts of the optimal risky portfolio).

EXAMPLE 5-10 Choosing the Right Portfolio

In Exhibit 5-24, the risk and return of the points marked are as follows:

Point	Return	Risk	Point	Return	Risk
A	15%	10%	B	11%	10%
C	15%	30%	D	25%	30%
F	4%	0%	G (gold)	10%	30%
P	16%	17%			

EXHIBIT 5-24

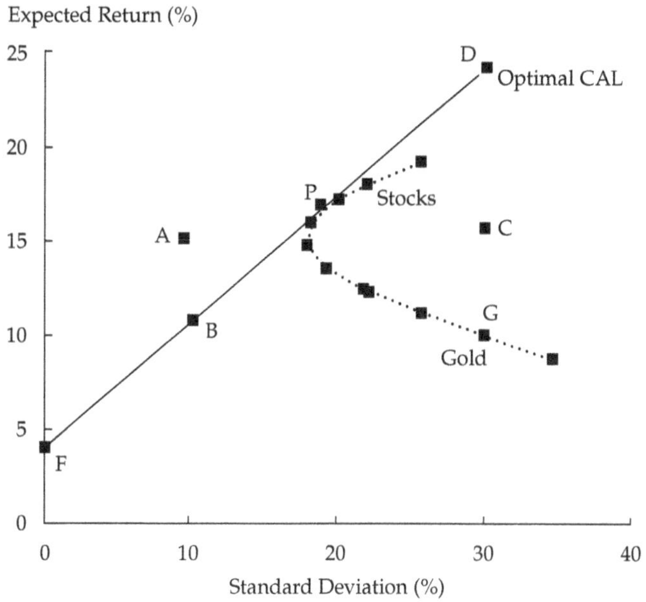

Answer the following questions with reference to the points plotted on Exhibit 5-24 and explain your answers. The investor is choosing one portfolio based on the graph.

1. Which of the preceding points is not achievable?
2. Which of these portfolios will not be chosen by a rational, risk-averse investor?
3. Which of these portfolios is most suitable for a risk-neutral investor?
4. Gold is on the inefficient part of the feasible set. Nonetheless, gold is owned by many rational investors as part of a larger portfolio. Why?
5. What is the utility of an investor at point P with a risk aversion coefficient of 3?

Solution to 1: Portfolio A is not attainable because it lies outside the feasible set and not on the capital allocation line.

Solution to 2: Portfolios G and C will not be chosen because D provides higher return for the same risk. G and C are the only investable points that do not lie on the capital allocation line.

Solution to 3: Portfolio D is most suitable because a risk-neutral investor cares only about return and portfolio D provides the highest return. A = 0 in the utility formula.

Solution to 4: Gold may be owned as part of a portfolio (not as *the* portfolio) because gold has low or negative correlation with many risky assets, such as stocks. Being part of a portfolio can thus reduce overall risk even though its standalone risk is high and return is low. Note that gold's price is not stable—its return is very risky (30 percent). Even risk seekers will choose D over G, which has the same risk but higher return.

Solution to 5: $U = E(r) - 0.5\ A\ \sigma^2 = 0.16 - 0.5 \times 3 \times 0.0289 = 0.1167 = 11.67\%$.

5.4. Optimal Investor Portfolio

The CAL(P) in Exhibits 5-23 and 5-25 contains the best possible portfolios available to investors. Each of those portfolios is a linear combination of the risk-free asset and the optimal risky portfolio. Among the available portfolios, the selection of each investor's optimal portfolio depends on the risk preferences of an investor. In section 3, we discussed that the individual investor's risk preferences are incorporated into their indifference curves. These can be used to select the optimal portfolio.

EXHIBIT 5-25 Optimal Investor Portfolio

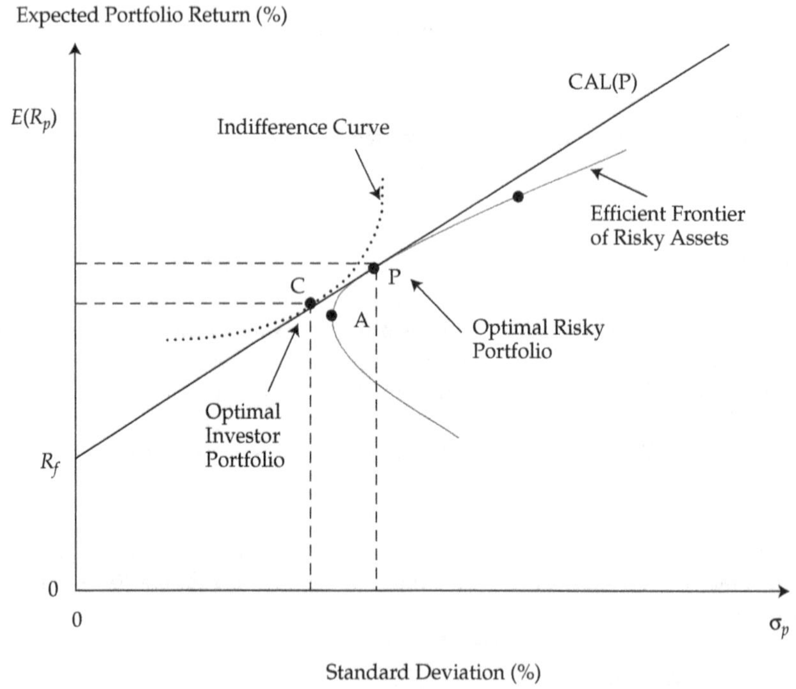

Exhibit 5-25 shows an indifference curve that is tangent to the capital allocation line, CAL(P). Indifference curves with higher utility than this one lie above the capital allocation line, so their portfolios are not achievable. Indifference curves that lie below this one are not preferred because they have lower utility. Thus, the optimal portfolio for the investor with this indifference curve is portfolio C on CAL(P), which is tangent to the indifference curve.

EXAMPLE 5-11 Comprehensive Example on Portfolio Selection

This comprehensive example reviews many concepts learned in this chapter. The example begins with simple information about available assets and builds an optimal investor portfolio for the Lohrmanns.

Suppose the Lohrmanns can invest in only two risky assets, A and B. The expected return and standard deviation for asset A are 20 percent and 50 percent, and the expected return and standard deviation for asset B are 15 percent and 33 percent. The two assets have zero correlation with one another.

1. Calculate portfolio expected return and portfolio risk (standard deviation) if an investor invests 10 percent in A and the remaining 90 percent in B.

   Solution to 1: The subscript "*rp*" means risky portfolio.

$$R_{rp} = [0.10 \times 20\%] + [(1 - 0.10) \times 15\%] = 0.155 = 15.50\%$$

$$\begin{aligned}\sigma_{rp} &= \sqrt{w_A^2\sigma_A^2 + w_B^2\sigma_B^2 + 2w_Aw_B\rho_{AB}\sigma_A\sigma_B} \\ &= \sqrt{(0.10^2 \times 0.50^2)+(0.90^2 \times 0.33^2)+(2 \times 0.10 \times 0.90 \times 0.0 \times 0.50 \times 0.33)} \\ &= 0.3012 = 30.12\%\end{aligned}$$

   Note that the correlation coefficient is 0, so the last term for standard deviation is zero.

2. Generalize the previous calculations for portfolio return and risk by assuming an investment of w_A in asset A and an investment of $(1 - w_A)$ in asset B.

   Solution to 2: $R_{rp} = w_A \times 20\% + (1 - w_A) \times 15\% = 0.05\, w_A + 0.15$

$$\begin{aligned}\sigma_{rp} &= \sqrt{w_A^2 \times 0.5^2 + (1 - w_A)^2 \times 0.33^2} = \sqrt{0.25w_A^2 + 0.1089(1 - 2w_A + w_A^2)} \\ &= \sqrt{0.3589w_A^2 - 0.2178w_A + 0.1089}\end{aligned}$$

   The investment opportunity set can be constructed by using different weights in the expressions for $E(R_{rp})$ and σ_{rp} in Part 1 of this example. Exhibit 5-26 on page 230 shows the combination of assets A and B.

3. Now introduce a risk-free asset with a return of 3 percent. Write an equation for the capital allocation line in terms of w_A that will connect the risk-free asset to the portfolio of risky assets. (Hint: use the equation in Section 3.3 and substitute the expressions for a risky portfolio's risk and return from the preceding part 2).

   Solution to 3: The equation of the line connecting the risk-free asset to the portfolio of risky assets is given next (see Section 3.3), where the subscript "*rp*" refers to the

EXHIBIT 5-26

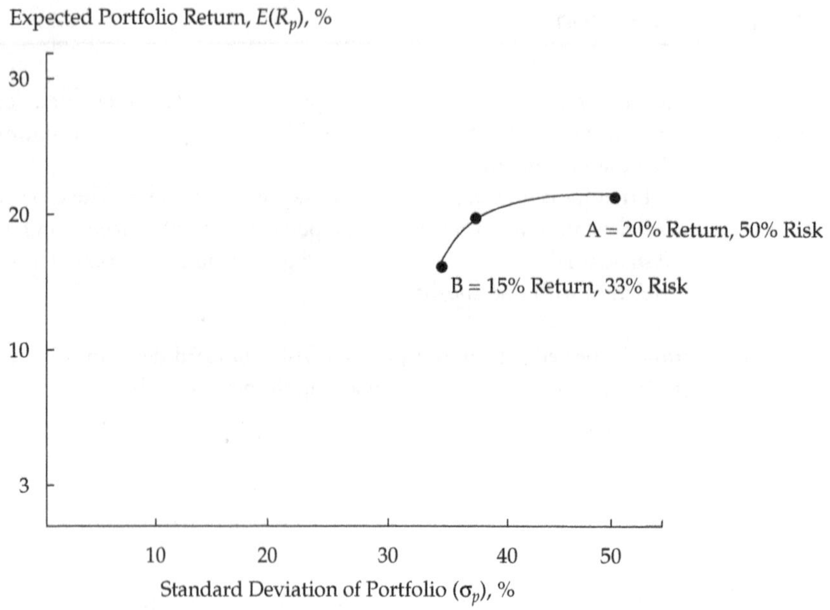

risky portfolio instead of "i", and the subscript "p" refers to the new portfolio of two risky assets and one risk-free asset.

$$E(R_p) = R_f + \frac{E(R_i) - R_f}{\sigma_i}\sigma_p, \text{ rewritten as}$$

$$E(R_p) = R_f + \frac{E(R_{rp}) - R_f}{\sigma_{rp}}\sigma_p$$

$$= 0.03 + \frac{0.05w_A + 0.15 - 0.03}{\sqrt{0.3589w_A^2 - 0.2178w_A + 0.1089}}$$

$$\sigma_p = 0.03 + \frac{0.05w_A + 0.12}{\sqrt{0.3589w_A^2 - 0.2178w_A + 0.1089}}\sigma_p$$

The capital allocation line is the line that has the maximum slope because it is tangent to the curve formed by portfolios of the two risky assets. Exhibit 5-27 shows the capital allocation line based on a risk-free asset added to the group of assets.

4. The slope of the capital allocation line is maximized when the weight in asset A is 38.20 percent.[10] What is the equation for the capital allocation line using w_A of 38.20 percent?

[10]You can maximize $\frac{0.05w_A + 0.12}{\sqrt{0.3589w_A^2 - 0.2178w_A + 0.1089}}$ by taking the first derivative of the slope with respect to w_A and setting it to 0.

EXHIBIT 5-27

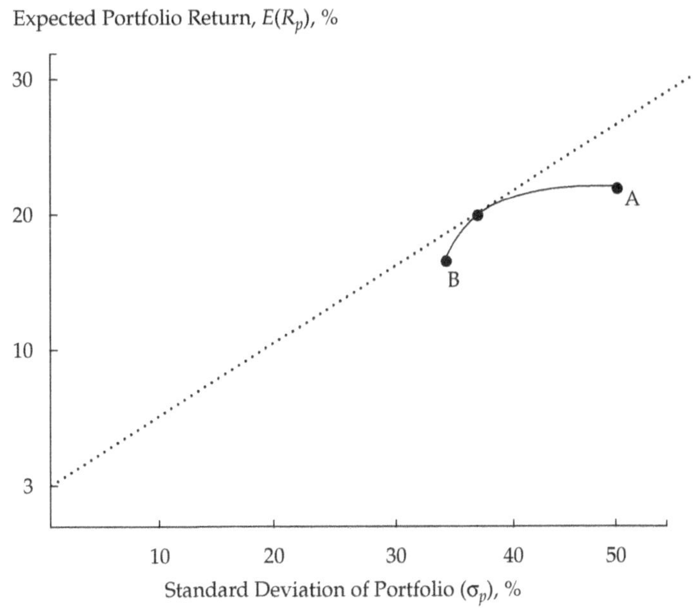

Solution to 4: By substituting 38.20 percent for w_A in the equation in Part 3, we get $E(R_p) = 0.03 + 0.4978\ \sigma_p$ as the capital allocation line.

5. Having created the capital allocation line, we turn to the Lohrmanns. What is the standard deviation of a portfolio that gives a 20 percent return and is on the capital allocation line? How does this portfolio compare with asset A?

   Solution to 5: Solve the equation for the capital allocation line to get the standard deviation: $0.20 = 0.03 + 0.4978\ \sigma_p$. $\sigma_p = 34.2\%$. The portfolio with a 20 percent return has the same return as asset A but a lower standard deviation, 34.2 percent instead of 50.0 percent.

6. What is the risk of portfolios with returns of 3 percent, 9 percent, 15 percent, and 20 percent?

   Solution to 6: You can find the risk of the portfolio using the equation for the capital allocation line: $E(R_p) = 0.03 + 0.4978\ \sigma_p$.

   For a portfolio with a return of 15 percent, write $0.15 = 0.03 + 0.4978\ \sigma_p$. Solving for σ_p gives 24.1 percent. You can similarly calculate risks of other portfolios with the given returns.

   The risk of the portfolio for a return of 3 percent is 0.0 percent, for a return of 9 percent is 12.1 percent, for a return of 15 percent is 24.1 percent, and for a return of 20 percent is 34.2 percent. The points are plotted in Exhibit 5-28.

EXHIBIT 5-28

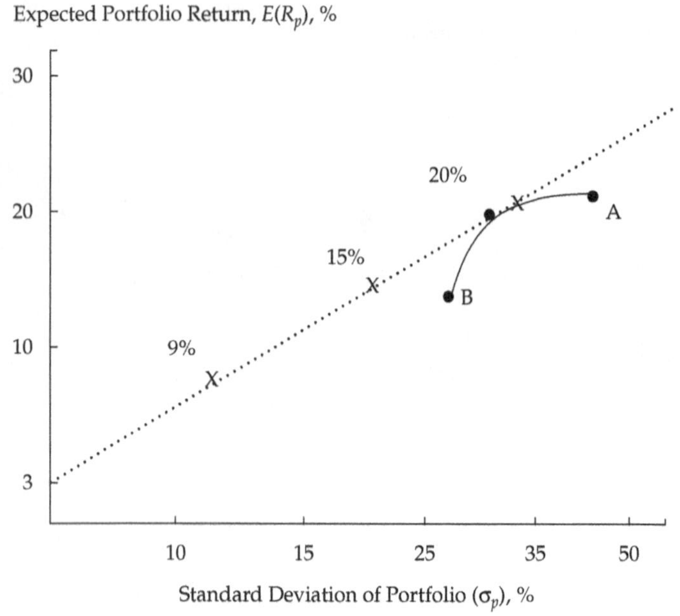

7. What is the utility that the Lohrmanns derive from a portfolio with a return of 3 percent, 9 percent, 15 percent, and 20 percent? The risk aversion coefficient for the Lohrmanns is 2.5.

Solution to 7: To find the utility, use the utility formula with a risk aversion coefficient of 2.5:

$$\begin{aligned}
Utility &= E(R_p) - 0.5 \times 2.5\sigma_p^2 \\
Utility\,(3\%) &= 0.0300 \\
Utility\,(9\%) &= 0.09 - 0.5 \times 2.5 \times 0.121^2 = +0.0717 \\
Utility\,(15\%) &= 0.15 - 0.5 \times 2.5 \times 0.241^2 = +0.0774 \\
Utility\,(20\%) &= 0.20 - 0.5 \times 2.5 \times 0.341^2 = +0.0546
\end{aligned}$$

Based on the preceding information, the Lohrmanns choose a portfolio with a return of 15 percent and a standard deviation of 24.1 percent because it has the highest utility: 0.0774. Finally, Exhibit 5-29 shows the indifference curve that is tangent to the capital allocation line to generate Lohrmanns' optimal investor portfolio.

EXHIBIT 5-29

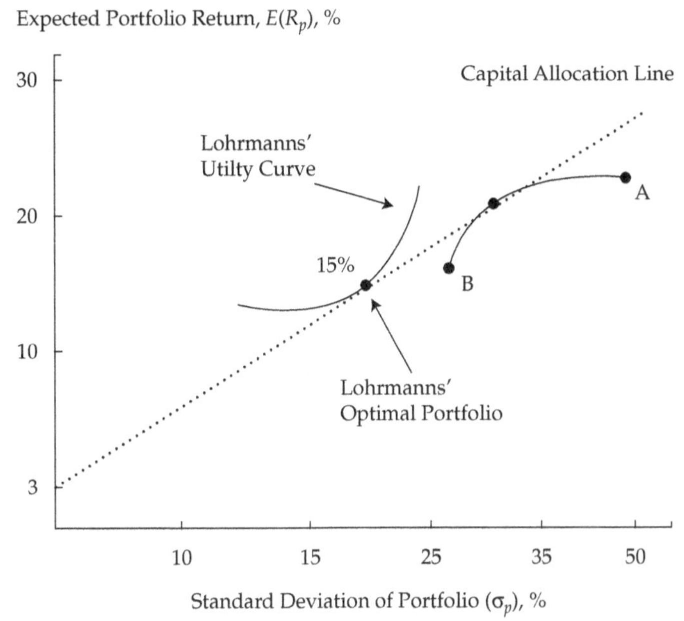

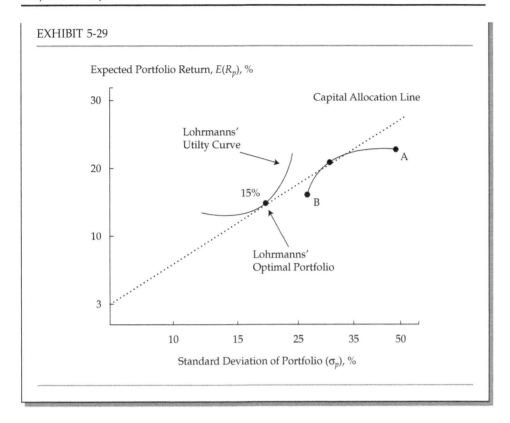

5.4.1. Investor Preferences and Optimal Portfolios

The location of an optimal investor portfolio depends on the investor's risk preferences. A highly risk-averse investor may invest a large proportion, even 100 percent, of his/her assets in the risk-free asset. The optimal portfolio in this investor's case will be located close to the *y*-axis. A less risk-averse investor, however, may invest a large portion of his/her wealth in the optimal risky asset. The optimal portfolio in this investor's case will lie closer to point P in Exhibit 5-25.

Some less risk-averse investors (i.e., with a high risk tolerance) may wish to accept even more risk because of the chance of higher return. Such an investor may borrow money to invest more in the risky portfolio. If the investor borrows 25 percent of his wealth, he/she can invest 125 percent in the optimal risky portfolio. The optimal investor portfolio for such an investor will lie to the right of point P on the capital allocation line.

Thus, moving from the risk-free asset along the capital allocation line, we encounter investors who are willing to accept more risk. At point P, the investor is 100 percent invested in the optimal risky portfolio. Beyond point P, the investor accepts even more risk by borrowing money and investing in the optimal risky portfolio.

Note that we are able to accommodate all types of investors with just two portfolios: the risk-free asset and the optimal risky portfolio. Exhibit 5-25 is also an illustration of the two-fund separation theorem. Portfolio P is the optimal risky portfolio that is selected without regard to investor preferences. The optimal investor portfolio is selected on the capital allocation line by overlaying the indifference curves that incorporate investor preferences.

6. SUMMARY

This chapter provides a description and computation of investment characteristics, such as risk and return, that investors use in evaluating assets for investment. This was followed by sections about portfolio construction, selection of an optimal risky portfolio, and an understanding of risk aversion and indifference curves. Finally, the tangency point of the indifference curves with the capital allocation line allows identification of the optimal investor portfolio. Key concepts covered in the chapter include the following:

- Holding period return is most appropriate for a single, predefined holding period.
- Multiperiod returns can be aggregated in many ways. Each return computation has special applications for evaluating investments.
- Risk-averse investors make investment decisions based on the risk–return trade-off, maximizing return for the same risk, and minimizing risk for the same return. They may be concerned, however, by deviations from a normal return distribution and from assumptions of financial markets' operational efficiency.
- Investors are risk averse, and historical data confirm that financial markets price assets for risk-averse investors.
- The risk of a two-asset portfolio is dependent on the proportions of each asset, their standard deviations, and the correlation (or covariance) between the asset's returns. As the number of assets in a portfolio increases, the correlation among asset risks becomes a more important determinant of portfolio risk.
- Combining assets with low correlations reduces portfolio risk.
- The two-fund separation theorem allows us to separate decision making into two steps. In the first step, the optimal risky portfolio and the capital allocation line are identified, which are the same for all investors. In the second step, investor risk preferences enable us to find a unique optimal investor portfolio for each investor.
- The addition of a risk-free asset creates portfolios that are dominant to portfolios of risky assets in all cases except for the optimal risky portfolio.

By successfully understanding the content of this chapter, you should be comfortable calculating an investor's optimal portfolio given the investor's risk preferences and universe of investable assets available.

PROBLEMS[11]

1. An investor purchased 100 shares of a stock for \$34.50 per share at the beginning of the quarter. If the investor sold all of the shares for \$30.50 per share after receiving a \$51.55 dividend payment at the end of the quarter, the holding period return is *closest* to:

   A. −13.0%.
   B. −11.6%.
   C. −10.1%.

[11]These practice questions were developed by Stephen P. Huffman, CFA (University of Wisconsin, Oshkosh).

2. An analyst obtains the following annual rates of return for a mutual fund:

Year	Return
2008	14%
2009	−10%
2010	−2%

The fund's holding period return over the three-year period is *closest* to:

A. 0.18%.
B. 0.55%.
C. 0.67%.

3. An analyst observes the following annual rates of return for a hedge fund:

Year	Return
2008	22%
2009	−25%
2010	11%

The hedge fund's annual geometric mean return is *closest* to:

A. 0.52%.
B. 1.02%.
C. 2.67%.

4. Which of the following return calculating methods is *best* for evaluating the annualized returns of a buy-and-hold strategy of an investor who has made annual deposits to an account for each of the last five years?

A. Geometric mean return.
B. Arithmetic mean return.
C. Money-weighted return.

5. An investor evaluating the returns of three recently formed exchange-traded funds gathers the following information:

ETF	Time since Inception	Return since Inception
1	146 days	4.61%
2	5 weeks	1.10%
3	15 months	14.35%

The ETF with the highest annualized rate of return is:

A. ETF 1.
B. ETF 2.
C. ETF 3.

6. With respect to capital market theory, which of the following asset characteristics is *least likely* to impact the variance of an investor's equally weighted portfolio?

   A. Return on the asset.
   B. Standard deviation of the asset.
   C. Covariances of the asset with the other assets in the portfolio.

7. A portfolio manager creates the following portfolio:

Security	Security Weight	Expected Standard Deviation
1	30%	20%
2	70%	12%

   If the correlation of returns between the two securities is 0.40, the expected standard deviation of the portfolio is *closest* to:

   A. 10.7%.
   B. 11.3%.
   C. 12.1%.

8. A portfolio manager creates the following portfolio:

Security	Security Weight	Expected Standard Deviation
1	30%	20%
2	70%	12%

   If the covariance of returns between the two securities is −0.0240, the expected standard deviation of the portfolio is *closest* to:

   A. 2.4%.
   B. 7.5%.
   C. 9.2%.

Use the following data to answer Questions 9 and 10.

A portfolio manager creates the following portfolio:

Security	Security Weight	Expected Standard Deviation
1	30%	20%
2	70%	12%

9. If the standard deviation of the portfolio is 14.40%, the correlation between the two securities is equal to:

   A. −1.0.
   B. 0.0.
   C. 1.0.

10. If the standard deviation of the portfolio is 14.40%, the covariance between the two securities is equal to:

    A. 0.0006.
    B. 0.0240.
    C. 1.0000.

Use the following data to answer Questions 11 through 14.

An analyst observes the following historic geometric returns:

Asset Class	Geometric Return
Equities	8.0%
Corporate Bonds	6.5%
Treasury Bills	2.5%
Inflation	2.1%

11. The real rate of return for equities is *closest* to:

    A. 5.4%.
    B. 5.8%.
    C. 5.9%.

12. The real rate of return for corporate bonds is *closest* to:

    A. 4.3%.
    B. 4.4%.
    C. 4.5%.

13. The risk premium for equities is *closest* to:

    A. 5.4%.
    B. 5.5%.
    C. 5.6%.

14. The risk premium for corporate bonds is *closest* to:

    A. 3.5%.
    B. 3.9%.
    C. 4.0%.

15. With respect to trading costs, liquidity is *least likely* to impact the:

    A. Stock price.
    B. Bid-ask spreads.
    C. Brokerage commissions.

16. Evidence of risk aversion is *best* illustrated by a risk-return relationship that is:

    A. Negative.
    B. Neutral.
    C. Positive.

17. With respect to risk-averse investors, a risk-free asset will generate a numerical utility that is:
    A. The same for all individuals.
    B. Positive for risk-averse investors.
    C. Equal to zero for risk-seeking investors.

18. With respect to utility theory, the most risk-averse investor will have an indifference curve with the:
    A. Most convexity.
    B. Smallest intercept value.
    C. Greatest slope coefficient.

19. With respect to an investor's utility function expressed as $U = E(r) - \frac{1}{2}A\sigma^2$, which of the following values for the measure for risk aversion has the *least* amount of risk-aversion?
    A. −4
    B. 0
    C. 4

Use the following data to answer Questions 20 through 23.

A financial planner has created the following data to illustrate the application of utility theory to portfolio selection:

Investment	Expected Return	Expected Standard Deviation
1	18%	2%
2	19%	8%
3	20%	15%
4	18%	30%

20. A risk-neutral investor is *most likely* to choose:
    A. Investment 1.
    B. Investment 2.
    C. Investment 3.

21. If an investor's utility function is expressed as $U = E(r) - \frac{1}{2}A\sigma^2$ and the measure for risk aversion has a value of −2, the risk-seeking investor is *most likely* to choose:
    A. Investment 2.
    B. Investment 3.
    C. Investment 4.

22. If an investor's utility function is expressed as $U = E(r) - \frac{1}{2}A\sigma^2$ and the measure for risk aversion has a value of 2, the risk-averse investor is *most likely* to choose:
    A. Investment 1.
    B. Investment 2.
    C. Investment 3.

23. If an investor's utility function is expressed as $U = E(r) - \frac{1}{2}A\sigma^2$ and the measure for risk aversion has a value of 4, the risk-averse investor is *most likely* to choose:

A. Investment 1.
B. Investment 2.
C. Investment 3.

24. With respect to the mean-variance portfolio theory, the capital allocation line, CAL, is the combination of the risk-free asset and a portfolio of all:

A. Risky assets.
B. Equity securities.
C. Feasible investments.

25. Two individual investors with different levels of risk aversion will have optimal portfolios that are:

A. Below the capital allocation line.
B. On the capital allocation line.
C. Above the capital allocation line.

Use the following data to answer Questions 26 through 28.

A portfolio manager creates the following portfolio:

Security	Expected Annual Return	Expected Standard Deviation
1	16%	20%
2	12%	20%

26. If the portfolio of the two securities has an expected return of 15%, the proportion invested in security 1 is:

A. 25%.
B. 50%.
C. 75%.

27. If the correlation of returns between the two securities is –0.15, the expected standard deviation of an equal-weighted portfolio is *closest* to:

A. 13.04%.
B. 13.60%.
C. 13.87%.

28. If the two securities are uncorrelated, the expected standard deviation of an equal-weighted portfolio is *closest* to:

A. 14.00%.
B. 14.14%.
C. 20.00%.

29. As the number of assets in an equally weighted portfolio increases, the contribution of each individual asset's variance to the volatility of the portfolio:

A. Increases.
B. Decreases.
C. Remains the same.

30. With respect to an equally weighted portfolio made up of a large number of assets, which of the following contributes the *most* to the volatility of the portfolio?

    A. Average variance of the individual assets.
    B. Standard deviation of the individual assets.
    C. Average covariance between all pairs of assets.

31. The correlation between assets in a two-asset portfolio increases during a market decline. If there is no change in the proportion of each asset held in the portfolio or the expected standard deviation of the individual assets, the volatility of the portfolio is *most likely* to:

    A. Increase.
    B. Decrease.
    C. Remain the same.

Use the following data to answer Questions 32 through 34.

An analyst has made the following return projections for each of three possible outcomes with an equal likelihood of occurrence:

Asset	Outcome 1	Outcome 2	Outcome 3	Expected Return
1	12%	0%	6%	6%
2	12%	6%	0%	6%
3	0%	6%	12%	6%

32. Which pair of assets is perfectly negatively correlated?

    A. Asset 1 and Asset 2.
    B. Asset 1 and Asset 3.
    C. Asset 2 and Asset 3.

33. If the analyst constructs two-asset portfolios that are equally weighted, which pair of assets has the *lowest* expected standard deviation?

    A. Asset 1 and Asset 2.
    B. Asset 1 and Asset 3.
    C. Asset 2 and Asset 3.

34. If the analyst constructs two-asset portfolios that are equally weighted, which pair of assets provides the *least* amount of risk reduction?

    A. Asset 1 and Asset 2.
    B. Asset 1 and Asset 3.
    C. Asset 2 and Asset 3.

35. Which of the following statements is *least* accurate? The efficient frontier is the set of all attainable risky assets with the:

    A. Highest expected return for a given level of risk.
    B. Lowest amount of risk for a given level of return.
    C. Highest expected return relative to the risk-free rate.

36. The portfolio on the minimum-variance frontier with the lowest standard deviation is:

    A. Unattainable.
    B. The optimal risky portfolio.
    C. The global minimum-variance portfolio.

37. The set of portfolios on the minimum-variance frontier that dominates all sets of portfolios below the global minimum-variance portfolio is the:

    A. Capital allocation line.
    B. Markowitz efficient frontier.
    C. Set of optimal risky portfolios.

38. The dominant capital allocation line is the combination of the risk-free asset and the:

    A. Optimal risky portfolio.
    B. Levered portfolio of risky assets.
    C. Global minimum-variance portfolio.

39. Compared to the efficient frontier of risky assets, the dominant capital allocation line has higher rates of return for levels of risk greater than the optimal risky portfolio because of the investor's ability to:

    A. Lend at the risk-free rate.
    B. Borrow at the risk-free rate.
    C. Purchase the risk-free asset.

40. With respect to the mean-variance theory, the optimal portfolio is determined by each individual investor's:

    A. Risk-free rate.
    B. Borrowing rate.
    C. Risk preference.

CHAPTER 6

PORTFOLIO RISK AND RETURN: PART II

Vijay Singal, CFA
Blacksburg, VA, U.S.A.

LEARNING OUTCOMES

After completing this chapter, you will be able to do the following:

- Discuss the implications of combining a risk-free asset with a portfolio of risky assets.
- Explain and interpret the capital allocation line (CAL) and the capital market line (CML).
- Explain systematic and nonsystematic risk and why an investor should not expect to receive additional return for bearing nonsystematic risk.
- Explain return-generating models (including the market model) and their uses.
- Calculate and interpret beta.
- Explain the capital asset pricing model (CAPM) including the required assumptions, and the security market line (SML).
- Calculate and interpret the expected return of an asset using the CAPM.
- Illustrate applications of the CAPM and the SML.

1. INTRODUCTION

Our objective in this chapter is to identify the optimal risky portfolio for all investors by using the capital asset pricing model (CAPM). The foundation of this chapter is the computation of risk and return of a portfolio and the role that correlation plays in diversifying portfolio risk and arriving at the efficient frontier. The efficient frontier and the capital allocation line consist of portfolios that are generally acceptable to all investors. By combining an investor's individual indifference curves with the market-determined capital allocation line, we are able to illustrate that the only optimal risky portfolio for an investor is the portfolio of all risky assets (i.e., the market).

Additionally, we discuss the capital market line, a special case of the capital allocation line that is used for passive investor portfolios. We also differentiate between systematic and nonsystematic risk, and explain why investors are compensated for bearing systematic risk but receive no compensation for bearing nonsystematic risk. We discuss in detail the CAPM, which is a simple model for estimating asset returns based only on the asset's systematic risk. Finally, we illustrate how the CAPM allows security selection to build an optimal portfolio for an investor by changing the asset mix beyond a passive market portfolio.

The chapter is organized as follows. In Section 2, we discuss the consequences of combining a risk-free asset with the market portfolio and provide an interpretation of the capital market line. Section 3 decomposes total risk into systematic and nonsystematic risk and discusses the characteristics of and differences between the two kinds of risk. We also introduce return-generating models, including the single-index model, and illustrate the calculation of beta by using formulas and graphically by using the security characteristic line. In Section 4, we introduce the capital asset pricing model and the security market line. We discuss many applications of the CAPM and the SML throughout the chapter, including the use of expected return in making capital budgeting decisions, the evaluation of portfolios using the CAPM's risk-adjusted return as the benchmark, security selection, and determining whether adding a new security to the current portfolio is appropriate. Our focus on the CAPM does not suggest that the CAPM is the only viable asset-pricing model. Although the CAPM is an excellent starting point, more advanced readings expand on these discussions and extend the analysis to other models that account for multiple explanatory factors. A preview of a number of these models is given in Section 5. Finally, in Section 6 we conclude the chapter and provide a summary.

2. CAPITAL MARKET THEORY

You have learned how to combine a risk-free asset with one risky asset and with many risky assets to create a capital allocation line. In this section, we will expand our discussion of multiple risky assets and consider a special case of the capital allocation line, called the capital market line. While discussing the capital market line, we will define the market and its role in passive portfolio management. Using these concepts, we will illustrate how leveraged portfolios can enhance both risk and return.

2.1. Portfolio of Risk-Free and Risky Assets

Although investors desire an asset that produces the highest return and carries the lowest risk, such an asset does not exist. As the risk–return capital market theory illustrates, one must assume higher risk in order to earn a higher return. We can improve an investor's portfolio, however, by expanding the opportunity set of risky assets because this allows the investor to choose a superior mix of assets.

Similarly, an investor's portfolio improves if a risk-free asset is added to the mix. In other words, a combination of the risk-free asset and a risky asset can result in a better risk–return trade-off than an investment in only one type of asset because the risk-free asset has zero correlation with the risky asset. The combination is called the **capital allocation line** (and is depicted in Exhibit 6-2). Superimposing an investor's indifference curves on the capital allocation line will lead to the optimal investor portfolio.

Investors with different levels of risk aversion will choose different portfolios. Highly risk-averse investors choose to invest most of their wealth in the risk-free asset and earn low returns because they are not willing to assume higher levels of risk. Less risk-averse investors, in contrast, invest more of their wealth in the risky asset, which is expected to yield a higher return. Obviously, the higher return cannot come without higher risk, but the less risk-averse investor is willing to accept the additional risk.

2.1.1. Combining a Risk-Free Asset with a Portfolio of Risky Assets

We can extend the analysis of one risky asset to a portfolio of risky assets. For convenience, assume that the portfolio contains all available risky assets,[1] although an investor may not wish to include all of these assets in the portfolio because of the investor's specific preferences. If an asset is not included in the portfolio, its weight will be zero. The risk–return characteristics of a portfolio of N risky assets are given by the following equations:

$$E(R_p) = \sum_{i=1}^{N} w_i E(R_i), \quad \sigma_p^2 = \left(\sum_{i=1,\, j=1}^{N} w_i w_j \text{cov}(i,j) \right), \text{ and } \sum_{i=1}^{N} w_i = 1$$

The expected return on the portfolio, $E(R_p)$, is the weighted average of the expected returns of individual assets, where w_i is the fractional weight in asset i and R_i is the expected return of asset i. The risk of the portfolio (σ_p), however, depends on the weights of the individual assets, the risk of the individual assets, and their interrelationships. The **covariance** between assets i and j, Cov(i, j), is a statistical measure of the interrelationship between each pair of assets in the portfolio and can be expressed as follows, where ρ_{ij} is the **correlation** between assets i and j and σ_i is the risk of asset i:

$$\text{Cov}(i,j) = \rho_{ij}\sigma_i\sigma_j$$

Note from the following equation that the correlation of an asset with itself is 1; therefore:

$$\text{Cov}(i,\, i) = \rho_{ij}\sigma_i\sigma_j = \sigma_i^2$$

By substituting the preceding expressions for covariance, we can rewrite the portfolio variance equation as

$$\sigma_p^2 = \left(\sum_{i=1}^{N} w_i^2 \sigma_i^2 + \sum_{i,j=1, i \neq j}^{N} w_i w_j \rho_{ij} \sigma_i \sigma_j \right)$$

The suggestion that portfolios have lower risk than the assets they contain may seem counterintuitive. These portfolios can be constructed, however, as long as the assets in the portfolio are not perfectly correlated. As an illustration of the effect of asset weights on portfolio characteristics, consider a simple two-asset portfolio with zero weights in all other assets. Assume that Asset 1 has a return of 10 percent and a standard deviation (risk) of 20 percent. Asset 2 has a return of 5 percent and a standard deviation (risk) of 10 percent. Furthermore, the correlation between the two assets is zero. Exhibit 6-1 shows risks and returns for Portfolio X with a weight of 25 percent in Asset 1 and 75 percent in Asset 2, Portfolio Y with a weight of 50 percent in each of the two assets, and Portfolio Z with a weight of 75 percent in Asset 1 and 25 percent in Asset 2.

---

[1] N risky assets.

EXHIBIT 6-1 Portfolio Risk and Return

Portfolio	Weight in Asset 1	Weight in Asset 2	Portfolio Return	Portfolio Standard Deviation
X	25.0%	75.0%	6.25%	9.01%
Y	50.0	50.0	7.50	11.18
Z	75.0	25.0	8.75	15.21
Return	10.0%	5.0%		
Standard deviation	20.0%	10.0%		
Correlation between Assets 1 and 2		0.0%		

From this example we observe that the three portfolios are quite different in terms of their risk and return. Portfolio X has a 6.25 percent return and only 9.01 percent standard deviation, whereas the standard deviation of Portfolio Z is more than two-thirds higher (15.21 percent), although the return is only slightly more than one-third higher (8.75 percent). These portfolios may become even more dissimilar as other assets are added to the mix.

Consider three portfolios of risky assets, A, B, and C, as in Exhibit 6-2, that may have been presented to a representative investor by three different investment advisers. Each portfolio is combined with the risk-free asset to create three capital allocation lines, CAL(A), CAL(B), and CAL(C). The exhibit shows that Portfolio C is superior to the other two portfolios because it has a greater expected return for any given level of risk. As a result, an investor will choose the portfolio that lies on the capital allocation line for Portfolio C. The combination of the risk-free asset and the risky Portfolio C that is selected for an investor depends on the investor's degree of risk aversion.

2.1.2. Does a Unique Optimal Risky Portfolio Exist?

We assume that all investors have the same economic expectation and thus have the same expectations of prices, cash flows, and other investment characteristics. This assumption is referred to as **homogeneity of expectations**. Given these investment characteristics, everyone goes through the same calculations and should arrive at the same optimal risky portfolio. Therefore, assuming homogeneous expectations, only one optimal portfolio exists. If investors have different expectations, however, they might arrive at different optimal risky portfolios. To illustrate, we begin with an expression for the price of an asset:

$$P = \sum_{t=0}^{T} \frac{CF_t}{(1 + r_t)^t}$$

where CF_t is the cash flow at the end of period t and r_t is the discount rate or the required rate of return for that asset for period t. Period t refers to all periods beginning from now until the asset ceases to exist at the end of time T. Because the current time is the end of period 0, which is the same as the beginning of period 1, there are $(T + 1)$ cash flows and $(T + 1)$ required rates of return. These conditions are based on the assumption that a cash flow, such as an initial investment, can occur now ($t = 0$). Ordinarily, however, CF_0 is zero.

We use the formula for the price of an asset to estimate the intrinsic value of an asset. For ease of reference, assume that the asset we are valuing is a share of HSBC Holdings (parent of

EXHIBIT 6-2 Risk-Free Asset and Portfolio of Risky Assets

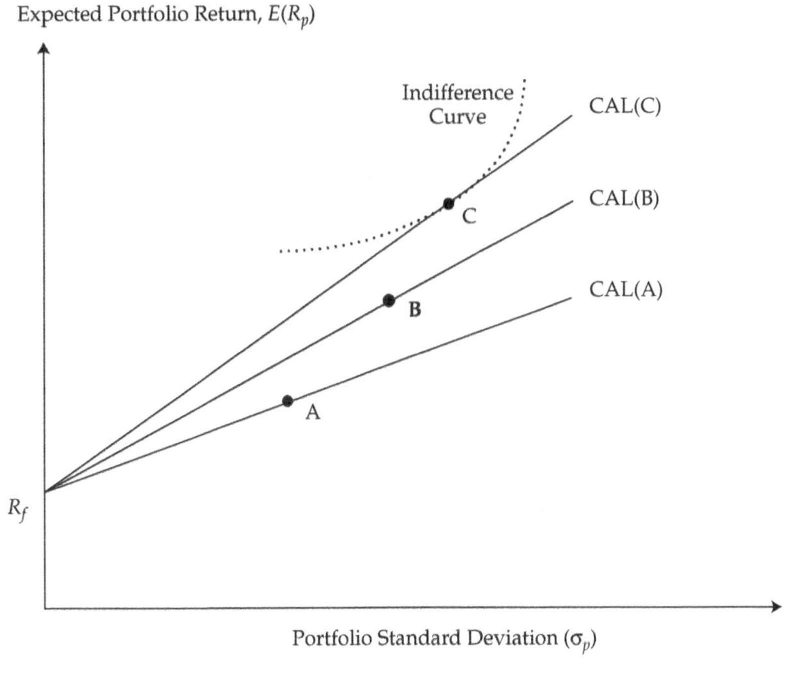

HSBC Bank), a British company that also trades on the Hong Kong Stock Exchange. In the case of corporate stock, there is no expiration date, so T could be extremely large, meaning we will need to estimate a large number of cash flows and rates of return. Fortunately, the denominator reduces the importance of distant cash flows, so it may be sufficient to estimate, say, 20 annual cash flows and 20 rates of returns. How much will HSBC earn next year and the year after next? What will the banking sector look like in five years' time? Different analysts and investors will have their own estimates that may be quite different from one another. Also, as we delve further into the future, more serious issues in estimating future revenue, expenses, and growth rates arise. Therefore, to assume that cash flow estimates for HSBC will vary among these investors is reasonable. In addition to the numerator (cash flows), it is also necessary to estimate the denominator, the required rates of return. We know that riskier companies will require higher returns because risk and return are positively correlated. HSBC stock is riskier than a risk-free asset, but by how much? And what should the compensation for that additional risk be? Again, it is evident that different analysts will view the riskiness of HSBC differently and, therefore, arrive at different required rates of return.

HSBC closed at HK$89.40 on 31 December 2009 on the Hong Kong Stock Exchange. The traded price represents the value that a marginal investor attaches to a share of HSBC, say, corresponding to Analyst A's expectation. Analyst B may think that the price should be HK$50, however, and Analyst C may think that the price should be HK$150. Given a current price of HK$89.40, the expected returns of HSBC are quite different for the three analysts. Analyst B, who believes the price should be HK$50, concludes that HSBC is overvalued and may assign a weight of zero to HSBC in the recommended portfolio even though the market capitalization of HSBC is in excess of HK$1 trillion. In contrast, Analyst C, with a valuation of HK$150, thinks HSBC is undervalued and will significantly overweight HSBC in a portfolio.

Our discussion illustrates that analysts can arrive at different valuations that necessitate the assignment of different asset weights in a portfolio. Given the existence of many asset classes and numerous assets in each asset class, one can visualize that each investor will have his or her own optimal risky portfolio depending on his or her assumptions underlying the valuation computations. Therefore, market participants will have their own and possibly different optimal risky portfolios.

If investors have different valuations of assets, then the construction of a unique optimal risky portfolio is not possible. If we make a simplifying assumption of homogeneity in investor expectations, we will have a single optimal risky portfolio as previously mentioned. Even if investors have different expectations, market prices are a proxy of what the marginal, informed investor expects, and the market portfolio becomes the base case, the benchmark, or the reference portfolio that other portfolios can be judged against. For HSBC, the market price is HK$89.40 per share and the market capitalization is HK$1.08 trillion. In constructing the market portfolio, HSBC's weight in the market portfolio will be equal to its market value divided by the value of all other assets included in the market portfolio.

2.2. The Capital Market Line

In the previous section, we discussed how the risk-free asset could be combined with a risky portfolio to create a capital allocation line. In this section, we discuss a specific CAL that uses the market portfolio as the optimal risky portfolio and is known as the capital market line. We also discuss the significance of the market portfolio and applications of the capital market line.

2.2.1. Passive and Active Portfolios

In the previous subsection, we arrived at three possible valuations for each share of HSBC: HK$50, HK$89.40, and HK$150. Which one is correct?

If the markets are **informationally efficient**, the price in the market, HK$89.40, is an unbiased estimate of all future discounted cash flows (recall the formula for the price of an asset). In other words, the price aggregates and reflects all information that is publicly available, and investors cannot expect to earn a return that is greater than the required rate of return for that asset. If, however, the price reflects all publicly available information and there is no way to outperform the market, then there is little point in investing time and money in evaluating HSBC to arrive at your price using your own estimates of cash flows and rates of return.

In that case, a simple and convenient approach to investing is to rely on the prices set by the market. Portfolios that are based on the assumption of unbiased market prices are referred to as passive portfolios. **Passive portfolios** most commonly replicate and track market indices, which are passively constructed on the basis of market prices and market capitalizations. Examples of market indices are the S&P 500 Index, the Nikkei 300, and the CAC 40. Passive portfolios based on market indices are called index funds and generally have low costs because no significant effort is expended in valuing securities that are included in an index.

In contrast to passive investors' reliance on market prices and index funds, active investors may not rely on market valuations. They have more confidence in their own ability to estimate cash flows, growth rates, and discount rates. Based on these estimates, they value assets and determine whether an asset is fairly valued. In an actively managed portfolio, assets that are undervalued, or have a chance of offering above-normal returns, will have a positive weight (i.e., overweight compared to the market weight in the benchmark index), whereas other assets will have a zero weight, or even a negative weight if short selling is permitted (i.e., some assets will be underweighted compared with the market weight in the benchmark index). This style of investing is called active investment management, and the portfolios are referred to as active portfolios. Most open-end mutual funds and hedge funds practice active investment management, and most analysts believe that active investing adds value. Whether these analysts are right or wrong is the subject of continuing debate.

2.2.2. What Is the "Market"?

In the previous discussion, we referred to the "market" on numerous occasions without actually defining the market. The optimal risky portfolio and the capital market line depend on the definition of the market. So what is the market?

Theoretically, the **market** includes all risky assets or anything that has value, which includes stocks, bonds, real estate, and even human capital. Not all assets are tradable, however, and not all tradable assets are investable. For example, the Taj Mahal in India is an asset but is not a tradable asset. Similarly, human capital is an asset that is not tradable. Moreover, assets may be tradable but not investable because of restrictions placed on certain kinds of investors. For example, all stocks listed on the Shanghai Stock Exchange are tradable. Class A shares, however, are available only to domestic investors, whereas Class B shares are available to both domestic and foreign investors. For investors not domiciled in China, Class A shares are not investable—that is, they are not available for investment.

If we consider all stocks, bonds, real estate assets, commodities, and so forth, probably hundreds of thousands of assets are tradable and investable. The "market" should contain as many assets as possible; we emphasize the word "possible" because it is not practical to include all assets in a single risky portfolio. Even though advancements in technology and interconnected markets have made it much easier to span the major equity markets, we are still not able to easily invest in other kinds of assets like bonds and real estate except in the most developed countries.

For the rest of this chapter, we will define the "market" quite narrowly because it is practical and convenient to do so. Typically, a local or regional stock market index is used as a proxy for the market because of active trading in stocks and because a local or regional market is most visible to the local investors. For our purposes, we will use the S&P 500 Index as the market's proxy. The S&P 500 is commonly used by analysts as a benchmark for market performance throughout the United States. It contains 500 of the largest stocks that are domiciled in the United States, and these stocks are weighted by their market capitalization (price times the number of outstanding shares).

The stocks in the S&P 500 account for approximately 80 percent of the total equity market capitalization in the United States, and because the U.S. stock markets represent about 32 percent of the world markets, the S&P 500 represents roughly 25 percent of worldwide publicly traded equity. Our definition of the market does not include non-U.S. stock markets, bond markets, real estate, and many other asset classes, and therefore, "market" return and the "market" risk premium refer to U.S. equity return and the U.S. equity risk premium, respectively. The use of this proxy, however, is sufficient for our discussion, and is relatively easy to expand to include other tradable assets.

2.2.3. The Capital Market Line (CML)

A capital allocation line includes all possible combinations of the risk-free asset and any risky portfolio. The **capital market line** is a special case of the capital allocation line, where the risky portfolio is the market portfolio. The risk-free asset is a debt security with no default risk, no inflation risk, no liquidity risk, no interest rate risk, and no risk of any other kind. U.S. Treasury bills are usually used as a proxy of the risk-free return, R_f.

The S&P 500 is a proxy of the market portfolio, which is the optimal risky portfolio. Therefore, the expected return on the risky portfolio is the expected market return, expressed as $E(R_m)$. The capital market line is shown in Exhibit 6-3, where the standard deviation (σ_p), or total risk, is on the *x*-axis and expected portfolio return, $E(R_p)$, is on the *y*-axis. Graphically, the market portfolio is the point on the Markowitz efficient frontier where a line from the risk-free asset is tangent to the Markowitz efficient frontier. All points on the interior of the Markowitz efficient frontier are inefficient portfolios in that they provide the same level of return with a higher level of risk or a lower level of return with the same amount of risk. When plotted together, the point at which the CML is tangent to the Markowitz efficient frontier is the optimal combination of risky and risk-free assets, on the basis of market prices and market capitalizations. The optimal risky portfolio is the market portfolio.

EXHIBIT 6-3 Capital Market Line

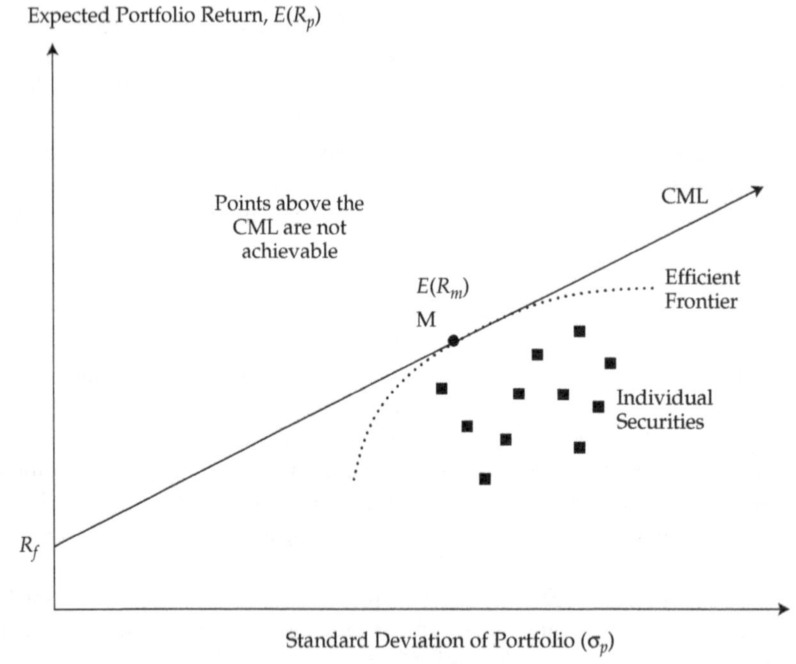

The CML's intercept on the *y*-axis is the risk-free return (R_f) because that is the return associated with zero risk. The CML passes through the point represented by the market return, $E(R_m)$. With respect to capital market theory, any point above the CML is not achievable and any point below the CML is dominated by and inferior to any point on the CML.

Note that we identify the CML and CAL as lines even though they are a combination of two assets. Unlike a combination of two risky assets, which is usually not a straight line, a combination of the risk-free asset and a risky portfolio is a straight line, as illustrated in the following by computing the combination's risk and return.

Risk and return characteristics of the portfolio represented by the CML can be computed by using the return and risk expressions for a two-asset portfolio:

$$E(R_p) = w_1 R_f + (1 - w_1)E(R_m)$$

and

$$\sigma_p = \sqrt{w_1^2\sigma_f^2 + (1 - w_1)^2\sigma_m^2 + 2w_1(1 - w_1)\text{Cov}(R_f, R_m)}$$

The proportion invested in the risk-free asset is given by w_1, and the balance is invested in the market portfolio, $(1 - w_1)$. The risk of the risk-free asset is given by σ_f, the risk of the market is given by σ_m, the risk of the portfolio is given by σ_p, and the covariance between the risk-free asset and the market portfolio is represented by $\text{Cov}(R_f, R_m)$.

By definition, the standard deviation of the risk-free asset is zero. Because its risk is zero, the risk-free asset does not co-vary or move with any other asset. Therefore, its covariance with all other assets, including the market portfolio, is zero, making the first and third terms under the square root sign zero. As a result, the portfolio return and portfolio standard deviation can be simplified and rewritten as:

$$E(R_p) = w_1 R_f + (1 - w_1)E(R_m)$$

and

$$\sigma_p = (1 - w_1)\sigma_m$$

By substitution, we can express $E(R_p)$ in terms of σ_p. Substituting for w_1, we get:

$$E(R_p) = R_f + \left(\frac{E(R_m) - R_f}{\sigma_m}\right) \times \sigma_p$$

Note that the expression is in the form of a line, $y = a + bx$. The y-intercept is the risk-free rate, and the slope of the line referred to as the market price of risk is $[E(R_m) - R_f]/\sigma_m$. The CML has a positive slope because the market's risky return is larger than the risk-free return. As the amount of the total investment devoted to the market increases—that is, as we move up the line—both standard deviation (risk) and expected return increase.

EXAMPLE 6-1 Risk and Return on the CML

Mr. Miles is a first-time investor and wants to build a portfolio using only U.S. T-bills and an index fund that closely tracks the S&P 500 Index. The T-bills have a return of 5 percent. The S&P 500 has a standard deviation of 20 percent and an expected return of 15 percent.

1. Draw the CML and mark the points where the investment in the market is 0 percent, 25 percent, 75 percent, and 100 percent.
2. Mr. Miles is also interested in determining the exact risk and return at each point.

Solution to 1: We calculate the equation for the CML as $E(R_p) = 5\% + 0.50 \times \sigma_p$ by substituting the given information into the general CML equation. The intercept of the line is 5 percent, and its slope is 0.50. We can draw the CML by arbitrarily taking any two points on the line that satisfy the previous equation.

Alternatively, the CML can be drawn by connecting the risk-free return of 5 percent on the *y*-axis with the market portfolio at (20 percent, 15 percent). The CML is shown in Exhibit 6-4.

EXHIBIT 6-4 Risk and Return on the CML

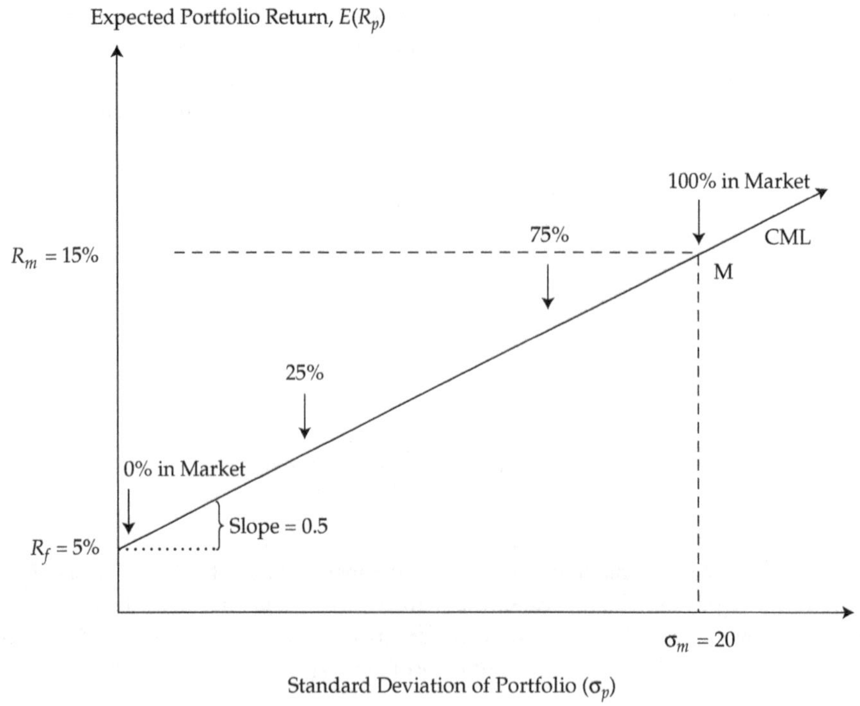

Solution to 2:

Return with 0 percent invested in the market = 5 percent, which is the risk-free return.

Standard deviation with 0 percent invested in the market = 0 percent because T-bills are not risky.

Return with 25 percent invested in the market = $(0.75 \times 5\%) + (0.25 \times 15\%) = 7.5\%$.

Standard deviation with 25 percent invested in the market = $0.25 \times 20\% = 5\%$.

Return with 75 percent invested in the market = (0.25 × 5%) + (0.75 × 15%) = 12.50%.
Standard deviation with 75 percent invested in the market = 0.75 × 20% = 15%.
Return with 100 percent invested in the market = 15 percent, which is the return on the S&P 500.
Standard deviation with 100 percent invested in the market = 20 percent, which is the risk of the S&P 500.

2.2.4. Leveraged Portfolios

In the previous example, Mr. Miles evaluated an investment of between 0 percent and 100 percent in the market and the balance in T-bills. The line connecting R_f and M (market portfolio) in Exhibit 6-4 illustrates these portfolios with their respective levels of investment. At R_f, an investor is investing all of his or her wealth into risk-free securities, which is equivalent to lending 100 percent at the risk-free rate. At point M he or she is holding the market portfolio and not lending any money at the risk-free rate. The combinations of the risk-free asset and the market portfolio, which may be achieved by the points between these two limits, are termed "lending" portfolios. In effect, the investor is lending part of his or her wealth at the risk-free rate.

If Mr. Miles is willing to take more risk, he may be able to move to the right of the market portfolio (point M in Exhibit 6-4) by borrowing money and purchasing more of Portfolio M. Assume that he is able to borrow money at the same risk-free rate of interest, R_f, at which he can invest. He can then supplement his available wealth with borrowed money and construct a borrowing portfolio. If the straight line joining R_f and M is extended to the right of point M, this extended section of the line represents borrowing portfolios. As one moves further to the right of point M, an increasing amount of borrowed money is being invested in the market. This means that there is *negative* investment in the risk-free asset, which is referred to as a *leveraged position* in the risky portfolio. The particular point chosen on the CML will depend on the individual's utility function, which, in turn, will be determined by his risk and return preferences.

EXAMPLE 6-2 Risk and Return of a Leveraged Portfolio with Equal Lending and Borrowing Rates

Mr. Miles decides to set aside a small part of his wealth for investment in a portfolio that has greater risk than his previous investments because he anticipates that the overall market will generate attractive returns in the future. He assumes that he can borrow money at 5 percent and achieve the same return on the S&P 500 as before: an expected return of 15 percent with a standard deviation of 20 percent.

Calculate his expected risk and return if he borrows 25 percent, 50 percent, and 100 percent of his initial investment amount.

Solution: The leveraged portfolio's standard deviation and return can be calculated in the same manner as before with the following equations:

$$E(R_p) = w_1 R_f + (1 - w_1) E(R_m)$$

and

$$\sigma_p = (1 - w_1)\sigma_m$$

The proportion invested in T-bills becomes negative instead of positive because Mr. Miles is borrowing money. If 25 percent of the initial investment is borrowed, $w_1 = -0.25$, and $(1 - w_1) = 1.25$, and so on.

Return with –25 percent invested in T-bills = (–0.25 × 5%) + (1.25 × 15%) = 17.5%.
Standard deviation with –25 percent invested in T-bills = 1.25 × 20% = 25%.
Return with –50 percent invested in T-bills = (–0.50 × 5%) + (1.50 × 15%) = 20.0%.
Standard deviation with –50 percent invested in T-bills = 1.50 × 20% = 30%.
Return with –100 percent invested in T-bills = (–1.00 × 5%) + (2.00 × 15%) = 25.0%.
Standard deviation with –100 percent invested in T-bills = 2.00 × 20% = 40%.

Note that negative investment (borrowing) in the risk-free asset provides a higher expected return for the portfolio but that higher return is also associated with higher risk.

2.2.4.1. Leveraged Portfolios with Different Lending and Borrowing Rates

Although we assumed that Mr. Miles can borrow at the same rate as the U.S. government, it is more likely that he will have to pay a higher interest rate than the government because his ability to repay is not as certain as that of the government. Now consider that although Mr. Miles can invest (lend) at R_f, he can borrow at only R_b, a rate that is higher than the risk-free rate.

With different lending and borrowing rates, the CML will no longer be a single straight line. The line will have a slope of $[E(R_m) - R_f]/\sigma_m$ between points R_f and M, where the lending rate is R_f, but will have a smaller slope of $[E(R_m) - R_b]/\sigma_m$ at points to the right of M, where the borrowing rate is R_b. Exhibit 6-5 illustrates the CML with different lending and borrowing rates.

The equations for the two lines are given next.

$$w_1 \geq 0 : E(R_p) = R_f + \left(\frac{E(R_m) - R_f}{\sigma_m}\right) \times \sigma_p$$

and

$$w_1 < 0 : E(R_p) = R_b + \left(\frac{E(R_m) - R_b}{\sigma_m}\right) \times \sigma_p$$

The first equation is for the line where the investment in the risk-free asset is zero or positive—that is, at M or to the left of M in Exhibit 6-5. The second equation is for the line where borrowing, or negative investment in the risk-free asset, occurs. Note that the only difference between the two equations is in the interest rates used for borrowing and lending.

EXHIBIT 6-5 CML with Different Lending and Borrowing Rates

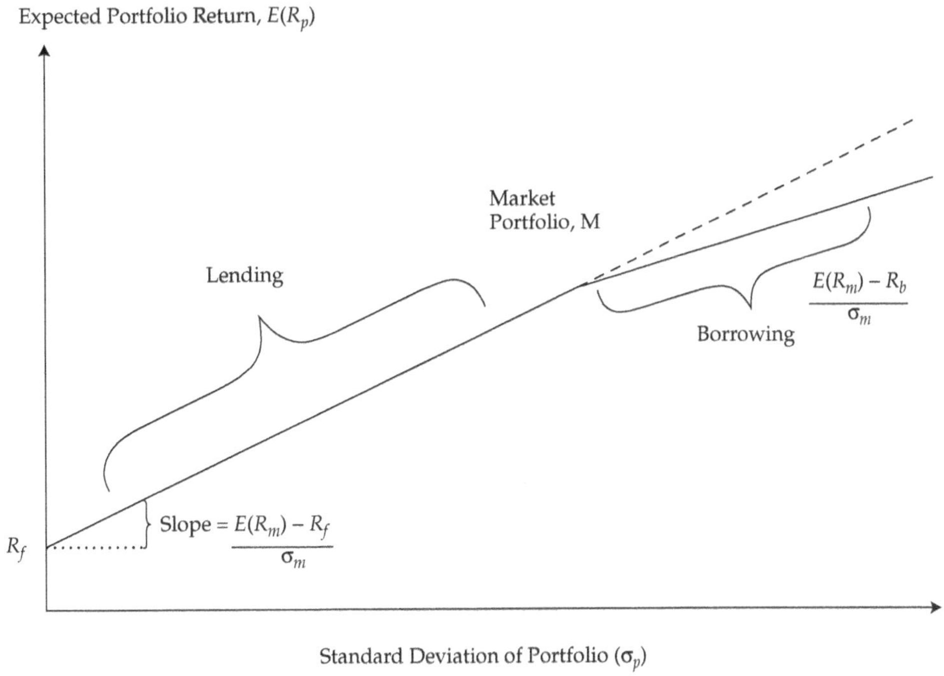

All passive portfolios will lie on the kinked CML, although the investment in the risk-free asset may be positive (lending), zero (no lending or borrowing), or negative (borrowing). Leverage allows less risk-averse investors to increase the amount of risk they take by borrowing money and investing more than 100 percent in the passive portfolio.

EXAMPLE 6-3 Leveraged Portfolio with Different Lending and Borrowing Rates

Mr. Miles approaches his broker to borrow money against securities held in his portfolio. Even though Mr. Miles' loan will be secured by the securities in his portfolio, the broker's rate for lending to customers is 7 percent. Assuming a risk-free rate of 5 percent and a market return of 15 percent with a standard deviation of 20 percent, estimate Mr. Miles' expected return and risk if he invests 25 percent and 75 percent in the risk-free asset and if he decides to borrow 25 percent and 75 percent of his initial investment and invest the money in the market.

Solution: The unleveraged portfolio's standard deviation and return are calculated using the same equations as before:

$$E(R_p) = w_1 R_f + (1 - w_1)E(R_m)$$

and

$$\sigma_p = (1 - w_1)\sigma_m$$

The results are unchanged. The slope of the line for the unleveraged portfolio is 0.50, just as before:

Return with 25 percent invested in the market = (0.75 × 5%) + (0.25 × 15%) = 7.5%.
Standard deviation with 25 percent invested in the market = 0.25 × 20% = 5%.
Return with 75 percent invested in the market = (0.25 × 5%) + (0.75 × 15%) = 12.5%.
Standard deviation with 75 percent invested in the market = 0.75 × 20% = 15%.

For the leveraged portfolio, everything remains the same except that R_f is replaced with R_b.

$$E(R_p) = w_1 R_b + (1 - w_1)E(R_m)$$

and

$$\sigma_p = (1 - w_1)\sigma_m$$

Return with –25 percent invested in T-bills = (–0.25 × 7%) + (1.25 × 15%) = 17.0%.
Standard deviation with –25 percent invested in T-bills = 1.25 × 20% = 25%.
Return with –75 percent invested in T-bills = (–0.75 × 7%) + (1.75 × 15%) = 21.0%.
Standard deviation with –75 percent invested in T-bills = 1.75 × 20% = 35%.

The risk and return of the leveraged portfolio is higher than that of the unleveraged portfolio. As Mr. Miles borrows more money to invest in the market, the expected return increases but so does the standard deviation of the portfolio. The slope of the line for the leveraged portfolio is 0.40, compared with 0.50 for the unleveraged portfolio, which means that for every 1 percent increase in risk, the investor gets a 0.40 percent increase in expected return in the leveraged part of the portfolio, compared with a 0.50 percent increase in expected return in the unleveraged part of the portfolio. Only investors who are less risk averse will choose leveraged portfolios.

3. PRICING OF RISK AND COMPUTATION OF EXPECTED RETURN

In constructing a portfolio, it is important to understand the concept of correlation and how less than perfect correlation can diversify the risk of a portfolio. As a consequence, the risk of an asset held alone may be greater than the risk of that same asset when it is part of a portfolio. Because the risk of an asset varies from one environment to another, which kind of risk should an investor consider and how should that risk be priced? This section addresses the question of pricing of risk by decomposing the total risk of a security or a portfolio into systematic and nonsystematic risk. The meaning of these risks, how they are computed, and their relevance to the pricing of assets are also discussed.

3.1. Systematic Risk and Nonsystematic Risk

Systematic risk, also known as nondiversifiable or market risk, is the risk that affects the entire market or economy. In contrast, nonsystematic risk is the risk that pertains to a single company or industry and is also known as company-specific, industry-specific, diversifiable, or idiosyncratic risk.

Systematic risk is risk that cannot be avoided and is inherent in the overall market. It is nondiversifiable because it includes risk factors that are innate within the market and affect the market as a whole. Examples of factors that constitute systematic risk include interest rates, inflation, economic cycles, political uncertainty, and widespread natural disasters. These events affect the entire market, and there is no way to avoid their effect. Systematic risk can be magnified through selection or by using leverage, or diminished by including securities that have a low correlation with the portfolio, assuming they are not already part of the portfolio.

Nonsystematic risk is risk that is local or limited to a particular asset or industry that need not affect assets outside of that asset class. Examples of nonsystematic risk could include the failure of a drug trial, major oil discoveries, or an airliner crash. All these events will directly affect their respective companies and possibly industries, but have no effect on assets that are far removed from these industries. Investors are capable of avoiding nonsystematic risk through diversification by forming a portfolio of assets that are not highly correlated with one another.

We will derive expressions for each kind of risk later in this chapter. You will see that the sum of systematic variance and nonsystematic variance equals the total variance of the security or portfolio:

$$\text{Total variance} = \text{Systematic variance} + \text{Nonsystematic variance}$$

Although the equality relationship is between variances, you will find frequent references to total risk as the sum of systematic risk and nonsystematic risk. In those cases, the statements refer to variance, not standard deviation.

3.1.1. Pricing of Risk

Pricing or valuing an asset is equivalent to estimating its expected rate of return. If an asset has a known terminal value, such as the face value of a bond, then a lower current price implies a higher future return and a higher current price implies a lower future return. The relationship between price and return can also be observed in the valuation expression shown in Section 2.1.2. Therefore, we will occasionally use price and return interchangeably when discussing the price of risk.

Consider an asset with both systematic and nonsystematic risk. Assume that both kinds of risk are priced—that is, you receive a return for both systematic risk and nonsystematic risk. What will you do? Realizing that nonsystematic risk can be diversified away, you would buy assets that have a large amount of nonsystematic risk. Once you have bought those assets with nonsystematic risk, you would diversify, or reduce that risk, by including other assets that are not highly correlated. In the process, you will minimize nonsystematic risk and eventually eliminate it altogether from your portfolio. Now, you would have a diversified portfolio with only systematic risk, yet you would be compensated for nonsystematic risk that you no longer have. Just like everyone else, you would have an incentive to take on more and more diversifiable risk because you are compensated for it even though you can get rid of it. The demand for diversifiable risk will keep increasing until its price becomes infinite and its expected return falls to zero. This means that our initial assumption of a nonzero return for diversifiable risk was incorrect and that the correct assumption is zero return for diversifiable risk. Therefore, we can assume that in an efficient market, no incremental reward can be earned for taking on diversifiable risk.

In the previous exercise we illustrated why investors should not be compensated for taking on nonsystematic risk. Therefore, investors who have nonsystematic risk must diversify it away by investing in many industries, many countries, and many asset classes. Because future returns are unknown and it is not possible to pick only winners, diversification helps in offsetting poor returns in one asset class by garnering good returns in another asset class, thereby reducing the overall risk of the portfolio. In contrast, investors must be compensated for accepting systematic risk because that risk cannot be diversified away. If investors do not receive a return commensurate with the amount of systematic risk they are taking, they will refuse to accept systematic risk.

In summary, systematic or nondiversifiable risk is priced and investors are compensated for holding assets or portfolios based only on that investment's systematic risk. Investors do not receive any return for accepting nonsystematic or diversifiable risk. Therefore, it is in the interest of risk-averse investors to hold only well-diversified portfolios.

EXAMPLE 6-4 Systematic and Nonsystematic Risk

1. Describe the systematic and nonsystematic risk components of the following assets:
   A. A risk-free asset, such as a three-month Treasury bill
   B. The market portfolio, such as the S&P 500, with total risk of 20 percent
2. Consider two assets, A and B. Asset A has total risk of 30 percent, half of which is nonsystematic risk. Asset B has total risk of 17 percent, all of which is systematic risk. Which asset should have a higher expected rate of return?

Solution to 1A: By definition, a risk-free asset has no risk. Therefore, a risk-free asset has zero systematic risk and zero nonsystematic risk.

Solution to 1B: As we mentioned earlier, a market portfolio is a diversified portfolio, one in which no more risk can be diversified away. We have also described it as an efficient portfolio. Therefore, a market portfolio does not contain any nonsystematic risk. All of its total risk, 20 percent, is systematic risk.

Solution to 2: The amount of systematic risk in Asset A is 15 percent, and the amount of systematic risk in Asset B is 17 percent. Because only systematic risk is priced or receives a return, the expected rate of return must be higher for Asset B.

3.2. Calculation and Interpretation of Beta

As previously mentioned, in order to form the market portfolio, you should combine all available assets. Knowledge of the correlations among those assets allows us to estimate portfolio risk. You also learned that a fully diversified portfolio will include all asset classes and essentially all assets in those asset classes. The work required for construction of the market portfolio is formidable. For example, for a portfolio of 1,000 assets, we will need 1,000 return estimates, 1,000 standard deviation estimates, and 499,500 (1,000 × 999 ÷ 2) correlations. Other related questions that arise with this analysis are whether we really need all 1,000 assets and what happens if there are errors in these estimates.

An alternate method of constructing an optimal portfolio is simpler and easier to implement. An investor begins with a known portfolio, such as the S&P 500, and then adds other assets one at a time on the basis of the asset's standard deviation, expected return, and impact on the portfolio's risk and return. This process continues until the addition of another asset does not have a significant impact on the performance of the portfolio. The process requires only estimates of systematic risk for each asset because investors will not be compensated for nonsystematic risk. Expected returns can be calculated by using return-generating models, as we will discuss in this section. In addition to using return-generating models, we will also decompose total variance into systematic variance and nonsystematic variance and establish a formal relationship between systematic risk and return. In the next section, we will expand on this discussion and introduce the CAPM as the preferred return-generating model.

3.2.1. Return-Generating Models

A **return-generating model** is a model that can provide an estimate of the expected return of a security given certain parameters. If systematic risk is the only relevant parameter for return, then the return-generating model will estimate the expected return for any asset given the level of systematic risk.

As with any model, the quality of estimates of expected return will depend on the quality of input estimates and the accuracy of the model. Because it is difficult to decide which factors are appropriate for generating returns, the most general form of a return-generating model is a multifactor model. A **multifactor model** allows more than one variable to be considered in estimating returns and can be built using different kinds of factors, such as macroeconomic, fundamental, and statistical factors.

Macroeconomic factor models use economic factors that are correlated with security returns. These factors may include economic growth, the interest rate, the inflation rate, productivity, employment, and consumer confidence. Past relationships with returns are estimated to obtain parameter estimates, which are, in turn, used for computing expected returns. Fundamental factor models analyze and use relationships between security returns and the company's underlying fundamentals, such as earnings, earnings growth, cash flow generation, investment in research, advertising, and number of patents. Finally, in a statistical factor model, historical and cross-sectional return data are analyzed to identify factors that explain variance or covariance in observed returns. These statistical factors, however, may or may not have an economic or fundamental connection to returns. For example, the conference to which the American football Super Bowl winner belongs, whether the American Football Conference or the National Football Conference, may be a factor in U.S. stock returns, but no obvious economic connection seems to exist between the winner's conference and U.S. stock returns. Moreover, data mining may generate many spurious factors that are devoid of any economic meaning. Because of this limitation, analysts prefer the macroeconomic and fundamental factor models for specifying and estimating return-generating models.

A general return-generating model is expressed in the following manner:

$$E(R_i) - R_f = \sum_{j=1}^{k} \beta_{ij} E(F_j) = \beta_{i1}[E(R_m) - R_f] + \sum_{j=2}^{k} \beta_{ij} E(F_j)$$

The model has k factors, $E(F_1)$, $E(F_2)$, ... $E(F_k)$. The coefficients, β_{ij}, are called factor weights or factor loadings associated with each factor. The left-hand side of the model has excess return, or return over the risk-free rate. The right-hand side provides the risk factors that would generate the return or premium required to assume that risk. We have separated out one factor, $E(R_m)$, which represents the market return. All models contain return on the market portfolio as a key factor.

3.2.1.2. Three-Factor and Four-Factor Models

Eugene Fama and Kenneth French[2] suggested that a return-generating model for stock returns should include relative size of the company and relative book-to-market value of the company in addition to beta. Fama and French found that past returns could be explained better with their model than with other models available at that time, most notably, the capital asset pricing model. Mark Carhart (1997) extended the Fama and French model by adding another factor: momentum, defined as relative past stock returns. We will discuss these models further in Section 5.3.2.

3.2.1.3. The Single-Index Model

The simplest form of a return-generating model is a single-factor linear model, in which only one factor is considered. The most common implementation is a single-index model, which uses the market factor in the following form: $E(R_i) - R_f = \beta_i[E(R_m) - R_f]$.

Although the single-index model is simple, it fits nicely with the capital market line. Recall that the CML is linear, with an intercept of R_f and a slope of $[E(R_m) - R_f]/\sigma_m$. We can rewrite the CML by moving the intercept to the left-hand side of the equation, rearranging the terms, and generalizing the subscript from p to i, for any security:

$$E(R_i) - R_f = \left(\frac{\sigma_i}{\sigma_m}\right)[E(R_m) - R_f]$$

The factor loading or factor weight, σ_i/σ_m, refers to the ratio of total security risk to total market risk. To obtain a better understanding of factor loading and to illustrate that the CML reduces to a single-index model, we decompose total risk into its components.

3.2.2. Decomposition of Total Risk for a Single-Index Model

With the introduction of return-generating models, particularly the single-index model, we are able to decompose total variance into systematic and nonsystematic variances. Instead of using expected returns in the single index, let us use realized returns. The difference between

[2]Fama and French (1992).

expected returns and realized returns is attributable to nonmarket changes, as an error term, e_i, in the second equation shown here:

$$E(R_i) - R_f = \beta_i[E(R_m) - R_f]$$

and

$$R_i - R_f = \beta_i(R_m - R_f) + e_i$$

The variance of realized returns can be expressed in the next equation (note that R_f is a constant). We can further drop the covariance term in this equation because, by definition, any nonmarket return is uncorrelated with the market. Thus, we are able to decompose total variance into systematic and nonsystematic variances in the second equation shown here:

$$\sigma_i^2 = \beta_i^2\sigma_m^2 + \sigma_e^2 + 2\text{Cov}(R_m, e_i).$$

Total variance = Systematic variance + Nonsystematic variance, which can be written as

$$\sigma_i^2 = \beta_i^2\sigma_m^2 + \sigma_e^2$$

Total risk can be expressed as

$$\sigma_i = \sqrt{\beta_i^2\sigma_m^2 + \sigma_e^2}.$$

Because nonsystematic risk is zero for well-diversified portfolios, such as the market portfolio, the total risk of a market portfolio and other similar portfolios is only systematic risk, which is $\beta_i\sigma_m$. We can now return to the CML discussed in the previous subsection and replace σ_i with $\beta_i\sigma_m$ because the CML assumes that the market is a diversified portfolio. By making this substitution for the previous equation, we get the following single-index model:

$$E(R_i) - R_f = \left(\frac{\sigma_i}{\sigma_m}\right) \times [E(R_m) - R_f] = \left(\frac{\beta_i\sigma_m}{\sigma_m}\right) \times [E(R_m) - R_f],$$

$$E(R_j) - R_f = \beta_i[E(R_m) - R_f]$$

Thus, the CML, which is only for well-diversified portfolios, is fully consistent with a single-index model.

In this section, you have learned how to decompose total variance into systematic and nonsystematic variances and how the CML is the same as a single-index model for diversified portfolios.

3.2.3. Return-Generating Models: The Market Model

The most common implementation of a single-index model is the **market model**, in which the market return is the single factor or single index. In principle, the market model and the single-index model are similar. The difference is that the market model is easier to work with and is normally used for estimating beta risk and computing abnormal returns. The market model is

$$R_i = \alpha_i + \beta_i R_m + e_i$$

To be consistent with the previous section, $\alpha_i = R_f(1 - \beta)$. The intercept, α_i, and slope coefficient, β_i, can be estimated by using historical security and market returns. These parameter estimates are then used to predict company-specific returns that a security may earn in a future period. Assume that a regression of Wal-Mart's historical daily returns on S&P 500 daily returns gives an α_i of 0.0001 and a β_i of 0.9. Thus, Wal-Mart's expected daily return $= 0.0001 + 0.90 \times R_m$. If on a given day the market rises by 1 percent and Wal-Mart's stock rises by 2 percent, then Wal-Mart's company-specific return (e_i) for that day $= R_i - E(R_i) = R_i - (\alpha_i + \beta_i R_m) = 0.02 - (0.0001 + 0.90 \times 0.01) = 0.0109$, or 1.09%. In other words, Wal-Mart earned an abnormal return of 1.09 percent on that day.

3.2.4. Calculation and Interpretation of Beta

We begin with the single-index model introduced in Section 3.2.2 using realized returns and rewrite it as

$$R_i = (1-\beta_i)R_f + \beta_i \times R_m + e_i$$

Because systematic risk depends on the correlation between the asset and the market, we can arrive at a measure of systematic risk from the covariance between R_i and R_m, where R_i is defined using the preceding equation. Note that the risk-free rate is a constant, so the first term in R_i drops out.

$$\begin{aligned}\text{Cov}(R_i, R_m) &= \text{Cov}(\beta_i \times R_m + e_i, R_m) \\ &= \beta_i \text{Cov}(R_m, R_m) + \text{Cov}(e_i, R_m) \\ &= \beta_i \sigma_m^2 + 0\end{aligned}$$

The first term is beta multiplied by the variance of R_m. Because the error term is uncorrelated with the market, the second term drops out. Then, we can rewrite the equation in terms of beta as follows:

$$\beta_i = \frac{\text{Cov}(R_i, R_m)}{\sigma_m^2} = \frac{\rho_{i,m}\sigma_i\sigma_m}{\sigma_m^2} = \frac{\rho_{i,m}\sigma_i}{\sigma_m}$$

The preceding formula shows the expression for beta, β_i, which is similar to the factor loading in the single-index model presented in Section 3.2.1. For example, if the correlation between an asset and the market is 0.70 and the asset and market have standard deviations of return of 0.25 and 0.15, respectively, the asset's beta would be (0.70)(0.25)/0.15 = 1.17. If the asset's covariance with the market and market variance were given as 0.026250 and 0.02250, respectively, the calculation would be 0.026250/0.02250 = 1.17. The beta in the market model includes an adjustment for the correlation between asset *i* and the market because the market model covers all assets whereas the CML works only for fully diversified portfolios.

As shown in the previous equation, **beta** is a measure of how sensitive an asset's return is to the market as a whole and is calculated as the covariance of the return on *i* and the return on the market divided by the variance of the market return; that expression is equivalent to the product of the asset's correlation with the market with a ratio of standard deviations of return (i.e., the ratio of the asset's standard deviation to the market's). As we have shown, beta captures an asset's systematic risk, or the portion of an asset's risk that cannot be eliminated by diversification. The variances and correlations required for the calculation of beta are usually based on historical returns.

A positive beta indicates that the return of an asset follows the general market trend, whereas a negative beta shows that the return of an asset generally follows a trend that is opposite to that of the market. In other words, a positive beta indicates that the return of an asset moves in the same direction of the market, whereas a negative beta indicates that the return of an asset moves in the opposite direction of the market. A risk-free asset's beta is zero because its covariance with other assets is zero. In other words, a beta of zero indicates that the asset's return has no correlation with movements in the market. The market's beta can be calculated by substituting σ_m for σ_i in the numerator. Also, any asset's correlation with itself is 1, so the beta of the market is 1:

$$\beta_i = \frac{\rho_{i,m}\sigma_i}{\sigma_m} = \frac{\rho_{m,m}\sigma_m}{\sigma_m} = 1.$$

Because the market's beta is 1, the average beta of stocks in the market, by definition, is 1. In terms of correlation, most stocks, especially in developed markets, tend to be highly correlated with the market, with correlations in excess of 0.70. Some U.S. broad market indices, such as the S&P 500, the Dow Jones 30, and the Nasdaq 100, have even higher correlations that are in excess of 0.90. The correlations among different sectors are also high, which shows that companies have similar reactions to the same economic and market changes. As a consequence and as a practical matter, finding assets that have a consistently negative beta because of the market's broad effects on all assets is unusual.

EXAMPLE 6-5 Calculation of Beta

Assuming that the risk (standard deviation) of the market is 25 percent, calculate the beta for the following assets:

1. A short-term U.S. Treasury bill.
2. Gold, which has a standard deviation equal to the standard deviation of the market but a zero correlation with the market.
3. A new emerging market that is not currently included in the definition of "market"—the emerging market's standard deviation is 60 percent, and the correlation with the market is –0.1.
4. An initial public offering or new issue of stock with a standard deviation of 40 percent and a correlation with the market of 0.7 (IPOs are usually very risky but have a relatively low correlation with the market).

We use the formula for beta in answering the preceding questions: $\beta_i = \dfrac{\rho_{i,m}\sigma_i}{\sigma_m}$.

Solution to 1: By definition, a short-term U.S. Treasury bill has zero risk. Therefore, its beta is zero.

Solution to 2: Because the correlation of gold with the market is zero, its beta is zero.

Solution to 3: Beta of the emerging market is $-0.1 \times 0.60 \div 0.25 = -0.24$.

Solution to 4: Beta of the initial public offering is $0.7 \times 0.40 \div 0.25 = 1.12$.

3.2.5. Estimation of Beta

An alternative and more practical approach is to estimate beta directly by using the market model described previously. The market model, $R_i = \alpha_i + \beta_i R_m + e_i$, is estimated by using regression analysis, which is a statistical process that evaluates the relationship between a given variable (the dependent variable) and one or more other (independent) variables. Historical security returns (R_i) and historical market returns (R_m) are inputs used for estimating the two parameters α_i and β_i.

Regression analysis is similar to plotting all combinations of the asset's return and the market return (R_i, R_m) and then drawing a line through all points such that it minimizes the sum of squared linear deviations from the line. Exhibit 6-6 illustrates the market model and the estimated parameters. The intercept, α_i (sometimes referred to as the constant), and the slope term, β_i, are all that is needed to define the security characteristic line and obtain beta estimates.

EXHIBIT 6-6 Beta Estimation Using a Plot of Security and Market Returns

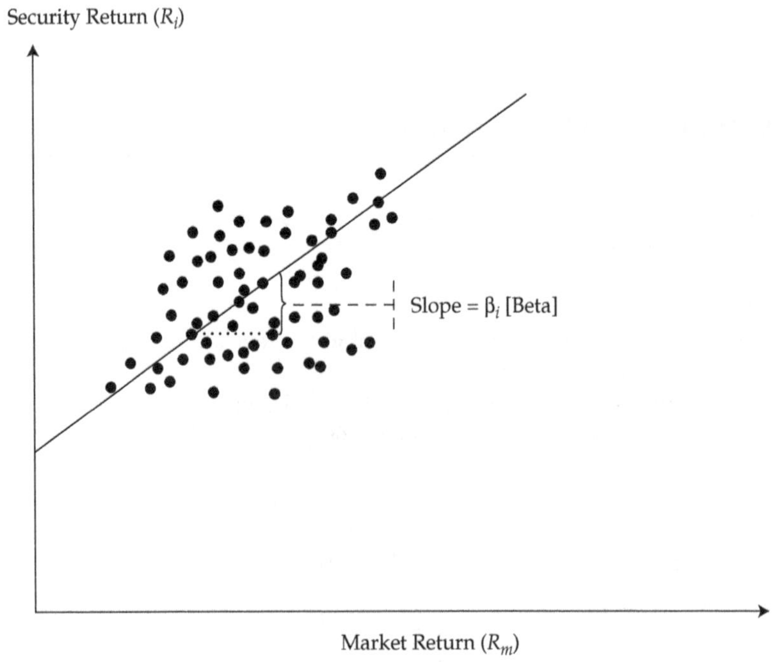

Although beta estimates are important for forecasting future levels of risk, there is much concern about their accuracy. In general, shorter periods of estimation (e.g., 12 months) represent betas that are closer to the asset's current level of systematic risk. Shorter period beta estimates, however, are also less accurate than beta estimates measured over three to five years because they may be affected by special events in that short period. Although longer period beta estimates are more accurate, they may be a poor representation of future expectations, especially if major changes in the asset have occurred. Therefore, it is necessary to recognize that estimates of beta, whether obtained through calculation or regression analysis, may or may not represent current or future levels of an asset's systematic risk.

3.2.6. Beta and Expected Return

Although the single-index model, also called the **capital asset pricing model** (CAPM), will be discussed in greater detail in the next section, we will use the CAPM in this section to estimate returns, given asset betas. The CAPM is usually written with the risk-free rate on the right-hand side:

$$E(R_i) = R_f + \beta_i[E(R_m) - R_f]$$

The model shows that the primary determinant of expected return for a security is its beta, or how well the security correlates with the market. The higher the beta of an asset, the higher its expected return will be. Assets with a beta greater than 1 have an expected return that is higher than the market return, whereas assets with a beta of less than 1 have an expected return that is less than the market return.

In certain cases, assets may require a return that is less than the risk-free return. For example, if an asset's beta is negative, the required return will be less than the risk-free rate. When combined with the market, the asset reduces the risk of the overall portfolio, which makes the asset very valuable. Insurance is one such asset. Insurance gives a positive return when the insured's wealth is reduced because of a catastrophic loss. In the absence of such a loss or when the insured's wealth is growing, the insured is required to pay an insurance premium. Thus, insurance has a negative beta and a negative expected return, but helps in reducing overall risk.

EXAMPLE 6-6 Calculation of Expected Return

1. Alpha Natural Resources (ANR), a coal producer, buys a large but privately held coal producer in China. As a result of the cross-border acquisition of a private company, ANR's standard deviation of returns is reduced from 50 percent to 30 percent and its correlation with the market falls from 0.95 to 0.75. Assume that the standard deviation and return of the market remain unchanged at 25 percent and 10 percent, respectively, and that the risk-free rate is 3 percent.
   A. Calculate the beta of ANR stock and its expected return before the acquisition.
   B. Calculate the expected return after the acquisition.

Solution to 1A: Using the formula for β_i, we can calculate β_i and then the return.

$$\beta_i = \frac{\rho_{i,m}\sigma_i}{\sigma_m} = \frac{0.95 \times 0.50}{0.25} = 1.90$$

$$E(R_i) = R_f + \beta_i[E(R_m) - R_f] = 0.03 + 1.90 \times (0.10 - 0.03) = 0.163 = 16.3\%$$

Solution to 1B: We follow the same procedure but with the after-acquisition correlation and risk.

$$\beta_i = \frac{\rho_{i,m}\sigma_i}{\sigma_m} = \frac{0.75 \times 0.30}{0.25} = 0.90$$

$$E(R_i) = R_f + \beta_i[E(R_m) - R_f] = 0.03 + 0.90 \times (0.10 - 0.03) = 0.093 = 9.3\%$$

The market risk premium is 7 percent (10% – 3%). As the beta changes, the change in the security's expected return is the market risk premium multiplied by the change in beta. In this scenario, ANR's beta decreased by 1.0, so the new expected return for ANR is 7 percentage points lower.

2. Mr. Miles observes the strong demand for iPods and iPhones and wants to invest in Apple stock. Unfortunately, Mr. Miles doesn't know the return he should expect from his investment. He has been given a risk-free rate of 3 percent, a market return of 10 percent, and Apple's beta of 1.5.
   A. Calculate Apple's expected return.
   B. An analyst looking at the same information decides that the past performance of Apple is not representative of its future performance. He decides that, given the increase in Apple's market capitalization, Apple acts much more like the market than before and thinks Apple's beta should be closer to 1.1. What is the analyst's expected return for Apple stock?

Solution to 2A:

$$E(R_i) = R_f + \beta_i[E(R_m) - R_f] = 0.03 + 1.5 \times (0.10 - 0.03) = 0.135 = 13.5\%$$

Solution to 2B:

$$E(R_i) = R_f + \beta_i[E(R_m) - R_f] = 0.03 + 1.1 \times (0.10 - 0.03) = 0.107 = 10.7\%$$

This example illustrates the lack of connection between estimation of past returns and projection into the future. Investors should be aware of the limitations of using past returns for estimating future returns.

4. THE CAPITAL ASSET PRICING MODEL

The capital asset pricing model is one of the most significant innovations in portfolio theory. The model is simple, yet powerful; is intuitive, yet profound; and uses only one factor, yet is broadly applicable. The CAPM was introduced independently by William Sharpe, John Lintner, Jack Treynor, and Jan Mossin and builds on Harry Markowitz's earlier work on diversification and modern portfolio theory.[3] The model provides a linear expected return–beta relationship that precisely determines the expected return given the beta of an asset. In doing so, it makes the transition from total risk to systematic risk, the primary determinant of expected return. Recall the following equation:

$$E(R_i) = R_f + \beta_i[E(R_m) - R_f]$$

The CAPM asserts that the expected returns of assets vary only by their systematic risk as measured by beta. Two assets with the same beta will have the same expected return irrespective of the nature of those assets. Given the relationship between risk and return, all assets are defined only by their beta risk, which we will explain as the assumptions are described.

In the remainder of this section, we will examine the assumptions made in arriving at the CAPM and the limitations those assumptions entail. Second, we will implement the CAPM through the security market line to price any portfolio or asset, both efficient and inefficient. Finally, we will discuss ways in which the CAPM can be applied to investments, valuation, and capital budgeting.

4.1. Assumptions of the CAPM

Similar to all other models, the CAPM ignores many of the complexities of financial markets by making simplifying assumptions. These assumptions allow us to gain important insights into how assets are priced without complicating the analysis. Once the basic relationships are established, we can relax the assumptions and examine how our insights need to be altered. Some of these assumptions are constraining, whereas others are benign. And other assumptions affect only a particular set of assets or only marginally affect the hypothesized relationships.

1. **Investors are risk-averse, utility-maximizing, rational individuals.**
   Risk aversion means that investors expect to be compensated for accepting risk. Note that the assumption does not require investors to have the same degree of risk aversion; it only requires that they are averse to risk. Utility maximization implies that investors want higher returns, not lower returns, and that investors always want more wealth (i.e., investors are never satisfied). Investors are understood to be rational in that they correctly evaluate and analyze available information to arrive at rational decisions. Although rational investors may use the same information to arrive at different estimates of expected risk and expected returns, homogeneity among investors (see Assumption 4) requires that investors be rational individuals.

   Risk aversion and utility maximization are generally accepted as reflecting a realistic view of the world. Yet, rationality among investors has been questioned because investors may allow their personal biases and experiences to disrupt their decision making, resulting

[3]See, for example, Markowitz (1952), Sharpe (1964), Lintner (1965a, 1965b), Treynor (1961, 1962), and Mossin (1966).

in suboptimal investments. Nonetheless, the model's results are unaffected by such irrational behavior as long as it does not affect prices in a significant manner (i.e., the trades of irrational investors cancel each other or are dominated by the trades of rational investors).

2. **Markets are frictionless, including no transaction costs and no taxes.**
   Frictionless markets allow us to abstract the analysis from the operational characteristics of markets. In doing so, we do not allow the risk–return relationship to be affected by, for example, the trading volume on the New York Stock Exchange or the difference between buying and selling prices. Specifically, frictionless markets do not have transaction costs, taxes, or any costs or restrictions on short selling. We also assume that borrowing and lending at the risk-free rate is possible.

   Transaction costs of many large institutions are negligible, and many institutions do not pay taxes. Even the presence of nonzero transaction costs, taxes, or the inability to borrow at the risk-free rate does not materially affect the general conclusions of the CAPM. Costs of short selling[4] or restrictions on short selling, however, can introduce an upward bias in asset prices, potentially jeopardizing important conclusions of the CAPM.
3. **Investors plan for the same single holding period.**
   The CAPM is a single-period model, and all investor decisions are made on the basis of that one period. The assumption of a single period is applied for convenience because working with multiperiod models is more difficult. A single-period model, however, does not allow learning to occur, and bad decisions can persist. In addition, maximizing utility at the end of a multiperiod horizon may require decisions in certain periods that may seem suboptimal when examined from a single-period perspective. Nonetheless, the single holding period does not severely limit the applicability of the CAPM to multiperiod settings.
4. **Investors have homogeneous expectations or beliefs.**
   This assumption means that all investors analyze securities in the same way using the same probability distributions and the same inputs for future cash flows. In addition, given that they are rational individuals, the investors will arrive at the same valuations. Because their valuations of all assets are identical, they will generate the same optimal risky portfolio, which we call the market portfolio.

   The assumption of homogeneous beliefs can be relaxed as long as the differences in expectations do not generate significantly different optimal risky portfolios.
5. **All investments are infinitely divisible.**
   This assumption implies that an individual can invest as little or as much as he or she wishes in an asset. This supposition allows the model to rely on continuous functions rather than on discrete jump functions. The assumption is made for convenience only and has an inconsequential impact on the conclusions of the model.
6. **Investors are price takers.**
   The CAPM assumes that there are many investors and that no investor is large enough to influence prices. Thus, investors are price takers, and we assume that security prices are unaffected by investor trades. This assumption is generally true because even though investors may be able to affect prices of small stocks, those stocks are not large enough to affect the primary results of the CAPM.

[4]**Short selling** shares involves selling shares that you do not own. Because you do not own the shares, you (or your broker) must borrow the shares before you can short sell. You sell the borrowed shares in the market hoping that you will be able to return the borrowed shares by buying them later in the market at a lower price. Brokerage houses and securities lenders lend shares to you to sell in return for a portion (or all) of the interest earned on the cash you receive for the shares that are short sold.

The main objective of these assumptions is to create a marginal investor who rationally chooses a mean–variance-efficient portfolio in a predictable fashion. We assume away any inefficiency in the market from both operational and informational perspectives. Although some of these assumptions may seem unrealistic, relaxing most of them will have only a minor influence on the model and its results. Moreover, the CAPM, with all its limitations and weaknesses, provides a benchmark for comparison and for generating initial return estimates.

4.2. The Security Market Line

In this subsection, we apply the CAPM to the pricing of securities. The **security market line** (SML) is a graphical representation of the capital asset pricing model with beta on the *x*-axis and expected return on the *y*-axis. Using the same concept as the capital market line, the SML intersects the *y*-axis at the risk-free rate of return, and the slope of this line is the market risk premium, $R_m - R_f$. Recall that the capital allocation line (CAL) and the capital market line (CML) do not apply to all securities or assets but only to efficient portfolios. In contrast, the security market line applies to any security, efficient or not. The difference occurs because the CAL and the CML use the total risk of the asset rather than its systematic risk. Because only systematic risk is priced and the CAL and the CML are based on total risk, the CAL and the CML can only be applied to those assets whose total risk is equal to systematic risk. Total risk and systematic risk are equal only for efficient portfolios because those portfolios have no diversifiable risk remaining. We are able to relax the requirement of efficient portfolios for the SML because the CAPM, which forms the basis for the SML, prices a security based only on its systematic risk, not its total risk.

EXHIBIT 6-7 The Security Market Line

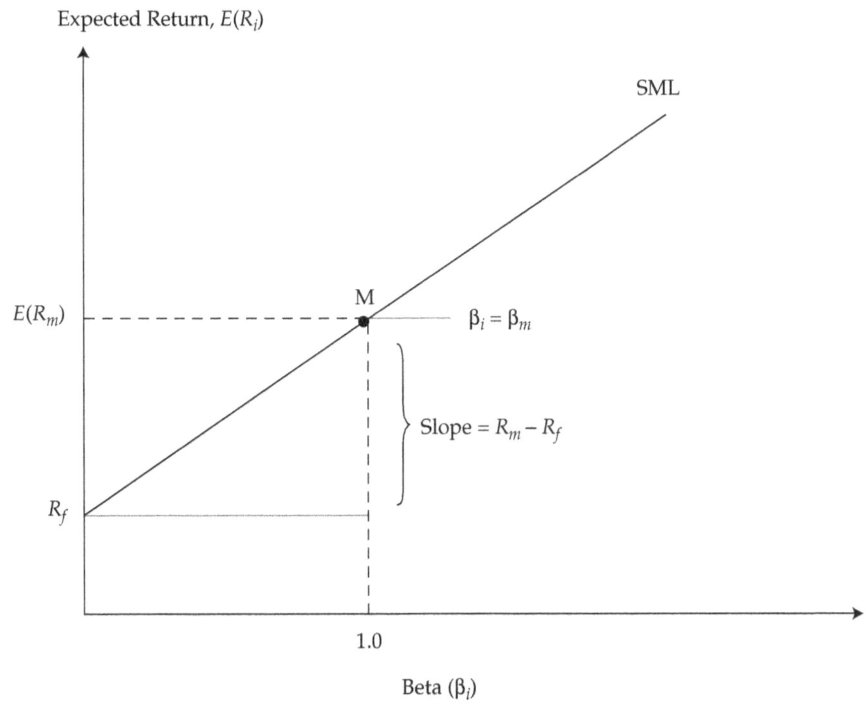

Exhibit 6-7 is a graphical representation of the CAPM, the security market line. As shown earlier in this chapter, the beta of the market is 1 (*x*-axis) and the market earns an expected return of R_m (*y*-axis). Using this line, it is possible to calculate the expected return of an asset. The next example illustrates the beta and return calculations.

EXAMPLE 6-7 Security Market Line and Expected Return

1. Suppose the risk-free rate is 3 percent, the expected return on the market portfolio is 13 percent, and its standard deviation is 23 percent. An Indian company, Bajaj Auto, has a standard deviation of 50 percent but is uncorrelated with the market. Calculate Bajaj Auto's beta and expected return.
2. Suppose the risk-free rate is 3 percent, the expected return on the market portfolio is 13 percent, and its standard deviation is 23 percent. A German company, Mueller Metals, has a standard deviation of 50 percent and a correlation of 0.65 with the market. Calculate Mueller Metal's beta and expected return.

Solution to 1: Using the formula for β_i, we can calculate β_i and then the return.

$$\beta_i = \frac{\rho_{i,m}\sigma_i}{\sigma_m} = \frac{0.0 \times 0.50}{0.23} = 0$$

$$E(R_i) = R_f + \beta_i[E(R_m) - R_f] = 0.03 + 0 \times (0.13 - 0.03) = 0.03 = 3.0\%$$

Because of its zero correlation with the market portfolio, Bajaj Auto's beta is zero. Because the beta is zero, the expected return for Bajaj Auto is the risk-free rate, which is 3 percent.

Solution to 2: Using the formula for β_i, we can calculate β_i and then the return.

$$\beta_i = \frac{\rho_{i,m}\sigma_i}{\sigma_m} = \frac{0.65 \times 0.50}{0.23} = 1.41$$

$$E(R_i) = R_f + \beta_i[E(R_m) - Rf] = 0.03 + 1.41 \times (0.13 - 0.03) = 0.171 = 17.1\%$$

Because of the high degree of correlation with the market, the beta for Mueller Metals is 1.41 and the expected return is 17.1 percent. Because Mueller Metals has systematic risk that is greater than that of the market, it has an expected return that exceeds the expected return of the market.

4.2.1. Portfolio Beta

As we stated previously, the security market line applies to all securities. But what about a combination of securities, such as a portfolio? Consider two securities, 1 and 2, with a weight of w_i in Security 1 and the balance in Security 2. The return for the two securities and return of the portfolio can be written as:

$$E(R_1) = R_f + \beta_1[E(R_m) - R_f]$$
$$E(R_2) = R_f + \beta_2[E(R_m) - R_f]$$
$$\begin{aligned} E(R_p) &= w_1 E(R_1) + w_2 E(R_2) \\ &= w_1 R_f + w_1\beta_1[E(R_m) - R_f] + w_2 R_f + w_2\beta_2[E(R_m) - R_f] \\ &= R_f + (w_1\beta_1 + w_2\beta_2)[E(R_m) - R_f] \end{aligned}$$

The last equation gives the expression for the portfolio's expected return. From this equation, we can conclude that the portfolio's beta $= w_1\beta_1 + w_2\beta_2$. In general, the portfolio beta is a weighted sum of the betas of the component securities and is given by:

$$\beta_p = \sum_{i=1}^{n} w_i\beta_i; \sum_{i=1}^{n} w_i = 1$$

The portfolio's return given by the CAPM is

$$E(R_p) = R_f + \beta_p[E(R_m) - R_f]$$

This equation shows that a linear relationship exists between the expected return of a portfolio and the systematic risk of the portfolio as measured by β_p.

EXAMPLE 6-8 Portfolio Beta and Return

You invest 20 percent of your money in the risk-free asset, 30 percent in the market portfolio, and 50 percent in RedHat, a U.S. stock that has a beta of 2.0. Given that the risk-free rate is 4 percent and the market return is 16 percent, what are the portfolio's beta and expected return?

Solution: The beta of the risk-free asset = 0, the beta of the market = 1, and the beta of RedHat is 2.0. The portfolio beta is

$$\beta_p = w_1\beta_1 + w_2\beta_2 + w_3\beta_3 = (0.20 \times 0.0) + (0.30 \times 1.0) + (0.50 \times 2.0) = 1.30$$

$$E(R_i) = R_f + \beta_i[E(R_m) - R_f] = 0.04 + 1.30 \times (0.16 - 0.04) = 0.196 = 19.6\%$$

The portfolio beta is 1.30, and its expected return is 19.6 percent.

Alternate Method: Another method for calculating the portfolio's return is to calculate individual security returns and then use the portfolio return formula (i.e., weighted average of security returns) to calculate the overall portfolio return.

Return of the risk-free asset = 4 percent.
Return of the market = 16 percent.

RedHat's return based on its beta = $0.04 + 2.0 \times (0.16 - 0.04) = 0.28$.
Portfolio return = $(0.20 \times 0.04) + (0.30 \times 0.16) + (0.50 \times 0.28) = 0.196 = 19.6\%$.

Not surprisingly, the portfolio return is 19.6 percent, as calculated in the first method.

4.3. Applications of the CAPM

The CAPM offers powerful and intuitively appealing predictions about risk and the relationship between risk and return. The CAPM is not only important from a theoretical perspective but is also used extensively in practice. In this section, we will discuss some common applications of the model. When applying these tools to different scenarios, it is important to understand that the CAPM and the SML are functions that give an indication of what the return in the market *should* be, given a certain level of risk. The actual return may be quite different from the expected return.

Applications of the CAPM include estimates of the expected return for capital budgeting, comparison of the actual return of a portfolio or portfolio manager with the CAPM return for performance appraisal, and the analysis of alternate return estimates and the CAPM returns as the basis for security selection. The applications are discussed in more detail in this section.

4.3.1. Estimate of Expected Return

Given an asset's systematic risk, the expected return can be calculated using the CAPM. Recall that the price of an asset is the sum of all future cash flows discounted at the required rate of return, where the discount rate or the required rate of return is commensurate with the asset's risk. The expected rate of return obtained from the CAPM is normally the first estimate that investors use for valuing assets, such as stocks, bonds, real estate, and other similar assets. The required rate of return from the CAPM is also used for capital budgeting and determining the economic feasibility of projects. Again, recall that when computing the net present value of a project, investments and net revenues are considered cash flows and are discounted at the required rate of return. The required rate of return, based on the project's risk, is calculated using the CAPM.

Because risk and return underlie almost all aspects of investment decision making, it is not surprising that the CAPM is used for estimating expected return in many scenarios. Other examples include calculating the cost of capital for regulated companies by regulatory commissions and setting fair insurance premiums. The next example shows an application of the CAPM to capital budgeting.

EXAMPLE 6-9 Application of the CAPM to Capital Budgeting

GlaxoSmithKline Plc is examining the economic feasibility of developing a new medicine. The initial investment in Year 1 is $500 million. The investment in Year 2 is $200 million. There is a 50 percent chance that the medicine will be developed and will be successful. If that happens, GlaxoSmithKline must spend another $100 million in

Year 3, but its income from the project in Year 3 will be \$500 million, not including the third-year investment. In Years 4, 5, and 6, it will earn \$400 million a year if the medicine is successful. At the end of Year 6, it intends to sell all rights to the medicine for \$600 million. If the medicine is unsuccessful, none of GlaxoSmithKline's investments can be salvaged. Assume that the market return is 12 percent, the risk-free rate is 2 percent, and the beta risk of the project is 2.3. All cash flows occur at the end of each year.

1. Calculate the annual cash flows using the probability of success.
2. Calculate the expected return.
3. Calculate the net present value.

Solution to 1: There is a 50 percent chance that the cash flows in Years 3–6 will occur. Taking that into account, the annual cash flows are:

Year 1: –\$500 million (outflow)
Year 2: –\$200 million (outflow)
Year 3: 50% of –\$100 million (outflow) + 50% of \$500 million = \$200 million
Year 4: 50% of \$400 million = \$200 million
Year 5: 50% of \$400 million = \$200 million
Year 6: 50% of \$400 million + 50% of \$600 million = \$500 million

Solution to 2: The expected or required return for the project can be calculated using the CAPM, which is = 0.02 + 2.3 × (0.12 – 0.02) = 0.25.

Solution to 3: The net present value is the discounted value of all cash flows:

$$
\begin{aligned}
NPV &= \sum_{t=0}^{T} \frac{CF_t}{(1+r_t)^t} \\
&= \frac{-500}{(1+0.25)} + \frac{-200}{(1+0.25)^2} + \frac{200}{(1+0.25)^3} + \frac{200}{(1+0.25)^4} \\
&\quad + \frac{200}{(1+0.25)^5} + \frac{500}{(1+0.25)^6} \\
&= -400 - 128 + 102.40 + 81.92 + 65.54 + 131.07 = -147.07
\end{aligned}
$$

Because the net present value is negative (–\$147.07 million), the project should not be accepted by GlaxoSmithKline.

4.3.2. Portfolio Performance Evaluation

Institutional money managers, pension fund managers, and mutual fund managers manage large amounts of money for other people. Are they doing a good job? How does their performance compare with a passively managed portfolio—that is, one in which the investor holds just the market portfolio? Evaluating the performance of a portfolio is of interest to all investors and money managers. Because active management costs significantly more than passive management, we expect active managers to perform better than passive managers or at least to cover the difference in expenses. For example, Fidelity's passively managed Spartan 500 Index fund has an expense ratio of only 0.10 percent whereas Fidelity's actively managed Contrafund has an expense ratio of 0.94 percent. Investors need a method for determining whether the manager of the Contrafund is worth the extra 0.84 percent in expenses.

In this chapter, **performance evaluation** is based only on the CAPM. However, it is easy to extend this analysis to multifactor models that may include industry or other special factors. Four ratios are commonly used in performance evaluation.

4.3.2.1. Sharpe and Treynor Ratios

Performance has two components, risk and return. Although return maximization is a laudable objective, comparing just the return of a portfolio with that of the market is not sufficient. Because investors are risk averse, they will require compensation for higher risk in the form of higher returns. A commonly used measure of performance is the **Sharpe ratio**, which is defined as the portfolio's risk premium divided by its risk:

$$\text{Sharpe ratio} = \frac{R_p - R_f}{\sigma_p}$$

Recalling the CAL from earlier in the chapter, one can see that the Sharpe ratio, also called the reward-to-variability ratio, is simply the slope of the capital allocation line; the greater the slope, the better the asset. Note, however, that the ratio uses the *total risk* of the portfolio, not its systematic risk. The use of total risk is appropriate if the portfolio is an investor's total portfolio—that is, the investor does not own any other assets. Sharpe ratios of the market and other portfolios can also be calculated in a similar manner. The portfolio with the highest Sharpe ratio has the best performance, and the one with the lowest Sharpe ratio has the worst performance, provided that the numerator is positive for all comparison portfolios. If the numerator is negative, the ratio will be less negative for riskier portfolios, resulting in incorrect rankings.

The Sharpe ratio, however, suffers from two limitations. First, it uses total risk as a measure of risk when only systematic risk is priced. Second, the ratio itself (e.g., 0.2 or 0.3) is not informative. To rank portfolios, the Sharpe ratio of one portfolio must be compared with the Sharpe ratio of another portfolio. Nonetheless, the ease of computation makes the Sharpe ratio a popular tool.

The **Treynor ratio** is a simple extension of the Sharpe ratio and resolves the Sharpe ratio's first limitation by substituting beta risk for total risk. The Treynor ratio is

$$\text{Treynor ratio} = \frac{R_p - R_f}{\beta_p}$$

Just like the Sharpe ratio, the numerators must be positive for the Treynor ratio to give meaningful results. In addition, the Treynor ratio does not work for negative-beta assets—that is, the denominator must also be positive for obtaining correct estimates and rankings. Although both the Sharpe and Treynor ratios allow for ranking of portfolios, neither ratio gives any information about the economic significance of differences in performance. For example, assume the Sharpe ratio of one portfolio is 0.75 and the Sharpe ratio for another portfolio is 0.80. The second portfolio is superior, but is that difference meaningful? In addition, we do not know whether either of the portfolios is better than the passive market portfolio. The remaining two measures, M^2 and Jensen's alpha, attempt to address that problem by comparing portfolios while also providing information about the extent of the overperformance or underperformance.

4.3.2.2. M-Squared (M^2)

M^2 was created by Franco Modigliani and his granddaughter, Leah Modigliani—hence the name *M*-squared. M^2 is an extension of the Sharpe ratio in that it is based on *total risk*, not beta risk. The idea behind the measure is to create a portfolio (P′) that mimics the risk of a market portfolio—that is, the mimicking portfolio (P′) alters the weights in Portfolio P and the risk-free asset until Portfolio P′ has the same total risk as the market (i.e., $\sigma_p' = \sigma_m$). Because the risks of the mimicking portfolio and the market portfolio are the same, we can obtain the return on the mimicking portfolio and directly compare it with the market return. The weight in Portfolio P, w_p, that makes the risks equal can be calculated as follows:

$$\sigma_{p'} = w_p\sigma_p + (1-w_p)\sigma_{Rf} = \sigma_m = w_p\sigma_p, \text{which gives}$$

$$w_p = \frac{\sigma_m}{\sigma_p}$$

Because the correlation between the market and the risk-free asset is zero, we get w_p as the weight invested in Portfolio P and the balance invested in the risk-free asset. The risk-adjusted return for the mimicking portfolio is:

$$R_{p'} = w_pR_p + (1-w_p)R_f = \left(\frac{\sigma_m}{\sigma_p}\right)R_p + \left(1-\frac{\sigma_m}{\sigma_p}\right)R_f$$

$$= R_f + \left(\frac{\sigma_m}{\sigma_p}\right)(R_p-R_f) = R_f + \sigma_m\left(\frac{R_p-R_f}{\sigma_p}\right)$$

The return of the mimicking portfolio based on excess returns is $(R_p-R_f)\frac{\sigma_m}{\sigma_p}$.[5] The difference in the return of the mimicking portfolio and the market return is M^2, which can be expressed as a formula:

$$M^2 = (R_p-R_f)\frac{\sigma_m}{\sigma_p} - (R_m-R_f)$$

M^2 gives us rankings that are identical to those of the Sharpe ratio. They are easier to interpret, however, because they are in percentage terms. A portfolio that matches the performance of the market will have an M^2 of zero, whereas a portfolio that outperforms the market will have an M^2 that is positive. By using M^2, we are not only able to determine the rank of a portfolio but also which, if any, of our portfolios beat the market on a risk-adjusted basis.

[5]Note that the last term within parentheses on the right-hand side of the previous equation is the Sharpe ratio.

4.3.2.3. Jensen's Alpha

Like the Treynor ratio, Jensen's alpha is based on systematic risk. We can measure a portfolio's systematic risk by estimating the market model, which is done by regressing the portfolio's daily return on the market's daily return. The coefficient on the market return is an estimate of the beta risk of the portfolio (see Section 3.2.5 for more details). We can calculate the risk-adjusted return of the portfolio using the beta of the portfolio and the CAPM. The difference between the actual portfolio return and the calculated risk-adjusted return is a measure of the portfolio's performance relative to the market portfolio and is called Jensen's alpha. By definition, α_m of the market is zero. Jensen's alpha is also the vertical distance from the SML measuring the excess return for the same risk as that of the market and is given by

$$\alpha_p = R_p - [R_f + \beta_p(R_m - R_f)]$$

If the period is long, it may contain different risk-free rates, in which case R_f represents the average risk-free rate. Furthermore, the returns in the equation are all realized actual returns. The sign of α_p indicates whether the portfolio has outperformed the market. If α_p is positive, then the portfolio has outperformed the market; if α_p is negative, the portfolio has underperformed the market. Jensen's alpha is commonly used for evaluating most institutional managers, pension funds, and mutual funds. Values of alpha can be used to rank different managers and the performance of their portfolios, as well as the magnitude of underperformance or overperformance. For example, if a portfolio's alpha is 2 percent and another portfolio's alpha is 5 percent, the second portfolio has outperformed the first portfolio by 3 percentage points and the market by 5 percentage points. Jensen's alpha is the maximum amount that you should be willing to pay the manager to manage your money.

EXAMPLE 6-10 Portfolio Performance Evaluation

A British pension fund has employed three investment managers, each of whom is responsible for investing in one-third of all asset classes so that the pension fund has a well-diversified portfolio. Information about the managers is given next.

Manager	Return	σ	β
X	10%	20%	1.1
Y	11	10	0.7
Z	12	25	0.6
Market (M)	9	19	
Risk-free rate (R_f)	3		

Calculate the expected return, Sharpe ratio, Treynor ratio, M^2, and Jensen's alpha. Analyze your results and plot the returns and betas of these portfolios.

Solution: In each case, the calculations are shown only for Manager X. All answers are tabulated next. Note that the β of the market is 1 and the σ and β of the risk-free rate are both zero.

Expected return: $E(R_X) = R_f + \beta_X[E(R_m) - R_f] = 0.03 + 1.10 \times (0.09 - 0.03) = 0.096 = 9.6\%$.

$$\text{Sharpe ratio} = \frac{R_X - R_f}{\sigma_X} = \frac{0.10 - 0.03}{0.20} = 0.35$$

$$\text{Treynor ratio} = \frac{R_X - R_f}{\beta_X} = \frac{0.10 - 0.03}{1.1} = 0.064$$

$$M^2 = (R_X - R_f)\frac{\sigma_m}{\sigma_X} - (R_m - R_f) = (0.10 - 0.03)\frac{0.19}{0.20} - (0.09 - 0.03) = 0.0065 = 0.65\%$$

$$\alpha_X = R_X - [R_f + \beta_X(R_m - R_f)] = 0.10 - (0.03 + 1.1 \times 0.06) = 0.004 = 0.40\%$$

EXHIBIT 6-8 Measures of Portfolio Performance Evaluation

Manager	R_i	σ_i	β_i	$E(R_i)$	Sharpe Ratio	Treynor Ratio	M^2	α_i
X	10.0%	20.0%	1.10	9.6%	0.35	0.064	0.65%	0.40%
Y	11.0	10.0	0.70	7.2	0.80	0.114	9.20	3.80
Z	12.0	25.0	0.60	6.6	0.36	0.150	0.84	5.40
M	9.0	19.0	1.00	9.0	0.32	0.060	0.00	0.00
R_f	3.0	0.0	0.00	3.0	–	–	–	0.00

Let us begin with an analysis of the risk-free asset. Because the risk-free asset has zero risk and a beta of zero, calculating the Sharpe ratio, Treynor ratio, or M^2 is not possible because they all require the portfolio risk in the denominator. The risk-free asset's alpha, however, is zero. Turning to the market portfolio, we see that the absolute measures of performance, the Sharpe ratio and the Treynor ratio, are positive for the market portfolio. These ratios are positive as long as the portfolio earns a return that is in excess of that of the risk-free asset. M^2 and α_i are performance measures relative to the market, so they are both equal to zero for the market portfolio.

All three managers have Sharpe and Treynor ratios greater than those of the market, and all three managers' M^2 and α_i are positive; therefore, the pension fund should be satisfied with their performance. Among the three managers, Manager X has the worst performance, irrespective of whether total risk or systematic risk is considered for measuring performance. The relative rankings are depicted in Exhibit 6-9.

EXHIBIT 6-9 Ranking of Portfolios by Performance Measure

Rank	Sharpe Ratio	Treynor Ratio	M^2	α_i
1	Y	Z	Y	Z
2	Z	Y	Z	Y
3	X	X	X	X
4	M	M	M	M
5	–	–	–	R_f

Comparing Y and Z, we can observe that Y performs much better than Z when total risk is considered. Y has a Sharpe ratio of 0.80, compared with a Sharpe ratio of 0.36 for Z. Similarly, M^2 is higher for Y (9.20 percent) than for Z (0.84 percent). In contrast, when systematic risk is used, Z outperforms Y. The Treynor ratio is higher for Z (0.150) than for Y (0.114), and Jensen's alpha is also higher for Z (5.40 percent) than for Y (3.80 percent), which indicates that Y has done a better job of generating excess return relative to total risk than Z because Y has diversified away more of the nonsystematic risk than Z.

Exhibit 6-10 confirms these observations in that all three managers outperform the benchmark because all three points lie above the SML. Among the three portfolios, Z performs the best when we consider risk-adjusted returns because it is the point in Exhibit 6-10 that is located northwest relative to the portfolios X and Y.

EXHIBIT 6-10 Portfolios along the SML

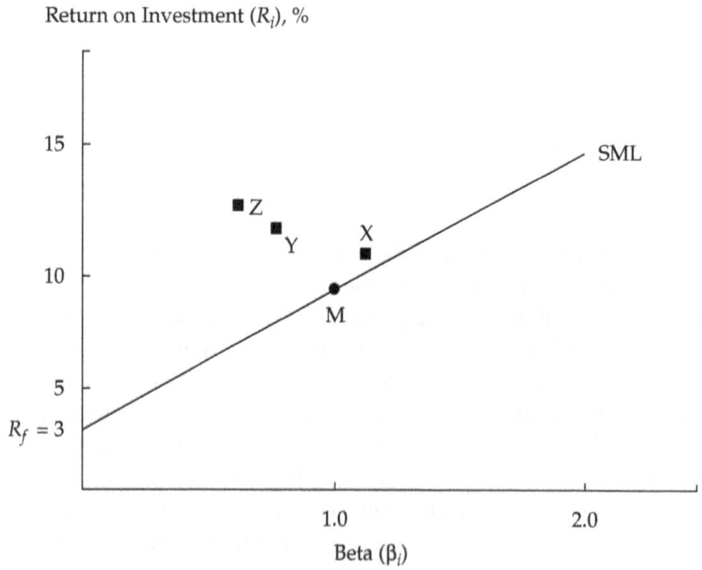

When do we use total risk performance measures like the Sharpe ratio and M^2, and when do we use beta risk performance measures like the Treynor ratio and Jensen's alpha? Total risk is relevant for an investor when he or she holds a portfolio that is not fully diversified, which is not a desirable portfolio. In such cases, the Sharpe ratio and M^2 are appropriate performance measures. Thus, if the pension fund were to choose only one fund manager to manage all its assets, it should choose Manager Y. Performance measures relative to beta risk—Treynor ratio and Jensen's alpha—are relevant when the investor holds a well-diversified portfolio with negligible diversifiable risk. In other words, if the pension fund is well diversified and only the systematic risk of the portfolio matters, the fund should choose Manager Z.

The measures of performance evaluation assume that the benchmark market portfolio is the correct portfolio. As a result, an error in the benchmark may cause the results to be misleading. For example, evaluating a real estate fund against the S&P 500 is incorrect because real estate has different characteristics than equity. In addition to errors in benchmarking, errors could occur in the measurement of risk and return of the market portfolio and the portfolios being evaluated. Finally, many estimates are based on historical data. Any projections based on such estimates assume that this level of performance will continue in the future.

4.3.3. Security Characteristic Line

Similar to the SML, we can draw a **security characteristic line** (SCL) for a security. The SCL is a plot of the excess return of the security on the excess return of the market. In Exhibit 6-11, Jensen's alpha is the intercept and the beta is the slope. The equation of the line can be obtained by rearranging the terms in the expression for Jensen's alpha and replacing the subscript p with i:

$$R_i - R_f = \alpha_i + \beta_i(R_m - R_f)$$

As an example, the SCL is drawn in Exhibit 6-11 using Manager X's portfolio from Exhibit 6-8. The security characteristic line can also be estimated by regressing the excess security return, $R_i - R_f$, on the excess market return, $R_m - R_f$.

4.3.4. Security Selection

When discussing the CAPM, we assumed that investors have homogeneous expectations and are rational, risk-averse, utility-maximizing investors. With these assumptions, we were able to state that all investors assign the same value to all assets and, therefore, have the same optimal risky portfolio, which is the market portfolio. In other words, we assumed that there is commonality among beliefs about an asset's future cash flows and the required rate of return. Given the required rate of return, we can discount the future cash flows of the asset to arrive at its current value, or price, which is agreed upon by all or most investors.

In this section, we introduce heterogeneity in beliefs of investors. Because investors are price takers, it is assumed that such heterogeneity does not significantly affect the market price of an asset. The difference in beliefs can relate to future cash flows, the systematic risk of the asset, or both. Because the current price of an asset is the discounted value of the future cash flows, the difference in beliefs could result in an investor-estimated price that is different from the CAPM-calculated price. The CAPM-calculated price is the current market price because it reflects the beliefs of all other investors in the market. If the investor-estimated current price is

EXHIBIT 6-11 The Security Characteristic Line

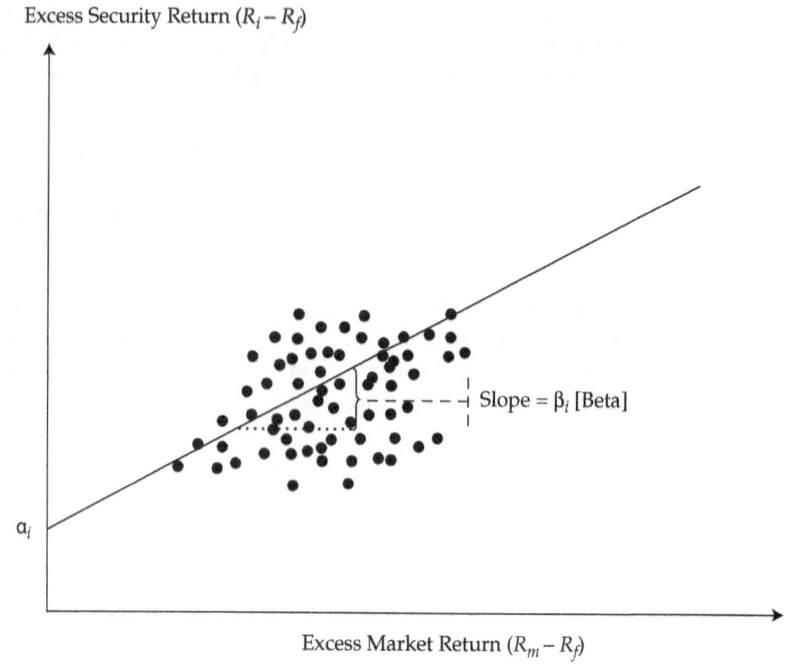

higher (lower) than the market price, the asset is considered undervalued (overvalued). Therefore, the CAPM is an effective tool for determining whether an asset is undervalued or overvalued and whether an investor should buy or sell the asset.

Although portfolio performance evaluation is backward looking and security selection is forward looking, we can apply the concepts of portfolio evaluation to security selection. The best measure to apply is Jensen's alpha because it uses systematic risk and is meaningful even on an absolute basis. A positive Jensen's alpha indicates a superior security, whereas a negative Jensen's alpha indicates a security that is likely to underperform the market when adjusted for risk.

Another way of presenting the same information is with the security market line. Potential investors can plot a security's expected return and beta against the SML and use this relationship to decide whether the security is overvalued or undervalued in the market.[6] Exhibit 6-12 shows a number of securities along with the SML. All securities that reflect the consensus market view are points directly on the SML (i.e., properly valued). If a point representing the estimated return of an asset is above the SML (Points A and C), the asset has a low level of risk relative to the amount of expected return and would be a good choice for investment. In contrast, if the point representing a particular asset is below the SML (Point

[6]In this chapter, we do not consider transaction costs, which are important whenever deviations from a passive portfolio are considered. Thus, the magnitude of undervaluation or overvaluation should be considered in relation to transaction costs prior to making an investment decision.

B), the stock is considered overvalued. Its return does not compensate for the level of risk and should not be considered for investment. Of course, a short position in Asset B can be taken if short selling is permitted.

EXHIBIT 6-12 Security Selection Using SML

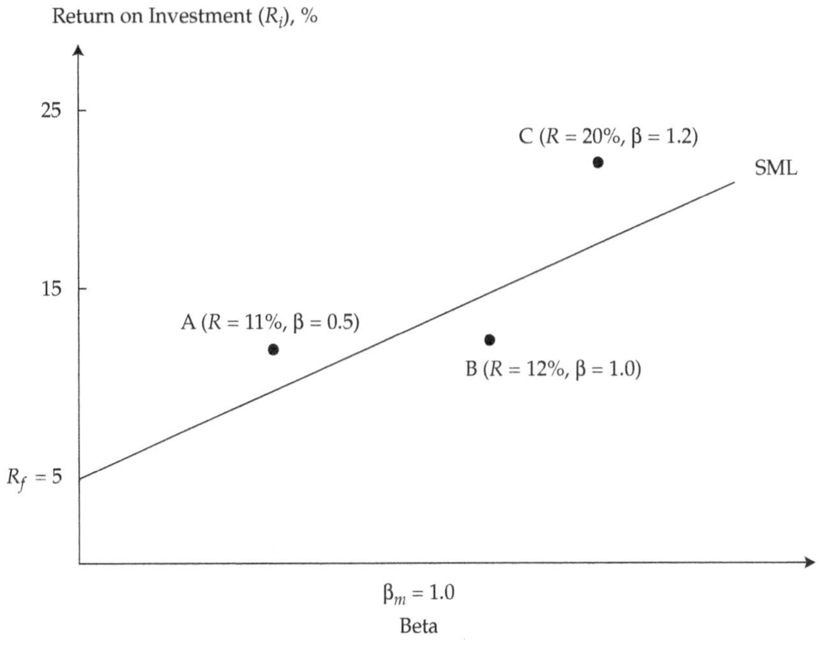

4.3.5. Constructing a Portfolio

Based on the CAPM, investors should hold a combination of the risk-free asset and the market portfolio. The true market portfolio consists of a large number of securities, and an investor would have to own all of them in order to be completely diversified. Because owning all existing securities is not practical, in this section we will consider an alternate method of constructing a portfolio that may not require a large number of securities and will still be sufficiently diversified. Exhibit 6-13 shows the reduction in risk as we add more and more securities to a portfolio. As can be seen from the exhibit, much of the nonsystematic risk can be diversified away in as few as 30 securities. These securities, however, should be randomly selected and represent different asset classes for the portfolio to effectively diversify risk. Otherwise, one may be better off using an index (e.g., the S&P 500 for a diversified large-cap equity portfolio and other indices for other asset classes).

Let's begin constructing the optimal portfolio with a portfolio of securities like the S&P 500. Although the S&P 500 is a portfolio of 500 securities, it is a good starting point because it is readily available as a single security for trading. In contrast, it represents only the large corporations that are traded on the U.S. stock markets and, therefore, does not encompass the global market entirely. Because the S&P 500 is the base portfolio, however, we treat it as the market for the CAPM.

EXHIBIT 6-13 Diversification with Number of Stocks

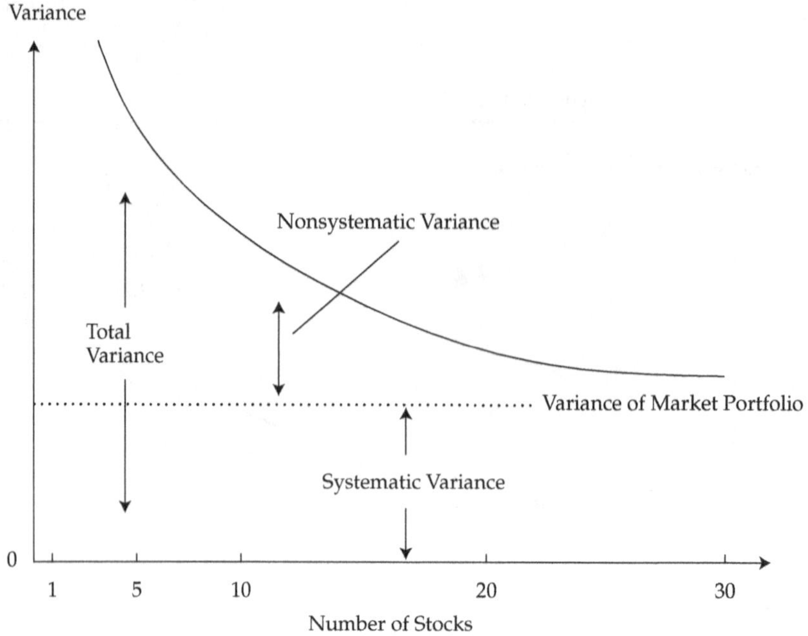

Any security not included in the S&P 500 can be evaluated to determine whether it should be integrated into the portfolio. That decision is based on the α_i of the security, which is calculated using the CAPM with the S&P 500 as the market portfolio. Note that security i may not necessarily be priced incorrectly for it to have a nonzero α_i; α_i can be positive merely because it is not well correlated with the S&P 500 and its return is sufficient for the amount of systematic risk it contains. For example, assume a new stock market, ABC, opens to foreign investors only and is being considered for inclusion in the portfolio. We estimate ABC's model parameters relative to the S&P 500 and find an α_i of approximately 3 percent, with a β_i of 0.60. Because α_i is positive, ABC should be added to the portfolio. Securities with a significantly negative α_i may be short sold to maximize risk-adjusted return. For convenience, however, we will assume that negative positions are not permitted in the portfolio.

In addition to the securities that are correctly priced but enter the portfolio because of their risk–return superiority, securities already in the portfolio (S&P 500) may be undervalued or overvalued based on investor expectations that are incongruent with the market. Securities in the S&P 500 that are overvalued (negative α_i) should be dropped from the S&P 500 portfolio, if it is possible to exclude individual securities, and positions in securities in the S&P 500 that are undervalued (positive α_i) should be increased.

This brings us to the next question: What should the relative weight of securities in the portfolio be? Because we are concerned with maximizing risk-adjusted return, securities with a higher α_i should have a higher weight, and securities with greater nonsystematic risk should be given less weight in the portfolio. A complete analysis of portfolio optimization is beyond the scope of this chapter, but the following principles are helpful. The weight in each nonmarket security should be proportional to $\frac{\alpha_i}{\sigma_{ei}^2}$, where the denominator is the nonsystematic variance of security i. The total weight of nonmarket securities in the portfolio is proportional to

$$\frac{\sum_{i=1}^{N} w_i \alpha_i}{\sum_{i=1}^{N} w_i^2 \sigma_{ei}^2}$$

The weight in the market portfolio is a function of

$$\frac{E(R_m)}{\sigma_m^2}$$

The information ratio, $\frac{\alpha_i}{\sigma_{ei}}$ (i.e., alpha divided by nonsystematic risk), measures the abnormal return per unit of risk added by the security to a well-diversified portfolio. The larger the information ratio is, the more valuable the security.

EXAMPLE 6-11 Optimal Investor Portfolio with Heterogeneous Beliefs

A Japanese investor is holding the Nikkei 225 index, which is her version of the market. She thinks that three stocks, P, Q, and R, which are not in the Nikkei 225, are undervalued and should form a part of her portfolio. She has the following information about the stocks, the Nikkei 225, and the risk-free rate (the information is given as expected return, standard deviation, and beta):

P: 15%, 30%, 1.5
Q: 18%, 25%, 1.2
R: 16%, 23%, 1.1
Nikkei 225: 12%, 18%, 1.0
Risk-free rate: 2%, 0%, 0.0

1. Calculate Jensen's alpha for P, Q, and R.
2. Calculate nonsystematic variance for P, Q, and R.
3. Should any of the three stocks be included in the portfolio? If so, which stock should have the highest weight in the portfolio?

Solution to 1:
Stock P's α: $R_i - [R_f + \beta_i(R_m - R_f)] = 0.15 - (0.02 + 1.5 \times 0.10) = -0.02$.
Stock Q's α: $R_i - [R_f + \beta_i(R_m - R_f)] = 0.18 - (0.02 + 1.2 \times 0.10) = 0.04$.
Stock R's α: $R_i - [R_f + \beta_i(R_m - R_f)] = 0.16 - (0.02 + 1.1 \times 0.10) = 0.03$.

Solution to 2: Total variance = Systematic variance + Nonsystematic variance. From Section 3.2.2, we write the equation as $\sigma_{ei}^2 = \sigma_i^2 - \beta_i^2\sigma_m^2$.

$$\begin{aligned}\text{Stock P's nonsystematic variance} &= (0.30 \times 0.30) - (1.5 \times 1.5 \times 0.18 \times 0.18)\\ &= 0.09 - 0.0729 = 0.0171\end{aligned}$$

$$\text{Stock Q's nonsystematic variance} = (0.25 \times 0.25) - (1.2 \times 1.2 \times 0.18 \times 0.18)$$
$$= 0.0625 - 0.0467 = 0.0158.$$
$$\text{Stock R's nonsystematic variance} = (0.23 \times 0.23) - (1.1 \times 1.1 \times 0.18 \times 0.18)$$
$$= 0.0529 - 0.0392 = 0.0137.$$

Solution to 3: Stock P has a negative α and should not be included in the portfolio, unless a negative position can be assumed through short selling. Stocks Q and R have a positive α; therefore, they should be included in the portfolio with positive weights.

The relative weight of Q is 0.04/0.0158 = 2.53.
The relative weight of R is 0.03/0.0137 = 2.19.

Stock Q will have the largest weight among the nonmarket securities to be added to the portfolio. In relative terms, the weight of Q will be 15.5 percent greater than the weight of R (2.53/2.19 = 1.155). As the number of securities increases, the analysis becomes more complex. However, the contribution of each additional security toward improvement in the risk–return trade-off will decrease and eventually disappear, resulting in a well-diversified portfolio.

5. BEYOND THE CAPITAL ASSET PRICING MODEL

In general, return-generating models allow us to estimate an asset's return given its characteristics, where the asset characteristics required for estimating the return are specified in the model. Estimating an asset's return is important for investment decision making. These models are also important as a benchmark for evaluating portfolio, security, or manager performance. The return-generating models were briefly introduced in Section 3.2.1, and one of those models, the capital asset pricing model, was discussed in detail in Section 4.

The purpose of this section is to make readers aware that, although the CAPM is an important concept and model, the CAPM is not the only return-generating model. In this section, we revisit and highlight the limitations of the CAPM and preview return-generating models that address some of those limitations.

5.1. The CAPM

The CAPM is a model that simplifies a complex investment environment and allows investors to understand the relationship between risk and return. Although the CAPM affords us this insight, its assumptions can be constraining and unrealistic, as mentioned in Section 5.2. In Section 5.3, we discuss other models that have been developed along with their own limitations.

5.2. Limitations of the CAPM

The CAPM is subject to theoretical and practical limitations. Theoretical limitations are inherent in the structure of the model, whereas practical limitations are those that arise in implementing the model.

5.2.1. Theoretical Limitations of the CAPM

- Single-factor model: Only systematic risk or beta risk is priced in the CAPM. Thus, the CAPM states that no other investment characteristics should be considered in estimating returns. As a consequence, it is prescriptive and easy to understand and apply, although it is very restrictive and inflexible.
- Single-period model: The CAPM is a single-period model that does not consider multi-period implications or investment objectives of future periods, which can lead to myopic and suboptimal investment decisions. For example, it may be optimal to default on interest payments in the current period to maximize current returns, but the consequences may be negative in the next period. A single-period model like the CAPM is unable to capture factors that vary over time and span several periods.

5.2.2. Practical Limitations of the CAPM

In addition to the theoretical limitations, implementation of the CAPM raises several practical concerns, some of which are listed next.

- Market portfolio: The true market portfolio according to the CAPM includes all assets, financial and nonfinancial, which means that it also includes many assets that are not investable, such as human capital and assets in closed economies. Richard Roll[7] noted that one reason the CAPM is not testable is that the true market portfolio is unobservable.
- Proxy for a market portfolio: In the absence of a true market portfolio, market participants generally use proxies. These proxies, however, vary among analysts, the country of the investor, and so on. and generate different return estimates for the same asset, which is impermissible in the CAPM.
- Estimation of beta risk: A long history of returns (three to five years) is required to estimate beta risk. The historical state of the company, however, may not be an accurate representation of the current or future state of the company. More generally, the CAPM is an *ex ante* model, yet it is usually applied using *ex post* data. In addition, using different periods for estimation results in different estimates of beta. For example, a three-year beta is unlikely to be the same as a five-year beta, and a beta estimated with daily returns is unlikely to be the same as the beta estimated with monthly returns. Thus, we are likely to estimate different returns for the same asset depending on the estimate of beta risk used in the model.
- The CAPM is a poor predictor of returns: If the CAPM is a good model, its estimate of asset returns should be closely associated with realized returns. However, empirical support for the CAPM is weak.[8] In other words, tests of the CAPM show that asset returns are not determined only by systematic risk. Poor predictability of returns when using the CAPM is a serious limitation because return-generating models are used to estimate future returns.
- Homogeneity in investor expectations: The CAPM assumes that homogeneity exists in investor expectations for the model to generate a single optimal risky portfolio (the market) and a single security market line. Without this assumption, there will be numerous optimal risky portfolios and numerous security market lines. Clearly, investors can process the same information in a rational manner and arrive at different optimal risky portfolios.

---

[7]Roll (1977).

[8]See, for example, Fama and French (1992).

5.3. Extensions to the CAPM

Given the limitations of the CAPM, it is not surprising that other models have been proposed to address some of these limitations. These new models are not without limitations of their own, which we will mention while discussing the models. We divide the models into two categories and provide one example of each type.

5.3.1. Theoretical Models

Theoretical models are based on the same principle as the CAPM but expand the number of risk factors. The best example of a theoretical model is the **arbitrage pricing theory** (APT), which was developed by Stephen Ross.[9] Like the CAPM, APT proposes a linear relationship between expected return and risk:

$$E(R_p) = R_F + \lambda_1\beta_{p,1} + \cdots + \lambda_K\beta_{p,K}$$

where

$E(R_p)$ = the expected return of portfolio p
R_F = the risk-free rate
λ_j = the risk premium (expected return in excess of the risk-free rate) for factor j
$\beta_{p,j}$ = the sensitivity of the portfolio to factor j
K = the number of risk factors

Unlike the CAPM, however, APT allows numerous risk factors—as many as are relevant to a particular asset. Moreover, other than the risk-free rate, the risk factors need not be common and may vary from one asset to another. A no-arbitrage condition in asset markets is used to determine the risk factors and estimate betas for the risk factors.

Although it is theoretically elegant, flexible, and superior to the CAPM, APT is not commonly used in practice because it does not specify any of the risk factors and it becomes difficult to identify risk factors and estimate betas for each asset in a portfolio. So from a practical standpoint, the CAPM is preferred to APT.

5.3.2. Practical Models

If beta risk in the CAPM does not explain returns, which factors do? Practical models seek to answer this question through extensive research. As mentioned in Section 3.2.1, the best example of such a model is the four-factor model proposed by Fama and French (1992) and Carhart (1997).

Based on an analysis of the relationship between past returns and a variety of different factors, Fama and French (1992) proposed that three factors seem to explain asset returns better than just systematic risk. Those three factors are relative size, relative book-to-market value, and beta of the asset. With Carhart's (1997) addition of relative past stock returns, the model can be written as follows:

$$E(R_{it}) = \alpha_i + \beta_{i,MKT}MKT_t + \beta_{i,SMB}SMB_t + \beta_{i,HML}HML_t + \beta_{i,UMD}UMD_t,$$

where

$E(R_i)$ = the return on an asset in excess of the one-month T-bill return
MKT = the excess return on the market portfolio

[9] Ross (1976).

SMB = the difference in returns between small-capitalization stocks and large-capitalization stocks (size)
HML = the difference in returns between high-book-to-market stocks and low-book-to-market stocks (value versus growth)
UMD = the difference in returns of the prior year's winners and losers (momentum).

Historical analysis shows that the coefficient on *MKT* is not significantly different from zero, which implies that stock return is unrelated to the market. The factors that explain stock returns are size (smaller companies outperform larger companies), book-to-market ratio (value companies outperform glamour companies), and momentum (past winners outperform past losers).

The four-factor model has been found to predict asset returns much better than the CAPM and is extensively used in estimating returns for *U.S. stocks*. Note the emphasis on U.S. stocks; because these factors were estimated for U.S. stocks, they have worked well for U.S. stocks over the past several years.

Three observations are in order. First, no strong economic arguments exist for the three additional risk factors. Second, the four-factor model does not necessarily apply to other assets or assets in other countries, and third, there is no expectation that the model will continue to work well in the future.

5.4. The CAPM and Beyond

The CAPM has limitations and, more importantly, is ineffective in modeling asset returns. However, it is a simple model that allows us to estimate returns and evaluate performance. The newer models provide alternatives to the CAPM, although they are not necessarily better in all situations or practical in their application in the real world.

6. SUMMARY

In this chapter, we discussed the capital asset pricing model in detail and covered related topics such as the capital market line. The chapter began with an interpretation of the CML, uses of the market portfolio as a passive management strategy, and leveraging of the market portfolio to obtain a higher expected return. Next, we discussed systematic and nonsystematic risk and why one should not expect to be compensated for taking on nonsystematic risk. The discussion of systematic and nonsystematic risk was followed by an introduction to beta and return-generating models. This broad topic was then broken down into a discussion of the CAPM and, more specifically, the relationship between beta and expected return. The final section included applications of the CAPM to capital budgeting, portfolio performance evaluation, and security selection. The highlights of the chapter are as follows.

- The capital market line is a special case of the capital allocation line, where the efficient portfolio is the market portfolio.
- Obtaining a unique optimal risky portfolio is not possible if investors are permitted to have heterogeneous beliefs because such beliefs will result in heterogeneous asset prices.
- Investors can leverage their portfolios by borrowing money and investing in the market.
- Systematic risk is the risk that affects the entire market or economy and is not diversifiable.
- Nonsystematic risk is local and can be diversified away by combining assets with low correlations.

- Beta risk, or systematic risk, is priced and earns a return, whereas nonsystematic risk is not priced.
- The expected return of an asset depends on its beta risk and can be computed using the CAPM, which is given by $E(R_i) = R_f + \beta_i[E(R_m) - R_f]$.
- The security market line is an implementation of the CAPM and applies to all securities, whether they are efficient or not.
- Expected return from the CAPM can be used for making capital budgeting decisions.
- Portfolios can be evaluated by several CAPM-based measures, such as the Sharpe ratio, the Treynor ratio, M^2, and Jensen's alpha.
- The SML can assist in security selection and optimal portfolio construction.

By successfully understanding the content of this chapter, you should feel comfortable decomposing total variance into systematic and nonsystematic variance, analyzing beta risk, using the CAPM, and evaluating portfolios and individual securities.

PROBLEMS[10]

1. The line depicting the risk and return of portfolio combinations of a risk-free asset and any risky asset is the:

   A. Security market line.
   B. Capital allocation line.
   C. Security characteristic line.

2. The portfolio of a risk-free asset and a risky asset has a better risk–return tradeoff than investing in only one asset type because the correlation between the risk-free asset and the risky asset is equal to:

   A. −1.0.
   B. 0.0.
   C. 1.0.

3. With respect to capital market theory, an investor's optimal portfolio is the combination of a risk-free asset and a risky asset with the highest:

   A. Expected return.
   B. Indifference curve.
   C. Capital allocation line slope.

4. Highly risk-averse investors will *most likely* invest the majority of their wealth in:

   A. Risky assets.
   B. Risk-free assets.
   C. The optimal risky portfolio.

5. The capital market line, CML, is the graph of the risk and return of portfolio combinations consisting of the risk-free asset and:

   A. Any risky portfolio.
   B. The market portfolio.
   C. The leveraged portfolio.

[10]Practice questions were developed by Stephen P. Huffman, CFA (University of Wisconsin, Oshkosh).

6. Which of the following statements *most accurately* defines the market portfolio in capital market theory? The market portfolio consists of all:

   A. Risky assets.
   B. Tradable assets.
   C. Investable assets.

7. With respect to capital market theory, the optimal risky portfolio:

   A. Is the market portfolio.
   B. Has the highest expected return.
   C. Has the lowest expected variance.

8. Relative to portfolios on the CML, any portfolio that plots above the CML is considered:

   A. Inferior.
   B. Inefficient.
   C. Unachievable.

9. A portfolio on the capital market line with returns greater than the returns on the market portfolio represents a(n):

   A. Lending portfolio.
   B. Borrowing portfolio.
   C. Unachievable portfolio.

10. With respect to the capital market line, a portfolio on the CML with returns less than the returns on the market portfolio represents a(n):

    A. Lending portfolio.
    B. Borrowing portfolio.
    C. Unachievable portfolio.

11. Which of the following types of risk is *most likely* avoided by forming a diversified portfolio?

    A. Total risk.
    B. Systematic risk.
    C. Nonsystematic risk.

12. Which of the following events is *most likely* an example of nonsystematic risk?

    A. A decline in interest rates.
    B. The resignation of chief executive officer.
    C. An increase in the value of the U.S. dollar.

13. With respect to the pricing of risk in capital market theory, which of the following statements is *most accurate*?

    A. All risk is priced.
    B. Systematic risk is priced.
    C. Nonsystematic risk is priced.

14. The sum of an asset's systematic variance and its nonsystematic variance of returns is equal to the asset's:

    A. Beta.
    B. Total risk.
    C. Total variance.

15. With respect to return-generating models, the intercept term of the market model is the asset's estimated:
    A. Beta.
    B. Alpha.
    C. Variance.

16. With respect to return-generating models, the slope term of the market model is an estimate of the asset's:
    A. Total risk.
    B. Systematic risk.
    C. Nonsystematic risk.

17. With respect to return-generating models, which of the following statements is *most accurate*? Return-generating models are used to directly estimate the:
    A. Expected return of a security.
    B. Weights of securities in a portfolio.
    C. Parameters of the capital market line.

Use the following data to answer questions 18 through 20:

An analyst gathers the following information:

Security	Expected Annual Return	Expected Standard Deviation	Correlation between Security and the Market
Security 1	11%	25%	0.6
Security 2	11%	20%	0.7
Security 3	14%	20%	0.8
Market	10%	15%	1.0

18. Which security has the *highest* total risk?
    A. Security 1.
    B. Security 2.
    C. Security 3.

19. Which security has the *highest* beta measure?
    A. Security 1.
    B. Security 2.
    C. Security 3.

20. Which security has the *least* amount of market risk?
    A. Security 1.
    B. Security 2.
    C. Security 3.

21. With respect to capital market theory, the average beta of all assets in the market is:
    A. Less than 1.0.
    B. Equal to 1.0.
    C. Greater than 1.0.
22. The slope of the security characteristic line is an asset's:
    A. Beta.
    B. Excess return.
    C. Risk premium.
23. The graph of the capital asset pricing model is the:
    A. Capital market line.
    B. Security market line.
    C. Security characteristic line.
24. With respect to capital market theory, correctly priced individual assets can be plotted on the:
    A. Capital market line.
    B. Security market line.
    C. Capital allocation line.
25. With respect to the capital asset pricing model, the primary determinant of expected return of an individual asset is the:
    A. Asset's beta.
    B. Market risk premium.
    C. Asset's standard deviation.
26. With respect to the capital asset pricing model, which of the following values of beta for an asset is *most likely* to have an expected return for the asset that is less than the risk-free rate?
    A. −0.5.
    B. 0.0.
    C. 0.5.
27. With respect to the capital asset pricing model, the market risk premium is:
    A. Less than the excess market return.
    B. Equal to the excess market return.
    C. Greater than the excess market return.

Use the following data to answer questions 28 through 31:

An analyst gathers the following information:

Security	Expected Standard Deviation	Beta
Security 1	25%	1.50
Security 2	15%	1.40
Security 3	20%	1.60

28. With respect to the capital asset pricing model, if the expected market risk premium is 6% and the risk-free rate is 3%, the expected return for Security 1 is *closest* to:

    A. 9.0%.
    B. 12.0%.
    C. 13.5%.

29. With respect to the capital asset pricing model, if expected return for Security 2 is equal to 11.4% and the risk-free rate is 3%, the expected return for the market is *closest* to:

    A. 8.4%.
    B. 9.0%.
    C. 10.3%.

30. With respect to the capital asset pricing model, if the expected market risk premium is 6% the security with the *highest* expected return is:

    A. Security 1.
    B. Security 2.
    C. Security 3.

31. With respect to the capital asset pricing model, a decline in the expected market return will have the *greatest* impact on the expected return of:

    A. Security 1.
    B. Security 2.
    C. Security 3.

32. Which of the following performance measures is consistent with the CAPM?

    A. *M*-squared.
    B. Sharpe ratio.
    C. Jensen's alpha.

33. Which of the following performance measures does *not* require the measure to be compared to another value?

    A. Sharpe ratio.
    B. Treynor ratio.
    C. Jensen's alpha.

34. Which of the following performance measures is *most* appropriate for an investor who is *not* fully diversified?

    A. *M*-squared.
    B. Treynor ratio.
    C. Jensen's alpha.

35. Analysts who have estimated returns of an asset to be greater than the expected returns generated by the capital asset pricing model should consider the asset to be:

    A. Overvalued.
    B. Undervalued.
    C. Properly valued.

36. With respect to capital market theory, which of the following statements *best* describes the effect of the homogeneity assumption? Because all investors have the same economic expectations of future cash flows for all assets, investors will invest in:

A. The same optimal risky portfolio.
B. The S&P 500 Index.
C. Assets with the same amount of risk.

37. With respect to capital market theory, which of the following assumptions allows for the existence of the market portfolio? All investors:

A. Are price takers.
B. Have homogeneous expectations.
C. Plan for the same, single holding period.

38. The intercept of the best fit line formed by plotting the excess returns of a manager's portfolio on the excess returns of the market is *best* described as Jensen's:

A. Beta.
B. Ratio.
C. Alpha.

39. Portfolio managers who are maximizing risk-adjusted returns will seek to invest *more* in securities with:

A. Lower values of Jensen's alpha.
B. Values of Jensen's alpha equal to 0.
C. Higher values of Jensen's alpha.

40. Portfolio managers, who are maximizing risk-adjusted returns, will seek to invest *less* in securities with:

A. Lower values for nonsystematic variance.
B. Values of nonsystematic variance equal to 0.
C. Higher values for nonsystematic variance.

CHAPTER 7

BASICS OF PORTFOLIO PLANNING AND CONSTRUCTION

Alistair Byrne, CFA
Edinburgh, U.K.

Frank E. Smudde, CFA
Amsterdam, The Netherlands

LEARNING OUTCOMES

After completing this chapter, you will be able to do the following:

- Explain the reasons for a written investment policy statement (IPS).
- List and explain the major components of an IPS.
- Discuss risk and return objectives, including their preparation.
- Distinguish between the willingness and the ability (capacity) to take risk in analyzing an investor's financial risk tolerance.
- Describe the investment constraints of liquidity, time horizon, tax concerns, legal and regulatory factors, and unique circumstances and their implications for the choice of portfolio assets.
- Explain the definition and specification of asset classes in relation to asset allocation.
- Discuss the principles of portfolio construction and the role of asset allocation in relation to the IPS.

1. INTRODUCTION

To build a suitable portfolio for a client, investment advisers should first seek to understand the client's investment goals, resources, circumstances, and constraints. Investors can be categorized into broad groups based on shared characteristics with respect to these factors (e.g., various types of individual investors and institutional investors). Even investors within a given type, however, will invariably have a number of distinctive requirements. In this chapter, we consider in detail the planning for investment success based on an individualized understanding of the client.

This chapter is organized as follows: Section 2 discusses the investment policy statement, a written document that captures the client's investment objectives and the constraints. Section 3 discusses the portfolio construction process, including the first step of specifying a strategic asset allocation for the client. Section 4 concludes and summarizes the chapter.

2. PORTFOLIO PLANNING

Portfolio planning can be defined as a program developed in advance of constructing a portfolio that is expected to satisfy the client's investment objectives. The written document governing this process is the investment policy statement (IPS).

2.1. The Investment Policy Statement

The IPS is the starting point of the portfolio management process. Without a full understanding of the client's situation and requirements, it is unlikely that successful results will be achieved. "Success" can be defined as a client achieving his or her important investment goals using means that he or she is comfortable with (in terms of risks taken and other concerns). The IPS essentially communicates a plan for achieving investment success.

The IPS will be developed following a fact-finding discussion with the client. This fact-finding discussion can include the use of a questionnaire designed to articulate the client's risk tolerance as well as specific circumstances. In the case of institutional clients, the fact-finding may involve asset–liability management studies, identification of liquidity needs, and a wide range of tax and legal considerations.

The IPS can take a variety of forms. A typical format will include the client's investment objectives and the constraints that apply to the client's portfolio.

The client's objectives are specified in terms of risk tolerance and return requirements. These must be consistent with each other: A client is unlikely to be able to find a portfolio that offers a relatively high expected return without taking on a relatively high level of risk.

The constraints section covers factors that need to be taken into account when constructing a portfolio for the client that meets the objectives. The typical constraint categories are liquidity requirements, time horizon, regulatory requirements, tax status, and unique needs. The constraints may be internal (i.e., set by the client), or external (i.e., set by law or regulation). These are discussed in detail next.

Having a well-constructed IPS for all clients should be standard procedure for a portfolio manager. The portfolio manager should have the IPS close at hand and be able to refer to it to assess the suitability of a particular investment for the client. In some cases, the need for the IPS goes beyond simply being a matter of standard procedure. In some countries, the IPS (or an equivalent document) is a legal or regulatory requirement. For example, U.K. pension schemes must have a statement of investment principles under the Pensions Act 1995 (Section 35), and this statement is in essence an IPS. The U.K. Financial Services Authority also has requirements for investment firms to "know their customers." The European Union's Markets in Financial Instruments Directive ("MiFID") requires firms to assign clients to categories, such as professional clients and retail clients.

In the case of an institution, such as a pension plan or university endowment, the IPS may set out the governance arrangements that apply to the investment funds. For example, this information could cover the investment committee's approach to appointing and reviewing investment managers for the portfolio, and the discretion that those managers have. The IPS could also set out the institution's approach to corporate governance, in terms of how it will approach the use of shareholder voting rights and other forms of engagement with corporate management.

The IPS should be reviewed on a regular basis to ensure that it remains consistent with the client's circumstances and requirements. For example, the U.K. Pensions Regulator suggests that a pension scheme's statements of investment principles—a form of IPS—should be reviewed at least every three years. The IPS should also be reviewed if the manager becomes aware of a material change in the client's circumstances, or on the initiative of the client when his or her objectives, time horizon, or liquidity needs change.

2.2. Major Components of an IPS

There is no single standard format for an IPS. Many IPSs, however, include the following sections:

- *Introduction.* This section describes the client.
- *Statement of Purpose.* This section states the purpose of the IPS.
- *Statement of Duties and Responsibilities.* This section details the duties and responsibilities of the client, the custodian of the client's assets, and the investment managers.
- *Procedures.* This section explains the steps to take to keep the IPS current and the procedures to follow to respond to various contingencies.
- *Investment Objectives.* This section explains the client's objectives in investing.
- *Investment Constraints.* This section presents the factors that constrain the client in seeking to achieve the investment objectives.
- *Investment Guidelines.* This section provides information about how policy should be executed (e.g., on the permissible use of leverage and derivatives) and on specific types of assets excluded from investment, if any.
- *Evaluation and Review.* This section provides guidance on obtaining feedback on investment results.
- *Appendices*: (A) Strategic Asset Allocation (B) Rebalancing Policy. Many investors specify a strategic asset allocation (SAA), also known as the policy portfolio, which is the baseline allocation of portfolio assets to asset classes in view of the investor's investment objectives and the investor's policy with respect to rebalancing asset class weights.

The sections that are most closely linked to the client's distinctive needs, and probably the most important from a planning perspective, are those dealing with investment objectives and constraints. An IPS focusing on these two elements has been called an IPS in an "objectives and constraints" format.

In the following sections, we discuss the investment objectives and constraints format of an IPS beginning with risk and return objectives. We follow a tradition of CFA Institute presentations in discussing risk objectives first. The process of developing the IPS is the basic mechanism for evaluating and trying to improve an investor's overall expected return–risk stance. In a portfolio context, "investors have learned to appreciate that their objective is not to manage reward but to control and manage risk."[1] Stated another way, return objectives and expectations must be tailored to be consistent with risk objectives. The risk and return objectives must also be consistent with the constraints that apply to the portfolio.

2.2.1. Risk Objectives

When constructing a portfolio for a client, it is important to ensure that the risk of the portfolio is suitable for the client. The IPS should state clearly the risk tolerance of the client.

Risk objectives are specifications for portfolio risk that reflect the risk tolerance of the client. Quantitative risk objectives can be absolute or relative or a combination of the two.

Examples of an absolute risk objective would be a desire not to suffer any loss of capital or not to lose more than a given percent of capital in any 12-month period. Note that these objectives are not related to investment market performance, good or bad, and are absolute in the sense of being self-standing. The fulfillment of such objectives could be achieved by not taking any risk; for example, by investing in an insured bank certificate of deposit at a creditworthy bank. If investments in risky assets are undertaken, however, such statements would need to be restated as a probability statement to be operational (i.e., practically useful). For example, the desire to not lose more than 4 percent of capital in any 12-month period might be restated as an objective that with 95 percent probability the portfolio not lose more than 4 percent in any 12-month period. Measures of absolute risk include the variance or standard deviation of returns and value at risk.[2]

Some clients may choose to express relative risk objectives, which relate risk relative to one or more benchmarks perceived to represent appropriate risk standards. For example, investments in large-cap U.K. equities could be benchmarked to an equity market index, such as the FTSE 100 Index. The S&P 500 Index could be used as a benchmark for large-cap U.S. equities, or, for investments with cash-like characteristics, the benchmark could be an interest rate such as LIBOR or a Treasury bill rate. For risk relative to a benchmark, the relevant measure is tracking risk, or tracking error.[3]

For institutional clients, the benchmark may be linked to some form of liability the institution has. For example, a pension plan must meet the pension payments as they come due and the risk objective will be to minimize the probability that it will fail to do so. (A related return objective might be to outperform the discount rate used in finding the present value of liabilities over a multiyear time horizon.)

When a policy portfolio (that is, a specified set of long-term asset class weightings) is used, the risk objective may be expressed as a desire for the portfolio return to be within a band of plus or minus X percent of the benchmark return calculated by assigning an index or benchmark to represent each asset class present in the policy portfolio. Again, this objective has to be interpreted as a statement of probability; for example, a 95 percent probability that the portfolio return will be within X percent of the benchmark return over a stated time period. Example 7-1 reviews this material.

[1] Maginn and Tuttle (1983), p. 23.

[2] **Value at risk** is a money measure of the minimum value of losses expected during a specified time period at a given level of probability.

[3] **Tracking risk** (sometimes called **tracking error**) is the standard deviation of the differences between a portfolio's returns and its benchmark's returns.

EXAMPLE 7-1 Types of Risk Objectives

A Japanese institutional investor has a portfolio valued at ¥10 billion. The investor expresses his first risk objective as a desire not to lose more than ¥1 billion in the coming 12-month period. The investor specifies a second risk objective of achieving returns within 4 percent of the return to the TOPIX stock market index, which is the investor's benchmark. Based on this information, address the following:

Problem 1:

A. Characterize the first risk objective as absolute or relative.
B. Give an example of how the risk objective could be restated in a practical manner.

Problem 2:

A. Characterize the second risk objective as absolute or relative.
B. Identify a measure for quantifying the risk objective.

Solution to 1:

A. This is an absolute risk objective.
B. This risk objective could be restated in a practical manner by specifying that the 12-month 95 percent value at risk of the portfolio must not be more than ¥1 billion.

Solution to 2:

A. This is a relative risk objective.
B. This risk objective could be quantified using the tracking risk as a measure. For example, assuming returns follow a normal distribution, an expected tracking risk of 2 percent would imply a return within 4 percent of the index return approximately 95 percent of the time. Remember that tracking risk is stated as a one standard deviation measure.

A client's overall risk tolerance is a function of the client's ability to bear (accept) risk and his or her "risk attitude," which might be considered as the client's willingness to take risk. For ease of expression, from this point on we will refer to ability to bear risk and willingness to take risk as the two components of risk tolerance. Above-average ability to bear risk and above-average willingness to take risk imply above-average risk tolerance. Below-average ability to bear risk and below-average willingness to take risk imply below-average risk tolerance.

The ability to bear risk is measured mainly in terms of objective factors, such as time horizon, expected income, and the level of wealth relative to liabilities. For example, an investor with a 20-year time horizon can be considered to have a greater ability to bear risk, other things being equal, than an investor with a two-year horizon. This difference is because over 20 years there is more scope for losses to be recovered or other adjustments to circumstances to be made than there is over two years.

Similarly, an investor whose assets are comfortably in excess of their liabilities has more ability to bear risk than an investor whose wealth and expected future expenditure are more closely balanced. For example, a wealthy individual who can sustain a comfortable lifestyle after a very substantial investment loss has a relatively high ability to bear risk. A pension plan that has a large surplus of assets over liabilities has a relatively high ability to bear risk.

Risk attitude, or willingness to take risk, is a more subjective factor based on the client's psychology and perhaps also his or her current circumstances. Although the list of factors that are related to an individual's risk attitude remains open to debate, it is believed that some psychological factors, such as personality type, self-esteem, and inclination to independent thinking, are correlated with risk attitude. Some individuals are comfortable taking financial and investment risk, whereas others find it distressing. Although there is no single agreed-upon method for measuring risk tolerance, a willingness to take risk may be gauged by discussing risk with the client or by asking the client to complete a psychometric questionnaire. For example, financial planning academic John Grable and collaborators have developed 13-item and 5-item risk attitude questionnaires that have undergone some level of technical validation. The five-item questionnaire is shown in Exhibit 7-1.

EXHIBIT 7-1 A Five-Item Risk Assessment Instrument

1. Investing is too difficult to understand.
   A. Strongly agree
   B. Tend to agree
   C. Tend to disagree
   D. Strongly disagree
2. I am more comfortable putting my money in a bank account than in the stock market.
   A. Strongly agree
   B. Tend to agree
   C. Tend to disagree
   D. Strongly disagree
3. When I think of the word "risk" the term "loss" comes to mind immediately.
   A. Strongly agree
   B. Tend to agree
   C. Tend to disagree
   D. Strongly disagree
4. Making money in stocks and bonds is based on luck.
   A. Strongly agree
   B. Tend to agree
   C. Tend to disagree
   D. Strongly disagree
5. In terms of investing, safety is more important than returns.
   A. Strongly agree
   B. Tend to agree
   C. Tend to disagree
   D. Strongly disagree

Source: Grable and Joo (2004).

The responses, (A), (B), (C), and (D), are coded 1, 2, 3, and 4, respectively, and summed. The lowest score is 5 and the highest score is 20, with higher scores indicating greater risk tolerance. For two random samples drawn from the faculty and staff of large U.S. universities ($n = 406$), the mean score was 12.86 with a standard deviation of 3.01 and a median (i.e., most frequently observed) score of 13.

Note that a question, such as the first one in Exhibit 7-1, indicates that risk attitude may be associated with nonpsychological factors (such as level of financial knowledge and understanding and decision-making style) as well as psychological factors.

The adviser needs to examine whether a client's ability to accept risk is consistent with the client's willingness to take risk. For example, a wealthy investor with a 20-year time horizon, who is thus able to take risk, may also be comfortable taking risk; in this case the factors are consistent. If the wealthy investor has a low willingness to take risk, there would be a conflict.

In the institutional context, there could also be conflict between ability and willingness to take risk. In addition, different stakeholders within the institution may take different views. For example, the trustees of a well-funded pension plan may desire a low-risk approach to safeguard the funding of the scheme and beneficiaries of the scheme may take a similar view. The sponsor, however, may wish a higher-risk/higher-return approach in an attempt to reduce future funding costs. When a trustee bears a fiduciary responsibility to pension beneficiaries and the interests of the pension sponsor and the pension beneficiaries conflict, the trustee should act in the best interests of the beneficiaries.

When ability to take risk and willingness to take risk are consistent, the investment adviser's task is the simplest. When ability to take risk is below average and willingness to take risk is above average, the investor's risk tolerance should be assessed as below average overall. When ability to take risk is above average but willingness is below average, the portfolio manager or adviser may seek to counsel the client and explain the conflict and its implications. For example, the adviser could outline the reasons why the client is considered to have a high ability to take risk and explain the likely consequences, in terms of reduced expected return, of not taking risk. The investment adviser, however, should not aim to change a client's willingness to take risk that is not a result of a miscalculation or misperception. Modification of elements of personality is not within the purview of the investment adviser's role. The prudent approach is to reach a conclusion about risk tolerance consistent with the lower of the two factors (ability and willingness) and to document the decisions made.

Example 7-2 is the first of a set that follows the analysis of a private wealth management client through the preparation of the major elements of an IPS.

EXAMPLE 7-2 The Case of Henri Gascon: Risk Tolerance

Henri Gascon is an energy trader who works for a major French oil company based in Paris. He is 30 years old and married with one son, aged five. Gascon has decided that it is time to review his financial situation and consults a financial adviser. The financial adviser notes the following aspects of Gascon's situation:

- Gascon's annual salary of €250,000 is more than sufficient to cover the family's outgoings.
- Gascon owns his apartment outright and has €1,000,000 of savings.

- Gascon perceives that his job is reasonably secure.
- Gascon has a good knowledge of financial matters and is confident that equity markets will deliver positive returns over the longer term.
- In the risk tolerance questionnaire, Gascon strongly disagrees with the statements that "making money in stocks and bonds is based on luck" and that "in terms of investing, safety is more important than returns."
- Gascon expects that most of his savings will be used to fund his retirement, which he hopes to start at age 50.

Based only on the information given, which of the following statements is *most* accurate?

A. Gascon has a low ability to take risk, but a high willingness to take risk.
B. Gascon has a high ability to take risk, but a low willingness to take risk.
C. Gascon has a high ability to take risk, and a high willingness to take risk.

Solution: C is correct. Gascon has a high income relative to outgoings, a high level of assets, a secure job, and a time horizon of 20 years. This information suggests a high *ability* to take risk. At the same time, Gascon is knowledgeable and confident about financial markets and responds to the questionnaire with answers that suggest risk tolerance. This result suggests he also has a high *willingness* to take risk.

EXAMPLE 7-3 The Case of Jacques Gascon: Risk Tolerance

Henri Gascon is so pleased with the services provided by the financial adviser, that he suggests to his brother Jacques that he should also consult the adviser. Jacques thinks it is a good idea. Jacques is a self-employed computer consultant also based in Paris. He is 40 years old and divorced with four children, aged between 12 and 16. The financial adviser notes the following aspects of Jacques' situation:

- Jacques' consultancy earnings average €40,000 per annum, but are quite volatile.
- Jacques is required to pay €10,000 per year to his ex-wife and children.
- Jacques has a mortgage on his apartment of €100,000 and €10,000 of savings.
- Jacques has a good knowledge of financial matters and expects that equity markets will deliver very high returns over the longer term.
- In the risk tolerance questionnaire, Jacques strongly disagrees with the statements "I am more comfortable putting my money in a bank account than in the stock market" and "When I think of the word "risk" the term "loss" comes to mind immediately."
- Jacques expects that most of his savings will be required to support his children at university.

Based on the preceding information, which statement is correct?

A. Jacques has a low ability to take risk, but a high willingness to take risk.
B. Jacques has a high ability to take risk, but a low willingness to take risk.
C. Jacques has a high ability to take risk, and a high willingness to take risk.

Solution: A is correct. Jacques does not have a particularly high income, his income is unstable, and he has reasonably high outgoings for his mortgage and maintenance payments. His investment time horizon is approximately two to six years given the ages of his children and his desire to support them at university. This finely balanced financial situation and short time horizon suggests a low ability to take risk. In contrast, his expectations for financial market returns and risk tolerance questionnaire answers suggest a high willingness to take risk. The financial adviser may wish to explain to Jacques how finely balanced his financial situation is and suggest that, despite his desire to take more risk, a relatively cautious portfolio might be the most appropriate approach to take.

2.2.2. Return Objectives

A client's return objectives can be stated in a number of ways. Similar to risk objectives, return objectives may be stated on an absolute or a relative basis.

As an example of an absolute objective, the client may want to achieve a particular percentage rate of return, for example, X percent. This could be a nominal rate of return or be expressed in real (inflation-adjusted) terms.

Alternatively, the return objective can be stated on a relative basis, for example, relative to a benchmark return. The benchmark could be an equity market index, such as the S&P 500 or the FTSE 100, or a cash rate of interest such as LIBOR. LIBOR might be appropriate when the investor has some liability that is linked to that rate; for example, a bank that has a particular cost of funding linked to LIBOR. A relative return objective might be stated as, for example, a desire to outperform the benchmark index by one percentage point per year.

Some institutions also set their return objective relative to a peer group or universe of managers; for example, an endowment aiming for a return that is in the top 50 percent of returns of similar institutions, or a private equity mandate aiming for returns in the top quartile among the private equity universe. This objective can be problematic when limited information is known about the investment strategies or the returns calculation methodology being used by peers, and we must bear in mind the impossibility of *all* institutions being "above average." Furthermore, a good benchmark should be investable—that is, able to be replicated by the investor—and a peer benchmark typically does not meet that criterion.

In each case, the return requirement can be stated before or after fees. Care should be taken that the fee basis used is clear and understood by both the manager and client. The return can also be stated on either a pre- or post-tax basis when the investor is required to pay tax. For a taxable investor, the baseline is to state and analyze returns on an after-tax basis.

The return objective could be a required return—that is, the amount the investor needs to earn to meet a particular future goal—such as a certain level of retirement income.

The manager or adviser must ensure that the return objective is realistic. Care should be taken that client and manager are in agreement on whether the return objective is nominal (which is more convenient for measurement purposes) or real (i.e., inflation-adjusted, which usually relates better to the objective). It must be consistent with the client's risk objective (high expected returns are unlikely to be possible without high levels of risk) and also with the current economic and market environment. For example, 15 percent nominal returns might be possible when inflation is 10 percent, but will be unlikely when inflation is 3 percent.

When a client has unrealistic return expectations, the manager or adviser will need to counsel them about what is achievable in the current market environment and within the client's tolerance for risk.

EXAMPLE 7-4 The Case of Henri Gascon: Return Objectives

Having assessed his risk tolerance, Henri Gascon now begins to discuss his retirement income needs with the financial adviser. He wishes to retire at age 50, which is 20 years from now. His salary meets current and expected future expenditure requirements, but he does not expect to be able to make any additional pension contributions to his fund. Gascon sets aside €100,000 of his savings as an emergency fund to be held in cash. The remaining €900,000 is invested for his retirement.

Gascon estimates that a before-tax amount of €2,000,000 in today's money will be sufficient to fund his retirement income needs. The financial adviser expects inflation to average 2 percent per year over the next 20 years. Pension fund contributions and pension fund returns in France are exempt from tax, but pension fund distributions are taxable upon retirement.

1. Which of the following is closest to the amount of money Gascon will have to accumulate in nominal terms by his retirement date to meet his retirement income objective (i.e., expressed in money of the day in 20 years)?
   A. €900,000
   B. €2,000,000
   C. €3,000,000
2. Which of the following is closest to the annual rate of return that Gascon must earn on his pension portfolio to meet his retirement income objective?
   A. 2.0%
   B. 6.2%
   C. 8.1%

Solution to 1: C is correct. At 2 percent annual inflation, €2,000,000 in today's money equates to €2,971,895 in 20 years measured in money of the day [$2\text{m} \times (1 + 2\%)^{20}$].

Solution to 2: B is correct. €900,000 growing at 6.2 percent per year for 20 years will accumulate to €2,997,318, which is just above the required amount. (The solution of 6.2 percent comes from $€2{,}997{,}318/€900{,}000 = (1 + X)^{20}$, where X is the required rate of return.)

In the following sections, we analyze five major types of constraints on portfolio selection: liquidity, time horizon, tax concerns, legal and regulatory factors, and unique circumstances.

2.2.3. Liquidity

The IPS should state what the likely requirements are to withdraw funds from the portfolio. Examples for an individual investor would be outlays for covering health care payments or tuition fees. For institutions, it could be spending rules and requirements for endowment funds, the existence of claims coming due in the case of property and casualty insurance, or benefit payments for pension funds and life insurance companies.

EXHIBIT 7-2 Asset Allocation of Sampo

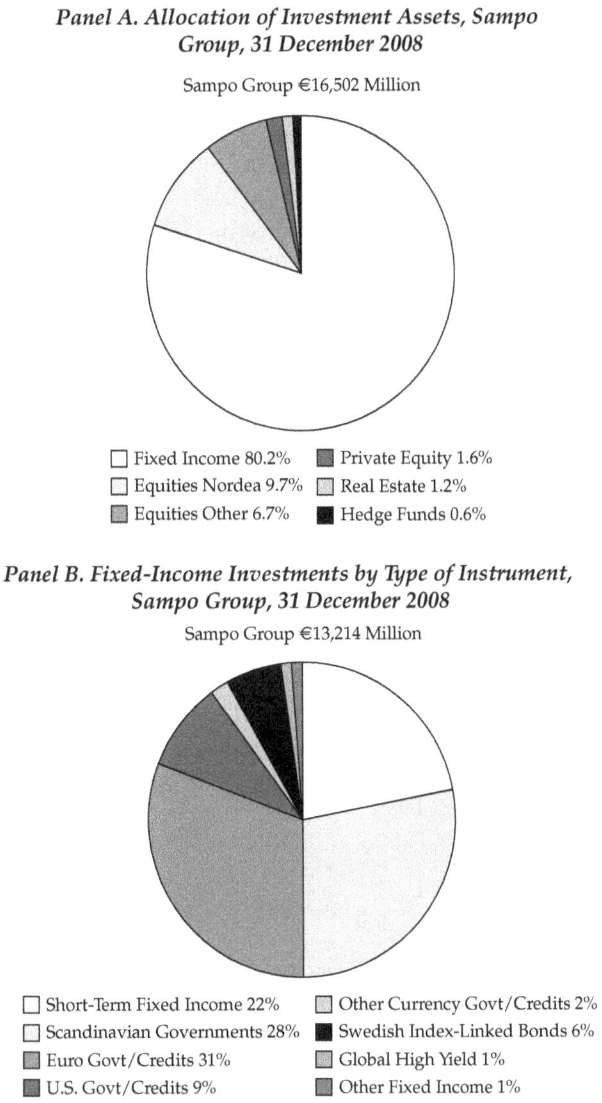

Source: Sampo Group, 2008 Annual Report, pp. 59–61.

When the client does have such a requirement, the manager should allocate part of the portfolio to cover the liability. This part of the portfolio will be invested in assets that are liquid—that is, easily converted to cash—and low risk at the point in time the liquidity need is actually present (e.g., a bond maturing at the time when private education expenses will be incurred), so that their value is known with reasonable certainty. For example, the asset allocation in the insurance portfolios of Finnish insurer Sampo (see Exhibit 7-2) shows a large allocation to fixed-income investments, some of which are either highly liquid or have a short maturity. These investments enable the company, in the case of property and casualty insurance, to pay out on potentially "lumpy" claims of which the timing is unpredictable, and in the case of life insurance, to pay out on life benefits, the size and timing of which are more predictable and can therefore be matched with the maturity profile of the fixed-income portfolio.

2.2.4. Time Horizon

The IPS should state the time horizon over which the investor is investing. It may be the period over which the portfolio is accumulating before any assets need to be withdrawn; it could also be the period until the client's circumstances are likely to change. For example, a 50-year-old pension plan investor hoping to retire at age 60 has a 10-year horizon. The portfolio may not be liquidated at age 60, but its structure may need to change, for example, as the investor begins to draw an income from the fund.

The time horizon of the investor will affect the nature of investments used in the portfolio. Illiquid or risky investments may be unsuitable for an investor with a short time horizon because the investor may not have enough time to recover from investment losses, for example. Such investments, however, may be suitable for an investor with a longer horizon, especially if the risky investments are expected to have higher returns.

EXAMPLE 7-5 Investment Time Horizon

1. Frank Johnson is investing for retirement and has a 20-year horizon. He has an average risk tolerance. Which investment is likely to be the *least* suitable for a major allocation in Johnson's portfolio?
   A. Listed equities.
   B. Private equity.
   C. U.S. Treasury bills.
2. Al Smith has to pay a large tax bill in six months and wants to invest the money in the meantime. Which investment is likely to be the *least* suitable for a major allocation in Smith's portfolio?
   A. Listed equities.
   B. Private equity.
   C. U.S. Treasury bills.

Solution to 1: C is correct. With a 20-year horizon and average risk tolerance, Johnson can accept the additional risk of listed equities and private equity compared with U.S. Treasury bills.

Solution to 2: B is correct. Private equity is risky, has no public market, and is the least liquid among the assets mentioned.

2.2.5. Tax Concerns

Tax status varies among investors. Some investors will be subject to taxation on investment returns and some will not. For example, in many countries returns to pension funds are exempt from tax. Some investors will face various rates of tax on income (dividends and interest payments) than they do on capital gains (associated with increases in asset prices). Typically, when there is a differential, income is taxed more highly than gains. Gains may be subject to a lower rate of tax or part or all of the gain may be exempt from taxation. Furthermore, income may be taxed as it is earned, whereas gains may be taxed when they are realized. Hence, in such cases there is a time value of money benefit in the deferment of taxation of gains relative to income.

In many cases, the portfolio should reflect the tax status of the client. For example, a taxable investor may wish to hold a portfolio that emphasizes capital gains and receives little income. A taxable investor based in the United States is also likely to consider including U.S. municipal bonds ("munis") in his or her portfolio because interest income from munis, unlike from treasuries and corporate bonds, is exempt from taxes. A tax-exempt investor, such as a pension fund, will be relatively indifferent to the form of returns.

2.2.6. Legal and Regulatory Factors

The IPS should state any legal and regulatory restrictions that constrain how the portfolio is invested.

In some countries, such institutional investors as pension funds are subject to restrictions on the composition of the portfolio. For example, there may be a limit on the proportion of equities or other risky assets in the portfolio, or on the proportion of the portfolio that may be invested overseas. The United States has no limits on pension fund asset allocation but some countries do, examples of which are shown in Exhibit 7-3. Pension funds also often face restrictions on the percentage of assets that can be invested in securities issued by the plan sponsor, so called **self-investment limits.**

EXHIBIT 7-3 Examples of Pension Fund Investment Restrictions

Country	Listed Equity	Real Estate	Government Bonds	Corporate Bonds	Foreign Assets
Switzerland	50%	50%	No limits	No limits	30%
Russia	65%	Not allowed	No limits	80%	10%
Japan	No limits	Not permitted	No limits	No limits	No limits
India	Minimum 25 percent in central government bonds; minimum 15 percent in state government bonds; minimum 30 percent invested in bonds of public sector enterprises				

Source: OECD Survey of Investment Regulations of Pension Funds, July 2008.

When an individual has access to material nonpublic information about a particular security, this situation may also form a constraint. For example, the directors of a public company may need to refrain from trading the company's stock at certain points of the year before financial results are published. The IPS should note this constraint so that the portfolio manager does not inadvertently trade the stock on the client's behalf.

2.2.7. Unique Circumstances

This section of the IPS should cover any other aspect of the client's circumstances that is likely to have a material impact on the composition of the portfolio. A client may have considerations derived from his or her religion or ethical values that could constrain investment choices. For instance, a Muslim investor seeking compliance with Shari'a (the Islamic law) will avoid investing in businesses and financial instruments inconsistent with Shari'a, such as casinos and bonds, because Shari'a prohibits gambling and lending money on interest. Similarly, a Christian investor may wish to avoid investments that he or she believes are inconsistent with their faith.

Whether rooted in religious beliefs or not, a client may have personal objections to certain products (e.g., pornography, weapons, tobacco, gambling) or practices (e.g., environmental impact of business activities, human impact of government policies, labor standards), which could lead to the exclusion of certain companies, countries, or types of securities (e.g., interest-bearing debt) from the investable universe as well as the client's benchmark. Such considerations are often referred to as ESG (environmental, social, governance), and investing in accordance with such considerations is referred to as SRI (socially responsible investing).

EXAMPLE 7-6 Ethical Preferences

The £3 billion F&C Stewardship Growth Fund is designed for investors who wish to have ethical and environmental principles applied to the selection of their investments. The fund's managers apply both positive (characteristics to be emphasized in the portfolio) and negative (characteristics to be avoided in the portfolio) screening criteria:

Positive Criteria

- Supplies the basic necessities of life (e.g., healthy food, housing, clothing, water, energy, communication, health care, public transport, safety, personal finance, education).
- Offers product choices for ethical and sustainable lifestyles (e.g., fair trade, organic).
- Improves quality of life through the responsible use of new technologies.
- Shows good environmental management.
- Actively addresses climate change (e.g., renewable energy, energy efficiency).
- Promotes and protects human rights.
- Supports good employment practices.
- Provides a positive impact on local communities.
- Maintains good relations with customers and suppliers.
- Applies effective anticorruption controls.
- Uses transparent communication.

Negative Criteria

- Tobacco production.
- Alcohol production.

- Gambling.
- Pornography or violent material.
- Manufacture and sale of weapons.
- Unnecessary exploitation of animals.
- Nuclear power generation.
- Poor environmental practices.
- Human rights abuses.
- Poor relations with employees, customers, or suppliers.

Source: Excerpted from F&C documents; www.fandc.com/new/Advisor/Default.aspx?ID=79620.

When the portfolio represents only part of the client's total wealth, there may be aspects or portions of wealth not under the control of the manager that have implications for the portfolio. For example, an employee of a public company whose labor income and retirement income provision are reliant on that company and who may have substantial investment exposure to the company through employee share options and stock holdings, may decide that their portfolio should not invest additional amounts in that stock. An entrepreneur may be reluctant to see his or her portfolio invested in the shares of competing businesses or in any business that has risk exposures aligned with his or her entrepreneurial venture.

A client's income may rely on a particular industry or asset class. Appropriate diversification requires that industry or asset class to be deemphasized in the client's investments. For example, a stockbroker should consider having a relatively low weighting in equities, as his skills and thus income-generating ability are worth less when equities do not perform well. Employees should similarly be wary of having concentrated share positions in the equity of the company they work for. If the employer encounters difficulties, not only may the employee lose his or her job, but their investment portfolio could also suffer a significant loss of value.

2.3. Gathering Client Information

As noted previously, it is important for portfolio managers and investment advisers to know their clients. For example, Dutch securities industry practice requires financial intermediaries to undertake substantial fact finding. This is required not only in the case of full-service wealth management or in the context of an IPS, but also in "lighter" forms of financial intermediation, such as advisory relationships (in which clients make investment decisions after consultation with their investment adviser or broker) or execution-only relationships (in which the client makes his investment decisions independently).

An exercise in fact-finding about the customer should take place at the beginning of the client relationship. This will involve gathering information about the client's circumstances as well as discussing the client's objectives and requirements.

Important data to gather from a client should cover family and employment situations as well as financial information. If the client is an individual, it may also be necessary to know about the situation and requirements of the client's spouse or other family members. The health of the client and his or her dependents is also relevant information. In an institutional relationship, it will be important to know about key stakeholders in the organization and what their perspective and requirements are. Information gathering may be done in an informal way or may involve structured interviews or questionnaires or analysis of data. Many advisers will capture data electronically and use special systems that record data and produce customized reports.

Good recordkeeping is very important, and may be crucial in a case in which any aspect of the client relationship comes into dispute at a later stage.

EXAMPLE 7-7 Henri Gascon: Description of Constraints

Henri Gascon continues to discuss his investment requirements with the financial adviser. The financial adviser begins to draft the constraints section of the IPS.

Gascon expects that he will continue to work for the oil company and that his relatively high income will continue for the foreseeable future. Gascon and his wife do not plan to have any additional children, but expect that their son will go to a university at age 18. They expect that their son's education costs can be met out of their salary income.

Gascon's emergency reserve of €100,000 is considered to be sufficient as a reserve for unforeseen expenditures and emergencies. His retirement savings of €900,000 has been contributed to his defined-contribution pension plan account to fund his retirement. Under French regulation, pension fund contributions are paid from gross income (i.e., income prior to deduction of tax) and pension fund returns are exempt from tax, but pension payments from a fund to retirees are taxed as income to the retiree.

With respect to Gascon's retirement savings portfolio, refer back to Example 7-2 as needed and address the following:

1. As concerns liquidity,
   A. A maximum of 50 percent of the portfolio should be invested in liquid assets.
   B. The portfolio should be invested entirely in liquid assets because of high spending needs.
   C. The portfolio has no need for liquidity because there are no short-term spending requirements.
2. The investment time horizon is closest to
   A. 5 years.
   B. 20 years.
   C. 40 years.
3. As concerns taxation, the portfolio
   A. Should emphasize capital gains because income is taxable.
   B. Should emphasize income because capital gains are taxable.
   C. Is tax exempt and thus indifferent between income and capital gains.
4. The principle legal and regulatory factors applying to the portfolio are
   A. U.S. Securities laws.
   B. European banking laws.
   C. French pension fund regulations.
5. As concerns unique needs, the portfolio should
   A. Have a high weighting in oil and other commodity stocks.
   B. Be invested only in responsible and sustainable investments.
   C. Not have significant exposure to oil and other commodity stocks.

Solution to 1: C is correct. The assets are for retirement use, which is 20 years away. Any short-term spending needs will be met from other assets or income.

Solution to 2: B is correct. The relevant time horizon is to the retirement date, which is 20 years away. The assets may not be liquidated at that point, but a restructuring of the portfolio is to be expected as Gascon starts to draw an income from it.

Solution to 3: C is correct. Because no tax is paid in the pension fund, it does not matter whether returns come in the form of income or capital gains.

Solution to 4: C is correct. The management of the portfolio will have to comply with any rules relating to the French pension funds.

Solution to 5: C is correct. Gascon's human capital (i.e., future labor income) is affected by the prospects of the oil industry. If his portfolio has significant exposure to oil stocks, he would be increasing a risk exposure he already has.

Example 7-8, the final one based on Henri Gascon, shows how the information obtained from the fact-finding exercises might be incorporated into the objectives and constraints section of an IPS.

EXAMPLE 7-8 Henri Gascon: Outline of an IPS

Following is a simplified excerpt from the IPS the adviser prepares for Henri Gascon, covering objectives and constraints.

Risk Objectives:

- The portfolio may take on relatively high amounts of risk in seeking to meet the return requirements. With a 20-year time horizon and significant assets and income, the client has an above-average ability to take risk. The client is a knowledgeable investor, with an above-average willingness to take risk. Hence, the client's risk tolerance is above average, explaining the above portfolio risk objective.
- The portfolio should be well diversified with respect to asset classes and concentration of positions within an asset class. Although the client has above-average risk tolerance, his investment assets should be diversified to control the risk of catastrophic loss.

Return Objectives:

The portfolio's long-term return requirement is 6.2 percent per year, in nominal terms and net of fees, to meet the client's retirement income goal.

Constraints:

- *Liquidity:* The portfolio consists of pension fund assets and there is no need for liquidity in the short to medium term.
- *Time horizon:* The portfolio will be invested with a 20-year time horizon. The client intends to retire in 20 years, at which time an income will be drawn from the portfolio.
- *Tax status:* Under French law, contributions to the fund are made gross of tax and returns in the fund are tax-free. Hence, the client is indifferent between income and capital gains in the fund.
- *Legal and regulatory factors:* The management of the portfolio must comply with French pension fund regulations.
- *Unique needs:* The client is an executive in the oil industry. The portfolio should strive to minimize additional exposures to oil and related stocks.

3. PORTFOLIO CONSTRUCTION

Once the IPS has been compiled, the investment manager can construct a suitable portfolio. Strategic asset allocation is a traditional focus of the first steps in portfolio construction. The strategic asset allocation is stated in terms of percent allocations to asset classes. An **asset class** is a category of assets that have similar characteristics, attributes, and risk/return relationships. The **strategic asset allocation** (SAA) is the set of exposures to IPS-permissible asset classes that is expected to achieve the client's long-term objectives given the client's investment constraints.

The focus on the SAA is the result of a number of important investment principles. One principle is that a portfolio's systematic risk accounts for most of its change in value over the long term. **Systematic risk** is risk related to the economic system (e.g., risk related to business cycle) that cannot be eliminated by holding a diversified portfolio. This risk is different from the particular risks of individual securities, which may be avoided by holding other securities with offsetting risks. A second principle is that the returns to groups of similar assets (e.g., long-term debt claims) predictably reflect exposures to certain sets of systematic factors (e.g., for the debt claims, unexpected changes in the inflation rate). Thus, the SAA is a means of providing the investor with exposure to the systematic risks of asset classes in proportions that meet the risk and return objectives.

The process of formulating a strategic asset allocation is based on the IPS, already discussed, and capital market expectations, introduced in Section 3.1. How to make the strategic asset allocation operational with a rebalancing policy and a translation into actual investment portfolios will be described in Section 3.3. Section 3.4 lists some alternatives to the approach chosen and describes some portfolio construction techniques.

3.1. Capital Market Expectations

Capital market expectations are the investor's expectations concerning the risk and return prospects of asset classes, however broadly or narrowly the investor defines those asset classes.[4]

[4] For an in-depth discussion of this topic see Calverley, Meder, Singer, and Staub (2007).

When associated with the client's investment objectives, the result is the strategic asset allocation that is expected to allow the client to achieve his or her investment objectives (at least under normal capital market conditions).

Traditionally, capital market expectations are quantified in terms of asset class expected returns, standard deviation of returns, and correlations among pairs of asset classes. Formally, the expected return of an asset class consists of the risk-free rate and one or more risk premium(s) associated with the asset class. Expected returns are in practice developed in a variety of ways, including the use of historical estimates, economic analysis, and various kinds of valuation models. Standard deviations and correlation estimates are frequently based on historical data.

3.2. The Strategic Asset Allocation

Traditionally, investors have distinguished cash, equities, bonds, and real estate as the major asset classes. In recent years, this list has been expanded with private equity, hedge funds, and commodities. In addition, such assets as art and intellectual property rights may be considered asset classes for those investors prepared to take a more innovative approach and to accept some illiquidity. Combining such new asset classes as well as hedge funds and private equity under the header "alternative investments" has become accepted practice.

As the strategic asset allocation is built up by asset classes, the decision about how to define those asset classes is an important one. Defining the asset classes also determines the extent to which the investor controls the risk and return characteristics of the eventual investment portfolio. For example, separating bonds into government bonds and corporate bonds, and then further separating corporate bonds into investment grade and non-investment grade (high yield) and government bonds into domestic and foreign government bonds, creates four bond categories for which risk–return expectations can be expressed and correlations with other asset classes (and, in an asset–liability management context, with the liabilities) can be estimated. An asset allocator who wants to explicitly consider the risk–return characteristics of those bond categories in the strategic asset allocation may choose to treat them as distinct asset classes. Similarly, in equities some investors distinguish between emerging market and developed market equities, between domestic and international equities, or between large-cap and small-cap equities. In some regulatory environments for institutional investors, asset class definitions are mandatory, thereby forcing asset allocators to articulate risk–return expectations (and apply risk management) on the asset classes specified.

When defining asset classes, a number of criteria apply. Intuitively, an asset class should contain relatively homogeneous assets while providing diversification relative to other asset classes. In statistical terms, risk and return expectations should be similar and paired correlations of assets should be relatively high within an asset class but should be lower versus assets in other asset classes.[5] Also, the asset classes, while being mutually exclusive, should add up to a sufficient approximation of the relevant investable universe. Applying these criteria ensures that the strategic asset allocation process has considered all available investment alternatives.

Using correlation as a metric, Example 7-9 tends to indicate that only emerging markets were well differentiated from European equities. So, why do investors still often subdivide

[5] A technically precise characterization other than one in terms of pairwise correlations is given by Kritzman (1999).

EXAMPLE 7-9 Specifying Asset Classes

The strategic asset allocations of many institutional investors make a distinction between domestic equities and international equities, or between developed market equities and emerging market equities. Often, equities are separated into different market capitalization brackets, resulting, for example, in an asset class such as domestic small-cap equity.

The correlation matrix in Exhibit 7-4 shows the paired correlations between different equity asset classes and other asset classes. These correlations are measured over 10 years of monthly returns through February 2009. In addition, the exhibit shows the annualized volatility of monthly returns.

EXHIBIT 7-4 Asset Class Correlation Matrix

	A	B	C	D	E	F	G	H	I	J	K	L
A. MSCI Europe	1.00	0.77	0.95	0.97	0.88	0.20	0.59	−0.08	−0.35	0.10	−0.29	0.01
B. MSCI Emerging Markets	0.77	1.00	0.82	0.83	0.76	0.35	0.63	0.18	−0.25	0.22	−0.20	0.11
C. MSCI World	0.95	0.82	1.00	0.96	0.97	0.25	0.69	0.00	−0.31	0.18	−0.27	0.06
D. MSCI EAFE	0.97	0.83	0.96	1.00	0.88	0.27	0.65	−0.01	−0.34	0.15	−0.29	0.05
E. MSCI U.S.	0.88	0.76	0.97	0.88	1.00	0.20	0.70	−0.01	−0.27	0.18	−0.24	0.06
F. Commodities	0.20	0.35	0.25	0.27	0.20	1.00	0.27	0.25	−0.04	0.14	−0.07	0.14
G. Real Estate	0.59	0.63	0.69	0.65	0.70	0.27	1.00	0.18	−0.01	0.40	0.02	0.32
H. Gold	−0.08	0.18	0.00	−0.01	−0.01	0.25	0.18	1.00	0.21	0.30	0.12	0.14
I. U.S. Treasuries	−0.35	−0.25	−0.31	−0.34	−0.27	−0.04	−0.01	0.21	1.00	0.67	0.78	0.55
J. U.S. Investment Grade	0.10	0.22	0.18	0.15	0.18	0.14	0.40	0.30	0.67	1.00	0.61	0.79
K. European Government Bonds	−0.29	−0.20	−0.27	−0.29	−0.24	−0.07	0.02	0.12	0.78	0.61	1.00	0.83
L. European Investment Grade Corporates	0.01	0.11	0.06	0.05	0.06	0.14	0.32	0.14	0.55	0.79	0.83	1.00
Annualized Volatility	16.6%	20.7%	15.0%	15.4%	15.7%	25.4%	18.9%	16.6%	5.0%	6.0%	3.1%	3.2%

Data based on monthly returns in local currencies from January 1999 to February 2009. Commodities, Real Estate, and Gold in US$.

Source: MSCI, NAREIT, Barclays Capital, Standard and Poor's.

Based only on the information given, address the following:

1. Contrast the correlations between equity asset classes with the correlations between equity asset classes and European government bonds.
2. Which equity asset class is most sharply distinguished from MSCI Europe?

Solution to 1: The matrix reveals very strong correlation between the equity asset classes (MSCI Europe, MSCI Emerging Markets, MSCI EAFE, and MSCI U.S.). For example, the correlation between European equities and U.S. equities is 0.88. The correlation of equities with bonds, however, is much lower. For example, both asset classes have a similar negative correlation with European government bonds (–0.29 and –0.24 respectively). It is worth noting, however, that correlations can vary through time and the values shown may be specific to the sample period used. In this particular case, extreme market conditions in 2008 resulted in negative correlations between equities and bonds.

Solution to 2: Correlations of emerging market equities with other categories of equities are 0.76 or higher, whereas all groupings of equities share similar correlations with commodities (between 0.20 and 0.35), gold (between –0.08 and 0.18), and real estate (between 0.59 and 0.70). These high-paired correlations between equity asset classes, combined with the similarity of the correlations between any of these asset classes and nonequity asset classes, suggests that defining the equity asset class more narrowly has limited added value in providing diversification. The case for treatment as a separate asset class can best be made for emerging markets stocks, which usually have the lowest correlation of all equity asset classes with other asset classes and have a volatility of returns far in excess of the other equity groupings.

equities? Apart from any regulatory reasons, one explanation might be that this decomposition into smaller asset classes corresponds to the way the asset allocation is structured in portfolios. Many investment managers have expertise exclusively in specific areas of the market, such as emerging market equities, U.S. small-cap equity, or international investment-grade credit. Bringing the asset class definitions of the asset allocation in line with investment products actually available in the market may simplify matters from an organizational perspective.

The risk–return profile of the strategic asset allocation depends on the expected returns and risks of the individual asset classes, as well as the correlation between those asset classes. In general, adding assets classes with low correlation improves the risk–return trade-off (more return for similar risk), as long as the stand-alone risk of such asset classes does not exceed its diversification effect. Typically, the strategic asset allocation for risk-averse investors will have a large weight in government bonds and cash, whereas those with more willingness and ability to take risk will have more of their assets in risky asset classes, such as equities and many types of alternative investments.

EXAMPLE 7-10 Objective of a Strategic Asset Allocation

ABP is a pension fund with approximately 2.6 million members. It manages a defined-benefit scheme for civil servants in the Netherlands, and its goal is to pay out a "real" pension (i.e., one that will increase through time in line with consumer price inflation).

With €173 billion under management at the end of 2008, ABP is one of the world's largest pension funds. It decides on its asset allocation in an investment plan that is reviewed every three years. The asset class terminology used by ABP is distinctive.* Exhibit 7-5 shows ABP's SAA under the plan for 2007–2009.

EXHIBIT 7-5 Strategic Asset Allocation for ABP

Real assets	
Equities, developed countries	27%
Equities, emerging markets	5%
Convertible bonds	2%
Private equity	5%
Hedge funds	5%
Commodities	3%
Real estate	9%
Infrastructure	2%
Innovation	2%
Total real assets	***60%***
Fixed-income securities	
Inflation-linked bonds	7%
Government bonds	10%
Corporate bonds	23%
Total fixed-income securities	***40%***
Total	100%

1. Discuss the way the asset classes have been defined.
2. How does the asset allocation relate to the pension fund's ambition to pay out a real (i.e., inflation-adjusted) pension?

Solution to 1: The asset allocation is fairly narrow in its definition of alternative asset classes, whereas the traditional asset classes, such as bonds and equities, are defined quite broadly. It appears that allocations within the broader groupings of government bonds, credits, and equities (developed and emerging) are not made on the strategic level.

Solution to 2: This asset allocation seems to reflect an attempt to control the risk of inflation: only 33 percent of the strategic asset allocation is in nominal bonds, whereas 7 percent is in inflation-linked bonds and 60 percent in "real" assets (assets believed to have a positive correlation with inflation and, therefore, hedging inflation to some degree).

**Note:* ABP defines an asset class category called "real assets," which contains asset classes (not fixed-income securities) that are expected to perform well in times of inflation, but are considered a major risk. The use of the term "real assets" may differ from the use elsewhere. The term "innovation" refers to alternative investments that are relatively new to ABP's portfolio. An example of such an investment is music rights. "Infrastructure" is investments in nonpublic equity of infrastructure projects such as toll roads. Inflation-linked bonds are fixed-income securities of which the payout depends on a measure of inflation in the issuing country. Some major issuers of such bonds are the United States, the United Kingdom, and France.

A strategic asset allocation results from combining the constraints and objectives articulated in the IPS and long-term capital market expectations regarding the asset classes. The strategic asset allocation or policy portfolio will subsequently be implemented into real portfolios. Exhibit 7-6 illustrates conceptually how investment objectives and constraints and long-term capital market expectations combine into a policy portfolio.

EXHIBIT 7-6 Strategic Asset Allocation Process

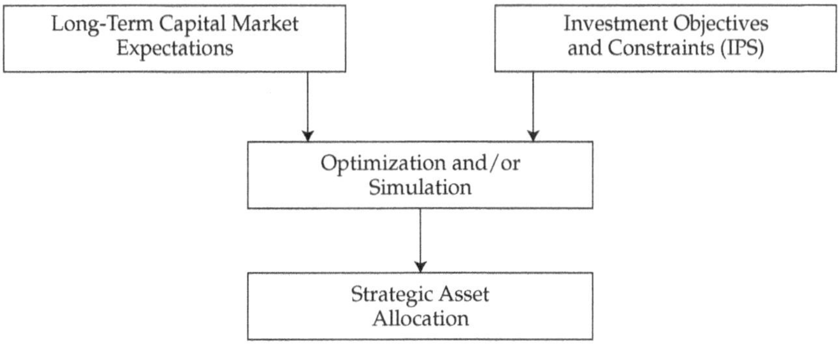

In some frameworks used in practice, the asset allocation is an integral part of the investment policy statement. This presentation, however, keeps the asset allocation separate from the investment policy statement because clients' investment objectives and constraints qualitatively differ in nature from capital market expectations, thus requiring different types of analysis, different sources of information, and different review cycles.

How will capital market expectations and investment objectives and constraints eventually translate into a strategic asset allocation? In general, investors choosing from a range of asset allocations with similar returns would prefer those with lower risk. Choosing from allocations with similar levels of risk, investors would prefer those with the highest return. Formally, investors' risk and return objectives can be described as a utility function, in which utility increases with higher expected returns and lower risk. The assumption that expected utility is increasing in expected return and decreasing in variance of return could yield an expected utility equation, such as that shown in Equation 7.1.[6]

[6] Sharpe, Chen, Pinto, and McLeavey (2007).

$$U_p = E(R_p) - \lambda_p^2 \tag{7.1}$$

where

U_p = the investor's expected utility from the portfolio
$E(R_p)$ = the expected return of the portfolio
σ_p = the standard deviation of returns of the portfolio
λ = a measure of the investor's risk aversion

This utility function expresses a positive relationship between utility and expected portfolio return (i.e., higher expected return increases utility, all else equal) and a negative relationship between utility and volatility of portfolio return as measured by the variance of portfolio returns. The stronger the negative relationship, the greater the investor's risk aversion. The portfolio is understood to represent a particular asset allocation. The asset allocation providing the highest expected utility is the one that is optimal for the investor given his or her risk aversion.

For different values of U_p, a line can be plotted that links those combinations of risk and expected return that produces that level of utility: an indifference curve. An investor would attain equal utility from all risk/return combinations on that curve.

Capital market expectations, specified in asset classes' expected returns, standard deviations of return, and correlations, translate into an efficient frontier of portfolios. A multiasset class portfolio's expected return is given by

$$E(R_p) = \sum\nolimits_{i=1}^{n} w_i E(R_i) \tag{7.2}$$

where w_i equals the weight of asset class i in the portfolio, and its risk is given by

$$\sigma_p = \sqrt{\sum\nolimits_{i=1}^{n} \sum\nolimits_{j=1}^{n} w_{p,i} w_{p,j} \text{Cov}(R_i, R_j)} \tag{7.3}$$

The covariance between the returns on asset classes i and j is given by the product of the correlation between the two asset classes and their standard deviations of return:

$$\text{Cov}(R_i, R_j) = \rho_{i,j} \sigma_i \sigma_j \tag{7.4}$$

where

$\text{Cov}(R_i,R_j)$ = the covariance between the return of asset classes i and j
$\rho_{i,j}$ = the correlation between the returns of asset classes i and j

The resulting portfolios can be represented as a scatter of dots in a chart depicting their risk and expected return. As a portfolio's risk is a positive function of the risk of its assets and the correlations among them, a portfolio consisting of lowly correlated risky assets has lower risk than one with similarly risky assets with high correlation. It is therefore possible to construct different portfolios with equal expected returns but with different levels of risk. The line that connects those portfolios with the minimal risk for each level of expected return (above that of the minimum variance portfolio) is the efficient frontier. Clearly, the efficient frontier will move "upward" as more lowly correlated assets with sufficient expected return are added to the mix because it lowers the risk in the portfolios. Similarly, when return expectations increase for asset classes while volatility and correlation assumptions remain unchanged, the efficient frontier will move upward because each portfolio is able to generate higher returns for the same level of risk.

Both the efficient frontier and a range of indifference curves can be plotted in the risk–return space. In Exhibit 7-7, the curves that are concave from below represent efficient frontiers associated with different assumed expected returns. The dashed curves are indifference curves. The point where the efficient frontier intersects with the indifference curve with the highest utility attainable (i.e., the point of tangency) represents the optimal asset allocation for the client/investor. In Exhibit 7-7, efficient frontier 1 has a point of tangency with indifference curve 1. Higher levels of utility, such as those associated with indifference curve 0, can apparently not be reached with the assets underlying the efficient frontier. It is clear that when capital market expectations change, this change moves the efficient frontier away from its original location. In the chart, this movement is illustrated by efficient frontier 2, which incorporates different capital market expectations. This new efficient frontier has a point of tangency with indifference curve 2, which is associated with a lower level of expected utility. Because the point of tangency represents the strategic asset allocation, it implies the asset allocation should be adjusted. Similarly, should investment objectives or constraints change, the indifference curves will change their shape and location. This change will again move the point of tangency, and hence change the asset allocation.

EXHIBIT 7-7 Strategic Asset Allocation Efficient Frontier

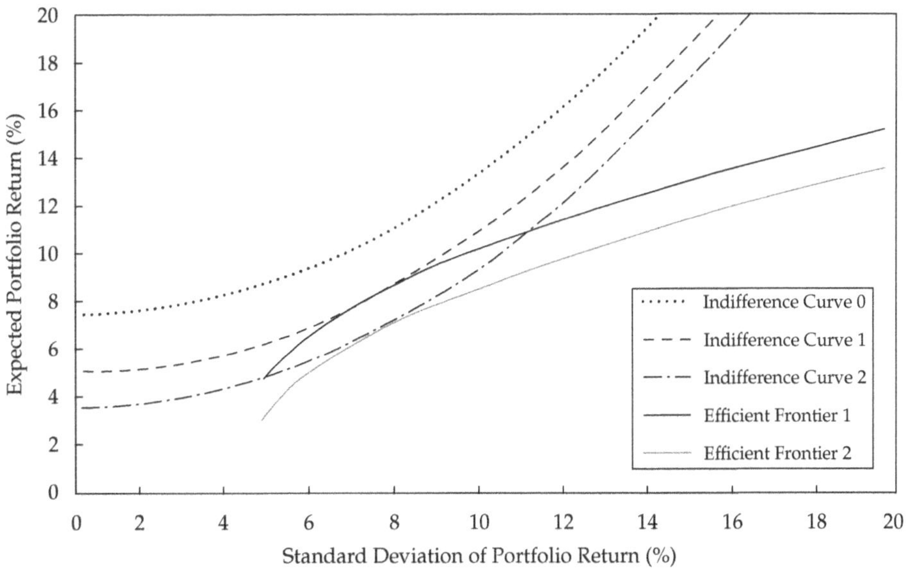

This framework describes how investor objectives and capital market expectations should theoretically be reconciled. It will, however, not be the exact procedure that in practice will be followed. First, an IPS does not necessarily translate the client's investment objectives and constraint into a utility function. Rather, an IPS gives threshold levels for risk and expected return, combined with a number of additional constraints that cannot be captured in this model. Second, the model illustrated is a single-period model, whereas in practice, the constraints from the IPS will make it more appropriate to use multiperiod models. Multiperiod problems can be more effectively addressed using simulation.

EXAMPLE 7-11 Approaching an SAA for a Private Investor

Rainer Gottschalk recently sold his local home construction company in the south of Germany to a large homebuilder with a nationwide reach. Upon selling his company, he accepted a job as regional manager for that nationwide homebuilder. He is now considering his and his family's financial future. He looks forward to his new job, where he likes his new role, and which provides him with income to fulfill his family's short-term and medium-term liquidity needs. He feels strongly that he should not invest the proceeds of the sale of his company in real estate because his income already depends on the state of the real estate market. He consults a financial adviser from his bank about how to invest his money to retire in good wealth in 20 years.

The IPS they develop suggests a return objective of 6 percent, with a standard deviation of 12 percent. The bank's asset management division provides Gottschalk and his adviser with the following data (Exhibit 7-8) on market expectations.

EXHIBIT 7-8 Risk, Return, and Correlation Estimates

			Correlation Matrix		
	Expected Return	Standard Deviation	European Equities	Emerging Mkt Equities	European Govt Bonds
European equities	8.40%	24%	1.00	0.86	–0.07
Emerging market equities	9.20%	28%	0.86	1.00	–0.07
European government bonds	3.50%	7%	–0.07	–0.07	1.00

Note: Standard deviation and correlation calculated over the period March 1999–December 2008. All data in unhedged euros.
Sources: Barclay's, MSCI, Bloomberg.

To illustrate the possibilities, the adviser presents Gottschalk with the following plot (Exhibit 7-9), in which the points forming the shaded curve outline the risk–return characteristics of the portfolios that can be constructed out of the three assets. An imaginary line linking the points with the lowest standard deviation for each attainable level of return would be the efficient frontier. The two straight lines show the risk and return objectives. Gottschalk should aim for portfolios that offer an expected return of at least 6 percent (the straight horizontal line or above) and a standard deviation of return of 12 percent or lower (the straight vertical line to the left).

EXHIBIT 7-9 Efficient Frontier

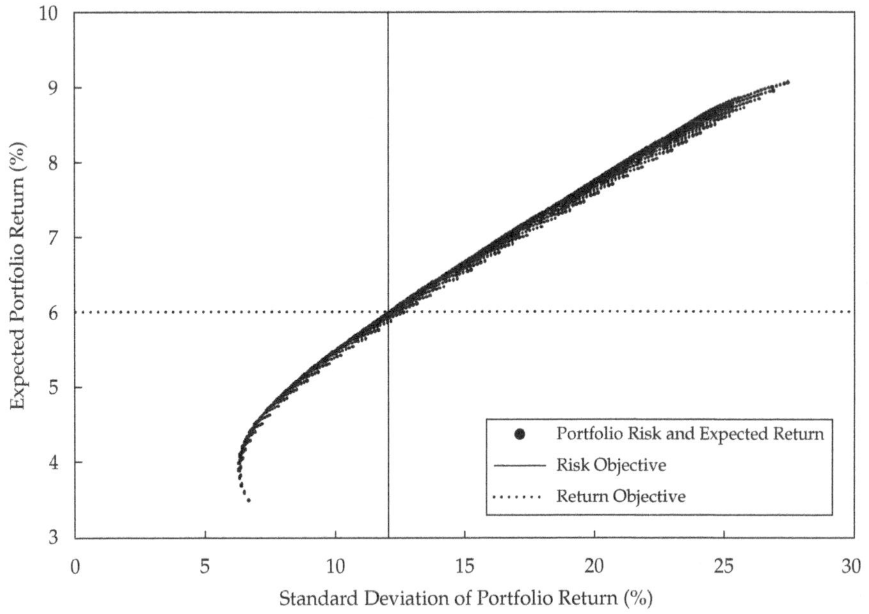

Exhibit 7-9 shows that a portfolio on the efficient frontier satisfies the two objectives. This portfolio consists of 28 percent European stocks, 20 percent emerging market equities, and 52 percent government bonds and gives a 6 percent expected return and a 12 percent standard deviation. This combination is what the adviser recommends to Gottschalk as his strategic asset allocation.

3.3. Steps toward an Actual Portfolio

The strategic asset allocation in itself does not yet represent an actual investment portfolio. It is the first step in implementing an investment strategy. For quantitatively oriented portfolio managers, the next step is often risk budgeting.

As used in this chapter, **risk budgeting** is the process of deciding on the amount of risk to assume in a portfolio (the overall risk budget), and subdividing that risk over the sources of investment return (e.g., strategic asset allocation, tactical asset allocation, and security selection).[7] Because the decision about the amount of risk to be taken is made in constructing the IPS, at this stage we are concerned about the subdivision of that risk.

[7] Some writers use risk budgeting to refer to allocating an amount or budget of tracking risk to active portfolio managers on a given asset class. See Waring, Whitney, Pirone, and Castille (2000).

Apart from the exposures to systematic risk factors specified in the strategic asset allocation, the returns of an investment strategy depend on two other sources: tactical asset allocation and security selection. **Tactical asset allocation** is the decision to deliberately deviate from the policy exposures to systematic risk factors (i.e., the policy weights of asset classes) with the intent to add value based on forecasts of the near-term returns of those asset classes. For instance, an investor may decide to temporarily invest more of the portfolio in equities than the SAA prescribes if the investor anticipates that equities will deliver a higher return over the short term than other asset classes. **Security selection** is an attempt to generate higher returns than the asset class benchmark by selecting securities with a higher expected return. For example, an investment manager may decide to add more IBM stock in his portfolio than the weight in his equity benchmark if he expects this stock to do better than the benchmark. To fund this purchase, he may sell another stock expected to do worse than either the benchmark or IBM. Obviously, deciding to deviate from policy weights or to select securities aiming to beat the benchmark creates additional uncertainty about returns. This risk is over and above the risk inherent in the policy portfolio. Hence, an investment policy should set risk limits and desired payoffs for each of these three activities.

Risk budgeting implies that the portfolio manager has to choose, for every asset class, whether to deploy security selection as a return generator. This choice is generally referred to as the choice between active or passive management. Contrary to strategic asset allocation, where exposures to sources of systematic risk are selected and sized, security selection is not rewarded with a long-run payoff to risk. Security selection is a zero-sum game: All investors in an asset class are competing with each to identify a typically limited number of assets that are misvalued. In total, the gross returns of all market participants average out to the market return (the reward for taking systematic risk). This implies that the average active investor will match the market return, and that one investor's gain versus the market return is the other investor's loss versus the market return. However, because active managers tend to trade more and have to pay people (including themselves) to generate investment ideas or information leading to such ideas, the average active manager will underperform the market, net of costs. This does not imply, however, that there are no skillful investment managers who, with some consistency, beat their benchmarks. Neither does it imply that all passive managers will be able to match the benchmark. The higher the turnover of an index, the more trading costs a passive manager will incur, making the task of effectively mimicking an index more difficult.

The likelihood of adding a significant amount of value from security selection depends on the skills of the manager and the informational efficiency of the market for the asset class his skill relates to. The more efficient an asset class or a subset of that asset class (such as a regional stock, bond, or real estate market or a size category within the stock market), the more skillful an asset manager has to be to add value. Broadly speaking, an efficient market is a market in which prices, on average, very quickly reflect newly available information. That requires a sizeable participation of mean–variance optimizing investors, acting on rational expectations, using the same or similar pricing models, and having equal opportunities to access relevant information. Clearly, the market for U.S. large-capitalization equities would be quite efficient. By contrast, some regional bond and equity markets do not have the technical and regulatory systems for information dissemination that are sufficient to serve all investors on a timely basis. Skilled managers should be able to exploit the resulting inefficiencies.

Sometimes, however, the choice between active and passive management is actually made implicitly when the asset class is included in the asset allocation. The markets for some assets—such as those for nonlisted real estate, art, and infrastructure assets—are so illiquid that it is very difficult to buy a diversified exposure. As a result, there is no way of taking exposure to the asset class without engaging in security selection.

As the portfolio is constructed and its value changes with the returns of the asset classes and securities in which it is invested, the weights of the asset classes will gradually deviate from the policy weights in the strategic asset allocation. This process is referred to as drift. Periodically, or when a certain threshold deviation from the policy weight (the bandwidth) has been breached, the portfolio should be rebalanced back to the policy weights. The set of rules that guide the process of restoring the portfolio's original exposures to systematic risk factors is known as the **rebalancing policy**. Even absent a formal risk budget, formulating a rebalancing policy is an important element of risk management.

EXAMPLE 7-12 Strategic Asset Allocation for a European Charity

A European charity has an asset allocation at the beginning of the year consisting of the asset classes and weights as shown in Exhibit 7-10.

EXHIBIT 7-10 Asset Allocation of a European Charity (beginning of year)

Asset Class	Policy Weight	Corridor (+/–)	Upper Limit	Lower Limit
European equities	30.0%	2.0%	32.0%	28.0%
International equities	15.0%	2.0%	17.0%	13.0%
European government bonds	20.0%	2.0%	22.0%	18.0%
Corporate bonds	20.0%	2.0%	22.0%	18.0%
Cash and money market instruments	15.0%	2.0%	17.0%	13.0%
Total	100.0%			

The charity has a policy that the asset class weights cannot deviate from the policy weights by more than 2 percent (the corridor). The resulting upper and lower limits for the asset class weights are shown in the rightmost columns of the table. There are two reasons for asset class actual weights to deviate from policy weights: by deliberate choice (tactical asset allocation or market timing) and as a result of divergence of the returns of the different asset classes (drift). In this example, the asset class weights start the year exactly in line with policy weights.

After half a year, the investment portfolio is as shown in Exhibit 7-11.

EXHIBIT 7-11 Asset Allocation for a European Charity (6 Months Later)

Asset Class	Policy Weight	Corridor (+/–)	Upper Limit	Lower Limit	Period Return	Ending Weight
European equities	30.0%	2.0%	32.0%	28.0%	15.0%	32.4%
International equities	15.0%	2.0%	17.0%	13.0%	10.0%	15.5%
European government bonds	20.0%	2.0%	22.0%	18.0%	0.5%	18.9%
Corporate bonds	20.0%	2.0%	22.0%	18.0%	1.5%	19.1%
Cash and money market instruments	15.0%	2.0%	17.0%	13.0%	1.0%	14.2%
Total	100.0%				6.6%	100.0%

1. Discuss the returns of the portfolio and comment on the main asset weight changes.

Solution to 1: The investment portfolio generated a return calculated on beginning (policy) weights of 6.55 percent or 6.6 percent ($= 0.30 \times 15\% + 0.15 \times 10\% + 0.20 \times 0.5\% + 0.20 \times 1.5\% + 0.15 \times 1.0\%$), mainly driven by a strong equity market. Bond returns were more subdued, leading to considerable drift in asset class weights. In particular, the European equity weight breached the upper limit of its allowed actual weight.

The investment committee decides against reducing European equities back to policy weight and adding to the fixed income and cash investments toward policy weights. Although this rebalancing would be prudent, the committee decides to engage in tactical asset allocation based on the view that this market will continue to be strong over the course of the year. It decides to just bring European equities back to within its bandwidth (a 32 percent portfolio weight) and add the proceeds to cash. Exhibit 7-12 shows the outcome after another half year.

EXHIBIT 7-12 Asset Allocation for a European Charity (an Additional 6 Months Later)

Asset Class	Policy Weight	Starting Weight	Corridor (+/−)	Upper Limit	Lower Limit	Period Return	Ending Weight
European equities	30.0%	32.0%	2.0%	32.0%	28.0%	–9.0%	29.7%
International equities	15.0%	15.5%	2.0%	17.0%	13.0%	–6.0%	14.9%
European government bonds	20.0%	18.9%	2.0%	22.0%	18.0%	4.0%	20.0%
Corporate bonds	20.0%	19.1%	2.0%	22.0%	18.0%	4.0%	20.2%
Cash and money market instruments	15.0%	14.6%	2.0%	17.0%	13.0%	2.0%	15.2%
Total	100.0%					–2.0%	100.0%

The prior decision not to rebalance to policy weights did not have a positive result. Contrary to the expectations of the investment committee, both European and international equities performed poorly while bonds recovered. The return of the portfolio was −2.0 percent.

2. How much of this return can be attributed to tactical asset allocation?

Solution to 2: Because tactical asset allocation is the deliberate decision to deviate from policy weights, the return contribution from tactical asset allocation is equal to the difference between the actual return and the return that would have been made if the asset class weights were equal to the policy weights. Exhibit 7-13 shows the difference to be −0.30 percent.

EXHIBIT 7-13 Returns to Tactical Asset Allocation

Asset Class	Policy Weight I	Starting Weight II	Weights Difference III (= II–I)	Period Return IV	TAA Contribution V (= III × IV)
European equities	30.0%	32.0%	2.0%	–9.0%	–0.18%
International equities	15.0%	15.5%	0.5%	–6.0%	–0.03%
European government bonds	20.0%	18.9%	–1.1%	4.0%	–0.05%
Corporate bonds	20.0%	19.1%	–0.9%	4.0%	–0.04%
Cash and money market instruments	15.0%	14.6%	–0.4%	2.0%	–0.01%
Total	100.0%			–2.0%	–0.30%

The process of executing an investment strategy continues with selecting the appropriate manager(s) for each asset class and allocating funds to them. The investment portfolio management process is then well into the execution stage.

The investment managers' performance will be monitored, as well as the results of the strategic asset allocation. When asset class weights move outside their corridors, money is transferred from the asset classes that have become too large compared with the SAA to those that fall short. Managers as well as the strategic asset allocation will be reviewed on the basis of the outcome of the monitoring process. In addition, capital market expectations may change, as may the circumstances and objectives of the client. These changes could result in an adjustment of the strategic asset allocation.

3.4. Additional Portfolio Organizing Principles

The top-down oriented framework laid out in earlier paragraphs is quite general. Other models of portfolio organization are also used in practice, and these are described briefly here. In addition, this section introduces some portfolio construction concepts in use to better capture the value of active management.

According to some practitioners, a top-down investment process as described earlier has two drawbacks. They both result from the fact that in a top-down process, a multitude of specialist managers may work for the same client within the same asset class. Each of these managers will manage risk versus the client's benchmark, and because these benchmarks may be similar to or overlapping with those of other managers, the aggregate of all the portfolios within one asset class may be less active than was intended. The resulting investment portfolio may underutilize its risk budget. Another drawback is that as the investment managers each engage in trading over the full extent (including the benchmark exposure) of their portfolio, the aggregate of all portfolios may not be efficient from a capital gains tax point of view. More trading results in more capital gains being realized, increasing the tax bill at the end of the year. To circumvent these issues, the core–satellite approach was developed. In this approach, a majority of the portfolio is invested on a passive or low active risk basis (usually a combination of a bond portfolio and an equity portfolio) while a minority of the assets is managed aggressively in smaller "satellite" portfolios. The aim of the satellite portfolios is to generate a high active return with little regard for benchmark exposure, whereas the core is managed with low turnover to capture the long-term systematic risk premium of its assets on a tax-optimal basis. The aggressive management in satellites can be executed with the objective of market timing (in which case tactical asset tilts are executed through long–short positions in asset class indices or derivatives), as well as security selection (in which case, highly active security selection vehicles act as satellites). A drawback of the core–satellite approach is that the assignment of asset class monies to actual portfolio managers—with their various expected alphas, risk surrounding those alphas, and correlations between those alphas—can be seen as an optimization process in its own right. The outcome of that process is not necessarily consistent with a core–satellite structure (Waring and Siegel, 2003).

4. SUMMARY

In this chapter, we have discussed construction of a client's investment policy statement, including discussion of risk and return objectives and the various constraints that will apply to the portfolio. We have also discussed the portfolio construction process, with emphasis on the strategic asset allocation decisions that must be made.

- The IPS is the starting point of the portfolio management process. Without a full understanding of the client's situation and requirements, it is unlikely that successful results will be achieved.
- The IPS can take a variety of forms. A typical format will include the client's investment objectives and also list the constraints that apply to the client's portfolio.
- The client's objectives are specified in terms of risk tolerance and return requirements.
- The constraints section covers factors that need to be considered when constructing a portfolio for the client that meets the objectives. The typical constraint categories are liquidity requirements, time horizon, regulatory requirements, tax status, and unique needs.
- Risk objectives are specifications for portfolio risk that reflect the risk tolerance of the client. Quantitative risk objectives can be absolute or relative or a combination of the two.
- The client's overall risk tolerance is a function of the client's ability to accept risk and their "risk attitude," which can be considered the client's willingness to take risk.

- The client's return objectives can be stated on an absolute or a relative basis. As an example of an absolute objective, the client may want to achieve a particular percentage rate of return. Alternatively, the return objective can be stated on a relative basis, for example, relative to a benchmark return.
- The liquidity section of the IPS should state what the client's requirements are to draw cash from the portfolio.
- The time horizon section of the IPS should state the time horizon over which the investor is investing. This horizon may be the period during which the portfolio is accumulating before any assets need to be withdrawn.
- Tax status varies among investors and a client's tax status should be stated in the IPS.
- The IPS should state any legal or regulatory restrictions that constrain the investment of the portfolio.
- The unique circumstances section of the IPS should cover any other aspect of a client's circumstances that is likely to have a material impact on the composition of the portfolio; for example, any religious or ethical preferences.
- Asset classes are the building blocks of an asset allocation. An asset class is a category of assets that have similar characteristics, attributes, and risk/return relationships. Traditionally, investors have distinguished cash, equities, bonds, and real estate as the major asset classes.
- A strategic asset allocation results from combining the constraints and objectives articulated in the IPS and capital market expectations regarding the asset classes.
- As time goes on, a client's asset allocation will drift from the target allocation, and the amount of allowable drift as well as a rebalancing policy should be formalized.
- In addition to taking systematic risk, an investment committee may choose to take tactical asset allocation risk or security selection risk. The amount of return attributable to these decisions can be measured.

PROBLEMS

1. Which of the following is *least* important as a reason for a written investment policy statement (IPS)?

   A. The IPS may be required by regulation.
   B. Having a written IPS is part of best practice for a portfolio manager.
   C. Having a written IPS ensures the client's risk and return objectives can be achieved.

2. Which of the following *best* describes the underlying rationale for a written investment policy statement (IPS)?

   A. A written IPS communicates a plan for trying to achieve investment success.
   B. A written IPS provides investment managers with a ready defense against client lawsuits.
   C. A written IPS allows investment managers to instruct clients about the proper use and purpose of investments.

3. A written investment policy statement (IPS) is *most* likely to succeed if:

   A. Created by a software program to assure consistent quality.
   B. It is a collaborative effort of the client and the portfolio manager.
   C. It reflects the investment philosophy of the portfolio manager.

4. The section of the investment policy statement (IPS) that provides information about how the policy may be executed, including investment constraints, is *best* described as the:
   A. Investment Objectives.
   B. Investment Guidelines.
   C. Statement of Duties and Responsibilities.

5. Which of the following is *least* likely to be placed in the appendices to an investment policy statement (IPS)?
   A. Rebalancing Policy.
   B. Strategic Asset Allocation.
   C. Statement of Duties and Responsibilities.

6. Which of the following typical topics in an investment policy statement (IPS) is *most* closely linked to the client's "distinctive needs"?
   A. Procedures.
   B. Investment Guidelines.
   C. Statement of Duties and Responsibilities.

7. An investment policy statement that includes a return objective of outperforming the FTSE 100 by 120 basis points is *best* characterized as having a(n):
   A. Relative return objective.
   B. Absolute return objective.
   C. Arbitrage-based return objective.

8. Risk assessment questionnaires for investment management clients are *most* useful in measuring:
   A. Value at risk.
   B. Ability to take risk.
   C. Willingness to take risk.

9. Which of the following is *best* characterized as a relative risk objective?
   A. Value at risk for the fund will not exceed US$3 million.
   B. The fund will not underperform the DAX by more than 250 basis points.
   C. The fund will not lose more than €2.5 million in the coming 12-month period.

10. In preparing an investment policy statement, which of the following is *most* difficult to quantify?
    A. Time horizon.
    B. Ability to accept risk.
    C. Willingness to accept risk.

11. After interviewing a client in order to prepare a written investment policy statement (IPS), you have established the following:
    - The client has earnings that vary dramatically between £30,000 and £70,000 (pre-tax) depending on weather patterns in Britain.
    - In three of the previous five years, the after-tax income of the client has been less than £20,000.

- The client's mother is dependent on her son (the client) for approximately £9,000 per year support.
- The client's own subsistence needs are approximately £12,000 per year.
- The client has more than 10 years experience trading investments including commodity futures, stock options, and selling stock short.
- The client's responses to a standard risk assessment questionnaire suggest he has above average risk tolerance.

The client is *best* described as having a:

A. Low ability to take risk, but a high willingness to take risk.
B. High ability to take risk, but a low willingness to take risk.
C. High ability to take risk and a high willingness to take risk.

12. After interviewing a client in order to prepare a written investment policy statement (IPS), you have established the following:

- The client has earnings that have exceeded €120,000 (pre-tax) each year for the past five years.
- She has no dependents.
- The client's subsistence needs are approximately €45,000 per year.
- The client states that she feels uncomfortable with her lack of understanding of securities markets.
- All of the client's current savings are invested in short-term securities guaranteed by an agency of her national government.
- The client's responses to a standard risk assessment questionnaire suggest she has low risk tolerance.

The client is *best* described as having a:

A. Low ability to take risk, but a high willingness to take risk.
B. High ability to take risk, but a low willingness to take risk.
C. High ability to take risk and a high willingness to take risk.

13. A client who is a 34-year-old widow with two healthy young children (aged 5 and 7) has asked you to help her form an investment policy statement. She has been employed as an administrative assistant in a bureau of her national government for the previous 12 years. She has two primary financial goals—her retirement and providing for the college education of her children. This client's time horizon is *best* described as being:

A. Long term.
B. Short term.
C. Medium term.

14. The timing of payouts for property and casualty insurers is unpredictable ("lumpy") in comparison with the timing of payouts for life insurance companies. Therefore, in general, property and casualty insurers have:

A. Lower liquidity needs than life insurance companies.
B. Greater liquidity needs than life insurance companies.
C. A higher return objective than life insurance companies.

15. A client who is a director of a publicly listed corporation is required by law to refrain from trading that company's stock at certain points of the year when disclosure of

financial results are pending. In preparing a written investment policy statement (IPS) for this client, this restriction on trading:

A. Is irrelevant to the IPS.
B. Should be included in the IPS.
C. Makes it illegal for the portfolio manager to work with this client.

16. Consider the pairwise correlations of monthly returns of the following asset classes:

	Brazilian Equities	East Asian Equities	European Equities	U.S. Equities
Brazilian equities	1.00	0.70	0.85	0.76
East Asian equities	0.70	1.00	0.91	0.88
European equities	0.85	0.91	1.00	0.90
U.S. equities	0.76	0.88	0.90	1.00

Based solely on the information in the preceding table, which equity asset class is *most* sharply distinguished from U.S. equities?

A. Brazilian equities.
B. European equities.
C. East Asian equities.

17. Returns on asset classes are *best* described as being a function of:

A. The failure of arbitrage.
B. Exposure to the idiosyncratic risks of those asset classes.
C. Exposure to sets of systematic factors relevant to those asset classes.

18. In defining asset classes as part of the strategic asset allocation decision, pairwise correlations within asset classes should generally be:

A. Equal to correlations among asset classes.
B. Lower than correlations among asset classes.
C. Higher than correlations among asset classes.

19. Tactical asset allocation is *best* described as:

A. Attempts to exploit arbitrage possibilities among asset classes.
B. The decision to deliberately deviate from the policy portfolio.
C. Selecting asset classes with the desired exposures to sources of systematic risk in an investment portfolio.

20. Investing the majority of the portfolio on a passive or low active risk basis while a minority of the assets is managed aggressively in smaller portfolios is *best* described as:

A. The core–satellite approach.
B. A top-down investment policy.
C. A delta-neutral hedge approach.

CHAPTER 8

OVERVIEW OF EQUITY SECURITIES

Ryan C. Fuhrmann, CFA
Westfield, IN, U.S.A.

Asjeet S. Lamba, CFA
Bulleen, Australia

LEARNING OUTCOMES

After completing this chapter, you will be able to do the following:

- Discuss the importance and relative performance of equity securities in global financial markets.
- Discuss the characteristics of various types of equity securities.
- Distinguish between public and private equity securities.
- Discuss the differences in voting rights and other ownership characteristics among various equity classes.
- Discuss the methods for investing in nondomestic equity securities.
- Compare and contrast the risk and return characteristics of various types of equity securities.
- Explain the role of equity securities in the financing of a company's assets and creating company value.
- Distinguish between the market value and book value of equity securities.
- Compare and contrast a company's cost of equity, its (accounting) return on equity, and investors' required rates of return.

1. INTRODUCTION

Equity securities represent ownership claims on a company's net assets. As an asset class, equity plays a fundamental role in investment analysis and portfolio management because it represents a significant portion of many individual and institutional investment portfolios.

The study of equity securities is important for many reasons. First, the decision on how much of a client's portfolio to allocate to equities affects the risk and return characteristics of the entire portfolio. Second, different types of equity securities have different ownership claims on a company's net assets, which affect their risk and return characteristics in different ways. Finally, variations in the features of equity securities are reflected in their market prices, so it is important to understand the valuation implications of these features.

This chapter provides an overview of equity securities and their different features and establishes the background required to analyze and value equity securities in a global context. It addresses the following questions:

- What distinguishes common shares from preference shares, and what purposes do these securities serve in financing a company's operations?
- What are convertible preference shares, and why are they often used to raise equity for unseasoned or highly risky companies?
- What are private equity securities, and how do they differ from public equity securities?
- What are depository receipts and their various types, and what is the rationale for investing in them?
- What are the risk factors involved in investing in equity securities?
- How do equity securities create company value?
- What is the relationship between a company's cost of equity, its return on equity, and investors' required rate of return?

The remainder of this chapter is organized as follows. Section 2 provides an overview of global equity markets and their historical performance. Section 3 examines the different types and characteristics of equity securities, and Section 4 outlines the differences between public and private equity securities. Section 5 provides an overview of the various types of equity securities listed and traded in global markets. Section 6 discusses the risk and return characteristics of equity securities. Section 7 examines the role of equity securities in creating company value and the relationship between a company's cost of equity, its return on equity, and investors' required rate of return. Section 8 concludes and summarizes the chapter.

2. EQUITY SECURITIES IN GLOBAL FINANCIAL MARKETS

This section highlights the relative importance and performance of equity securities as an asset class. We examine the total market capitalization and trading volume of global equity markets and the prevalence of equity ownership across various geographic regions. We also examine historical returns on equities and compare them to the returns on government bonds and bills.

Exhibit 8-1 summarizes the contributions of selected countries and geographic regions to global gross domestic product (GDP) and global equity market capitalization. Analysts can examine the relationship between equity market capitalization and GDP as an indicator of whether the global equity market (or a specific country's or region's equity market) is under, over, or fairly valued. Global equity markets expanded at twice the rate of global GDP between 1993 and 2004. At the beginning of 2008, global GDP and equity market capitalization were nearly equal at approximately US$55 trillion.[1] This implies an equity

[1] EconomyWatch.com, www.economywatch.com/gdp/world-gdp/.

EXHIBIT 8-1 Country and Regional Contributions to Global GDP and Equity Market Capitalization (2007)

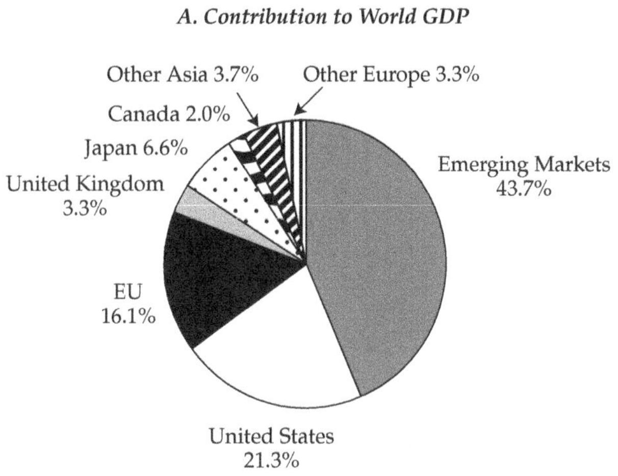

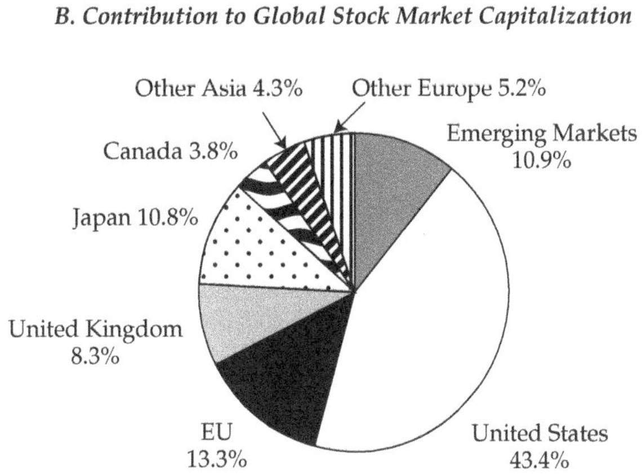

Sources: MacroMavens, *IMF World Economic Outlook 2008*, Standard & Poor's BMI Global Index weights.

market capitalization to GDP ratio of 100 percent, which was almost twice the long-run average of 50 percent and indicates that global equity markets were overvalued at that time.

Exhibit 8-1 illustrates the significant value that investors attach to publicly traded equities relative to the sum of goods and services produced globally every year. It shows the continued significance, and the potential overrepresentation, of U.S. equity markets relative to their contribution to global GDP. That is, while U.S. equity markets contribute around 43 percent to the total capitalization of global equity markets, their contribution to the global GDP is only around 21 percent. Following the stock market turmoil in 2008, however, the market

EXHIBIT 8-2 Equity Markets Ranked by Total Market Capitalization at the End of 2008 (billions of U.S. dollars)

Rank	Name of Market	Total U.S. Dollar Market Capitalization	Total U.S. Dollar Trading Volume	Number of Listed Companies
1	NYSE Euronext (U.S.)	$9,208.9	$33,638.9	3,011
2	Tokyo Stock Exchange Group	$3,115.8	$5,607.3	2,390
3	NASDAQ OMX	$2,396.3	$36,446.5	2,952
4	NYSE Euronext (Europe)	$2,101.7	$4,411.2	1,002
5	London Stock Exchange	$1,868.2	$6,271.5	3,096
6	Shanghai Stock Exchange	$1,425.4	$2,600.2	864
7	Hong Kong Exchanges	$1,328.8	$1,629.8	1,261
8	Deutsche Börse	$1,110.6	$4,678.8	832
9	TSX Group	$1,033.4	$1,716.2	3,841
10	BME Spanish Exchanges	$948.4	$2,410.7	3,576

Note that market capitalization by company is calculated by multiplying its stock price by the number of shares outstanding. The market's overall capitalization is the aggregate of the market capitalizations of all companies traded on that market. The number of listed companies includes both domestic and foreign companies whose shares trade on these markets.

Source: Adapted from the *World Federation of Exchanges 2008 Report* (see www.world-exchanges.org).

capitalization to GDP ratio of the United States fell to 59 percent, which is significantly lower than its long-run average of 79 percent.[2]

As equity markets outside the United States develop and become increasingly global, their total capitalization levels are expected to grow closer to their respective world GDP contributions. Therefore, it is important to understand and analyze equity securities from a global perspective.

Exhibit 8-2 lists the top 10 equity markets at the end of 2008 based on total market capitalization (in billions of U.S. dollars), trading volume, and the number of listed companies.[3] Note that the rankings differ based on the criteria used. For example, the top three markets based on total market capitalization are the NYSE Euronext (U.S.), Tokyo Stock Exchange Group, and NASDAQ OMX; however, the top three markets based on total U.S. dollar trading volume are the Nasdaq OMX, NYSE Euronext (U.S.), and London Stock Exchange, respectively.[4] A relatively new entrant to this top 10 list is China's Shanghai Stock Exchange, which is the only emerging equity market represented on this list.

[2] For further details, see Bary (2008).

[3] The market capitalization of an individual stock is computed as the share price multiplied by the number of shares outstanding. The total market capitalization of an equity market is the sum of the market capitalizations of each individual stock listed on that market. Similarly, the total trading volume of an equity market is computed by value weighting the total trading volume of each individual stock listed on that market. Total dollar trading volume is computed as the average share price multiplied by the number of shares traded.

[4] NASDAQ is the acronym for the National Association of Securities Dealers Automated Quotations.

EXHIBIT 8-3 Real Returns on Global Equity Securities, Bonds, and Bills during 1900–2008

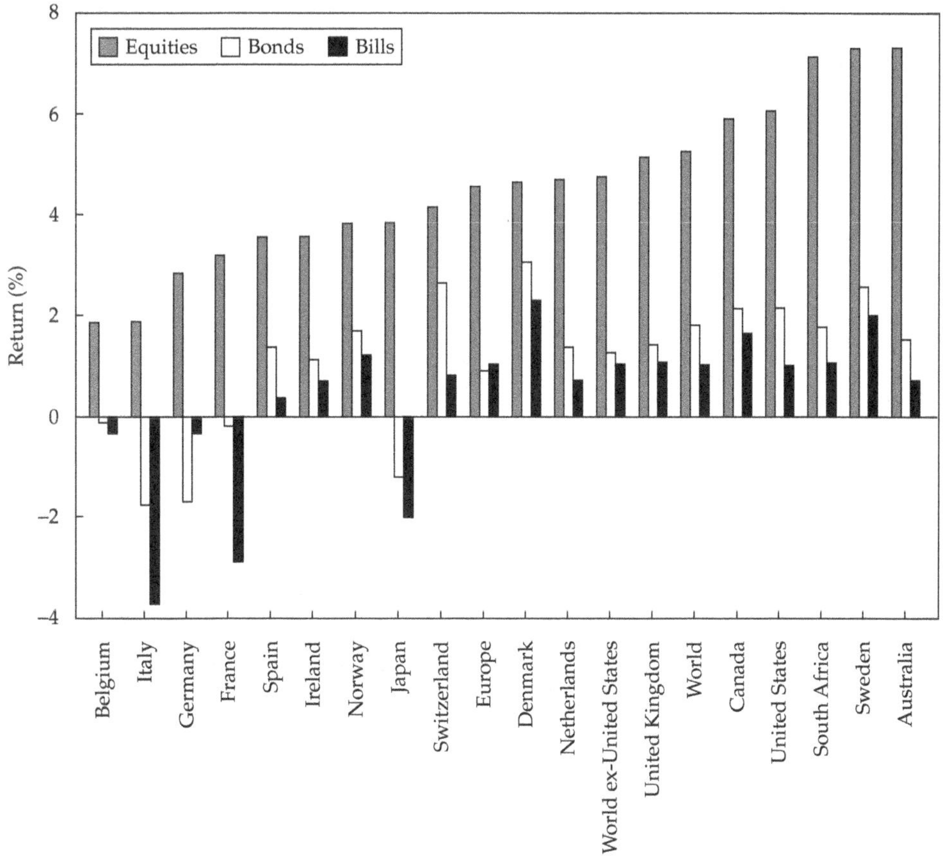

Source: Dimson, Marsh, and Staunton (2009).

Exhibit 8-3 compares the *real* (or inflation-adjusted) compounded returns on government bonds, government bills, and equity securities in 17 countries during 1900–2008.[5] In real terms, government bonds and bills have essentially kept pace with the inflation rate, earning annualized real returns of 1 percent to 2 percent in most countries.[6] By comparison, real returns in equity markets have generally been above 4 percent per year in most markets—with a world average return just over 5 percent and a world average return excluding the United States just under 5 percent. During this period, Australia and Sweden were the best performing markets followed by South Africa, the United States, and Canada.

[5] The real return for a country is computed by taking the nominal return and subtracting the observed inflation rate in that country.

[6] The exceptions are Belgium, Italy, Germany, France, and Japan—where the average real returns on government bonds have been negative. This is due to the very high inflation rates in these countries during the world war years.

Exhibit 8-4 focuses on the real compounded rates of return on equity securities in the same 17 countries during 1900–2008 as well as during the more recent time periods of 1990–1999 and 2000–2008. During 2000–2008, with the exception of Australia, Norway, and South Africa, real returns were negative or close to zero in all markets including the world average. This is in sharp contrast to the performance of these markets during 1990–1999, when inflation rates and interest rates were at record lows in most countries and growth in corporate profits was at record highs.[7]

EXHIBIT 8-4 Real Returns on Global Equity Securities during 1900–2008, 1990–1999, and 2000–2008

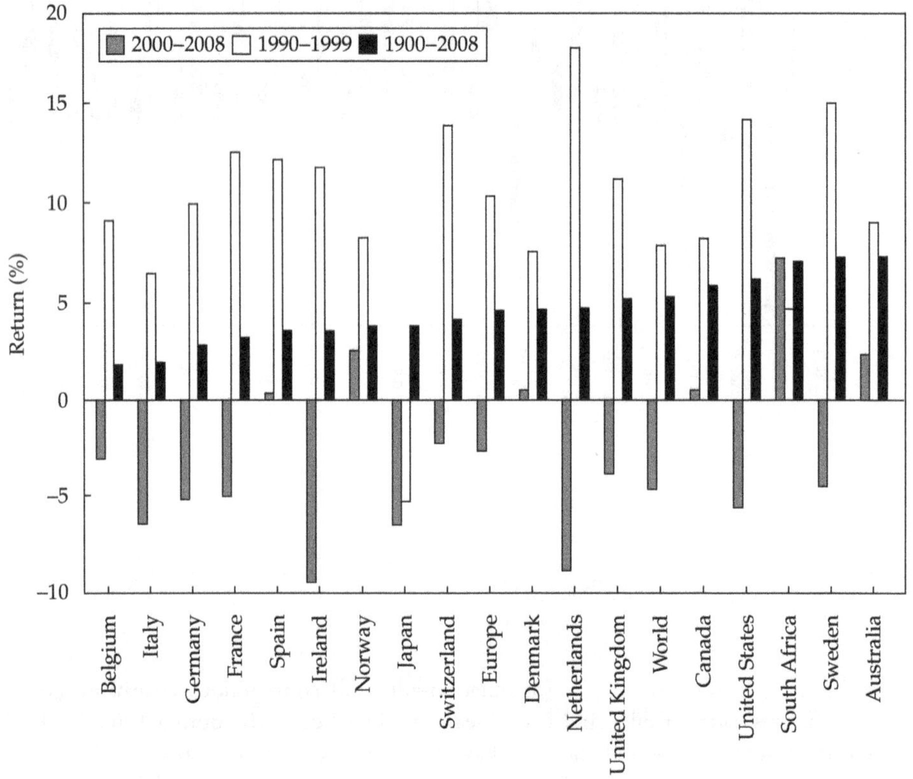

Source: Dimson, Marsh, and Staunton (2009).

The volatility in equity market returns is further highlighted in Exhibit 8-5, which shows the average performance of world equity markets and the worst performing equity market during World War I, World War II, the technology crash, the oil crisis, the Wall

[7] The only exception to this was the Japanese equity market, which experienced negative real returns in the 1990s as well. Even in the case of Japan, however, the average real compounded return over the much longer 1900–2008 period has been around 4 percent per year.

Street crash, and the more recent banking/credit crash. Note that in each period the losses suffered by the worst affected equity market were much larger than the average global losses. The data for the credit crash is as of the end of 2008 and thus does not fully capture the extent of its effects on world equity markets. It is more than likely that in the future, the credit crash of 2007–2008 will be viewed as being the worst of all the extreme market losses.

These observations and historical data are consistent with the concept that the return on securities is directly related to risk level. That is, equity securities have higher risk levels when compared with government bonds and bills, they earn higher rates of return to compensate investors for these higher risk levels, and they also tend to be more volatile over time.

EXHIBIT 8-5 Extreme Losses in Global Equity Markets during 1900–2008

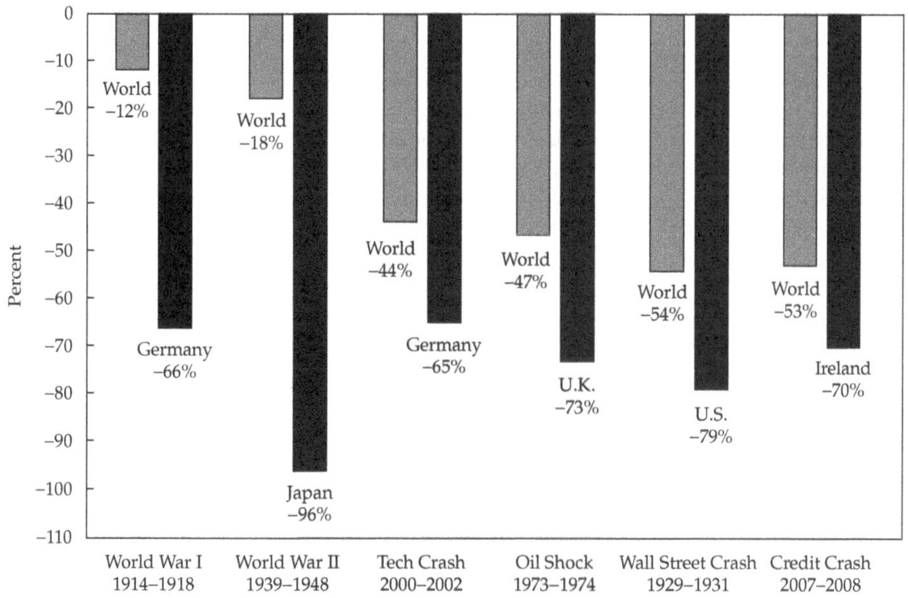

Source: Adapted from Dimson, Marsh, and Staunton (2009).

Given the high risk levels associated with equity securities, it is reasonable to expect that investors' tolerance for risk will tend to differ across equity markets. This is illustrated in Exhibit 8-6, which shows the results of a series of studies conducted by the Australian Securities Exchange on international differences in equity ownership. During the 2000–2008 period, equity ownership as a percentage of the population was lowest in South Korea (averaging 7.5 percent), followed by Germany (16.6 percent) and Sweden (21 percent). In contrast, Australia, Canada, and the United States had the highest equity ownership as a percentage of the population (averaging almost 50 percent). In addition, there has been a relative decline in share ownership in several countries over recent years, which is not surprising given the recent overall uncertainty in global economies and the volatility in equity markets that this uncertainty has created.

EXHIBIT 8-6 International Comparisons of Stock Ownership in Selected Countries: 2000–2008

	2000	2002	2004	2006	2008
Australia—Direct/Indirect	52%	50%	55%	46%	41%
Canada—Shares/Funds	49	46	49	N/A	N/A
Germany—Shares/Funds	19	18	16	16	14
Hong Kong—Shares	22	20	24	N/A	22
New Zealand	24	N/A	23	26	N/A
South Korea—Shares	7	8	8	7	N/A
Switzerland—Shares/Funds	34	25	21	21	21
Sweden—Shares	22	23	22	20	18
U.K.—Shares/Funds	26	25	22	20	18
U.S.—Direct/Indirect	N/A	50	49	N/A	45

The percentages reported in the exhibit are based on samples of the adult population in each country who own equity securities either directly or indirectly through investment or retirement funds. For example, 41 percent of the adult population of Australia in 2008 (approximately 6.7 million people) owned equity securities either directly or indirectly. As noted in the study, it is not appropriate to make absolute comparisons across countries given the differences in methodology, sampling, timing, and definitions that have been used in different countries. However, trends across different countries can be identified.

Source: Adapted from the *2008 Australian Share Ownership Study* conducted by the Australian Securities Exchange (see www.asx.com.au). For Australia and the United States, the data pertain to direct and indirect ownership in equity markets; for other countries, the data pertain to direct ownership in shares and share funds. Data not available in specific years are shown as "N/A."

An important implication from the above discussion is that equity securities represent a key asset class for global investors because of their unique return and risk characteristics. We next examine the various types of equity securities traded on global markets and their salient characteristics.

3. TYPES AND CHARACTERISTICS OF EQUITY SECURITIES

Companies finance their operations by issuing either debt or equity securities. A key difference between these securities is that debt is a liability of the issuing company, whereas equity is not. This means that when a company issues debt, it is contractually obligated to repay the amount it borrows (i.e., the principal or face value of the debt) at a specified future date. The cost of using these funds is called interest, which the company is contractually obligated to pay until the debt matures or is retired.

When the company issues equity securities, it is not contractually obligated to repay the amount it receives from shareholders, nor is it contractually obligated to make periodic payments to shareholders for the use of their funds. Instead, shareholders have a claim on the company's assets after all liabilities have been paid. Because of this residual claim, equity shareholders are considered to be owners of the company. Investors who purchase equity securities are seeking total return (i.e., capital or price appreciation and dividend income), whereas investors who purchase debt securities (and hold until maturity) are seeking interest income. As a result, equity investors expect the company's management to act in their best interest by making operating decisions that will maximize the market price of their shares (i.e., shareholder wealth).

In addition to common shares (also known as ordinary shares or common stock), companies may also issue preference shares (also known as preferred stock), the other type of equity security. The following sections discuss the different types and characteristics of common and preference securities.

3.1. Common Shares

Common shares represent an ownership interest in a company and are the predominant type of equity security. As a result, investors share in the operating performance of the company, participate in the governance process through voting rights, and have a claim on the company's net assets in the case of liquidation. Companies may choose to pay out some, or all, of their net income in the form of cash dividends to common shareholders, but they are not contractually obligated to do so.[8]

Voting rights provide shareholders with the opportunity to participate in major corporate governance decisions, including the election of its board of directors, the decision to merge with or take over another company, and the selection of outside auditors. Shareholder voting generally takes place during a company's annual meeting. As a result of geographic limitations and the large number of shareholders, it is often not feasible for shareholders to attend the annual meeting in person. For this reason, shareholders may **vote by proxy**, which allows a designated party—such as another shareholder, a shareholder representative, or management—to vote on the shareholders' behalf.

Regular shareholder voting, where each share represents one vote, is referred to as **statutory voting**. Although it is the common method of voting, it is not always the most appropriate one to use to elect a board of directors. To better serve shareholders who own a small number of shares, **cumulative voting** is often used. Cumulative voting allows shareholders to direct their total voting rights to specific candidates, as opposed to having to allocate their voting rights evenly among all candidates. Total voting rights are based on the number of shares owned multiplied by the number of board directors being elected. For example, under cumulative voting, if four board directors are to be elected, a shareholder who owns 100 shares is entitled to 400 votes and can either cast all 400 votes in favor of a single candidate or spread them across the candidates in any proportion. In contrast, under statutory voting, a shareholder would be able to cast only a maximum of 100 votes for each candidate.

The key benefit to cumulative voting is that it allows shareholders with a small number of shares to apply all of their votes to one candidate, thus providing the opportunity for a higher level of representation on the board than would be allowed under statutory voting.

Exhibit 8-7 describes the rights of Viacom Corporation's shareholders. In this case, a dual-share arrangement allows the founding chairman and his family to control more than 70 percent of the voting rights through the ownership of Class A shares. This arrangement gives them the ability to exert control over the board of director election process, corporate decision making,

[8] It is also possible for companies to pay more than the current period's net income as dividends. Such payout policies are, however, generally not sustainable in the long run.

and other important aspects of managing the company. A cumulative voting arrangement for any minority shareholders of Class A shares would improve their board representation.

EXHIBIT 8-7 Share Class Arrangements at Viacom Corporation

Viacom has two classes of common stock: Class A, which is the voting stock, and Class B, which is the nonvoting stock. There is no difference between the two classes except for voting rights; they generally trade within a close price range of each other. There are, however, far more shares of Class B outstanding, so most of the trading occurs in that class.

Voting Rights—Holders of Class A common stock are entitled to one vote per share. Holders of Class B common stock do not have any voting rights, except as required by Delaware law. Generally, all matters to be voted on by Viacom stockholders must be approved by a majority of the aggregate voting power of the shares of Class A common stock present in person or represented by proxy, except as required by Delaware law.

Dividends—Stockholders of Class A common stock and Class B common stock will share ratably in any cash dividend declared by the Board of Directors, subject to any preferential rights of any outstanding preferred stock. Viacom does not currently pay a cash dividend, and any decision to pay a cash dividend in the future will be at the discretion of the Board of Directors and will depend on many factors.

Conversion—So long as there are 5,000 shares of Class A common stock outstanding, each share of Class A common stock will be convertible at the option of the holder of such share into one share of Class B common stock.

Liquidation Rights—In the event of liquidation, dissolution, or winding-up of Viacom, all stockholders of common stock, regardless of class, will be entitled to share ratably in any assets available for distributions to stockholders of shares of Viacom common stock subject to the preferential rights of any outstanding preferred stock.

Split, Subdivisions, or Combination—In the event of a split, subdivision, or combination of the outstanding shares of Class A common stock or Class B common stock, the outstanding shares of the other class of common stock will be divided proportionally.

Preemptive Rights—Shares of Class A common stock and Class B common stock do not entitle a stockholder to any preemptive rights enabling a stockholder to subscribe for or receive shares of stock of any class or any other securities convertible into shares of stock of any class of Viacom.

This information has been adapted from Viacom's investor relations web site and its 10-K filing with the U.S. Securities and Exchange Commission; see www.viacom.com.

As seen in Exhibit 8-7, companies can issue different classes of common shares (Class A and Class B shares), with each class offering different ownership rights.[9] For example, as shown in Exhibit 8-8, the Ford Motor Company has Class A shares ("Common Stock"), which are owned by the investing public. It also has Class B shares, which are owned only by the Ford family. The exhibit contains an excerpt from Ford's *2008 Annual Report* (p. 115). Class A shareholders have 60 percent voting rights, whereas Class B shareholders have

[9] In some countries, including the United States, companies can issue different classes of shares, with Class A shares being the most common. The role and function of different classes of shares is described in more detail in Exhibit 8-7.

40 percent. In the case of liquidation, however, Class B shareholders will not only receive the first US$0.50 per share that is available for distribution (as will Class A shareholders), but they will also receive the next US$1.00 per share that is available for distribution before Class A shareholders receive anything else. Thus, Class B shareholders have an opportunity to receive a larger proportion of distributions upon liquidation than do Class A shareholders.[10]

EXHIBIT 8-8 Share Class Arrangements at Ford Motor Company

NOTE 21. CAPITAL STOCK AND AMOUNTS PER SHARE

All general voting power is vested in the holders of Common Stock and Class B Stock. Holders of our Common Stock have 60% of the general voting power and holders of our Class B Stock are entitled to such number of votes per share as will give them the remaining 40%. Shares of Common Stock and Class B Stock share equally in dividends when and as paid, with stock dividends payable in shares of stock of the class held. As discussed in Note 16, we are prohibited from paying dividends (other than dividends payable in stock) under the terms of the Credit Agreement.

If liquidated, each share of Common Stock will be entitled to the first $0.50 available for distribution to holders of Common Stock and Class B Stock, each share of Class B Stock will be entitled to the next $1.00 so available, each share of Common Stock will be entitled to the next $0.50 so available and each share of Common and Class B Stock will be entitled to an equal amount thereafter.

Extracted from Ford Motor Company's *2008 Annual Report* (http://virtual.stivesonline.com/publication/?i=14030).

Common shares may also be callable or putable. **Callable common shares** (also known as redeemable common shares) give the issuing company the option (or right), but not the obligation, to buy back shares from investors at a call price that is specified when the shares are originally issued. It is most common for companies to call (or redeem) their common shares when the market price is above the prespecified call price. The company benefits because it can buy back its shares below the current market price and later resell them at a higher market price, and it can also reduce dividend payments to preserve capital, if required. Investors benefit because they receive a guaranteed return when their shares are called. Exhibit 8-9 provides an example of callable common shares issued by Genomic Solutions in the U.S. market. The exhibit provides details on the creation of callable common shares used to consummate a strategic alliance between PerkinElmer and Genomic Solutions. The arrangement contains provisions more favorable to PerkinElmer because at the time it was a more established and better capitalized company than Genomic Solutions.

[10] For example, if US$2.00 per share is available for distribution, the Common Stock (Class A) shareholders will receive US$0.50 per share, while the Class B shareholders will receive US$1.50 per share. However, if there is US$3.50 per share available for distribution, the Common Stock shareholders will receive a total of US$1.50 per share and the Class B shareholders will receive a total of US$2.00 per share.

EXHIBIT 8-9 Callable Stock Arrangement from Genomic Solutions

The following information assumes that the underwriters do not exercise the overallotment option granted by us to purchase additional shares in the offering:

Callable common stock offered by us:	7,000,000 shares
Callable common stock to be outstanding after the offering:	22,718,888 shares
Common stock to be outstanding after the offering:	1,269,841 shares
Proposed Nasdaq National Market symbol:	GNSL
Use of proceeds:	General corporate purposes and possible future acquisitions

For two years from the completion of this offering, we may require all holders of our callable common stock to sell their shares back to us. We must exercise this right at PerkinElmer's direction. The price for repurchase of our callable common stock generally will be 20% over the market price. PerkinElmer also has a right to match any third party offer for our callable common stock or our business that our board of directors is prepared to accept.

Genomic Solutions Form S-1 as filed with the U.S. SEC (14 May 2000); see www.edgar-online.com.

Putable common shares give investors the option or right to sell their shares (i.e., "put" them) back to the issuing company at a price that is specified when the shares are originally issued. Investors will generally sell their shares back to the issuing company when the market price is below the prespecified put price. Thus, the put option feature limits the potential loss for investors. From the issuing company's perspective, the put option facilitates raising capital because the shares are more appealing to investors.

Exhibit 8-10 provides an example of putable common shares issued by Dreyer's, now a subsidiary of Switzerland-based Nestlé. In this case, shareholders had the right to sell their shares to Dreyer's for US $83.10, the prespecified put price.

EXHIBIT 8-10 Putable Stock Arrangement for Dreyer's Grand Ice Cream

Dreyer's Grand Ice Cream Holdings, Inc. ("Dreyer's") (NNM: DRYR) announced today that the period during which holders of shares of Dreyer's Class A Callable Putable Common Stock (the "Class A Shares") could require Dreyer's to purchase their Class A Shares (the "Put Right") for a cash payment of $83.10 per Class A Share (the "Purchase Price") expired at 5:00 p.m. New York City time on January 13, 2006 (the "Expiration Time"). According to the report of the depositary agent for the Put Right, holders of an aggregate of 30,518,885 Class A Shares (including 1,792,193 shares subject to guaranteed delivery procedures) properly exercised the Put Right.

"Dreyer's Announces Expiration of Put Period and Anticipated Merger with Nestle," *Business Wire* (14 January 2006): www.findarticles.com/p/articles/mi_m0EIN/is_2006_Jan_14/ai_n16001349.

3.2. Preference Shares

Preference shares (or preferred stock) rank above common shares with respect to the payment of dividends and the distribution of the company's net assets upon liquidation.[11] However, preference shareholders do not share in the operating performance of the company and generally do not have any voting rights, unless explicitly allowed for at issuance. Preference shares have characteristics of both debt securities and common shares. Similar to the interest payments on debt securities, the dividends on preference shares are fixed and are generally higher than the dividends on common shares. However, unlike interest payments, preference dividends are not contractual obligations of the company. Similar to common shares, preference shares can be perpetual (i.e., no fixed maturity date), can pay dividends indefinitely, and can be callable or putable.

Exhibit 8-11 provides an example of callable preference shares issued by Goldman Sachs to raise capital during the credit crisis of 2008. In this case, Berkshire Hathaway, the purchaser of the shares, will receive an ongoing dividend from Goldman Sachs. If Goldman Sachs chooses to buy back the shares, it must do so at a 10 percent premium above their par value.

EXHIBIT 8-11 Callable Stock Arrangement between Goldman Sachs and Berkshire Hathaway

> New York, NY, September 23, 2008—The Goldman Sachs Group, Inc. (NYSE: GS) announced today that it has reached an agreement to sell $5 billion of perpetual preferred stock to Berkshire Hathaway, Inc. in a private offering. The preferred stock has a dividend of 10 percent and is callable at any time at a 10 percent premium. In conjunction with this offering, Berkshire Hathaway will also receive warrants to purchase $5 billion of common stock with a strike price of $115 per share, which are exercisable at any time for a five year term. In addition, Goldman Sachs is raising at least $2.5 billion in common equity in a public offering.

Goldman Sachs, "Berkshire Hathaway to Invest $5 billion in Goldman Sachs," (23 September 2008): www.goldmansachs.com/our-firm/press/press-releases/archived/2008/berkshire-hathaway-invest.html.

Dividends on preference shares can be cumulative, noncumulative, participating, nonparticipating, or some combination thereof (i.e., cumulative participating, cumulative nonparticipating, noncumulative participating, noncumulative nonparticipating).

Dividends on **cumulative preference shares** accrue so that if the company decides not to pay a dividend in one or more periods, the unpaid dividends accrue and must be paid in full before dividends on common shares can be paid. In contrast, **noncumulative preference shares** have no such provision. This means that any dividends that are not paid in the current or subsequent periods are forfeited permanently and are not accrued over time to be paid at a later date. However, the company is still not permitted to pay any dividends to common shareholders in the current period unless preferred dividends have been paid first.

[11] Preference shares have a lower priority than debt in the case of liquidation. That is, debt holders have a higher claim on a firm's assets in the event of liquidation and will receive what is owed to them first, followed by preference shareholders and then common shareholders.

Participating preference shares entitle the shareholders to receive the standard preferred dividend plus the opportunity to receive an additional dividend if the company's profits exceed a prespecified level. In addition, participating preference shares can also contain provisions that entitle shareholders to an additional distribution of the company's assets upon liquidation, above the par (or face) value of the preference shares. **Nonparticipating preference shares** do not allow shareholders to share in the profits of the company. Instead, shareholders are entitled to receive only a fixed dividend payment and the par value of the shares in the event of liquidation. The use of participating preference shares is much more common for smaller, riskier companies where the possibility of future liquidation is more of a concern to investors.

Preference shares can also be convertible. **Convertible preference shares** entitle shareholders to convert their shares into a specified number of common shares. This conversion ratio is determined at issuance. Convertible preference shares have the following advantages:

- They allow investors to earn a higher dividend than if they invested in the company's common shares.
- They allow investors the opportunity to share in the profits of the company.
- They allow investors to benefit from a rise in the price of the common shares through the conversion option.
- Their price is less volatile than the underlying common shares because the dividend payments are known and more stable.

As a result, the use of convertible preference shares is a popular financing option in venture capital and private equity transactions in which the issuing companies are considered to be of higher risk and when it may be years before the issuing company "goes public" (i.e., issues common shares to the public).

Exhibit 8-12 provides examples of the types and characteristics of preference shares as issued by DBS Bank of Singapore.

EXHIBIT 8-12 Examples of Preference Shares Issued by DBS Bank

SINGAPORE, MAY 12—DBS Bank said today it plans to offer S$700 million in preference shares and make it available to both retail and institutional investors in Singapore. Called the DBS Preferred Investment Issue, it will yield investors a fixed noncumulative gross dividend rate of 6% for the first ten years and a floating rate thereafter. The DBS Preferred Investment Issue will be offered in two tranches, consisting of a S$100 million tranche to retail investors via ATMs and a S$600 million placement tranche available to both retail and institutional investors. Depending on investor demand, DBS could increase the offering amount.

Jackson Tai, President and Chief Operating Officer of DBS Group Holdings, said that following the success of the hybrid Tier 1 issue in March, DBS decided to make this new issue available to the local retail investors. "We consider these issues as an important capital management tool. We were pleased with the success of our hybrid Tier 1 issue for institutional investors and wanted to introduce a capital instrument that would be available to retail investors as well."

DBS Preferred Investment Issues are perpetual securities, redeemable after ten years at the option of DBS Bank and at every dividend date thereafter subject to certain redemption

EXHIBIT 8-12 (*Continued*)

conditions. They are issued by DBS Bank and are considered to be core Tier 1 capital under the Monetary Authority of Singapore and Bank of International Settlement's guidelines. They will be listed on the Singapore Exchange Securities Trading Limited and can be traded on the secondary market through a broker. Holders of the DBS Preferred Investment Issue will receive the dividend net of the 24.5% income tax. Investors may claim the tax credit in their tax returns.

DBS Bank, "DBS Follows US$850 Million Offering of Subordinated Notes to International Markets with Singapore Dollar Market Financing" (12 May 2001): www.dbs.com/newsroom/2001/Pages/press010512.aspx.

4. PRIVATE VERSUS PUBLIC EQUITY SECURITIES

Our discussion so far has focused on equity securities that are issued and traded in public markets and on exchanges. Equity securities can also be issued and traded in private equity markets. **Private equity securities** are issued primarily to institutional investors via nonpublic offerings, such as private placements. Because they are not listed on public exchanges, there is no active secondary market for these securities. As a result, private equity securities do not have "market determined" quoted prices, are highly illiquid, and require negotiations between investors in order to be traded. In addition, financial statements and other important information needed to determine the fair value of private equity securities may be difficult to obtain because the issuing companies are typically not required by regulatory authorities to publish this information.

There are three primary types of private equity investments: venture capital, leveraged buyouts, and private investment in public equity. **Venture capital** investments provide "seed" or start-up capital, early-stage financing, or mezzanine financing to companies that are in the early stages of development and require additional capital for expansion. These funds are then used to finance the company's product development and growth. Venture capitalists range from family and friends to wealthy individuals and private equity funds. Because the equity securities issued to venture capitalists are not publicly traded, they generally require a commitment of funds for a relatively long period of time; the opportunity to "exit" the investment is typically within 3 to 10 years from the initial start-up. The exit return earned by these private equity investors is based on the price that the securities can be sold for if and when the start-up company first goes public, either via an **initial public offering** (IPO) on the stock market or by being sold to other investors.

A **leveraged buyout** (LBO) occurs when a group of investors (such as the company's management or a private equity partnership) uses a large amount of debt to purchase all of the outstanding common shares of a publicly traded company. In cases where the group of investors acquiring the company is primarily comprised of the company's existing management, the transaction is referred to as a **management buyout** (MBO). After the shares are purchased, they cease to trade on an exchange and the investor group takes full control of the company. In other words, the company is taken "private" or has been privatized. Companies that are candidates for these types of transactions generally have large amounts of undervalued assets (which can be sold to reduce debt) and generate high levels of cash flows (which are used to make interest and principal payments on the debt). The ultimate objective of a buyout (LBO or MBO) is to restructure the acquired company and later take it "public" again by issuing new shares to the public in the primary market.

The third type of private investment is a **private investment in public equity**, or PIPE.[12] This type of investment is generally sought by a public company that is in need of additional capital quickly and is willing to sell a sizeable ownership position to a private investor or investor group. For example, a company may require a large investment of new equity funds in a short period of time because it has significant expansion opportunities, is facing high levels of indebtedness, or is experiencing a rapid deterioration in its operations. Depending on how urgent the need is and the size of the capital requirement, the private investor may be able to purchase shares in the company at a significant discount to the publicly quoted market price. Exhibit 8-13 contains a recent PIPE transaction for the electronics retailer hhgregg, which also included the issuance of additional common shares to the public.

EXHIBIT 8-13 Example of a PIPE Transaction

> On July 20, 2009, hhgregg completed a public stock offering of 4,025,000 shares of its common stock at $16.50 per share. Concurrently with the public offering, investment funds affiliated with Freeman Spogli & Co. purchased an additional 1,000,000 shares of common stock, in a private placement transaction, at the price per share paid by the public in the offering. Proceeds, net of underwriting fees, from the public stock offering and private placement, totaled approximately $78.6 million. These proceeds will be used for general corporate purposes, including funding the Company's accelerated new store growth plans.

This information was obtained from hhgregg's first quarter fiscal 2009 earnings report (http://ir.hhgregg.com/releasedetail.cfm?ReleaseID=401980).

While the global private equity market is relatively small in comparison to the global public equity market, it has experienced considerable growth over the past three decades. According to a study of the private equity market sponsored by the *World Economic Forum* and spanning the period 1970–2007, approximately US$3.6 trillion in debt and equity were acquired in leveraged buyouts. Of this amount, approximately 75 percent or US$2.7 trillion worth of transactions occurred during 2001–2007.[13] While the U.S. and the U.K markets were the focus of most private equity investments during the 1980s and 1990s, private equity investments outside of these markets have grown substantially in recent years. In addition, the number of companies operating under private equity ownership has also grown. For example, during the mid-1990s, fewer than 2,000 companies were under LBO ownership compared to close to 14,000 companies that were under LBO ownership globally at the beginning of 2007. The holding period for private equity investments has also increased during this time period from three to five years (1980s and 1990s) to approximately 10 years.[14]

The move to longer holding periods has given private equity investors the opportunity to more effectively and patiently address any underlying operational issues facing the company and to better manage it for long-term value creation. Because of the longer holding periods, more private equity firms are issuing convertible preference shares because they provide investors with greater total return potential through their dividend payments and the ability to convert their shares into common shares during an IPO.

[12] The term PIPE is widely used in the United States; it is referred to as a private finance initiative (PFI) in the United Kingdom. The more generic term of public–private partnership is used in other markets.
[13] Stromberg (2008).
[14] See, for example, Bailey, Wirth, and Zapol (2005).

In operating a publicly traded company, management often feels pressured to focus on short-term results[15] (e.g., meeting quarterly sales and earnings targets from analysts biased toward near-term price performance) instead of operating the company to obtain long-term sustainable revenue and earnings growth. By "going private," management can adopt a more long-term focus and can eliminate certain costs that are necessary to operate a publicly traded company—such as the cost of meeting regulatory and stock exchange filing requirements, the cost of maintaining investor relations departments to communicate with shareholders and the media, and the cost of holding quarterly analyst conference calls.

As described previously, public equity markets are much larger than private equity networks and allow companies more opportunities to raise capital that is subsequently actively traded in secondary markets. By operating under public scrutiny, companies are incentivized to be more open in terms of corporate governance and executive compensation to ensure that they are acting for the benefit of shareholders. In fact, some studies have shown that private equity firms score lower in terms of corporate governance effectiveness, which may be attributed to the fact that shareholders, analysts, and other stakeholders are able to influence management when corporate governance and other policies are public.

5. INVESTING IN NONDOMESTIC EQUITY SECURITIES

Technological innovations and the growth of electronic information exchanges (electronic trading networks, the Internet, etc.) have accelerated the integration and growth of global financial markets. As detailed previously, global capital markets have expanded at a much more rapid rate than global GDP in recent years; both primary and secondary international markets have benefited from the enhanced ability to rapidly and openly exchange information. Increased integration of equity markets has made it easier and less expensive for companies to raise capital and to expand their shareholder base beyond their local market. Integration has also made it easier for investors to invest in companies that are located outside of their domestic markets. This has enabled investors to further diversify and improve the risk and return characteristics of their portfolios by adding a class of assets with lower correlations to local country assets.

One barrier to investing globally is that many countries still impose "foreign restrictions" on individuals and companies from other countries that want to invest in their domestic companies. There are three primary reasons for these restrictions. The first is to limit the amount of control that foreign investors can exert on domestic companies. For example, some countries prevent foreign investors from acquiring a majority interest in domestic companies. The second is to give domestic investors the opportunity to own shares in the foreign companies that are conducting business in their country. For example, the Swedish home furnishings retailer IKEA abandoned efforts to invest in parts of the Asia/Pacific region because local governments did not want IKEA to maintain complete ownership of its stores. The third reason is to reduce the volatility of capital flows into and out of domestic equity markets. For example, one of the main consequences of the Asian Financial Crisis in 1997–1998 was the large outflow of capital from such emerging market countries as Thailand, Indonesia, and South Korea. These outflows led to dramatic declines in the equity markets of these countries and significant currency devaluations and resulted in many governments placing restrictions on capital flows. Today, many of these same markets have built up

[15] For further information, see "Overcoming Short-Termism: A Call for a More Responsible Approach to Investment and Business Management" (www.aspeninstitute.org/bsp/cvsg/policy2009).

currency reserves to better withstand capital outflows inherent in economic contractions and periods of financial market turmoil.

Studies have shown that reducing restrictions on foreign ownership has led to improved equity market performance over the long term.[16] Although restrictions vary widely, more countries are allowing increasing levels of foreign ownership. For example, Australia has sought tax reforms as a means to encourage international demand for its managed funds in order to increase its role as an international financial center. China recently announced plans to allow designated foreign institutional investors to invest up to US$1 billion in its domestic yuan-denominated A shares (up from a previous US$800 million) as it seeks to slowly liberalize its stock markets.

Over the past two decades, three trends have emerged: (1) an increasing number of companies have issued shares in markets outside of their home country; (2) the number of companies whose shares are traded in markets outside of their home has increased; and (3) an increasing number of companies are dual listed, which means that their shares are simultaneously issued and traded in two or more markets. Companies located in emerging markets have particularly benefited from these trends because they no longer have to be concerned with capital constraints or lack of liquidity in their domestic markets. These companies have found it easier to raise capital in the markets of developed countries because these markets generally have higher levels of liquidity and more stringent financial reporting requirements and accounting standards. Being listed on an international exchange has a number of benefits. It can increase investor awareness about the company's products and services, enhance the liquidity of the company's shares, and increase corporate transparency because of the additional market exposure and the need to meet a greater number of filing requirements.

Technological advancements have made it easier for investors to trade shares in foreign markets. The German insurance company Allianz SE recently delisted its shares from the NYSE and certain European markets because international investors increasingly traded its shares on the Frankfurt Stock Exchange. Exhibit 8-14 illustrates the extent to which the institutional shareholder base at BASF, a large German chemical corporation, has become increasingly global in nature.

5.1. Direct Investing

Investors can use a variety of methods to invest in the equity of companies outside of their local market. The most obvious is to buy and sell securities directly in foreign markets. However, this means that all transactions—including the purchase and sale of shares, dividend payments, and capital gains—are in the company's, not the investor's, domestic currency. In addition, investors must be familiar with the trading, clearing, and settlement regulations and procedures of that market. Investing directly often results in less transparency and more volatility because audited financial information may not be provided on a regular basis and the market may be less liquid. Alternatively, investors can use such securities as depository receipts and global registered shares, which represent the equity of international companies and are traded on local exchanges and in the local currencies. With these securities, investors have to worry less about currency conversions (price quotations and dividend payments are in the investor's local currency), unfamiliar market practices, and differences in accounting standards. The sections that follow discuss various securities that investors can invest in outside of their home market.

[16] See, for example, Henry and Chari (2007).

EXHIBIT 8-14 Example of Increased Globalization of Share Ownership

BASF is one of the largest publicly owned companies with around 460,000 shareholders and a high free float. An analysis of the shareholder structure carried out in September 2008 showed that, at 22% of share capital, the United States and Canada made up the largest regional group of institutional investors. Institutional investors from Germany made up 13%. Shareholders from Great Britain and Ireland held 14% of BASF shares, while a further 14% are held by institutional investors from the rest of Europe. Around 28% of the company's share capital is held by private investors, most of whom are resident in Germany

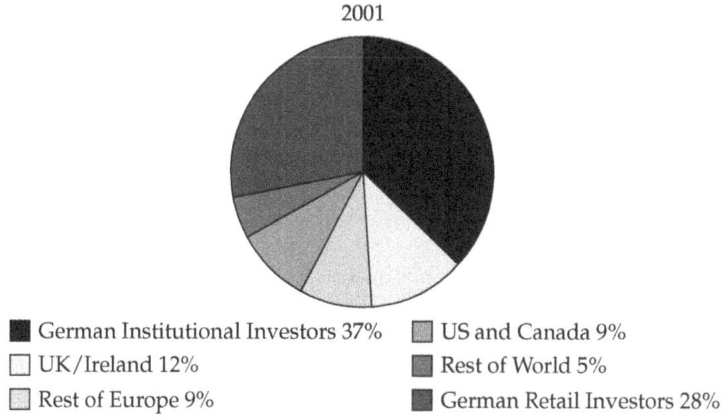

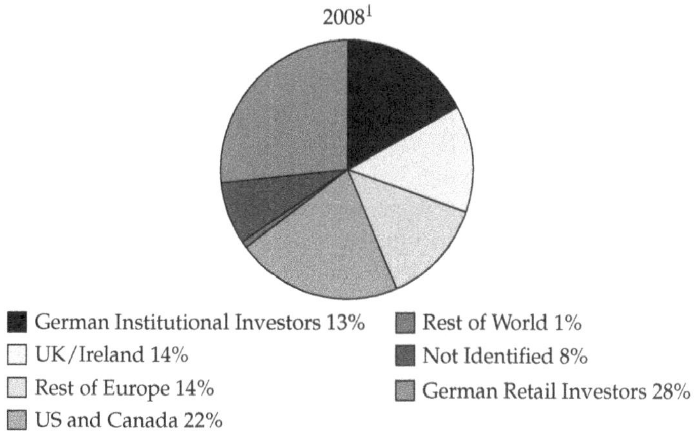

[1]As of September 30, 2008.

Adapted from BASF's investor relations web site (www.basf.com). **Free float** refers to the extent that shares are readily and freely tradable in the secondary market.

5.2. Depository Receipts

A **depository**[17] **receipt** (DR) is a security that trades like an ordinary share on a local exchange and represents an economic interest in a foreign company. It allows the publicly listed shares of a

[17] Note that the spellings *depositary* and *depository* are used interchangeably in financial markets. In this chapter, we use the spelling *depository* throughout.

EXHIBIT 8-15 Sponsored versus Unsponsored Depository Receipts

> The Japan Airlines (JAL) Group, Asia's biggest airline grouping, has picked the Bank of New York as the depository bank to make its previously unsponsored American depository receipts (ADRs) sponsored. By taking this action and by boosting investor relations activities in the U.S., the JAL group aims to increase the number of overseas shareholders. The JAL Group's sponsored ADRs became effective on August 19th, 2004 and dealing will start on August 25th. The JAL Group's American depository receipts had been previously issued in the U.S. as unsponsored ADRs by several U.S. depository banks since the 1970s. However, as unsponsored ADRs are issued without the involvement of the company itself, the company has difficulty in identifying ADR holders and controlling ADRs. From now, the JAL Group will be able to better serve its ADR holders and, at the same time, the JAL Group intends to increase its overseas investors.

Adapted from Japan Airlines Group's investor relations web site (www.jal.com/en/press/2004/082301/img/ADRS.pdf).

foreign company to be traded on an exchange outside its domestic market. A depository receipt is created when the equity shares of a foreign company are deposited in a bank (i.e., the depository) in the country on whose exchange the shares will trade. The depository then issues receipts that represent the shares that were deposited. The number of receipts issued and the price of each DR is based on a ratio, which specifies the number of depository receipts to the underlying shares. Consequently, a DR may represent one share of the underlying stock, many shares of the underlying stock, or a fractional share of the underlying stock. The price of each DR will be affected by factors that affect the price of the underlying shares, such as company fundamentals, market conditions, analysts' recommendations, and exchange rate movements. In addition, any short-term valuation discrepancies between shares traded on multiple exchanges represent a quick arbitrage profit opportunity for astute traders to exploit. The responsibilities of the depository bank that issues the receipts include acting as custodian and as a registrar. This entails handling dividend payments, other taxable events, stock splits, and serving as the transfer agent for the foreign company whose securities the DR represents. The Bank of New York Mellon is the largest depository bank; however, Deutsche Bank, JPMorgan, and Citibank also offer depository services.[18]

A DR can be **sponsored** or **unsponsored**. A sponsored DR is when the foreign company whose shares are held by the depository has a direct involvement in the issuance of the receipts. Investors in sponsored DRs have the same rights as the direct owners of the common shares (e.g., the right to vote and the right to receive dividends). In contrast, with an unsponsored DR, the underlying foreign company has no involvement with the issuance of the receipts. Instead, the depository purchases the foreign company's shares in its domestic market and then issues the receipts through brokerage firms in the depository's local market. In this case, the depository bank, not the investors in the DR, retains the voting rights. Sponsored DRs are generally subject to greater reporting requirements than unsponsored DRs. In the United States, for example, sponsored DRs must be registered (meet the reporting requirements) with the U.S. Securities and Exchange Commission (SEC). Exhibit 8-15 contains an example of a sponsored DR issued by Japan Airlines.

[18] Boubakri, Cosset, and Samet (2008).

There are two types of depository receipts: Global depository receipts (GDRs) and American depository receipts (ADRs), which are described next.

5.2.1. Global Depository Receipts

A **global depository receipt** (GDR) is issued outside of the company's home country and outside of the United States. The depository bank that issues GDRs is generally located (or has branches) in the countries on whose exchanges the shares are traded. A key advantage of GDRs is that they are not subject to the foreign ownership and capital flow restrictions that may be imposed by the issuing company's home country because they are sold outside of that country. The issuing company selects the exchange where the GDR is to be traded based on such factors as investors' familiarity with the company or the existence of a large international investor base. The London and Luxembourg exchanges were the first ones to trade GDRs. Other stock exchanges trading GDRs are the Dubai International Financial Exchange, the Singapore Stock Exchange, and the Hong Kong Stock Exchange. Currently, the London and Luxembourg exchanges are where most GDRs are traded because they can be issued in a more timely manner and at a lower cost. Regardless of the exchange they are traded on, the majority of GDRs are denominated in U.S. dollars, although the number of GDRs denominated in pound sterling and euros is increasing. Note that although GDRs cannot be listed on U.S. exchanges, they can be privately placed with institutional investors based in the United States.

5.2.2. American Depository Receipts

An **American depository receipt** (ADR) is a U.S. dollar-denominated security that trades like a common share on U.S. exchanges. First created in 1927, ADRs are the oldest type of depository receipts and are currently the most commonly traded depository receipts. They enable foreign companies to raise capital from U.S. investors. Note that an ADR is one form of a GDR; however, not all GDRs are ADRs because GDRs cannot be publicly traded in the United States. The term **American depository share** (ADS) is often used in tandem with the term ADR. A depository share is a security that is actually traded in the issuing company's domestic market. That is, while American depository receipts are the certificates that are traded on U.S. markets, American depository shares are the underlying shares on which these receipts are based.

There are four primary types of ADRs, with each type having different levels of corporate governance and filing requirements. Level I Sponsored ADRs trade in the over-the-counter (OTC) market and do not require full registration with the Securities and Exchange Commission (SEC). Level II and Level III Sponsored ADRs can trade on the New York Stock Exchange (NYSE), NASDAQ, and American Stock Exchange (AMEX). Level II and III ADRs allow companies to raise capital and make acquisitions using these securities. However, the issuing companies must fulfill all SEC requirements.

The fourth type of ADR, an SEC Rule 144A or a Regulation S depository receipt, does not require SEC registration. Instead, foreign companies are able to raise capital by privately placing these depository receipts with qualified institutional investors or to offshore non-U.S. investors. Exhibit 8-16 summarizes the main features of ADRs.

EXHIBIT 8-16 Summary of the Main Features of American Depository Receipts

	Level I (Unlisted)	Level II (Listed)	Level III (Listed)	Rule 144A (Unlisted)
Objectives	Develop and broaden U.S. investor base with existing shares	Develop and broaden U.S. investor base with existing shares	Develop and broaden U.S. investor base with existing/new shares	Access qualified institutional buyers (QIBs)
Raising capital on U.S. markets?	No	No	Yes, through public offerings	Yes, through private placements to QIBs
SEC registration	Form F-6	Form F-6	Forms F-1 and F-6	None
Trading	Over the counter (OTC)	NYSE, NASDAQ, or AMEX	NYSE, NASDAQ, or AMEX	Private offerings, resales, and trading through automated linkages such as PORTAL
Listing fees	Low	High	High	Low
Size and earnings requirements	None	Yes	Yes	None

Source: Adapted from Boubakri, Cosset, and Samet (2008): Table 1.

More than 2,000 DRs, from over 80 countries, currently trade on U.S. exchanges. Based on current statistics, the total market value of DRs issued and traded is estimated at approximately US$2 trillion, or 15 percent of the total dollar value of equities traded in U.S. markets.[19]

5.2.3. Global Registered Share

A **global registered share** (GRS) is a common share that is traded on different stock exchanges around the world in different currencies. Currency conversions are not needed to purchase or sell them, because identical shares are quoted and traded in different currencies. Thus, the same share purchased on the Swiss exchange in Swiss francs can be sold on the Tokyo exchange for Japanese yen. As a result, GRSs offer more flexibility than depository receipts because the shares represent an actual ownership interest in the company that can be traded anywhere and currency conversions are not needed to purchase or sell them. GRSs were created and issued by Daimler Chrysler in 1998.

5.2.4. Basket of Listed Depository Receipts

Another type of global security is a **basket of listed depository receipts** (BLDR), which is an exchange-traded fund (ETF) that represents a portfolio of depository receipts. An ETF is a security that tracks an index but trades like an individual share on an exchange. An equity-ETF is a security that contains a portfolio of equities that tracks an index. It trades throughout

[19] JPMorgan Depositary Receipt Guide (2005):4.

the day and can be bought, sold, or sold short, just like an individual share. Like ordinary shares, ETFs can also be purchased on margin and used in hedging or arbitrage strategies. The BLDR is a specific class of ETF security that consists of an underlying portfolio of DRs and is designed to track the price performance of an underlying DR index. For example, the Asia 50 ADR Index Fund is a capitalization-weighted ETF designed to track the performance of 50 Asian market-based ADRs.

6. RISK AND RETURN CHARACTERISTICS OF EQUITY SECURITIES

Different types of equity securities have different ownership claims on a company's net assets. The type of equity security and its features affect its risk and return characteristics. The following sections discuss the different return and risk characteristics of equity securities.

6.1. Return Characteristics of Equity Securities

There are two main sources of equity securities' total return: price change (or capital gain) and dividend income. The price change represents the difference between the purchase price (P_{t-1}) and the sale price (P_t) of a share at the end of time $t - 1$ and t, respectively. Cash or stock dividends (D_t) represent distributions that the company makes to its shareholders during period t. Therefore, an equity security's total return is calculated as:

$$\text{Total return}, R_t = (P_t - P_{t-1} + D_t)/P_{t-1} \tag{8.1}$$

For non-dividend-paying stocks, the total return consists of price appreciation only. Companies that are in the early stages of their life cycle generally do not pay dividends because earnings and cash flows are reinvested to finance the company's growth. In contrast, companies that are in the mature phase of their life cycle may not have as many profitable growth opportunities; therefore, excess cash flows are often returned to investors via the payment of regular dividends or through share repurchases.

For investors who purchase depository receipts or foreign shares directly, there is a third source of return: **foreign exchange gains** (or losses). Foreign exchange gains arise because of the change in the exchange rate between the investor's currency and the currency that the foreign shares are denominated in. For example, U.S. investors who purchase the ADRs of a Japanese company will earn an additional return if the yen appreciates relative to the U.S. dollar. Conversely, these investors will earn a lower total return if the yen depreciates relative to the U.S. dollar. For example, if the total return for a Japanese company was 10 percent in Japan and the yen depreciated by 10 percent against the U.S. dollar, the total return of the ADR would be (approximately) 0 percent. If the yen had instead appreciated by 10 percent against the U.S. dollar, the total return of the ADR would be (approximately) 20 percent.

Investors who only consider price appreciation overlook an important source of return: the compounding that results from reinvested dividends. Reinvested dividends are cash dividends that the investor receives and uses to purchase additional shares. As Exhibit 8-17 shows, in the long run total returns on equity securities are dramatically influenced by the compounding effect of reinvested dividends. Between 1900 and 2008, US$1 invested in U.S. equities in 1900 would have grown in *real* terms to US$582 with dividends reinvested, but to just US$6 when taking only the price appreciation or capital gain into account. This corresponds to a real compounded return of 6 percent per year with dividends reinvested versus only 1.7 percent per year without dividends reinvested. As a comparison, Exhibit 8-17 shows the ending real wealth for bonds and bills, which are US$9.90 and US$2.90, respectively. These ending real wealth figures correspond to annualized real compounded returns of 2.1 percent on bonds and 1.0 percent on bills. This exhibit also shows the various bear markets (the lower boxes) over these periods, which were described in detail in Exhibit 8-5. In addition, it shows that each bear market was followed by a significant upward trend in the U.S. (and other) equity markets (the upper boxes).

EXHIBIT 8-17 Impact of Reinvested Dividends on Cumulative Real Returns in the U.S. Equity Market: 1900–2008

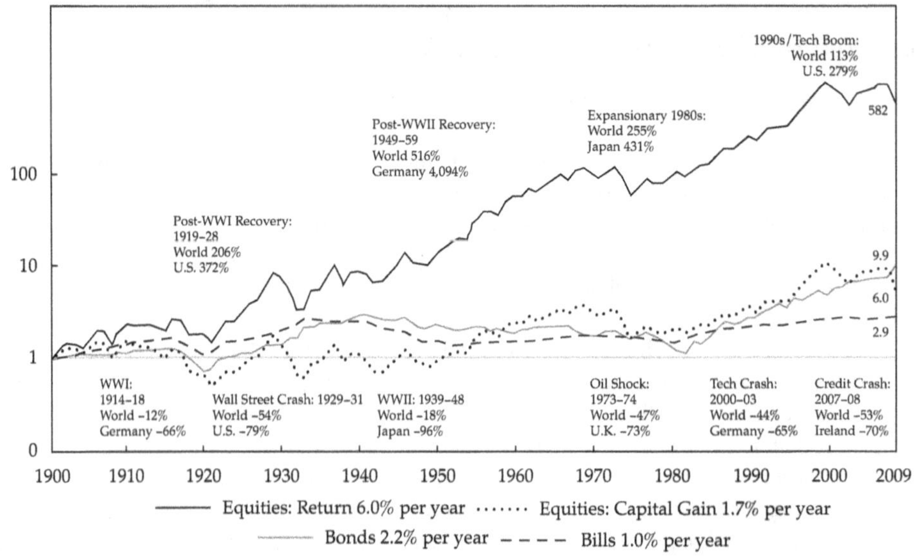

Source: Dimson, Marsh, and Staunton (2009).

6.2. Risk of Equity Securities

The risk of any security is based on the uncertainty of its future cash flows. The greater the uncertainty of its future cash flows, the greater the risk and the more variable or volatile the security's price. As discussed previously, an equity security's total return is determined by its price change and dividends. Therefore, the risk of an equity security can be defined as the uncertainty of its expected (or future) total return. Risk is most often measured by calculating the standard deviation of the equity's expected total return.

A variety of different methods can be used to estimate an equity's expected total return and risk. One method uses the equity's average historical return and the standard deviation of this return as proxies for its expected future return and risk. Another method involves estimating a range of future returns over a specified period of time, assigning probabilities to those returns, and then calculating an expected return and a standard deviation of return based on this information.

The type of equity security, as well as its characteristics, affects the uncertainty of its future cash flows and therefore its risk. In general, preference shares are less risky than common shares for three main reasons:

1. Dividends on preference shares are known and fixed, and they account for a large portion of the preference shares' total return. Therefore, there is less uncertainty about future cash flows.
2. Preference shareholders receive dividends and other distributions before common shareholders.
3. The amount preference shareholders will receive if the company is liquidated is known and fixed as the par (or face) value of their shares. However, there is no guarantee that investors will receive that amount if the company experiences financial difficulty.

With common shares, however, a larger portion of shareholders' total return (or all of their total return for nondividend shares) is based on future price appreciation, and future dividends are unknown. If the company is liquidated, common shareholders will receive whatever amount (if any) is remaining after the company's creditors and preference shareholders have been paid. In summary, because the uncertainty surrounding the total return of preference shares is less than common shares, preference shares have lower risk and lower expected return than common shares.

It is important to note that some preference shares and common shares can be riskier than others because of their associated characteristics. For example, from an investor's point of view, putable common or preference shares are less risky than their callable or noncallable counterparts because they give the investor the option to sell the shares to the issuer at a predetermined price. This predetermined price establishes a minimum price that investors will receive and reduces the uncertainty associated with the security's future cash flow. As a result, putable shares generally pay a lower dividend than nonputable shares.

Because the major source of total return for preference shares is dividend income, the primary risk affecting all preference shares is the uncertainty of future dividend payments. Regardless of the preference shares' features (callable, putable, cumulative, etc.), the greater the uncertainty surrounding the issuer's ability to pay dividends, the greater the risk. Because the ability of a company to pay dividends is based on its future cash flows and net income, investors try to estimate these amounts by examining past trends or forecasting future amounts. The more earnings and the greater amount of cash flow that the company has had, or is expected to have, the lower the uncertainty and risk associated with its ability to pay future dividends.

Callable common or preference shares are riskier than their noncallable counterparts because the issuer has the option to redeem the shares at a predetermined price. Because the call price limits investors' potential future total return, callable shares generally pay a higher dividend to compensate investors for the risk that the shares could be called in the future. Similarly, putable preference shares have lower risk than nonputable preference shares. Cumulative preference shares have lower risk than noncumulative preference shares because the cumulative feature gives investors the right to receive any unpaid dividends before any dividends can be paid to common shareholders.

7. EQUITY SECURITIES AND COMPANY VALUE

Companies issue equity securities on primary markets to raise capital and increase liquidity. This additional liquidity also provides the corporation an additional "currency" (its equity), which it can use to make acquisitions and provide stock option-based incentives to employees. The primary goal of raising capital is to finance the company's revenue-generating activities in order to increase its net income and maximize the wealth of its shareholders. In most cases, the capital that is raised is used to finance the purchase of long-lived assets, capital expansion projects, research and development, the entry into new product or geographic regions, and the acquisition of other companies. Alternatively, a company may be forced to raise capital to ensure that it continues to operate as a going concern. In these cases, capital is raised to fulfill regulatory requirements, improve capital adequacy ratios, or to ensure that debt covenants are met.

The ultimate goal of management is to increase the book value (shareholders' equity on a company's balance sheet) of the company and maximize the market value of its equity. Although management actions can directly affect the book value of the company (by increasing net income or by selling or purchasing its own shares), they can only indirectly affect the market value of its equity. The book value of a company's equity—the difference between its total assets and total liabilities—increases when the company retains its net income. The more net income that is earned and retained, the greater the company's book value of equity. Because management's decisions directly influence a company's net income, they also directly influence its book value of equity.

The market value of the company's equity, however, reflects the collective and differing expectations of investors concerning the amount, timing, and uncertainty of the company's future cash flows. Rarely will book value and market value be equal. Although management may be accomplishing its objective of increasing the company's book value, this increase may not be reflected in the market value of the company's equity because it does not affect investors' expectations about the company's future cash flows. A key measure that investors use to evaluate the effectiveness of management in increasing the company's book value is the accounting return on equity.

7.1. Accounting Return on Equity

Return on equity (ROE) is the primary measure that equity investors use to determine whether the management of a company is effectively and efficiently using the capital they have provided to generate profits. It measures the total amount of net income available to common shareholders generated by the total equity capital invested in the company. It is computed as net income available to ordinary shareholders (i.e., after preferred dividends have been deducted) divided by the average total book value of equity (BVE). That is:

$$\text{ROE}_t = \frac{\text{NI}_t}{\text{Average BVE}_t} = \frac{\text{NI}_t}{(\text{BVE}_t + \text{BVE}_{t-1})/2} \qquad (8.2)$$

where NI_t is the net income in year t and the average book value of equity is computed as the book values at the beginning and end of year t divided by 2. Return on equity assumes that the net income produced in the current year is generated by the equity existing at the beginning of the year and any new equity that was invested during the year. Note that some formulas only use shareholders' equity at the beginning of year t (that is, the end of year $t-1$)

EXHIBIT 8-18 Net Income and Book Value of Equity for Pfizer, Novartis AG, and GlaxoSmithKline (in thousands of U.S. dollars)

	Financial Year Ending		
	31 Dec 2008	31 Dec 2007	31 Dec 2006
Pfizer			
Net income	\$8,104,000	\$8,144,000	\$19,337,000
Total stockholders' equity	\$57,556,000	\$65,010,000	\$71,358,000
Novartis AG			
Net income	\$8,233,000	\$11,968,000	\$5,264,000
Total stockholders' equity	\$50,437,000	\$49,396,000	\$41,670,000
GlaxoSmithKline			
Net income	\$6,822,505	\$10,605,663	\$8,747,382
Total stockholders' equity	\$11,483,295	\$19,180,072	\$67,888,692

in the denominator. This assumes that only the equity existing at the beginning of the year was used to generate the company's net income during the year. That is:

$$ROE_t = \frac{NI_t}{BVE_{t-1}} \tag{8.3}$$

Both formulas are appropriate to use as long as they are applied consistently. For example, using beginning of the year book value is appropriate when book values are relatively stable over time or when computing ROE for a company annually over a period of time. Average book value is more appropriate if a company experiences more volatile year-end book values or if the industry convention is to use average book values in calculating ROE.

One caveat to be aware of when computing and analyzing ROE is that net income and the book value of equity are directly affected by management's choice of accounting methods, such as those relating to depreciation (straight line versus accelerated methods) or inventories (first in, first out versus weighted average cost). Different accounting methods can make it difficult to compare the return on equity of companies even if they operate in the same industry. It may also be difficult to compare the ROE of the same company over time if its accounting methods have changed during that time.

Exhibit 8-18 contains information on the net income and total book value of shareholders' equity for three **blue chip** (widely held large market capitalization companies that are considered financially sound and are leaders in their respective industry or local stock market) pharmaceutical companies: Pfizer, Novartis AG, and GlaxoSmithKline. The data are for their financial years ending December 2006 through December 2008.[20]

[20] Pfizer uses U.S. GAAP to prepare its financial statements; Novartis and GlaxoSmithKline use International Financial Reporting Standards. Therefore, it would be inappropriate to compare the ROE of Pfizer to that of Novartis or GlaxoSmithKline.

Using the average book value of equity, the return on equity for Pfizer for the years ending December 2007 and 2008 can be calculated as:

Return on equity for the year ending December 2007

$$ROE_{2007} = \frac{NI_{2007}}{(BVE_{2006} + BVE_{2007})/2} = \frac{8,144,000}{(71,358,000 + 65,010,000)/2} = 11.9\%$$

Return on equity for the year ending December 2008

$$ROE_{2008} = \frac{NI_{2008}}{(BVE_{2007} + BVE_{2008})/2} = \frac{8,104,000}{(65,010,000 + 57,556,000)/2} = 13.2\%$$

Exhibit 8-19 summarizes the return on equity for Novartis and GlaxoSmithKline in addition to Pfizer for 2007 and 2008.

EXHIBIT 8-19 Return on Equity for Pfizer, Novartis AG, and GlaxoSmithKline

	31 Dec 2008	31 Dec 2007
Pfizer	13.2%	11.9%
Novartis AG	16.5%	26.3%
GlaxoSmithKline	44.5%	24.4%

In the case of Novartis, the ROE of 26.3 percent in 2007 indicates that the company was able to generate a return (profit) of US$0.263 on every US$1.00 of capital invested by shareholders. In 2008, its operating performance deteriorated because it was only able to generate a 16.5 percent return on its equity. In contrast, GlaxoSmithKline almost doubled its return on equity over this period, from 24.4 percent to 44.5 percent. Pfizer's ROE remained relatively unchanged.

ROE can increase if net income increases at a faster rate than shareholders' equity or if net income decreases at a slower rate than shareholders' equity. In the case of Novartis, ROE fell in 2008 because its net income decreased by over 30 percent while shareholders' equity remained relatively stable. Stated differently, Novartis was less effective in using its equity capital to generate profits in 2008 than in 2007. In the case of GlaxoSmithKline, its ROE increased dramatically from 24.4 percent to 44.5 percent in 2007 versus 2008 even though its net income fell over 35 percent because its average shareholder equity decreased dramatically from 2006–2007 to 2007–2008.

An important question to ask is whether an increasing ROE is always good. The short answer is, "it depends." One reason ROE can increase is if net income decreases at a slower rate than shareholders' equity, which is not a positive sign. In addition, ROE can increase if the company issues debt and then uses the proceeds to repurchase some of its outstanding shares. This action will increase the company's leverage and make its equity riskier. Therefore, it is important to examine the source of changes in the company's net income *and* shareholders' equity over time. The DuPont formula, which is discussed in a separate chapter, can be used to analyze the sources of changes in a company's ROE.

The book value of a company's equity reflects the historical operating and financing decisions of its management. The market value of the company's equity reflects these decisions as well as investors' collective assessment and expectations about the company's future cash flows generated by its positive net present value investment opportunities. If investors believe that the company has a large number of these future cash flow-generating investment opportunities, the market value of the company's equity will exceed its book value. Exhibit 8-20 shows the market price per share, the total number of shares outstanding, and the total book value of shareholders' equity for Pfizer, Novartis AG, and GlaxoSmithKline at the end of December 2008. This exhibit also shows the total market value of equity (or market capitalization) computed as the number of shares outstanding multiplied by the market price per share.

EXHIBIT 8-20 Market Information for Pfizer, Novartis AG, and GlaxoSmithKline (in thousands of U.S. dollars, except Market Price)

	Pfizer	Novartis AG	GlaxoSmithKline
Market price	$16.97	$47.64	$35.84
Total shares outstanding	6,750,000	2,260,000	2,530,000
Total shareholders' equity	$57,556,000	$50,437,000	$11,483,295
Total market value of equity	$114,547,500	$107,666,400	$90,675,200

Note that in Exhibit 8-20, the total market value of equity for Pfizer is computed as:

$$\text{Market value of equity} = \text{Market price per share} \times \text{Shares outstanding}$$

$$\text{Market value of equity} = \text{US\$}16.97 \times 6{,}750{,}000 = \text{US\$}114{,}547{,}500$$

The book value of equity per share for Pfizer can be computed as:

$$\text{Book value of equity per share} = \text{Total shareholders' equity}/\text{Shares outstanding}$$

$$\text{Book value of equity per share} = \text{US\$}57{,}556{,}000/6{,}750{,}000 = \text{US\$}8.53$$

A useful ratio to compute is a company's price-to-book ratio, which is also referred to as the market-to-book ratio. This ratio provides an indication of investors' expectations about a company's future investment and cash flow–generating opportunities. The larger the price-to-book ratio (i.e., the greater the divergence between market value per share and book value per share), the more favorably investors will view the company's future investment opportunities. For Pfizer the price-to-book ratio is:

$$\text{Price-to-book ratio} = \text{Market price per share}/\text{Book value of equity per share}$$

$$\text{Price-to-book ratio} = \text{US\$}16.97/\text{US\$}8.53 = 1.99$$

Exhibit 8-21 contains the market price per share, book value of equity per share, and price-to-book ratios for Novartis and GlaxoSmithKline in addition to Pfizer.

EXHIBIT 8-21 Pfizer, Novartis AG, and GlaxoSmithKline

	Pfizer	Novartis AG	GlaxoSmithKline
Market price per share	$16.97	$47.64	$35.84
Book value of equity per share	$8.53	$22.32	$4.54
Price-to-book ratio	1.99	2.13	7.89

The market price per share of all three companies exceeds their respective book values, so their price-to-book ratios are all greater than 1.00. However, there are significant differences in the sizes of their price-to-book ratios. GlaxoSmithKline has the largest price-to-book ratio, while the price-to-book ratios of Pfizer and Novartis are similar to each other. This suggests that investors believe that GlaxoSmithKline has substantially higher future growth opportunities than either Pfizer or Novartis.

It is not appropriate to compare the price-to-book ratios of companies in different industries because their price-to-book ratios also reflect investors' outlooks for the industry. Companies in high growth industries, such as technology, will generally have higher price-to-book ratios than companies in slower growth (i.e., mature) industries, such as heavy equipment. Therefore, it is more appropriate to compare the price-to-book ratios of companies in the same industry. A company with relatively high growth opportunities compared to its industry peers would likely have a higher price-to-book ratio than the average price-to-book ratio of the industry.

Book value and return on equity are useful in helping analysts determine value but can be limited as a primary means to estimate a company's true or intrinsic value, which is the present value of its future projected cash flows. In Exhibit 8-22, Warren Buffett, one of the most successful investors in the world and CEO of Berkshire Hathaway, provides an explanation of the differences between the book value of a company and its intrinsic value in a letter to shareholders. As discussed previously, market value reflects the collective and differing expectations of investors concerning the amount, timing, and uncertainty of a company's future cash flows. A company's intrinsic value can only be estimated because it is impossible to predict the amount and timing of its future cash flows. However, astute investors—such as Buffett—have been able to profit from discrepancies between their estimates of a company's intrinsic value and the market value of its equity.

EXHIBIT 8-22 Book Value versus Intrinsic Value

> We regularly report our per-share book value, an easily calculable number, though one of limited use. Just as regularly, we tell you that what counts is intrinsic value, a number that is impossible to pinpoint but essential to estimate.
>
> For example, in 1964, we could state with certitude that Berkshire's per-share book value was $19.46. However, that figure considerably overstated the stock's intrinsic value since all of the company's resources were tied up in a sub-profitable textile business. Our textile assets had neither going-concern nor liquidation values equal to their carrying values. In 1964, then, anyone inquiring into the soundness of Berkshire's balance sheet might well have deserved the answer once offered up by a Hollywood mogul of dubious reputation: "Don't worry, the liabilities are solid."

EXHIBIT 8-22 (*Continued*)

> Today, Berkshire's situation has reversed: Many of the businesses we control are worth far more than their carrying value. (Those we don't control, such as Coca-Cola or Gillette, are carried at current market values.) We continue to give you book value figures, however, because they serve as a rough, understated, tracking measure for Berkshire's intrinsic value.
>
> We define intrinsic value as the discounted value of the cash that can be taken out of a business during its remaining life. Anyone calculating intrinsic value necessarily comes up with a highly subjective figure that will change both as estimates of future cash flows are revised and as interest rates move. Despite its fuzziness, however, intrinsic value is all-important and is the only logical way to evaluate the relative attractiveness of investments and businesses.
>
> To see how historical input (book value) and future output (intrinsic value) can diverge, let's look at another form of investment, a college education. Think of the education's cost as its "book value." If it is to be accurate, the cost should include the earnings that were foregone by the student because he chose college rather than a job.
>
> For this exercise, we will ignore the important non-economic benefits of an education and focus strictly on its economic value. First, we must estimate the earnings that the graduate will receive over his lifetime and subtract from that figure an estimate of what he would have earned had he lacked his education. That gives us an excess earnings figure, which must then be discounted, at an appropriate interest rate, back to graduation day. The dollar result equals the intrinsic economic value of the education.

Extracts from Berkshire Hathaway's *2008 Annual Report* (www.berkshirehathaway.com).

7.2. The Cost of Equity and Investors' Required Rates of Return

When companies issue debt (or borrow from a bank) or equity securities, there is a cost associated with the capital that is raised. In order to maximize profitability and shareholder wealth, companies attempt to raise capital efficiently so as to minimize these costs.

When a company issues debt, the cost it incurs for the use of these funds is called the cost of debt. The cost of debt is relatively easy to estimate because it reflects the periodic interest (or coupon) rate that the company is contractually obligated to pay to its bondholders (lenders). When a company raises capital by issuing equity, the cost it incurs is called the cost of equity. Unlike debt, however, the company is not contractually obligated to make any payments to its shareholders for the use of their funds. As a result, the cost of equity is more difficult to estimate.

Investors require a return on the funds they provide to the company. This return is called the investor's minimum required rate of return. When investors purchase the company's debt securities, their minimum required rate of return is the periodic rate of interest they charge the company for the use of their funds. Because all of the bondholders receive the same periodic rate of interest, their required rate of return is the same. Therefore, the company's cost of debt and the investors' minimum required rate of return on the debt are the same.

When investors purchase the company's equity securities, their minimum required rate of return is based on the future cash flows they expect to receive. Because these future cash flows are both uncertain and unknown, the investors' minimum required rate of return must be estimated. In addition, the minimum required return may differ across investors based on their expectations about the company's future cash flows. As a result, the company's cost of equity may be different from the investors' minimum required rate of return on equity.[21] Because companies try to raise capital at the lowest possible cost, the company's cost of equity is often used as a proxy for the investors' *minimum* required rate of return.

In other words, the cost of equity can be thought of as the minimum expected rate of return that a company must offer its investors to purchase its shares in the primary market and to maintain its share price in the secondary market. If this expected rate of return is not maintained in the secondary market, then the share price will adjust so that it meets the minimum required rate of return demanded by investors. For example, if investors require a higher rate of return on equity than the company's cost of equity, they would sell their shares and invest their funds elsewhere resulting in a decline in the company's share price. As the share price declined, the cost of equity would increase to reach the higher rate of return that investors require.

Two models commonly used to estimate a company's cost of equity (or investors' minimum required rate of return) are the dividend discount model (DDM) and the capital asset pricing model (CAPM). These models are discussed in detail in other chapters.

The cost of debt (after tax) and the cost of equity (i.e., the minimum required rates of return on debt and equity) are integral components of the capital budgeting process because they are used to estimate a company's weighted average cost of capital (WACC). Capital budgeting is the decision-making process that companies use to evaluate potential long-term investments. The WACC represents the minimum required rate of return that the company must earn on its long-term investments to satisfy all providers of capital. The company then chooses among those long-term investments with expected returns that are greater than its WACC.

8. SUMMARY

Equity securities play a fundamental role in investment analysis and portfolio management. The importance of this asset class continues to grow on a global scale because of the need for equity capital in developed and emerging markets, technological innovation, and the growing sophistication of electronic information exchange. Given their absolute return potential and ability to impact the risk and return characteristics of portfolios, equity securities are of importance to both individual and institutional investors.

This chapter introduces equity securities and provides an overview of global equity markets. A detailed analysis of their historical performance shows that equity securities have offered average real annual returns superior to government bills and bonds, which have provided average real annual returns that have only kept pace with inflation. The different types and characteristics of common and preference equity securities are examined, and the primary differences between public and private equity securities are outlined. An overview of the various types of equity securities listed and traded in global markets is provided, including a discussion of their risk and return characteristics. Finally, the role of equity securities in creating company value is examined as well as the relationship between a company's cost of equity, its accounting return on equity, investors' required rate of return, and the company's intrinsic value.

[21] Another important factor that can cause a firm's cost of equity to differ from investors' required rate of return on equity is the flotation cost associated with equity.

We conclude with a summary of the key components of this chapter:

- Common shares represent an ownership interest in a company and give investors a claim on its operating performance, the opportunity to participate in the corporate decision-making process, and a claim on the company's net assets in the case of liquidation.
- Callable common shares give the issuer the right to buy back the shares from shareholders at a price determined when the shares are originally issued.
- Putable common shares give shareholders the right to sell the shares back to the issuer at a price specified when the shares are originally issued.
- Preference shares are a form of equity in which payments made to preference shareholders take precedence over any payments made to common stockholders.
- Cumulative preference shares are preference shares on which dividend payments are accrued so that any payments omitted by the company must be paid before another dividend can be paid to common shareholders. Noncumulative preference shares have no such provisions, implying that the dividend payments are at the company's discretion and are thus similar to payments made to common shareholders.
- Participating preference shares allow investors to receive the standard preferred dividend plus the opportunity to receive a share of corporate profits above a prespecified amount. Nonparticipating preference shares allow investors to simply receive the initial investment plus any accrued dividends in the event of liquidation.
- Callable and putable preference shares provide issuers and investors with the same rights and obligations as their common share counterparts.
- Private equity securities are issued primarily to institutional investors in private placements and do not trade in secondary equity markets. There are three types of private equity investments: venture capital, leveraged buyouts, and private investments in public equity (PIPEs).
- The objective of private equity investing is to increase the ability of the company's management to focus on its operating activities for long-term value creation. The strategy is to take the "private" company "public" after certain profit and other benchmarks have been met.
- Depository receipts are securities that trade like ordinary shares on a local exchange but which represent an economic interest in a foreign company. They allow the publicly listed shares of foreign companies to be traded on an exchange outside their domestic market.
- American depository receipts are U.S. dollar-denominated securities trading much like standard U.S. securities on U.S. markets. Global depository receipts are similar to ADRs but contain certain restrictions in terms of their ability to be resold among investors.
- Underlying characteristics of equity securities can greatly affect their risk and return.
- A company's accounting return on equity is the total return that it earns on shareholders' book equity.
- A company's cost of equity is the minimum rate of return that stockholders require the company to pay them for investing in its equity.

PROBLEMS

1. Which of the following is *not* a characteristic of common equity?

   A. It represents an ownership interest in the company.
   B. Shareholders participate in the decision-making process.
   C. The company is obligated to make periodic dividend payments.

2. The type of equity voting right that grants one vote for each share of equity owned is referred to as:
   A. Proxy voting.
   B. Statutory voting.
   C. Cumulative voting.
3. All of the following are characteristics of preference shares *except*:
   A. They are either callable or putable.
   B. They generally do not have voting rights.
   C. They do not share in the operating performance of the company.
4. Participating preference shares entitle shareholders to:
   A. Participate in the decision-making process of the company.
   B. Convert their shares into a specified number of common shares.
   C. Receive an additional dividend if the company's profits exceed a predetermined level.
5. Which of the following statements about private equity securities is *incorrect*?
   A. They cannot be sold on secondary markets.
   B. They have market-determined quoted prices.
   C. They are primarily issued to institutional investors.
6. Venture capital investments:
   A. Can be publicly traded.
   B. Do not require a long-term commitment of funds.
   C. Provide mezzanine financing to early-stage companies.
7. Which of the following statements *most accurately* describes one difference between private and public equity firms?
   A. Private equity firms are focused more on short-term results than public firms.
   B. Private equity firms' regulatory and investor relations operations are less costly than those of public firms.
   C. Private equity firms are incentivized to be more open with investors about governance and compensation than public firms.
8. Emerging markets have benefited from recent trends in international markets. Which of the following has *not* been a benefit of these trends?
   A. Emerging market companies do not have to worry about a lack of liquidity in their home equity markets.
   B. Emerging market companies have found it easier to raise capital in the markets of developed countries.
   C. Emerging market companies have benefited from the stability of foreign exchange markets.
9. When investing in unsponsored depository receipts, the voting rights to the shares in the trust belong to:
   A. The depository bank.
   B. The investors in the depository receipts.
   C. The issuer of the shares held in the trust.

10. With respect to Level III sponsored ADRs, which of the following is *least likely* to be accurate? They:

    A. Have low listing fees.
    B. Are traded on the NYSE, NASDAQ, and AMEX.
    C. Are used to raise equity capital in U.S. markets.

11. A basket of listed depository receipts, or an exchange-traded fund, would *most likely* be used for:

    A. Gaining exposure to a single equity.
    B. Hedging exposure to a single equity.
    C. Gaining exposure to multiple equities.

12. Calculate the total return on a share of equity using the following data:
    Purchase price: $50
    Sale price: $42
    Dividend paid during holding period: $2

    A. –12.0%
    B. –14.3%
    C. –16.0%

13. If a U.S.-based investor purchases a euro-denominated ETF and the euro subsequently depreciates in value relative to the dollar, the investor will have a total return that is:

    A. Lower than the ETF's total return.
    B. Higher than the ETF's total return.
    C. The same as the ETF's total return.

14. Which of the following is *incorrect* about the risk of an equity security? The risk of an equity security is:

    A. Based on the uncertainty of its cash flows.
    B. Based on the uncertainty of its future price.
    C. Measured using the standard deviation of its dividends.

15. From an investor's point of view, which of the following equity securities is the *least* risky?

    A. Putable preference shares.
    B. Callable preference shares.
    C. Noncallable preference shares.

16. Which of the following is *least likely* to be a reason for a company to issue equity securities on the primary market?

    A. To raise capital.
    B. To increase liquidity.
    C. To increase return on equity.

17. Which of the following is *not* a primary goal of raising equity capital?

    A. To finance the purchase of long-lived assets.
    B. To finance the company's revenue-generating activities.
    C. To ensure that the company continues as a going concern.

18. Which of the following statements is *most accurate* in describing a company's book value?
    A. Book value increases when a company retains its net income.
    B. Book value is usually equal to the company's market value.
    C. The ultimate goal of management is to maximize book value.

19. Calculate the book value of a company using the following information:

Number of shares outstanding	100,000
Price per share	€52
Total assets	€12,000,000
Total liabilities	€7,500,000
Net income	€2,000,000

    A. €4,500,000
    B. €5,200,000
    C. €6,500,000

20. Which of the following statements is *least accurate* in describing a company's market value?
    A. Management's decisions do not influence the company's market value.
    B. Increases in book value may not be reflected in the company's market value.
    C. Market value reflects the collective and differing expectations of investors.

21. Calculate the 2009 return on equity (ROE) of a stable company using the following data:

Total sales	£2,500,000
Net income	£2,000,000
Beginning of year total assets	£50,000,000
Beginning of year total liabilities	£35,000,000
Number of shares outstanding at the end of 2009	1,000,000
Price per share at the end of 2009	£20

    A. 10.0%
    B. 13.3%
    C. 16.7%

22. Holding all other factors constant, which of the following situations will *most likely* lead to an increase in a company's return on equity?
    A. The market price of the company's shares increases.
    B. Net income increases at a slower rate than shareholders' equity.
    C. The company issues debt to repurchase outstanding shares of equity.

23. Which of the following measures is the *most difficult* to estimate?
    A. The cost of debt.
    B. The cost of equity.
    C. Investors' required rate of return on debt.
24. A company's cost of equity is often used as a proxy for investors':
    A. Average required rate of return.
    B. Minimum required rate of return.
    C. Maximum required rate of return.

CHAPTER 9

INTRODUCTION TO INDUSTRY AND COMPANY ANALYSIS

Patrick W. Dorsey, CFA
Chicago, IL, U.S.A.

Anthony M. Fiore, CFA
New York City, NY, U.S.A.

Ian Rossa O'Reilly, CFA
Toronto, Canada

LEARNING OUTCOMES

After completing this chapter, you will be able to do the following:

- Explain the uses of industry analysis and the relation of industry analysis to company analysis.
- Compare and contrast the methods by which companies can be grouped, current industry classification systems, and classify a company, given a description of its activities and the classification system.
- Explain the factors that affect the sensitivity of a company to the business cycle and the uses and limitations of industry and company descriptors such as "growth," "defensive," and "cyclical."
- Explain the relation of "peer group," as used in equity valuation, to a company's industry classification.
- Discuss the elements that need to be covered in a thorough industry analysis.
- Illustrate demographic, governmental, social, and technological influences on industry growth, profitability, and risk.
- Describe product and industry life-cycle models, classify an industry as to life-cycle phase (e.g., embryonic, growth, shakeout, maturity, or decline) based on a description of it, and discuss the limitations of the life-cycle concept in forecasting industry performance.

- Explain the effects of industry concentration, ease of entry, and capacity on return on invested capital and pricing power.
- Discuss the principles of strategic analysis of an industry.
- Compare and contrast the characteristics of representative industries from the various economic sectors.
- Describe the elements that should be covered in a thorough company analysis.

1. INTRODUCTION

Industry analysis is the analysis of a specific branch of manufacturing, service, or trade. Understanding the industry in which a company operates provides an essential framework for the analysis of the individual company—that is, **company analysis**. Equity analysis and credit analysis are often conducted by analysts who concentrate on one or several industries, which results in synergies and efficiencies in gathering and interpreting information.

Among the questions we address in this chapter are the following:

- What are the similarities and differences among industry classification systems?
- How does an analyst go about choosing a peer group of companies?
- What are the key factors to consider when analyzing an industry?
- What advantages are enjoyed by companies in strategically well-positioned industries?

After discussing the uses of industry analysis in the next section, Sections 3 and 4 discuss, respectively, approaches to identifying similar companies and industry classification systems. Section 5 covers the description and analysis of industries. Also, Section 5, which includes an introduction to competitive analysis, provides a background to Section 6, which introduces company analysis. Section 7 contains conclusions and a summary. Practice problems follow the text.

2. USES OF INDUSTRY ANALYSIS

Industry analysis is useful in a number of investment applications that make use of fundamental analysis. Its uses include the following:

- *Understanding a company's business and business environment.* Industry analysis is often a critical early step in stock selection and valuation because it provides insights into the issuer's growth opportunities, competitive dynamics, and business risks. For a credit analyst, industry analysis provides insights into the appropriateness of a company's use of debt financing and into its ability to meet its promised payments during economic contractions.
- *Identifying active equity investment opportunities.* Investors taking a top-down investing approach use industry analysis to identify industries with positive, neutral, or negative outlooks for profitability and growth. Generally, investors will then overweight, market weight, or underweight those industries (as appropriate to their outlooks) relative to the investor's benchmark if the investor judges that the industry's perceived prospects are not fully incorporated in market prices. Apart from security selection, some investors attempt

to outperform their benchmarks by industry or sector rotation—that is, timing investments in industries in relation to an analysis of industry fundamentals and/or business-cycle conditions (technical analysis may also play a role in such strategies). Several studies have underscored the importance of industry analysis by suggesting that the industry factor in stock returns is at least as important as the country factor (e.g., Cavaglia, Diermeier, Moroz, and De Zordo, 2004). In addition, industry membership has been found to account for about 20 percent of the variability of a company's profitability in the United States (McGahan and Porter 1995).
- *Portfolio performance attribution.* Performance attribution, which addresses the sources of a portfolio's returns, usually in relation to the portfolio's benchmark, includes industry or sector selection. Industry classification schemes play a role in such performance attribution.

Later in this chapter we explore the considerations involved in understanding a company's business and business environment. The next section addresses how companies may be grouped into industries.

3. APPROACHES TO IDENTIFYING SIMILAR COMPANIES

Industry classification attempts to place companies into groups on the basis of commonalities. In the following sections, we discuss the three major approaches to industry classification:

- Products and/or services supplied.
- Business-cycle sensitivities.
- Statistical similarities.

3.1. Products and/or Services Supplied

Modern classification schemes are most commonly based on grouping companies by similar products and/or services. According to this perspective, an **industry** is defined as a group of companies offering similar products and/or services. For example, major companies in the global heavy truck industry include Volvo, Daimler AG, Paccar, and Navistar, all of which make large commercial vehicles for the on-highway truck market. Similarly, some of the large players in the global automobile industry are Toyota, General Motors, Volkswagen, Ford, Honda, Nissan, PSA Peugeot Citroën, and Hyundai, all of which produce light vehicles that are close substitutes for one another.

Industry classification schemes typically provide multiple levels of aggregation. The term **sector** is often used to refer to a group of related industries. The health care sector, for example, consists of a number of related industries, including the pharmaceutical, biotechnology, medical device, medical supply, hospital, and managed care industries.

These classification schemes typically place a company in an industry on the basis of a determination of its principal business activity. A company's **principal business activity** is the source from which the company derives a majority of its revenues and/or earnings. For example, companies that derive a majority of their revenues from the sale of pharmaceuticals include Novartis AG, Pfizer Inc., Roche Holding AG, GlaxoSmithKline, and Sanofi-aventis S.A., all of which could be grouped together as part of the global pharmaceutical industry. Companies that engage in more than one significant business activity usually report the revenues (and, in many cases, operating profits) of the different business segments in their financial statements.[1]

Examples of classification systems based on products and/or services include the commercial classification systems that will be discussed later, namely, the Global Industry Classification Standard (GICS), Russell Global Sectors (RGS), and Industry Classification Benchmark. In addition to grouping companies by product and/or service, some of the major classification systems, including GICS and RGS, group consumer-related companies into cyclical and noncyclical categories depending on the company's sensitivity to the business cycle. The next section addresses how companies can be categorized on the basis of economic sensitivity.

3.2. Business-Cycle Sensitivities

Companies are sometimes grouped on the basis of their relative sensitivity to the business cycle. This method often results in two broad groupings of companies—cyclical and noncyclical.

A **cyclical** company is one whose profits are strongly correlated with the strength of the overall economy. Such companies experience wider-than-average fluctuations in demand—high demand during periods of economic expansion and low demand during periods of economic contraction—and/or are subject to greater-than-average profit variability related to high operating leverage (i.e., high fixed costs). Concerning demand, cyclical products and services are often relatively expensive and/or represent purchases that can be delayed if necessary (e.g., because of declining disposable income). Examples of cyclical industries are autos, housing, basic materials, industrials, and technology. A **noncyclical** company is one whose performance is largely independent of the business cycle. Noncyclical companies produce goods or services for which demand remains relatively stable throughout the business cycle. Examples of noncyclical industries are food and beverage, household and personal care products, health care, and utilities.

EXAMPLE 9-1 Descriptions Related to the Cyclical/ Noncyclical Distinction

Analysts commonly encounter a number of labels related to the cyclical/noncyclical distinction. For example, noncyclical industries have sometimes been sorted into **defensive** (or **stable**) versus **growth**. Defensive industries and companies are those whose revenues and profits are least affected by fluctuations in overall economic activity. These industries/companies tend to produce staple consumer goods (e.g., bread), to provide basic services (grocery stores, drug stores, fast food outlets), or to have their rates and revenues determined by contracts or government regulation (e.g., cost-of-service, rate-of-return regulated public utilities). Growth industries would include industries with specific demand dynamics that are so strong that they override

[1]For more information, see International Financial Reporting Standard (IFRS) 8: Operating Segments. In IFRS 8, *business segments* are called *operating segments.*

the significance of broad economic or other external factors and generate growth regardless of overall economic conditions, although their rates of growth may slow during an economic downturn.[2]

The usefulness of industry and company labels such as cyclical, growth, and defensive is limited. Cyclical industries as well as growth industries often have growth companies within them. A cyclical industry itself, although exposed to the effects of fluctuations in overall economic activity, may grow at an above-average rate for periods spanning multiple business cycles.[3] Furthermore, when fluctuations in economic activity are large, as in the deep recession of 2008–2009, few companies escape the effects of the cyclical weakness in overall economic activity.

The defensive label is also problematic. Industries may include both companies that are growth and companies that are defensive in character, making the choice between a "growth" and a "defensive" label difficult. Moreover, "defensive" cannot be understood as necessarily being descriptive of investment characteristics. Food supermarkets, for example, would typically be described as defensive but can be subject to profit-damaging price wars. So-called defensive industries/companies may sometimes face industry dynamics that make them far from defensive in the sense of preserving shareholders' capital.

Although the classification systems we will discuss do not label their categories as cyclical or noncyclical, certain sectors tend to experience greater economic sensitivity than others. Sectors that tend to exhibit a relatively high degree of economic sensitivity include consumer discretionary, energy, financials, industrials, technology, and materials. In contrast, sectors that exhibit relatively less economic sensitivity include consumer staples, health care, telecommunications, and utilities.

One limitation of the cyclical/noncyclical classification is that business-cycle sensitivity is a continuous spectrum rather than an "either/or" issue, so placement of companies in one of the two major groups is somewhat arbitrary. The impact of severe recessions usually reaches all parts of the economy, so noncyclical is better understood as a relative term.

Another limitation of a business-cycle classification for global investing is that different countries and regions of the world frequently progress through the various stages of the business cycle at different times. While one region of the world may be experiencing economic expansion, other regions or countries may be in recession, which complicates the application of a business-cycle approach to industry analysis. For example, a jewelry retailer (i.e., a cyclical company) that is selling domestically into a weak economy will exhibit markedly different fundamental performance relative to a jewelry company operating in an environment where demand is robust. Comparing these two companies—that is, similar companies that are currently exposed to different demand environments—could suggest

[2]Sometimes the "growth" label is attached to countries or regions in which economic growth is so strong that the fluctuations in local economic activity do not produce an actual decline in economic output, merely variation from high to low rates of real growth (e.g., China, India).

[3]The label **growth cyclical** is sometimes used to describe companies that are growing rapidly on a long-term basis but that still experience above-average fluctuation in their revenues and profits over the course of a business cycle.

investment opportunities. Combining fundamental data from such companies, however, to establish industry benchmark values would be misleading.

3.3. Statistical Similarities

Statistical approaches to grouping companies are typically based on the correlations of past securities' returns. For example, using the technique known as cluster analysis, companies are separated (on the basis of historical correlations of stock returns) into groups *in which* correlations are relatively high but *between which* correlations are relatively low. This method of aggregation often results in nonintuitive groups of companies, and the composition of the groups may vary significantly by time period and region of the world. Moreover, statistical approaches rely on historical data, but analysts have no guarantee that past correlation values will continue in the future. In addition, such approaches carry the inherent dangers of all statistical methods, namely, (1) falsely indicating a relationship that arose because of chance or (2) falsely excluding a relationship that actually is significant.

4. INDUSTRY CLASSIFICATION SYSTEMS

A well-designed classification system often serves as a useful starting point for industry analysis. It allows analysts to compare industry trends and relative valuations among companies in a group. Classification systems that take a global perspective enable portfolio managers and research analysts to make global comparisons of companies in the same industry. For example, given the global nature of the automobile industry, a thorough analysis of the industry would include auto companies from many different countries and regions of the world.

4.1. Commercial Industry Classification Systems

Major index providers, including Standard & Poor's, MSCI Barra, Russell Investments, Dow Jones, and FTSE, classify companies in their equity indices into industry groupings. Most classification schemes used by these index providers contain multiple levels of classification that start at the broadest level with a general sector grouping, then, in several further steps, subdivide or disaggregate the sectors into more "granular" (i.e., more narrowly defined) subindustry groups.

4.1.1. Global Industry Classification Standard

GICS was jointly developed by Standard & Poor's and MSCI Barra, two of the largest providers of global equity indices, in 1999. As the name implies, GICS was designed to facilitate global comparisons of industries, and it classifies companies in both developed and developing economies. Each company is assigned to a subindustry according to its principal business activity. Each subindustry belongs to a particular industry; each industry belongs to an industry group; and each group belongs to a sector. In June 2009, the GICS classification structure comprised four levels of detail consisting of 154 subindustries, 68 industries, 24 industry groups, and 10 sectors. The composition of GICS has historically been adjusted over time to reflect changes in the global equity markets.

4.1.2. Russell Global Sectors

The RGS classification system uses a three-tier structure to classify companies globally on the basis of the products or services a company produces. In June 2009, the RGS classification system consisted of 9 sectors, 32 subsectors, and 141 industries. Besides the number of tiers, another difference between the RGS and GICS classification systems is that the RGS system contains 9 sectors, whereas GICS consists of 10. For example, the RGS system does not provide a separate sector for telecommunication service companies. Many companies that GICS classifies as "Telecommunication Services," including China Mobile Ltd., AT&T, and Telefonica, are assigned by RGS to its more broadly defined "Utilities" sector.

4.1.3. Industry Classification Benchmark

The Industry Classification Benchmark (ICB), which was jointly developed by Dow Jones and FTSE, uses a four-tier structure to categorize companies globally on the basis of the source from which a company derives the majority of its revenue. In June 2009, the ICB classification system consisted of 10 industries, 19 supersectors, 41 sectors, and 114 subsectors. Although the ICB is similar to GICS in the number of tiers and the method by which companies are assigned to particular groups, the two systems use significantly different nomenclature. For example, whereas GICS uses the term "sector" to describe its broadest grouping of companies, ICB uses the term "industry." Another difference between the two systems is that ICB distinguishes between consumer goods and consumer services companies, whereas both GICS and the RGS systems group consumer products companies and consumer services companies together into sectors on the basis of economic sensitivity. These stylistic distinctions tend to be less obvious at the more granular levels of the different hierarchies.

Despite these subtle differences, the three commercial classification systems use common methodologies for assigning companies to groups. Also, the broadest level of grouping for all three systems is quite similar. Specifically, GICS, the RGS, and the ICB each identify 9 or 10 broad groupings below which all other categories reside. Next, we describe sectors that are fairly representative of how the broadest level of industry classification is viewed by GICS, RGS, and ICB.

4.1.4. Description of Representative Sectors

Basic Materials and Processing—companies engaged in the production of building materials, chemicals, paper and forest products, containers and packaging, and metal, mineral, and mining companies.

Consumer Discretionary—companies that derive a majority of revenue from the sale of consumer-related products or services for which demand tends to exhibit a relatively high degree of economic sensitivity. Examples of business activities that frequently fall into this category are automotive, apparel, hotel, and restaurant businesses.

Consumer Staples—consumer-related companies whose business tends to exhibit less economic sensitivity than other companies; for example, manufacturers of food, beverage, tobacco, and personal care products.

Energy—companies whose primary line of business involves the exploration, production, or refining of natural resources used to produce energy; companies that derive a majority of revenue from the sale of equipment or through the provision of services to energy companies would also fall into this category.

Financial Services—companies whose primary line of business involves banking, finance, insurance, real estate, asset management, and/or brokerage services.

Health Care—manufacturers of pharmaceutical and biotech products, medical devices, health care equipment, and medical supplies and providers of health care services.

Industrial/Producer Durables—manufacturers of capital goods and providers of commercial services; for example, business activities would include heavy machinery and equipment manufacture, aerospace and defense, transportation services, and commercial services and supplies.

Technology—companies involved in the manufacture or sale of computers, software, semiconductors, and communications equipment; other business activities that frequently fall into this category are electronic entertainment, Internet services, and technology consulting and services.

Telecommunications—companies that provide fixed-line and wireless communication services; some vendors prefer to combine telecommunication and utility companies together into a single "utilities" category.

Utilities—electric, gas, and water utilities; telecommunication companies are sometimes included in this category.

To classify a company accurately in a particular classification scheme requires definitions of the classification categories, a statement about the criteria used in classification, and detailed information about the subject company. Example 9-2 introduces an exercise in such classification. In addressing the question, the reader can make use of the widely applicable sector descriptions just given and familiarity with available business products and services.

EXAMPLE 9-2 Classifying Companies into Industries

The text defines 10 representative sectors, repeated here in Exhibit 9-1. Suppose the classification system is based on the criterion of a company's principal business activity as judged primarily by source of revenue.

EXHIBIT 9-1 Ten Sectors

Sector
Basic Materials and Processing
Consumer Discretionary
Consumer Staples
Energy
Financial Services
Health Care
Industrial/Producer Durables
Technology
Telecommunications
Utilities

Based on the information given, determine an appropriate industry membership for each of the following hypothetical companies:

1. A natural gas transporter and marketer
2. A manufacturer of heavy construction equipment
3. A provider of regional telephone services
4. A semiconductor company
5. A manufacturer of medical devices
6. A chain of supermarkets
7. A manufacturer of chemicals and plastics
8. A manufacturer of automobiles
9. An investment management company
10. A manufacturer of luxury leather goods
11. A regulated supplier of electricity
12. A provider of wireless broadband services
13. A manufacturer of soaps and detergents
14. A software development company
15. An insurer
16. A regulated provider of water/wastewater services
17. A petroleum (oil) service company
18. A manufacturer of pharmaceuticals
19. A provider of rail transportation services
20. A metals mining company

Solution:

Sector	Company Number
Basic Materials and Processing	7, 20
Consumer Discretionary	8, 10
Consumer Staples	6, 13
Energy	1, 17
Financial Services	9, 15
Health Care	5, 18
Industrial/Producer Durables	2, 19
Technology	4, 14
Telecommunications	3, 12
Utilities	11, 16

Example 9-3 reviews some major concepts in industry classification.

EXAMPLE 9-3 Industry Classification Schemes

1. The GICS classification system classifies companies on the basis of a company's primary business activity as measured primarily by:
   A. Assets.
   B. Income.
   C. Revenue.
2. Which of the following is *least likely* to be accurately described as a cyclical company? A(n)
   A. Automobile manufacturer.
   B. Producer of breakfast cereals.
   C. Apparel company producing the newest trendy clothes for teenage girls.
3. Which of the following is the *most accurate* statement? A statistical approach to grouping companies into industries:
   A. Is based on historical correlations of the securities' returns.
   B. Frequently produces industry groups whose composition is similar worldwide.
   C. Emphasizes the descriptive statistics of industries consisting of companies producing similar products and/or services.

Solution to 1: C is correct.

Solution to 2: B is correct. A producer of staple foods such as cereals is a classic example of a noncyclical company. Demand for automobiles is cyclical—that is, relatively high during economic expansions and relatively low during economic contractions. Also, demand for teenage fashions is likely to be more sensitive to the business cycle than demand for standard food items such as breakfast cereals. When budgets have been reduced, families may try to avoid expensive clothing or extend the life of existing wardrobes.

Solution to 3: A is correct.

4.2. Governmental Industry Classification Systems

A number of classification systems in use by various governmental agencies today organize statistical data according to type of industrial or economic activity. A common goal of each government classification system is to facilitate the comparison of data—both over time and among countries that use the same system. Continuity of the data is critical to the measurement and evaluation of economic performance over time.

4.2.1. International Standard Industrial Classification of All Economic Activities

The International Standard Industrial Classification of All Economic Activities (ISIC) was adopted by the United Nations in 1948 to address the need for international comparability of economic statistics. ISIC classifies entities into various categories on the basis of the principal type of economic activity the entity performs. ISIC is organized into 11 categories, 21 sections, 88 divisions, 233 groups, and more than 400 classes. According to the United Nations, a majority of the countries around the world have either used ISIC as their national activity classification system or have developed national classifications derived from ISIC. Some of the organizations currently using the ISIC are the UN and its specialized agencies, the International Monetary Fund, the World Bank, and other international bodies.

4.2.2. Statistical Classification of Economic Activities in the European Community

Often regarded as the European version of ISIC, Statistical Classification of Economic Activities in the European Community (NACE) is the classification of economic activities that correspond to ISIC at the European level. Similar to ISIC, NACE classification is organized according to economic activity. NACE is composed of four levels—namely, sections (identified by alphabetical letters A through U), divisions (identified by two-digit numerical codes 01 through 99), groups (identified by three-digit numerical codes 01.1 through 99.0), and classes (identified by four-digit numerical codes 01.11 through 99.00).

4.2.3. Australian and New Zealand Standard Industrial Classification

The Australian and New Zealand Standard Industrial Classification (ANZSIC) was jointly developed by the Australian Bureau of Statistics and Statistics New Zealand in 1993 to facilitate the comparison of industry statistics of the two countries and comparisons with the rest of the world. International comparability was achieved by aligning ANZSIC with the international standards used by ISIC. ANZSIC has a structure comprising five levels—namely, divisions (the broadest level), subdivisions, groups, classes, and at the most granular level, subclasses (New Zealand only).

4.2.4. North American Industry Classification System

Jointly developed by the United States, Canada, and Mexico, the North American Industry Classification System (NAICS) replaced the Standard Industrial Classification (SIC) system in 1997. NAICS distinguishes between establishments and enterprises. NAICS classifies establishments into industries according to the primary business activity of the establishment. In the NAICS system, an *establishment* is defined as "a single physical location where business is conducted or where services or industrial operations are performed" (e.g., factory, store, hotel, movie theater, farm, office). An *enterprise* may consist of more than one location performing the same or different types of economic activities. Each establishment of that enterprise is assigned a NAICS code on the basis of its own primary business activity.[4]

NAICS uses a two-digit through six-digit code to structure its categories into five levels of detail. The greater the number of digits in the code, the more narrowly defined the category. The five levels of categories, from broadest to narrowest, are sector (signified by the first two digits of the code), subsector (third digit of the code), industry group (fourth digit), NAICS industry (fifth digit), and national industry (sixth digit). The five-digit code is the level of greatest amount of comparability among countries; a six-digit code provides for more country-specific detail.

[4]For more information, see www.census.gov/eos/www/naics/faqs/faqs.html#q2.

Although differences exist, the structures of ISIC, NACE, ANZSIC, and NAICS are similar enough that many of the categories from each of the different classification systems are compatible with one another. The U.S. Census Bureau has published tables showing how the various categories of the classification systems relate to one another.[5]

4.3. Strengths and Weaknesses of Current Systems

Unlike commercial classification systems, most government systems do not disclose information about a specific business or company, so an analyst cannot know all of the constituents of a particular category. For example, in the United States, federal law prohibits the Census Bureau from disclosing individual company activities, so their NAICS and SIC codes are unknown.

Most government and commercial classification systems are reviewed and, if necessary, updated from time to time. Generally, commercial classification systems are adjusted more frequently than government classification systems, which may be updated only every five years or so. NAICS, for example, is reviewed for potential revisions every five years.

Government classification systems generally do not distinguish between small and large businesses, between for-profit and not-for-profit organizations, or between public and private companies. Many commercial classification systems have the ability to distinguish between large and small companies by virtue of association with a particular equity index, and these systems include only for-profit and publicly traded organizations.

Another limitation of current systems is that the narrowest classification unit assigned to a company generally cannot be assumed to be its peer group for the purposes of detailed fundamental comparisons or valuation. A **peer group** is a group of companies engaged in similar business activities whose economics and valuation are influenced by closely related factors. Comparisons of a company in relation to a well-defined peer group can provide valuable insights into the company's performance and its relative valuation.

4.4. Constructing a Peer Group

The construction of a peer group is a subjective process; the result often differs significantly from even the most narrowly defined categories given by the commercial classification systems. However, commercial classification systems do provide a starting point for the construction of a relevant peer group because, by using such systems, an analyst can quickly discover the public companies operating in the chosen industry.

In fact, one approach to constructing a peer group is to start by identifying other companies operating in the same industry. Analysts who subscribe to one or more of the commercial classification systems that were discussed in Section 4.1 can quickly generate a list of other companies in the industry in which the company operates according to that particular service provider's definition of the industry. An analyst can then investigate the business activities of these companies and make adjustments as necessary to ensure that the businesses truly are comparable. The following lists of suggested steps and questions are given as practical aids to analysts in identifying peer companies.

Steps in constructing a preliminary list of peer companies:

- Examine commercial classification systems, if available to the analyst. These systems often provide a useful starting point for identifying companies operating in the same industry.

[5]For more information, see www.census.gov/eos/www/naics/concordances/concordances.html.

- Review the subject company's annual report for a discussion of the competitive environment. Companies frequently cite specific competitors.
- Review competitors' annual reports to identify other potential comparable companies.
- Review industry trade publications to identify comparable companies.
- Confirm that each comparable company derives a significant portion of its revenue and operating profit from a business activity similar to the primary business of the subject company.

Questions that may improve the list of peer companies:

- What proportion of revenue and operating profit is derived from business activities similar to those of the subject company? In general, a higher percentage results in a more meaningful comparison.
- Does a potential peer company face a demand environment similar to that of the subject company? For example, a comparison of growth rates, margins, and valuations may be of limited value when comparing companies that are exposed to different stages of the business cycle. (As mentioned, such differences may be the result of conducting business in geographically different markets.)
- Does a potential company have a finance subsidiary? Some companies operate a finance division to facilitate the sale of their products (e.g., Caterpillar Inc. and John Deere). To make a meaningful comparison of companies, the analyst should make adjustments to the financial statements to lessen the impact that the finance subsidiaries have on the various financial metrics being compared.

Example 9-4 illustrates the process of identifying a peer group of companies and shows some of the practical hurdles to determining a peer group.

EXAMPLE 9-4 An Analyst Researches the Peer Group of Brink's Home Security

Suppose that an analyst needs to identify the peer group of companies for Brink's Home Security for use in the valuation section of a company report. Brink's is a provider of electronic security and alarm monitoring services primarily to residential customers in North America. The analyst starts by looking at Brink's industry classification according to GICS. As previously discussed, the most narrowly defined category that GICS uses is the subindustry level, and in June 2009, Brink's was in the GICS subindustry called Specialized Consumer Services, together with the companies listed here:

GICS Sector: Consumer Discretionary
  GICS Industry Group: Consumer Services
    GICS Industry: Diversified Consumer Services
      GICS Subindustry: Specialized Consumer Services
        Brink's Home Security Holdings, Inc.

Coinstar, Inc.
H&R Block Inc.
Hillenbrand Inc.
Mathews International Corporation
Pre-Paid Legal Services Inc.
Regis Corporation
Service Corporation International
Sotheby's

After looking over the list of companies, the analyst quickly realizes that some adjustments need to be made to the list to end up with a peer group of companies that are comparable to Brink's. For example, Brink's has little in common with the hair care salon services of Regis or, for that matter, with the funeral service operations of Hillenbrand, Mathews, or Service Corporation. In fact, after careful inspection, the analyst concludes that none of the other companies included in the GICS subindustry are particularly good "comparables" for Brink's.

Next, the analyst reviews the latest annual report for Brink's to find management statements concerning its competitors. On page 6 of Brink's 2008 10-K, in the section titled "Industry Trends and Competition," is a list of other companies with comparable business activities: "We believe our primary competitors with national scope include: ADT Security Services, Inc. (part of Tyco International, Ltd.), Protection One, Inc., Monitronics International, Inc., and Stanley Security Solutions (part of The Stanley Works)." The analyst notes that Protection One on this list is another publicly held security services company and a likely candidate for inclusion in the peer group for Brink's. Monitronics International is privately held, so the analyst excludes it from the peer group; up-to-date, detailed fundamental data are not available for it.

The analyst discovers that ADT represents a significant portion of Tyco International's sales and profits (more than 40 percent of 2008 sales and profits); therefore, an argument could be made to include Tyco International in the peer group. The analyst might also consider including Stanley Works in the peer group because that company derived roughly a third of its revenue and close to half of its operating profit from its security division in 2008. Just as the analyst reviewed the latest annual report for Brink's to identify additional potential comparables, the analyst should also scan the annual reports of the other companies listed to see if other comparables exist. In checking these three companies' annual reports, the analyst finds that Protection One is the only one that cites specific competitors; Tyco and Stanley Works discuss competition only broadly.

After scanning all of the annual reports, the analyst finds no additional comparables.

The analyst decides that Brink's peer group consists of ADT Security Services, Protection One, and Stanley Security Solutions but also decides to give extra weight to the comparison with Protection One in valuation because the comparison with Protection One has the fewest complicating factors.

In connection with this discussion, note that International Financial Reporting Standards and U.S. GAAP require companies to disclose financial information about their operating segments (subject to certain qualifications). Such disclosures provide analysts with operational and financial information that can be helpful in peer-group determination.

Although companies with limited lines of business may neatly be categorized into a single peer group, companies with multiple divisions may be included in more than one category. For example, Belgium-based Anheuser-Busch InBev primarily makes and sells various brands of beer. It can easily be grouped together with other beverage companies (the theme park business constitutes a relatively immaterial part of total revenue). However, U.S.-based Hewlett-Packard Company (HP), a global provider of technology and software solutions, might reasonably be included in more than one category. Investors interested in the personal computer (PC) industry, for example, would probably include HP in their peer group, but investors constructing a peer group of providers of information technology services would probably include HP in that group also.

In summary, analysts must distinguish between a company's industry—as defined by one or more of the various classification systems—and its peer group. A company's peer group should consist of companies with similar business activities whose economic activity depends on similar drivers of demand and similar factors related to cost structure and access to financial capital. In practice, these necessities frequently result in a smaller group (even a different group) of companies than the most narrowly defined categories used by the common commercial classification systems. Example 9-5 illustrates various aspects of developing and using peer groups.

EXAMPLE 9-5 The Semiconductor Industry: Business-Cycle Sensitivity and Peer-Group Determination

The GICS semiconductor and semiconductor equipment industry (453010) has two subindustries—the semiconductor equipment subindustry (45301010) and the semiconductors subindustry (45301020). Members of the semiconductor equipment subindustry include equipment suppliers such as Lam Research Corporation and ASML Holdings NV; the semiconductors subindustry includes integrated circuit manufacturers Intel Corporation and Taiwan Semiconductor Manufacturing Company Ltd.

Lam Research is a leading supplier of wafer fabrication equipment and services to the world's semiconductor industry. Lam also offers wafer-cleaning equipment that is used after many of the individual steps required to manufacture a finished wafer. Often, the technical advances that Lam introduces in its wafer-etching and wafer-cleaning products are also available as upgrades to its installed base. This benefit provides customers with a cost-effective way to extend the performance and capabilities of their existing wafer fabrication lines.

ASML describes itself as the world's leading provider of lithography systems (etching and printing on wafers) for the semiconductor industry. ASML manufactures complex machines that are critical to the production of integrated circuits or microchips. ASML designs, develops, integrates, markets, and services these advanced systems, which help chip makers reduce the size and increase the functionality of microchips and consumer electronic equipment. The machines are costly and thus represent a substantial capital investment for a purchaser.

Based on revenue, Intel is the world's largest semiconductor chip maker and has the dominant share of microprocessors for the personal computer market. Intel has made significant investments in research and development (R&D) to introduce and produce new chips for new applications.

Established in 1987, Taiwan Semiconductor Manufacturing (TSM) is the world's largest dedicated semiconductor foundry (a semiconductor fabrication plant that executes the designs of other companies). TSM describes itself as offering cutting-edge process technologies, pioneering design services, manufacturing efficiency, and product quality. The company's revenues represent about 50 percent of the dedicated foundry segment in the semiconductor industry.

The questions that follow take the perspective of early 2009, when many economies around the world were in a recession. Based only on the information given, answer the following questions:

1. If the weak economy of early 2009 were to recover within the next 12–18 months, which of the two subindustries of the semiconductor and semiconductor equipment industry would most likely be the first to experience a positive improvement in business?
2. Explain whether Intel and TSM should be considered members of the same peer group.
3. Explain whether Lam Research and ASML should be considered members of the same peer group.

Solution to 1: In the most likely scenario, improvement in the business of the equipment makers (Lam and ASML) would lag that of semiconductor companies (Intel and TSM). Because of the weak economy of early 2009, excess manufacturing capacity should be available to meet increased demand for integrated circuits in the near term without additional equipment, which is a major capital investment. When semiconductor manufacturers believe the longer-term outlook has improved, they should begin to place orders for additional equipment.

Solution to 2: Intel and TSM are not likely to be considered comparable members of the same peer group because they have different sets of customers and different business models. Intel designs and produces its own proprietary semiconductors for direct sale to customers, such as personal computer makers. TSM provides design and production services to a diverse group of integrated circuit suppliers that generally do not have their own in-house manufacturing capabilities. In mid-2009, Standard & Poor's did not group Intel and TSM in the same peer group; Intel was in the Semiconductors, Logic, Larger Companies group and TSM was in the Semiconductors, Foundry Services group.

Solution to 3: Both Lam Research and ASML are leading companies that design and manufacture equipment to produce semiconductor chips. The companies are comparable because they both depend on the same economic factors that drive demand for their products. Their major customers are the semiconductor chip companies. In mid-2009, Standard & Poor's grouped both companies in the same peer group—Semiconductor Equipment, Larger Front End.

The next section addresses fundamental skills in describing and analyzing an industry.

5. DESCRIBING AND ANALYZING AN INDUSTRY

In their work, analysts study statistical relationships between industry trends and a range of economic and business variables. Analysts use economic, industry, and business publications and Internet resources as sources of information. They also seek information from industry associations, from the individual subject companies they are analyzing, and from these companies' competitors, suppliers, and customers. An analyst with a superior knowledge about an industry's characteristics, conditions, and trends has a competitive edge in evaluating the investment merits of the companies in the industry.

Analysts attempt to develop practical, reliable industry forecasts by using various approaches to forecasting. They often estimate a range of projections for a variable reflecting various possible scenarios. Analysts may seek to compare their projections with the projections of other analysts, partly to study differences in methodology and conclusions but also to identify differences between their forecasts and consensus forecasts. These latter differences are extremely important for uncovering investment opportunities because, to be the basis for superior investment performance, the forecast for a value-relevant variable must be both correct and sufficiently different from the consensus reflected in the price of publicly traded securities. Note that, although some information on analysts' revenue projections, EPS estimates, and ratings are accessible in some markets, analysts may have limited access to details about other analysts' work and assumptions because such details are kept confidential for competitive reasons.

Investment managers and analysts also examine industry performance (1) in relation to other industries to identify industries with superior/inferior returns and (2) to determine the degree of consistency, stability, and risk in the returns in the industry over time. The objective of this analysis is to identify industries that offer the highest potential for investment returns on a risk-adjusted basis. The investment time horizon can be either long or short, as is the case for a rotation strategy in which portfolios are rotated into the industry groups that are expected to benefit from the next stage in the business cycle.

Often, analysts examine **strategic groups** (groups sharing distinct business models or catering to specific market segments in an industry) almost as separate industries within industries. Criteria for selecting a strategic group might include the complexity of the product or service, its mode of delivery, and "barriers to entry." For example, charter airlines form a strategic group among "airlines" that is quite distinct from scheduled airlines; full-service hotels form a strategic group that is separate from limited-service or budget hotels; and companies that sell proprietary drugs (which are protected by patents) would be in a separate group from companies that sell generic drugs (which do not have patent protection) partly because the two groups pursue different strategies and use different business models.

Analysts often consider and classify industries according to industry **life-cycle stage**. The analyst determines whether an industry is in the embryonic, growth, shakeout, mature, or declining stage of the industry life cycle. During the stages of the life cycle of a product or industry, its position on the experience curve is often analyzed. The **experience curve** shows direct cost per unit of good or service produced or delivered as a typically declining function of cumulative output. The curve declines (1) because as the utilization of capital equipment increases, fixed costs (administration, overhead, advertising, etc.) are spread over a larger number of units of production; (2) because of improvements in labor efficiency and management of facilities; and (3) because of advances in production methods and product design. Examples exist in virtually all industries, but the experience curve is especially important in industries with high fixed overhead costs and/or repetitive production operations, such as electronics and appliance, automobile, and aircraft manufacturing. The industry life cycle is discussed in depth later in this chapter.

Exhibit 9-2 provides a framework designed to help analysts check that they have considered the range of forces that may affect the evolution of an industry. It shows, at the macro level, macroeconomic, demographic, governmental, social, and technological influences affecting the industry. It then depicts how an industry is affected by the forces driving industry competition (threat of new entrants, substitution threats, customer and supplier bargaining forces), the competitive forces in the industry, life-cycle issues, business-cycle considerations, and position of the industry on the experience curve. Exhibit 9-2 summarizes and brings together pictorially topics and concepts discussed in this section.

5.1. Principles of Strategic Analysis

When analyzing an industry, the analyst must recognize that the economic fundamentals can vary markedly among industries. Some industries are highly competitive, with most players struggling to earn adequate returns on capital, whereas other industries have attractive characteristics that allow almost all industry participants to generate healthy profits. Exhibit 9-3 makes this point graphically. It shows the average spread between return on invested capital (ROIC) and the cost of capital for 54 industries from 2006 through 2008.[6] Industries earning positive spreads appear to be earning **economic profits**, in the sense that they are achieving returns on investment above the opportunity cost of funds. This result should create value—that is, should increase the wealth of the investors, who are the providers of capital. In contrast, industries that are realizing negative spreads are destroying value. As can be seen, some industries struggled to generate positive economic returns (i.e., to create value) even during this period of synchronized global growth, while other industries did very well in earning such returns.

Differing competitive environments are often tied to the structural attributes of an industry, which is one reason industry analysis is a vital complement to company analysis. To thoroughly analyze a company itself, the analyst needs to understand the context in which the company operates. Needless to say, industry analysis must be forward looking. Many of the industries in Exhibit 9-3 were very different 10 or 15 years ago and would have been placed differently with respect to value creation; many will look very different 10 or 15 years from now. As analysts examine the competitive structure of an industry, they should always be thinking about what attributes could change in the future.

Analysis of the competitive environment with an emphasis on the implications of the environment for corporate strategy is known as **strategic analysis**. Michael Porter's "five forces" framework is the classic starting point for strategic analysis;[7] although it was originally aimed more at internal managers of businesses than at external security analysts, the framework is useful to both.[8]

Porter focused on five determinants of the intensity of competition in an industry:

[6]Return on invested capital can be defined as net operating profit after tax divided by the sum of common and preferred equity, long-term debt, and minority interests.

[7]See Porter (2008) for a recent presentation.

[8]What aspects of a company are important may be different for internal and external analysts. Whether information about competitive positions is accurately reflected in market prices, for example, would be relatively more important to external analysts.

EXHIBIT 9-2 A Framework for Industry Analysis

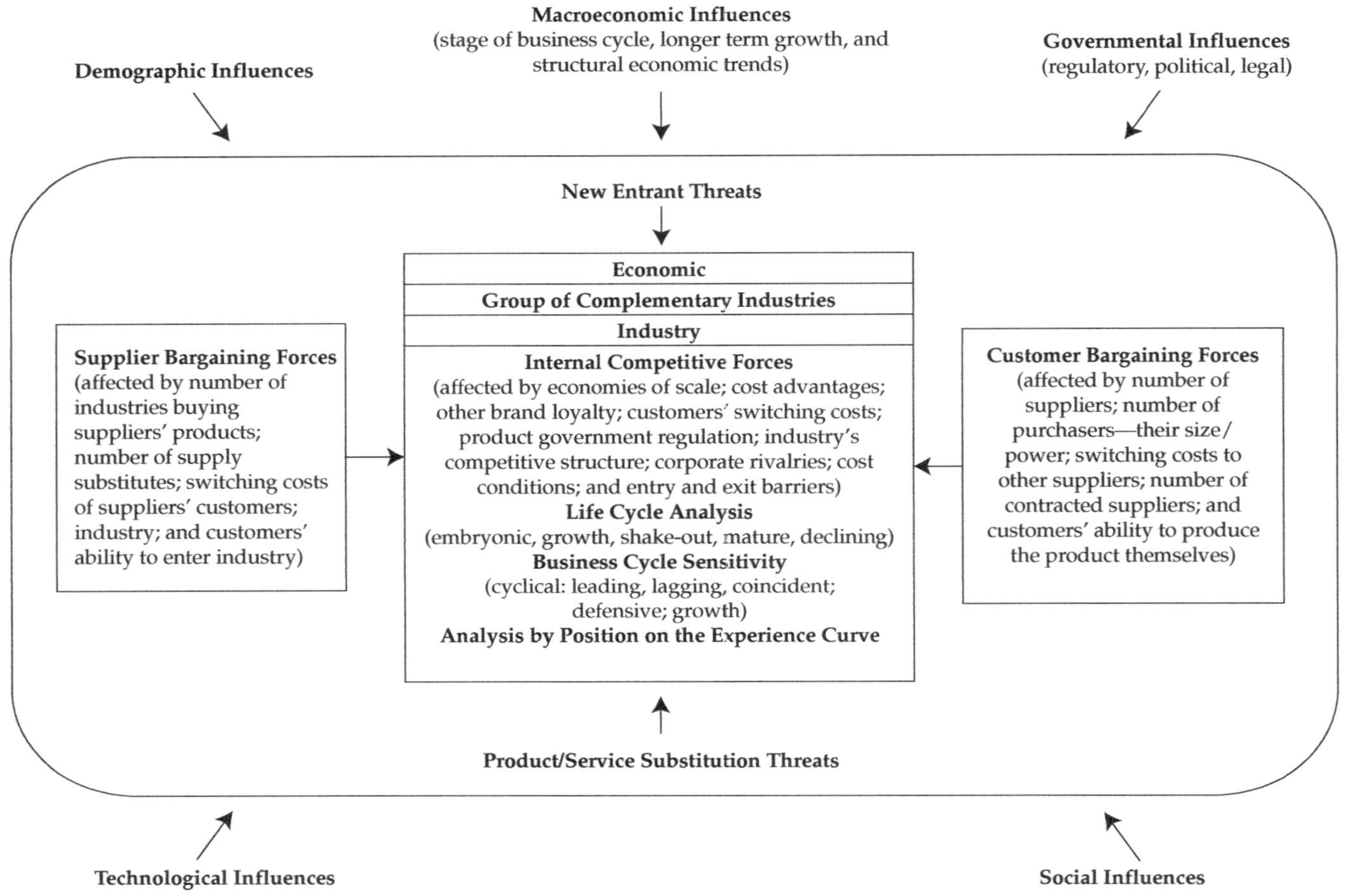

Demographic Influences
Macroeconomic Influences
(stage of business cycle, longer term growth, and structural economic trends)
Governmental Influences
(regulatory, political, legal)
New Entrant Threats
Economic
Group of Complementary Industries
Industry
Internal Competitive Forces
(affected by economies of scale; cost advantages; other brand loyalty; customers' switching costs; product government regulation; industry's competitive structure; corporate rivalries; cost conditions; and entry and exit barriers)
Life Cycle Analysis
(embryonic, growth, shake-out, mature, declining)
Business Cycle Sensitivity
(cyclical: leading, lagging, coincident; defensive; growth)
Analysis by Position on the Experience Curve
Supplier Bargaining Forces
(affected by number of industries buying suppliers' products; number of supply substitutes; switching costs of suppliers' customers; industry; and customers' ability to enter industry)
Customer Bargaining Forces
(affected by number of suppliers; number of purchasers—their size/power; switching costs to other suppliers; number of contracted suppliers; and customers' ability to produce the product themselves)
Product/Service Substitution Threats
Technological Influences
Social Influences

EXHIBIT 9-3 Some Industries Create Value, Others Destroy It

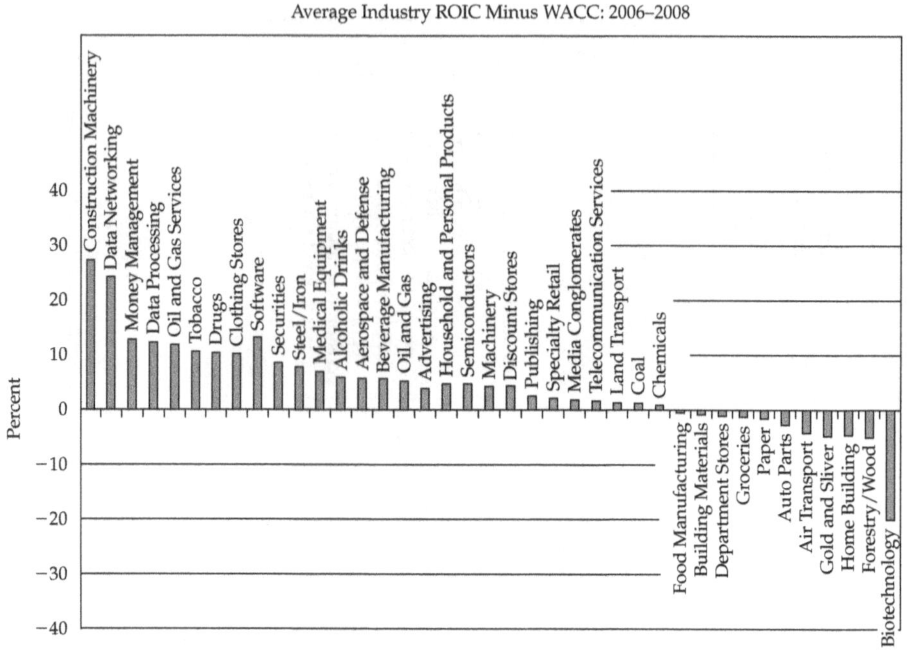

Source for data: Morningstar, Inc.

- The **threat of substitute products**, which can negatively affect demand if customers choose other ways of satisfying their needs. For example, consumers may trade down from premium beers to discount brands during recessions. Low-priced brands may be close substitutes for premium brands, which, when consumer budgets are constrained, reduces the ability of premium brands to maintain or increase prices.
- The **bargaining power of customers**, which can affect the intensity of competition by exerting influence on suppliers regarding prices (and possibly other factors such as product quality). For example, auto parts companies generally sell to a small number of auto manufacturers, which allows those customers, the auto manufacturers, to be tough negotiators when it comes to setting prices.
- The **bargaining power of suppliers**, which may be able to raise prices or restrict the supply of key inputs to a company. For example, workers at a heavily unionized company may have greater bargaining power as suppliers of labor than workers at a comparable nonunionized company. Suppliers of scarce or limited parts or elements often possess significant pricing power.
- The **threat of new entrants** to the industry, which depends on barriers to entry, or how difficult it would be for new competitors to enter the industry. Industries that are easy to enter will generally be more competitive than industries with high barriers to entry.
- The **intensity of rivalry** among incumbent companies (i.e., the current companies in the industry), which is a function of the industry's competitive structure. Industries that are fragmented among many small competitors, have high fixed costs, provide undifferentiated (commodity-like) products, or have high exit barriers usually experience more intense rivalry than industries without these characteristics.

Although all five of these forces merit attention, the fourth and fifth are particularly recommended as a first focus for analysis. The two factors are broadly applicable because all companies have competitors and must worry about new entrants to their industries. Also, in investigating these two forces, the analyst may become familiar in detail with an industry's incumbents and potential entrants, and all these companies' relative competitive prospects.

Addressing the following questions should help the analyst evaluate the threat of new entrants and the level of competition in an industry and thereby provide an effective base for describing and analyzing the industry:

- What are the barriers to entry? Is it difficult or easy for a new competitor to challenge incumbents? Relatively high (low) barriers to entry imply that the threat of new entrants is relatively low (high).
- How concentrated is the industry? Do a small number of companies control a relatively large share of the market, or does the industry have many players, each with a small market share?
- What are capacity levels? That is, based on existing investment, how much of the goods or services can be delivered in a given time frame? Does the industry suffer chronic over- or undercapacity, or do supply and demand tend to come into balance reasonably quickly in the industry?
- How stable are market shares? Do companies tend to rapidly gain or lose share, or is the industry stable?
- Where is the industry in its life cycle? Does it have meaningful growth prospects, or is demand stagnant/declining?
- How important is price to the customer's purchase decision?

The answers to these questions are elements of any thorough industry analysis.

5.1.1. Barriers to Entry

When a company is earning economic profits, the chances that it will be able to sustain them through time are greater, all else being equal, if the industry has high barriers to entry. The ease with which new competitors can challenge incumbents is often an important factor in determining the competitive landscape of an industry. If new competitors can easily enter the industry, the industry is likely to be highly competitive because high returns on invested capital will quickly be competed away by new entrants eager to grab their share of economic profits. As a result, industries with low barriers to entry often have little pricing power because price increases that raise companies' returns on capital will eventually attract new competitors to the industry.

If incumbents are protected by barriers to entry, the threat of new entrants is lower, and incumbents may enjoy a more benign competitive environment. Often, these barriers to entry can lead to greater pricing power, because potential competitors would find it difficult to enter the industry and undercut incumbents' prices. Of course, high barriers to entry do not guarantee pricing power, because incumbents may compete fiercely among each other.

A classic example of an industry with low barriers to entry is restaurants. Anyone with a modest amount of capital and some culinary skill can open a restaurant, and popular restaurants quickly attract competition. As a result, the industry is very competitive, and many restaurants fail in their first few years of business.

At the other end of the spectrum of barriers to entry are the global credit card networks such as MasterCard and Visa, both of which often post operating margins greater than

30 percent. Such high profits should attract competition, but the barriers to entry are extremely high. Capital costs are one hurdle; also, building a massive data-processing network would not be cheap. Imagine for a moment that a venture capitalist was willing to fund the construction of a network that would replicate the physical infrastructure of the incumbents. The new card-processing company would have to convince millions of consumers to use the new card and convince thousands of merchants to accept the card. Consumers would not want to use a card that merchants did not accept, and merchants would not want to accept a card that few consumers carried. This problem would be difficult to solve, which is why the barriers to entering this industry are quite high. The barriers help preserve the profitability of the incumbent players.

One way of understanding barriers to entry is simply by thinking about what it would take for new players to compete in an industry. How much money would they need to spend? What kind of intellectual capital would they need to acquire? How easy would it be to attract enough customers to become successful?

Another way to investigate the issue is by looking at historical data. How often have new companies tried to enter the industry? Is a list of industry participants today markedly different from what it was five or ten years ago? These kinds of data can be very helpful because the information is based on the real-world experience of many entrepreneurs and businesses making capital allocation decisions. If an industry has seen a flood of new entrants over the past several years, odds are good that the barriers are low; conversely, if the same ten companies that dominate an industry today dominated it ten years ago, barriers to entry are probably fairly high.

Do not confuse barriers to *entry*, however, with barriers to *success*. In some industries, entering may be easy but becoming successful enough to threaten the incumbents might be quite hard. For example, in the United States, starting a mutual fund requires a capital investment of perhaps US$150,000—not much of a barrier to an industry with historically high returns on capital. But once one has started a mutual fund, how does the company gather assets? Financial intermediaries are unlikely to sell a mutual fund with no track record. So, the fund may need to incur operational losses for a few years until it has established a good track record. Even with a track record, the fund will be competing in a crowded marketplace against companies with massive advertising budgets and well-paid salespeople. In this industry, good distribution can be even more valuable than good performance. So, although entering the asset management industry may be relatively easy, succeeding is another thing altogether.

Also, high barriers to entry do not automatically lead to good pricing power and attractive industry economics. Consider the cases of auto making, commercial aircraft manufacturing, and refining industries. Starting up a new company in any of these industries would be tremendously difficult. Aside from the massive capital costs, there would be significant other barriers to entry: A new automaker would need manufacturing expertise and a dealer network; an aircraft manufacturer would need a tremendous amount of intellectual capital; and a refiner would need process expertise and regulatory approvals.

Yet, all of these industries are quite competitive, with limited or nonexistent pricing power, and few industry participants reliably generate returns on capital in excess of their costs of capital. Among the reasons for this seeming paradox of high barriers to entry plus poor pricing power, two stand out.

- First, price is a large component of the customer's purchase decision when buying from these companies in these industries. In some cases, the reason is that the companies (e.g., refiners) sell a commodity; in other cases, the product is expensive but has easily available substitutes. For example, most airlines choose between purchasing Boeing and Airbus airplanes not on brand but on cost-related considerations: Airlines need to transport people and cargo at the lowest possible cost per mile because the airlines have limited ability to pass along higher costs to customers. That consideration makes price a huge component of their purchase decision. Most airlines purchase whichever plane is the most cost efficient at any point in time. The result is that the Boeing Company and Airbus have limited ability to price their planes at a level that generates good returns on invested capital.[9]

- Second, these industries all have high barriers to exit, which means they are prone to overcapacity. A refinery or automobile plant cannot be used for anything other than, respectively, refining oil or producing cars, which makes it hard to redeploy the capital elsewhere and exit the industry if conditions become unprofitable. This barrier gives owners of these types of assets a strong incentive to attempt to keep those loss-making plants operating, which, of course, prolongs conditions of overcapacity.

A final consideration when analyzing barriers to entry is that they can change over time. Years ago, a potential new entrant to the semiconductor industry would have needed the capital and expertise to build a "fab" (the industry term for a semiconductor manufacturing plant). Chip fabs are hugely expensive and technologically complex, which deterred potential new entrants. Starting in the mid-1990s, however, the outsourcing of chip making to contract semiconductor manufacturers became feasible, which meant that designers of chips could challenge the manufacturers without the need to build their own plants. As a result, the industry became much more fragmented through the late 1990s and into the first decade of the twenty-first century.

So, in general, high barriers to entry can lead to better pricing and less competitive industry conditions, but important exceptions are worth bearing in mind.

5.1.2. Industry Concentration

Much like industries with barriers to entry, industries that are concentrated among a relatively small number of players often experience relatively less price competition. Again, there are important exceptions, so the reader should not automatically assume that concentrated industries always have pricing power or that fragmented industries do not.

An analysis of industry concentration should start with market share: What percentage of the market does each of the largest players have, and how large are those shares relative to each other and relative to the remainder of the market? Often, the *relative* market shares of competitors matter as much as their ***absolute*** market shares.

For example, the global market for long-haul commercial aircraft is extremely concentrated—only Boeing and Airbus manufacture these types of planes. The two companies have roughly similar market shares, however, and control essentially the entire market. Because neither enjoys a scale advantage relative to its competitor and because any business gained by one is lost by the other, competition tends to be fierce.

This situation contrasts with the market for home improvement products in the United States, which is dominated by Home Depot and Lowe's. These two companies have

[9]Neither company's commercial aircraft segment has reliably generated returns on capital comfortably in excess of the company's cost of capital for many years. Boeing's returns on capital have been respectable overall, but the company's military segment is much more profitable than its commercial aircraft segment.

11 percent and 7 percent market share, respectively, which doesn't sound very large. However, the next largest competitor has only 2 percent of the market, and most market participants are tiny with miniscule market shares. Both Home Depot and Lowe's have historically posted high returns on invested capital, in part because they could profitably grow by targeting smaller competitors rather than engaging in fierce competition with each other.

Fragmented industries tend to be highly price competitive for several reasons. First, the large number of companies makes coordination difficult because there are too many competitors for each industry member to monitor effectively. Second, each player has such a small piece of the market that even a small gain in market share can make a meaningful difference to its fortunes, which increases the incentive of each company to undercut prices and attempt to steal share. Finally, the large number of players encourages industry members to think of themselves individualistically rather than as members of a larger group, which can lead to fierce competitive behavior.

In concentrated industries, in contrast, each player can relatively easily keep track of what its competitors are doing, which makes tacit coordination much more feasible. Also, leading industry members are large, which means they have more to lose—and proportionately less to gain—by destructive price behavior. Large companies are also more tied to the fortunes of the industry as a whole, making them more likely to consider the long-run effects of a price war on overall industry economics.

As with barriers to entry, the level of industry concentration is a guideline rather than a hard and fast rule when thinking about the level of pricing power in an industry. For example, Exhibit 9-4 shows a rough classification of industries compiled by Morningstar after asking its equity analysts whether industries were characterized by strong or weak pricing power and whether those industries were concentrated or fragmented. Examples of companies in industries are included in parentheses. In the upper right quadrant ("concentrated with weak pricing power"), those industries that are capital intensive and sell commodity-like products are shown in boldface.

EXHIBIT 9-4 Two-Factor Analysis of Industries

Concentrated with Strong Pricing Power	Concentrated with Weak Pricing Power
Soft drinks (Coca-Cola Co., PepsiCo)	**Commercial aircraft (Boeing, Airbus)**
Orthopedic devices (Zimmer, Smith & Nephew)	**Automobiles (General Motors, Toyota, Daimler)**
Laboratory services (Quest Diagnostics, LabCorp)	**Memory (DRAM & Flash Product, Samsung, Hynix)**
Biotech (Amgen, Genzyme)	**Semiconductor equipment (Applied Materials, Tokyo Electron)**
Pharmaceuticals (Merck & Co., Novartis)	Generic drugs (Teva Pharmaceutical Industries, Sandoz)
Microprocessors (Intel, Advanced Micro Devices)	Consumer electronics (Sony Electronics, Koninklijke Philips Electronics)
Industrial gases (Praxair, Air Products and Chemicals)	PCs (Dell, Acer, Lenovo)
Enterprise storage (EMC)	Printers/office machines (HP, Lexmark)
Enterprise networking (Cisco Systems)	
Integrated shippers (UPS, FedEx, DHL International)	

EXHIBIT 9-4 *(Continued)*

Concentrated with Strong Pricing Power	Concentrated with Weak Pricing Power
U.S. railroads (Burlington Northern)	**Refiners (Valero, Marathon Oil)**
U.S. defense (General Dynamics)	**Major integrated oil (BP, ExxonMobil)**
Heavy construction equipment (Caterpillar, Komatsu)	Equity exchanges (NYSE, Deutsche Börse Group)
Seaborne iron ore (Vale, Rio Tinto)	
Confections (Cadbury, Mars/Wrigley)	
Credit card networks (MasterCard, Visa)	
Custody and asset administration (BNY Mellon, State Street)	
Investment banking/mergers and acquisitions (Goldman Sachs, UBS)	
Futures exchanges (Chicago Mercantile Exchange, Intercontinental Exchange)	
Canadian banking (RBC Bank, TD Bank)	
Australian banking	
Tobacco (Philip Morris, British American Tobacco)	
Alcoholic beverages (Diageo, Pernod Ricard)	

Fragmented with Strong Pricing Power	Fragmented with Weak Pricing Power
Asset management (BlackRock, Fidelity)	Consumer packaged goods (Procter & Gamble, Unilever)
For-profit education (Apollo Group, DeVry University)	Retail (Wal-Mart, Carrefour Group)
Analog chips (Texas Instruments, STMicroelectronics)	Marine transportation (Maersk Line, Frontline)
Industrial distribution (Fastenal, W.W. Grainger)	Solar panels
Propane distribution (AmeriGas, Ferrellgas)	Homebuilding
Private banking (Northern Trust, Credit Suisse)	Airlines
	Mining (metals)
	Chemicals
	Engineering and construction
	Metal service centers
	Commercial printing
	Restaurants
	Radio broadcasting
	Oil services
	Life insurance
	Reinsurance
	Exploration and production (E&P)
	U.S. banking
	Specialty finance
	Property/casualty insurance
	Household and personal products

Source: Morningstar Equity Research.

The industries in the top right quadrant defy the "concentration is good for pricing" guideline. We discussed the commercial aircraft manufacturing example in the preceding section, but many other industries are dominated by a small number of players yet have difficult competitive environments and limited pricing power.

When we examine these concentrated-yet-competitive industries, a clear theme emerges: Many industries in this quadrant (the boldface ones) are highly capital intensive and sell commodity-like products. As we saw in the discussion of exit barriers, capital-intensive industries can be prone to overcapacity, which mitigates the benefits of industry concentration. Also, if the industry sells a commodity product that is difficult—or impossible—to differentiate, the incentive to compete on price increases because a lower price frequently results in greater market share.[10]

The computer memory market is a perfect example of a concentrated-yet-competitive industry. Dynamic random access memory (DRAM) is widely used in PCs, and the industry is concentrated, with about three-quarters of global market share held by the top four companies. The industry is also highly capital intensive; a new fab costs upwards of US$3 billion. But one DRAM chip is much like another, and players in this market have a huge economic incentive to capture market share because of the large scale economies involved in running a semiconductor manufacturing plant. As a result, price competition tends to be extremely fierce and industry concentration is essentially a moot point in the face of these other competitive dynamics.

The global soft drink market is also highly concentrated, of course, but capital requirements are relatively low and industry participants sell a differentiated product. Pepsi and Coca-Cola do not own their own bottling facilities, so a drop in market share does not affect them as much as it would a memory-chip maker. Moreover, although memory-chip companies are assured of gaining market share and increasing sales volumes by cutting prices, a sizable proportion of consumers would not switch from Pepsi to Coke (or vice-versa) even if one cost much less than the other.

Generally, industry concentration is a good indicator that an industry has pricing power and rational competition, but other factors may override the importance of concentration. Industry fragmentation is a much stronger signal that the industry is competitive with limited pricing power. Notice how few fragmented industries are in the bottom left quadrant in Exhibit 9-4.

The industry characteristics discussed here are guidelines meant to steer the analyst in a particular direction, not rules that should cause the analyst to ignore other relevant analytical factors.

5.1.3. Industry Capacity

The effect on pricing of industry capacity (the maximum amount of a good or service that can be supplied in a given time period) is clear: Tight, or limited, capacity gives participants more pricing power as demand for the product or service exceeds supply, whereas overcapacity leads to price-cutting and a very competitive environment as excess supply chases demand. An analyst should think about not only current capacity conditions but future changes in capacity levels. How quickly can companies in the industry adjust to fluctuations in demand? How flexible is the industry in bringing supply and demand into balance? What will be the effect of that process on industry pricing power or on industry margins?

[10]There are a small number of concentrated and rational commodity industries, such as potash (a type of fertilizer) and seaborne iron ore. What sets these industries apart is that they are *hyper*-concentrated: The top two players control 60 percent of the global potash market, and the top three players control two-thirds of the global market for seaborne iron ore.

Generally, capacity is fixed in the short term and variable in the long term because capacity can be increased—for example, new factories can be built—if time is sufficient. What is considered "sufficient" time—and, therefore, the duration of the short term, in which capacity cannot be increased—may vary dramatically among industries. Sometimes, adding capacity takes years to complete, as in the case of the construction of a "greenfield" (new) manufacturing plant for pharmaceuticals or for paper, which is complex and subject to regulatory requirements (e.g., relating to the plant's waste). In other situations, capacity may be added or reduced relatively quickly, as is the case with service industries, such as advertising. In cyclical markets, such as commercial paper and paperboard, capacity conditions can change rapidly. Strong demand in the early stages of an economic recovery can result in the addition of supply. Given the long lead times to build manufacturing plants, new supply may reach the market just as demand slows, rapidly changing capacity conditions from tight to loose. Such considerations underscore the importance of forecasting long-term industry demand in evaluating industry investments in capacity.

One of the more dramatic examples of this process in recent years occurred in the market for maritime dry-bulk shipping during the commodity boom of 2003–2008. Rapid industrialization in China—combined with synchronized global economic growth—increased demand for cargo ships that could transport iron ore, coal, grains, and other high-volume/low-value commodities. Given that the supply of cargo ships could not be increased very quickly (because ships take time to build and large commercial shipyards typically have multiyear backlogs), shippers naturally raised prices to take advantage of the tight global cargo capacity. In fact, the price to charter the largest type of dry-bulk vessel—a Capesize-class ship too big to fit through the Panama Canal—increased more than fivefold in only a year, from approximately US$30,000 per day in early 2006 to almost US$160,000 per day by late 2007.

As one would expect, orders for new dry-bulk carriers skyrocketed during this period as the industry scrambled to add shipping capacity to take advantage of seemingly insatiable demand and very favorable pricing. In early 2006, the number of dry-bulk carriers on order from shipyards represented approximately 20 percent of the worldwide fleet. By late 2008, the number of bulk ships on order represented almost 70 percent of the global bulk fleet.[11] Of course, the prospect of this additional capacity, combined with a dramatic slump in aggregate global demand for commodities, caused a massive decline in shipping rates. Capesize charter rates plummeted from the US$160,000/day high of late 2007 to a low of under US$10,000 per day just one year later.

In this example, the conditions of tight supply that were driving strong dry-bulk pricing were quite clear, and these high prices drove attractive returns on capital—and share-price performance—for dry-bulk-shipping companies. However, the careful analyst would have looked at future additions to supply in the form of new ships on order and would have forecasted that the tight supply conditions were not sustainable and thus that the pricing power of dry-bulk shippers was short lived. These predictions are, in fact, precisely what occurred.

Note that capacity need not be physical. After Hurricane Katrina caused enormous damage to the southeastern United States in 2005, reinsurance rates quickly spiked as customers sought to increase their financial protection from future hurricanes. However, these high reinsurance rates enticed a flood of fresh capital into the reinsurance market, and a number of new reinsurance companies were founded, which brought rates back down.

Generally, if new capacity is physical—for example, an auto manufacturing plant or a massive cargo ship—it will take longer for new capacity to come on line to meet an increase in

[11]From "RS Platou Monthly" (November 2008): www.platou.com/loadfileservlet/loadfiledb?id=1228989312093PUBLISHER&key=1228989321421.

demand, resulting in a longer period of tight conditions. Unfortunately, capacity additions frequently overshoot long-run demand, and because physical capital is often hard to re-deploy, industries reliant on physical capacity may get stuck in conditions of excess capacity and diminished pricing power for an extended period.

Financial and human capital, in contrast, can be quickly shifted to new uses. In the reinsurance example, for instance, financial capital was quick to enter the reinsurance market and take advantage of tight capacity conditions, but if too much capital had entered the market, some portion of that capital could easily have left to seek higher returns elsewhere. Money can be used for many things, but massive bulk cargo vessels are not useful for much more than transporting heavy goods across oceans.

5.1.4. Market Share Stability

Examining the stability of industry market shares over time is similar to thinking about barriers to entry and the frequency with which new players enter an industry. In fact, barriers to entry and the frequency of new product introductions, together with such factors as product differentiation, all affect market shares. Stable market shares typically indicate less competitive industries; unstable market shares often indicate highly competitive industries that have limited pricing power.

A comparison of two noncommodity markets in the health care sector illustrates this point. Over the past decade, the orthopedic device industry—mainly artificial hips and knees—has been a relatively stable global oligopoly. As Exhibit 9-5 indicates, five companies control about 95 percent of the worldwide market, and the market shares of those companies have changed by only small amounts over the past several years.

EXHIBIT 9-5 Market Share Stability in Global Orthopedic Devices (entries are market share)

Worldwide Knee/Hip Market Share	2005	2006	2007	2008
Zimmer	27.9%	27.5%	27.2%	26.0%
Johnson & Johnson (DePuy)	24.0%	23.9%	22.9%	22.9%
Stryker	21.6%	21.4%	21.5%	21.3%
Smith & Nephew	9.4%	9.8%	11.5%	12.6%
Biomet	11.5%	10.9%	10.9%	11.3%

Source: Company reports and Morningstar estimates.

In contrast, although the U.S. market for stents—small metal mesh devices used to prop open blocked arteries—is also controlled by a handful of companies, market shares recently have gone from being very stable to being marked by rapid change. Johnson & Johnson, which together with Boston Scientific, dominated the U.S. stent market for many years, went from having about half the market in 2007 to having only 15 percent in early 2009; over the same period, Abbott Laboratories increased its market share from zero to 25 percent. The reason for this change was the launch of new stents by Abbott and Medtronic, which took market share from Johnson & Johnson and Boston Scientific's established stents.

Orthopedic device companies have experienced more stability in their market shares for two reasons. First, artificial hips and knees are complicated to implant, and each manufacturer's products are slightly different. As a result, orthopedic surgeons become proficient at using one or several companies' devices and may be reluctant to incur the time and cost of learning how to implant products from a competing company. The second reason is the relatively slow pace of innovation in the orthopedic device industry, which tends to be evolutionary rather than revolutionary, making the benefit of switching among product lines relatively low. In addition, the number of orthopedic device companies has remained fairly static over many years.

In contrast, the U.S. stent market has experienced rapid shifts in market shares because of several factors. First, interventional cardiologists seem to be more open than orthopedic surgeons to implanting stents from different manufacturers; that tendency may reflect lower switching costs for stents relative to orthopedic devices. More importantly, however, the pace of innovation in the stent market has become quite rapid, giving cardiologists added incentive to switch to newer stents, with potentially better patient outcomes, as they became available.

Low switching costs plus a relatively high benefit from switching caused market shares to change quickly in the stent market. High switching costs for orthopedic devices coupled with slow innovation resulted in a lower benefit from switching, which led to greater market share stability in orthopedic devices.

5.1.5. Industry Life Cycle

An industry's life-cycle position often has a large impact on its competitive dynamics, making this position an important component of the strategic analysis of an industry.

5.1.5.1. Description of an Industry Life-Cycle Model

Industries, like individual companies, tend to evolve over time, and usually experience significant changes in the rate of growth and levels of profitability along the way. Just as an investment in an individual company requires careful monitoring, industry analysis is a continuous process to identify changes that may be occurring or be likely to occur. A useful framework for analyzing the evolution of an industry is an industry life-cycle model, which identifies the sequential stages that an industry typically goes through. The five stages of an industry life-cycle model are embryonic, growth, shakeout, mature, and decline. Each stage is characterized by different opportunities and threats.[12] Exhibit 9-6 shows the model as a curve illustrating the level and growth rate of demand at each stage.

Embryonic. An embryonic industry is one that is just beginning to develop. For example, in the 1960s, the global semiconductor industry was in the embryonic stage (it has grown to become a US$249 billion industry in 2008)[13] and in the early 1980s, the global mobile phone industry was in the embryonic stage (it now produces and sells more than a billion handsets annually). Characteristics of the embryonic stage include slow growth and high prices because customers tend to be unfamiliar with the industry's product and volumes are not yet sufficient to achieve meaningful economies of scale. Increasing product awareness and developing distribution channels are key strategic initiatives of companies during this stage. Substantial investment is generally required, and the risk of failure is high. A majority of start-up companies do not succeed.

Growth. A growth industry tends to be characterized by rapidly increasing demand, improving profitability, falling prices, and relativity low competition among companies in the industry. Demand is fueled by new customers entering the market, and prices fall as economies of scale

[12]Much of the discussion that follows regarding life-cycle stages owes a debt to the discussion in Hill and Jones (2008).

[13]Semiconductor Industry Association Factsheet: www.sia-online.org/cs/industry_resources/industry_fact_sheet.

EXHIBIT 9-6 An Industry Life-Cycle Model

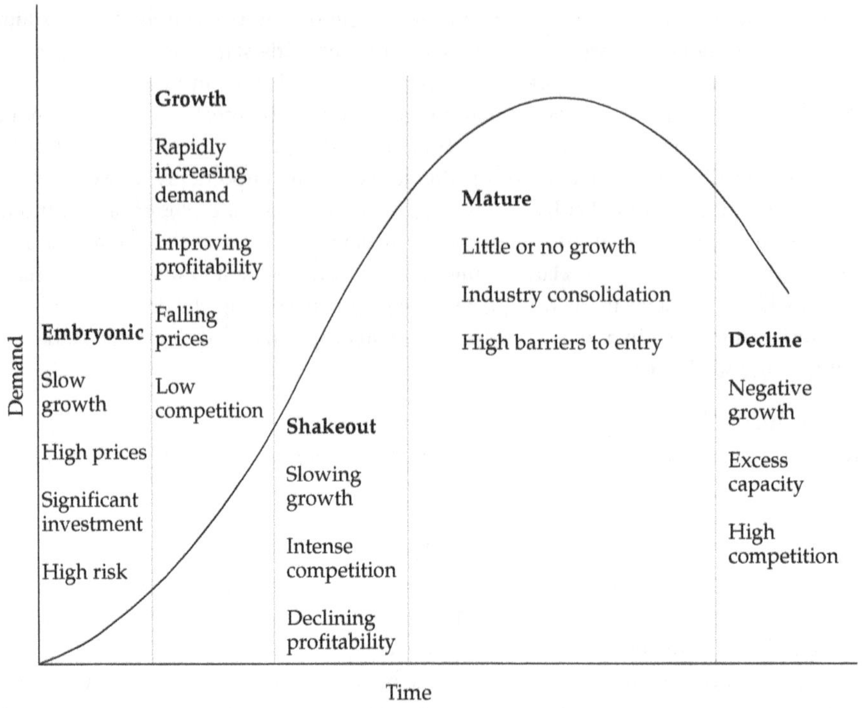

Source: Based on Figure 2.4 in Hill and Jones (2008).

are achieved and as distribution channels develop. The threat of new competitors entering the industry is usually highest during the growth stage, when barriers to entry are relatively low. Competition tends to be relatively limited, however, because rapidly expanding demand provides companies with an opportunity to grow without needing to capture market share from competitors. Industry profitability improves as volumes rise and economies of scale are attained.

Shakeout. The shakeout stage is usually characterized by slowing growth, intense competition, and declining profitability. During the shakeout stage, demand approaches market saturation levels because few new customers are left to enter the market. Competition is intense as growth becomes increasingly dependent on market share gains. Excess industry capacity begins to develop as the rate at which companies continue to invest exceeds the overall growth of industry demand. In an effort to boost volumes to fill excess capacity, companies often cut prices, so industry profitability begins to decline. During the shakeout stage, companies increasingly focus on reducing their cost structure (restructuring) and building brand loyalty. Marginal companies may fail or merge with others.

Mature. Characteristics of a mature industry include little or no growth, industry consolidation, and relatively high barriers to entry. Industry growth tends to be limited to replacement demand and population expansion because the market at this stage is completely saturated. As a result of the shakeout, mature industries often consolidate and become oligopolies. The surviving companies tend to have brand loyalty and relatively efficient cost structures, both of which are significant barriers to entry. During periods of stable demand, companies in mature industries tend to recognize their interdependence and try to avoid price wars. Periodic price wars do occur, however, most notably during periods of declining demand (such as during economic downturns). Companies with superior products or services are likely to gain market share and experience above-industry-average growth and profitability.

Decline. During the decline stage, industry growth turns negative, excess capacity develops, and competition increases. Industry demand at this stage may decline for a variety of reasons, including technological substitution (for example, the newspaper industry has been declining for years as more people turn to the Internet and 24-hour cable news networks for information), social changes, and global competition (for example, low-cost foreign manufacturers pushing the U.S. textile industry into decline). As demand falls, excess capacity in the industry forms and companies respond by cutting prices, which often leads to price wars. At this point, the weaker companies often exit the industry, merge, or redeploy capital into different products and services.

When overall demand for an industry's products or services is declining, the opportunity for individual companies to earn above-average returns on invested capital tends to be less than when demand is stable or increasing, because of price-cutting and higher per-unit costs as production is cut back. Example 9-6 deals with industry life cycles.

EXAMPLE 9-6 Industry Growth and Company Growth

U.S. shipments of prefabricated housing (precut, modular housing) declined sharply in 1999–2004 as the abundant availability of low-cost mortgage financing and other factors led individuals to purchase site-built housing. In 1998, however, some forecasts had projected that prefabricated housing would gain market share at the expense of site-built housing. What would have been the probable impact on market share of a typical company in the prefabricated housing industry under the 1998 optimistic forecast and under actual conditions?

Solution: Increasing industry demand as forecasted in 1998 would have given companies in the prefabricated housing industry the opportunity to grow without taking market share from one another, mitigating the intensity of competition in this industry. Under actual industry circumstances of declining demand and a shrinking market, in contrast, revenue growth for a prefabricated housing company could happen only through market share gains from its competitors.

5.1.5.2. Using an Industry Life-Cycle Model

In general, new industries tend to be more competitive (with lots of players entering and exiting) than mature industries, which often have stable competitive environments and players that are more interested in protecting what they have than in gaining lots of market share. However, as industries move from maturity to decline, competitive pressures may increase again as industry participants perceive a zero-sum environment and fight over pieces of an ever-shrinking pie.

An important point for the analyst to think about is whether a company is "acting its age" relative to where its industry sits in the life cycle. Companies in growth industries should be building customer loyalty as they introduce consumers to new products or services, building scale, and reinvesting heavily in their operations to capitalize on increasing demand. They are probably not focusing strongly on internal efficiency. These companies are rather like young adults, who are reinvesting their human and financial capital with the goal of becoming more successful in life. Growth companies typically reinvest their cash flows in new products and product platforms rather than returning cash flows to shareholders because these companies still have many opportunities to deploy their capital to make positive returns. Although this analogy to the human life cycle is a helpful way to think about the model, the analyst should also be aware that the analogy is not exact in detail. Long-established companies sometimes find a way to accelerate growth through innovation or by expansion into new markets. Humans cannot really move back to the days of youth. So, a more precise formulation may be "acting its stage" rather than acting its age.

Companies in mature industries are likely to be pursuing replacement demand rather than new buyers and are probably focused on extending successful product lines rather than introducing revolutionary new products. They are also probably focusing on cost rationalization and efficiency gains rather than on taking lots of market share. Importantly, these companies have fewer growth opportunities than in the previous stage, and thus more limited avenues for profitably reinvesting capital, but they often have strong cash flows. Given their strong cash flows and relatively limited reinvestment opportunities, such companies should be, according to a common perspective, returning capital to shareholders via share repurchases or dividends. These companies are rather like middle-aged adults who are harvesting the fruits of their success earlier in life.

What can be a concern is a middle-aged company acting like a young, growth company and pouring capital into projects with low ROIC prospects in an effort to pursue size for its own sake. Many companies have a difficult time managing the transition from growth to maturity, and their returns on capital—and shareholder returns—may suffer until management decides to allocate capital in a manner more appropriate to the company's life-cycle stage.

For example, three large U.S. retailers—Wal-Mart, Home Depot, and McDonald's—all went through the transition to maturity in the first decade of the twenty-first century. At various times between 2002 and 2005, these companies realized that their size and industry dominance meant that the days of double-digit growth that was driven largely by new store (restaurant) openings were a thing of the past. All three reallocated capital away from opening new stores to other areas—namely, increased inventory efficiency (Home Depot), improving the customer experience (McDonald's), and increased dividends and share repurchases (all three). As a result, returns on capital for each improved, as did shareholder returns.

5.1.5.3. Limitations of Industry Life-Cycle Analysis

Although models can provide a useful framework for thinking about an industry, the evolution of an industry does not always follow a predictable pattern. Various external factors may significantly affect the shape of the pattern, causing some stages to be longer or shorter than expected and, in certain cases, causing some stages to be skipped altogether.

Technological changes may cause an industry to experience an abrupt shift from growth to decline, thus skipping the shakeout and mature stages. For example, transistors replaced vacuum tubes in the 1960s at a time when the vacuum tube industry was still in its growth stage; word processors replaced typewriters in the 1980s; and today the movie rental industry is experiencing rapid change as consumers increasingly turn to on-demand services such as downloading movies from the Internet or through their cable providers.

Regulatory changes can also have a profound impact on the structure of an industry. A prime example is the deregulation of the U.S. telecommunications industry in the 1990s, which transformed a monopolistic industry into an intensely competitive one. AT&T was broken into regional service providers, and many new long distance telephone service entrants, such as Sprint, emerged. The result was a wider range of product and service offerings and lower consumer prices. Changes in government reimbursement rates for health-care products and services may (and have) affected the profitability of companies in the health care industry globally.

Social changes also have the ability to affect the profile of an industry. The casual dining industry has benefited over the past 30 years from the increase in the number of dual-income families, who often have more income but less time to cook meals to eat at home.

Demographics also play an important role. As the Baby Boom generation ages, for instance, industry demand for health care services is likely to increase.

Thus, life-cycle models tend to be most useful for analyzing industries during periods of relative stability. They are less practical when the industry may be experiencing rapid change because of external or other special circumstances.

Another limiting factor of models is that not all companies in an industry experience similar performances. The key objective for the analyst is to identify the potential winners while avoiding potential losers. Highly profitable companies can exist in competitive industries with below-average profitability—and vice versa. For example, Nokia has historically been able to use its scale to generate levels of profitability that are well above average despite operating in a highly competitive industry. In contrast, despite the historically above-average growth and profitability of the software industry, countless examples exist of software companies that failed to ever generate a profit and eventually went out of business.

EXAMPLE 9-7 Industry Life Cycle

1. An industry experiencing slow growth and high prices is best characterized as being in the:
   A. Mature stage.
   B. Shakeout stage.
   C. Embryonic stage.
2. Which of the following statements about the industry life-cycle model is *least* accurate?
   A. The model is more appropriately used during a period of rapid change than during a period of relative stability.
   B. External factors may cause some stages of the model to be longer or shorter than expected, and in certain cases, a stage may be skipped entirely.
   C. Not all companies in an industry will experience similar performance, and very profitable companies can exist in an industry with below-average profitability.

Solution to 1: C is correct. Both slow growth and high prices are associated with the embryonic stage. High price is not a characteristic of the mature or shakeout stages.

Solution to 2: A is correct. The statement is the least accurate. The model is best used during a period of relative stability rather than during a period of rapid change.

5.1.6. Price Competition

A highly useful tool for analyzing an industry is attempting to think like a customer of the industry. Whatever factor most influences customer purchase decisions is likely to also be the focus of competitive rivalry in the industry. In general, industries for which price is a large factor in customer purchase decisions tend to be more competitive than industries in which customers value other attributes more highly.

Although this depiction may sound like the description of a commodity industry versus a noncommodity industry, it is, in fact, a bit more subtle. Commercial aircraft and passenger cars are certainly more differentiated than lumps of coal or gallons of gasoline, but price nonetheless weighs heavily in the purchase decisions of buyers of aircraft and cars, because fairly good substitutes are easily available. If Airbus charges too much for an A320, an airline can buy a Boeing 737.[14] If BMW's price for a four-door luxury sedan rises too high, customers can switch to a Mercedes or other luxury brand with similar features. Similar switching can be expected as a result of a unilateral price increase in the case of most industries in the "Weak Pricing Power" column of Exhibit 9-4.

Contrast these industries with asset management, one of a handful of industries that is both fragmented and characterized by strong pricing power. Despite the well-documented impact of fees on future investment returns, the vast majority of asset management customers do not make decisions on the basis of price. Instead, asset management customers focus on historical returns, which allow this highly fragmented industry to maintain strong pricing power. Granted, the index fund arena is very price competitive, because any index fund is a perfect substitute for another fund tracking the same benchmark. But the active management segment of the industry has generally been able to price its products in an implicitly cooperative fashion that enables most players to generate consistently high returns on capital, presumably because price is not uppermost in the mind of a prospective mutual fund investor.

Returning to a more capital-intensive industry, consider heavy equipment manufacturers, such as Caterpillar, John Deere, and Komatsu. A large wheel loader or combine harvester requires a large capital outlay, so price certainly plays a part in the buyers' decisions. However, other factors are important enough to customers to allow these companies a small amount of pricing power. Construction equipment is typically used as a complement to other gear on a large project, which means that downtime for repairs increases costs because, for example, hourly laborers must wait for a bulldozer to be fixed. Broken equipment is also expensive for agricultural users, who may have only a few days in which to harvest a season's crop. Because of the importance to users of their products' reliability and their large service networks—which are important "differentiators" or factors bestowing a competitive advantage—Caterpillar, Komatsu, and John Deere have historically been able to price their equipment at levels that have generated solid returns on invested capital.

5.1.7. Industry Comparison

To illustrate how these elements might be applied, Exhibit 9-7 uses the factors discussed in this chapter to examine three industries.

[14]A small amount of "path dependence" characterizes the airline industry, in that an airline with a large fleet of a particular Airbus model will be marginally more likely to stick with that model for a new purchase than it will be to buy a Boeing, but the aircraft manufacturers' ability to exploit this likelihood is minimal.

EXHIBIT 9-7 Elements of a Strategic Analysis for Three Industries

	Branded Pharmaceuticals	Oil Services	Confections/Candy
Major Companies	Pfizer, Novartis, Merck, GlaxoSmithKline	Schlumberger, Baker Hughes, Halliburton	Cadbury, Hershey, Mars/Wrigley, Nestle
Barriers to entry/success	*Very High:* Substantial financial and intellectual capital required to compete effectively. A potential new entrant would need to create a sizable R&D operation, a global distribution network, and large-scale manufacturing capacity.	*Medium:* Technological expertise is required, but high level of innovation allows niche companies to enter the industry and compete in specific areas.	*Very High:* Low financial or technological hurdles, but new players would lack the established brands that drive consumer purchase decisions.
Level of concentration	*Concentrated:* A small number of companies control the bulk of the global market for branded drugs. Recent mergers have increased level of concentration.	*Fragmented:* Although only a small number of companies provide a full range of services, many smaller players compete effectively in specific areas. Service arms of national oil companies may control significant market share in their own countries, and some product lines are concentrated in the mature U.S. market.	*Very Concentrated:* Top four companies have a large proportion of global market share. Recent mergers have increased level of concentration.
Impact of industry capacity	*NA:* Pharmaceutical pricing is primarily determined by patent protection and regulatory issues, including government approvals of drugs and of manufacturing facilities. Manufacturing capacity is of little importance.	*Medium/High:* Demand can fluctuate quickly depending on commodity prices, and industry players often find themselves with too few (or too many) employees on the payroll.	*NA:* Pricing is driven primarily by brand strength. Manufacturing capacity has little effect.
Industry stability	*Stable:* The branded pharmaceutical market is dominated by major companies and consolidation via megamergers. Market shares shift quickly, however, as new drugs are approved and gain acceptance or lose patent protection.	*Unstable:* Market shares may shift frequently depending on technology offerings and demand levels.	*Very Stable:* Market shares change glacially.
Life cycle	*Mature:* Overall demand does not change greatly from year to year.	*Mature:* Demand does fluctuate with energy prices, but normalized revenue growth is only mid-single digits.	*Very Mature:* Growth is driven by population trends and pricing.

(Continued)

EXHIBIT 9-7 (*Continued*)

	Branded Pharmaceuticals	Oil Services	Confections/Candy
Price competition	*Low/Medium:* In the United States, price is a minimal factor because of consumer- and provider-driven, deregulated health care system. Price is a larger part of the decision process in single-payer systems, where efficacy hurdles are higher.	*High:* Price is a major factor in purchasers' decisions. Some companies have modest pricing power because of a wide range of services or best-in-class technology, but primary customers (major oil companies) can usually substitute with in-house services if prices are too high. Also, innovation tends to diffuse quickly throughout the industry.	*Low:* A lack of private-label competition keeps pricing stable among established players, and brand/familiarity plays a much larger role in consumer purchase decisions than price.
Demographic influences	*Positive:* Populations of developed markets are aging, which slightly increases demand.	NA	NA
Government and regulatory influences	*Very High:* All drugs must be approved for sale by national safety regulators. Patent regimes may differ among countries. Also, health care is heavily regulated in most countries.	*Medium:* Regulatory frameworks can affect energy demand at the margin. Also, governments play an important role in allocating exploration opportunities to E&P companies, which can indirectly affect the amount of work flowing down to service companies.	*Low:* Industry is not regulated, but childhood obesity concerns in developed markets are a low-level potential threat. Also, high-growth emerging markets may block entry of established players into their markets, possibly limiting growth.
Social influences	NA	NA	NA
Technological influences	*Medium/High:* Biologic (large-molecule) drugs are pushing new therapeutic boundaries, and many large pharmaceutical companies have a relatively small presence in biotech.	*Medium/High:* Industry is reasonably innovative, and players must reinvest in R&D to remain competitive. Temporary competitive advantages are possible via commercialization of new processes or exploitation of accumulated expertise.	*Very Low:* Innovation does not play a major role in the industry.
Growth versus defensive versus cyclical	*Defensive:* Demand for most health care services does not fluctuate with the economic cycle, but demand is not strong enough to be considered "growth."	*Cyclical:* Demand is highly variable and depends on oil prices, exploration budgets, and the economic cycle.	*Defensive:* Demand for candy and gum is extremely stable.

Note: "NA" in this exhibit stands for "not applicable."

Example 9-8 reviews some of the information presented in Exhibit 9-7.

EXAMPLE 9-8 External Influences

1. Which of the following industries is *most* affected by government regulation?
   A. Oil services.
   B. Pharmaceuticals.
   C. Confections and candy.
2. Which of the following industries is *least* affected by technological innovation?
   A. Oil services.
   B. Pharmaceuticals.
   C. Confections and candy.
3. Which of the following statements about industry characteristics is *least* accurate?
   A. Manufacturing capacity has little effect on pricing in the confections/candy industry.
   B. The branded pharmaceutical industry is considered to be defensive rather than a growth industry.
   C. With respect to the worldwide market, the oil services industry has a high level of concentration with a limited number of service providers.

Solution to 1: B is correct. Exhibit 9-7 states that the pharmaceutical industry has high amount of government and regulatory influences.

Solution to 2: C is correct. Exhibit 9-7 states that innovation does not play a large role in the candy industry.

Solution to 3: C is correct; it is a false statement. From a worldwide perspective, the industry is considered fragmented. Although a small number of companies provide the full range of services, competition by many smaller players occurs in niche areas. In addition, national oil service companies control significant market share in their home countries.

5.2. External Influences on Industry Growth, Profitability, and Risk

External factors affecting an industry's growth include macroeconomic, technological, demographic, governmental, and social influences.

5.2.1. Macroeconomic Influences

Trends in overall economic activity generally have significant effects on the demand for an industry's products or services. These trends can be cyclical (i.e., related to the changes in economic activity caused by the business cycle) or structural (i.e., related to enduring changes in the composition or magnitude of economic activity). Among the economic variables that usually affect an industry's revenues and profits are the following:

- Gross domestic product or the measure of the value of goods and services produced by an economy, either in current or constant currency (inflation-adjusted) terms.
- Interest rates, which represent the cost of debt to consumers and businesses and are important ingredients in financial institutions' revenues and costs.
- The availability of credit, which affects business and consumer spending and financial solvency.
- Inflation, which reflects the changes in prices of goods and services and influences costs, interest rates, and consumer and business confidence.

5.2.2. Technological Influences

New technologies create new or improved products that can radically change an industry and can also change how other industries that use the products conduct their operations.

The computer hardware industry provides one of the best examples of how technological change can affect industries. The 1958 invention of the microchip (also known as an "integrated circuit," which is effectively a computer etched on a sliver of silicon) enabled the computer hardware industry to eventually create a new market of personal computing for the general public and radically extended the use of computers in business, government, and educational institutions.

Moore's law states that the number of transistors that can be inexpensively placed on an integrated circuit doubles approximately every two years. Several other measures of digital technology have improved at exponential rates related to Moore's law, including the size, cost, density and speed of components. As a result of these trends, the computer hardware industry encroached upon and, in time, came to dominate the fields of hardware for word processing and many forms of electronic communication and home entertainment. The computing industry's integrated circuit innovation increased economies of scale and erected large barriers to new entrants because the capital costs of innovation and production became very high. Intel capitalized on both factors, which allowed it to garner an industry market leadership position and to become the dominant supplier of the PC industry's highest value component (the microprocessor). Thus, Intel became dominant because of its cost advantage, brand power, and access to capital.

Along the way, the computer hardware industry was supported and greatly assisted by the complementary industries of computer software and telecommunications (particularly in regard to development of the Internet); also important were other industries—entertainment (television, movies, games), retailing, and the print media. Ever more powerful integrated circuits and advances in wireless technology, as well as the convergence of media, which the Internet and new wireless technology have facilitated, continue to reshape the uses and the roles of PC hardware in business and personal life. In the middle of the twentieth century, few people in the world would have imagined they would ever have any use for a home computer. Today, the estimate is that about 1.6 billion people, or almost a quarter of the world's population, have access to connected computing. For the United States, the estimate is at least 76 percent of the population; it is much less in emerging and underdeveloped countries. More than 4 billion mobile cellular telephone subscriptions exist in the world today,[15] and the

[15] See www.itu.int/newsroom/press_releases/2009/39.html.

advances of mobile telephony appear poised to increase this figure dramatically in the years ahead as mobile phone and computer hardware technologies merge to provide new hand-held computing and communication capabilities.

Another example of the effects of technology on an industry is the impact of digital imaging technology on the photographic film industry. Digital imaging uses an electronic image sensor to record an image as electronic data rather than as chemical changes on film. This difference allows a much greater degree of image processing and transmission than in film photography. Since their invention in 1981, digital cameras have become extremely popular and now widely outsell traditional film cameras (although many professional photographers continue to use film for esthetic reasons for certain applications). Digital cameras include such features as video and audio recording. The effects of this major change in photographic technology have caused film and camera manufacturers—including Kodak, Fujifilm, Nikon Corporation, and Pentax Imaging Company—to completely restructure and redesign their products to adapt to the new technology's appeal to consumers.

5.2.3. Demographic Influences

Changes in population size, in the distributions of age and gender, and in other demographic characteristics may have significant effects on economic growth and on the amounts and types of goods and services consumed.

The effects of demographics on industries are well exemplified by the impact of the post–World War II Baby Boom in North America on demand for goods and services. Born between 1946 and 1964, this bulge of 76 million people in the North American population has influenced the composition of numerous products and services it needs in its passage from the cradle through childhood, adolescence, early adulthood, middle age, and into retirement. The teenage pop culture of the late 1950s and 1960s and all the products (records, movies, clothes, fashions) associated with it, the surge in demand for housing in the 1970s and 1980s, and the increasing demand for retirement-oriented investment products in the 1990s and early 2000s are all examples of the range of industries affected by this demographic bulge working its way through age categories of the population.

Another example of the effects of demographics on industries is the impact of an aging population in Japan, which has one of the highest percentages of elderly residents (21 percent over the age of 65) and a very low birth rate. Japan's ministry of health estimates that by 2055, the percentage of the population over 65 will rise to 40 percent and the total population will fall by 25 percent. These demographic changes are expected by some observers to have negative effects on the overall economy because, essentially, they imply a declining workforce. However, some sectors of the economy stand to benefit from these trends—for example, the heath care industry.

EXAMPLE 9-9 The Post–World War II Baby Boom and Its Effects on U.S. Housing Industry

In the United States, Canada, and Australia, the end of World War II marked the beginning of a sustained period of elevated birth rates per thousand in the population. This rise reflected the relief from the hardships of the Great Depression of the 1930s and World War II, increased levels of immigration (immigrants tend to be younger and hence more fertile than average), and a protracted period of postwar economic prosperity. The rate of births in the United States rose from 18.7 per thousand in 1935 and 20.4 per thousand in 1945 to 24.1 per thousand in 1950 and a peak of more than 25.0 per thousand in 1955–1957. Twenty years later, when the babies born during the period 1946–1964 entered adulthood, the housing industry experienced a surge in demand that led to a period of high sales of new homes. The rate of new housing starts in this period rose from 20.1 per thousand of population in 1966 to a peak of 35.3 per thousand in 1972 and remained elevated, except during the economic recession of 1974–1975, until the end of the 1970s.

Another demographic effect on the housing industry arising from the post–World War II Baby Boom came from the children of the Baby Boom generation (the so-called Echo Boomers). The Echo Boomers started to enter their most fertile years in the late 1970s and caused an increase in the number of births per thousand from a post–World War II low of 14.8 in 1975 to a peak of 16.7 in 1990. The Echo Boomers did not have as large an effect on housing demand 20 years later as their parents had had, but there was still a significant increase in new housing starts from 13.7 per thousand in 1995 to a high of 18.8 per thousand in 2005; easily available mortgage financing contributed to the increase.

5.2.4. Governmental Influences

Governmental influence on industries' revenues and profits is pervasive and important. In setting tax rates and rules for corporations and individuals, governments affect profits and incomes, which in turn, affect corporate and personal spending. Governments are also major purchasers of goods and services from a range of industries.

Example 9-10 illustrates the sudden shifts in wealth that can occur when governments step in to support or quash a securities market innovation. In the example, an **income trust** refers to a type of equity ownership vehicle established as a trust issuing ownership shares known as units. Income trusts became extremely popular among income-oriented investors in Canada in the late 1990s and early 2000s because under then-current regulation, such trusts could avoid taxation on income distributed to unit-holders (investors)—that is, avoid double taxation (once at the corporate level and once at the investor level). As Example 9-10 describes, the tax advantage that regulations permitted was eventually removed.

EXAMPLE 9-10 The Effects of Tax Increases on Income Trusts in Canada

On 31 October 2006, in an effort to halt the rapid growth of income trust structures in the Canadian stock market, Canada's Minister of Finance James Flaherty announced that these tax-exempt flow-through entities would in the future be taxable on the income, with exemptions only for passive rent-collecting real estate investment trusts.

A five-year hiatus was established for existing trusts to adapt. He stated that the government needed to clamp down on trusts because too many companies were converting to the high-yield securities, primarily to save taxes. The S&P/TSX Capped Income Trust Index declined 12 percent on the day after the announcement, wiping out C$24 billion in market value.

Often, governments exert their influence indirectly by empowering other regulatory or self-regulatory organizations (e.g., stock exchanges, medical associations, utility rate setters, and other regulatory commissions) to govern the affairs of an industry. By setting the terms of entry into various sectors, such as financial services and health care, and the rules that companies and individuals must adhere to in these fields, governments control the supply, quality, and nature of many products and services and the public's access to them. For example, in the financial industry, the acceptance of savings deposits from and the issuance of securities to the investing public are usually tightly controlled by governments and their agencies. This control is imposed through rules designed to protect investors from fraudulent operators and to ensure that investors receive adequate disclosure about the nature and risks of their investments. Another example is that medical patients in most developed countries are treated by doctors who are trained according to standards set by medical associations acting as self-regulatory organizations empowered under government laws. In addition, the medications that patients receive must be approved by government agencies. In a somewhat different vein, users of tobacco products purchase items for which the marketing and sales taxes are heavily controlled by governments in most developed countries and for which warnings to consumers about the dangers of smoking are mandated by governments. In the case of industries that supply branches of government, such as the military, public works, and law enforcement departments, government contracts directly affect the revenues and profits of the suppliers.

EXAMPLE 9-11 The Effects of Government Purchases on the Aerospace Industry

The aerospace, construction, and firearms industries are prime examples of industries for which governments are major customers and whose revenues and profits are significantly—in some cases, predominantly—affected by their sales to governments. An example is the European Aeronautic Defence and Space Company (EADS), a global leader in aerospace, defense, and related services with head offices in Paris and Ottobrunn, Germany. In 2008, EADS generated revenues of €43.3 billion and employed an international workforce of about 118,000. EADS includes Airbus, a leading manufacturer of commercial aircraft; Airbus Military, providing tanker, transport, and mission aircraft; Eurocopter, the world's largest helicopter supplier; and EADS Astrium, the European leader in space programs, including Ariane and Galileo. Its Defence & Security Division is a provider of comprehensive systems solutions and makes EADS the major partner in the Eurofighter consortium and a stakeholder in missile systems provider MBDA. On 3 March 2008, EADS shares rose 9.2 percent after the U.S. Air Force chose its Airbus A330 over Boeing's 767 for an airborne refueling plane contract worth as much as US$35 billion.

5.2.5. Social Influences

Societal changes involving how people work, spend their money, enjoy their leisure time, and conduct other aspects of their lives can have significant effects on the sales of various industries.

Tobacco consumption in the United Kingdom provides a good example of the effects of social influences on an industry. Although the role of government in curbing tobacco advertising, legislating health warnings on the purchases of tobacco products, and banning smoking in public places (such as restaurants, bars, public houses, and transportation vehicles) probably has been the most powerful apparent instrument of changes in tobacco consumption, the forces underlying that change have really been social in nature—namely, increasing consciousness on the part of the population of the damage to the health of tobacco users and those in their vicinity from smoking, the increasing cost to individuals and governments of the chronic illnesses caused by tobacco consumption, and the accompanying shift in public perception of smokers from socially correct to socially incorrect—even inconsiderate or reckless. As a result of these changes in society's views of smoking, cigarette consumption in the United Kingdom declined from 102.5 billion cigarettes in 1990 to less than 65.0 billion in 2009, placing downward pressure on tobacco companies' unit sales.

EXAMPLE 9-12 The Effects on Various Industries of More Women Entering the Workforce

In 1870, women accounted for only 15 percent of the workforce in the United States outside the home. By 1950, after two world wars and the Great Depression, this figure had risen to 30 percent (it had been even higher temporarily during World War II because of high levels of war-mandated production) and by 2008, to 48 percent. Based on economic reasoning, identify four industries that should have benefited from the social change that saw women shift from their most frequent historical roles in Western society as full-time homemakers to becoming more frequently full-time participants in the workforce.

Solution: Industries include the following:

1. The restaurant business. The restaurant business stands to benefit from an increased demand given that women, because of their work responsibilities, may not have the time and energy to prepare meals. Restaurant industry growth was actually high in this period: From accounting for only 25 percent of every food dollar in the United States in 1950, the restaurant industry today consumes more than 44 percent of

every food dollar, with 45 percent of current industry revenues arising from a category of restaurant that did not exist in 1950, namely, fast food.
2. Manufacturers of work clothing for women.
3. Home and child care services.
4. Automobile manufacturers. Extra vehicles became necessary to transport two members of the family to work, for instance, and children to school or day care.
5. Housing for the aging. With increasing workforce participation by women, aged family members requiring care or supervision became increasingly unable to rely on nonworking female family members to provide care in their homes.

EXAMPLE 9-13 The Airline Industry: A Case Study of Many Influences

The global airline industry exemplifies many of the concepts and influences we have discussed.

Life-Cycle Stage

The industry can be described as having some mature characteristics because average annual growth in global passenger traffic has remained relatively stable at 4.5 percent in the 2000s (compared with 4.7 percent in the 1990s). Some market segments in the industry, however, are still in their growth phase—notably, the markets of the Middle East and Asia, which are expected to grow at 6.5 percent compared with projected North American growth of 3.2 percent over the next 20 years.

Sensitivity to Business Cycle

The airline industry is a cyclical industry; global economic activity produces swings in revenues and, especially, profitability, because of the industry's high fixed costs and operating leverage. In 2009, for example, global passenger traffic is expected to have declined by approximately 8 percent and airlines are expected to report significant net losses—close to US$9.0 billion, which is down from a global industry profit of US $12.9 billion in 2007. The industry tends to respond early to upward and downward moves in economic cycles; depending on the region, air travel changes at 1.5 times to 2.0 times GDP growth. It is highly regulated, with governments and airport authorities playing a large role in allocating routes and airport slots. Government agencies and the International Airline Transport Association set rules for aircraft and flight safety. Airline customers tend to have low brand loyalty (except at the extremes of high and low prices and service); leisure travelers focus mainly on price, and business travelers focus mostly on schedules and service. Product and service differentiation at particular price points is low because aircraft, cabin configuration, and catering tend to be quite similar in most cases. For leisure travelers, the price competition is intense and is led by low-cost discount carriers, including Southwest Airlines in the United States, Ryanair in Europe, and Air Asia in Asia. For business travelers, the major scheduled airlines and a few service-quality specialists, such as Singapore Airlines, are the main contenders. Fuel costs (typically more than 25 percent of total costs and highly volatile) and labor costs (around 10 percent of total costs) have been the focus of management cost-reduction efforts. The airline industry is highly unionized, and labor strife has frequently been a source of costly disruptions to the industry. Technology has always played a major role in the airline industry, from its origins with small propeller-driven planes through the advent of the jet age to the drive for greater fuel efficiency since the oil price increases of the 1970s. Technology also poses a threat to the growth of business air travel in the form of improved telecommunications—notably, videoconferencing and webcasting. Arguably, the airline industry has been a great force in shaping demography by permitting difficult-to-access geographical areas to be settled with large populations. At the same time, large numbers of post–World War II Baby Boomers have been a factor in generating the growth in demand for air travel in the past half-century. In recent years, social issues have started to play a role in the airline industry; carbon emissions, for example, have come under scrutiny by environmentalists and governments.

6. COMPANY ANALYSIS

Company analysis includes an analysis of the company's financial position, products and/or services, and **competitive strategy** (its plans for responding to the threats and opportunities presented by the external environment). Company analysis takes place after the analyst has gained an understanding of a company's external environment—the macroeconomic, demographic, governmental, technological, and social forces influencing the industry's competitive structure. The analyst should seek to determine whether the strategy is primarily defensive or offensive in its nature and how the company intends to implement the strategy.

Porter identifies two chief competitive strategies: a low-cost strategy (cost leadership) and a product/service differentiation strategy.

In a low-cost strategy, companies strive to become the low-cost producers and to gain market share by offering their products and services at lower prices than their competition while still making a profit margin sufficient to generate a superior rate of return based on the higher revenues achieved. Low-cost strategies may be pursued defensively to protect market positions and returns or offensively to gain market share and increase returns. Pricing also can be defensive (when the competitive environment is one of low rivalry) or aggressive (when rivalry is intense). In the case of intense rivalry, pricing may even become predatory—that is, aimed at rapidly driving competitors out of business at the expense of near-term profitability. The hope in such a strategy is that having achieved a larger market share, the company can later increase prices to generate higher returns than before. For example, the predatory strategy has been alleged by some analysts to have been followed by major airlines trying to protect lucrative routes from discount airlines. Although laws concerning anticompetitive practices often prohibit predatory pricing to gain market share, in most cases, it is difficult to accurately ascribe the costs of products or services with sufficient precision to demonstrate that predatory pricing (as opposed to intense but fair price competition) is occurring. Companies seeking to follow low-cost strategies must have tight cost controls, efficient operating and reporting systems, and appropriate managerial incentives. In addition, they must commit themselves to painstaking scrutiny of production systems and their labor forces and to low-cost designs and product distribution. They must be able to invest in productivity-improving capital equipment and to finance that investment at a low cost of capital.

In differentiation strategies, companies attempt to establish themselves as the suppliers or producers of products and services that are unique either in quality, type, or means of distribution. To be successful, their price premiums must be above their costs of differentiation and the differentiation must be appealing to customers and sustainable over time. Corporate managers who successfully pursue differentiation strategies tend to have strong market research teams to identify and match customer needs with product development and marketing. Such a strategy puts a premium on employing creative and inventive people.

6.1. Elements That Should Be Covered in a Company Analysis

A thorough company analysis, particularly as presented in a research report, should

- Provide an overview of the company (corporate profile), including a basic understanding of its businesses, investment activities, corporate governance, and perceived strengths and weaknesses.
- Explain relevant industry characteristics.
- Analyze the demand for the company's products and services.
- Analyze the supply of products and services, which includes an analysis of costs.
- Explain the company's pricing environment.
- Present and interpret relevant financial ratios, including comparisons over time and comparisons with competitors.

Company analysis often includes forecasting the company's financial statements, particularly when the purpose of the analysis is to use a discounted cash flow method to value the company's common equity.

Exhibit 9-8 provides a checklist of points to cover in a company analysis. The list may need to be adapted to serve the needs of a particular company analysis and is not exhaustive.

EXHIBIT 9-8 A Checklist for Company Analysis

Corporate Profile

☐ Identity of company's major products and services; current position in industry; and history

☐ Composition of sales

☐ Product life-cycle stages/experience curve effects*

☐ Research and development activities

☐ Past and planned capital expenditures

☐ Board structure, composition, and electoral system; antitakeover provisions; and other corporate governance issues

EXHIBIT 9-8 (*Continued*)

- ☐ Management strengths, weaknesses, compensation, turnover, and corporate culture
- ☐ Benefits, retirement plans, and their influence on shareholder value
- ☐ Labor relations
- ☐ Insider ownership levels and changes
- ☐ Legal actions and the company's state of preparedness
- ☐ Other special strengths or weaknesses

Industry Characteristics

- ☐ Stage in its life cycle
- ☐ Business-cycle sensitivity or economic characteristics
- ☐ Typical product life cycles in the industry (short and marked by technological obsolescence or long, such as pharmaceuticals protected by patents)
- ☐ Brand loyalty, customer switching costs, and intensity of competition
- ☐ Entry and exit barriers
- ☐ Industry supplier considerations (concentration of sources, ability to switch suppliers or enter suppliers' business)
- ☐ Number of companies in the industry and whether it is, as determined by market shares, fragmented or concentrated
- ☐ Opportunity to differentiate product/service and relative product/service price, cost, and quality advantages/disadvantages
- ☐ Technologies used
- ☐ Government regulation
- ☐ State and history of labor relations
- ☐ Other industry problems/opportunities

Analysis of Demand for Products/Services

- ☐ Sources of demand
- ☐ Product differentiation
- ☐ Past record; sensitivities; and correlations with social, demographic, economic, and other variables
- ☐ Outlook—short, medium, and long term, including new product and business opportunities

Analysis of Supply of Products/Services

- ☐ Sources (concentration, competition, and substitutes)
- ☐ Industry capacity outlook—short, medium, and long term
- ☐ Company's capacity and cost structure
- ☐ Import/export considerations
- ☐ Proprietary products or trademarks

EXHIBIT 9-8 (*Continued*)

Analysis of Pricing

- ☐ Past relationships among demand, supply, and prices
- ☐ Significance of raw material and labor costs and the outlook for their cost and availability
- ☐ Outlook for selling prices, demand, and profitability based on current and anticipated future trends

Financial Ratios and Measures (in multiyear spreadsheets with historical and forecast data)

I. **Activity ratios:** measuring how efficiently a company performs such functions as the collection of receivables and inventory management.
   - ☐ Days of sales outstanding (DSO)
   - ☐ Days of inventory on hand (DOH)
   - ☐ Days of payables outstanding (DPO)

II. **Liquidity ratios:** measuring a company's ability to meet its short-term obligations.
   - ☐ Current ratio
   - ☐ Quick ratio
   - ☐ Cash ratio
   - ☐ Cash conversion cycle (DOH + DSO − DPO)

III. **Solvency ratios:** measuring a company's ability to meet its debt obligations. (In the following, "net debt" is the amount of interest-bearing liabilities after subtracting cash and cash equivalents.)
   - ☐ Net debt to EBITDA (earnings before interest, taxes, depreciation, and amortization)
   - ☐ Net debt to capital
   - ☐ Debt to assets
   - ☐ Debt to capital (at book and market values)
   - ☐ Financial leverage ratio (average total assets/average total equity)
   - ☐ Cash flow to debt
   - ☐ Interest coverage ratio
   - ☐ Off-balance-sheet liabilities and contingent liabilities
   - ☐ Non-arm's-length financial dealings

IV. **Profitability ratios:** measuring a company's ability to generate profitable sales from its resources (assets).
   - ☐ Gross profit margin
   - ☐ Operating profit margin
   - ☐ Pretax profit margin
   - ☐ Net profit margin
   - ☐ Return on invested capital or ROIC (net operating profits after tax/average invested capital)
   - ☐ Return on assets or ROA (net income/average total assets)
   - ☐ Return on equity or ROE (net income/average total equity)

EXHIBIT 9-8 (*Continued*)

V. **Financial statistics and related considerations:** quantities and facts about a company's finances that an analyst should understand.

- ☐ Growth rate of net sales
- ☐ Growth rate of gross profit
- ☐ EBITDA
- ☐ Net income
- ☐ Operating cash flow
- ☐ EPS
- ☐ Operating cash flow per share
- ☐ Operating cash flow in relation to maintenance and total capital expenditures
- ☐ Expected rate of return on retained cash flow
- ☐ Debt maturities and ability of company to refinance and/or repay debt
- ☐ Dividend payout ratio (common dividends/net income available to common shareholders)
- ☐ Off-balance-sheet liabilities and contingent liabilities
- ☐ Non-arm's-length financial dealings

*A *product life cycle* relates to stages in the sales of a product. *Experience curve effects* refer to the tendency for the cost of producing a good or service to decline with cumulative output.

To evaluate a company's performance, the key measures presented in Exhibit 9-8 should be compared over time and between companies (particularly peer companies). The following formula can be used to analyze how and why a company's ROE differs from that of other companies or its own ROE in other periods by tracing the differences to changes in its profit margin, the productivity of its assets, or its financial leverage:

$$\begin{aligned}\text{ROE} = {} & (\text{Net profit margin: Net earnings/Net sales}) \\ & \times (\text{Asset turnover: Net sales/Average total assets}) \\ & \times (\text{Financial leverage: Average total assets/Average common equity})\end{aligned}$$

The financial statements of a company over time provide numerous insights into the effects of industry conditions on its performance and the success or failure of its strategies. They also provide a framework for forecasting the company's operating performance when given the analyst's assumptions for numerous variables in the future. The financial ratios listed in Exhibit 9-8 are applicable to a wide range of companies and industries, but other statistics and ratios are often also used.

6.2. Spreadsheet Modeling

Spreadsheet modeling of financial statements to analyze and forecast revenues, operating and net income, and cash flows has become one of the most widely used tools in company analysis. Although spreadsheet models are a valuable tool for understanding past financial performance and forecasting future performance, the complexity of such models can at times be a problem. Because modeling requires the analyst to predict and input numerous items in financial statements, there is a risk of errors—either in assumptions made or in formulas in the model—which can compound, leading to erroneous forecasts. Yet, those forecasts may seem precise because of the sheer complexity of the model. The result is often a false sense of understanding and security on the part of those who rely on the models. To guard against this, before or after a model is completed, a "reality check" of the model is useful.

Such testing for reasonableness can be done by first, asking what the few most important changes in income statement items are likely to be from last year to this year and the next year and, second, attempting to quantify the effects of these significant changes or "swing factors" on the bottom line. If an analyst cannot summarize in a few points what factors are realistically expected to change income from year to year and is not convinced that these assumptions are correct, then he or she does not really understand the output of the computer modeling efforts. In general, financial models should be in a format that matches the company's reporting of its financial results or supplementary disclosures or that can be accurately derived from these reports. Otherwise, there will be no natural reality check when the company issues its financial results and the analyst will not be able to compare his or her estimates with actual reported results.

7. SUMMARY

In this chapter, we have provided an overview of industry analysis and illustrated approaches that are widely used by analysts to examine an industry.

- Company analysis and industry analysis are closely interrelated. Company and industry analysis together can provide insight into sources of industry revenue growth and competitors' market shares and thus the future of an individual company's top-line growth and bottom-line profitability.
- Industry analysis is useful for
  - Understanding a company's business and business environment.
  - Identifying active equity investment opportunities.
  - Formulating an industry or sector rotation strategy.
  - Portfolio performance attribution.
- The three main approaches to classifying companies are
  - Products and/or services supplied.
  - Business-cycle sensitivities.
  - Statistical similarities.
- Commercial industry classification systems include
  - Global Industry Classification Standard.
  - Russell Global Sectors.
  - Industry Classification Benchmark.
- Governmental industry classification systems include
  - International Standard Industrial Classification of All Economic Activities.
  - Statistical Classification of Economic Activities in the European Community.

- Australian and New Zealand Standard Industrial Classification.
- North American Industry Classification System.

- A limitation of current classification systems is that the narrowest classification unit assigned to a company generally cannot be assumed to constitute its peer group for the purposes of detailed fundamental comparisons or valuation.
- A peer group is a group of companies engaged in similar business activities whose economics and valuation are influenced by closely related factors.
- Steps in constructing a preliminary list of peer companies:
  - Examine commercial classification systems if available. These systems often provide a useful starting point for identifying companies operating in the same industry.
  - Review the subject company's annual report for a discussion of the competitive environment. Companies frequently cite specific competitors.
  - Review competitors' annual reports to identify other potential comparables.
  - Review industry trade publications to identify additional peer companies.
  - Confirm that each comparable or peer company derives a significant portion of its revenue and operating profit from a similar business activity as the subject company.
- Not all industries are created equal. Some are highly competitive, with many companies struggling to earn returns in excess of their cost of capital, and other industries have attractive characteristics that enable a majority of industry participants to generate healthy profits.
- Differing competitive environments are determined by the structural attributes of the industry. For this important reason, industry analysis is a vital complement to company analysis. The analyst needs to understand the context in which a company operates to fully understand the opportunities and threats that a company faces.
- The framework for strategic analysis known as "Porter's five forces" can provide a useful starting point. Porter maintains that the profitability of companies in an industry is determined by five forces: (1) The influence or threat of new entrants, which in turn is determined by economies of scale, brand loyalty, absolute cost advantages, customer switching costs, and government regulation; (2) the influence or threat of substitute products; (3) the bargaining power of customers, which is a function of switching costs among customers and the ability of customers to produce their own product; (4) the bargaining power of suppliers, which is a function of the feasibility of product substitution, the concentration of the buyer and supplier groups, and switching costs and entry costs in each case; and (5) the intensity of rivalry among established companies, which in turn is a function of industry competitive structure, demand conditions, cost conditions, and the height of exit barriers.
- The concept of barriers to entry refers to the ease with which new competitors can challenge incumbents and can be an important factor in determining the competitive environment of an industry. If new competitors can easily enter the industry, the industry is likely to be highly competitive because incumbents that attempt to raise prices will be undercut by newcomers. As a result, industries with low barriers to entry tend to have low pricing power. Conversely, if incumbents are protected by barriers to entry, they may enjoy a more benign competitive environment that gives them greater pricing power over their customers because they do not have to worry about being undercut by upstarts.
- Industry concentration is often, although not always, a sign that an industry may have pricing power and rational competition. Industry fragmentation is a much stronger signal, however, that the industry is competitive and pricing power is limited.

- The effect of industry capacity on pricing is clear: Tight capacity gives participants more pricing power because demand for products or services exceeds supply; overcapacity leads to price-cutting and a highly competitive environment as excess supply chases demand. The analyst should think about not only current capacity conditions but also future changes in capacity levels—how long it takes for supply and demand to come into balance and what effect that process has on industry pricing power and returns.
- Examining the market share stability of an industry over time is similar to thinking about barriers to entry and the frequency with which new players enter an industry. Stable market shares typically indicate less competitive industries, whereas unstable market shares often indicate highly competitive industries with limited pricing power.
- An industry's position in its life cycle often has a large impact on its competitive dynamics, so it is important to keep this positioning in mind when performing strategic analysis of an industry. Industries, like individual companies, tend to evolve over time and usually experience significant changes in the rate of growth and levels of profitability along the way. Just as an investment in an individual company requires careful monitoring, industry analysis is a continuous process that must be repeated over time to identify changes that may be occurring.
- A useful framework for analyzing the evolution of an industry is an industry life-cycle model, which identifies the sequential stages that an industry typically goes through. The five stages of an industry life cycle according to the Hill and Jones model are
  - Embryonic.
  - Growth.
  - Shakeout.
  - Mature.
  - Decline.
- Price competition and thinking like a customer are important factors that are often overlooked when analyzing an industry. Whatever factors most influence customer purchasing decisions are also likely to be the focus of competitive rivalry in the industry. Broadly, industries for which price is a large factor in customer purchase decisions tend to be more competitive than industries in which customers value other attributes more highly.
- External influences on industry growth, profitability, and risk include
  - Technology.
  - Demographics.
  - Government.
  - Social factors.
- Company analysis takes place after the analyst has gained an understanding of the company's external environment and includes answering questions about how the company will respond to the threats and opportunities presented by the external environment. This intended response is the individual company's competitive strategy. The analyst should seek to determine whether the strategy is primarily defensive or offensive in its nature and how the company intends to implement it.
- Porter identifies two chief competitive strategies:
  - A low-cost strategy (cost leadership) is one in which companies strive to become the low-cost producers and to gain market share by offering their products and services at lower prices than their competition while still making a profit margin sufficient to generate a superior rate of return based on the higher revenues achieved.

  - A product/service differentiation strategy is one in which companies attempt to establish themselves as the suppliers or producers of products and services that are unique either in quality, type, or means of distribution. To be successful, the companies' price premiums must be above their costs of differentiation and the differentiation must be appealing to customers and sustainable over time.
- A checklist for company analysis includes a thorough investigation of
  - Corporate profile.
  - Industry characteristics.
  - Demand for products/services.
  - Supply of products/services.
  - Pricing.
  - Financial ratios.
- Spreadsheet modeling of financial statements to analyze and forecast revenues, operating and net income, and cash flows has become one of the most widely used tools in company analysis. Spreadsheet modeling can be used to quantify the effects of the changes in certain swing factors on the various financial statements. The analyst should be aware that the output of the model will depend significantly on the assumptions that are made.

PROBLEMS

1. Which of the following is *least likely* to involve industry analysis?

   A. Sector rotation strategy.
   B. Top-down fundamental investing.
   C. Tactical asset allocation strategy.

2. A sector rotation strategy involves investing in a sector by:

   A. Making regular investments in it.
   B. Investing in a preselected group of sectors on a rotating basis.
   C. Timing investment to take advantage of business-cycle conditions.

3. Which of the following information about a company would *most likely* depend on an industry analysis? The company's:

   A. Dividend policy.
   B. Competitive environment.
   C. Trends in corporate expenses.

4. Which industry classification system uses a three-tier classification system?

   A. Russell Global Sectors.
   B. Industry Classification Benchmark.
   C. Global Industry Classification Standard.

5. In which sector would a manufacturer of personal care products be classified?

   A. Health care.
   B. Consumer staples.
   C. Consumer discretionary.

6. Which of the following statements about commercial and government industry classification systems is *most* accurate?
   A. Many commercial classification systems include private for-profit companies.
   B. Both commercial and government classification systems exclude not-for-profit companies.
   C. Commercial classification systems are generally updated more frequently than government classification systems.

7. Which of the following is *not* a limitation of the cyclical/noncyclical descriptive approach to classifying companies?
   A. A cyclical company may have a growth component in it.
   B. Business-cycle sensitivity is a discrete phenomenon rather than a continuous spectrum.
   C. A global company can experience economic expansion in one part of the world while experiencing recession in another part.

8. A company that is sensitive to the business cycle would *most likely*:
   A. Not have growth opportunities.
   B. Experience below-average fluctuation in demand.
   C. Sell products that the customer can purchase at a later date if necessary.

9. Which of the following factors would *most likely* be a limitation of applying business-cycle analysis to global industry analysis?
   A. Some industries are relatively insensitive to the business cycle.
   B. Correlations of security returns between different world markets are relatively low.
   C. One region or country of the world may experience recession while another region experiences expansion.

10. Which of the following statements about peer groups is *most* accurate?
    A. Constructing a peer group for a company follows a standardized process.
    B. Commercial industry classification systems often provide a starting point for constructing a peer group.
    C. A peer group is generally composed of all the companies in the most narrowly defined category used by the commercial industry classification system.

11. With regard to forming a company's peer group, which of the following statements is *not* correct?
    A. Comments from the management of the company about competitors are generally not used when selecting the peer group.
    B. The higher the proportion of revenue and operating profit of the peer company derived from business activities similar to the subject company, the more meaningful the comparison.
    C. Comparing the company's performance measures with those for a potential peer-group company is of limited value when the companies are exposed to different stages of the business cycle.

12. When selecting companies for inclusion in a peer group, a company operating in three different business segments would:

    A. Be in only one peer group.
    B. Possibly be in more than one peer group.
    C. Not be included in any peer group.

13. An industry that *most likely* has both high barriers to entry and high barriers to exit is the:

    A. Restaurant industry.
    B. Advertising industry.
    C. Automobile industry.

14. Which factor is *most likely* associated with stable market share?

    A. Low switching costs.
    B. Low barriers to entry.
    C. Slow pace of product innovation.

15. Which of the following companies *most likely* has the greatest ability to quickly increase its capacity?

    A. Restaurant.
    B. Steel producer.
    C. Legal services provider.

16. A population that is rapidly aging would *most likely* cause the growth rate of the industry producing eyeglasses and contact lenses to:

    A. Decrease.
    B. Increase.
    C. Not change.

17. If over a long period of time a country's average level of educational accomplishment increases, this development would *most likely* lead to the country's amount of income spent on consumer discretionary goods to:

    A. Decrease.
    B. Increase.
    C. Not change.

18. If the technology for an industry involves high fixed capital investment, then one way to seek higher profit growth is by pursuing:

    A. Economies of scale.
    B. Diseconomies of scale.
    C. Removal of features that differentiate the product or service provided.

19. Which of the following life-cycle phases is typically characterized by high prices?

    A. Mature.
    B. Growth.
    C. Embryonic.

20. In which of the following life-cycle phases are price wars *most likely* to be absent?

    A. Mature.
    B. Decline.
    C. Growth.

21. When graphically depicting the life-cycle model for an industry as a curve, the variables on the axes are:

    A. Price and time.
    B. Demand and time.
    C. Demand and stage of the life cycle.

22. Which of the following is *most likely* a characteristic of a concentrated industry?

    A. Infrequent, tacit coordination.
    B. Difficulty in monitoring other industry members.
    C. Industry members attempting to avoid competition on price.

23. Which of the following industry characteristics is generally *least likely* to produce high returns on capital?

    A. High barriers to entry.
    B. High degree of concentration.
    C. Short lead time to build new plants.

24. An industry with high barriers to entry and weak pricing power *most likely* has:

    A. High barriers to exit.
    B. Stable market shares.
    C. Significant numbers of issued patents.

25. Economic value is created for an industry's shareholders when the industry earns a return:

    A. Below the cost of capital.
    B. Equal to the cost of capital.
    C. Above the cost of capital.

26. Which of the following is *not* one of Porter's five forces?

    A. Intensity of rivalry.
    B. Bargaining power of suppliers.
    C. Threat of government intervention.

27. Which of the following industries is *most likely* to be characterized as concentrated with strong pricing power?

    A. Asset management.
    B. Alcoholic beverages.
    C. Household and personal products.

28. Which of the following industries is *most likely* to be considered to have the lowest barriers to entry?

    A. Oil services.
    B. Confections and candy.
    C. Branded pharmaceuticals.

29. With respect to competitive strategy, a company with a successful cost leadership strategy is *most likely* characterized by:

    A. A low cost of capital.
    B. Reduced market share.
    C. The ability to offer products at higher prices than competitors.

30. When conducting a company analysis, the analysis of demand for a company's product is *least likely* to consider the:

    A. Company's cost structure.
    B. Motivations of the customer base.
    C. Product's differentiating characteristics.

31. Which of the following statements about company analysis is *most* accurate?

    A. The complexity of spreadsheet modeling ensures precise forecasts of financial statements.
    B. The interpretation of financial ratios should focus on comparing the company's results over time but not with competitors.
    C. The corporate profile would include a description of the company's business, investment activities, governance, and strengths and weaknesses.

CHAPTER 10

EQUITY VALUATION: CONCEPTS AND BASIC TOOLS

John J. Nagorniak, CFA
Foxboro, MA, U.S.A.

Stephen E. Wilcox, CFA
Mankato, MN, U.S.A.

LEARNING OUTCOMES

After completing this chapter, you will be able to do the following:

- Evaluate whether a security, given its current market price and a value estimate, is overvalued, fairly valued, or undervalued by the market.
- Describe major categories of equity valuation models.
- Explain the rationale for using present value of cash flow models to value equity and describe the dividend discount and free cash flow to equity models.
- Calculate the intrinsic value of a noncallable, nonconvertible preferred stock.
- Calculate and interpret the intrinsic value of an equity security based on the Gordon (constant) growth dividend discount model or a two-stage dividend discount model, as appropriate.
- Identify companies for which the constant growth or a multistage dividend discount model is appropriate.
- Explain the rationale for using price multiples to value equity and distinguish between multiples based on comparables versus multiples based on fundamentals.
- Calculate and interpret the following multiples: price-to-earnings, price to an estimate of operating cash flow, price-to-sales, and price-to-book value.
- Explain the use of enterprise value multiples in equity valuation and demonstrate the use of enterprise value multiples to estimate equity value.
- Explain asset-based valuation models and demonstrate the use of asset-based models to calculate equity value.
- Explain the advantages and disadvantages of each category of valuation model.

1. INTRODUCTION

Analysts gather and process information to make investment decisions, including buy and sell recommendations. What information is gathered and how it is processed depend on the analyst and the purpose of the analysis. Technical analysis uses such information as stock price and trading volume as the basis for investment decisions. Fundamental analysis uses information about the economy, industry, and company as the basis for investment decisions. Examples of fundamentals are unemployment rates, gross domestic product (GDP) growth, industry growth, and quality of and growth in company earnings. Whereas technical analysts use information to predict price movements and base investment decisions on the direction of predicted change in prices, fundamental analysts use information to estimate the value of a security and to compare the estimated value to the market price and then base investment decisions on that comparison.

This chapter introduces equity valuation models used to estimate the **intrinsic value** (synonym: **fundamental value**) of a security; intrinsic value is based on an analysis of investment fundamentals and characteristics. The fundamentals to be considered depend on the analyst's approach to valuation. In a top-down approach, an analyst examines the economic environment, identifies sectors that are expected to prosper in that environment, and analyzes securities of companies from previously identified attractive sectors. In a bottom-up approach, an analyst typically follows an industry or industries and forecasts fundamentals for the companies in those industries in order to determine valuation. Whatever the approach, an analyst who estimates the intrinsic value of an equity security is implicitly questioning the accuracy of the market price as an estimate of value. Valuation is particularly important in active equity portfolio management, which aims to improve on the return–risk trade-off of a portfolio's benchmark by identifying mispriced securities.

This chapter is organized as follows. Section 2 discusses the implications of differences between estimated value and market price. Section 3 introduces three major categories of valuation model. Section 4 presents an overview of present value models with a focus on the dividend discount model. Section 5 describes and examines the use of multiples in valuation. Section 6 explains asset-based valuation and demonstrates how these models can be used to estimate value. Section 7 states conclusions and summarizes the chapter.

2. ESTIMATED VALUE AND MARKET PRICE

By comparing estimates of value and market price, an analyst can arrive at one of three conclusions: The security is *undervalued*, *overvalued*, or *fairly valued* in the market place. For example, if the market price of an asset is $10 and the analyst estimates intrinsic value at $10, a logical conclusion is that the security is fairly valued. If the security is selling for $20, the security would be considered overvalued. If the security is selling for $5, the security would be considered undervalued. Basically, by estimating value, the analyst is assuming that the market price is not necessarily the best estimate of intrinsic value. If the estimated value exceeds the market price, the analyst infers the security is *undervalued*. If the estimated value equals the market price, the analyst infers the security is *fairly valued*. If the estimated value is less than the market price, the analyst infers the security is *overvalued*.

In practice, the conclusion is not so straightforward. Analysts must cope with uncertainties related to model appropriateness and the correct value of inputs. An analyst's final conclusion depends not only on the comparison of the estimated value and the market price but also on the analyst's confidence in the estimated value (i.e., in the model selected and the inputs used in it). One can envision a spectrum running from relatively high confidence in the valuation model *and* the inputs to relatively low confidence in the valuation model *and/or* the inputs. When confidence is relatively low, the analyst might demand a substantial divergence between his or her own value estimate and the market price before acting on an apparent mispricing. For instance, if the estimate of intrinsic value is $10 and the market price is $10.05, the analyst might reasonably conclude that the security is fairly valued and that the ½ of 1 percent market price difference from the estimated value is within the analyst's confidence interval.

Confidence in the convergence of the market price to the intrinsic value over the investment time horizon relevant to the objectives of the portfolio must also be taken into account before an analyst acts on an apparent mispricing or makes a buy, sell, or hold recommendation: The ability to benefit from identifying a mispriced security depends on the market price converging to the estimated intrinsic value.

In seeking to identify mispricing and attractive investments, analysts are treating market prices with skepticism, but they are also treating market prices with respect. For example, an analyst who finds that many securities examined appear to be overvalued will typically recheck models and inputs before acting on a conclusion of overvaluation. Analysts also often recognize and factor into recommendations that different market segments—such as securities closely followed by analysts versus securities relatively neglected by analysts—may differ in how common or persistent mispricing is. Mispricing may be more likely in securities neglected by analysts.

EXAMPLE 10-1 Valuation and Analyst Response

1. An analyst finds that all the securities analyzed have estimated values higher than their market prices. The securities all appear to be:
   A. Overvalued.
   B. Undervalued.
   C. Fairly valued.
2. An analyst finds that nearly all companies in a market segment have common shares that are trading at market prices above the analyst's estimate of the shares' values. This market segment is widely followed by analysts. Which of the following statements describes the analyst's *most appropriate* first action?
   A. Issue a sell recommendation for each share issue.
   B. Issue a buy recommendation for each share issue.
   C. Reexamine the models and inputs used for the valuations.
3. An analyst, using a number of models and a range of inputs, estimates a security's value to be between ¥250 and ¥270. The security is trading at ¥265. The security appears to be:
   A. Overvalued.
   B. Undervalued.
   C. Fairly valued.

Solution to 1: B is correct. The estimated intrinsic value for each security is greater than the market price. The securities all appear to be undervalued in the market. Note, however, that the analyst may wish to reexamine the model and inputs to check that the conclusion is valid.

Solution to 2: C is correct. It seems improbable that all the share issues analyzed are overvalued, as indicated by market prices in excess of estimated value—particularly because the market segment is widely followed by analysts. Thus, the analyst will not issue a sell recommendation for each issue. The analyst will *most appropriately* re-examine the models and inputs prior to issuing any recommendations. A buy recommendation is not an appropriate response to an overvalued security.

Solution to 3: C is correct. The security's market price of ¥265 is within the range estimated by the analyst. The security appears to be fairly valued.

Analysts often use a variety of models and inputs to achieve greater confidence in their estimates of intrinsic value. The use of more than one model and a range of inputs also helps the analyst understand the sensitivity of value estimates to different models and inputs.

3. MAJOR CATEGORIES OF EQUITY VALUATION MODELS

Three major categories of equity valuation models are as follows:

- **Present value models** (synonym: **discounted cash flow models**). These models estimate the intrinsic value of a security as the present value of the future benefits expected to be received from the security. In present value models, benefits are often defined in terms of cash expected to be distributed to shareholders (**dividend discount models**) or in terms of cash flows available to be distributed to shareholders after meeting capital expenditure and working capital needs (**free-cash-flow-to-equity models**). Many models fall within this category, ranging from the relatively simple to the very complex. In Section 4, we discuss in detail two of the simpler models, the Gordon (constant) growth model and the two-stage dividend discount models.
- **Multiplier models** (synonym: **market multiple models**). These models are based chiefly on share price multiples or enterprise value multiples. The former model estimates intrinsic value of a common share from a price multiple for some fundamental variable, such as revenues, earnings, cash flows, or book value. Examples of the multiples include price to earnings (P/E, share price divided by earnings per share) and price to sales (P/S, share price divided by sales per share). The fundamental variable may be stated on a forward basis (e.g., forecasted EPS for the next year) or a trailing basis (e.g., EPS for the past year), as long as the usage is consistent across companies being examined. Price multiples are also used to compare relative values. The use of the ratio of share price to EPS—that is, the P/E multiple—to judge relative value is an example of this approach to equity valuation. **Enterprise value** (EV) multiples have the form (Enterprise value)/(Value of a fundamental variable). Two possible choices for the denominator are earnings before interest,

taxes, depreciation, and amortization (EBITDA) and total revenue. Enterprise value, the numerator, is a measure of a company's total market value from which cash and short-term investments have been subtracted (because an acquirer could use those assets to pay for acquiring the company). An estimate of common share value can be calculated indirectly from the EV multiple; the value of liabilities and preferred shares can be subtracted from the EV to arrive at the value of common equity.

- **Asset-based valuation models.** These models estimate intrinsic value of a common share from the estimated value of the assets of a corporation minus the estimated value of its liabilities and preferred shares. The estimated market value of the assets is often determined by making adjustments to the **book value** (synonym: **carrying value**) of assets and liabilities. The theory underlying the asset-based approach is that the value of a business is equal to the sum of the value of the business's assets.

As already mentioned, many analysts use more than one type of model to estimate value. Analysts recognize that each model is a simplification of the real world and that there are uncertainties related to model appropriateness and the inputs to the models. The choice of model(s) will depend on the availability of information to input into the model(s) and the analyst's confidence in the information and in the appropriateness of the model(s).

EXAMPLE 10-2 Categories of Equity Valuation Models

1. An analyst is estimating the intrinsic value of a new company. The analyst has one year of financial statements for the company and has calculated the average values of a variety of price multiples for the industry in which the company operates. The analyst plans to use at least one model from each of the three categories of valuation models. The analyst is *least likely* to rely on the estimate(s) from the:
   A. Multiplier model(s).
   B. Present value model(s).
   C. Asset-based valuation model(s).
2. Based on a company's EPS of €1.35, an analyst estimates the intrinsic value of a security to be €16.60. Which type of model is the analyst *most likely* to be using to estimate intrinsic value?
   A. Multiplier model.
   B. Present value model.
   C. Asset-based valuation model.

Solution to 1: B is correct. Because the company has only one year of data available, the analyst is *least likely* to be confident in the inputs for a present value model. The values on the balance sheet, even before adjustment, are likely to be close to market values because the assets are all relatively new. The multiplier models are based on average multiples from the industry.

Solution to 2: A is correct. The analyst is using a multiplier model based on the P/E multiple. The P/E multiple used was 16.60/1.35 = 12.3.

As you begin the study of specific equity valuation models in the next section, you must bear in mind that any model of value is, by necessity, a simplification of the real world. Never forget this simple fact! You may encounter models much more complicated than the ones discussed here, but even those models will be simplifications of reality.

4. PRESENT VALUE MODELS: THE DIVIDEND DISCOUNT MODEL

Present value models follow a fundamental tenet of economics stating that individuals defer consumption—that is, they invest—for the future benefits expected. Individuals and companies make an investment because they expect a rate of return over the investment period. Logically, the value of an investment should be equal to the present value of the expected future benefits. For common shares, an analyst can equate benefits to the cash flows to be generated by the investment. The simplest present value model of equity valuation is the dividend discount model (DDM), which specifies cash flows from a common stock investment to be dividends.[1] If the issuing company is assumed to be a going concern, the intrinsic value of a share is the present value of expected future dividends. If a constant required rate of return is also assumed, then the DDM expression for the intrinsic value of a share is Equation 10.1:

$$V_0 = \sum_{t=1}^{\infty} \frac{D_t}{(1+r)^t} \tag{10.1}$$

where

V_0 = value of a share of stock today, at $t = 0$
D_t = expected dividend in year t, assumed to be paid at the end of the year
r = required rate of return on the stock

At the shareholder level, cash received from a common stock investment includes any dividends received and the proceeds when shares are sold. If an investor intends to buy and hold a share for one year, the value of the share today is the present value of two cash flows—namely, the expected dividend *plus* the expected selling price in one year:

$$V_0 = \frac{D_1 + P_1}{(1+r)^1} = \frac{D_1}{(1+r)^1} + \frac{P_1}{(1+r)^1} \tag{10.2}$$

where P_1 = the expected price per share at $t = 1$.

To estimate the expected selling price, P_1, the analyst could estimate the price another investor with a one-year holding period would pay for the share in one year. If V_0 is based on D_1 and P_1, it follows that P_1 could be estimated from D_2 and P_2:

$$P_1 = \frac{D_2 + P_2}{(1+r)}$$

Substituting the right side of this equation for P_1 in Equation 10.2 results in V_0 estimated as

[1]Companies may also distribute cash to common shareholders by means of share repurchases.

$$V_0 = \frac{D_1}{(1+r)} + \frac{D_2 + P_2}{(1+r)^2} = \frac{D_1}{(1+r)} + \frac{D_2}{(1+r)^2} + \frac{P_2}{(1+r)^2}$$

Repeating this process, we find the value for n holding periods is the present value of the expected dividends for the n periods plus the present value of the expected price in n periods:

$$V_0 = \frac{D_1}{(1+r)^1} + \dots + \frac{D_n}{(1+r)^n} + \frac{P_n}{(1+r)^n}$$

Using summation notation to represent the present value of the n expected dividends, we arrive at the general expression for an n-period holding period or investment horizon:

$$V_0 = \sum_{t=1}^{n} \frac{D_t}{(1+r)^t} + \frac{P_n}{(1+r)^n} \qquad (10.3)$$

The expected value of a share at the end of the investment horizon—in effect, the expected selling price—is often referred to as the **terminal stock value** (or **terminal value**).

EXAMPLE 10-3 Estimating Share Value for a Three-Year Investment Horizon see notes

For the next three years, the annual dividends of a stock are expected to be €2.00, €2.10, and €2.20. The stock price is expected to be €20.00 at the end of three years. If the required rate of return on the shares is 10 percent, what is the estimated value of a share?

Solution: The present values of the expected future cash flows can be written as follows:

$$V_0 = \frac{2.00}{(1.10)^1} + \frac{2.10}{(1.10)^2} + \frac{2.20}{(1.10)^3} + \frac{20.00}{(1.10)^3}$$

Calculating and summing these present values gives an estimated share value of $V_0 = 1.818 + 1.736 + 1.653 + 15.026 =$ €20.23.

The three dividends have a total present value of €5.207, and the terminal stock value has a present value of €15.026, for a total estimated value of €20.23.

Extending the holding period into the indefinite future, we can say that a stock's estimated value is the present value of all expected future dividends as shown in Equation 10.1.

Consideration of an indefinite future is valid because businesses established as corporations are generally set up to operate indefinitely. This general form of the DDM applies even in the case in which the investor has a finite investment horizon. For that investor, stock value today depends *directly* on the dividends the investor expects to receive before the stock is sold and depends *indirectly* on the expected dividends for periods subsequent to that sale, because those expected future dividends determine the expected selling price. Thus, the general expression given by Equation 10.1 holds irrespective of the investor's holding period.

In practice, many analysts prefer to use a free-cash-flow-to-equity (FCFE) valuation model. These analysts assume that dividend-paying *capacity* should be reflected in the cash flow estimates rather than *expected dividends*. FCFE is a measure of dividend-paying capacity. Analysts may also use FCFE valuation models for a non-dividend-paying stock. To use a DDM, the analyst needs to predict the timing and amount of the first dividend and all the dividends or dividend growth thereafter. Making these predictions for non-dividend-paying stock accurately is typically difficult, so in such cases, analysts often resort to FCFE models.

The calculation of FCFE starts with the calculation of cash flow from operations (CFO). CFO is simply defined as net income plus noncash expenses minus investment in working capital. FCFE is a measure of cash flow generated in a period that is available for distribution to common shareholders. What does "available for distribution" mean? The entire CFO is *not* available for distribution; the portion of the CFO needed for fixed capital investment (FCInv) during the period to maintain the value of the company as a going concern is *not* viewed as available for distribution to common shareholders. Net amounts borrowed (borrowings minus repayments) are considered to be available for distribution to common shareholders. Thus, FCFE can be expressed as

$$\text{FCFE} = \text{CFO} - \text{FCInv} + \text{Net borrowing} \tag{10.4}$$

The information needed to calculate historical FCFE is available from a company's statement of cash flows and financial disclosures. Frequently, under the assumption that management is acting in the interest of maintaining the value of the company as a going concern, reported capital expenditure is taken to represent FCInv. Analysts must make projections of financials to forecast future FCFE. Valuation obtained by using FCFE involves discounting expected future FCFE by the required rate of return on equity; the expression parallels Equation 10.1:

$$V_0 = \sum_{t=1}^{\infty} \frac{\text{FCFE}_t}{(1+r)^t}$$

EXAMPLE 10-4 Present Value Models

1. An investor expects a share to pay dividends of $3.00 and $3.15 at the end of Years 1 and 2, respectively. At the end of the second year, the investor expects the shares to trade at $40.00. The required rate of return on the shares is 8 percent. If the investor's forecasts are accurate and the market price of the shares is currently $30, the *most likely* conclusion is that the shares are:
   A. Overvalued.
   B. Undervalued.
   C. Fairly valued.

see notes

2. Two investors with different holding periods but the same expectations and required rate of return for a company are estimating the intrinsic value of a common share of the company. The investor with the shorter holding period will *most likely* estimate a:
   A. Lower intrinsic value.
   B. Higher intrinsic value.
   C. Similar intrinsic value.
3. An equity valuation model that focuses on expected dividends rather than the capacity to pay dividends is the
   A. Dividend discount model.
   B. Free-cash-flow-to-equity model.
   C. Cash flow return on investment model.

Solution to 1: B is correct.

$$V_0 = \frac{3.00}{(1.08)^1} + \frac{3.15}{(1.08)^2} + \frac{40.00}{(1.08)^2} = 39.77$$

The value estimate of \$39.77 exceeds the market price of \$30, so the conclusion is that the shares are undervalued.

Solution to 2: C is correct. The intrinsic value of a security is independent of the investor's holding period.

Solution to 3: A is correct. Dividend discount models focus on expected dividends.

How is the required rate of return for use in present value models estimated? To estimate the required rate of return on a share, analysts frequently use the capital asset pricing model (CAPM):

$$\text{Required rate of return on share } i = \text{Current expected risk-free rate of return} + \text{Beta}_i[\text{Market (equity) risk premium}] \quad (10.5)$$

Equation 10.5 states that the required rate of return on a share is the sum of the current expected risk-free rate plus a risk premium that equals the product of the stock's beta (a measure of nondiversifiable risk) and the market risk premium (the expected return of the market in excess of the risk-free return, where in practice, the "market" is often represented by a broad stock market index). However, even if analysts agree that the CAPM is an appropriate model, their inputs into the CAPM may differ. Thus, there is no uniquely correct answer to the question: What is the required rate of return?

Other common methods for estimating the required rate of return for the stock of a company include adding a risk premium that is based on economic judgments, rather than the CAPM, to an appropriate risk-free rate (usually a government bond) and adding a risk premium to the yield on the company's bonds. Good business and economic judgment is paramount in estimating the required rate of return. In many investment firms, required rates of return are determined by firm policy.

4.1. Preferred Stock Valuation

General dividend discount models are relatively easy to apply to preferred shares. In its simplest form, **preferred stock** is a form of equity (generally, nonvoting) that has priority over common stock in the receipt of dividends and on the issuer's assets in the event of a company's liquidation. It may have a stated maturity date at which time payment of the stock's par (face) value is made or it may be perpetual with no maturity date; additionally, it may be callable or convertible.

For a noncallable, nonconvertible perpetual preferred share paying a level dividend D and assuming a constant required rate of return over time, Equation 10.1 reduces to the formula for the present value of a perpetuity. Its value is:

$$V_0 = \frac{D_0}{r} \tag{10.6}$$

For example, a \$100 par value noncallable perpetual preferred stock offers an annual dividend of \$5.50. If its required rate of return is 6 percent, the value estimate would be \$5.50/0.06 = \$91.67.

For a noncallable, nonconvertible preferred stock with maturity at time n, the estimated intrinsic value can be estimated by using Equation 10.3 but using the preferred stock's par value, F, instead of P_n:

$$V_0 = \sum_{t=1}^{n} \frac{D_t}{(1+r)^t} + \frac{F}{(1+r)^n} \tag{10.7}$$

When Equation 10.7 is used, the most precise approach is to use values for n, r, and D that reflect the payment schedule of the dividends. This method is similar to the practice of fixed-income analysts in valuing a bond. For example, a nonconvertible preferred stock with a par value of £20.00, maturity in six years, a nominal required rate of return of 8.20 percent, and semiannual dividends of £2.00 would be valued by using an n of 12, an r of 4.10 percent, a D of £2.00, and an F of £20.00. The result would be an estimated value of £31.01. Assuming payments are annual rather than semiannual (i.e., assuming that $n = 6$, $r = 8.20$ percent, and $D = £4.00$) would result in an estimated value of £30.84.

Preferred stock issues are frequently callable (redeemable) by the issuer at some point prior to maturity, often at par value or at prices in excess of par value that decline to par value as the maturity date approaches. Such call options tend to reduce the value of a preferred issue to an investor because the option to redeem will be exercised by the issuer when it is in the issuer's favor and ignored when it is not. For example, if an issuer can redeem shares at par value that would otherwise trade (on the basis of dividends, maturity, and required rate of return) above par value, the issuer has motivation to redeem the shares.

Preferred stock issues can also include a retraction option that enables the holder of the preferred stock to sell the shares back to the issuer prior to maturity on prespecified terms. Essentially, the holder of the shares has a put option. Such put options tend to increase the value of a preferred issue to an investor because the option to retract will be exercised by the investor when it is in the investor's favor and ignored when it is not. Although the precise valuation of issues with such embedded options is beyond the scope of this chapter, Example 10-5 includes a case in which Equation 10.7 can be used to approximate the value of a callable, retractable preferred share.

EXAMPLE 10-5 Preferred Share Valuation: Two Cases

Case 1: Noncallable, Nonconvertible, Perpetual Preferred Shares

The following facts concerning the Union Electric Company 4.75 percent perpetual preferred shares (CUSIP identifier: 906548821) are as follows:

- Issuer: Union Electric Co. (owned by Ameren)
- Par value: US$100
- Dividend: US$4.75 per year
- Maturity: perpetual
- Embedded options: none
- Credit rating: Moody's Investors Service/Standard & Poor's Ba1/BB
- Required rate of return on Ba1/BB rated preferred shares as of valuation date: 7.5 percent.

A. Estimate the intrinsic value of this preferred share.
B. Explain whether the intrinsic value of this issue would be higher or lower if the issue were callable (with all other facts remaining unchanged).

Solution to 1A: Basing the discount rate on the required rate of return on Ba1/BB rated preferred shares of 7.5 percent gives an intrinsic value estimate of US$4.75/0.075 = US $63.33.

Solution to 1B: The intrinsic value would be lower if the issue were callable. The option to redeem or call the issue is valuable to the issuer because the call will be exercised when doing so is in the issuer's interest. The intrinsic value of the shares to the investor will typically be lower if the issue is callable. In this case, because the intrinsic value without the call is much less than the par value, the issuer would be unlikely to redeem the issue if it were callable; thus, callability would reduce intrinsic value, but only slightly.

Case 2: Retractable Term Preferred Shares

Retractable term preferred shares are a type of preferred share that has been issued by Canadian companies. This type of issue specifies a "retraction date" when the preferred shareholders have the option to sell back their shares to the issuer at par value (i.e., the shares are "retractable" or "putable" at that date).[2] At predetermined dates prior to the retraction date, the issuer has the option to redeem the preferred issue at predetermined prices (which are always at or above par value).

An example of a retractable term preferred share currently outstanding is YPG (Yellow Pages) Holdings, series 2, 5 percent first preferreds (TSX: YPG.PR.B). YPG Holdings is Canada's leading local commercial search provider and largest telephone directory publisher. The issue is in Canadian dollars. The shares have a $25 par

[2] "Retraction" refers to this option, which is a put option. The terminology is not completely settled: The type of share being called "retractable term preferred" is also known as "hard retractable preferred," with "hard" referring to payment in cash rather than common shares at the retraction date. See the 2009 ScotiaMcLeod report, www.ritceyteam.com/pdf/guide_to_preferred_shares.pdf.

value and pay a quarterly dividend of \$0.3125 [= (5 percent × \$25)/4]. As of 29 December 2008, shares were priced at \$12.01 and carried ratings from Dominion Bond Rating Service (DBRS) and Standard & Poor's of Pfd-3H and P3, respectively. Thus, the shares are viewed by DBRS as having "adequate" credit quality, qualified by "H," which means relatively high quality within that group. The shares are redeemable at the option of YPG Holdings in June 2009 at \$26.75, with redemption prices eventually declining to par value at later dates. The retraction date is 30 June 2017, or eight and one-half years (34 quarters) from the date (31 December 2008) the shares were being valued. Similarly rated preferred issues had an estimated nominal required rate of return of 15.5 percent (3.875 percent per quarter). Because the issue's market price is so far below the prices at which YPG could redeem or call the issue, redemption is considered to be unlikely and the redemption option is assumed here to have minimal value for an investor.

A. Assume that the issue will be retracted in June 2017; the holders of the shares will put the shares to the company in June 2017. Based on the information given, estimate the intrinsic value of a share.

Solution to 2A: An intrinsic value estimate of a share of this preferred issue is \$12.71:

$$V_0 = \left[\frac{\$0.3125}{(1+0.03875)} + \frac{\$0.3125}{(1+0.03875)^2} + \ldots. + \frac{\$0.3125}{(1+0.03875)^{34}}\right] + \frac{\$25}{(1+0.03875)^{34}}$$

$$\approx \$12.71$$

4.2. The Gordon Growth Model

A rather obvious problem when one is trying to implement Equation 10.1 for common equity is that it requires the analyst to estimate an infinite series of expected dividends. To simplify this process, analysts frequently make assumptions about how dividends will grow or change over time. The Gordon (constant) growth model (Gordon, 1962) is a simple and well-recognized DDM. The model assumes dividends grow indefinitely at a constant rate.

Because of its assumption of a constant growth rate, the Gordon growth model is particularly appropriate for valuing the equity of dividend-paying companies that are relatively insensitive to the business cycle and in a mature growth phase. Examples might include an electric utility serving a slowly growing area or a producer of a staple food product (e.g., bread). A history of increasing the dividend at a stable growth rate is another practical criterion if the analyst believes that pattern will hold in the future.

With a constant growth assumption, Equation 10.1 can be written as Equation 10.8, where g is the constant growth rate:

$$V_0 = \sum_{t=1}^{\infty} \frac{D_0(1+g)^t}{(1+r)^t} = D_0\left[\frac{(1+g)}{(1+r)} + \frac{(1+g)^2}{(1+r)^2} + \ldots + \frac{(1+g)^{\infty}}{(1+r)^{\infty}}\right] \quad (10.8)$$

If required return r is assumed to be strictly greater than growth rate g, then the square-bracketed term in Equation 10.8 is an infinite geometric series and sums to $[(1+g)/(r-g)]$.

Substituting into Equation 10.8 produces the Gordon growth model as presented in Equation 10.9:

$$V_0 = \frac{D_0(1+g)}{r-g} = \frac{D_1}{r-g} \tag{10.9}$$

For an illustration of the expression, suppose the current (most recent) annual dividend on a share is €5.00 and dividends are expected to grow at 4 percent per year. The required rate of return on equity is 8 percent. The Gordon growth model estimate of intrinsic value is, therefore, €5.00(1.04)/(0.08 – 0.04) = €5.20/0.04 = €130 per share. Note that the numerator is D_1 not D_0. (Using the wrong numerator is a common error.)

The Gordon growth model estimates intrinsic value as the present value of a growing perpetuity. If the growth rate, g, is assumed to be zero, Equation 10.8 reduces to the expression for the present value of a perpetuity, given earlier as Equation 10.6.

In estimating a long-term growth rate, analysts use a variety of methods, including assessing the growth in dividends or earnings over time, using the industry median growth rate, and using the relationship shown in Equation 10.10 to estimate the sustainable growth rate:

$$g = b \times \text{ROE} \tag{10.10}$$

where

g = dividend growth rate
b = earnings retention rate = (1 – Dividend payout ratio)
ROE = return on equity

Example 10-6 illustrates the application of the Gordon growth model to the shares of an integrated petroleum company. The analyst believes it will not continue to grow at the relatively fast growth rate of its past but will moderate to a lower and stable growth rate in the future. The example asks how much the dividend growth assumption adds to the intrinsic value estimate. The question is relevant to valuation because if the amount is high on a percentage basis, a large part of the value of the share depends on the realization of the growth estimate. One can answer the question by subtracting from the intrinsic value estimate determined by Equation 10.9 the value determined by Equation 10.6, which assumes no dividend growth.[3]

see notes

EXAMPLE 10-6 Applying the Gordon Growth Model

Total S.A. (Euronext Paris: FP), one of France's largest corporations and the world's fifth-largest publicly traded integrated petroleum company, operates in more than 130 countries. Total engages in all aspects of the petroleum industry, produces base chemicals and specialty chemicals for the industrial and consumer markets, and has

[3]A related concept, the present value of growth opportunities (PVGO), is discussed in more advanced readings.

interests in the coal mining and power generation sectors. To meet growing energy needs on a long-term basis, Total considers sustainability when making decisions. Selected financial information for Total appears in Exhibit 10-1.

EXHIBIT 10-1 Selected Financial Information for Total S.A.

Year	2008	2007	2006	2005	2004
EPS	€6.20	€5.37	€5.44	€5.08	€3.76
DPS	€2.28	€2.07	€1.87	€1.62	€1.35
Payout ratio	37%	39%	34%	32%	36%
ROE	32%	31%	33%	35%	33%
Share price (Paris Bourse)	€38.910	€56.830	€54.650	€52.367	€39.657

Note: DPS stands for "dividends per share."
Source: Company web site: www.total.com.

The analyst estimates the growth rate to be approximately 14 percent based on the dividend growth rate over the period 2004 to 2008 [$1.35(1+g)^4 = 2.28$, so $g = 14\%$]. To verify that the estimated growth rate of 14 percent is feasible in the future, the analyst also uses the average of Total's retention rate and ROE for the previous five years ($g \approx 0.64 \times 33\% \approx 21\%$) to estimate the sustainable growth rate.

Using a number of approaches, including adding a risk premium to a long-term French government bond and using the CAPM, the analyst estimates a required return of 19 percent. The most recent dividend of €2.28 is used for D_0.

1. Use the Gordon growth model to estimate Total's intrinsic value.
2. How much does the dividend growth assumption add to the intrinsic value estimate?
3. Based on the estimated intrinsic value, is a share of Total undervalued, overvalued, or fairly valued?
4. What is the intrinsic value if the growth rate estimate is lowered to 13 percent?
5. What is the intrinsic value if the growth rate estimate is lowered to 13 percent and the required rate of return estimate is increased to 20 percent?

Solution to 1: $V_0 = \dfrac{€2.28(1+0.14)}{0.19-0.14} = €51.98$

Solution to 2: $€51.98 - \dfrac{€2.28}{0.19} = €39.98$

Solution to 3: A share of Total appears to be undervalued. The analyst, before making a recommendation, might consider how realistic the estimated inputs are and check the sensitivity of the estimated value to changes in the inputs.

Solution to 4: $V_0 = \dfrac{€2.28(1+0.13)}{0.19-0.13} = €42.94$

Solution to 5: $V_0 = \dfrac{€2.28(1 + 0.13)}{0.20 - 0.13} = €36.81$

The Gordon growth model estimate of intrinsic value is extremely sensitive to the choice of required rate of return r and growth rate g. It is likely that the growth rate assumption and the required return assumption used initially were too high. Worldwide economic growth is typically in the low single digits, making it highly unlikely that Total's dividend can grow at 14 percent into perpetuity. Exhibit 10-2 presents a further sensitivity analysis of Total's intrinsic value to the required return and growth estimates. Note that no value is shown when the growth rate exceeds the required rate of return. The Gordon growth model assumes that the growth rate cannot be greater than the required rate of return.

EXHIBIT 10-2 Sensitivity Analysis of the Intrinsic-Value Estimate for Total S.A.

	$g = 2\%$	$g = 5\%$	$g = 8\%$	$g = 11\%$	$g = 14\%$
$r = 7\%$	€46.512	€119.700	—	—	—
$r = 10\%$	€29.070	€47.880	€123.120	—	—
$r = 13\%$	€21.142	€29.925	€49.248	€126.540	—
$r = 16\%$	€16.611	€21.764	€30.780	€50.616	€129.960
$r = 19\%$	€13.680	€17.100	€22.385	€31.635	€51.984

The assumptions of the Gordon model are as follows:

- Dividends are the correct metric to use for valuation purposes.
- The dividend growth rate is forever: It is perpetual and never changes.
- The required rate of return is also constant over time.
- The dividend growth rate is strictly less than the required rate of return.

An analyst might be dissatisfied with these assumptions for many reasons. The equities being examined might not currently pay a dividend. The Gordon assumptions might be too simplistic to reflect the characteristics of the companies being evaluated. Some alternatives to using the Gordon model are as follows:

- Use a more robust DDM that allows for varying patterns of growth.
- Use a cash flow measure other than dividends for valuation purposes.
- Use some other approach (such as a multiplier method) to valuation.

Applying a DDM is difficult if the company being analyzed is not currently paying a dividend. A company may not be paying a dividend if (1) the investment opportunities the company has are all so attractive that the retention and reinvestment of funds is preferable, from a return perspective, to the distribution of a dividend to shareholders or (2) the company is in such shaky financial condition that it cannot afford to pay a dividend. An analyst might still use a DDM to value such companies by assuming that dividends will begin at some future point in time. The analyst might further assume that constant growth occurs after that date and use the Gordon growth model for valuation. Extrapolating from no current dividend, however, generally yields highly uncertain forecasts. Analysts typically choose to use one or more of the alternatives instead of or as a supplement to the Gordon growth model.

EXAMPLE 10-7 Gordon Growth Model in the Case of No Current Dividend See notes

A company does not currently pay a dividend but is expected to begin to do so in five years (at $t = 5$). The first dividend is expected to be \$4.00 and to be received five years from today. That dividend is expected to grow at 6 percent into perpetuity. The required return is 10 percent. What is the estimated current intrinsic value?

Solution: The analyst can value the share in two pieces:

1. The analyst uses the Gordon growth model to estimate the value at $t = 5$; in the model, the year-ahead dividend is \$4(1.06). Then the analyst finds the present value of this value as of $t = 0$.
2. The analyst finds the present value of the \$4 dividend not "counted" in the estimate in Piece 1 (which values dividends from $t = 6$ onward). Note that the statement of the problem implies that D_0, D_1, D_2, D_3, and D_4 are zero.
   Piece 1: The value of this piece is \$65.818:

$$V_n = \frac{D_n(1+g)}{r-g} = \frac{D_{n+1}}{r-g}$$

$$V_5 = \frac{\$4(1+0.06)}{0.10-0.06} = \frac{\$4.24}{0.04} = \$106$$

$$V_0 = \frac{\$106}{(1+0.10)^5} = \$65.818$$

Piece 2: The value of this piece is \$2.484:

$$V_0 = \frac{\$4}{(1+0.10)^5} = \$2.484$$

The sum of the two pieces is \$65.818 + \$2.484 = \$68.30.

Alternatively, the analyst could value the share at $t = 4$, the point at which dividends are expected to be paid in the following year and from which point they are expected to grow at a constant rate.

$$V4 = \frac{\$4.00}{0.10 - 0.06} = \frac{\$4.00}{0.04} = \$100$$

$$V_0 = \frac{\$100}{(1 + 0.10)^4} = \$68.30$$

The next section addresses the application of the DDM with more flexible assumptions as to the dividend growth rate.

4.3. Multistage Dividend Discount Models

Multistage growth models are often used to model rapidly growing companies. The *two-stage DDM* assumes that at some point the company will begin to pay dividends that grow at a constant rate, but prior to that time the company will pay dividends that are growing at a higher rate than can be sustained in the long run. That is, the company is assumed to experience an initial, finite period of high growth, perhaps prior to the entry of competitors, followed by an infinite period of sustainable growth. The two-stage DDM thus makes use of two growth rates: a high growth rate for an initial, finite period followed by a lower, sustainable growth rate into perpetuity. The Gordon growth model is used to estimate a terminal value at time n that reflects the present value at time n of the dividends received during the sustainable growth period.

Equation 10.11 will be used here as the starting point for a two-stage valuation model. The two-stage valuation model is similar to Example 10-7 except that instead of assuming zero dividends for the initial period, the analyst assumes that dividends will exhibit a high rate of growth during the initial period. Equation 10.11 values the dividends over the short-term period of high growth and the terminal value at the end of the period of high growth. The short-term growth rate, g_S, lasts for n years. The intrinsic value per share in year n, V_n, represents the year n value of the dividends received during the sustainable growth period or the terminal value at time n. V_n can be estimated by using the Gordon growth model as shown in Equation 10.12, where g_L is the long-term or sustainable growth rate. The dividend in year $n + 1$, D_{n+1}, can be determined by using Equation 10.13:

$$V_0 = \sum_{t=1}^{n} \frac{D_0(1 + g_S)^t}{(1 + r)^t} + \frac{V_n}{(1 + r)^n} \tag{10.11}$$

$$V_n = \frac{D_{n+1}}{r - g_L} \tag{10.12}$$

$$D_{n+1} = D_0(1 + g_S)^n(1 + g_L) \tag{10.13}$$

The DDM can be extended to as many stages as deemed appropriate. For most publicly traded companies (that is, companies beyond the start-up stage), practitioners assume growth

EXAMPLE 10-8 Applying the Two-Stage Dividend Discount Model

The current dividend, D_0, is \$5.00. Growth is expected to be 10 percent a year for three years and then 5 percent thereafter. The required rate of return is 15 percent. Estimate the intrinsic value.

will ultimately fall into three stages:[4] (1) growth, (2) transition, and (3) maturity. This assumption supports the use of a *three-stage DDM*, which makes use of three growth rates: a high growth rate for an initial finite period, followed by a lower growth rate for a finite second period, followed by a lower, sustainable growth rate into perpetuity.

One can make the case that a three-stage DDM would be most appropriate for a fairly young company, one that is just entering the growth phase. The two-stage DDM would be appropriate to estimate the value of an older company that has already moved through its growth phase and is currently in the transition phase (a period with a higher growth rate than the sustainable growth rate) prior to moving to the maturity phase (the period with a lower, sustainable growth rate).

However, the choice of a two-stage DDM need not rely solely on the age of a company. Long-established companies sometimes manage to restart above-average growth through, for example, innovation, expansion to new markets, or acquisitions. Or a company's long-run growth rate may be interrupted by a period of subnormal performance. If growth is expected to moderate (in the first case) or improve (in the second case) toward some long-term growth rate, a two-stage DDM may be appropriate. Thus, we chose a two-stage DDM to value Brown-Forman in Example 10-9.

[4]Sharpe, Alexander, and Bailey (1999).

EXAMPLE 10-9 Two-Stage Dividend Discount Model: Brown-Forman

Brown-Forman Corporation (NYSE: BFB) is a diversified producer of wines and spirits. It was founded in 1870 by George Garvin Brown in Louisville, Kentucky, USA. His original brand, Old Forester Kentucky Straight Bourbon Whisky, was America's first bottled bourbon. Brown-Forman, one of the largest American-owned spirits and wine companies and among the top 10 largest global spirits companies, sells its brands in more than 135 countries and has offices in cities across the globe. In all, Brown-Forman has more than 35 brands in its portfolio of wines and spirits.

The 30 January 2009 *Value Line* report on Brown-Forman appears in Exhibit 10-3. Brown-Forman has increased its dividends every year except 2000, when the dividend remained at US$0.50 as it was in 1999. On the left side of the report, in the section titled "Annual Rates," dividend growth is shown as 7.5 percent for the past 10 years, 11 percent for the past five years, and estimated 5 percent for 2005–2007 to 2011–2013. After a period of growth through acquisition and merger, the pattern suggests that Brown-Forman may be transitioning to a mature growth phase.

The two-stage DDM is arguably a good choice for valuing Brown Forman because the company appears to be transitioning from a high-growth phase (note the 11 percent dividend growth for the past five years) to a lower-growth phase (note the forecast of 5 percent dividend growth to 2011–2013). The analyst discussion refers to the company facing "short-term obstacles" and states that the company's "capital appreciation potential for the three- to five-year time frame is well below average."

The CAPM can be used to estimate the required return, r, for Brown-Forman. The *Value Line* report (in the upper left corner) estimates beta to be 0.70. Using the yield of about 3.1 percent on 10-year U.S. Treasury notes as a proxy for the risk-free rate and assuming an equity risk premium of 5.0 percent, we find the estimate for r would be 6.6 percent [3.1% + 0.70(5.0%)].

To estimate the intrinsic value at the end of 2008, we use the 2008 dividend of US $1.08 from the *Value Line* report. The dividend is assumed to grow at a rate of 6.5 percent for two years and then 4.0 percent thereafter. The growth rate assumption for the first stage is consistent with the *Value Line* forecast for 2008 to 2009 growth. The assumption of a 4.0 percent perpetual growth rate produces a five-year growth rate assumption near 5 percent,* which is consistent with the *Value Line* forecast of 5 percent growth to 2011–2013. Thus:

$$D_{2009} = \text{US\$}1.08(1 + 0.065) = \text{US\$}1.1502$$

$$D_{2010} = \text{US\$}1.08(1 + 0.065)^2 = \text{US\$}1.224963$$

$$D_{2011} = \text{US\$}1.08(1 + 0.065)^2(1 + 0.04) = \text{US\$}1.273962$$

$$V_{2010} = \frac{\text{US\$}1.273962}{0.066 - 0.04} = \text{US\$}48.99854$$

*The exact geometric average annual growth rate can be determined as $[(1 + 0.065)(1 + 0.065)(1 + 0.04)(1 + 0.04)(1.04)]^{1/5} - 1 = 0.049929 \approx 5.0\%$.

$$V_{2008} = \frac{\text{US\$}1.1502}{(1+0.066)} + \frac{\text{US\$}1.224963}{(1+0.066)^2} + \frac{\text{US\$}48.99854}{(1+0.066)^2} \approx \text{US\$}45.28$$

Given a recent price of US$47.88, as noted at the top of the *Value Line* report, the intrinsic-value estimate of US$45.28 suggests that Brown-Forman is modestly overvalued.

EXHIBIT 10-3 *Value Line* Report on Brown-Forman

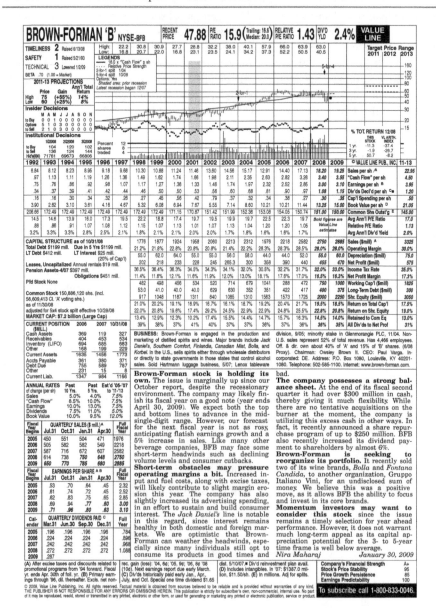

BROWN-FORMAN 'B' NYSE-BFB | RECENT PRICE 47.88 | P/E RATIO 15.9 (Trailing: 16.6 Median: 20.0) | RELATIVE P/E RATIO 1.43 | DIV'D YLD 2.4% | VALUE LINE

TIMELINESS 2 Raised 6/13/08
SAFETY 1 Raised 5/21/93
TECHNICAL 3 Lowered 1/2/09
BETA .70 (1.00 = Market)

2011-13 PROJECTIONS	Price	Gain	Ann'l Total Return
High	75	(+55%)	14%
Low	60	(+25%)	8%

Insider Decisions

	M	A	M	J	J	A	S	O	N
to Buy	0	0	1	0	0	0	0	0	0
Options	5	1	0	3	0	0	0	0	0
to Sell	2	1	0	3	0	0	0	0	0

Institutional Decisions

	1Q2008	2Q2008	3Q2008
to Buy	104	120	102
to Sell	136	124	144
Hld's(000)	71761	69673	66806

	1997	1998	1999	2000	2001	2002	2003	2004	2005	2006	2007	2008
High:	22.2	30.8	30.9	27.7	28.8	32.2	38.0	40.1	57.9	66.0	63.9	63.0
Low:	16.8	20.7	22.0	16.8	23.1	23.5	24.1	34.2	37.3	52.2	50.5	40.5

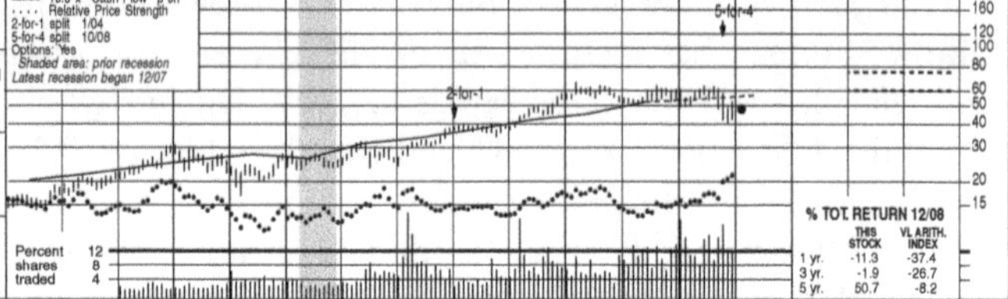

1992	1993	1994	1995	1996	1997	1998	1999	2000	2001	2002	2003	2004	2005	2006	2007	2008	2009	© VALUE LINE PUB., INC.	11-13
6.84	8.12	8.23	8.95	9.18	9.68	10.30	10.88	11.24	11.46	13.60	14.56	15.17	12.91	14.40	17.13	*18.20*	*19.25*	Sales per sh A	*22.95*
.97	1.13	1.11	1.19	1.26	1.36	1.49	1.62	1.74	1.66	1.98	2.11	2.35	2.63	2.82	3.26	*3.40*	*3.55*	"Cash Flow" per sh	*4.50*
.75	.76	.86	.92	.98	1.07	1.17	1.27	1.36	1.33	1.46	1.74	1.97	2.32	2.52	2.85	*3.00*	*3.10*	Earnings per sh B	*3.95*
.34	.37	.39	.41	.42	.44	.46	.50	.50	.53	.56	.60	.68	.81	.90	.97	*1.08*	*1.15*	Div'ds Decl'd per sh C■	*1.20*
.16	.16	.30	.34	.32	.26	.27	.45	.56	.42	.79	.37	.32	.34	.38	.27	*.30*	*.35*	Cap'l Spending per sh	*.50*
3.90	2.62	3.10	3.61	4.16	4.67	5.32	6.08	6.94	7.67	5.55	7.14	8.60	10.21	10.21	11.44	*13.25*	*15.00*	Book Value per sh D	*21.05*
206.66	172.49	172.49	172.49	172.49	172.49	172.49	172.49	171.15	170.87	151.42	151.99	152.36	153.08	154.05	150.74	*151.00*	*150.00*	Common Shs Outst'g E	*145.00*
14.5	14.6	13.9	16.0	17.3	19.5	22.2	18.8	17.4	19.7	19.5	19.9	19.7	22.5	22.3	19.7	*Bold figures are*		Avg Ann'l P/E Ratio	*17.0*
.88	.86	.91	1.07	1.08	1.12	1.15	1.07	1.13	1.01	1.07	1.13	1.04	1.20	1.20	1.05	*Value Line*		Relative P/E Ratio	*1.13*
3.2%	3.3%	3.3%	2.8%	2.5%	2.1%	1.8%	2.1%	2.1%	2.0%	2.0%	1.7%	1.8%	1.6%	1.6%	1.7%	*estimates*		Avg Ann'l Div'd Yield	*2.0%*
						1776	1877	1924	1958	2060	2213	2312	1976	2218	2582	*2750*	*2885*	Sales ($mill) A	*3325*
						21.2%	21.8%	22.8%	20.8%	20.8%	21.4%	22.2%	28.3%	28.3%	28.5%	*28.0%*	*28.0%*	Operating Margin	*30.0%*
						55.0	62.0	64.0	55.0	55.0	56.0	58.0	44.0	44.0	52.0	*55.0*	*60.0*	Depreciation ($mill)	*75.0*
						202	218	233	228	245	265.3	300	358	390	440	*455*	*470*	Net Profit ($mill)	*575*
						36.5%	36.4%	36.3%	34.5%	34.3%	34.1%	32.0%	30.5%	32.2%	31.7%	*32.0%*	*33.0%*	Income Tax Rate	*35.0%*
						11.4%	11.6%	12.1%	11.6%	11.9%	12.0%	13.0%	18.1%	17.6%	17.0%	*16.5%*	*16.3%*	Net Profit Margin	*17.3%*
						482	498	456	534	520	714	679	1041	288	472	*750*	*1000*	Working Cap'l ($mill)	*1825*
						53.0	41.0	40.0	40.0	629	630	352	351	422	417	*400*	*375*	Long-Term Debt ($mill)	*300*
						917	1048	1187	1311	840	1085	1310	1563	1573	1725	*2000*	*2250*	Shr. Equity ($mill)	*3050*
						21.0%	20.2%	19.1%	16.9%	16.7%	16.1%	18.7%	19.2%	20.4%	21.7%	*19.5%*	*18.5%*	Return on Total Cap'l	*17.5%*
						22.0%	20.8%	19.6%	17.4%	29.2%	24.5%	22.9%	22.9%	24.8%	25.5%	*22.8%*	*20.8%*	Return on Shr. Equity	*19.0%*
						13.4%	12.9%	12.3%	10.2%	17.4%	15.5%	14.4%	14.7%	15.7%	16.3%	*14.5%*	*14.0%*	Retained to Com Eq	*13.0%*
						39%	38%	37%	41%	40%	37%	37%	36%	37%	36%	*36%*	*35%*	All Div'ds to Net Prof	*31%*

CAPITAL STRUCTURE as of 10/31/08
Total Debt $1199 mill. **Due in 5 Yrs** $1199 mill.
LT Debt $412 mill. **LT Interest** $25 mill.
(20% of Cap'l)
Leases, Uncapitalized Annual rentals $19 mill.
Pension Assets-4/07 $397 mill.
Obligations $451 mill.
Pfd Stock None

Common Stock 150,886,120 shs. (incl. 56,609,413 Cl. 'A' voting shs.) as of 11/30/08
adjusted for 5x4 stock split effective 10/28/08
MARKET CAP: $7.2 billion (Large Cap)

CURRENT POSITION ($MILL.)	2006	2007	10/31/08
Cash Assets	369	119	327
Receivables	404	453	534
Inventory (LIFO)	694	685	683
Other	168	199	229
Current Assets	1635	1456	1773
Accts Payable	361	380	371
Debt Due	755	589	787
Other	231	15	8
Current Liab.	1347	984	1166

ANNUAL RATES of change (per sh)	Past 10 Yrs.	Past 5 Yrs.	Est'd '05-'07 to '11-'13
Sales	5.0%	4.0%	*7.5%*
"Cash Flow"	8.5%	10.0%	*7.5%*
Earnings	10.0%	13.0%	*7.5%*
Dividends	7.5%	11.0%	*5.0%*
Book Value	10.0%	9.5%	*12.0%*

Fiscal Year Begins	QUARTERLY SALES ($ mill.) A Jul.31	Oct.31	Jan.31	Apr.30	Full Fiscal Year
2005	450	551	504	471	1976
2006	505	582	582	549	2218
2007	587	716	672	607	2582
2008	614	738	*750*	*648*	*2750*
2009	*650*	*770*	*785*	*680*	*2885*

Fiscal Year Begins	EARNINGS PER SHARE A B Jul.31	Oct.31	Jan.31	Apr.30	Full Fiscal Year
2005	.53	.70	.64	.45	2.32
2006	.61	.74	.72	.45	2.52
2007	.62	.83	.75	.65	2.85
2008	.69	.94	*.77*	*.60*	*3.00*
2009	*.71*	*.96*	*.80*	*.63*	*3.10*

Cal-endar	QUARTERLY DIVIDENDS PAID C Mar.31	Jun.30	Sep.30	Dec.31	Full Year
2005	.196	.196	.196	.196	.784
2006	.224	.224	.224	.224	.896
2007	.242	.242	.242	.242	.968
2008	.272	.272	.272	.272	1.088
2009	.287				

BUSINESS: Brown-Forman is engaged in the production and marketing of distilled spirits and wines. Major brands include *Jack Daniel's*, *Southern Comfort*, *Finlandia*, *Canadian Mist*, *Bolla*, and *Korbel*. In the U.S., sells spirits either through wholesale distributors or directly to state governments in those states that control alcohol sales. Sold Hartmann luggage business, 5/07; Lenox tableware division, 9/05; minority stake in Glenmorangie PLC, 11/04. Non-U.S. sales represent 52% of total revenue. Has 4,466 employees. Off. & dir. own about 40% of 'A' and 15% of 'B' shares. (6/08 Proxy). Chairman: Owsley Brown II. CEO: Paul Varga. Incorporated: DE. Address: P.O. Box 1080, Louisville, KY 40201-1080. Telephone: 502-585-1100. Internet: www.brown-forman.com.

Brown-Forman stock is holding its own. The issue is marginally up since our October report, despite the recessionary environment. The company may likely finish its fiscal year on a good note (year ends April 30, 2009). We expect both the top and bottom lines to advance in the mid-single-digit range. However, our forecast for the next fiscal year is not as rosy, anticipating flatish earnings growth and a 5% increase in sales. Like many other beverage companies, BFB may face some short-term headwinds such as declining volume levels and consumer cutbacks.

Short-term obstacles may pressure operating margins a bit. Increased input and fuel costs, along with excise taxes, will likely contribute to slight margin erosion this year. The company has also slightly increased its advertising spending, in an effort to sustain and build consumer interest. The *Jack Daniel's* line is notable in this regard, since interest remains healthy in both domestic and foreign markets. We are optimistic that Brown-Forman can weather the headwinds, especially since many individuals still opt to consume its products in good times and bad.

The company possesses a strong balance sheet. At the end of its fiscal second quarter it had over $300 million in cash, thereby giving it much flexibility. While there are no tentative acquisitions on the burner at the moment, the company is utilizing this excess cash in other ways. In fact, it recently announced a share repurchase program of up to $250 million. BFB also recently increased its dividend payment to shareholders by almost 6%.

Brown-Forman is seeking to reorganize its portfolio. It recently sold two of its wine brands, *Bolla* and *Fontana Candida*, to another organization, Gruppo Italiano Vini, for an undisclosed sum of money. We believe this was a positive move, as it allows BFB the ability to focus and invest in its core brands.

Momentum investors may want to consider this stock since the issue remains a timely selection for year ahead performance. However, it does not warrant much long-term appeal as its capital appreciation potential for the 3- to 5-year time frame is well below average.

Nira Maharaj *January 30, 2009*

(A) After excise taxes and discounts related to promotional programs from '94 forward. Fiscal yr. ends Apr. 30th of foll. yr. (B) Primary earnings through '96, dil. thereafter. Excls. net nonrec. gain (loss): '04, 6¢; '05, 9¢; '06, 8¢ '08 (10¢). Next earnings report due early March. (C) Div'ds historically paid early Jan., Apr., July, and Oct. Special one time dividend $1.65 dist. 5/10/07.■ Div'd reinvestment plan avail. (D) Includes intangibles. In '07: $1387.0 million, $11.50/sh. (E) In millions. Adj for splits.

Company's Financial Strength	A+
Stock's Price Stability	95
Price Growth Persistence	85
Earnings Predictability	100

5. MULTIPLIER MODELS

The term **price multiple** refers to a ratio that compares the share price with some sort of monetary flow or value to allow evaluation of the relative worth of a company's stock. Some practitioners use price ratios as a screening mechanism. If the ratio falls below a specified value, the shares are identified as candidates for purchase, and if the ratio exceeds a specified value, the shares are identified as candidates for sale. Many practitioners use ratios when examining a group or sector of stocks and consider the shares for which the ratio is relatively low to be attractively valued securities.

Price multiples that are used by security analysts include the following:

- Price-to-earnings ratio (P/E). This measure is the ratio of the stock price to earnings per share. P/E is arguably the price multiple most frequently cited by the media and used by analysts and investors (Block 1999). The seminal works of McWilliams (1966), Miller and Widmann (1966), Nicholson (1968), Dreman (1977), and Basu (1977) presented evidence of a return advantage to low-P/E stocks.
- Price-to-book ratio (P/B). The ratio of the stock price to book value per share. Considerable evidence suggests that P/B multiples are inversely related to future rates of return (Fama and French 1995).
- Price-to-sales ratio (P/S). This measure is the ratio of stock price to sales per share. O'Shaughnessy (2005) provided evidence that a low P/S multiple is the most useful multiple for predicting future returns.
- Price-to-cash-flow ratio (P/CF). This measure is the ratio of stock price to some per-share measure of cash flow. The measures of cash flow include free cash flow (FCF) and operating cash flow (OCF).

A common criticism of all of these multiples is that they do not consider the future. This criticism is true if the multiple is calculated from trailing or current values of the divisor. Practitioners seek to counter this criticism by a variety of techniques, including forecasting fundamental values (the divisors) one or more years into the future. The resulting forward (leading or prospective) price multiples may differ markedly from the trailing price multiples. In the absence of an explicit forecast of fundamental values, the analyst is making an implicit forecast of the future when implementing such models. The choice of price multiple—trailing or forward—should be used consistently for companies being compared.

Besides the traditional price multiples used in valuation, just presented, analysts need to know how to calculate and interpret other ratios. Such ratios include those used to analyze business performance and financial condition based on data reported in financial statements. In addition, many industries have specialized measures of business performance that analysts covering those industries should be familiar with. In analyzing cable television companies, for example, the ratio of total market value of the company to the total number of subscribers is commonly used. Another common measure is revenue per subscriber. In the oil industry, a commonly cited ratio is proved reserves per common share. Industry-specific or sector-specific ratios such as these can be used to understand the key business variables in an industry or sector as well as to highlight attractively valued securities.

5.1. Relationships among Price Multiples, Present Value Models, and Fundamentals

Price multiples are frequently used independently of present value models. One price multiple valuation approach, the method of comparables, does not involve cash flow forecasts or discounting to present value. A price multiple is often related to fundamentals through a discounted cash flow model, however, such as the Gordon growth model. Understanding such connections can deepen the analyst's appreciation of the factors that affect the value of a multiple and often can help explain reasons for differences in multiples that do not involve mispricing. The expressions that are developed can be interpreted as the *justified value* of a multiple—that is, the value justified by (based on) fundamentals or a set of cash flow predictions. These expressions are an alternative way of presenting intrinsic-value estimates.

As an example, using the Gordon growth model identified previously in Equation 10.9 and assuming that price equals intrinsic value ($P_0 = V_0$), we can restate Equation 10.9 as follows:

$$P_0 = \frac{D_1}{r-g} \tag{10.9'}$$

To arrive at the model for the justified forward P/E given in Equation 10.14, we divide both sides of Equation (10.9′) by a forecast for next year's earnings, E_1. In Equation 10.14, the dividend payout ratio, p, is the ratio of dividends to earnings:

$$\frac{P_0}{E_1} = \frac{D_1/E_1}{r-g} = \frac{p}{r-g} \tag{10.14}$$

Equation 10.14 indicates that the P/E is inversely related to the required rate of return and positively related to the growth rate; that is, as the required rate of return increases, the P/E declines, and as the growth rate increases, the P/E increases. The P/E and the payout ratio appear to be positively related. This relationship may not be true, however, because a higher payout ratio may imply a slower growth rate as a result of the company retaining a lower proportion of earnings for reinvestment. This phenomenon is referred to as the dividend displacement of earnings.

EXAMPLE 10-10 A Value Estimate Based on Fundamentals

Petroleo Brasileiro SA, commonly known as Petrobras (BOVESPA: PETR), was once labeled "the most expensive oil company" by Bloomberg.com. Data for Petrobras and the oil industry, including the trailing twelve-month (TTM) P/E and payout ratios, follow.

	Petrobras	Industry
P/E ratio (TTM)	11.77	7.23
Payout ratio (TTM) (%)	24.40	21.66
EPS five-year growth rate (%)	26.35	15.46
EPS (MRQ) vs. Qtr. 1 yr. ago (% change)	−41.44	−127.53

Note: MRQ stands for "most recent quarter."
Source: Reuters.

Explain how the information shown supports a higher P/E for Petrobras than for the industry.

Solution: The data support a higher P/E for Petrobras because its payout ratio and five-year EPS growth rate exceed those of the industry. Equation 10.14 implies a positive relationship between the payout ratio and the P/E multiple. A higher payout ratio supports a higher P/E. Furthermore, to the extent that higher EPS growth implies a high growth rate in dividends, the high EPS growth rate supports a high P/E. Although the Petrobras quarterly EPS have declined relative to EPS of a year ago, the decline is less than that of the industry.

EXAMPLE 10-11 Determining Justified Forward P/E

Heinrich Gladisch, CFA, is estimating the justified forward P/E for Nestlé (SIX: NESN), one of the world's leading nutrition and health companies. Gladisch notes that sales for 2008 were SFr109.9 billion (US$101.6 billion) and that net income was SFr18.0 billion (US$16.6 billion). He organizes the data for EPS, dividends per share, and the dividend payout ratio for the years 2004–2008 in the following table:

	2004	2005	2006	2007	2008
Earnings per share	SFr1.70	SFr2.08	SFr2.39	SFr2.78	SFr4.87
Year over year % change		22.4%	14.9%	16.3%	75.2%
Dividend per share	SFr0.80	SFr0.90	SFr1.04	SFr1.22	SFr1.40
Year over year % change		12.5%	15.6%	17.3%	14.8%
Dividend payout ratio	47.1%	43.3%	43.5%	43.9%	28.7%

Gladisch calculates that ROE averaged slightly more than 19 percent in the period 2004–2007 but jumped to about 35 percent in 2008. In 2008, however, Nestlé's reported net income included a large nonrecurring component. The company reported 2008 "underlying earnings," which it defined as net income "from continuing operations before impairments, restructuring costs, results on disposals and significant one-off items," to be SFr2.82. Predicting increasing pressure on Nestlé's profit margins from lower-priced goods, particularly in developed markets, Gladisch estimates a long-run ROE of 16 percent.

Gladisch decides that the dividend payout ratios of the 2004–2007 period—averaging 44.5 percent—are more representative of Nestlé's future payout ratio than is the low 2008 dividend payout ratio. The dividend payout ratio in 2008 was lower because management apparently based the 2008 dividend on the components of net income that were expected to continue into the future. Basing a dividend on net income including nonrecurring items creates the potential need to reduce dividends in the future. Rounding up the 2004–2007 average, Gladisch settles on an estimate of 45 percent for the dividend payout ratio for use in calculating a justified forward P/E using Equation 10.14.

Gladisch's firm estimates that the required rate of return for Nestlé's shares is 12 percent per year. Gladisch also finds the following data in UBS and Credit Suisse analyst reports dated, respectively, 9 December 2009 and 16 October 2009:

	2009E	2010E
UBS forecast:		
EPS	SFr2.86	SFr3.10
Year over year % change	–41.3%	8.39%
P/E (based on a price of SFr48.82)	17.1	15.6
Credit Suisse forecast:		
EPS	SFr2.82	SFr3.05
Year over year % change	–42.1%	8.16%
P/E (based on a price of SFr47.88)	16.9	15.6

1. Based only on information and estimates developed by Gladisch and his firm, estimate Nestlé's justified forward P/E.
2. Compare and contrast the justified forward P/E estimate from Question 1 to the estimates from UBS and Credit Suisse.

Solution to 1: The estimate of the justified forward P/E is 14.1. The dividend growth rate can be estimated by using Equation 10.10 as (1 – Dividend payout ratio) × ROE = (1 – 0.45) × 0.16 = 0.088, or 8.8 percent. Therefore,

$$\frac{P_0}{E_1} = \frac{p}{r-g} = \frac{0.45}{0.12-0.088} = 14.1$$

Solution to 2: The estimated justified forward P/E of 14.1 is lower than the 2009 P/E estimates of 17.1 by UBS and 16.9 by Credit Suisse. Using a required rate of return of 11.5 percent rather than 12 percent results in a justified forward P/E estimate of 16.7 = (0.45/(0.115 – 0.088). Using an ROE of 19 percent (the average ROE of the 2004–2007 period) rather than 16 percent results in a justified forward P/E estimate of 30.0 = 0.45/[0.12 – (0.55)(0.19)] = 0.45/(0.12 – 0.105). The justified forward P/E is very sensitive to changes in the inputs.

Justified forward P/E estimates can be sensitive to small changes in assumptions. Therefore, analysts can benefit from carrying out a sensitivity analysis, as shown in Exhibit 10-4, which is based on Example 10-11. Exhibit 10-4 shows how the justified forward P/E varies with changes in the estimates for the dividend payout ratio (columns) and return on equity. The dividend growth rate (rows) changes because of changes in the retention rate (1 − Payout rate) and ROE. Recall g = ROE times retention rate.

EXHIBIT 10-4 Estimates for Nestlé's Justified Forward P/E (required rate of return = 12 percent)

	Dividend Payout Ratio				
Constant Dividend Growth Rate	40.0%	42.5%	45.0%	47.5%	50.0%
7.0%	8.0	8.5	9.0	9.5	10.0
7.5%	8.9	9.4	10.0	10.6	11.1
8.0%	10.0	10.6	11.3	11.9	12.5
8.5%	11.4	12.1	12.9	13.6	14.3
9.0%	13.3	14.2	15.0	15.8	16.7
9.5%	16.0	17.0	18.0	19.0	20.0
10.0%	20.0	21.3	22.5	23.8	25.0
10.5%	26.7	28.3	30.0	31.7	33.3

5.2. The Method of Comparables

The method of comparables is the most widely used approach for analysts reporting valuation judgments on the basis of price multiples. This method essentially compares relative values estimated using multiples or the relative values of multiples. The economic rationale underlying the method of comparables is the **law of one price**: Identical assets should sell for the same price. The methodology involves using a price multiple to evaluate whether an asset is fairly valued, undervalued, or overvalued in relation to a benchmark value of the multiple. Choices for the benchmark multiple include the multiple of a closely matched individual stock or the average or median value of the multiple for the stock's industry. Some analysts perform trend or time-series analyses and use past or average values of a price multiple as a benchmark.

Identifying individual companies or even an industry as the "comparable" may present a challenge. Many large corporations operate in several lines of business, so the scale and scope of their operations can vary significantly. When identifying comparables (sometimes referred to as "comps"), the analyst should be careful to identify companies that are most similar according to a number of dimensions. These dimensions include (but are not limited to) overall size, product lines, and growth rate. The type of analysis shown in Section 5.1 relating multiples to fundamentals is a productive way to identify the fundamental variables that should be taken into account in identifying comparables.

EXAMPLE 10-12 Method of Comparables (1)

As noted previously, P/E is a price multiple frequently used by analysts. Using P/E in the method of comparables can be problematic, however, as a result of business cycle effects on EPS. An alternative valuation tool that is useful during periods of economic slowdown or extraordinary growth is the P/S multiple. Although sales will decline during a recession and increase during a period of economic growth, the change in sales will be less than the change in earnings in percentage terms because earnings are heavily influenced by fixed operating and financing costs (operating and financial leverage).

The following data provide the P/S for most of the major automobile manufacturers in early 2009 (from the *Value Line* stock screener):

Company	P/S
General Motors	0.01
Ford Motor	0.14
Daimler	0.27
Nissan Motor	0.32
Honda Motor	0.49
Toyota Motor	0.66

Which stock appears to be undervalued when compared with the others?

Solution: The P/S analysis suggests that General Motors shares offer the best value. When the information shown was published, however, General Motors was on the brink of bankruptcy and had submitted several business plans to the U.S. government that included plant closings and elimination of the Pontiac brand. An analyst must be alert for potential explanations of apparently low or high multiples when performing comparables analysis, rather than just assuming a relative mispricing.

EXAMPLE 10-13 Method of Comparables (2)

Incorporated in the Netherlands, the European Aeronautic Defense and Space Company, or EADS (Euronext Paris: EAD) is a dominant aerospace company in Europe. Its largest subsidiary, Airbus S.A.S., is an aircraft manufacturing company with bases in several European countries. The majority of EADS's profits arise from Airbus operations. Airbus and its primary competitor, Boeing (NYSE: BA), control most of the commercial airplane industry.

Comparisons are frequently made between EADS and Boeing. As noted in Exhibit 10-5, the companies are about equal in size as measured by total revenues in 2008. Converting total revenues from euros to U.S. dollars using the average daily exchange rate for 2008 of US$1.4726/€ results in a value of $64,242 million for EADS's total revenues. Thus, total revenues for EADS are only 5.5 percent higher than those for Boeing.

The companies do differ, however, in several important areas. EADS derives a greater share of its revenue from commercial aircraft production than does Boeing. Also, the book value of shareholders' equity was negative for Boeing at year-end 2008. Finally, the order backlog for EADS is much higher than that for Boeing. Converting the EADS order backlog from euros to U.S. dollars using the year-end rate for 2008 of \$1.3919/€ results in a value of \$557,105 million for EADS's order backlog. Thus, the order backlog for EADS is 72.0 percent higher than the backlog for Boeing.*

EXHIBIT 10-5 Data for EADS and Boeing

	EADS	Boeing
Total revenues (millions)	€43,625	\$60,909
12-month revenue growth	10.6%	–8.3%
Percent of revenues from commercial aircraft	69.3%	46.4%
Debt ratio (Total liabilities/Equity)	85.4%	102.4%
Order backlog	€400,248	\$323,860
Share price, 31/Dec/08	€12.03	\$42.67
EPS (basic)	€1.95	\$3.68
DPS	€0.20	\$1.62
Dividend payout ratio	10.3%	44.0%
P/E ratio	6.2	11.6

Sources: Company web sites: www.eads.com and www.boeing.com.

What data shown in Exhibit 10-5 support a higher P/E for Boeing than for EADS?

Solution: Recall from Equation 10.14 and the discussion that followed it that P/E is directly related to the payout ratio and the dividend growth rate. The P/E is inversely related to the required rate of return. The only data presented in Exhibit 10-5 that support a higher P/E for Boeing is that company's higher dividend payout ratio (44.0 percent versus 10.3 percent for EADS).

The following implicitly supports a higher P/E for EADS: EADS has higher 12-month revenue growth and a higher backlog of orders, suggesting that it will have a higher future growth rate. Boeing also has a higher debt ratio, which implies greater financial risk and a higher required return.

*Exchange rate data are available from FRED (Federal Reserve Economic Data) at http://research.stlouisfed.org/fred2/.

EXAMPLE 10-14 Method of Comparables (3)

Canon Inc. (TSE: 7751) is a leading worldwide manufacturer of business machines, cameras, and optical products. Canon was founded in 1937 as a camera manufacturer and is incorporated in Tokyo. The corporate philosophy of Canon is *kyosei* or "living and working together for the common good." The following data can be used to determine a P/E for Canon over the time period 2004–2008. Analyze the P/E of Canon over time and discuss the valuation of Canon.

Year	Price (a)	EPS (b)	P/E (a) ÷ (b)
2004	¥5,546	¥387.8	14.3
2005	¥6,883	¥432.9	15.9
2006	¥6,703	¥342.0	19.6
2007	¥5,211	¥377.6	13.8
2008	¥2,782	¥246.2	11.3

Source: EPS and P/E data are from Canon's web site: www.canon.com. P/E is based on share price data from the Tokyo Stock Exchange.

5.3. Illustration of a Valuation Based on Price Multiples

Telefónica S.A. (LSE: TDE), a world leader in the telecommunication sector, provides communication, information, and entertainment products and services in Europe, Africa, and Latin America. It has operated in its home country of Spain since 1924, but as of 2008, more than 60 percent of its business was outside its home market.

Deutsche Telekom AG (FWB: DTE) provides network access, communication services, and value-added services via fixed and mobile networks. It generates more than half of its revenues outside its home country, Germany.

Exhibit 10-6 provides comparable data for these two communication giants for 2006–2008.

Time-series analysis of all price multiples in Exhibit 10-6 suggests that both companies are currently attractively valued. For example, the 2008 price-to-revenue ratio (P/R) of 1.3 for Telefónica is below the 2006–2008 average for this ratio of approximately 1.6. The 2008 P/CF of 3.0 for Deutsche Telekom is below the 2006–2008 average for this ratio of approximately 4.0.

A comparative analysis produces somewhat mixed results. The 2008 values for Deutsche Telekom for the P/R, P/CF, P/B multiples are lower than those for Telefónica. This result suggests that Deutsche Telekom is attractively valued when compared with Telefónica. The 2008 P/E for Telefónica, however, is much lower than for Deutsche Telekom.

An analyst investigating these contradictory results would look for information not reported in Exhibit 10-6. For example, the earnings before interest, taxes, depreciation, and

EXHIBIT 10-6 Data for Telefónica and Deutsche Telekom

	Telefónica			Deutsche Telekom		
	2008	2007	2006	2008	2007	2006
(1) Total assets (€ billions)	99.9	105.9	109.0	123.1	120.7	130.2
Asset growth	−5.7%	−2.8%	—	2.0%	−7.3%	—
(2) Net revenues (€ billions)	57.9	56.4	52.9	61.7	62.5	61.3
Revenue growth	2.7%	6.6%	—	−1.3%	2.0%	—
(3) Net cash flow from operating activities (€ billions)	16.4	15.6	15.4	15.4	13.7	14.2
Cash flow growth	5.1%	1.3%	—	12.4%	−3.5%	—
(4) Book value of common shareholders' equity (€ billions)	19.6	22.9	20.0	43.1	45.2	49.7
Debt ratio: 1 − [(4) ÷ (1)]	80.4%	78.4%	81.7%	65.0%	62.6%	61.8%
(5) Net profit (€ billions)	7.8	9.1	6.6	1.5	0.6	3.2
Earnings growth	−14.3%	37.9%	—	150.0%	−81.3%	—
(6) Weighted average number of shares outstanding (millions)	4,646	4,759	4,779	4,340	4,339	4,353
(7) Price per share (€)	15.85	22.22	16.22	10.75	15.02	13.84
Price-to-revenue ratio (P/R): (7) ÷ [(2) ÷ (6)]	1.3	1.9	1.5	0.8	1.0	1.0
P/CF: (7) ÷ [(3) ÷ (6)]	4.5	6.8	5.0	3.0	4.8	4.2
P/B: (7) ÷ [(4) ÷ (6)]	3.8	4.6	3.9	1.1	1.4	1.2
P/E: (7) ÷ [(5) ÷ (6)]	9.4	11.6	11.7	31.1	108.6	18.8

Sources: Company web sites: www.telefonica.es and www.deutschetelekom.com.

amortization (EBITDA) for Telefónica was €22.9 billion in 2008. The EBITDA value for Deutsche Telekom was €18.0 billion in 2008. The 2008 price-to-EBITDA ratio for Telefónica is [(15.85 × 4,646)/22,900] or [15.85/(22,900/4,646)] = 3.2, whereas the 2008 price-to-EBITDA ratio for Deutsche Telekom is 2.6. Thus, the higher P/E for Deutsche Telekom may be explained by higher depreciation charges, higher interest costs, and/or a greater tax burden.

In summary, the major advantage of using price multiples is that they allow for relative comparisons, both cross-sectional (versus the market or another comparable) and in time series. The approach can be especially beneficial for analysts who are assigned to a particular industry or sector and need to identify the expected best performing stocks within that sector. Price multiples are popular with investors because the multiples can be calculated easily and many multiples are readily available from financial web sites and newspapers.

Caution is necessary. A stock may be relatively undervalued when compared with its benchmarks but overvalued when compared with an estimate of intrinsic value as determined by one of the discounted cash flow methodologies. Furthermore, differences in reporting rules among different markets and in chosen accounting methods can result in revenues, earnings, book values, and cash flows that are not easily comparable. These differences can, in turn, result in multiples that are not easily comparable. Finally, the multiples for cyclical companies may be highly influenced by current economic conditions.

5.4. Enterprise Value

An alternative to estimating the value of equity is to estimate the value of the enterprise. Enterprise value is most frequently determined as market capitalization plus market value of preferred stock plus market value of debt minus cash and investments (cash equivalents and short-term investments). Enterprise value is often viewed as the cost of a takeover: In the event of a buyout, the acquiring company assumes the acquired company's debt but also receives its cash. Enterprise value is most useful when comparing companies with significant differences in capital structure.

Enterprise value (EV) multiples are widely used in Europe, with EV/EBITDA arguably the most common. EBITDA is a proxy for operating cash flow because it excludes depreciation and amortization. EBITDA may include other noncash expenses, however, and noncash revenues. EBITDA can be viewed as a source of funds to pay interest, dividends, and taxes. Because EBITDA is calculated prior to payment to any of the company's financial stakeholders, using it to estimate enterprise value is logically appropriate.

Using enterprise value instead of market capitalization to determine a multiple can be useful to analysts. Even where the P/E is problematic because of negative earnings, the EV/EBITDA multiple can generally be computed because EBITDA is usually positive. An alternative to using EBITDA in EV multiples is to use operating income.

In practice, analysts may have difficulty accurately assessing enterprise value if they do not have access to market quotations for the company's debt. When current market quotations are not available, bond values may be estimated from current quotations for bonds with similar maturity, sector, and credit characteristics. Substituting the book value of debt for the market value of debt provides only a rough estimate of the debt's market value. This is because market interest rates change and investors' perception of the issuer's credit risk may have changed since the debt was issued.

EXAMPLE 10-15 Estimating the Market Value of Debt and Enterprise Value

Cameco Corporation (NYSE: CCJ) is one of the world's largest uranium producers; it accounts for 15 percent of world production from its mines in Canada and the United States. Cameco estimates it has about 226,796,185 kilograms of proven and probable reserves and holds premier land positions in the world's most promising areas for new uranium discoveries in Canada and Australia. Cameco is also a leading provider of processing services required to produce fuel for nuclear power plants. It generates 1,000 megawatts of electricity through a partnership in North America's largest nuclear generating station located in Ontario, Canada.

For simplicity of exposition in this example, we will present share counts in thousands and all dollar amounts in thousands of Canadian dollars. In 2008, Cameco had 350,130 shares outstanding. Its 2008 year-end share price was $20.99. Therefore, Cameco's 2008 year-end market capitalization was $7,349,229.

In its 2008 Annual Report (available at www.cameco.com), Cameco reported total debt and other liabilities of $2,716,475. The company presented the following schedule for long-term debt payments:

Year	Payment
2009	$10,175
2010	453,288
2011	13,272
2012	317,452
2013	16,325
Thereafter	412,645
Total	$1,223,157

Cameco's longest maturity debt matures in 2018. We will assume that the $412,645 to be paid "thereafter" will be paid in equal amounts of $82,529 over the 2014 to 2018 time period. A yield curve for zero-coupon Canadian government securities was available from the Bank of Canada. The yield-curve data and assumed risk premiums in Exhibit 10-7 were used to estimate the market value of Cameco's long-term debt:

EXHIBIT 10-7 Estimated Market Value

Year	Yield on Zero-Coupon Government Security	Assumed Risk Premium	Discount Rate	Book Value	Market Value
2009	0.89%	0.50%	1.39%	$10,175	$10,036
2010	1.11%	1.00%	2.11%	$453,288	$434,748
2011	1.39%	1.50%	2.89%	$13,272	$12,185
2012	1.65%	2.00%	3.65%	$317,452	$275,043
2013	1.88%	2.50%	4.38%	$16,325	$13,175
2014	2.10%	3.00%	5.10%	$82,529	$61,234
2015	2.30%	3.50%	5.80%	$82,529	$55,617
2016	2.50%	4.00%	6.50%	$82,529	$49,867
2017	2.71%	4.50%	7.21%	$82,529	$44,105
2018	2.92%	5.00%	7.92%	$82,529	$38,511
				$1,223,157	$994,521

Note from Exhibit 10-7 that the book value of long-term debt is $1,223,157 and its estimated market value is $994,521. The book value of total debt and liabilities of $2,716,475 minus the book value of long-term debt of $1,223,157 is $1,493,318. If we assume that the market value of that remaining debt is equal to its book value of $1,493,318, an estimate of the market value of total debt and liabilities is that amount plus the estimated market value of long-term debt of $994,521 or $2,487,839.

At the end of 2008, Cameco had cash and equivalents of $269,176. Enterprise value can be estimated as the $7,349,229 market value of stock plus the $2,487,839 market value of debt minus the $269,176 cash and equivalents, or $9,567,892. Cameco's 2008 EBITDA was $1,078,606; an estimate of EV/EBITDA is, therefore, $9,567,892 divided by $1,078,606, or 8.9.

EXAMPLE 10-16 EV/Operating Income

Exhibit 10-8 presents data for nine major mining companies. Based on the information in Exhibit 10-8, which two mining companies seem to be the *most* undervalued?

EXHIBIT 10-8 Data for Nine Major Mining Companies

Company	Ticker Symbol	EV (C$millions)	Operating Income (OI) (C$millions)	EV/OI
BHP Billiton	BHP	197,112.00	9,794.00	20.1
Rio Tinto	RIO	65,049.60	7,905.00	8.2
Anglo American	AAL	48,927.30	6,208.00	7.9
Barrick Gold	ABX	35,288.00	1,779.00	19.8
Goldcorp	G	28,278.00	616.66	45.9
Newmont Mining	NEM	22,040.80	1,385.00	15.9
AngloGold Ashanti	AU	19,918.30	−362.00	−55.0
Alcoa	AA	17,570.40	4,166.00	4.2
Freeport-McMoRan Copper & Gold	FCX	11,168.40	2,868.75	3.9

Source: www.miningnerds.com.

Solution: Alcoa and Freeport-McMoRan Copper & Gold have the lowest EV/OI and thus appear to be the *most* undervalued or favorably priced on the basis of the EV/OI. Note the negative ratio for AngloGold Ashanti. Negative ratios are difficult to interpret, so other means are used to evaluate companies with negative ratios.

6. ASSET-BASED VALUATION

An asset-based valuation of a company uses estimates of the market or fair value of the company's assets and liabilities. Thus, asset-based valuations work well for companies that do not have a high proportion of intangible or "off the books" assets and that do have a high proportion of current assets and current liabilities. The analyst may be able to value these companies' assets and liabilities in a reasonable fashion by starting with balance sheet items. For most companies, however, balance sheet values are different from market (fair) values, and the market (fair) values can be difficult to determine.

Asset-based valuation models are frequently used together with multiplier models to value private companies. As public companies increase reporting or disclosure of fair values, asset-based valuation may be increasingly used to supplement present value and multiplier models of valuation. Important facts that the practitioner should realize are as follows:

- Companies with assets that do not have easily determinable market (fair) values—such as those with significant property, plant, and equipment—are very difficult to analyze using asset valuation methods.
- Asset and liability fair values can be very different from the values at which they are carried on the balance sheet of a company.
- Some assets that are "intangible" are shown on the books of the company. Other intangible assets, such as the value from synergies or the value of a good business reputation, may not be shown on the books. Because asset-based valuation may not consider some intangibles, it can give a "floor" value for a situation involving a significant amount of intangibles. When a company has significant intangibles, the analyst should prefer a forward-looking cash flow valuation.
- Asset values may be more difficult to estimate in a hyperinflationary environment.

We begin by discussing asset-based valuation for hypothetical nonpublic companies and then move on to a public company example. Analysts should consider the difficulties and rewards of using asset-based valuation for companies that are suited to this measure. Owners of small privately held businesses are familiar with valuations arrived at by valuing the assets of the company and then subtracting any relevant liabilities.

EXAMPLE 10-17 An Asset-Based Valuation of a Family-Owned Laundry

A family owns a laundry and the real estate on which the laundry stands. The real estate is collateral for an outstanding loan of $100,000. How can asset-based valuation be used to value this business?

Solution: The analyst should get at least two market appraisals for the real estate (building and land) and estimate the cost to extinguish the $100,000 loan. This information would provide estimated values for everything except the laundry as a going concern. That is, the analyst has market values for the building and land and the loan but needs to value the laundry business. The analyst can value the assets of the laundry: the equipment and inventory. The equipment can be valued at depreciated value, inflation-adjusted depreciated value, or replacement cost. Replacement cost in this case means the amount that would have to be spent to buy equivalent used machines. This amount is the market value of the used machines. The analyst will recognize that any intangible value of the laundry (prime location, clever marketing, etc.) is being excluded, which will result in an inaccurate asset-based valuation.

Example 10-17 shows some of the subtleties present in applying asset-based valuation to determine company value. It also shows how asset-based valuation does not deal with intangibles. Example 10-18 emphasizes this point.

EXAMPLE 10-18 An Asset-Based Valuation of a Restaurant

The business being valued is a restaurant that serves breakfast and lunch. The owner/proprietor wants to sell the business and retire. The restaurant space is rented, not owned. This particular restaurant is hugely popular because of the proprietor's cooking skills and secret recipes. How can the analyst value this business?

Solution: Because of the intangibles, setting a value on this business is challenging. A multiple of income or revenue might be considered. But even those approaches overlook the fact that the proprietor may not be selling his secret recipes and, furthermore, does not intend to continue cooking. Some (or all) of the intangible assets may vanish when the business is sold. Asset-based valuation for this restaurant would begin with estimating the value of the restaurant equipment and inventory and subtracting the value of any liabilities. This approach will provide only a good baseline, however, for a minimum valuation.

For public companies, the assets will typically be so extensive that a piece-by-piece analysis will be impossible, and the transition from book value to market value is a nontrivial task. The asset-based valuation approach is most applicable when the market value of the corporate assets is readily determinable and the intangible assets, which are typically difficult to value, are a relatively small proportion of corporate assets. Asset-based valuation has also been applied to financial companies, natural resource companies, and formerly going concerns that are being liquidated. Even for other types of companies, however, asset-based valuation of tangible assets may provide a baseline for a minimal valuation.

EXAMPLE 10-19 An Asset-Based Valuation of an Airline

Consider the value of an airline company that has few routes, high labor and other operating costs, has stopped paying dividends, and is losing millions of dollars each year. Using most valuation approaches, the company will have a negative value. Why might an asset-based valuation approach be appropriate for use by one of the company's competitors that is considering acquisition of this airline?

Solution: The airline's routes, landing rights, leases of airport facilities, and ground equipment and airplanes may have substantial value to a competitor. An asset-based approach to valuing this company would value the company's assets separately and aside from the money-losing business in which they are presently being utilized.

Analysts recognizing the uncertainties related to model appropriateness and the inputs to the models frequently use more than one model or type of model in valuation to increase their confidence in their estimates of intrinsic value. The choice of models will depend on the availability of information to put into the models. Example 10-20 illustrates the use of three valuation methods.

EXAMPLE 10-20 A Simple Example of the Use of Three Major Equity Valuation Models

Company data for dividend per share (DPS), earnings per share (EPS), share price, and price-to-earnings ratio (P/E) for the most recent five years are presented in Exhibit 10-9. In addition, estimates (indicated by an "E" after the amount) of DPS and EPS for the next five years are shown. The valuation date is at the end of Year 5. The company has 1,000 shares outstanding.

EXHIBIT 10-9 Company DPS, EPS, Share Price, and P/E Data

Year	DPS	EPS	Share price	TTM P/E
10	$3.10E	$5.20E	—	—
9	$2.91E	$4.85E	—	—
8	$2.79E	$4.65E	—	—
7	$2.65E	$4.37E	—	—
6	$2.55E	$4.30E	—	—
5	$2.43	$4.00	$50.80	12.7

EXHIBIT 10-9 (*Continued*)

Year	DPS	EPS	Share price	TTM P/E
4	$2.32	$3.90	$51.48	13.2
3	$2.19	$3.65	$59.86	16.4
2	$2.14	$3.60	$54.72	15.2
1	$2.00	$3.30	$46.20	14.0

The company's balance sheet at the end of Year 5 is given in Exhibit 10-10.

EXHIBIT 10-10 Balance Sheet as of End of Year 5

Cash	$ 5,000
Accounts receivable	15,000
Inventories	30,000
Net fixed assets	50,000
Total assets	$100,000
Accounts payable	$ 3,000
Notes payable	17,000
Term loans	25,000
Common shareholders' equity	55,000
Total liabilities and equity	$100,000

1. Using a Gordon growth model, estimate intrinsic value. Use a discount rate of 10 percent and an estimate of growth based on growth in dividends over the next five years.
2. Using a multiplier approach, estimate intrinsic value. Assume that a reasonable estimate of P/E is the average trailing twelve-month (TTM) P/E ratio over Years 1 through 4.
3. Using an asset-based valuation approach, estimate value per share from adjusted book values. Assume that the market values of accounts receivable and inventories are as reported, the market value of net fixed assets is 110 percent of reported book value, and the reported book values of liabilities reflect their market values.

Solution to 1:
$D_5\ (1+g)^5 = D_{10}2.43(1+g)^5 = 3.10$
$g \approx 5.0\%$
Estimate of value $= V_5 = 2.55/(0.10 - 0.05) = \$51.00$

Solution to 2:
Average P/E $= (14.0 + 15.2 + 16.4 + 13.2)/4 = 14.7$
Estimate of value $= \$4.00 \times 14.7 = \$58.80$

Solution to 3:
Market value of assets = 5,000 + 15,000 + 30,000 + 1.1(50,000) = \$105,000
Market value of liabilities = \$3,000 + 17,000 + 25,000 = \$45,000
Adjusted book value = \$105,000 − 45,000 = \$60,000
Estimated value (adjusted book value per share) = \$60,000 ÷ 1,000 shares = \$60.00

Given the current share price of \$50.80, the multiplier and the asset-based valuation approaches indicate that the stock is undervalued. Given the intrinsic value estimated using the Gordon growth model, the analyst is likely to conclude that the stock is fairly priced. The analyst might examine the assumptions in the multiplier and the asset-based valuation approaches to determine why their estimated values differ from the estimated value provided by the Gordon growth model and the market price.

7. SUMMARY

The equity valuation models used to estimate intrinsic value—present value models, multiplier models, and asset-based valuation—are widely used and serve an important purpose. The valuation models presented here are a foundation on which to base analysis and research but must be applied wisely. Valuation is not simply a numerical analysis. The choice of model and the derivation of inputs require skill and judgment.

When valuing a company or group of companies, the analyst wants to choose a valuation model that is appropriate for the information available to be used as inputs. The available data will, in most instances, restrict the choice of model and influence the way it is used. Complex models exist that may improve on the simple valuation models described in this chapter; but before using those models and assuming that complexity increases accuracy, the analyst would do well to consider the "law of parsimony": A model should be kept as simple as possible in light of the available inputs. Valuation is a fallible discipline, and any method will result in an inaccurate forecast at some time. The goal is to minimize the inaccuracy of the forecast.

Among the points made in this chapter are the following:

- An analyst estimating intrinsic value is implicitly questioning the market's estimate of value.
- If the estimated value exceeds the market price, the analyst infers the security is *undervalued.* If the estimated value equals the market price, the analyst infers the security is *fairly valued.* If the estimated value is less than the market price, the analyst infers the security is *overvalued.* Because of the uncertainties involved in valuation, an analyst may require that value estimates differ markedly from market price before concluding that a misvaluation exists.
- Analysts often use more than one valuation model because of concerns about the applicability of any particular model and the variability in estimates that result from changes in inputs.
- Three major categories of equity valuation models are present value, multiplier, and asset-based valuation models.

- Present value models estimate value as the present value of expected future benefits.
- Multiplier models estimate intrinsic value based on a multiple of some fundamental variable.
- Asset-based valuation models estimate value based on the estimated value of assets and liabilities.
- The choice of model will depend upon the availability of information to input into the model and the analyst's confidence in both the information and the appropriateness of the model.
- In the dividend discount model, value is estimated as the present value of expected future dividends.
- In the free-cash-flow-to-equity model, value is estimated as the present value of expected future free cash flow to equity.
- The Gordon growth model, a simple DDM, estimates value as $D_1/(r - g)$.
- The two-stage dividend discount model estimates value as the sum of the present values of dividends over a short-term period of high growth and the present value of the terminal value at the end of the period of high growth. The terminal value is estimated using the Gordon growth model.
- The choice of dividend model is based upon the patterns assumed with respect to future dividends.
- Multiplier models typically use multiples of the form: P/measure of fundamental variable or EV/measure of fundamental variable.
- Multiples can be based upon fundamentals or comparables.
- Asset-based valuation models estimate value of equity as the value of the assets less the value of liabilities.

PROBLEMS

1. An analyst estimates the intrinsic value of a stock to be in the range of €17.85 to €21.45. The current market price of the stock is €24.35. This stock is *most likely*:
   A. Overvalued.
   B. Undervalued.
   C. Fairly valued.

2. An analyst determines the intrinsic value of an equity security to be equal to $55. If the current price is $47, the equity is *most likely*:
   A. Undervalued.
   B. Fairly valued.
   C. Overvalued.

3. In asset-based valuation models, the intrinsic value of a common share of stock is based on the:
   A. Estimated market value of the company's assets.
   B. Estimated market value of the company's assets plus liabilities.
   C. Estimated market value of the company's assets minus liabilities.

4. Which of the following is *most likely* used in a present value model?
   A. Enterprise value.
   B. Price to free cash flow.
   C. Free cash flow to equity.

5. Book value is *least likely* to be considered when using:
   A. A multiplier model.
   B. An asset-based valuation model.
   C. A present value model.

6. An analyst is attempting to calculate the intrinsic value of a company and has gathered the following company data: EBITDA, total market value, and market value of cash and short-term investments, liabilities, and preferred shares. The analyst is *least likely* to use:
   A. A multiplier model.
   B. A discounted cash flow model.
   C. An asset-based valuation model.

7. An analyst who bases the calculation of intrinsic value on dividend-paying capacity rather than expected dividends will *most likely* use the:
   A. Dividend discount model.
   B. Free cash flow to equity model.
   C. Cash flow from operations model.

8. An investor expects to purchase shares of common stock today and sell them after two years. The investor has estimated dividends for the next two years, D_1 and D_2, and the selling price of the stock two years from now, P_2. According to the dividend discount model, the intrinsic value of the stock today is the present value of:
   A. Next year's dividend, D_1.
   B. Future expected dividends, D_1 and D_2.
   C. Future expected dividends and price—D_1, D_2, and P_2.

9. In the free-cash-flow-to-equity (FCFE) model, the intrinsic value of a share of stock is calculated as:
   A. The present value of future expected FCFE.
   B. The present value of future expected FCFE plus net borrowing.
   C. The present value of future expected FCFE minus fixed capital investment.

10. With respect to present value models, which of the following statements is *most accurate*?
    A. Present value models can be used only if a stock pays a dividend.
    B. Present value models can be used only if a stock pays a dividend or is expected to pay a dividend.
    C. Present value models can be used for stocks that currently pay a dividend, are expected to pay a dividend, or are not expected to pay a dividend.

11. A Canadian life insurance company has an issue of 4.80 percent, $25 par value, perpetual, nonconvertible, noncallable preferred shares outstanding. The required rate of return on similar issues is 4.49 percent. The intrinsic value of a preferred share is *closest to*:
    A. $25.00.
    B. $26.75.
    C. $28.50.

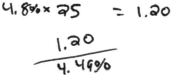

4.8% × 25 = 1.20

$\frac{1.20}{4.49\%}$

12. Two analysts estimating the value of a nonconvertible, noncallable, perpetual preferred stock with a constant dividend arrive at different estimated values. The *most likely* reason for the difference is that the analysts used different:

    A. Time horizons.
    B. Required rates of return.
    C. Estimated dividend growth rates.

13. The Beasley Corporation has just paid a dividend of $1.75 per share. If the required rate of return is 12.3 percent per year and dividends are expected to grow indefinitely at a constant rate of 9.2 percent per year, the intrinsic value of Beasley Corporation stock is *closest* to:

    A. $15.54.
    B. $56.45.
    C. $61.65.

14. An investor is considering the purchase of a common stock with a $2.00 annual dividend. The dividend is expected to grow at a rate of 4 percent annually. If the investor's required rate of return is 7 percent, the intrinsic value of the stock is *closest* to:

    A. $50.00.
    B. $66.67.
    C. $69.33.

15. An analyst gathers or estimates the following information about a stock:

Current price per share	€22.56
Current annual dividend per share	€1.60
Annual dividend growth rate for Years 1–4	9.00%
Annual dividend growth rate for Years 5 +	4.00%
Required rate of return	12%

    Based on a dividend discount model, the stock is *most likely*:

    A. Undervalued.
    B. Fairly valued.
    C. Overvalued.

16. An analyst is attempting to value shares of the Dominion Company. The company has just paid a dividend of $0.58 per share. Dividends are expected to grow by 20 percent next year and 15 percent the year after that. From the third year onward, dividends are expected to grow at 5.6 percent per year indefinitely. If the required rate of return is 8.3 percent, the intrinsic value of the stock is *closest* to:

    A. $26.00.
    B. $27.00.
    C. $28.00.

17. Hideki Corporation has just paid a dividend of ¥450 per share. Annual dividends are expected to grow at the rate of 4 percent per year over the next four years. At the end

of four years, shares of Hideki Corporation are expected to sell for ¥9,000. If the required rate of return is 12 percent, the intrinsic value of a share of Hideki Corporation is *closest* to:

A. ¥5,850.
B. ¥7,220.
C. ¥7,670.

18. The Gordon growth model can be used to value dividend-paying companies that are:

A. Expected to grow very fast.
B. In a mature phase of growth.
C. Very sensitive to the business cycle.

19. The best model to use when valuing a young dividend-paying company that is just entering the growth phase is *most likely* the:

A. Gordon growth model.
B. Two-stage dividend discount model.
C. Three-stage dividend discount model.

20. An equity analyst has been asked to estimate the intrinsic value of the common stock of Omega Corporation, a leading manufacturer of automobile seats. Omega is in a mature industry, and both its earnings and dividends are expected to grow at a rate of 3 percent annually. Which of the following is *most likely* to be the best model for determining the intrinsic value of an Omega share?

A. Gordon growth model.
B. Free-cash-flow-to-equity model.
C. Multistage dividend discount model.

21. A price-to-earnings ratio that is derived from the Gordon growth model is inversely related to the:

A. Growth rate.
B. Dividend payout ratio.
C. Required rate of return.

22. The primary difference between P/E multiples based on comparables and P/E multiples based on fundamentals is that fundamentals-based P/Es take into account:

A. Future expectations.
B. The law of one price.
C. Historical information.

23. An analyst makes the following statement: "Use of P/E and other multiples for analysis is not effective because the multiples are based on historical data and because not all companies have positive accounting earnings." The analyst's statement is *most likely*:

A. Inaccurate with respect to both historical data and earnings.
B. Accurate with respect to historical data and inaccurate with respect to earnings.
C. Inaccurate with respect to historical data and accurate with respect to earnings.

24. An analyst has prepared a table of the average trailing 12-month price-to-earning (P/E), price-to-cash flow (P/CF), and price-to-sales (P/S) for the Tanaka Corporation for the years 2005 to 2008.

Year	P/E	P/CF	P/S
2005	4.9	5.4	1.2
2006	6.1	8.6	1.5
2007	8.3	7.3	1.9
2008	9.2	7.9	2.3

As of the date of the valuation in 2009, the trailing 12-month P/E, P/CF, and P/S are, respectively, 9.2, 8.0, and 2.5. Based on the information provided, the analyst may reasonably conclude that Tanaka shares are *most likely*:

A. Overvalued.
B. Undervalued.
C. Fairly valued.

25. An analyst has gathered the following information for the Oudin Corporation:
Expected earnings per share = €5.70
Expected dividends per share = €2.70
Dividends are expected to grow at 2.75 percent per year indefinitely
The required rate of return is 8.35 percent
Based on the information provided, the price/earnings multiple for Oudin is *closest* to:

A. 5.7.
B. 8.5.
C. 9.4.

26. An analyst gathers the following information about two companies:

	Alpha Corp.	Delta Co.
Current price per share	$57.32	$18.93
Last year's EPS	$3.82	$ 1.35
Current year's estimated EPS	$4.75	$ 1.40

Which of the following statements is *most accurate*?

A. Delta has the higher trailing P/E multiple and lower current estimated P/E multiple.
B. Alpha has the higher trailing P/E multiple and lower current estimated P/E multiple.
C. Alpha has the higher trailing P/E multiple and higher current estimated P/E multiple.

27. An analyst gathers the following information about similar companies in the banking sector:

	First Bank	Prime Bank	Pioneer Trust
P/B	1.10	0.60	0.60
P/E	8.40	11.10	8.30

Which of the companies is *most likely* to be undervalued?

A. First Bank.
B. Prime Bank.
C. Pioneer Trust.

28. The market value of equity for a company can be calculated as enterprise value:

A. Minus market value of debt, preferred stock, and short-term investments.
B. Plus market value of debt and preferred stock minus short-term investments.
C. Minus market value of debt and preferred stock plus short-term investments.

29. Which of the following statements regarding the calculation of the enterprise value multiple is *most likely* correct?

A. Operating income may be used instead of EBITDA.
B. EBITDA may not be used if company earnings are negative.
C. Book value of debt may be used instead of market value of debt.

30. An analyst has determined that the appropriate EV/EBITDA for Rainbow Company is 10.2. The analyst has also collected the following forecasted information for Rainbow Company:
EBITDA = $22,000,000
Market value of debt = $56,000,000
Cash = $1,500,000
The value of equity for Rainbow Company is *closest* to:

A. $169 million.
B. $224 million.
C. $281 million.

31. Enterprise value is most often determined as market capitalization of common equity and preferred stock minus the value of cash equivalents plus the:

A. Book value of debt.
B. Market value of debt.
C. Market value of long-term debt.

32. Asset-based valuation models are best suited to companies where the capital structure does not have a high proportion of:

A. Debt.
B. Intangible assets.
C. Current assets and liabilities.

33. Which of the following is *most likely* a reason for using asset-based valuation?

A. The analyst is valuing a privately held company.
B. The company has a relatively high level of intangible assets.
C. The market values of assets and liabilities are different from the balance sheet values.

34. A disadvantage of the EV method for valuing equity is that the following information may be difficult to obtain:

A. Operating income.
B. Market value of debt.
C. Market value of equity.

35. Which type of equity valuation model is *most likely* to be preferable when one is comparing similar companies?

    A. A multiplier model.
    B. A present value model.
    C. An asset-based valuation model.

36. Which of the following is *most likely* considered a weakness of present value models?

    A. Present value models cannot be used for companies that do not pay dividends.
    B. Small changes in model assumptions and inputs can result in large changes in the computed intrinsic value of the security.
    C. The value of the security depends on the investor's holding period; thus, comparing valuations of different companies for different investors is difficult.

CHAPTER 11

EQUITY MARKET VALUATION

Peter C. Stimes, CFA
Altadena, CA, U.S.A.

Stephen E. Wilcox, CFA
Mankato, MN, U.S.A.

LEARNING OUTCOMES

After completing this chapter, you will be able to do the following:

- Explain the terms of the Cobb-Douglas production function and demonstrate how the function can be used to model growth in real output under the assumption of constant returns to scale.
- Evaluate the relative importance of growth in total factor productivity, in capital stock, and in labor input given relevant historical data.
- Demonstrate the use of the Cobb-Douglas production function in obtaining a discounted dividend model estimate of the intrinsic value of an equity market.
- Evaluate the sensitivity of equity market value estimates to changes in assumptions.
- Contrast top-down and bottom-up forecasts of the earnings per share of an equity market index.
- Explain and critique models of relative equity market valuation based on earnings and assets.
- Judge whether an equity market is under-, fairly, or overvalued based on a relative equity valuation model.

1. INTRODUCTION

Economic strength or weakness affects equity prices through its effect on risk-free rates, risk premiums, and corporate earnings. These economic drivers of security prices are often considered fundamental because they will affect security returns throughout most investment horizons. It is widely accepted that equity prices are negatively related to risk-free rates and risk premiums and positively related to earnings growth.

There are, of course, other drivers of equity returns and most of these can be considered behavioral. The cognitive and emotional factors experienced by investors can create both positive and negative feedback mechanisms. Market momentum may thus result in both bull market rallies and bear market declines lasting longer than may be justified by fundamental factors. This chapter does not deal specifically with such behavioral drivers. Rather, this chapter illustrates the application of economic forecasts to the valuation of equity markets. While many factors interact to determine whether equity prices are currently rising or falling, economic fundamentals will ultimately dictate secular equity market price trends.

Section 2 uses GDP forecasts for a developing country, China, to develop inputs for a discounted cash flow valuation of that country's equity market.[1] Section 3 contrasts the top-down and bottom-up valuation approaches. Section 4 explains and critiques popular earnings- and asset-based models to relative equity market valuation. Section 5 summarizes the chapter, and practice problems in the CFA Institute format follow.

2. ESTIMATING A JUSTIFIED P/E RATIO

Investors commonly use the market's price-to-earnings (P/E) ratio or multiple to gauge the prospects for future equity returns. Sections 2.1 through 2.3 develop the Cobb-Douglas production function (also called the Cobb-Douglas model) for obtaining growth rates for an economy and, thus, the dividend growth rate trajectories for a corresponding equity market. This model is particularly useful in the case of developing markets such as China, where the structure of the underlying economy has experienced, and may experience, fundamental changes (as compared with the relatively stable growth rates of more developed economies).

In Section 2.4 we apply a form of the dividend discount model known as the H-model to the complicated dividend growth trajectory because it is well suited to instances where near term growth rates can diverge significantly from the ultimately sustainable dividend growth rate. We also standardize the results in justified P/E form. This facilitates intertemporal and cross-border market value comparisons. The difference between prevailing P/Es and justified P/Es is a measure of potential investment attractiveness.

As will be shown, the Cobb-Douglas and dividend discount models may also be applied to developed economies and equity markets.

2.1. Neoclassical Approach to Growth Accounting

Growth accounting is used in economics to measure the contribution of different factors—usually broadly defined as capital and labor—to economic growth and, indirectly, to compute the rate of an economy's technological progress. The neoclassical approach to growth accounting uses the Cobb-Douglas production function.[2] This approach can be useful to financial analysts because it gives insights into the long-term potential economic growth in individual countries, in larger regions, and for the world as a whole. The Cobb-Douglas

[1] Forecasts and opinions offered in this chapter are those of the authors (or the writers cited) and are not positions of CFA Institute.

[2] See Cobb and Douglas (1928).

estimate of the growth of total production can help to estimate corporate profit growth and develop corporate cash flow projections for stock market composites.

The basic form of the Cobb-Douglas production function is set forth as Equation 11.1, where Y represents total real economic output, A is total factor productivity, K is capital stock, α is output elasticity of K, L is labor input, and β is the output elasticity of L. **Total factor productivity** (TFP) is a variable which accounts for that part of Y not directly accounted for by the levels of the production factors (K and L).

$$Y = AK^{\alpha}L^{\beta} \tag{11.1}$$

If we assume that the production function exhibits **constant returns to scale** (i.e., a given percentage increase in capital stock and labor input results in an equal percentage increase in output), we can substitute $\beta = (1 - \alpha)$ into Equation 11.1.[3] Taking the natural logarithm of both sides of the equation gives

$$\ln(Y) = \ln(A) + \alpha \ln(K) + (1 - \alpha)\ln(L) \tag{11.2}$$

Taking first differences of Equation 11.2 and utilizing the fact that, for small changes in any variable x,

$$\ln(x + \Delta x) - \ln(x) = \ln\left(\frac{x + \Delta x}{x}\right) \approx \frac{\Delta x}{x}$$

we obtain the expression:

$$\frac{\Delta Y}{Y} \approx \frac{\Delta A}{A} + \alpha\frac{\Delta K}{K} + (1 - \alpha)\frac{\Delta L}{L} \tag{11.3}$$

Equation 11.3 is the expression which we will employ in our analysis. In Equation 11.3, the percentage growth in real output (or gross domestic product, GDP) is shown as $\Delta Y/Y$ and it is decomposed into its components: $\Delta A/A$ is growth in TFP; $\Delta K/K$ is the growth in the capital stock; $\Delta L/L$ is the growth in the labor input; α is the output elasticity of capital; and $1 - \alpha$ is the output elasticity of labor where $0 < \alpha < 1$.

In practice, all the variables in Equation 11.3, with the exception of the growth in TFP, are directly observable or can be derived from national income and product accounts.[4] However, growth in TFP is determined using the other inputs as noted by Equation 11.3 and is commonly referred to as the **Solow residual**.[5]

TFP growth means that aggregate output (i.e., GDP) can grow at a faster rate than would be predicted simply from growth in accumulated capital stock and the labor force. Interpreting TFP as a measure of the level of technology, growth in TFP is often described as a measure of "technical progress" and linked to innovation. As examples, such technological advances as the introduction of the steam engine, electricity, the internal combustion engine, telecommunications, microchips, penicillin, and the Internet are thought to have contributed to growth in TFP. However, growth in TFP, as a residual in the sense described, can be driven by factors other than improvements in technology. These factors could be particularly significant

[3]As a result, if both capital and labor change by a percentage x, then the total change in output is $\alpha x + (1 - \alpha)x = x$. The use of constant returns to scale is predicated on empirical results from several large economies over various time periods during the nineteenth and twentieth centuries.

[4]Capital, α, and labor, $(1 - \alpha)$, output elasticities may differ across national economies.

[5]See Solow (1957). The Solow residual is thus simply: $\frac{\Delta A}{A} \approx \frac{\Delta Y}{Y} - \alpha\frac{\Delta K}{K} - (1 - \alpha)\frac{\Delta L}{L}$

in economies which are experiencing major changes in political and/or regulatory structures. As examples, liberalization of trade policies, abolition of restrictions on the movement and ownership of capital and labor, the establishment of peace and the predictable rule of law, and even the dismantling of punitive taxation policies, would be expected to contribute to growth in TFP. Finally, growth in TFP can benefit from improvements in the division of labor that arise from the growth of the economy itself. By contrast, developments such as the depletion and degradation of natural resources would detract from growth in TFP.

The robustness and simplicity of the approach we have presented can be tested against the complex and important case of valuing the equity markets in mainland China.

2.2. The China Economic Experience

China has been widely regarded as the most influential emerging economy, and its growth performance since reform has been hailed as an economic miracle. Historical growth accounting results, as presented in Zheng, Hu, and Bigsten (2009), are reported in Exhibit 11-1. Note particularly the comparisons of China's growth in the capital stock, $\Delta K/K$, and growth in the labor input, $\Delta L/L$, to those of the (former) Soviet Union, United States, and European Union. The growth in capital stock stands out particularly for China and is most apparent during the period of economic liberalization that commenced in the early 1990s. According to estimates by the World Bank and other institutions, the gross effective savings in China (loosely defined as investment in plant, property, equipment, and inventories) divided by economic output have been in the neighborhood of 40 percent. This compares with 15 to 20 percent over the comparable periods for the other countries in Exhibit 11-1.

EXHIBIT 11-1 Historical Growth Accounting for China, the (Former) Soviet Union, United States, and European Union

Countries	Time Period	Real GDP Growth $\Delta Y/Y$	Growth in Total Factor Productivity $\Delta A/A$	Growth in Capital Stock $\Delta K/K$	Growth in Labor Input $\Delta L/L$
China	1978–1995	10.11%	3.80%	9.12%	3.49%
	1995–2007	9.25%	1.45%	12.81%	2.78%
Soviet Union	1950–1970	5.4%	1.6%	8.8%	1.8%
	1970–1985	2.7%	−0.4%	7.0%	1.1%
United States	1950–1972	3.9%	1.6%	2.6%	1.4%
	1972–1996	3.3%	0.6%	3.1%	1.7%
	1996–2004	3.6%	1.5%	2.6%	0.7%
European Union	1960–1973	5.1%	3.2%	—	4.8%
	1973–2003	2.2%	1.0%	0.5%	2.8%

Source: Zheng, Hu, and Bigsten (2009). China's output elasticity for capital (α) and output elasticity for labor ($1 - \alpha$) were both estimated to be 0.5.

Concerns over the sustainability of China's growth have emerged in recent years because, as is evident from Exhibit 11-1, the growth in TFP has slowed. Zheng, Bigsten, and Hu (2006)

studied the Chinese economy and found that reform measures had a significant positive impact on TFP, but this impact should be considered a one-time event. Those authors make a case that China should now focus on achieving sustained increases in productivity.

Exhibit 11-1 also shows that Chinese economic growth has been largely driven by growth in the capital stock. Zheng, Bigsten, and Hu note that government policies in the mid- to late 1990s supported this extraordinary growth in investments. Key input prices were kept low through subsidies, and controlled pricing and a high savings rate allowed for the availability of cheap credit. A huge trade surplus has been another side effect of both high investment[6] and an unsustainably low fixed exchange-rate policy designed to support exports. China's foreign reserves are currently the world's largest by a considerable amount and have recently surpassed $2 trillion.[7] Because of this, China is facing excessive growth in its money supply and there are concerns about potential bubbles in both real estate and share prices. (Recent year-over-year growth in the broad M2 measure of the money supply has been over 25 percent.[8]) A necessary, eventual "course correction" in exchange rate and monetary policies would reduce or reverse the forces that contributed to a de facto subsidization of capital formation.

In addition to the foregoing structural factors, changes in consumer behavior are also likely to cause the Chinese savings/investment rate to moderate. Altogether, government policy changes, structural imbalances, and an increased propensity to consume all point to an eventual reduction from the double-digit growth rates of capital stock. At the same time, while the labor force of China has grown at a much more rapid pace than for European and American economies, this has been attributable both to higher population growth rates and to a rise in labor force participation rates. The Chinese population growth rate has slowed to less than 1.0 percent per year in recent years, according to the World Bank. Furthermore, major changes in labor force participation rates, largely due to more people leaving rural occupations and household/childcare activities, represent one-time changes rather than sustainable trends. In sum, these considerations suggest that Chinese economic growth will eventually moderate, which is consistent with the economic history for the Soviet Union, United States, and European Union presented in Exhibit 11-1.

Finally, in addition to these factors, an investment analyst might wish to consider other, more qualitative factors in producing a long-term growth forecast (e.g., China's educational system or pollution side effects of China's strategy of rapid capital formation). Because adjustments for such factors would typically have a large judgmental element, this chapter does not address them.

EXAMPLE 11-1 The Neoclassical Approach to Growth

1. The savings rate for a national economy is comparatively stable. The economy faces a sharp uptick in energy prices and at the same time imposes stringent restrictions on environmental pollution. The combined impact of energy and

[6]In lieu of higher consumption spending, particularly on imported goods.
[7]Preston (2009).
[8]Xin and Rabinovitch (2009).

environmental factors renders a large portion of the existing stock of manufacturing equipment and structures economically obsolescent. What is the impact on the economy according to Equation 11.3?

2. A country experiences a sharp demographic rise in the divorce rate and single-parent households. Using the framework of Equations 11.1 and 11.3, what is likely to happen to total national production, total per capita income, and total income per household?

Solution to 1: The sudden, unexpected obsolescence of a significant portion of the capital stock means that the percentage growth rate in capital stock in that period will be negative, that is, $\Delta K/K < 0$. All other things being equal, this implies a one-time reduction in economic output. Assuming no change in technological innovation, savings rates, and labor force growth trends, the subsequent long-term growth rates should be relatively close to the previously prevailing growth rates, starting from the lower base value for Y.

Solution to 2: The change in demographics implies an increase in the aggregate labor force as stay-at-home parents and spouses re-enter the workforce. That is, the labor force will grow, for some period of time, at a pace faster than underlying population growth until a new steady-state labor force participation rate is attained. Total economic production (and income) will thus also rise at an above-trend rate during this adjustment period. Above-trend growth in national income, holding population trends constant, means that per capita income will also grow above trend during this period of demographic adjustment. Per household income, by contrast, will grow at a below-trend rate (and may even decline) due to an uptick in new household formation during the shift in divorce and separation rates to ultimately prevailing steady-state levels.

2.3. Quantifying China's Future Economic Growth

Now that we have covered a simple model for estimating an economy's growth rate, the next step is to apply the model using our best estimates of the model inputs. As in any forecasting exercise, the specific forecasts must be based on currently available information. Any forecast has an "as of" date associated with it. Comparing the forecasts to actual outcomes subsequently, some inputs or elements of the forecast may appear to be misjudged or dated. With that caution in mind, we can proceed to develop our economic growth projections for China.

Zheng, Hu, and Bigsten (2009) offer the GDP growth projections presented in Exhibit 11-2 for China, the United States, and the European Union. The forecast of an 8 percent GDP growth rate for China is consistent with the Chinese government's 8 percent GDP growth target as presented by Premier Wen Jiabao. Zheng, Hu, and Bigsten note their own projections rely heavily on two basic assumptions: (1) growth in the capital stock cannot exceed GDP growth and (2) a TFP growth rate of 2 to 3 percent will prevail for the foreseeable future. These authors believe that the potential for China to absorb new technologies from developed nations is double that for the United States and European Union. Given the history of other developing countries and the record of economic recovery of developed countries after World War II, this does not seem unreasonable.

EXHIBIT 11-2 Growth Projections (2009–2030)

Country	Real GDP Growth, $\Delta Y/Y$	Growth in Total Factor Productivity, $\Delta A/A$	Output Elasticity of Capital, α	Growth in Capital Stock, $\Delta K/K$	Output Elasticity of Labor, $1-\alpha$	Growth in Labor Input, $\Delta L/L$
China	8.0%	2.5%	0.5	8.0%	0.5	3.0%
United States	2.75%	1.2%	0.3	4.0%	0.7	0.5%
European Union	2.2%	1.0%	0.4	3.0%	0.6	0.0%

Source: Zheng, Hu, and Bigsten (2009).

The neoclassical framework we have presented permits analysts to apply their own forecasts of factors of production and with particular emphasis on how such factor trajectories might change over time. Once the analyst has developed a long-term macro forecast, it can then be used in conjunction with traditional valuation models.

In applying the framework, we modify the Zheng, Hu, and Bigsten ("ZHB") projections by using a lower estimate of the growth rate in the labor force, since World Bank data indicate that population growth in China now appears to have declined to below 1.0 percent annually. At the same time, we are inclined to think that savings and investment rates will only decline gradually from over 35 percent of GDP, thereby keeping the growth rate of capital stock much higher than the 8 percent per annum assumed by ZHB. We have no disagreement with the ZHB projection of 2.5 percent per year for TFP growth. If we utilize the labor and capital elasticities from the ZHB study, a reasonable projection for economic growth would therefore be:

Total factor productivity	plus	Growth in capital stock	plus	Labor force growth		
2.5%	+	$0.5 \times 12\%$	+	$0.5 \times 1.5\%$	=	9.25%

This near-term rate is higher than the ZHB forecast, the official forecast of the Chinese government, and the consensus of many economic forecasters. We note, however, that there are several factors that are consistent with our higher near-term forecast. First, actual real growth has cumulatively exceeded the 8 percent Chinese official growth target of the past several years. Second, and more importantly, our forecast is to be thought of as a normalized forecast of sustainable cash flow growth potential.

While our near-term forecast for economic growth is higher than ZHB and the Chinese government, the reasoning set forth in the preceding section leads us to believe that economic growth will gradually decline to levels lower than the ZHB analysis.[9] This is because, as economies develop and as the stock of accumulated capital per person rises, savings rates tend to decline and TFP trends fall to levels closer to those of more highly developed countries. Finally, although labor force growth can exceed population growth for some time (as labor force participation rates increase), in the long run, labor force growth is constrained by

[9]Our forecast is for a 30-year time period and was made in the summer of 2009. As noted in Exhibit 11-2, the ZHB forecast was for 2009–2030. We believe the choice of a longer time horizon for our forecast is also supportive of the choice of a lower terminal growth rate.

population growth. China appears to be on its way toward zero population growth (much like Japan and Western Europe). With this in mind, an ultimately sustainable economic growth rate might be:

Total factor productivity	plus	Growth in capital stock	plus	Labor force growth		
1.25%	+	0.5 × 6%	+	0.5 × 0.0%	=	4.25%

2.4. Equity Market Valuation

In this section we translate macroeconomic forecasts into corporate cash flow forecasts and combine those corporate forecasts with an appropriate discounted cash flow model to estimate the intrinsic value of an equity market in terms of justified P/E ratios.

The growth rate of corporate earnings and dividend cash flow, adjusted for inflation, should bear a close relationship with real GDP growth over the long term. For purposes of this analysis, we assume that earnings and dividend cash flow for the underlying comprehensive stock composite grow at the same rate as the core growth rate of Chinese GDP.[10]

In theory, we would like to be able to forecast, year by year, each of the underlying factors of production and the change in TFP. In practice, however, we recognize that a less complicated cash flow representation might be more suitable, because it lessens the possibility of compounding forecast errors. Fuller and Hsia (1984) developed a valuation model, known as the **H-model**, in which dividend *growth rates* are expected to decline in a linear fashion, over a finite horizon, toward an ultimately sustainable rate from the end of that horizon into perpetuity. It incorporates a growth rate in dividends that is expected to prevail in the initial period g_S, a period of years, N, where the dividend growth rate declines in a linear fashion, and a long-term dividend growth rate g_L that is expected to prevail to perpetuity beginning at the end of period N. With an initial annualized dividend rate at time zero of D_0 and a discount rate to perpetuity of r, the H–model estimate of value, V_0, is given by Equation 11.4:

$$V_0 = \frac{D_0}{r - g_L}\left[(1 + g_L) + \frac{N}{2}(g_S - g_L)\right] \tag{11.4}$$

The H-model provides a convenient means for modeling initially high ("supernormal") dividend growth rates that gradually transition to a lower, long-run growth at a constant mature-stage growth rate. The H-model involves an approximation to the value estimate that would result from period-by-period discounting of cash flows in the phase prior to the mature or terminal phase when a constant growth rate is assumed. The approximation is generally very good in most practical situations and the gain from using an approximation is an easy to evaluate expression.[11] In the case of valuation of mature developed equity markets, the

[10] In principle, the sector of publicly traded companies could grow somewhat above or below the overall growth rate of GDP, because it is a subset of the overall economy. However, the approach used in the text should serve as a good approximation for analytical purposes.

[11] Valuation differences between the H-Model and a period-by-period approach should be minimal so long as the differences between long-term and interim growth rates are of single-digit magnitude and the "interim" period length is not much longer than 30–40 years. In any event, the possible valuation error from adopting a simpler model is reasonable in comparison with the incremental valuation error that can arise from introducing an excessive number of valuation parameters, i.e., year-by-year cash flows.

Gordon (constant) growth dividend discount model would be more commonly used than the H-model because supernormal growth would not generally need to be modeled in such cases.

In our valuation analysis, we express the discount rate and both growth factors in real, that is, inflation-adjusted terms. A key to valuation is consistency: stating variables consistently on a nominal basis or consistently on a real basis are both feasible approaches. Economists, however, typically prefer to use real variables as they tend to be more stable and, therefore, easier to predict than their nominal counterparts.

We use our growth rate trajectory and apply the H-model to the S&P China BMI Index. This index underlies the SPDR S&P China ETF, which is an exchange-traded fund designed to track the investment performance of the mainland China and (to a much lesser extent) Hong Kong stock markets. Both the underlying stocks and the ETF itself are avenues in which both Chinese and non-Chinese investors may obtain participation in the Chinese equity markets. The index underlying the ETF and the information provided by the ETF's sponsor (State Street Global Advisors) provide up-to-date information that can enter traditional valuation models.

In evaluating the investment attractiveness of a market index, we utilize a price–earnings ratio or P/E approach. Because of the behavioral factors mentioned in the introduction, prices of equities and equity market composites tend to vary more than underlying normalized earnings and growth prospects. P/E analysis permits us to make useful intertemporal valuation comparisons and has the additional benefit of providing intuition when making comparisons across international borders. As of 15 July 2009, the forward or prospective P/E ratio for the underlying S&P China BMI Index was 19.1 (this P/E is the level of the S&P China BMI Index divided by year-ahead expected earnings for that index). In the following analysis, we estimate what justified P/E ratios should be under differing inflation-adjusted equity discount rates and for different estimates of the ultimately prevailing terminal inflation-adjusted dividend growth rate to perpetuity.

The (forward) **justified P/E** is the estimated intrinsic value divided by year-ahead expected earnings; in this case we are estimating intrinsic value using the H-model. Reflecting the meaning of *justified* here as *warranted by fundamentals*, price in the justified P/E ratio is assumed in this discussion to equal intrinsic value as estimated by the valuation model, that is, P_0 (or P) = V_0.[12] In all instances, we assume that core inflation-adjusted growth rates decline in a linear fashion over a 30-year time horizon from the 9.25 percent per year we estimate for year one.[13] The 30-year time horizon is selected both because it is a round number and because it is not unlike other historical instances where national economies experienced fundamental changes in political and economic structure, the notable examples being post–World War II European economies and Japan both in the late nineteenth century and after World War II.

[12]Analysts and practitioners may, if desired, proceed directly to forecasting a justified market index *level* based on the H-Model, the current dividend rate, and the growth-factor inputs. (Strictly speaking, the H-Model does not directly utilize earnings per share, although, indirectly, the trajectory of dividend growth is assumed to be supported by growth in EPS.) Under our approach, the relative differences in P/E ratios in Exhibits 11-3 and 11-4 translate directly into the relative differences between observed and justified market levels.

[13]The geometric average growth rate during the 30-year period is around 6.7 percent. Also of interest, the *average* compound growth rate for the first 20 years is not far off from the ZHB 20-year 8 percent annual growth rate.

EXHIBIT 11-3 Justified P/E Ratios for Chinese Equity Market at Mid-Year 2009

Terminal Real Growth Rate	Real Equity Discount Rate 6.00%	6.50%	7.00%	7.50%	8.00%	8.50%	9.00%	9.50%
3%	26.8	23.0	20.1	17.9	16.1	14.6	13.4	12.4
4%	37.3	29.9	24.9	21.3	18.7	16.6	14.9	13.6
5%	69.0	46.0	34.5	27.6	23.0	19.7	17.2	15.3

EXHIBIT 11-4 Justified Chinese Equity Market Valuation Multiples

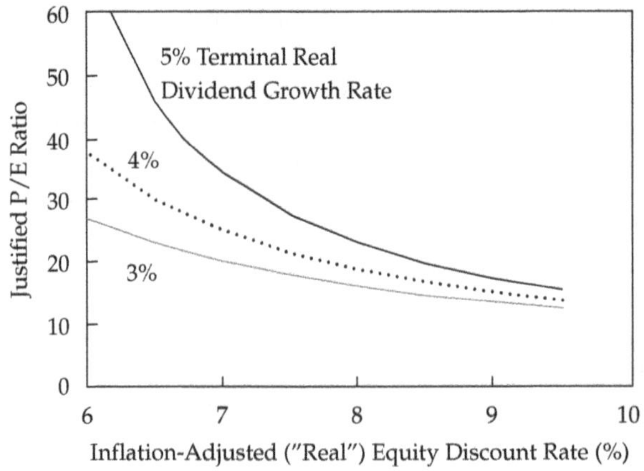

Note: Chinese equity markets justified P/Es: 30-year transition from 9.25 percent real dividend growth rate to various terminal growth rates to perpetuity.

In Exhibit 11-3 and Exhibit 11-4, we have presented justified P/E ratios. Interpolating visually, the observed 19.1 P/E ratio on 15 July 2009, assuming a terminal 4.25 percent real dividend growth rate to perpetuity, is consistent with a real equity discount rate just under 8.0 percent.

This leads immediately to the question of what the proper discount rate should be. To answer this we would like to know a little bit about both the volatility of Chinese equity prices and how such return/volatility prospects compare with other world equity markets.

In Exhibit 11-5, we present cumulative return data for both the S&P China BMI Index and the S&P 500. The data series commence in 2001, the point at which the China BMI Index data are first available, and a point by which mainland Chinese equity markets had become seasoned and widely accessible to non-Chinese investors.[14]

[14]To check the reasonableness of the data, we computed the cumulative total returns for the Morgan Stanley Capital International (MSCI) China Index and found them in good accord with the S&P China BMI Index.

EXHIBIT 11-5 Cumulative Performance Comparison for Chinese and U.S. Stock Markets (in RMB for China, USD for S&P 500)

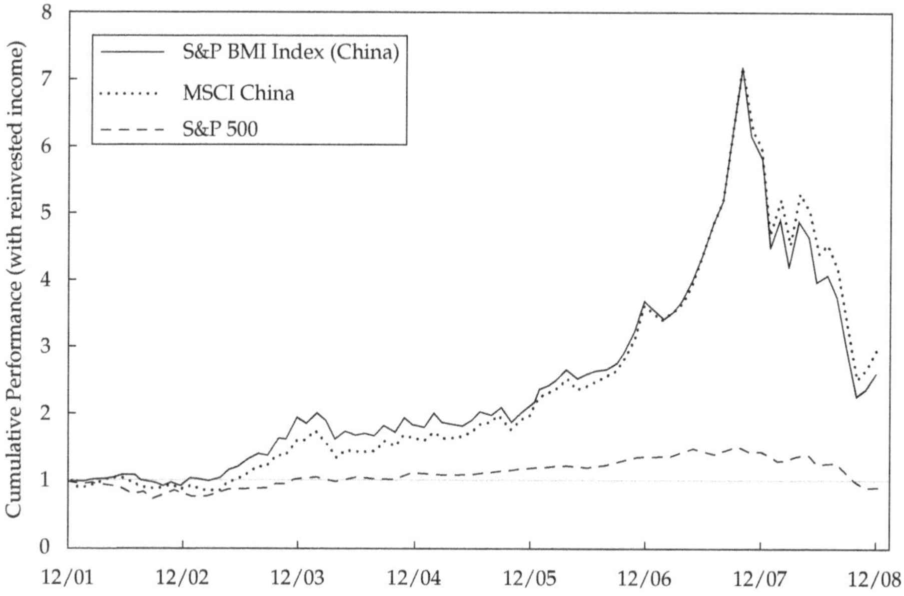

Sources for data: Standard & Poor's, Morgan Stanley.

Over the seven-year period, the cumulative return of Chinese equities far outpaced those of the United States. However, Chinese markets also experienced more of a bubble and subsequent collapse, resulting in a much higher volatility of returns. For China, the annualized return over this time frame approached an inflation-adjusted 13 percent. This outpaced the return one would have expected even from coupling a 2 to 2.5 percent dividend yield with an aggressive core dividend real growth rate of 9 percent. The cumulative return benefited from a positive shift in P/E ratios between the beginning and end of the measurement period. In fact, the P/E expansion and subsequent contraction appear to be the chief cause of the 2007 Chinese bubble and the following collapse.

By comparison, the equity markets in the United States were much less volatile, although the cumulative return, particularly net of inflation, was negative. Assuming a 6 percent inflation-adjusted discount rate for the U.S. equity market (in line with long-term historical realized returns), the cumulative nominal return—incorporating the 2.6 percent average inflation rate—would have resulted in an ending cumulative return index value of around 1.80 in December 2008 (compared with the 2.61 achieved by the S&P China BMI Index). The explanation for the poor performance by U.S. equities was largely attributable to a contraction from the high normalized P/E valuation relationships prevailing in 2001 to the below-average levels at the end of the period. Additional evidence is presented in Exhibit 11-6.

In establishing a reasonable discount rate to apply to our cash flow forecasts, we should take into account the higher volatility of Chinese markets, which has arisen in part because of structural macroeconomic instabilities (discussed previously) and the evolution of their legal and regulatory systems.

EXHIBIT 11-6 Return and Volatility Data, 31 December 2001–31 December 2008

	S&P China BMI	MSCI China	S&P 500
Annualized nominal total return (1)	14.7%	16.6%	–1.5%
Annualized standard deviation of total returns (2)	29.4%	29.4%	14.3%
Annualized inflation rate (3)	3.7%	3.7%	2.6%

(1) In RMB for Chinese composites, USD for S&P 500
(2) Based on monthly observations
(3) Data through 2007 reflects changes in GDP deflator
Sources for data: Standard & Poor's, Morgan Stanley, Bloomberg, World Bank.

The higher observed volatility also has arisen from behavioral shifts in P/E relationships that are more pronounced than those usually seen in U.S. and European markets. Such valuation-induced price volatility is not unusual for any market that is new by historical standards and has been experienced in the past by U.S., European, and Japanese markets in their own long paths to economic maturity. Furthermore, because the bulk of mainland equities are still 75 percent owned (directly or indirectly) by the mainland Chinese government, there is an overhanging risk of intervention or divestiture that might be occasioned by noneconomic motives. However, the possibility of denationalization, such as carried out by the United Kingdom in the 1980s, might be viewed more as a market opportunity than as a risk.

The effect of higher volatility on required returns might be somewhat mitigated to the extent (1) market returns are less than perfectly correlated with other international equity markets and (2) cross-border investing and divesting of equities is freely achievable by investors both inside and outside of China.

On balance, the foregoing factors suggest that the required real equity discount rate be higher in China than, for example, in the United States. This naturally leads us to investigate both what the realized real equity discount rate has been in the United States and what real equity discount rates are predicted based on alternative theoretical models. Historical studies have been undertaken[15] which indicate that a prospective inflation-adjusted equity discount rate[16] in the area of 5–7 percent is reasonable. Work based on macroeconomic, corporate finance, and financial market equilibrium[17] suggests that a slightly higher range might be possible in equilibrium. Purely theoretical models have had mixed results. The utility function models,[18] for example, find that real discount rates in the 5–7 percent area are well above what can be justified by underlying market volatility. On the other hand, a theoretical approach[19] simply based on prospective wealth accumulation under different volatility assumptions is consistent with the results actually realized in the U.S. historical record.

In the volatile economic and market conditions at the time (2009) this chapter is being written, the higher end of the discount rate estimates seem to be in order for the United States. If we place these at 6–7 percent, the additional relative risk considerations for the Chinese market suggest that a required discount rate for that market might be in the range of

[15]Ibbotson and Sinquefield (1989), Siegel (1992), Arnott and Bernstein (2002), Siegel (2005).
[16]Geometrically compounded.
[17]Ibbotson, Diermeier, and Siegel (1984), Stimes (2008).
[18]Mehra and Prescott (1985), Mehra (2003).
[19]Arnott (2004).

7.5–8.5 percent. This is a necessarily judgmental adjustment but should (1) reflect an analyst's view of differential riskiness (in the context of a well-diversified international portfolio) and (2) reflect congruence with historical realized return differentials between markets that were then seasoned and those that were then developing.

Referring back to Exhibit 11-4 and integrating our view of the real (i.e., inflation-adjusted) equity discount rate with the sustainable dividend growth rates obtained from our macroeconomic framework, we can conclude that the currently observed 19.1 forward P/E ratio for Chinese equities is not unreasonable. As a further check, we note that a 19.1 P/E would be somewhat on the high side for seasoned U.S. and European stock markets. However, reflecting much higher growth prospects over the next several decades, a much higher Chinese P/E ratio would be warranted (although the impact would be somewhat offset by a greater discount rate reflecting higher volatility in China) as compared with U.S. and European markets.

Inherent in our analysis of equity composites is the difficulty of specifying precise price or P/E ratios at which a "buy" or "sell" recommendation is to be made. However, the strength of this kind of relative value approach is that, in a diversified portfolio context, investors can usually make reasonable decisions—at the margin—whether it is then appropriate to raise or lower market exposures relative to the investable universe in the aggregate. The price/value relationships prevailing at the date of the analysis were such that those investing on a fundamental basis should have a weighting in Chinese equities close to their baseline or normal-strategy allocation.[20] Stated differently, only those with a very optimistic long-term dividend growth rate forecast and/or a low required discount rate would find the Chinese market to have substantially better than average current attractiveness.

EXAMPLE 11-2 Equity Market Valuation Using Dividend Discount Models

1. The S&P China BMI Index on 30 September 2009 is 358. Forecasted 12-month earnings per share for the composite are 18.00 RMB and the current annual dividend rate for the composite is 7.90 RMB. Assuming an 8.0 percent inflation-adjusted equity discount rate, a thirty-year decline in dividend growth rates from an initial growth rate of 8.25 percent, and a terminal sustainable growth rate to perpetuity of 4.25 percent, compute the composite index price level implied by the H-Model (Equation 11.4). Next compute the justified P/E ratio implied by such price level.
2. Assuming the same annualized dividend rate of 7.90 RMB, using the Gordon growth model compute the discount rate required to reproduce the prevailing index level of 358 under different growth assumptions, specifically assuming an 8 percent real growth rate of dividends to perpetuity, rather than a gradually slackening rate of growth as in Question 1. Evaluate the result.
3. Assuming the same information in Question 1, what would be the appropriate composite index price level and justified P/E ratio, if the period at which the 4.25 percent growth rate to perpetuity is reached (a) at year 20, (b) at year 40?

[20] Which could, of course, be zero.

Solution to 1: The H-Model states that:

$$V_0 = \frac{D_0}{r - g_L}\left[(1 + g_L) + \frac{N}{2}(g_S - g_L)\right]$$

Inserting the information given, we get

$$V_0 = \frac{7.90}{0.08 - 0.0425}\left[(1 + 0.0425) + \frac{30}{2}(0.0825 - 0.0425)\right] = 346.02$$

Dividing this result by forecasted earnings of 18.00 produces a justified P/E ratio of 19.2.

Solution to 2: The standard Gordon growth model states that:

$$V_0 = \frac{D_0(1 + g)}{r - g}$$

which can be rearranged as

$$r = \frac{D_0(1 + g)}{V_0} + g$$

Substituting in the given values, we obtain:

$$r = \frac{7.90(1 + 0.08)}{358} + 0.08 = 0.1038 \approx 10.4\%$$

This result, which assumes no slackening in core growth rates, produces an implied discount rate that appears unusually large relative to the prospects of other world equity markets. Given the ability of international portfolio reallocation, even on a constrained basis, capital market equilibrium does not seem consistent with a real equity discount to perpetuity rate almost twice that of mature equity markets. The implication is that Chinese market participants are pricing the index at a lower discount rate, consistent with other worldwide investment opportunities, but also with a more restrained long-term growth outlook relative to those growth rates expected over the next few years.

Solution to 3:
Assuming an interim period of 20 years, Equation 11.4 produces:

$$V_0 = \frac{7.90}{0.08 - 0.0425}\left[(1 + 0.0425) + \frac{20}{2}(0.0825 - 0.0425)\right] = 303.89$$

and a P/E = 303.89 ÷ 18 = 16.9.
Assuming an interim period of 40 years, Equation 11.4 produces:

$$V_0 = \frac{7.90}{0.08 - 0.0425}\left[(1 + 0.0425) + \frac{40}{2}(0.0825 - 0.0425)\right] = 388.15$$

and a justified P/E = 388.15 ÷ 18 = 21.6.

The possible criticisms of our approach should not be overlooked. From a practical perspective, there may be severe problems with the accuracy of data inputs. It is difficult enough to obtain macroeconomic data in developed countries with long-established methods and facilities. In developing markets or in economies experiencing profound governmental and structural change, such as the Eastern Bloc after the fall of the Berlin Wall, the problems of obtaining accurate and, more importantly, historically consistent, data are multiplied. The same fluidity in political and demographic fundamentals also calls into question whether companies' growth rates will track GDP growth rates. In certain instances, there can be long departures between growth rates, meaning that for long periods of time the share of corporate profits may be rising or declining relative to GDP.

The analysis in this chapter has also focused on inflation-adjusted income, cash flow, and discount rates. In a global economy with reasonably robust currency exchange markets and where monetary growth is targeted to keep inflation at manageable levels, this is probably appropriate. However, hyperinflation, currency instability, and other trade disequilibria have occurred far too frequently from a historical perspective to be overlooked. In the presence of such factors, the confidence of our model's approach could be diminished.

EXAMPLE 11-3 Applying Valuation Methodology to a Developed Economy

In the following, assume that all growth and discount rates are stated in real terms.

1. Assume the Eurozone inflation-adjusted average growth in capital stock is 3.0 percent per annum into perpetuity. Long-term labor force growth is expected to remain stable at 0.0 percent, while TFP growth is projected to average 1.0 percent per annum over time. If the output elasticity of capital is 0.4 and the output elasticity of labor is 0.6, calculate the implied growth rate of Eurozone GDP.
2. The Dow Jones Euro Stoxx 50 Index is comprised of mature, large capital common equities domiciled in the Euro currency zone. At 30 September 2009 the index level stood at 2450. Forecasted 12-month dividends per share for the composite (net of withholding tax) are €125.00. Because of the mature nature of the economy and the particular market composite, you project that growth in both inflation-adjusted earnings and dividends will equal that of GDP. Using the Gordon constant dividend growth rate model solved for the discount rate, estimate the implied inflation-adjusted discount rate to perpetuity.
3. A. Applying the Gordon growth model to value the DJ Euro Stoxx 50 Index, you assume that the appropriate discount rate to perpetuity should be 6.0 percent. If this assumption is correct, what is the fair value of the DJ Euro Stoxx 50 Index?
   B. As of the end of September 2009, the DJ Euro Stoxx 50 Index was trading almost 30 percent below its high of twelve months earlier. What is the likely major cause for the price decline?

Solution to 1: In the context of Equation 11.1 from the text, total growth in GDP is:

$$\frac{\Delta Y}{Y} \approx \frac{\Delta A}{A} + \alpha\frac{\Delta K}{K} + (1-\alpha)\frac{\Delta L}{L}$$

Substituting the information given, the GDP growth rate is 2.2 percent computed as follows:

$$\frac{\Delta Y}{Y} \approx 1.0\% + 0.4 \times 3.0\% + 0.6 \times 0.0\% = 2.2\%$$

Solution to 2: The Gordon growth model can be rearranged as

$$r = \frac{D_1}{P_0} + g$$

Substituting in the given values for dividends, the index level, and our forecast for dividend growth, we obtain:

$$r = \frac{125}{2450} + 0.022 = 0.051 + 0.022 = 0.073 = 7.3\%$$

Solution to 3.A: The constant growth model gives us the following estimate of the fair value of the DJ Euro Stoxx 50:

$$V_0 = \frac{D_1}{r-g} = \frac{125}{0.06-0.022} = 3,289$$

This estimate is more than 34 percent above the level observed at 30 September 2009.

Solution to 3.B: Given the mature nature of the underlying economic region and the companies in the composite, it is unlikely that the estimate of long-term, real dividend growth changed much, if at all. If the actual dividends paid also did not change much, the most likely major cause of the price decline is an increase in the discount rate over the period.

3. TOP-DOWN AND BOTTOM-UP FORECASTING

When it comes to predicting equity returns, analytical approaches can be divided into two major categories: top-down and bottom-up. In top-down forecasting, analysts use *macroeconomic* projections to produce return expectations for large stock market composites, such as the S&P 500, the Nikkei 225, or the FTSE 100. These can then be further refined into return expectations for various market sectors and industry groups within the composites. At the final stage, such information can, if desired, be distilled into projected returns for individual securities.

By contrast, bottom-up forecasting begins with the *microeconomic* outlook for the fundamentals of individual companies. An analyst can use this information to develop predicted investment returns for each security. If desired, the forecasts for individual security returns can be aggregated into expected returns for industry groupings, market sectors, and for the equity market as a whole.

Exhibit 11-7 sets forth the manner in which top-down and bottom-up approaches are typically implemented. Top-down can be characterized as moving from the general to the specific, while bottom-up forecasting moves from the specific to the general. Depending on the investment strategy and portfolio context, one of the types of forecasting may be more suitable. In other instances, both types of forecasting may be useful. In those cases where both top-down and bottom-up are used, the additional work involved may provide valuable insights.

EXHIBIT 11-7 Comparison of Top-Down and Bottom-Up Analysis

Top-Down Analysis

- Market analysis: Examine valuations in different equity markets to identify those with superior expected returns.
  - Compare relative value measures for each equity market to their historical values to identify those markets where equities are relatively cheap or expensive.
  - Examine the trends in relative value measures for each equity market to identify market momentum.
  - Compare the expected returns for those equity markets expected to provide superior performance to the expected returns for other asset classes, such as bonds, real estate, and commodities.
- Industry analysis: Evaluate domestic and global economic cycles to determine those industries expected to be top performers in the best-performing equity markets.
  - Compare relative growth rates and expected profit margins across industries.
  - Identify those industries that will be favorably impacted by expected trends in interest rates, exchange rates, and inflation.
- Company analysis: Identify the best stocks in those industries that are expected to be top performers in the best-performing equity markets.

Bottom-Up Analysis

- Company analysis: Identify a rationale for why certain stocks should be expected to outperform, without regard to the prevailing macroeconomic conditions.
  - Identify reasons why a company's products, technology, or services should be expected to be successful.
  - Evaluate the company's management, history, business model, and growth prospects.
  - Use discounted cash flow models to determine expected returns for individual securities.
- Industry analysis: Aggregate expected returns for stocks within an industry to identify the industries that are expected to be the best performers.
- Market analysis: Aggregate expected industry returns to identify the expected returns for every equity market.

3.1. Portfolio Suitability of Each Forecasting Type

In theory and practice, it is not necessary for either top-down or bottom-up forecasting to be carried to the final step shown for each method in Exhibit 11-7. For example, if a portfolio focuses primarily on tactical asset allocation among different market composites (and/or different industry groups within such composites), a top-down forecast may not need to focus all the way down to the relative merits of individual securities.

Likewise, there are instances where either the investment strategy or specific portfolio constraints dictate a focus primarily on individual security returns. In such instances, the unique factors pertaining to particular securities may render the need to study industry and market composite unnecessary. In such cases, the bottom-up method stops well short of the top. The partial application of each method is developed in the following examples.

EXAMPLE 11-4 Growth Model Questions

Explain whether top-down or bottom-up forecasting is more appropriate for each of the different investors.

1. The MegaCosmos Mutual Fund has a stated goal of investing in the stock market composites of developed country economies in North America, Western Europe, and Japan. Its return target is expressed in euros. The fund may or may not hedge individual country currency returns depending on its outlook for foreign exchange rates. Furthermore, the fund attempts to track individual country stock market composites while minimizing tracking error via the use of index baskets wherever possible.
2. EMF Advisers is a boutique firm that manages a dedicated portfolio of electric, gas, and water utility companies domiciled in the United States. The portfolio EMF oversees is, in turn, a small part of the American Pipefitters Union Pension Plan.
3. Bocage International is a hedge fund that actively bets on the relative attractiveness of stocks, interest rates, currencies, and commodities. Its investment in equities is limited to futures and options on exchange-traded equity indexes.
4. Alpha Bet Partnership is an investment vehicle featuring a U.S. long/short overlay. Specifically, the partnership may keep short positions in U.S. equities in an amount not to exceed 30 percent of the net value of the partnership. All short positions must be invested in U.S. equities to maintain an overall beta of 1.0. The partnership hopes for the stocks it owns to outperform the stocks it has sold short in order to generate a respectable alpha. The partnership specifies that with the objective of minimizing tracking error, every stock sold short must be matched by a stock bought in the same industry.

Solution to 1: MegaCosmos' ability to carry out its strategy will depend on its ability to forecast economic factors at a very "macro" scale. It would employ a top-down approach involving an examination of the economic strength of different international economies, different fiscal and tax policies among the governments involved, and international trade patterns and currency flows. MegaCosmos' desire to track underlying national markets quite closely means that its holdings will not diverge materially from the particular market composites selected. Individual security selection will not be much of a focus, thereby minimizing the need for continuing the top-down analysis as low as individual market sectors, industry groups, or securities.

Solution to 2: EMF Advisers' ability to carry out its strategy will depend on its ability to select among different securities within the very specific niche to which it has been assigned by the pension plan sponsor. As a result, bottom-up forecasting is most appropriate and probably no higher than the industry level in any great detail. The plan sponsor, however, will need to be concerned with top-down forecasting to determine the appropriate allocation to EMF's strategy.

Solution to 3: Bocage's situation is very similar to that of MegaCosmos in Question 1 and top-down forecasting is thus appropriate. In Bocage's case, exposure to individual stocks is not permitted so the analysis need not be carried down to the level of industry groups or market sectors.

Solution to 4: There are two parts to the answer for Alpha Bet. Because the underlying beta is targeted at 1.0, this portion of the strategy can be considered passive and very little or no top-down forecasting is required. In contrast, the remaining portion of the strategy, the long/short overlay, involves pure security selection on a "matched" or "paired trades" basis. Within each long/short combination, aggregate factors (global, market, industry) cancel each other out, because both long and short candidates must be matched to the same country, market, and industry. Only specific factors affecting each of the two paired companies matter. Therefore, a bottom-up forecast is necessary—and one that likely does not need to go above the level of individual securities.

3.2. Using Both Forecasting Types

When engaged in fundamental securities analysis, it can be wise to use both top-down and bottom-up forecasting. However, when we use both approaches, we often find ourselves in the situation of the person with two clocks, each displaying a different time. They may both be wrong, but they cannot both be right!

It is frequently the case that top-down and bottom-up forecasts provide significantly different results. In such instances, the analyst should investigate the underlying data, assumptions, and forecast methods before employing them as a basis for investment decisions. After all, if forecasts cannot be consistent with each other, at least one of them cannot be consistent with underlying reality.

Because we are fallible human beings, most forecasting discrepancies arise from our own limited knowledge, errors, and incomplete assumptions. Reconciling top-down and bottom-up forecasts is therefore a discipline that can help prevent us from taking inappropriate investment actions. In other words, most of the time, the aggregate market consensus will tend to be more accurate than the individual forecasts that comprise the consensus. The reconciling and revision process is therefore useful in helping us better understand the market consensus.

However, in rare and significant instances, we will find that carefully retracing the steps reveals a gap between the two forecast types that gives rise to significant market opportunities. In such instances, the process of reconciling the two types of forecasts creates instances where we differ significantly and correctly from the consensus.

Recent years have provided major examples of this. In the early 2000s, top-down forecasts provided much more subdued outlooks compared to bottom-up projections for corporate profits, both in the aggregate and for particular industries. In the tech area, both consumer and capital spending on computer equipment were below the projected sales growth that companies, and analysts following them, were individually expecting. After all, individual companies were optimistic about their own prospects. However, in the aggregate, many of their technologies and products competed with each other. Thus, the success of some companies meant the failure of others and this natural, competitive offsetting tendency was correctly reflected in aggregate, top-down sales growth for the industry.

Aggregating the bottom-up forecasts of individual companies, however, produced a wildly inflated forecast of both sales quantities and average prices and profit margins. Thus, the high-tech "bubble" originated from the mistaken principle that *all* the companies could be above average. For those who recognized the inconsistency of the top-down and bottom-up forecasts, and the accuracy of the top-down forecast, much of the carnage of the bubble collapse was avoided.

More recently, the collapse of equity markets in developed countries was a case where bottom-up forecasts proved their superiority over top-down approaches. In both the United States and the United Kingdom, some banking and real estate analysts perceived the excesses in residential real estate in a microeconomic sense. Those who pushed their analyses to a macro conclusion realized that certain large financial institutions were imperiled, particularly the highly-levered Fannie Mae and Freddie Mac in the United States. Those who understood the pressure on these and other large financial institutions correctly foresaw that then-prevailing worldwide forecasts of economic activity and equity market returns were dramatically overstated.

3.3. Top-Down and Bottom-Up Forecasting of Market Earnings per Share

Two different methods are employed when estimating earnings for a market index, such as the S&P 500 Index. The first is to add up the individual estimates of the companies in the index. This is referred to as the bottom-up earnings estimate. The top-down estimate relies on forecasts for various macroeconomic variables and a model that fits these forecasts to past trends in aggregate earnings.

EXAMPLE 11-5 Comparing and Evaluating Top-Down and Bottom-Up Forecasts

Standard and Poor's' July 2009 top-down and bottom-up forecasts for operating earnings per share appear in Exhibit 11-8. Note that the bottom-up forecasts are more optimistic than the top-down forecasts.

The bottom-up projection starts from a June 2009 level of earnings that is some 27 percent above the top-down estimate. Furthermore, the annualized growth of estimated earnings over the subsequent 18 months is 28.1 percent for the bottom-up forecast and a much lower 8.6 percent for the top-down projection.

EXHIBIT 11-8 Standard and Poor's Forecasts: July 2009

Quarter Ending	Operating Earnings per Share (estimates are bottom up)	Operating Earnings per Share (estimates are top down)	Difference
31 Dec 2010	$20.39	$12.50	$7.89
30 Sep 2010	19.11	11.42	7.69
30 Jun 2010	18.00	11.18	6.82
31 Mar 2010	16.59	10.86	5.73
31 Dec 2009	16.25	11.72	4.53
30 Sep 2009	15.05	11.68	3.37
30 Jun 2009	14.06	11.05	3.01

There are several possible reasons for the forecast discrepancies. First, the bottom-up estimates may be influenced by managers believing that their own company's earnings prospects are better than that for the economy as a whole.[21] This is simple human nature as confirmed by survey results, which consistently report that 85 percent of all drivers think they are better than average.

Alternatively, the bottom-up estimates may be correctly detecting signs of a cyclical economic and profit upturn. Most top-down models are of the econometric type and rely on historical relationships to be the basis for assumptions about the future. Thus, top-down models can be slow in detecting cyclical turns. This would be particularly true if the current statistical relationships between economic variables deviate significantly from their historic norms.

In short, the data indicate that we need to investigate both forecasts in greater detail. Without further analysis, we might be unable to distinguish whether the S&P 500 composite is overvalued, undervalued, or somewhere in between due to the disparity in the two earnings forecasts.

EXAMPLE 11-6 Earnings Forecast Revisions

The information in Exhibit 11-9 was collected from the Standard and Poor's web site. Note that actual Q2 2008 EPS for the S&P 500 was $17.02. The percentages for the S&P 500 represent how much Q2 2009 EPS were expected to change from the Q2

[21]For company EPS estimates, Darrough and Russell (2002) showed bottom-up forecasts are systematically more optimistic than top-down forecasts. The authors contend this occurs because analysts rely heavily on management's assessment of future profitability and such estimates often are overly optimistic.

2008 amount of \$17.02 on a particular forecast date. For example, the estimate for Q2 2009 EPS on 30 September 2008 was that the year-over-year change would be an increase of 49.47 percent:

$$\$17.02(1 + 0.4947) \approx \$25.44$$

On 30 June 2009, the estimate for Q2 2009 EPS was that the year-over-year change would be a decrease of 17.38 percent:

$$\$17.02(1 - 0.1738) \approx \$14.06$$

Similarly, the percentages for the various industry sectors noted in Exhibit 11-9 reflect how much Q2 2009 EPS were expected to change from the Q2 2008 amount on a particular forecast date. Exhibit 11-9 shows that earnings forecast revisions can be significant.

EXHIBIT 11-9 Revisions to Bottom-Up Estimates of Operating Earnings per Share, Standard and Poor's Forecasts–July 2009

Q2 Estimates	9/30/2008	12/31/2008	3/30/2009	6/30/2009	7/7/2009
S&P 500	49.47%	17.04%	–12.82%	–17.38%	–17.42%
Consumer Discretionary	134.52%	72.02%	–40.30%	36.61%	36.61%
Consumer Staples	14.52%	12.88%	6.83%	2.96%	4.12%
Energy	16.91%	–17.06%	–43.35%	–65.11%	–65.11%
Financials	691.43%	450.48%	289.93%	297.10%	293.35%
Health Care	13.56%	10.41%	4.51%	3.06%	3.06%
Industrials	1.17%	–14.07%	–34.53%	–42.89%	–42.89%
Information Technology	24.12%	–5.04%	–28.02%	–26.31%	–26.31%
Materials	9.30%	–26.85%	–51.13%	–69.52%	–69.52%
Telecommunication Services	26.22%	6.67%	–9.77%	–5.64%	–5.44%
Utilities	14.61%	8.99%	–1.10%	–4.80%	–4.80%
S&P 500 EPS	\$25.44	\$19.92	\$14.84	\$14.06	\$14.06

EXAMPLE 11-7 Bottom-Up and Top-Down Market EPS Forecasts

What considerations might encourage a market analyst to rely more on a top-down or bottom-up forecast of S&P 500 operating earnings?

Solution: Bottom-up forecasts are based on consensus earnings estimates from equity research analysts covering the S&P 500 stocks. Top-down estimates are often based on econometric methods rather than fundamental analysis of the companies comprising the index.

Analysts frequently wait for information from the companies they follow to change their forecasts. Thus, bottom-up estimates may be more optimistic than top-down heading into a recession, and more pessimistic than top-down coming out. If the belief exists that companies are reacting slowly to changes in economic conditions, then a market analyst may prefer a top-down forecast.

However, top-down earnings forecasting models also have limitations. Most such models rely on the extrapolation of past trends in economic data. As a result, the impact of a significant contemporaneous change in a key economic variable or variables on the stock market may not be accurately predicted by the model. If the belief exists that the economy is on the brink of a significant change, then a market analyst may prefer the bottom-up forecast.

4. RELATIVE VALUE MODELS

Relative value investing is consistent with the popular trading maxim that investors should buy what is cheap and sell what is expensive. The relative value models presented in this section can be used to support the tactical asset allocation decision. They can help to identify times when investors would be well served switching from bonds to stocks, or vice-versa. As an investor, it is important to focus on the markets in a comparative fashion.

4.1. Earnings-Based Models

In its 22 July 1997 Humphrey-Hawkins report to Congress, the United States Federal Reserve compared 1982–1997 10-year Treasury note yields to the earnings yield of the S&P 500 and showed a very close correlation between the two. The **Fed model**, so named by Edward Yardeni of (at the time) Prudential Securities, was based primarily on the results of this report. However, use of the term "Fed model" is somewhat misleading, as the model has never been formally adopted by the Federal Reserve as a policy-making tool.

The Fed model is a theory of equity valuation that hypothesizes that the yield on long-term U.S. Treasury securities (usually defined as the 10-year T-note yield) should be equal to the S&P 500 earnings yield (usually defined as forward operating earnings divided by the index level) in equilibrium. Differences in these yields identify an overpriced or underpriced equity market. The model predicts:

- U.S. stocks are undervalued if the forward earnings yield on the S&P 500 is greater than the yield on U.S. Treasury bonds.
- U.S. stocks are overvalued if the forward earnings yield on the S&P 500 is less than the yield on U.S. Treasury bonds.

For example, if the S&P 500 forward earnings yield is 5 percent and the 10-year T-note yield is 4.5 percent, stocks would be considered undervalued according to the Fed model.

EXAMPLE 11-8 Fed Model with U.S. Data

The difference between the S&P 500 earnings yield (based on forward operating earnings estimates) and the 10-year T-note yield for the time period January 1979 through December 2008 is presented in Exhibit 11-10.

The Fed model predicts that investors will be indifferent between investing in equities and investing in government bonds when the difference between the two yields is zero. Note that the average difference between the two yields was 0.70 percent during this time period. The positive difference between the two yields was at its greatest in December 2008. Thus, the model predicted that equities were significantly undervalued at that time, following the stock market sell-off during the second half of 2008. Similarly, the largest negative differences occurred prior to the collapse of the stock market bubbles in October 1987 and early 2000.

EXHIBIT 11-10 The Fed Model: Difference between the S&P 500 Forward Earnings Yield and Yield on 10-Year T-Note, Monthly Data: January 1979–December 2008

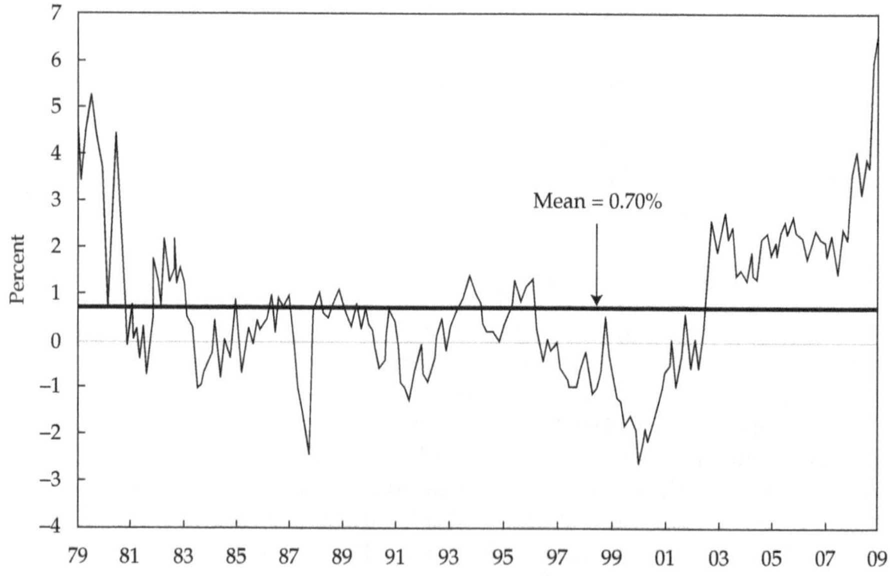

Source for data: www.yardeni.com.

The key criticism of the Fed model is that it ignores the equity risk premium. (Informally, the **equity risk premium** is the compensation demanded by investors for the greater risk of investing in equities compared to investing in default-risk-free debt.) The validity of this criticism is apparent if one understands the assumptions necessary to derive the Fed model from the Gordon growth model. Equation 11.5 presents the Gordon growth model where V_0 is intrinsic value, D_1 is the dividend per share to be received one-year from today, r is the required return, and the constant annual dividend growth rate is g.

$$V_0 = \frac{D_1}{r - g} \tag{11.5}$$

Assuming markets correctly set price, P_0, equal to intrinsic value, then $P_0 = V_0$. The expected dividend, D_1, can be determined as the payout ratio, p, times expected earnings, E_1. Sustainable growth, g, can be estimated as return on equity, ROE, times the earnings retention rate, $(1 - p)$.

Substituting $D_1 = pE_1$ and $g = \text{ROE}(1 - p)$ into Equation 11.5 and noting that $P_0 = V_0$ we are able to derive Equation 11.6. Equation 11.6 provides a Gordon growth model estimate for the forward earnings yield, E_1/P_0.

$$\frac{E_1}{P_0} = \frac{r - \text{ROE}(1 - p)}{p} \tag{11.6}$$

The Fed model hypothesizes that the earnings yield, E_1/P_0, and the yield on Treasury bonds, y_T, are equal in equilibrium. One way to produce this equilibrium using Equation 11.6 is to assume that the required return, r, and the return on equity, ROE, are equal to the Treasury bond yield, y_T. Making these substitutions in Equation 11.6 shows this result:

$$\frac{E_1}{P_0} = \frac{r - \text{ROE}(1 - p)}{p} = \frac{y_T - y_T(1 - p)}{p} = y_T \tag{11.7}$$

Thus, implicit in the Fed model equilibrium are the assumptions that the required return, r, and the accounting rate of return on equity, ROE, for risky equity securities are equal to the Treasury bond yield, y_T. Historical evidence and financial theory resoundingly reject the notion that either assumption is true. For example, the long-run average return on U.S. equities has exceeded the long-run average return on T-bonds by a significant amount.[22] Because of this, many analysts consider the Fed model flawed.

Two additional criticisms of the Fed model are that they ignore inflation and earnings growth opportunities. Asness (2003) criticized the Fed model because it compares an arguably real variable, the earnings yield, to a nominal variable, the T-bond yield. According to this argument, the earnings yield is real because it is a ratio of current period prices.[23] The T-bond yield is nominal because it is reflective of the expected rate of inflation as first noted by Fisher (1930). In the presence of inflation, investors should compare the earnings yield with a real interest rate. Asness provides evidence that the Fed model has often been a poor predictor of future equity returns.

Another criticism of the Fed model is that it ignores any earnings growth opportunities available to equity holders beyond those forecasted for the next year (as reflected by expected earnings, E_1). In the United States, long-term compound average earnings growth has been

[22]Bodie, Kane, and Marcus (2007) show that the geometric average annual return on U.S. large capitalization stocks was 10.23 percent over the 1926 to 2003 time period. The geometric average annual return on long-term Treasury bonds was 5.10 percent during this same time period.

[23]Wilcox (2007) and Palkar and Wilcox (2009) note that accounting and debt adjustments must be made to GAAP-based reported earnings before they can be considered real.

3–4 percent nominal and 1–2 percent real.[24] Thus, the model ignores a significant portion of total equity return.[25]

In spite of the several criticisms, the Fed model still can provide some useful insights. It does suggest that equities become more attractive as an asset class when interest rates decline. This is consistent with the predictions of any discounted cash flow model and is supported by market evidence. In practice, the model typically makes use of expected earnings (a future cash flow) as an input, which is again consistent with traditional discounted cash flow analysis.

Some analysts find a comparison of the earnings yield and Treasury bond yield to be most useful when the relationship is toward the extremes of its typical range. For example, some analysts compare the current difference between the earnings yield and the Treasury bond yield with the historical average difference. Stocks are viewed as more attractive as an investment when the current period difference significantly exceeds the historical average difference.

EXAMPLE 11-9 Fed Model with U.K. Data

The Fed model can be applied to the valuation of non-U.S. equity markets. In early 2009, the Fed model produced a very bullish prediction for British stocks. The forecasted earnings yield on the FTSE 100 was 10.1 percent and the yield on 10-year U.K. government debt was 3.6 percent. The difference between these yields was much greater than the long-term average, according to Citigroup data, of 4.5 percent.

Analysts should always question the inputs to any valuation model. Reasonable questions for these results include "Can the government bond yield be expected to rise?" and "Can the forecast for earnings be expected to decline?" Most would likely agree that the latter question was of greater concern in early 2009.

EXAMPLE 11-10 Fed Model Questions

1. Assume the S&P 500 forward earnings yield is 5 percent and the 10-year T-note yield is 4.6 percent. Are stocks overvalued or undervalued according to the Fed model?
2. Why might the earnings yield be considered a poor measure for the true worth of equities?

---

[24]Based on a dataset maintained by Professor Shiller (www.econ.yale.edu/~shiller/data.htm), the compound (geometric mean) annual earnings growth rate was 3.52 percent from 1872–2008. In the more recent shorter term, the growth rate has been higher: from 1990–2008, the rate was 3.55 percent but stopping at 2007 (i.e., from 1990–2007), reflecting an unusually long period of sustained growth, it was 6.89 percent. The long run rate is probably most appropriate here.

[25]The required return on equity for a no-growth company that pays all of its earnings out as dividends is the earnings yield (based on a constant EPS).

Solution to 1: According to the Fed model, stocks are undervalued because the forward S&P 500 earnings yield exceeds the 10-year T-note yield. However, recall from Example 11-1 that the average difference between the S&P 500 earnings yield and the 10-year T-note yield for the time period January 1979–December 2008 was 0.70 percent. In this question, the difference between the two yields is 0.40 percent. Analysts who compare the difference in yields to this average difference would contend that equities are overvalued.

Solution to 2: The forward earnings yield measure used in the Fed model to assess the worth of equities fails to accurately capture the long-term growth opportunities available to equity investors. Although studies show that the dividend yield has been the major determinant of long-term equity returns, the impact of earnings growth has been significant and arguably should not be ignored.

The **Yardeni model** addresses some of the criticisms of the Fed model. In creating the model, Yardeni (2002) assumed investors valued earnings rather than dividends. With the assumption that markets set price equal to intrinsic value, $P_0 = V_0$, a constant growth valuation model that values earnings is presented in Equation 11.8. E_1 is an estimate of next year's earnings, r is the required return, and g is the earnings growth rate. Equation 11.8 shows that, given the assumptions of the model, the earnings yield, E_1/P_0, is equal to the required return, r, minus the growth rate, g.

$$P_0 = \frac{E_1}{r-g} \Rightarrow \frac{E_1}{P_0} = r - g \tag{11.8}$$

As a data input for the required return, r, Yardeni used the Moody's A-rated corporate bond yield, y_B, which allowed for risk to be incorporated into the model. The risk premium captured by the model, however, is largely a default risk premium (the credit spread between the A-rated bond, y_B, and the yield on a Treasury bond, y_T), not the unobservable equity risk premium. Thus, while an improvement over the Fed model, the Yardeni model still does not fully capture the risk of equities.

As an input for the growth rate, g, Yardeni used the consensus five-year earnings growth forecast for the S&P 500 from Thomson Financial, LTEG. Note that g is truly a perpetual or sustainable growth rate and that a five-year forecast for growth may not be sustainable.

The Yardeni model introduces an additional variable, the coefficient d. It represents a weighting factor measuring the importance the market assigns to the earnings projections. Yardeni (2000) found that the historical values for d averaged about 0.10.[26] However, depending on market conditions, d can vary considerably from its historical average. Equation 11.9 presents the Yardeni model stated as the justified (forward) earnings yield on equities.

$$\frac{E_1}{P_0} = y_B - d \times \text{LTEG} \tag{11.9}$$

[26]Note that rearranging the terms in Equation 11.9 so that they produce a formula for d results in

$$d = \frac{y_B - \frac{E_1}{P_0}}{\text{LTEG}}$$

Thus historical values for d can be estimated from market data.

A justified forward earnings yield that is below, equal to, or greater than the forward earnings yield value implied by current equity market index values (using consensus forward earnings estimates, for example) would indicate that equities are undervalued, fairly valued, or overvalued in the marketplace. A valuation judgment can also be made by using Equation 11.9 solved for P_0, which gives the Yardeni model expression for the fair value of the equity market: $E_1/(y_B - d \times \text{LTEG})$. The judgment would be that the equity market is undervalued, fairly valued, or overvalued if the fair value estimate is above, equal to, or below the current equity market level. Example 11-11 shows such an analysis.

EXAMPLE 11-11 The Yardeni Model (1)

Exhibit 11-11 presents in logarithmic ("log") scale the actual S&P 500 Index and a fair value estimate of the S&P 500 using the Yardeni model assuming $d = 0.10$. The time period is January 1985 to December 2008.

As Exhibit 11-12 shows, the Yardeni model predicted the S&P 500 was undervalued by 39.25 percent in December 2008. The Yardeni model also did a good job predicting the overvaluation and subsequent pullbacks of October 1987 and the early 2000s. However, the model signaled the equity market was significantly undervalued in 2007 even though U.S. and other world equity markets collapsed dramatically in the wake of a major financial crisis.

EXHIBIT 11-11 S&P 500 Index and Fair Value Estimate Using Yardeni Model with $d = 0.10$ (log scale). Monthly Data: January 1985–December 2008

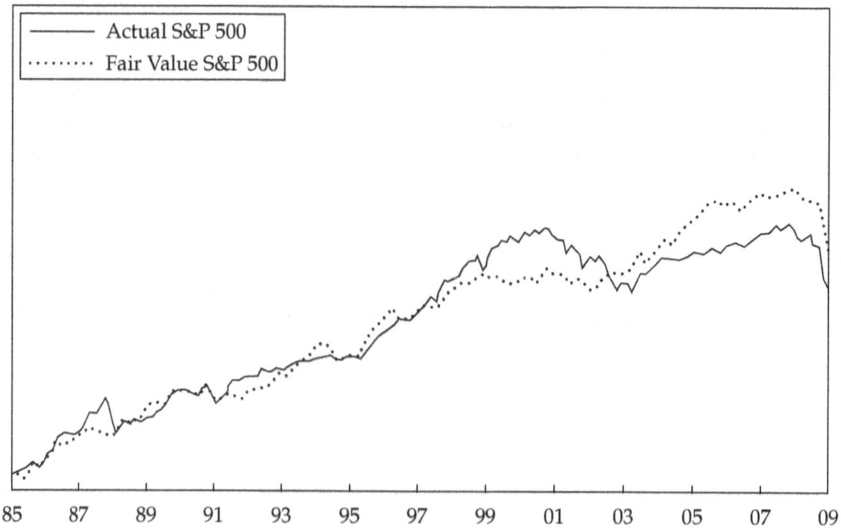

Source for data: www.yardeni.com.

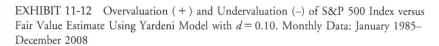

EXHIBIT 11-12 Overvaluation (+) and Undervaluation (–) of S&P 500 Index versus Fair Value Estimate Using Yardeni Model with $d = 0.10$. Monthly Data: January 1985–December 2008

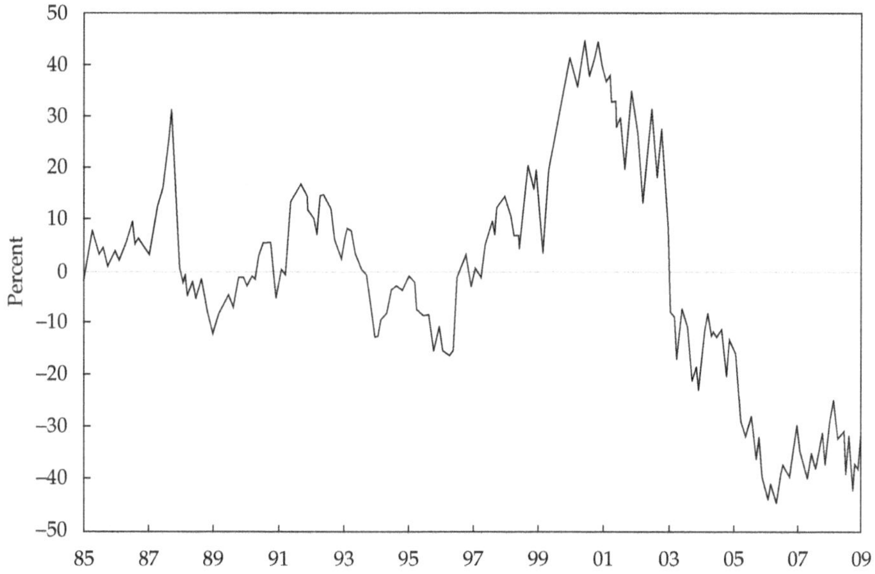

Source for data: www.yardeni.com.

EXAMPLE 11-12 Yardeni Model (2)

1. Assume the Moody's A-rated corporate bond yield is 6.49 percent and the forecast for long-term earnings growth is 11.95 percent. Determine the Yardeni model estimate of the fair value earnings yield assuming $d = 0.05$ and $d = 0.10$. Are equities overvalued or undervalued if the S&P 500 earnings yield is 5.5 percent?
2. Assume the Moody's A-rated corporate bond yield is 6.32 percent and the forecast for long-term earnings growth is 11.5 percent. Determine the Yardeni model estimate of the fair value price–earnings (P/E) ratio assuming $d = 0.10$. When would equities be undervalued? When would equities be overvalued?
3. A. Indicate the directional relationship predicted by the Yardeni model between changes in y_B, LTEG, and d and changes in the earnings yield.
   B. Indicate the directional relationship predicted by the Yardeni model between changes in y_B, LTEG, and d and changes in the P/E ratio.

Solution to 1:
For $d = 0.05$: $0.0649 - 0.05(0.1195) \approx 0.0589 \approx 5.89$ percent is the Yardeni model estimate. Equities are overvalued as 5.5 percent $<$ 5.89 percent.
For $d = 0.10$: $0.0649 - 0.10(0.1195) \approx 0.530 \approx 5.30$ percent is the Yardeni model estimate. Equities are undervalued as 5.5 percent $>$ 5.30 percent.

Solution to 2: P/E is the reciprocal of the earnings yield. The Yardeni estimate of the fair value P/E ratio would be $1 \div [0.0632 - 0.10(0.115)]$ or approximately 19.3. Stocks would be undervalued if the actual P/E ratio for the S&P 500 is less than 19.3. Stocks would be overvalued if the actual P/E ratio for the S&P 500 is greater than 19.3.

Solution to 3:
A. Increases in y_B and decreases in *d* and LTEG produce higher fair value estimates of the earnings yield.
B. Decreases in y_B and increases in *d* and LTEG produce higher fair value estimates of the P/E ratio.

Examples 11-11 and 11-12 were taken from U.S. equity markets. To date, nearly all analysis using the Yardeni model has been limited to the U.S. equity market. If adequate data are available, especially for forecasted earnings growth, the Yardeni model could be applied in any equity market.

Campbell and Shiller's (1998, 2005) 10-year Moving Average Price/Earnings [P/10-year MA(E)] has become a popular measure of market valuation. The authors defined the numerator of P/10-year MA(E) as the real S&P 500 price index and the denominator as the moving average of the preceding 10 years of real reported earnings. "Real" denotes that the stock index and earnings are adjusted for inflation using the Consumer Price Index (CPI). The purpose of the 10-year moving average of real reported earnings is to control for business cycle effects on earnings and is based on recommendations from the seminal Graham and Dodd (1934) text.

EXAMPLE 11-13 Determining P/10-Year MA(E): An Historical Exercise

For the purpose of illustrating the calculation of P/10-year MA(E) one can use data from any period. Exhibit 11-13 is a historical exercise showing the calculation of P/10-year MA(E) for U.S. equities as of 1881. The real stock price index and real earnings are priced in 2009 U.S. dollars and are determined using the January 2009 CPI value of 211.143. Note that:

$$\text{Real Stock Price Index}_t = \text{Nominal Stock Price Index}_t \times \text{CPI}_{2009} \div \text{CPI}_t$$

$$\text{Real Earnings}_t = \text{Nominal Earnings}_t \times \text{CPI}_{2009} \div \text{CPI}_{t+1}$$

$$\text{Real Stock Price Index}_{1871} = 4.44 \times 211.143 \div 12.464061 = 75.21424358$$

$$\text{Real Earnings}_{1871} = 0.4 \times 211.143 \div 12.654392 = 6.674141278$$

The P/10-year MA(E) in 1881 of 18.21479737 is the Real Stock Price Index in 1881 of 138.7532563 divided by average Real Earnings from 1871 to 1880 of 7.617411851.

$$\text{Average Real Earnings}_{1871 \rightarrow 1880} = (6.674141278 + \ldots + 10.9836988) \div 10$$
$$= 7.617611851$$

$$\text{P/10-year MA(E)}_{1881} = 138.7532563 \div 7.617611851 = 18.21479737$$

EXHIBIT 11-13 Determining P/10-Year MA(E) in 1881

Year	Stock Price Index (January)	Earnings Accruing to Index	Consumer Price Index	Real Stock Price Index	Real Earnings	P/10-Year MA(E)
1871	4.44	0.40	12.464061	75.21424358	6.674141278	
1872	4.86	0.43	12.654392	81.09081653	7.016448545	
1873	5.11	0.46	12.939807	83.38151643	7.852421105	
1874	4.66	0.46	12.368896	79.54843989	8.436439183	
1875	4.54	0.36	11.5126510	83.26398672	7.007878524	
1876	4.46	0.28	10.8465750	86.81982838	5.403166224	
1877	3.55	0.30	10.9417400	68.50442891	6.863396587	
1878	3.25	0.31	9.2290893	74.35346302	7.907328567	
1879	3.58	0.38	8.2776793	91.31689120	8.031199688	
1880	5.11	0.49	9.9903306	107.99850110	10.983698800	
1881	6.19	0.44	9.4194198	138.75325630		18.21479737

The number of decimal places shown reflects the precision given in the Shiller dataset referenced.
Source for data: www.econ.yale.edu/~shiller/data.htm.

Real earnings in 1880 exceeded the 10-year moving average by a considerable amount, and this is a typical result. This discrepancy undoubtedly reflects the real growth in corporate earnings. If some smoothing for business cycle effects is necessary, the case can be made that it would be better to compute a moving average of the P/E ratio (current period price divided by current period earnings).

Many analysts believe that P/10-year MA(E) should be considered a mean-reverting series. Exhibit 11-14 presents P/10-year MA(E) from January 1881 to January 2009. The mean value of P/10-year MA(E) for this time period was 16.3 and the January 2009 P/10-year MA(E) was 15.8 suggesting the U.S. equity market was slightly undervalued at that time. The highest value for P/10-year MA(E) was 42.5 in 2000 and the lowest value for P/10-year MA(E) was 5.3 in 1921.

Campbell and Shiller (1998, 2005) made the case that the U.S. equity market was extremely overvalued in the late 1990s and provided evidence that future 10-year real price-growth was negatively related to P/10-year MA(E). Exhibit 11-15 updates the Campbell-Shiller results through 2009. Each plotted data point represents an annual observation for real price growth for the next 10 years and P/10-year MA(E) for that same year. A trend line is plotted and shows the ordinary least squares regression relationship between 10-year real price growth and P/10-year MA(E).

The table in the upper right-hand corner of Exhibit 11-15 shows the predicted 10-year real price growth given some value for the explanatory variable P/10-year MA(E). The regression results predict that 10-year real price growth will be 17.9 percent given the January 2009 P/10-year MA(E) of 15.8. The R-squared for the regression is 0.1488, which indicates that P/10-year MA(E) explains only 14.88 percent of the variation in 10-year real price growth. Furthermore, the traditional regression statistics for this regression are unreliable because of the serial correlation induced by the overlapping time periods used to compute returns.

EXHIBIT 11-14 P/10-Year MA(E), Annual Data: 1881–2009

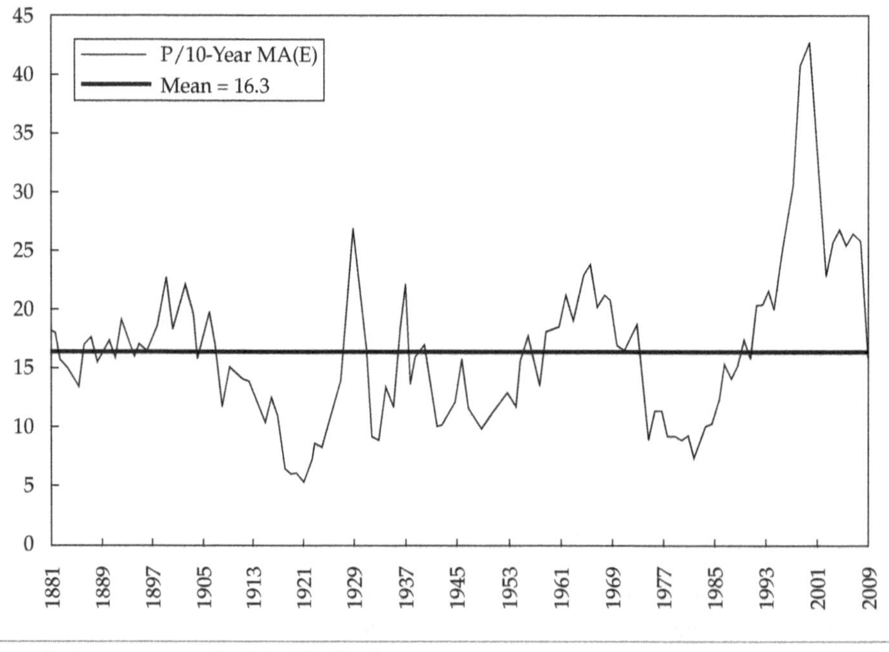

Source for data: www.econ.yale.edu/~shiller/data.htm.

With a 10-year projected real price growth of 17.9 percent, the annualized growth rate is less than 1.7 percent per year. Given a dividend yield of about 2.9 percent and assuming share repurchases effectively add 1 percent to the annual real cash flow to shareholders, the inflation-adjusted expected return would be approximately 5.6 percent, which is below the 6–7 percent compounded average inflation-adjusted return over long periods in the United States (Siegel 2005). Thus, in contrast to the Fed model and the Yardeni model, the Campbell and Shiller model implies below-average prospective returns.

The conflicting signals between and among various valuation models may provide valuable insights, especially if they cause us to rethink how the parameter estimates and the numerical inputs give rise to the different results. For example, assume that changes in accounting rules lead to significant differences in how earnings are reported over time. Thus, the P/10-year MA(E) at some given point in time might not be comparable with other time periods. A high or low P/10-year MA(E) relative to the long-term average at present could be due to differences in prior accounting rules, thereby resulting in stocks actually being more undervalued or overvalued than they currently appear.

EXHIBIT 11-15 P/10-Year MA(E) and Predicted Ten-Year Real Price Growth

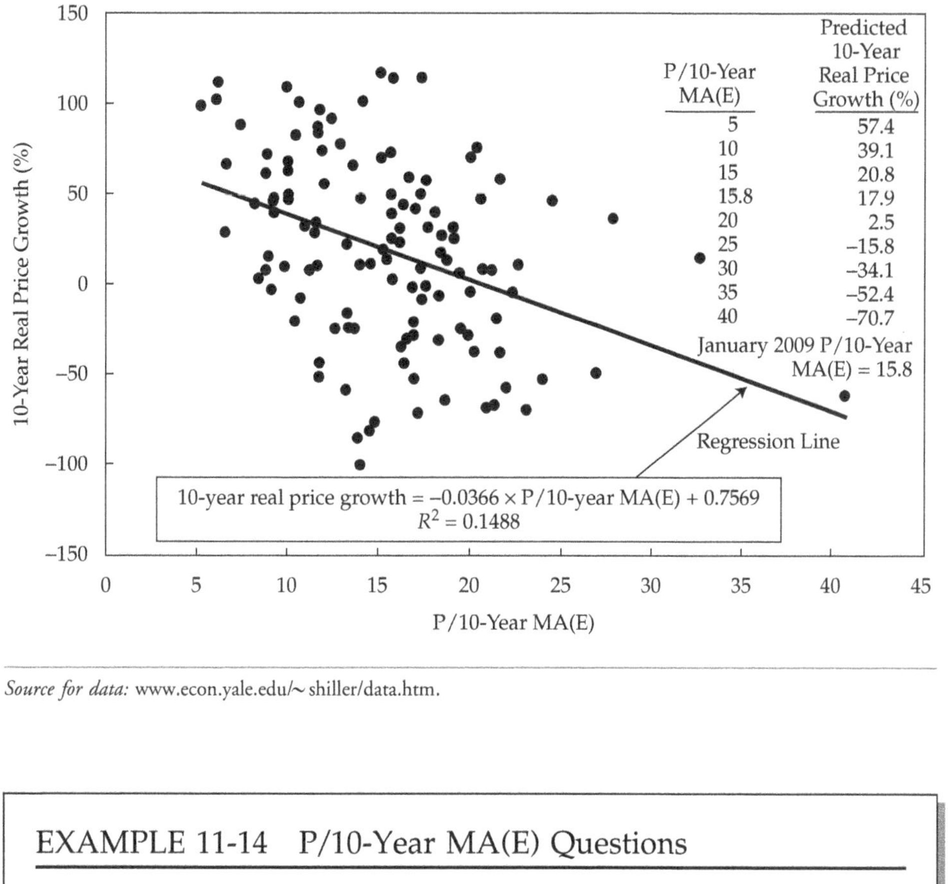

Source for data: www.econ.yale.edu/~shiller/data.htm.

EXAMPLE 11-14 P/10-Year MA(E) Questions

1. What adjustments are made to earnings in determining P/10-year MA(E)?
2. Assume P/10-year MA(E) reached an all-time high of 42.5 in 2000. Use the regression results in Exhibit 11-15 to determine predicted real price growth for the time period 2000–2009.

Solution to 1: Following Graham and Dodd, Campbell and Shiller averaged earnings over a 10-year time period. Their goal was to normalize earnings by providing an estimate of what earnings would be under mid-cyclical conditions. The implicit assumption is that the typical business cycle lasts 10 years.

Campbell and Shiller also control for inflation by adjusting past earnings to current period dollars using the Consumer Price Index.

Solution to 2: Ten-year real price growth $= -0.0366 \times 42.5 + 0.7569 = -0.7986 = -79.86$ percent.

4.2. Asset-Based Models

Tobin's *q* ratio, pioneered in Brainard and Tobin (1968) and Tobin (1969), is an asset-based valuation measure. Tobin's q has been used for several purposes, including decision-making concerning physical capital investment and equity market valuation. The first application is the simplest: At the company level, Tobin's q is calculated as the market value of a company (i.e., the market value of its debt and equity) divided by the replacement cost of its assets. According to economic theory, Tobin's q is approximately equal to 1 in equilibrium. If it is greater than 1 for a company, the marketplace values the company's assets at more than their replacement costs so additional capital investment should be profitable for the company's suppliers of financing. By contrast, a Tobin's q below 1 indicates that further capital investment is unprofitable.

Tobin's q has also been calculated at an overall market level. In that case, the denominator involves an estimate of the replacement cost of aggregate corporate assets and the numerator involves estimates of aggregate equity and debt market values. Some analysts have used a market-level Tobin's q to judge whether an equity market is misvalued. This application involves a comparison of the current value of market-level Tobin's q with its presumed equilibrium value of 1 or with its historical mean value. Assuming that Tobin's q will revert to the comparison value, a Tobin's q below, at, or above the comparison values is interpreted as the market being undervalued, fairly valued, or overvalued. Strong economic arguments exist that both Tobin's q and equity q, discussed later, should be mean-reverting series.

The calculation of Tobin's q often poses difficulties. At the company level, it is usually possible to get a fairly accurate estimate of market value (the numerator of Tobin's q) by summing the values of the securities a company has issued, such as its stocks and bonds. It is much more difficult to obtain an accurate estimate of replacement costs of the company's assets (the denominator of Tobin's q). Liquid markets for many assets (e.g., many kinds of industrial equipment) do not exist. Moreover, such items as human capital, trade secrets, copyrights and patents, and brand equity are intangible assets that are often difficult to value. Typically, researchers who try to construct Tobin's q ignore the replacement cost of intangible assets in their calculations.

Smithers and Wright (2000) created an **equity *q*** that is the ratio of a company's equity market capitalization divided by net worth measured at replacement cost. Their measure differs from the price-to-book value ratio because net worth is based on replacement cost rather than the historic or book value of equity. Based on a market-level equity q, Smithers and Wright made the case that the U.S. equity market was extremely overvalued in the late 1990s. The principles of that application parallel those given for Tobin's q.

To date, much of the market-level analysis using Tobin's q or equity q has been conducted in the U.S. equity market, but analysis based on European and Asian equity markets is increasingly available.

EXAMPLE 11-15 Market-Level Analysis of Tobin's q and Equity q

Data from which Tobin's q and equity q can be calculated are published in the *Flow of Funds Accounts of the United States-Z.1*, published quarterly by the Federal Reserve.* This data source is available from 1952 onward. Following is data for Nonfarm Nonfinancial Corporate Business for the fourth quarter of 2008 (billions of U.S. dollars). Based on this data, determine Tobin's q and equity q.

Assets at Market Value or Replacement Cost	Liabilities	Market Value of Equities Outstanding
28,277.33	12,887.51	9,554.05

Source for data: www.federalreserve.gov/releases/z1/.

Solution:

$$\text{Tobin's } q = (12,877.51 + 9,554.05) \div 28,277.33 = 0.793623726$$

$$\text{Equity } q = 9,554.05 \div (28,277.33 - 12,877.51) = 0.620803232$$

Using this data, the long-term average for Tobin's q and equity q are both significantly below 1.0. Smithers and Wright suggest this is due to the true economic rate of depreciation being underestimated, which leads to the replacement cost of assets being overstated. Such overstatement means that the denominator in both formulations of the q ratio is too high and that the correctly measured ratios should be much higher.

*Specifically, the data currently appear in Table B.102 of that publication.

Exhibit 11-16 presents quarterly Tobin's q data and quarterly equity q data for the U.S. equity market over the time period 1952 to 2008. Last quarter 2008 values for these two variables relative to their respective means suggest that the U.S. equity market was slightly undervalued at that time. However, both series had declined to significantly lower levels relative to their means in the early 1950s and early 1980s.

EXHIBIT 11-16 Equity q and Tobin's q Quarterly Data: 1952 Q1 to 2008 Q4

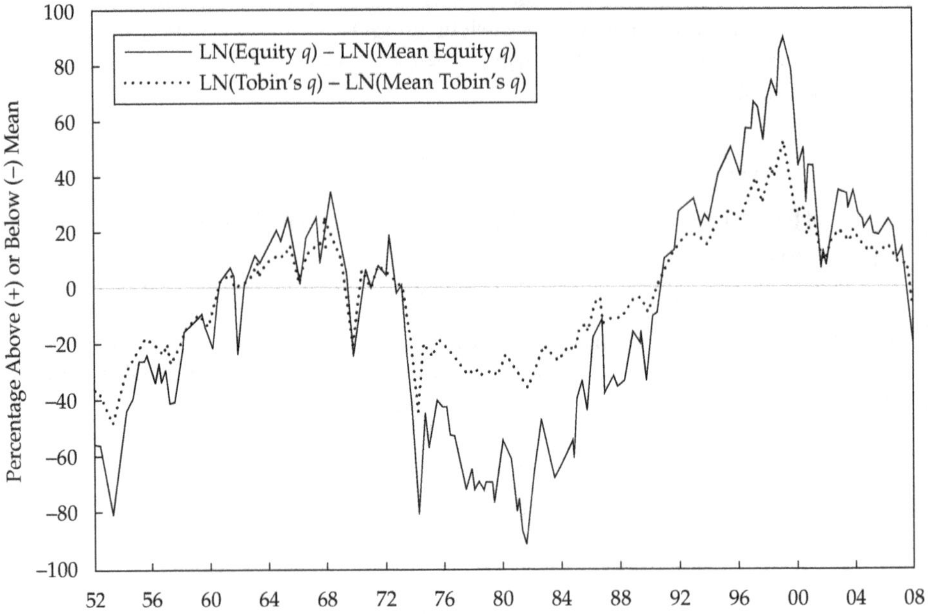

Note: 2008 Q4 values: Equity's $q = -19.1\%$, Tobin's $q = -5.50\%$.
Source for data: www.federalreserve.gov/releases/z1/.

EXAMPLE 11-16 Tobin's q and Equity q

1. Why should Tobin's q be expected to mean revert?
2. How does equity q differ from the price-to-book ratio?

Solution to 1: If Tobin's q is greater than 1.0, then the market is valuing a company at more than it costs to replace its assets. Either security prices must fall or the company should continue to invest in new assets until the ratio returns to its equilibrium. If Tobin's q is below 1.0, then security prices are undervalued because new businesses can't be created as cheaply as they can be bought in the open market. Either security prices must rise or the company should sell some of its assets until the ratio returns to its equilibrium.

Solution to 2: Book value in the price-to-book ratio reflects the value of equity that is reported on the company's balance sheet. The denominator of equity q reflects the difference between the replacement cost of assets and the market value of liabilities. Most financial reporting standards require the use of acquisition cost as a measure of asset value. Thus, the book value of assets is typically less than their replacement cost and this is particularly true during periods of rising prices.

A summary of the relative value models appears in Exhibit 11-17.

EXHIBIT 11-17 Summary of Relative Value Models

Model	Predictions of the Model	Strengths	Limitations
Fed model	The equity market is undervalued if its earnings yield exceeds the yield on government securities.	• Easy to understand and apply. • Consistent with discounted cash flow models that show an inverse relationship between value and the discount rate.	• Ignores the equity risk premium. • Compares a real variable to a nominal variable. • Ignores earnings growth.
Yardeni model	Equities are overvalued if the fair value estimate of the earnings yield provided by the model exceeds the actual earnings yield for the market index.	• Improves on the Fed model by including the yield on risky debt and a measure of expected earnings growth as determinants of value.	• Risk premium captured by the model is largely a default risk premium that does not accurately measure equity risk. • The forecast for earnings growth may not be accurate or sustainable. • The estimate of fair value assumes the discount factor investors apply to the earnings forecast remains constant over time.
P/10-year MA (E)	Future equity returns will be higher when P/10-year MA(E) is low.	• Controls for inflation and business cycle effects by using a 10-year moving average of real earnings. • Historical data supports an inverse relationship between P/10-year MA(E) and future equity returns.	• Changes in the accounting methods used to determine reported earnings may lead to comparison problems. • Current period or other measures of earnings may provide a better estimate for equity prices than the 10-year moving average of real earnings. • Evidence suggests that both low and high levels of P/10-year MA(E) can persist for extended periods of time.
Tobin's *q* and equity *q*	Future equity returns will be higher when Tobin's *q* and equity *q* are low.	• Both measures rely on a comparison of security values to asset replacement costs (minus the debt market value, in the case of equity *q*); economic theory suggests this relationship is mean-reverting. • Historical data support an inverse relationship between both measures and future equity returns.	• It is difficult to obtain an accurate measure of replacement cost for many assets because liquid markets for these assets do not exist and intangible assets are often difficult to value. • Evidence suggests that both low and high levels of Tobin's *q* and equity *q* can persist for extended periods of time.

EXAMPLE 11-17 Questions Regarding the Relative Value Models

1. Which of the models ignore the current level of market interest rates as determinants of equity market value?
2. Under what conditions might the Fed model and Yardeni model provide a different assessment of the value of the equity market?
3. Which of the models use some measure of earnings as an input? How might this lead to comparison issues?

Solution to 1: In assessing equity market value, P/10-year MA(E), Tobin's q, and equity q are typically compared to their long-term averages and not to market interest rates. While the Yardeni model compares the fair value earnings yield predicted by the model to the actual earnings yield, the A-rated corporate bond yield is an input to the model.

Solution to 2: The Fed model compares the earnings yield to the Treasury bond yield. The Yardeni model uses the A-rated corporate bond yield and the consensus five-year earnings growth forecast to determine a fair value earnings yield. One scenario where the two models might differ in their predictions would be if the default risk premium on the A-rated corporate bond was currently high, the Treasury bond yield was currently low, and earnings were forecasted to grow at a slow rate. Given these assumptions, the Fed model might indicate that equities are undervalued while the Yardeni model indicates equities are overvalued.

Solution to 3: The Fed model, Yardeni model, and P/10-year MA(E) all use some measure of earnings as a determinant of value. Time series comparisons will be problematic if the accounting methods used to determine earnings change over time.

5. SUMMARY

In this chapter we have investigated several ways in which economic theory can be applied to the valuation of equity markets. Among the major points are the following:

- The growth accounting equation allows one to decompose real GDP growth, $\Delta Y/Y$, into components that can be attributed to the observable factors: the growth of the capital stock, $\Delta K/K$, the output elasticity of capital, α, the growth in the labor force, $\Delta L/L$, the output elasticity of labor, $1 - \alpha$, and a residual factor—often called the Solow residual—that is the portion of growth left unaccounted for by increases in the standard factors of production, $\Delta A/A$.

$$\frac{\Delta Y}{Y} \approx \frac{\Delta A}{A} + \alpha\frac{\Delta K}{K} + (1-\alpha)\frac{\Delta L}{L}$$

- The existence of TFP growth, $\Delta A/A$, means that total output can grow at a faster rate than would be predicted simply from growth in accumulated capital stock and the labor force. TFP is typically linked to innovation and technical progress. However, changes in work organization, government regulation, and the literacy and skills of the work force, as well as many other factors, also affect TFP.
- The inputs for the H-model include the initial growth rate, g_S, a period of years, N, where the dividend growth rate declines in a linear fashion, and a long-term dividend growth rate, g_L, that is expected to prevail to perpetuity beginning at the end of period N. With an initial annualized dividend rate D_0 and a discount rate to perpetuity of r, the formula for intrinsic value, V_0 according to the H-model is:

$$V_0 = \frac{D_0}{r - g_L}\left[(1 + g_L) + \frac{N}{2}(g_S - g_L)\right]$$

- In top-down forecasting, analysts use macroeconomic forecasts to develop market forecasts and then make industry and security forecasts consistent with the market forecasts. In bottom-up forecasting, individual company forecasts are aggregated to industry forecasts, which in turn are aggregated to produce a market forecast.
- Bottom-up forecasts tend to be more optimistic than top-down forecasts. Top-down models can be slow in detecting cyclical turns if the current statistical relationships between economic variables deviate significantly from their historic norms.
- The Fed model is a theory of equity valuation that hypothesizes that the yield on long-term U.S. Treasury securities (usually defined as the 10-year T-note yield) should be equal to the S&P 500 earnings yield (usually defined as forward operating earnings divided by the index level) in equilibrium.
- A common criticism of the Fed model equilibrium is that it fails to incorporate the equity risk premium. The earnings yield can also be a poor measure of the true value of equities if significant growth opportunities exist. Some authors have also argued that the Fed model comparison is flawed because the earnings yield is real while the Treasury yield is nominal.
- The Yardeni model addresses some of the criticisms of the Fed model. As inputs, Yardeni used the Moody's A-rated corporate bond yield, y_B, the consensus five-year earnings growth forecast for the S&P 500 from Thomson Financial, LTEG, and the coefficient d, which represents a weighting factor measuring the importance the market assigns to the earnings projections. Yardeni found that the historical values for d averaged about 0.10. The formula for the Yardeni model is:

$$\frac{E_1}{P_0} = y_B - d \times \text{LTEG}$$

- Limitations of the Yardeni model include that the risk premium captured by the model is largely a default risk premium and not the future equity risk premium, which is unobservable. Also, the consensus five-year earnings growth forecast for the S&P 500 from Thomson Financial may not be sustainable and evidence suggests that the weighting factor varies significantly over time.
- Campbell and Shiller's P/10-year MA(E) has become a popular measure of market valuation. The numerator of P/10-year MA(E) is the real S&P 500 and the denominator is

the moving average of the preceding 10 years of real reported earnings. "Real" denotes that the stock index and earnings are adjusted for inflation using the Consumer Price Index (CPI). The purpose of the 10-year moving average of real reported earnings is to control for business cycle effects on earnings and is based on recommendations from the seminal work of Graham and Dodd.
- Tobin's q is calculated at the individual company level as the market value of a company divided by the replacement cost of its assets. Smithers and Wright created an equity q that is the ratio of a company's market capitalization divided by net worth measured at replacement cost. Market-level measures may be computed for Tobin's q and equity q by a process of aggregation; these market-level measures may be used to form a valuation judgment about an equity market. Assuming that Tobin's q will revert to the comparison value, a Tobin's q below, at, or above the comparison value is interpreted as the market being under-, fairly, or overvalued. Strong economic arguments exist that both Tobin's q and equity q should be mean-reverting series.
- In practice, estimating replacement cost can be problematic due to the lack of liquid markets for many assets. Moreover, such items as human capital, trade secrets, copyrights and patents, and brand equity are intangible assets that are difficult to value.

PROBLEMS

1. Elizabeth Villeneuve is a senior economist at Proplus Financial Economics Consulting (Proplus). She is responsible for the valuation of equity markets in developing countries and is reviewing the preliminary report on Emerge Country prepared by one of her analysts, Danielle DeLaroche. Emerge Country is now experiencing stronger economic growth than most developed countries.

   DeLaroche has summarized in Exhibit A some of the assumptions contained in the report. In modeling the growth in the country's real output, she has used the Cobb-Douglas production function under the assumption of constant returns to scale and, in valuing the equity market, she has used the standard Gordon growth model with constant dividend growth rate.

EXHIBIT A Assumptions for the Equity Index of Emerge Country

Annual dividend per share in 2008	450 CU*
Forecasted earnings per share in 2009	750 CU*
Forecasted annual growth in TFP	1.5%
Expected real growth rate of dividends to perpetuity	5.5%
Required real discount rate to perpetuity	7.5%

*CU = currency unit of Emerge Country

A. Based on the information in Exhibit A, calculate the equity index price level of Emerge Country implied by the Gordon growth model, as of 31 December 2008. Villeneuve is familiar with the Gordon growth model but not the H-model.

B. Identify *two* variables that are needed in the H-model and not needed in the Gordon growth model.

As an illustration of a relative value approach that can be used to support tactical asset allocation, DeLaroche has estimated that the forward operating earnings yield of the equity index in Emerge Country is 6 percent and that the medium-term government bond yield is 7 percent. She then applies the Fed model to the situation in Emerge Country.

C. Based on the Fed model, determine whether the equity market is undervalued or overvalued and identify three criticisms of the Fed model.

Because most of Proplus's clients use strategies that require fundamental security analysis, Proplus uses both top-down and bottom-up approaches in all reports dealing with equity return forecasts.

D. Contrast the two forecasting approaches used by DeLaroche as they relate to industry analysis.

2. Don Murray, an economist, is president of the investment committee of a large U.S. pension plan. He is reviewing the plan's recent investment returns and finds that non-U.S. equity returns have been much higher than U.S. equity returns. Before making any changes to the plan's asset allocation, he has asked to meet with Susan McLean, CFA, who is responsible for the equity portion of the pension plan assets. Murray wants to discuss with McLean the current valuation levels of various equity markets.

   Murray develops his own growth projections for the United States and for a hypothetical country (Hyp Country) that enjoys a well-developed economy but whose population is aging. These projections are shown in Exhibit B. In addition, Murray projects that output elasticity of capital equals 0.3 and 0.5 for the United States and Hyp Country, respectively.

EXHIBIT B Growth Projections (2010–2029)

Country	Growth in Total Factor Productivity	Growth in Capital Stock	Growth in Labor Input
United States	0.6%	3.5%	0.4%
Hyp Country	1.0%	3.3%	0.1%

A. Based on the information in Exhibit B, calculate the projected GDP growth for the United States for the period 2010–2029. Use the Cobb-Douglas production function and assume constant returns to scale.

Murray identifies two possible measures that the government of Hyp Country could implement and he wants to know how these measures would affect projected GDP growth for Hyp Country.

Measure 1: Lower the retirement age from 65 to 63, gradually over the next four-year period

Measure 2: Reduce subsidies to higher education over the next five years

B. For each of the growth measures identified by Murray in Exhibit B, indicate which growth factor is *most* affected. Justify your answers.

Murray is surprised that the bottom-up forecasts produced by McLean for the United States in the last five years have been consistently more optimistic than her top-down forecasts. As a result, he expresses doubt about the validity of either approach.

C. State *one* justification for using both top-down and bottom-up models even when these models produce different forecasts and state one justification for using the bottom-up approach by itself.

Murray suggests replacing earnings-based models with asset-based models in valuing equity markets. In response, McLean recommends using Tobin's q ratio and equity q ratio, although both are subject to estimation errors when applied to valuing a particular company.

D. Identify *two* problems that McLean may have in estimating the Tobin's q ratio and the equity q ratio for the pension plan assets that she manages.

Use the following information to answer Questions 3 through 10.

Claudia Atkinson, CFA, is chief economist of an investment management firm. In analyzing equity markets, the firm has always used a bottom-up approach but now Atkinson is in the process of implementing a top-down approach. She is discussing this topic with her assistant, Nicholas Ryan.

At Atkinson's request, Ryan has prepared a memo comparing the top-down approach and the bottom-up approach. Ryan presents three conclusions:

Conclusion 1: The top-down approach is less optimistic when the economy is heading into a recession than the bottom-up approach.
Conclusion 2: The top-down approach is more often based on consensus earnings estimates from equity analysts than the bottom-up approach.
Conclusion 3: The top-down approach is often more accurate in predicting the effect on the stock market of a contemporaneous change in a key economic variable than is the bottom-up approach.

Atkinson explains to Ryan how the Cobb-Douglas function can be used to model GDP growth under assumptions of constant returns to scale. For illustrative purposes, she uses the data shown in Exhibit C.

EXHIBIT C Hypothetical Data for a Developing Country

Time Period	Growth in Total Factor Productivity	Output Elasticity of Capital	Growth in Capital Stock	Growth in Labor Input
1970–1989	2.5%	0.4	4.8%	3.0%
1990–2009	2.8%	0.4	4.4%	4.6%

Atkinson wants to use the data shown in Exhibit C as an input for estimating justified P/E ratios. Ryan expresses some criticisms about using such historical data:

- "In a context of hyperinflation, the approach may not be appropriate."
- "The companies' growth rates may not match GDP growth for long periods."
- "Government-implemented measures may not be taken into account in any of the growth factors."

Atkinson intends to use relative value models in order to support the firm's asset allocation recommendation. The earnings-based approach that she studies is the Fed model. She asks Ryan to write a summary of the advantages of that model. Ryan's report makes the following assertions about the Fed model:

- "The model can be used for non-U.S. equity markets."
- "The model captures the net present value of growth investment opportunities available to investors."
- "The model is most informative when the excess of the earnings yield over the Treasury bond yield is close to the historical average."

Atkinson thinks that the Yardeni model might address some of the criticisms of the Fed model and bring certain improvements. She will use that model as an alternate approach.

Because different results from various equity market valuation models may provide relevant information, Atkinson will present a third earnings-based approach, namely the P/10-year MA(E) model. Ryan identifies many positive features in that model, including the following:

- "The model controls for inflation."
- "The model is independent of changes in accounting rules."
- "The model controls for business cycle effects on earnings."

When evaluating the equity market in the United States, Atkinson uses the following asset-based models: Tobin's q ratio and equity q ratio. She calculates the equity q ratio of Nonfarm Nonfinancial Corporate Business based on the Federal Reserve data shown in Exhibit D.

EXHIBIT D Nonfarm Nonfinancial Corporate Business for Fourth Quarter of 2008 (billions of U.S. dollars)

Assets at market value or replacement cost	27.3
Assets at book value	23.4
Liabilities	13.3
Equities at market value	9.0

Atkinson notes that the Tobin's q ratio that could be derived from Exhibit D is less than 1. She asks Ryan what conclusion could be drawn from such a low ratio if it had been obtained for a specific company.

3. Which conclusion presented by Ryan about the top-down approach and the bottom-up approach is *most likely* correct?

   A. Conclusion 1.
   B. Conclusion 2.
   C. Conclusion 3.

4. Based on Exhibit C, which of the components of economic growth has contributed most to GDP growth during the 1970–1989 time period?

   A. Labor input.
   B. Capital stock.
   C. Total factor productivity.

5. Which of the following criticisms expressed by Ryan about the use of historical data is the *least* valid?

   A. In a context of hyperinflation, the approach may not be appropriate.
   B. The companies' growth rates may not match GDP growth for long periods.
   C. Government-implemented measures may not be taken into account in any of the growth factors.

6. Which of the following advantages listed by Ryan with respect to the earnings-based approach studied by Atkinson is *most likely* correct? The model

   A. Can be used for non-U.S. equity markets.
   B. Captures the net present value of growth investment opportunities available to investors.
   C. Is most informative when the excess of the earnings yield over the Treasury bond yield is close to the historical average.

7. The *most likely* improvement from using the Yardeni model instead of the Fed model is that the Yardeni model captures:

   A. A pure equity risk premium.
   B. A pure default risk premium.
   C. The effect of long-term earnings growth on equity market values.

8. Which of the following features of the P/10-year MA(E) model as stated by Ryan is *least likely* to be correct? The model

   A. Controls for inflation.
   B. Is independent of changes in accounting rules.
   C. Controls for business cycle effects on earnings.

9. Based on the data shown in Exhibit D, the equity q ratio is closest to:

   A. 0.6429.
   B. 0.8168.
   C. 0.8911.

10. The best conclusion that Ryan can provide to Atkinson regarding the calculated value for Tobin's q ratio is that, based on comparing it to an equilibrium value of 1:

    A. The replacement cost of assets is understated.
    B. The company appears to be overvalued in the marketplace.
    C. The company appears to be undervalued in the marketplace.

Use the following information to answer Questions 11 through 16.

Egon Carmichael, CFA, is a senior analyst at Supranational Investment Management (Supranational), a firm specializing in global investment analysis. He is meeting with Nicolas Schmidt, a potential client representing a life insurance company, discussing a report prepared by Supranational on the U.S. equity market. The report contains valuations of the U.S. equity market based on two approaches: the justified P/E model and the Fed model.

When Carmichael informs Schmidt that Supranational applies the neoclassical approach to growth accounting, Schmidt makes the following statements about what he considers to be some limitations of that approach:

Statement 1: The growth in total factor productivity is not directly observable.
Statement 2: The growth factors must be stated in nominal (i.e., not inflation-adjusted) terms.
Statement 3: The total output may not grow at a rate faster than predicted by the growth in capital stock and in labor force.

For use in estimating the justified P/E based on the Gordon constant growth model, Carmichael develops the assumptions displayed in Exhibit E.

EXHIBIT E Justified P/E Ratio for the U.S. Equity Market: Assumptions

Required real rate of return	5.0%
Inflation-adjusted dividend growth rate	2.5%

Using these assumptions, Carmichael's estimate of the justified P/E ratio for the U.S. equity market is 13.2. Schmidt asks Carmichael, "All else equal, what would cause the justified P/E for the U.S. equity market to fall?"

Supranational's report concludes that the U.S. equity market is currently undervalued, based on the Fed model. Schmidt asks Carmichael, "Which of the following scenarios would result in the Fed model most likely indicating that the U.S. equity market is overvalued?"

Scenario 1: The S&P 500 forward earnings yield is 4.5 percent and the 10-year T-note yield is 4.75 percent.
Scenario 2: The S&P 500 forward earnings yield is 4.5 percent, the 10-year T-note yield is 4.0 percent, and the average difference between the S&P 500 forward earnings yield and the 10-year T-note over the last 20 years has been 0.25 percent.
Scenario 3: The long-term inflation rate is expected to be 2 percent and the long-term average earnings growth is expected to be 1 percent real.

Schmidt points out that the Fed model has been the subject of criticism and recommends that Carmichael use the Yardeni model to value the U.S. equity market. Before employing the Yardeni model, Carmichael asks Schmidt to identify criticisms of the Fed model that are addressed by the Yardeni model.

Finally, Carmichael presents a third earnings-based approach, the P/10-year MA(E) model, and describes many positive features of that model.

Schmidt mentions that the international life insurance company that he represents might be interested in the equity forecasts produced by Supranational. He says that his company's objective is to accumulate sufficient assets to fulfill the firm's obligations under its long term insurance and annuity contracts. For competitive reasons, the company wants to quickly detect significant cyclical turns in equity markets and to minimize tracking errors with respect to the equity index. Schmidt asks Carmichael to identify the forecasting approach that is most appropriate.

11. Which of the statements expressed by Schmidt about the neoclassical approach to growth accounting is correct?
    A. Statement 1.
    B. Statement 2.
    C. Statement 3.

12. Carmichael's *most appropriate* response to Schmidt's question about the justified P/E ratio is:

    A. Lower volatility of the U.S. equity market.
    B. Higher inflation-adjusted dividend growth rate.
    C. Higher correlation of U.S. equity market with international equity markets.

13. Carmichael's *most appropriate* response to Schmidt's question about the Fed model is:

    A. Scenario 1.
    B. Scenario 2.
    C. Scenario 3.

14. In response to Carmichael's question about which criticisms of the Fed model are addressed by the Yardeni model, Schmidt's *most appropriate* response is that the Yardeni model does take account of the criticism that the Fed model:

    A. Assumes that investors value earnings rather than dividends.
    B. Ignores long-term earnings growth opportunities available to shareholders.
    C. Assumes that the required rate of return on equity equals the Treasury bill rate.

15. Which of the following features is *least* applicable to the third earnings-based approach presented by Carmichael? The model:

    A. Controls for inflation.
    B. Is independent of changes in accounting rules.
    C. Controls for business cycle effects on earnings.

16. Carmichael's *best* answer to Schmidt's question about a recommended forecasting approach is to use:

    A. A top-down approach.
    B. A bottom-up approach.
    C. Both top-down and bottom-up approaches.

CHAPTER 12

TECHNICAL ANALYSIS

Barry M. Sine, CFA
Miami Beach, FL, U.S.A.

Robert A. Strong, CFA
Orono, ME, U.S.A.

LEARNING OUTCOMES

After completing this chapter, you will be able to do the following:

- Explain the principles of technical analysis, its applications, and its underlying assumptions.
- Discuss the construction and interpretation of different types of technical analysis charts.
- Demonstrate the uses of trend, support and resistance lines, and change in polarity.
- Identify and interpret common chart patterns.
- Discuss common technical analysis indicators: price-based indicators, momentum oscillators, sentiment, and flow of funds.
- Explain the use of cycles by technical analysts.
- Discuss the key tenets of Elliott Wave Theory and the importance of Fibonacci numbers.
- Describe intermarket analysis as it relates to technical analysis and asset allocation.

1. INTRODUCTION

Technical analysis has been used by traders and analysts for centuries, but it has only recently achieved broad acceptance among regulators and the academic community. This chapter gives a brief overview of the field, compares technical analysis with other schools of analysis, and describes some of the main tools in technical analysis. Some applications of technical analysis are subjective. That is, although certain aspects, such as the calculation of indicators, have specific rules, the interpretation of findings is often subjective and based on the long-term context of the security being analyzed. This aspect is similar to fundamental analysis, which has specific rules for calculating ratios, for example, but introduces subjectivity in the evaluation phase.

2. TECHNICAL ANALYSIS: DEFINITION AND SCOPE

Technical analysis is a form of security analysis that uses price and volume data, which is often graphically displayed, in decision making. Technical analysis can be used for securities in any freely traded market around the globe. A freely traded market is one where willing buyers trade with willing sellers without external intervention or impediment. Prices are the result of the interaction of supply and demand in real time. Technical analysis is used on a wide range of financial instruments, including equities, bonds, commodity futures, and currency futures.

The underlying logic of technical analysis is simple:

- Supply and demand determine prices.
- Changes in supply and demand cause changes in prices.
- Prices can be projected with charts and other technical tools.

Technical analysis of any financial instrument does not require detailed knowledge of that instrument. As long as the chart represents the action in a freely traded market, a technician does not even need to know the name or type of the security to conduct the analysis. Technical analysis can also be applied over any time frame—from short-term price movements to long-term movements of annual closing prices. Trends that are apparent in short-term charts may also appear over longer time frames. Because fundamental analysis is more time consuming than technical analysis, investors with short-term time horizons, such as traders, tend to prefer technical analysis—but not always. For example, fundamental analysts with long time frames often perform technical analysis to time the purchase and sale of the securities they have analyzed.

2.1. Principles and Assumptions

Technical analysis can be thought of as the study of collective investor psychology, or sentiment. Prices in any freely traded market are set by human beings or their automated proxies (such as computerized trading programs), and price is set at the equilibrium between supply and demand at any instant in time. Various fundamental theorists have proposed that markets are efficient and rational, but technicians believe that humans are often irrational and emotional and that they tend to behave similarly in similar circumstances.

Although fundamental data are key inputs into the determination of value, these data are analyzed by humans, who may be driven, at least partially, by factors other than rational factors.[1] Human behavior is often erratic and driven by emotion in many aspects of one's life, so technicians conclude that it is unreasonable to believe that investing is the one exception where humans always behave rationally. Technicians believe that market trends and patterns reflect this irrational human behavior. Thus, technical analysis is the study of market trends or patterns. And technicians believe the trends and patterns tend to repeat themselves and are, therefore, somewhat predictable. So, technicians rely on recognition of patterns that have occurred in the past in an attempt to project future patterns of security prices.

[1]Fundamental analysts use a wide variety of inputs, including financial statements, legal documents, economic data, first-hand observations from visiting the facilities of subject companies, and interviews with corporate managers, customers, suppliers, and competitors.

Another tenet of technical analysis is that the market reflects the collective knowledge and sentiment of many varied participants and the amount of buying and selling activity in a particular security. In a freely traded market, only those market participants who actually buy or sell a security have an impact on price. And the greater the volume of a participant's trades, the more impact that market participant will have on price. Those with the best information and most conviction have more say in setting prices than others because the informed traders trade higher volumes. To make use of their information, however, they must trade. Technical analysis relies on knowledgeable market participants putting this knowledge to work by trading in the market, thereby influencing prices and volume. Without trading, the information is not captured in the charts. Arguably, although insider trading is illegal for a variety of reasons, it improves the efficiency of technical analysis.

Trades determine volume and price. The impact occurs instantaneously and frequently anticipates fundamental developments correctly. So, by studying market technical data—price and volume trends—the technician is seeking to understand investor sentiment. The technician is benefiting from the wide range of knowledge of market participants and the collective conclusion of market participants about a security. In contrast, the fundamental analyst must wait for the release of financial statements to conduct financial statement analysis, so a time lag occurs between the market's activities and the analyst's conclusions.

Charles Dow, creator in 1896 of what is now known as the Dow Jones Industrial Average, described the collective action of participants in the markets as follows:

> *The market reflects all the jobber knows about the condition of the textile trade; all the banker knows about the money market; all that the best-informed president knows of his own business, together with his knowledge of all other businesses; it sees the general condition of transportation in a way that the president of no single railroad can ever see; it is better informed on crops than the farmer or even the Department of Agriculture. In fact, the market reduces to a bloodless verdict all knowledge bearing on finance, both domestic and foreign.*

A similar notion was expressed by George A. Akerlof and Robert J. Shiller:

> *To understand how economies work and how we can manage them and prosper, we must pay attention to the thought patterns that animate people's ideas and feelings, their animal spirits. We will never really understand important economic events unless we confront the fact that their causes are largely mental in nature.*[2]

Market participants use many inputs and analytical tools before trading. Fundamental analysis is a key input in determining security prices, but it is not the only one. Technical analysts believe that emotions play a role. Investors with a favorable fundamental view may nonetheless sell a financial instrument for other reasons, including pessimistic investor sentiment, margin calls, and requirements for their capital—for example, to pay for a child's college tuition. Technicians do not care why market participants are buying or selling, just that they are doing so.

Some financial instruments have an associated income stream that contributes to the security's intrinsic value. Bonds have regular coupon payments, and equity shares may have

[2]Akerlof and Shiller (2009).

underlying cash flows or dividend streams. A fundamental analyst can adjust these cash flows for risk and use standard time value of money techniques to determine a present value. Other assets, such as a bushel of wheat, gallon of crude oil, or ounce of silver, do not have underlying financial statements or an income stream, so valuation models cannot be used to derive their fundamental intrinsic values. For these assets, technical analysis is the only form of analysis possible. So, whereas fundamental analysis is widely used in the analysis of fixed-income and equity securities, technical analysis is widely used in the analysis of commodities, currencies, and futures.

Market participants attempt to anticipate economic developments and enter into trades to profit from them. Technicians believe that security price movements occur before fundamental developments unfold—certainly before they are reported. This belief is reflected in the fact that stock prices are one of the 12 components of the National Bureau of Economic Research's Index of Leading Economic Indicators. A key tenet of technical analysis is that the equity market moves roughly six months ahead of inflection points in the broad economy.

2.2. Technical and Fundamental Analysis

Technical analysis and fundamental analysis are both useful and valid, but they approach the market in different ways. Technicians focus solely on analyzing markets and the trading of financial instruments. Fundamental analysis is a much wider field, encompassing financial and economic analysis as well as analysis of societal and political trends. Technicians analyze the result of this extensive fundamental analysis in terms of how it affects market prices. A technician's analysis is derived solely from price and volume data, whereas a fundamental equity analyst analyzes a company and incorporates data that are external to the market and then uses this analysis to predict security price movements. As the quotation from Dow in Section 2.1 illustrates, technical analysis assumes that all of the factors considered by a fundamental analyst are reflected in the price of a financial instrument through buying and selling activity.

A key distinction between technical analysis and fundamental analysis is that the technician has more concrete data, primarily price and volume data, to work with. The financial statements analyzed by fundamental analysts are not objective data but are the result of numerous estimates and assumptions that have been added together to arrive at the line items in the financial statements. Even the cash line on a balance sheet is subject to corporate management's opinion about which securities are liquid enough to be considered "cash." This opinion must be agreed to by auditors and, in many countries, regulators (who sometimes differ with the auditors). Financial statements are subject to restatements because of such issues as changes in accounting assumptions and even fraud. But the price and volume data used in technical analysis are objective. When the data become subject to analysis, however, both types of analysis become subjective because judgment is exercised when a technician analyzes a price chart and when a fundamental analyst analyzes an income statement.

Fundamental analysis can be considered to be the more theoretical approach because it seeks to determine the underlying long-term (or intrinsic) value of a security. Technical analysis can be considered to be the more practical because a technician studies the markets and financial instruments as they exist, even if trading activity appears, at times, to be irrational. Technicians seek to project the level at which a financial instrument *will* trade, whereas fundamental analysts seek to predict where it *should* trade.

Being a fundamental analyst can be lonely if the analyst is the first to arrive at a fundamental conclusion, even though it is correct, because deviations from intrinsic value can persist for long periods. The reason these deviations may persist is that it takes buying activity to raise (or lower) the price of a security in a freely traded market.

A drawback of technical analysis is that technicians are limited to studying market movements and do not use other predictive analytical methods, such as interviewing the customers of a subject company, to determine future demand for a company's products. Technicians study market trends and are mainly concerned with a security's price trend: Is the security trading up, down, or sideways? Trends are driven by collective investor psychology, however, and can change without warning. Additionally, it can take some time for a trend to become evident. Thus, technicians may make wrong calls and have to change their opinions. Technicians are better at identifying market moves after the moves are already under way.

Moreover, trends and patterns must be in place for some time before they are recognizable, so a key shortcoming of technical analysis is that it can be late in identifying changes in trends or patterns. This shortcoming mirrors a key shortcoming of fundamental analysis in that securities often overshoot fundamental fair values in an uptrend and undershoot fundamental fair values in a downtrend. Strictly relying on price targets obtained by fundamental analysis can lead to closing profitable investment positions too early because investors may irrationally bid securities prices well above or well below intrinsic value.

Fundamental analysis is a younger field than technical analysis because reliable fundamental data are a relatively new phenomenon. In contrast, the first recorded use of technical analysis was in Japan in the 1700s, where it was used to analyze trading in the rice market. The Japanese developed a detailed field of technical analysis with their own chart design and patterns. These tools were translated and widely understood outside Japan only in the 1980s.

Western use of technical analysis was pioneered by Dow, who was also the first editor of the *Wall Street Journal*, in the 1890s. At the time, publicly traded companies were under no requirement to release their financial information even to shareholders, and insider trading was common and legal. Dow created the Dow Jones Industrial Average and the Dow Jones Railroad Average (now the Transportation Average) as a proxy to gauge the health of the economy, because fundamental data were not available. By his logic, if industrial stocks were doing well, industrial companies themselves must be doing well and if railroad stocks were doing well, railroad companies must be doing well. And if both manufacturers and the companies that transported goods to market were prospering, the economy as a whole must be prospering.

Not until the Securities Exchange Act of 1934 were public companies in the United States required to regularly file financial statements that were available to the public. In that year, Benjamin Graham published his seminal work, *Security Analysis*, and three years later, he and several others founded one of the first societies devoted to fundamental analysis, the New York Society of Security Analysts.[3] Fundamental analysis quickly overtook technical analysis in terms of acceptance by practitioners, regulators, and academics.

Acceptance of technical analysis by practitioners was revived in the 1970s with the creation of the Market Technicians Association in New York and the International Federation of Technical Analysts a few years later. Only in the last decade, however, has the field started to achieve widespread acceptance by regulators and academics. An important impediment to acceptance by academics is the difficulty of capturing the subjectivity involved in technical analysis. The human brain can recognize, analyze, and interpret technical information that is difficult for statistical computer models to recognize and test.

[3]The New York Society of Security Analysts was a successor to the New York Society of Financial Statisticians, which was founded in 1916.

Although technical analysis can be applied to any freely traded security, it does have its limits. In markets that are subject to large outside manipulation, the application of technical analysis is limited. For example, the central banks of many countries intervene in their currency markets from time to time to maintain exchange rate stability. Interestingly, traders claim to have been able to successfully predict interventions in some countries, especially those where the central bank is itself using technical analysis. Technical analysis is also limited in illiquid markets, where even modestly sized trades can have an inordinate impact on prices. For example, in considering a thinly traded American Depositary Receipt (ADR), analyzing the more heavily traded local security frequently yields a better analysis.[4] Another example of when technical analysis may give an incorrect reading is in the case of a company that has declared bankruptcy and announced that its shares will have zero value in a restructuring. A positive technical trend may appear in such cases as investors who hold short positions buy shares to close out their positions.

A good example of when technical analysis is a superior tool to fundamental analysis is in the case of securities fraud, such as occurred at Enron Corporation and WorldCom. These companies were issuing fraudulent financial statements, but many fundamental analysts continued to hold favorable views of the companies' equity securities even as the share prices declined. Simultaneously, a small group of investors came to the opposite view and expressed this view through high-volume sales of the securities. The result was clearly negative chart patterns that could then be discerned by technical analysis.

3. TECHNICAL ANALYSIS TOOLS

The primary tools used in technical analysis are charts and indicators. Charts are the graphical display of price and volume data, and the display may be done in a number of ways. Charts are then subjected to various analyses, including the identification of trends, patterns, and cycles. Technical indicators include a variety of measures of relative price level—for example, price momentum, market sentiment, and funds flow. We will discuss charts first.

3.1. Charts

Charts are an essential component of the technical analyst's toolkit. Charts provide information about past price behavior and provide a basis for inferring likely future price behavior. A variety of charts can be useful in studying the markets. The selection of the chart to use in technical analysis is determined by the intended purpose of the analysis.

3.1.1. Line Chart

Line charts are familiar to all types of analysts and are a simple graphic display of price trends over time. Usually, the chart is a plot of data points, such as share price, with a line connecting these points. Line charts are typically drawn with closing prices as the data points. The vertical axis (*y*-axis) reflects price level, and the horizontal axis (*x*-axis) is time. Even though the line chart is the simplest chart, an analyst can quickly glean information from this chart.

[4]An American Depositary Receipt is a negotiable certificate issued by a depositary bank that represents ownership in a non-U.S. company's deposited equity (i.e., equity held in custody by the depositary bank in the company's home market).

The chart in Exhibit 12-1 is a quarterly chart of the FTSE 100 Index from 1984 through mid-2009. Up years and down years are clearly evident. The strong rally from 1984 through 1999 and the market decline from late 1999 to late 2002 are also clearly visible. The 2003–2007 rally did not exceed the high reached in 1999, which suggests that investors were not willing to pay as high a price for stocks on the London Stock Exchange during that rally as they were in the prior rally. This information provides a broad overview of investor sentiment and can lead to further analysis. Importantly, the analyst can access and analyze this information quickly. Collecting and analyzing the full array of data normally incorporated in fundamental analysis would take much longer.

EXHIBIT 12-1 Line Chart: FTSE 100 Quarterly Price Data, 1984–2009 (price measured in British pounds sterling)

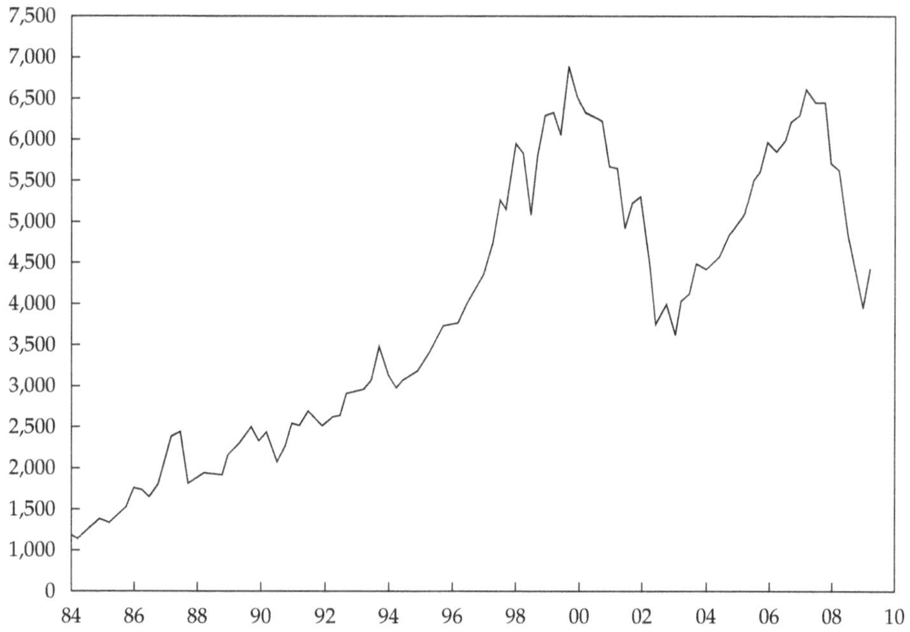

3.1.2. Bar Chart

A line chart has one data point per time interval. A **bar chart**, in contrast, has four bits of data in each entry—the high and low price encountered during the time interval plus the opening and closing prices. Such charts can be constructed for any time period, but they are customarily constructed from daily data.

As Exhibit 12-2 shows, a vertical line connects the high and low price of the day; a cross-hatch to the right indicates the closing price, and a cross-hatch to the left indicates the opening price. The appeal of this chart is that the analyst immediately gets a sense of the nature of that day's trading. A short bar indicates little price movement during the day; that is, the high, low, and close were near the opening price. A long bar indicates a wide divergence between the high and the low for the day.

EXHIBIT 12-2 Bar Chart Notation

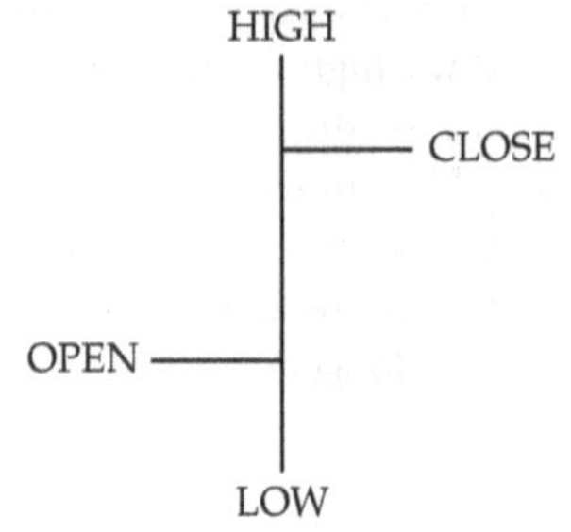

Exhibit 12-3 shows daily performance of the Brazilian Bovespa Index (BVSP) from late 2007 through late 2009. The top part provides the price open, close, high, and low; the bottom part shows volume, which will be discussed in Section 3.1.6. The downturn in the second half of 2008 is obvious, but also notable are the extreme price movements in the fourth quarter of 2008. There were 40 trading days from 29 September to 24 November. On 20 of those days, the closing value of the index changed from the previous close by at least 4 percent, a huge move by historical standards. During the same period, the average daily price range (high to low) was 7 percent, compared with 3.7 percent in the previous two months. This potentially important information would not be captured in a line chart.

EXHIBIT 12-3 Bar Chart: Bovespa Index, November 2007–November 2009 (price in Brazilian reais)

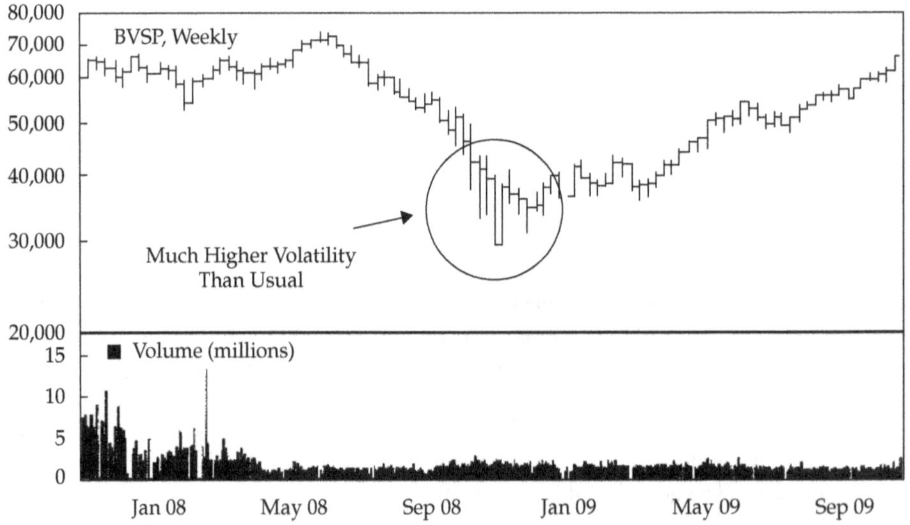

3.1.3. Candlestick Chart

Candlestick charts trace their roots to Japan, where technical analysis has been in use for centuries. Like a bar chart, a **candlestick chart** also provides four prices per data point entry: the opening and closing prices and the high and low prices during the period. As shown in Exhibit 12-4, a vertical line represents the range through which the security price traveled during the time period. The line is known as the wick or shadow. The body of the candle is shaded if the opening price was higher than the closing price, and the body is clear if the opening price was lower than the closing price.

EXHIBIT 12-4 Construction of a Candlestick Chart

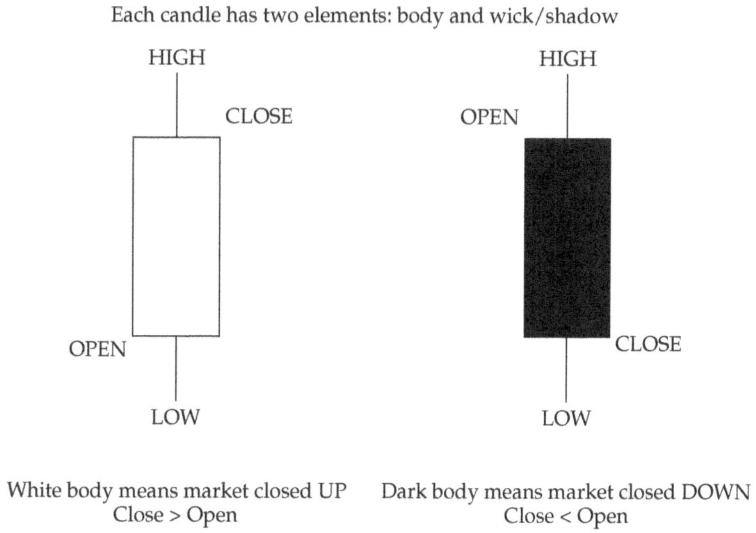

Exhibit 12-5 shows a weekly candlestick chart for Companhia Vale do Rio Doce for the period 1 January through 15 June 2009.

The advantage of the candlestick chart over the bar chart is that price moves are much more visible in the candlestick chart, which allows faster analysis. The bar chart indicates market volatility only by the height of each bar, but in candlestick charts, the difference between opening and closing prices and their relationship to the highs and lows of the day are clearly apparent. Compare the sixth candle with the twelfth in Exhibit 12-5. In the sixth candle, the analyst can see significant volatility because the high of the day and low of the day are so far apart. The stock opened near the low of the day and closed near the high, suggesting a steady rally during the day. In contrast, the twelfth candle shows no difference between the high and low, and the shares opened and closed at the same price, creating a cross pattern. In Japanese terminology used in candlestick charting, this pattern is called a doji. The doji signifies that after a full day of trading, the positive price influence of buyers and the negative price influence of sellers exactly counteracted each other, which tells the analyst that this market is in balance. If a doji occurs at the end of a long uptrend or downtrend, it signals that the trend will probably reverse.

EXHIBIT 12-5 Candlestick Chart: Companhia Vale do Rio Doce, 1 January–15 June 2009 (prices in U.S. dollars)

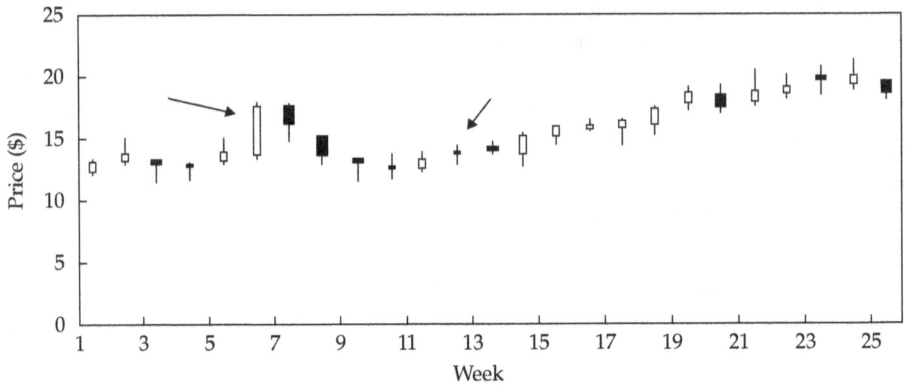

3.1.4. Point and Figure Chart

Point and figure charts were widely used in the United States in the early 1900s and were favored because they were easy to create and update manually in the era before computers. As with any technical analysis tool, these charts can be used with equities, fixed-income securities, commodities, or foreign exchange.

Where the point and figure chart originated is unclear; the chart is referred to in a number of books in the United States dating back to 1898. The methodology evolved until 1934 when the first book was published on the topic: *The Point and Figure Method of Anticipating Stock Price Movements* by Victor de Villiers and Owen Taylor. With the advent of powerful charting software and Internet web sites, complex chart types, such as the candlestick chart, have become more popular. But point and figure charts still offer tremendous value if one knows their limitations and their advantages. The key reason this knowledge is necessary, as explained next, is that point and figure charts are constructed differently from other charts; they have a clear focus on entry and exit levels but no focus on holding periods.

As illustrated in Exhibit 12-6, a point and figure chart is drawn on a grid and consists of columns of X's alternating with columns of O's. Neither time nor volume is represented on this type of chart, and *the horizontal axis represents the number of changes in price, not time.* Movement along the horizontal axis does reflect the passage of time, but not in any uniform fashion. The analyst makes entries on a point and figure chart only when the price changes by the "box size," which is explained below. This lack of a normal time dimension is perhaps the most unusual characteristic of a point and figure chart.

To construct a point and figure chart, the analyst must determine both the box size and the reversal size. Box size refers to the change in price represented by the height of each box (boxes are generally square, but the width has no meaning). In Exhibit 12-6, the box size is HK$1. The reversal size is used to determine when to create a new column. In Exhibit 12-6, the reversal size is three, meaning a reversal in price of three or more boxes.

Although a point and figure chart can be constructed in several ways, these charts are always drawn on graph paper to facilitate seeing the "columns and rows" nature of the data. The vertical axis measures *discrete increments of price.* For example, an analyst in Europe might draw a €1 chart, a €2 chart, or any other increment. In a €1 chart, boxes would be €1 apart

EXHIBIT 12-6 Point and Figure Chart: Wharf Holdings Daily Price Chart, 2007–2009 (in Hong Kong dollars)

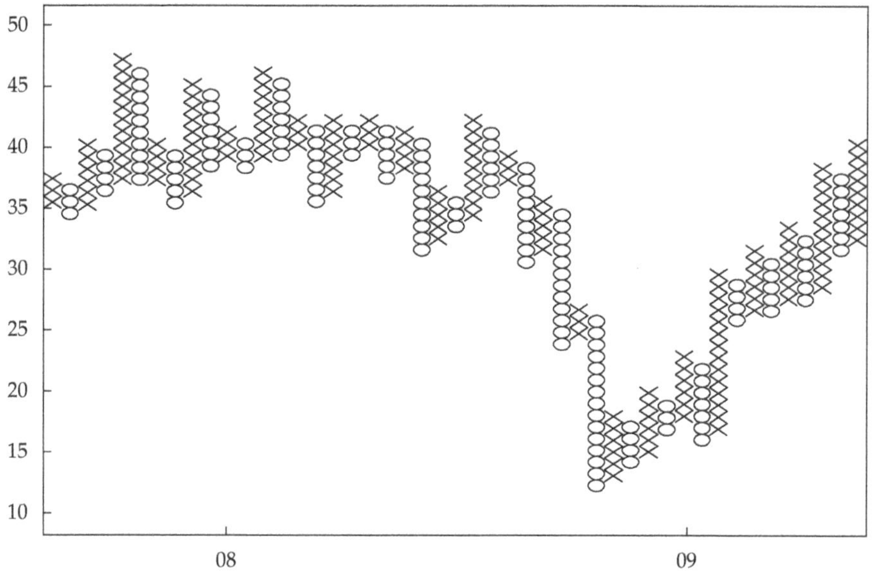

Note: The box size is HK$1, and the reversal size is three.

(e.g., €40, €41, €42), whereas in a €2 chart they would be €2 apart (€40, €42, €44). The most commonly used box size is 1 unit of currency, which is used when prices range from 20 to 100 per share of the currency.

The next decision the technician needs to make is the reversal size. The most common size is three, meaning a reversal in price of three or more boxes (€3 in the case of a box size of €1). This use of a multibox reversal helps eliminate "noise" in the price data. (*Noise* refers to short-term trading volatility that does not alter the long-term trend of the security.)

In a point and figure chart, X represents an increase in price and O represents a decline in price. In constructing a chart, the technician draws an X in a column of boxes every time the security price closes up by the amount of the box size. (Ideally, all security prices are considered on an intraday basis, but this practice has given way to using closing prices only.) If the price increases by twice the box size, the technician draws two X's to fill in two boxes, one on top of the other. The technician fills in more boxes for larger price moves. The resulting column starts at the opening price level and extends to the closing price level. As long as the security keeps closing at higher prices, the technician keeps filling in boxes with X's, which makes the column higher and higher. If the price does not increase by at least the box size, no indication is made on the chart. Thus, in some cases, the chart is not updated for long periods, but no indication of this passage of time is made on the chart.

The reversal size determines when to create a new column. In the case of a €1 box size, and three-box reversal size, a decline of €3 or more would result in the technician shifting to the next column over and beginning a column of O's. The first box to be filled in is to the right and below the highest X in the prior column. The technician then fills in an O to bring the column down to the price level at the close. Again, each filled-in box (if the box size is €1) represents a €1 decline in the security price. As long as the downtrend continues, without a €3 increase in price, the technician continues adding O's to the column below the prior O's. A reversal in the downtrend by at least the amount of the reversal size prompts the technician to move to the next column and begin drawing a series of X's again. Computer technology makes the process easy, but many technicians prefer to keep point and figure charts on their wall and update them manually because doing so provides a vivid reminder of the market trend.

Point and figure charts are particularly useful for making trading decisions because they clearly illustrate price levels that may signal the end of a decline or advance. They also clearly show price levels at which a security may frequently trade. In using the point size and reversal size to make trading decisions, for uptrends, or columns of X's, the practitioner would maintain long positions. The reversal size could be considered the amount of loss that would prompt the closing of a long position and the establishment of a new short position. The larger the reversal size, the fewer columns in the chart and the longer uptrends and downtrends will run.

The box size can be varied in relation to the security price. For a security with a very low price—say, below €5—a €1 box size might mean few or no updates on the chart because the price would only rarely change by this amount. Thus, the technician could reduce the box size to cents. For highly priced securities, much larger box sizes could be used. The reversal size is a multiple of the box size, so if the box size is changed, the reversal size changes. Practitioners who want fewer columns or trade signals can use a large reversal size.

Analysis of a point and figure chart is relatively straightforward as long as the technician understands its construction and limitations. The chart is relatively simple, and repeated high and low prices are evident. Congestion areas, where a security trades up and down in a narrow range, are evidenced by a series of short columns of X's and O's spanning roughly the same price range. Major, sustained price moves are represented by long columns of X's (when prices are moving up) or O's (when prices are moving down).

3.1.5. Scale

For any chart—line, bar, or candlestick—the vertical axis can be constructed with either a **linear scale** (also known as an arithmetic scale) or a **logarithmic scale**, depending on how you want to view the data. With a logarithmic scale, equal vertical distances on the chart correspond to an equal percentage change. A logarithmic scale is appropriate when the data move through a range of values representing several orders of magnitude (e.g., from 10 to 10,000); a linear scale is better suited for narrower ranges (e.g., prices from $35 to $50). The share price history of a particular company, for instance, is usually best suited to a linear scale because the data range is usually narrow.

The horizontal axis shows the passage of time. The appropriate time interval depends on the nature of the underlying data and the specific use of the chart. An active trader, for instance, may find 10-minute, 5-minute, or even tick-by-tick data useful, but other technical analysts may prefer daily or weekly data. In general, the greater the volatility of the data, the greater the likelihood that an analyst can find useful information in more-frequent data sampling.

Consider Exhibits 12-7 and 12-8, which both show the yearly history of the Dow Jones Industrial Average (DJIA) from 1928 to 2010. Plotting the index on a linear scale, as in Exhibit 12-7, makes it difficult to gather much information from the first 50 years of the data series. Analysts can see a slight uptrend but not much else. The eye is drawn to the bull market of the 1980s, the subsequent dot-com bubble, and the recent era of the subprime crisis. When plotted on a logarithmic scale, as in Exhibit 12-8, however, many people would find that the data tell a more comprehensive story. The Great Depression of the 1930s stands out, but over the following 75 years, the data follow a relatively stable upward trend.

EXHIBIT 12-7 Dow Jones Industrial Average on Linear Scale, 1928–2010 (in U.S. dollars)

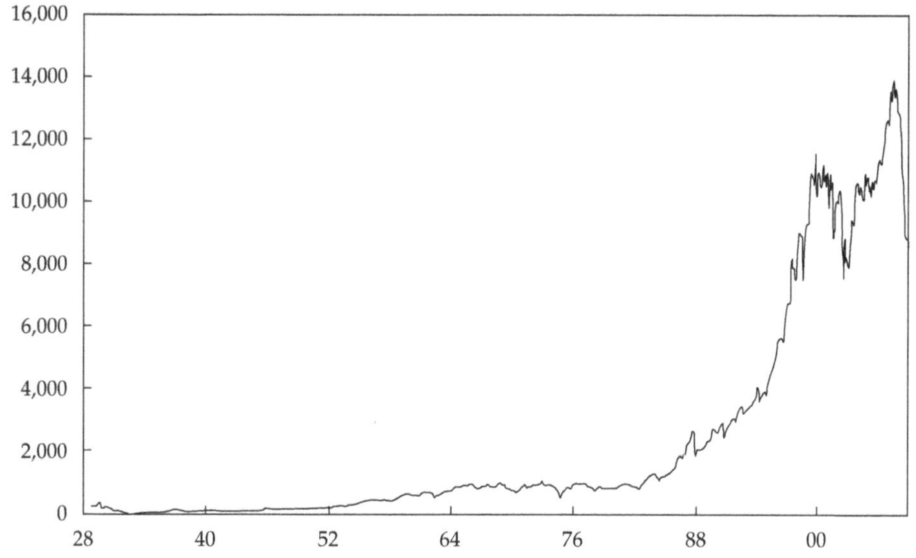

EXHIBIT 12-8 Dow Jones Industrial Average on Logarithmic Scale, 1928–2010 (in U.S. dollars)

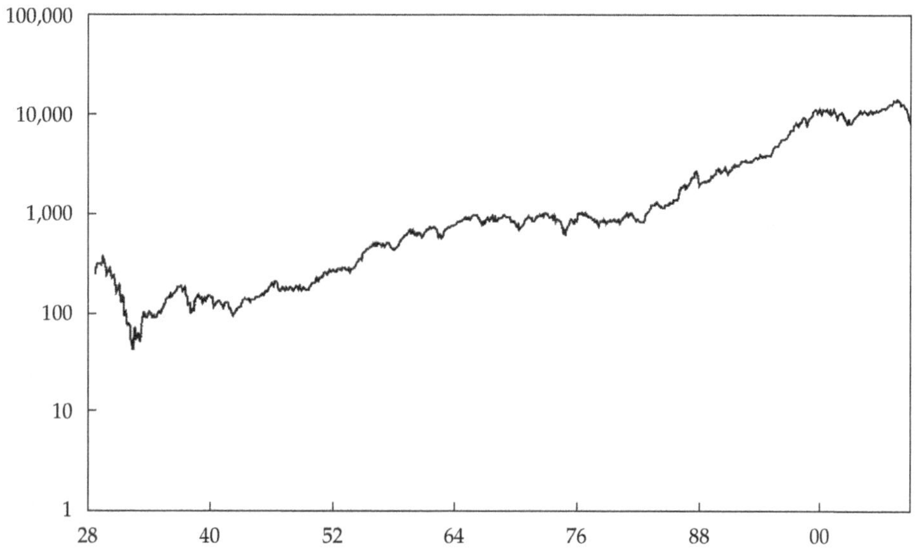

3.1.6. Volume

Volume is an important characteristic that is included at the bottom of many charts; see, for example, Exhibit 12-3. Volume is used to assess the strength or conviction of buyers and sellers in determining a security's price. For example, on a daily price chart, below the price section would be a column chart showing the volume traded for that day.

Some technicians consider volume information to be crucial. If volume increases during a time frame in which price is also increasing, that combination is considered positive and the two indicators are said to "confirm" each other. The signal would be interpreted to mean that over time, more and more investors are buying the financial instrument and they are doing so at higher and higher prices. This pattern is considered a positive technical development.

Conversely, if volume and price diverge—for example, if a stock's price rises while its volume declines—the implication is that fewer and fewer market participants are willing to buy that stock at the new price. If this trend in volume continues, the price rally will soon end because demand for the security at higher prices will cease. Exhibit 12-9 shows a bar chart for Toronto-Dominion Bank (TD Bank) with volume displayed separately.

EXHIBIT 12-9 Daily Candlestick Price Chart and Volume Bar Chart: TD Bank, November 2007–November 2009 (price in Canadian dollars)

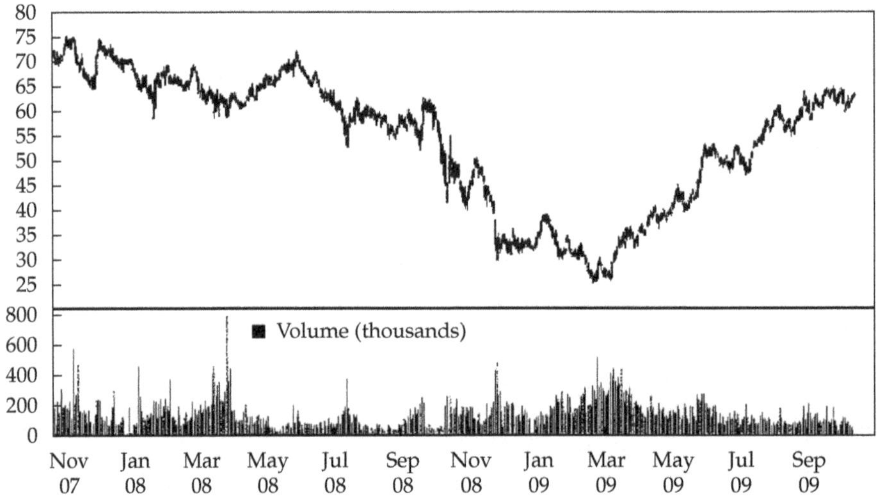

3.1.7. Time Intervals

Most of the chart examples in this chapter are daily price charts in that they show the price and volume on a daily basis. Daily frequency is not required, however, because charts can be constructed by using any time interval. For short-term trading, the analyst can create charts with one-minute or shorter intervals. For long-term investing, the analyst can use weekly, monthly, or even annual intervals. The same analytical approach applies irrespective of the time interval. Using long intervals allows the analyst to chart longer time periods than does using short time intervals for the simple reason that long intervals contain fewer data points, so a longer time frame can be presented on the chart. Using short intervals allows the analyst to see more detail. A useful step for many analysts is to begin the analysis of a security with the chart for a long time frame, such as a weekly or monthly chart, and then construct charts with shorter and shorter time intervals, such as daily or hourly charts.

3.1.8. Relative Strength Analysis

Relative strength analysis is widely used to compare the performance of a particular asset, such as a common stock, with that of some benchmark—such as, in the case of common stocks, the FTSE 100, the Nikkei 225, or the S&P 500 Index—or the performance of another security. The intent is to show out- or underperformance of the individual issue relative to some other index or asset. Typically, the analyst prepares a line chart of the ratio of two prices, with the asset under analysis as the numerator and with the benchmark or other security as the denominator. A rising line shows the asset is performing better than the index or other stock; a declining line shows the opposite. A flat line shows neutral performance.

Suppose a private investor is researching two investment ideas she read about. Harley-Davidson Motor Company (HOG) is a well-known motorcycle company; Rodman and Renshaw (RODM) is a small investment bank. The investor wants to determine which of these two has been the stronger performer (relative to the S&P 500) over the past few months. Exhibit 12-10 shows relative strength lines for the two stocks for the first six months of 2009. Each point on the relative strength plot is simply the ratio of a share price to the S&P 500. For example, on 9 March 2009, HOG closed at US$8.42 and the S&P 500 closed at $676.53. The relative strength data point is, therefore, 8.42/676.53, or 0.0124. On 27 April, HOG closed at US$19.45, with the S&P 500 at $857.51. The relative strength value is 19.45/857.51, or 0.0227, nearly double the 9 March value.

EXHIBIT 12-10 Relative Strength Analysis: HOG versus the S&P 500 and RODM versus the S&P 500, January–June 2009

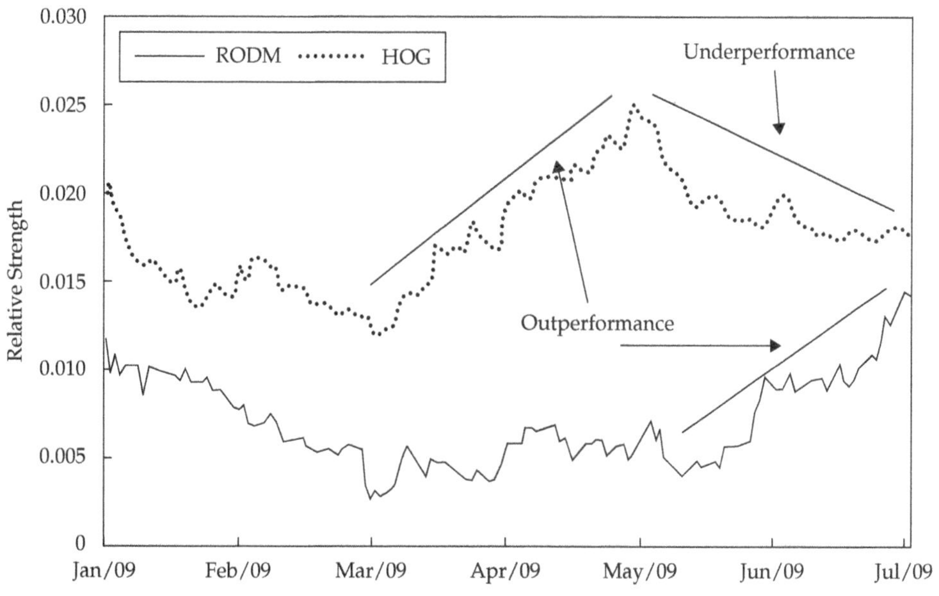

The units on the vertical axis are not significant; the ratio is a function of the relative prices of the assets under consideration. The important information is how the ratio has changed. This type of chart allows an analyst to make a visual determination of that change. As Exhibit 12-10 illustrates, Harley-Davidson was a strong performer in March and April but lagged the index beginning in May. In contrast, the stock of Rodman and Renshaw began a significant rise in mid-May that outperformed the market average.

3.2. Trend

The concept of a **trend** is perhaps the most important aspect of technical analysis. Trend analysis is based on the observation that market participants tend to act in herds and that trends tend to stay in place for some time. A security can be considered to be in an upward trend, a downward trend, a sideways trend, or no apparent trend. Not all securities are in a trend, and little useful forecasting information can be gleaned from technical analysis when a security is not in a trend. Not every chart will have obvious or clear implications, so the analyst must avoid the temptation to force a conclusion from every chart and thus reach a wrong interpretation.

An uptrend for a security is when the price goes to higher highs and higher lows. As the security moves up in price, each subsequent new high is higher than the prior high and each time there is a **retracement**, which is a reversal in the movement of the security's price, it must stop at a higher low than the prior lows in the trend period. To draw an uptrend line, a technician draws a line connecting the lows of the price chart. Major breakdowns in price, however, when the price drops through and below the trendline by a significant amount (many technicians use 5–10 percent below the trendline) indicate that the uptrend is over and may signal a further decline in the price. Minor breakthroughs below previous lows simply call for the line to be moderately adjusted over time. Time is also a consideration in trends: The longer the security price stays below the trendline, the more meaningful the breakdown is considered to be.

In an uptrend, the forces of demand are greater than the forces of supply. So, traders are willing to pay higher and higher prices for the same asset over time. Presumably, the strong demand indicates that investors believe the intrinsic value of the security is increasing.

A downtrend is when a security makes lower lows and lower highs. As the security moves down in price, each subsequent new high must be lower than the prior high and each time there is a retracement, it must stop at a lower low than the prior lows in the trend period. To draw a downtrend line, a technician draws a line connecting the highs of the price chart. Major breakouts above the downtrend line (e.g., 5–10 percent) indicate that the downtrend is over and a rise in the security's price may occur. And as with an uptrend, the longer the security price stays above the trendline, the more meaningful the breakout is considered to be.

In a downtrend, supply is overwhelming demand. Over time, sellers are willing to accept lower and lower prices to exit long positions or enter new short positions. Both motives of the sellers generally indicate deteriorating investor sentiment about the asset. However, selling may be prompted by factors not related to the fundamental or intrinsic value of the stock. For example, investors may be forced to sell to meet margin calls in their portfolios. From a purely technical standpoint, the reason is irrelevant. The downtrend is assumed to continue until contrary technical evidence appears. Combining fundamental analysis with technical analysis in such a case, however, might reveal a security that has attractive fundamentals but a currently negative technical position. In uptrends, however, a security with an attractive technical position but unattractive fundamentals is rare because most buying activity is driven by traders who expect the security price to increase in the future. The rare exception is covering short positions after a sizable decline in the share price.

A security may trade in a fairly narrow range, moving sideways on the price chart without much upward or downward movement. This pattern indicates a relative balance between supply and demand. A technical analyst may not expect to profit from long or short trades in such securities but might devise profitable option strategies for short-term investors with the ability to accept the risks.

Exhibit 12-11 shows the application of trend analysis. Depicted is an uptrend line for the shares of China Mobile Limited. Note that through late 2007, every rally took the shares to a new high whereas sell-offs stopped at increasingly higher levels. The first sign of trouble came in the spring of 2008 when the rally terminated at a lower price point than the prior rally of late 2007. This movement was followed by the shares breaking through the trendline.

EXHIBIT 12-11 Trend Analysis: China Mobile Weekly Price Chart, 2002–2010 (prices in Hong Kong dollars)

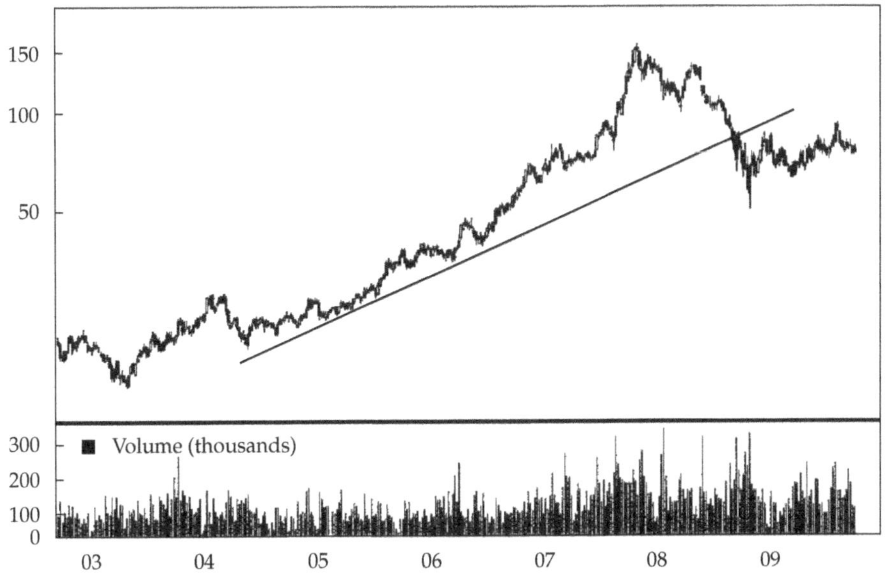

The chart in Exhibit 12-11 covers roughly seven years and would most likely be used by investors with a long time horizon. Investors with a shorter horizon might use a chart with a shorter time frame and would thus obtain a different trendline as well as a different trendline breakdown.

Two concepts related to trend are support and resistance. **Support** is defined as a low price range in which buying activity is sufficient to stop the decline in price. It is the opposite of **resistance**, which is a price range in which selling is sufficient to stop the rise in price. The psychology behind the concepts of support and resistance is that investors have come to a collective consensus about the price of a security. Support and resistance levels can be sloped lines, as in trendlines, or horizontal lines.

A key tenet of support and resistance as a part of technical analysis is the **change in polarity principle**, which states that once a support level is breached, it becomes a resistance level. The same holds true for resistance levels; once breached, they become support levels. For example, if the price of a security never rises above SFr10 over a long period of time and begins to decline each time it reaches this level but then finally breaks through this level by a significant amount, the point to which the price rises becomes a support level.

Support and resistance levels are commonly round numbers. Support indicates that at some price level, investors consider a security to be an attractive investment and are willing to buy, even in the wake of a sharp decline (and for resistance, at some level, investors are not willing to buy, even in an uptrend). The fact that these price points tend to be round numbers strongly suggests that human sentiment is at work.

One of the most widely publicized examples of support and resistance is when the DJIA broke through the 10,000 mark in 1999, shown in Exhibit 12-12. Previously, 10,000 had been viewed as a resistance line, but from 1999 through the end of the chart in 2001, 10,000 served as a support level.

EXHIBIT 12-12 Support Level: DJIA Weekly Price Chart, 1990–2001 (price in U.S. dollars ÷ 100)

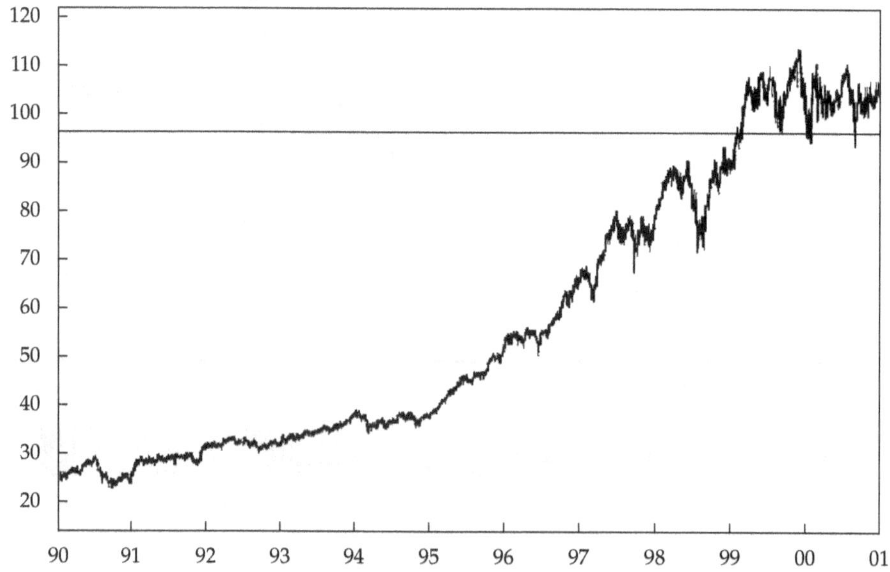

3.3. Chart Patterns

Chart patterns are formations that appear in price charts that create some type of recognizable shape. Common patterns appear repeatedly and often lead to similar subsequent price movements. Thus, the identification and analysis of chart patterns is a common aspect of technical analysis used to predict security prices. An important connection to understand is that patterns form as a result of the behavior of market participants and that these patterns represent graphical depictions of the collective psychology of the market at a given time.

The recurring patterns that appear in charts can be used as a basis for market forecasting. The reason chart patterns have predictive value is that they are graphic representations of human trading activity and human behavior is frequently repeated, especially trading activity that is driven by fear (in market sell-offs) or hope and greed (as evidenced in bubbles—that is, rallies that extend well beyond valuation levels that would be derived by fundamental values). An example of a rally driven by greed is the recent real estate bubble, which took home prices to unsustainably high levels. This bubble started a few years after the Internet stock bubble of the 1990s, which also took prices to unsustainably high levels. In bubbles, investors, driven by hope and greed, drive the price of an asset to irrationally high levels, in the expectation that another buyer will be willing to pay an even higher price for the asset. The housing bubble was notable because it so closely followed the Internet stock bubble, despite all that had been written about the "irrational exuberance" of the Internet bubble of the 1990s.

Chart patterns can be divided into two categories: **reversal patterns** and **continuation patterns**. These terms refer to the trend for the security in question prior to the formation of the pattern. The most important concept to understand in using chart patterns is that without a clear trend in place prior to the pattern, the pattern has no predictive value. This aspect is frequently forgotten by investors who are so eager to identify and use patterns that they forget the proper application of charts.

3.3.1. Reversal Patterns

As the name implies, a reversal pattern signals the end of a trend, a change in direction of the financial instrument's price. Evidence that the trend is about to change direction is obviously important, so reversal patterns are noteworthy.

3.3.1.1. Head and Shoulders

Perhaps the most widely recognized reversal pattern is the **head and shoulders pattern**. The pattern consists of three segments. Volume is an important characteristic in interpreting this pattern. Because head and shoulders indicates a trend reversal, a clear trend must exist prior to the formation of the pattern in order for the pattern to have predictive validity. For a head and shoulders pattern, the prior trend must be an uptrend. Later, we will discuss the *inverse* head and shoulders pattern (preceded by a downtrend).

Exhibit 12-13 depicts a head and shoulders pattern for Marvell Technology Group during 2006. The three parts of the pattern are as follows:

- **Left shoulder:** This part appears to show a strong rally, with the slope of the rally being greater than the prior uptrend, on strong volume. The rally then reverses back to the price level where it started, forming an inverted V pattern, but on lower volume.
- **Head:** The head is a more pronounced version of the left shoulder. A rally following the first shoulder takes the security to a higher high than the left shoulder by a significant enough margin to be clearly evident on the price chart. Volume is typically lower in this rally, however, than in the one that formed the first, upward side of the left shoulder. This second rally also fails, with price falling back to the same level at which the left shoulder began and ended. This price level is called the neckline. This price level also will be below the uptrend line formed by connecting the low prices in the uptrend preceding the beginning of the head and shoulders pattern. This head pattern is the first signal that the rally may be coming to an end and that a reversal may be starting.
- **Right shoulder:** The right shoulder is a mirror image (or close to a mirror image) of the left shoulder but on lower volume, signifying less buying enthusiasm. The price rallies up

to roughly the same level as the first shoulder, but the rally reverses at a lower high price than the rally that formed the head.

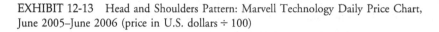

EXHIBIT 12-13 Head and Shoulders Pattern: Marvell Technology Daily Price Chart, June 2005–June 2006 (price in U.S. dollars ÷ 100)

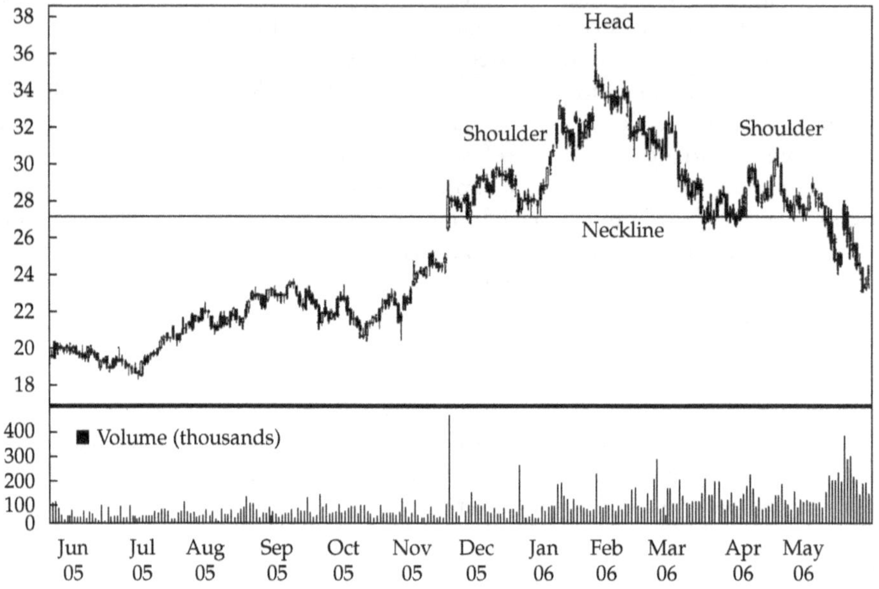

Rarely will an analyst see a perfectly formed head and shoulders pattern; variations include two tops on the shoulders or on the head. The head, however, should rise to a higher price level than either shoulder, whereas the shoulders should be roughly symmetrical. In terms of the neckline price level, the first rally should begin at this level and the left shoulder and head should also decline to roughly this level. But necklines may not always form exactly horizontal lines. These imperfect variations make this (and other) technical patterns difficult for quantitative analysts or academicians to model, but the human brain can detect the pattern even if it is imperfectly formed.

Volume is important in analyzing head and shoulders patterns. A new high in price at the top of the head without a new high in volume signals fewer bullish market participants. When one indicator is making a new high (or low) but another is not, this situation is called divergence. In divergence, the right shoulder will have even lower volume, signaling that buying interest or demand is tapering off and will soon be overwhelmed by supply. The result will be a price decline.

Once the head and shoulders pattern has formed, the expectation is that the share price will decline down through the neckline price. Technicians tend to use filtering rules to make sure that a clear breakdown of the neckline has occurred. These rules may take the form of waiting to trade until the price falls to a meaningful level below the neckline (3 percent or 5 percent are commonly used) and/or a time limit for the price to remain below the neckline before trading; when a daily price chart is used, the rule may be several days to a week. Prices commonly rebound to the neckline levels, even after a decline has exceeded the filter levels.

Prices generally stop, however, at or around the neckline. The neckline was a support level, and under the change in polarity principle, once a support level is breached, it becomes a resistance level.

3.3.1.2. Inverse Head and Shoulders

The head and shoulders pattern can also form upside down and act as a reversal pattern for a preceding downtrend. The three parts of the inverse head and shoulders are as follows:

- **Left shoulder:** This shoulder appears to show a strong decline, with the slope of the decline greater than the prior downtrend, on strong volume. The rally then reverses back to the price level where it started, forming a V pattern, but on lower volume.
- **Head:** The head is a more pronounced version of the left shoulder. Another decline follows but on diminishing volume, which takes the price to a lower low than the prior shoulder by a significant enough margin that it is clearly evident on the price chart. This second decline also reverses, with price rising to the same level at which the left shoulder began and ended. This price level, the neckline, will also be above the uptrend line formed by connecting the high prices in the downtrend preceding the beginning of the inverse head and shoulders pattern. This pattern is the first signal that the decline may be coming to an end and that a reversal may be near.
- **Right shoulder:** The right shoulder is roughly a mirror image of the left shoulder but on lower volume, signifying less selling enthusiasm. The price declines down to roughly the same level as the first shoulder, but the rally reverses at a higher low price than the rally that formed the head.

3.3.1.3. Setting Price Targets with Head and Shoulders Pattern

As with all technical patterns, the head and shoulders pattern must be analyzed from the perspective of the security's long-term price trend. The rally that happened before the formation of the pattern must be large enough for there to be something to reverse. The stronger and more pronounced the rally was, the stronger and more pronounced the reversal is likely to be. Similarly, once the neckline is breached, the security is expected to decline by the same amount as the change in price from the neckline to the top of the head. If the preceding rally started at a price higher than the neckline, however, the correction is unlikely to bring the price lower than the price level at the start of the rally. Because a head and shoulders formation is a bearish indicator (i.e., a technician would expect the previously established uptrend to end and a downtrend to commence), a technician would seek to profit by shorting the security under analysis. When attempting to profit from the head and shoulders pattern, a technician will often use the price differences between the head and the neckline to set a price target, which is the price at which the technician anticipates closing the investment position. The price target for the head and shoulders pattern is calculated as follows:

$$\text{Price target} = \text{Neckline} - (\text{Head} - \text{Neckline})$$

For example, in Exhibit 12-14, the high price reached at the top of the head is roughly \$37 and the neckline formed at roughly \$27 for a difference of \$10. So a technician would expect the price to decline to a level \$10 below the neckline, or to \$17; that is,

$$\text{Price target} = \$27 - (\$37 - \$27) = \$17$$

EXHIBIT 12-14 Calculating Price Target: Marvell Technology Daily Price Chart, June 2005–November 2006 (price in U.S. dollars)

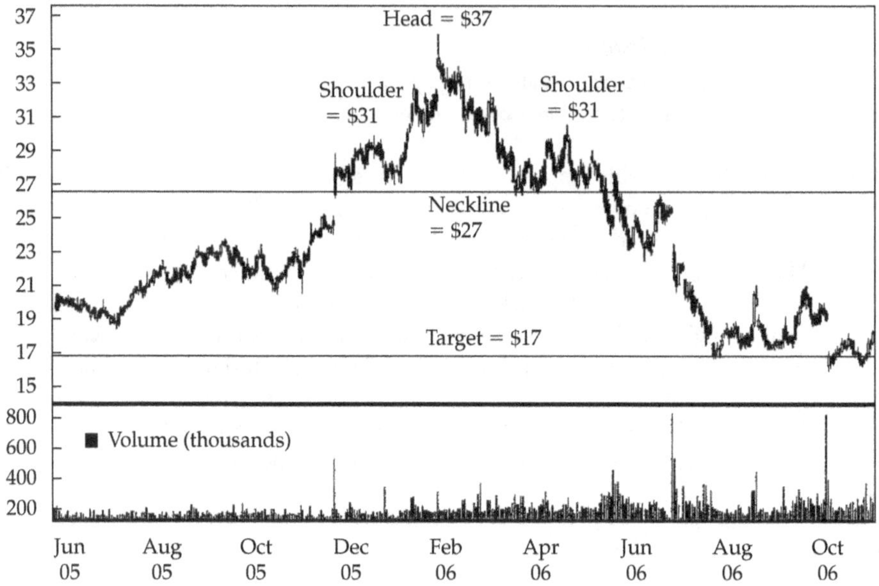

EXAMPLE 12-1 Determining a Price Target from a Head and Shoulders Pattern

Danielle Waterhouse is the technical analyst at Kanektok Securities. One of the companies her firm follows is LPA Petroleum. Waterhouse believes that a graph of LPA's share prices over the past six months reveals a classic head and shoulders pattern. The share price peaked at US$108, and she estimates the neckline at US$79. At today's close, the shares traded at US$78. Based on the head and shoulders pattern, what price target should Waterhouse estimate?

Solution: Waterhouse estimates the neckline at US$79, which is US$108 minus US$79, or US$29 lower than the head. Her price target is thus US$79 minus US$29, which is US$50. Waterhouse would attempt to sell LPA short at today's price of US$78 and anticipate closing the position at US$50 for a profit of US$28 per share (not accounting for transaction costs).

3.3.1.4. Setting Price Targets with Inverse Head and Shoulders Pattern

Calculating price targets for inverse head and shoulders patterns is similar to the process for head and shoulders patterns, but in this case, because the pattern predicts the end of a downtrend, the technician calculates how high the price is expected to rise once it breaches the neckline. Exhibit 12-15 illustrates an inverse head and shoulders pattern.

EXHIBIT 12-15 Calculating Price Target for Inverse Head and Shoulders Pattern: DJIA Daily Price Chart, February 2002–January 2004 (price in U.S. dollars ÷ 100)

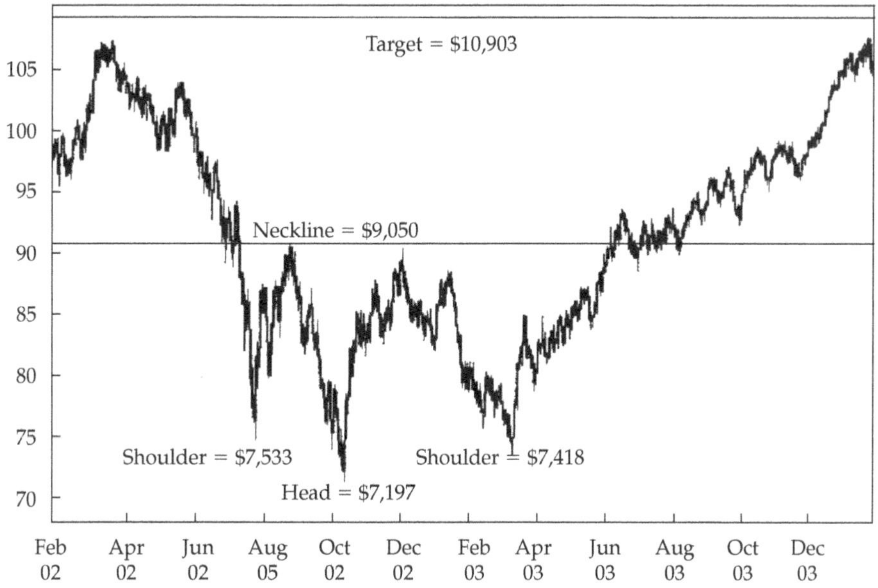

For an inverse head and shoulders pattern, the formula is similar to a head and shoulders pattern:

$$\text{Price target} = \text{Neckline} + (\text{Head} - \text{Neckline})$$

For example, in the price chart in Exhibit 12-15, the low price reached at the bottom of the head is roughly US$7,197 and the neckline formed at roughly US$9,050. The target can thus be found as $9,050 + (9,050 – $7,197) = $10,903. In this case, a technician might have taken a long position in the summer of 2003 with the hope of eventually exiting the position at about US$10,903 for a profit.

3.3.1.5. Double Tops and Bottoms

A **double top** is when an uptrend reverses twice at roughly the same high price level. Typically, volume is lower on the second high than on the first high, signaling a diminishing of demand. The longer the time is between the two tops and the deeper the sell-off is after the first top, the more significant the pattern is considered to be. Price targets can be calculated from this pattern in a manner similar to the calculation for the head and shoulders pattern. For a double top, price is expected to decline below the low of the valley between the two tops by at least the distance from the valley low to the high of the double tops.

EXAMPLE 12-2 Determining a Price Target from a Double-Top Pattern

Richard Dupuis is a technician who trades Eurodollar futures for his own account. He analyzes charts based on one-minute time intervals looking for short-term trading opportunities. Eurodollar futures contracts have been trending upward most of the morning, but Dupuis now observes what he believes is a double-top pattern: After peaking at US$97.03, the futures contract price fell to US$96.42, climbed again to US $97.02, and then started a decline. Because of the double top, Dupuis anticipates a reversal from the uptrend to a downtrend. Dupuis decides to open a short position to capitalize on the anticipated trend reversal. What price target should Dupuis estimate for closing the position?

Solution: Dupuis estimates the price target as \$96.42 – (\$97.02 – \$96.42) = \$95.82.

Double bottoms are formed when the price reaches a low, rebounds, and then sells off back to the first low level. Exhibit 12-16 depicts a double bottom pattern for Time Warner. Technicians use the double bottom to predict a change from a downtrend to an uptrend in security prices. For double bottoms, the price is expected to appreciate above the peak between the two bottoms by at least the distance from the valley lows to the peak.

EXHIBIT 12-16 Double-Bottom Pattern: Time Warner Daily Price Chart, November 2007–October 2009 (price in U.S. dollars)

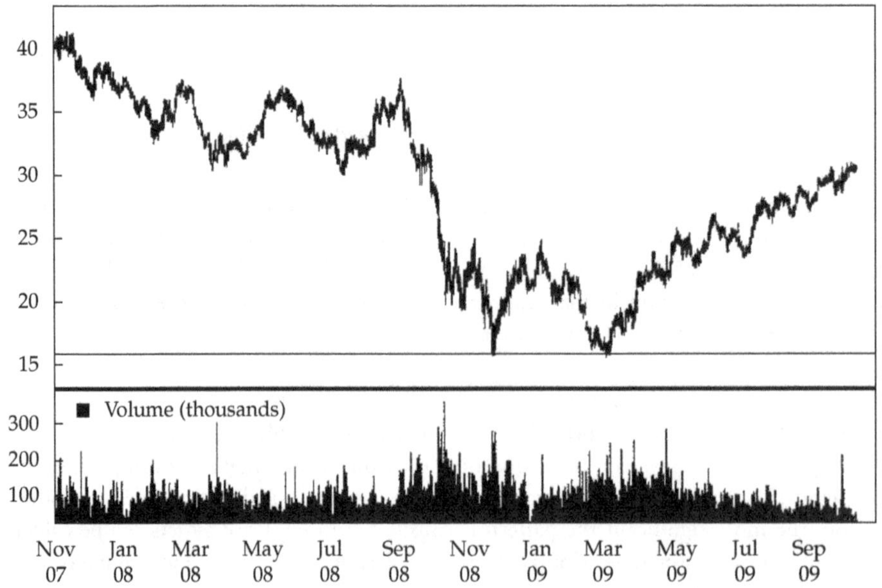

The reason these patterns are significant is that they show that at some price point, investors step in to reverse trends that are under way. For an uptrend, a double top implies that at some price point, enough traders are willing to either sell positions (or enter new short positions) that their activities overwhelm and reverse the uptrend created by demand for the shares. A reasonable conclusion is that this price level has been fundamentally derived and that it represents the intrinsic value of the security that is the consensus of investors. With double bottoms, if a security ceases to decline at the same price point on two separate occasions, the analyst can conclude that the market consensus is that at that price point, the security is now cheap enough that it is an attractive investment.

3.3.1.6. Triple Tops and Bottoms

Triple tops consist of three peaks at roughly the same price level, and **triple bottoms** consist of three troughs at roughly the same price level. A triple top for Rockwell Automation during 1999 is shown in Exhibit 12-17.

EXHIBIT 12-17 Triple-Top Pattern: Rockwell Automation Daily Price Chart, 1999 (price in U.S. dollars)

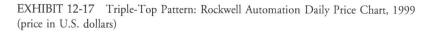

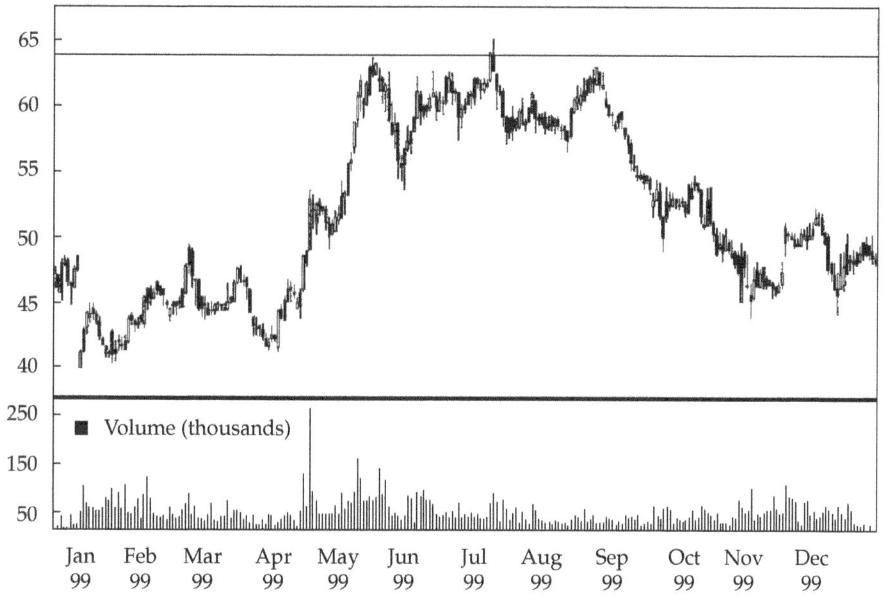

One of the challenges in double-top and triple-top patterns, and one of the valid criticisms of technical analysis in general, is that an analyst cannot know which pattern will result until after the fact. For example, after the broad equity market sell-off in the first quarter of 2009, a number of investment professionals were quoted as calling for a "retest of the lows"—in technical terms, a double bottom.

There is no evidence that market corrections (or rallies) must end with a double bottom (or double top in the case of an uptrend), and there is no generally accepted technical theory that predicts whether a low will be repeated once or even twice before a reversal occurs. A double bottom is considered to be a more significant pattern than a single bottom because traders have stepped in on two occasions to halt declines. However, traders have no way to determine whether a double top or bottom will be followed by a third top or bottom. Triple tops and triple bottoms are rare, but when they occur, they are more significant reversal patterns than double tops or double bottoms. On three separate occasions, traders stepped in to sell or buy shares with enough volume to end a rally or decline under way at the time. Nevertheless, the greater the number of times the price reverses at the same level, and the greater the time interval over which this pattern occurs, the greater the significance of the pattern.

3.3.2. Continuation Patterns

A continuation pattern is used to predict the resumption of a market trend that was in place prior to the formation of a pattern. From a supply-and-demand standpoint, a continuation pattern indicates a change in ownership from one group of investors to another. For example, if a positive trend was in place prior to a pattern and then one group of investors begins selling, the negative impact on price is quickly offset by other investors buying, so the forces of supply and demand go back and forth in terms of their impact on price. But neither has an overwhelming advantage. This type of pattern is often called "a healthy correction" because the long-term market trend does not change and because while one set of investors is seeking to exit, they are replaced by another set of investors willing to take their positions at roughly the same share price.

3.3.2.1. Triangles

Triangle patterns are a type of continuation pattern. They come in three forms, symmetrical triangles, ascending triangles, and descending triangles. A triangle pattern forms as the range between high and low prices narrows, visually forming a triangle. In old terminology, triangles were referred to as "coils" (which was also synonymous with "springs") because a triangle was considered analogous to a spring being wound up tighter and tighter and storing energy that would at some point be released. In a triangle, a trendline connects the highs and a trendline connects the lows. As the distance between the highs and lows narrows, the trendlines meet, forming a triangle. In a daily price chart, a triangle pattern usually forms over a period of several weeks.

In an ascending triangle, as shown in Exhibit 12-18, the trendline connecting the high prices is horizontal and the trendline connecting the low prices forms an uptrend. What this pattern means is that market participants are selling the stock at the same price level over a period of time, putting a halt to rallies at the same price point, but that buyers are getting more and more bullish and stepping in at increasingly higher prices to halt sell-offs instead of waiting for further price declines. An ascending triangle typically forms in an uptrend. The horizontal line represents sellers taking profits at around the same price point, presumably because they believe that this price represents the fundamental, intrinsic value of the security. The fact that the rally continues beyond the triangle may be a bullish signal; it means that another set of investors is presumably willing to buy at an even higher price because their analysis suggests the intrinsic value of the security is higher. Alternatively, the fundamental facts themselves may have changed; that is, the security's fundamental value may be increasing over time. The technician does not care which explanation is true; the technician is relying solely on the information conveyed by the security price itself, not the underlying reason.

EXHIBIT 12-18 Ascending Triangle Pattern

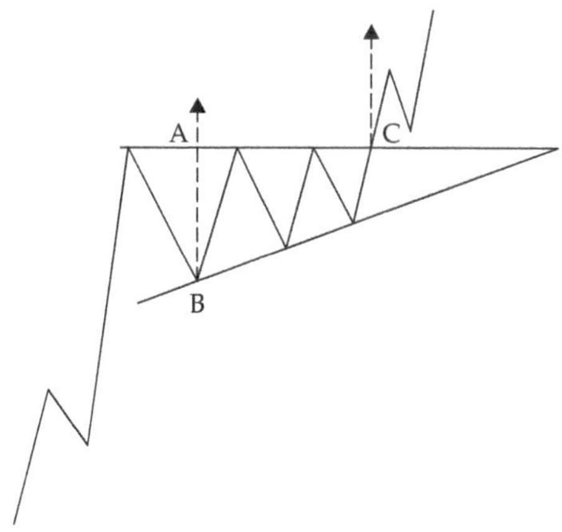

In the descending triangle, shown in Exhibit 12-19, the low prices form a horizontal trendline and the high prices form a series of lower and lower highs. Typically, a descending triangle will form in a downtrend. At some point in the sell-offs, buyers appear with enough demand to halt sell-offs each time they occur, at around the same price. Again, this phenomenon may be the result of fundamental analysts believing that the security has reached a price where it represents a significant discount to its intrinsic value and these analysts step in and buy. As the triangle forms, each rally ceases at a lower and lower high price point, suggesting that the selling demand is exerting greater price influence than the buying demand.

EXHIBIT 12-19 Descending Triangle

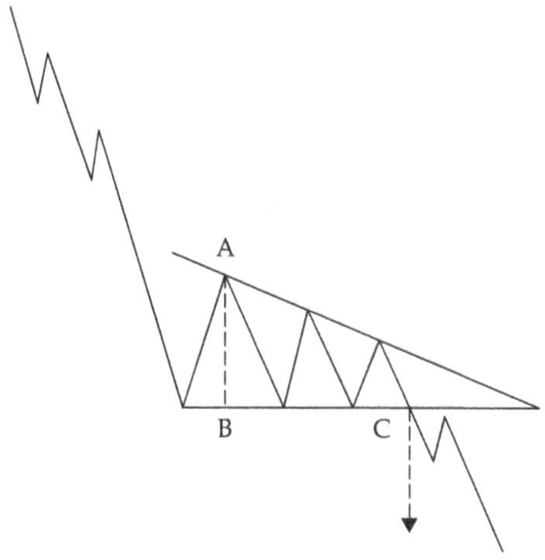

EXHIBIT 12-20 Symmetrical Triangle Pattern: Transocean Weekly Price Chart, June 1999–June 2000 (price in U.S. dollars)

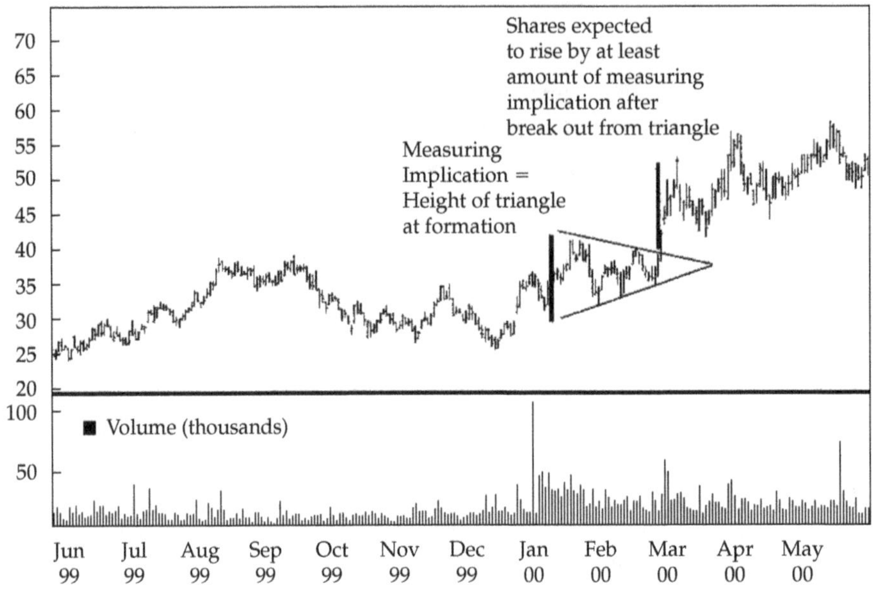

In a symmetrical triangle, the trendline formed by the highs angles down and the trendline formed by the lows angles up, both at roughly the same angle, forming a symmetrical pattern. Exhibit 12-20 contains a symmetrical triangle formed by the price for Transocean in early 2000. What this triangle indicates is that buyers are becoming more bullish while, simultaneously, sellers are becoming more bearish, so they are moving toward a point of consensus. Because the sellers are often dominated by long investors exiting positions (as opposed to short sellers creating new short positions), the pressure to sell diminishes once the sellers have sold the security. Thus, the pattern ends in the same direction as the trend that preceded it, either uptrend or downtrend.

The term "measuring implication" refers to the height of a triangle, as illustrated with a dark vertical bar in Exhibit 12-20. The measuring implication is derived by calculating the difference in price from the two trendlines at the start of the triangle. Once the pattern is broken and the price breaks through one of the trendlines that form the triangle, the analyst expects the price to move by at least the amount of the breakthrough above or below the trendline. Typically, price breaks out of a triangle pattern between halfway and three-quarters of the way through the pattern. The longer the triangle pattern persists, the more volatile and sustained the subsequent price movement is likely to be.

3.3.2.2. Rectangle Pattern

A rectangle pattern is a continuation pattern formed by two parallel trendlines, one formed by connecting the high prices during the pattern, and the other formed by the lows. Exhibit 12-21 shows two rectangle patterns. As is the case with other patterns, the rectangle pattern is a graphical representation of what has been occurring in terms of collective market sentiment. The horizontal resistance line that forms the top of the rectangle shows that investors are repeatedly selling shares at a specific price level, bringing rallies to an end. The horizontal support line forming the bottom of the rectangle indicates that traders are repeatedly making large enough purchases at the same price level to reverse declines. The support level in a bullish rectangle is natural because the long-term trend in the market is bullish. The resistance line may simply represent investors taking profits. Conversely, in a bearish rectangle, the support level may represent investors buying the security. Again, the technician is not concerned with why a pattern has formed, only with the likely next price movement once the price breaks out of the pattern.

EXHIBIT 12-21 Rectangle Patterns

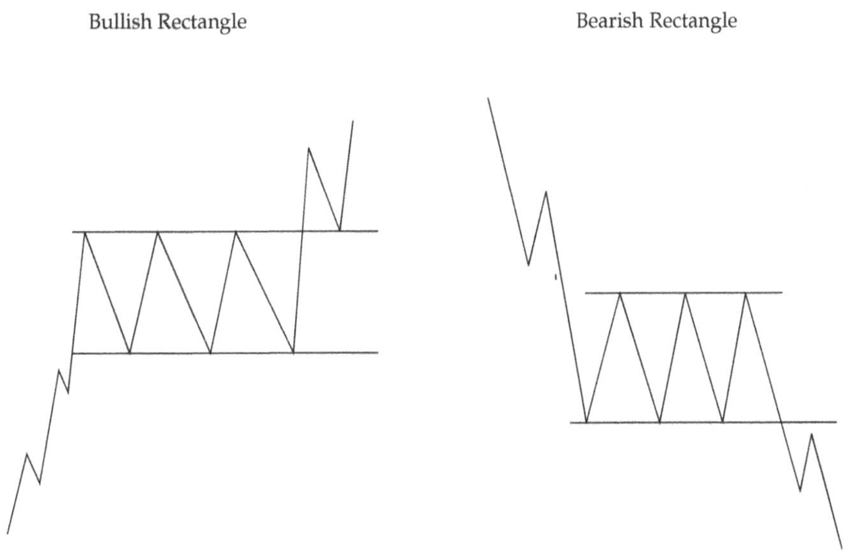

3.3.2.3. Flags and Pennants

Flags and **pennants** are considered minor continuation patterns because they form over short periods of time—on a daily price chart, typically over a week. They are similar to each other and have the same uses. A flag is formed by parallel trendlines, in the same way that most countries' flags are rectangular and create a parallelogram. Typically, the trendlines slope in a direction opposite to the trend up to that time; for example, in an uptrend, they slope down. A pennant formation is similar except that the trendlines converge to form a triangle, similar to the pennants of many sports teams or pennants flown on ships. The key difference between a triangle and pennant is that a pennant is a short-term formation whereas a triangle is a long-term formation.

The expectation for both flags and pennants is that the trend will continue after the pattern in the same direction it was going prior to the pattern. The price is expected to change by at least the same amount as the price change from the start of the trend to the formation of the flag or pennant. In Exhibit 12-22, a downtrend begins at point A, which is \$104. At point B, which is \$70, a pennant begins to form. The distance from point A to point B is \$34. The pennant ends at point C, which is \$76. The price target is \$76 minus \$34, which is \$42, the line labeled D.

EXHIBIT 12-22 Pennant Formation: China Mobile ADR, November 2006–July 2009 (price in U.S. dollars)

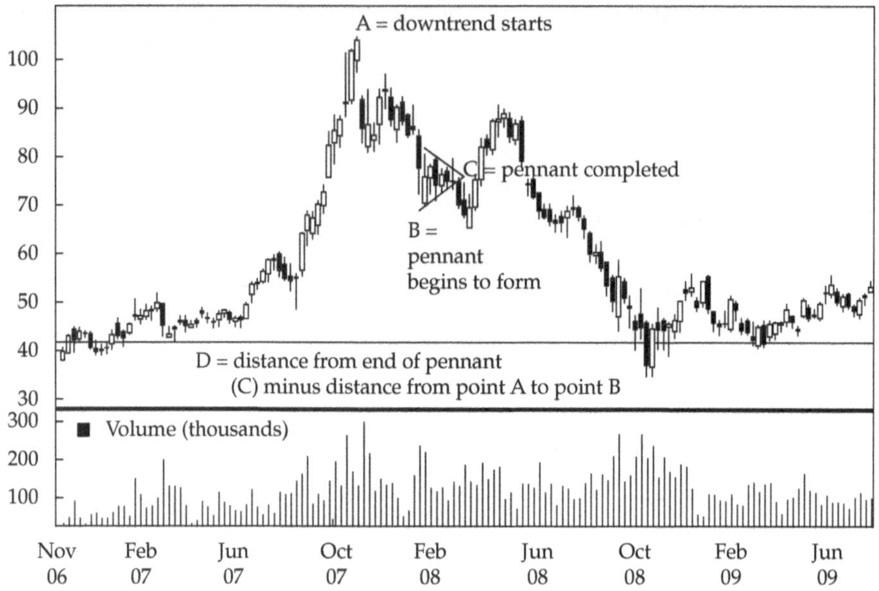

3.4. Technical Indicators

The technical analyst uses a variety of **technical indicators** to supplement the information gleaned from charts. A technical indicator is any measure based on price, market sentiment, or funds flow that can be used to predict changes in price. These indicators often have a supply-and-demand underpinning; that is, they measure how potential changes in supply and demand might affect a security's price.

3.4.1. Price-Based Indicators

Price-based indicators somehow incorporate information contained in the current and past history of market prices. Indicators of this type range from simple (e.g., a moving average) to complex (e.g., a stochastic oscillator).

3.4.1.1. Moving Average

A **moving average** is the average of the closing price of a security over a specified number of periods. Moving averages smooth out short-term price fluctuations, giving the technician a clearer image of market trend. Technicians commonly use a simple moving average, which weights each price equally in the calculation of the average price. Some technicians prefer to use an exponential moving average (also called an exponentially smoothed moving average), which gives the greatest weight to recent prices while giving exponentially less weight to older prices.

The number of data points included in the moving average depends on the intended use of the moving average. A 20-day moving average is commonly used because a month contains roughly 20 trading days. Also, 60 days is commonly used because it represents a quarter year (three months) of trading activity.

Moving averages can be used in conjunction with a price trend or in conjunction with one another. Moving averages are also used to determine support and resistance.

Because a moving average is less volatile than price, this tool can be used in several ways. First, whether price is above or below its moving average is important. A security that has been trending down in price will trade below its moving average, and a security that has been trending up will trade above its moving average. Second, the distance between the moving-average line and price is also significant. Once price begins to move back up toward its moving-average line, this line can serve as a resistance level. The 65-day moving-average line is commonly cited in the press, and when the price approaches the moving-average line, many investors become concerned that a rally will stall, so they sell the security.

Two or more moving averages can be used in conjunction. Exhibit 12-23 shows the price chart of Gazprom SP European Depositary Receipts (EDRs) on the Frankfurt Stock Exchange overlaid with 20-day and 60-day EDR moving averages for late 2007 to mid-2009.[5] Note that the longer the time frame used in the creation of a moving average, the smoother and less volatile the line. Investors often use moving-average crossovers as a buy or sell signal. When a short-term moving average crosses from underneath a longer-term average, this movement is considered bullish and is termed a **golden cross**. Conversely, when a short-term moving average crosses from above a longer-term moving average, this movement is considered bearish and is called a **dead cross**. In the case shown in Exhibit 12-23, a trading strategy of buying on golden crosses and selling on dead crosses would have been profitable.

EXHIBIT 12-23 Daily Price Chart with 20-Day and 60-Day Moving Averages: Gazprom EDR, November 2007–August 2009 (price in euros)

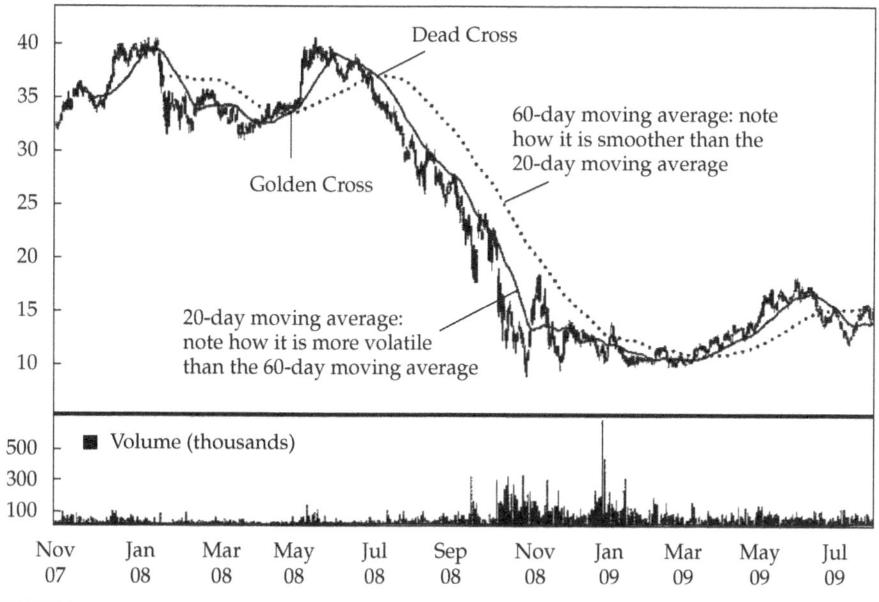

[5]A European Depositary Receipt is a negotiable certificate issued by a depositary bank in one country against equity that is traded on the stock exchange of another country.

Moving averages are easy to construct, and simple trading rules can be derived for using them. Computers can optimize what time lengths to set when using two moving averages. This optimization may take the form of changing the number of days included in each moving average or adding filter rules, such as waiting several days after a trade signal is given to make a trade. Reasons for optimization include the desire to manage capital drawdowns, to maximize gains, or to minimize losses. Once the moving average is optimized, even if a profitable trading system is devised for that security, the strategy is unlikely to work for other securities, especially if they are dissimilar. Also, as market conditions change, a previously optimized trading system may no longer work.

3.4.1.2. Bollinger Bands

Market veteran John Bollinger combined his knowledge of technical analysis with his knowledge of statistics to create an indicator called **Bollinger Bands**. Bollinger Bands consist of a moving average plus a higher line representing the moving average plus a set number of standard deviations from average price (for the same number of periods as used to calculate the moving average) and a lower line that is a moving average minus the same number of standard deviations. Exhibit 12-24 depicts Bollinger Bands for the Gazprom EDR.

The more volatile the security being analyzed becomes, the wider the range becomes between the two outer lines or bands. Similar to moving averages, Bollinger Bands can be used to create trading strategies that can be easily computerized and tested. A common use is as a contrarian strategy, in which the investor sells when a security price reaches the upper band and buys when it reaches the lower band. This strategy assumes that the security price will stay within the bands.

EXHIBIT 12-24 Bollinger Band Using 60-Day Moving Average and Two Standard Deviations: Gazprom EDR Daily Price Chart, November 2007–August 2009 (price in euros)

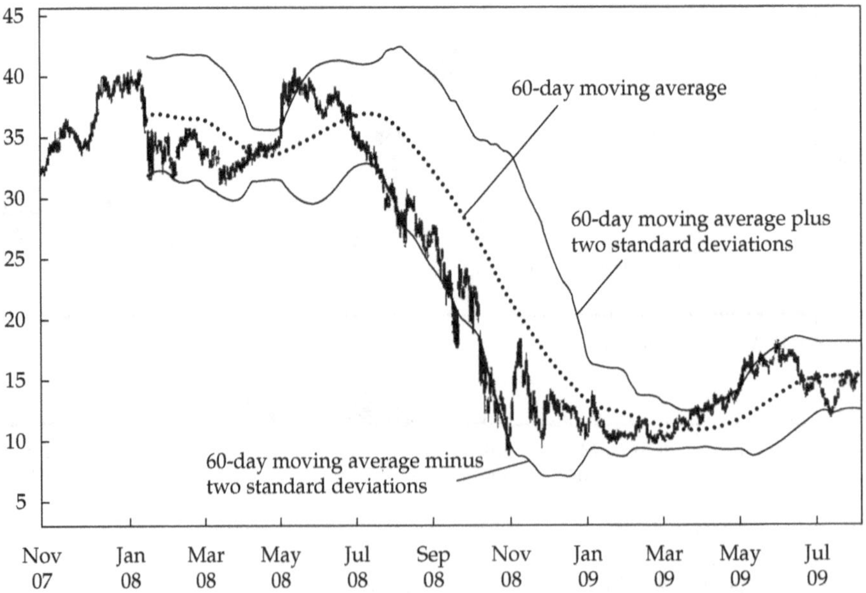

This type of strategy is likely to lead to a large number of trades, but it also limits risk because the trader can quickly exit unprofitable trades. In the event of a sharp price move and a change in trend, however, a contrarian strategy based on Bollinger Bands would be unprofitable. So, long-term investors might actually buy on a significant breakout above the upper boundary band because a major breakout would imply a change in trend likely to persist for some time. The long-term investor would sell on a significant breakout below the lower band. In this strategy, significance would be defined as breaking above or below the band by a certain percentage (say, 5 percent or 10 percent) and/or for a certain period of time (say, a week for a daily price chart). Again, such rules can easily be computerized and tested.

3.4.2. Momentum Oscillators

One of the key challenges in using indicators overlaid on a price chart is the difficulty of discerning changes in market sentiment that are out of the ordinary. **Momentum oscillators** are intended to alleviate this problem. They are constructed from price data, but they are calculated so that they either oscillate between a high and low (typically 0 and 100) or oscillate around a number (such as 0 or 100). Because of this construction, extreme highs or lows are easily discernible. These extremes can be viewed as graphic representations of market sentiment when selling or buying activity is more aggressive than historically typical. Because they are price based, momentum oscillators also can be analyzed by using the same tools technicians use to analyze price, such as the concepts of trend, support, and resistance.

Technicians also look for **convergence** or **divergence** between oscillators and price. Convergence is when the oscillator moves in the same manner as the security being analyzed, and divergence is when the oscillator moves differently from the security. For example, when price reaches a new high, this sign is considered bullish, but if the momentum oscillator being used does not also reach a new high at the same time, this pattern is divergence. It is considered to be an early warning of weakness, an indication that the uptrend may soon end.

Momentum oscillators should be used in conjunction with an understanding of the existing market (price) trend. Oscillators alert a trader to **overbought** or **oversold** conditions. In an overbought condition, market sentiment is unsustainably bullish. In an oversold condition, market sentiment is unsustainably bearish. In other words, the oscillator *range* must be considered separately for every security. Some securities may experience wide variations, and others may experience only minor variations.

Oscillators have three main uses. First, oscillators can be used to determine the strength of a trend. Extreme overbought levels are warning signals for uptrends, and extreme oversold levels are warning signals for downtrends. Second, when oscillators reach historically high or low levels, they may be signaling a pending trend reversal. For oscillators that move above and below 0, crossing the 0 level signals a change in the direction of the trend. For oscillators that move above and below 100, crossing the 100 level signals a change in the direction of the trend. Third, in a non-trending market, oscillators can be used for short-term trading decisions—that is, to sell at overbought levels and to buy at oversold levels.

3.4.2.1. Momentum or Rate of Change Oscillator

The terms *momentum oscillator* and *rate of change oscillator* are synonymous. "Rate of change" is often abbreviated ROC. The ROC oscillator is calculated by taking the most recent closing price, subtracting the closing price from a prior date that is a set number of days in the past, and multiplying the result by 100:

$$M = (V - Vx) \times 100$$

where

M = momentum oscillator value
V = last closing price
Vx = closing price x days ago, typically 10 days

When the ROC oscillator crosses zero in the same direction as the direction of the trend, this movement is considered a buy or sell signal. For example, if the ROC oscillator crosses into positive territory during an uptrend, it is a buy signal. If it enters into negative territory during a downtrend, it is considered a sell signal. The technician will ignore crossovers in opposition to the trend because the technician must *always* first take into account the general trend when using oscillators.

An alternative method of constructing this oscillator it to set it so that it oscillates above and below 100, instead of 0, as follows:

$$M = \frac{V}{Vx} \times 100$$

This approach is shown in Exhibit 12-25 for Toyota Motor Corporation.

EXHIBIT 12-25 Momentum Oscillator with 100 as Midpoint: Toyota Motor, May 2008–October 2009 (price in Japanese yen)

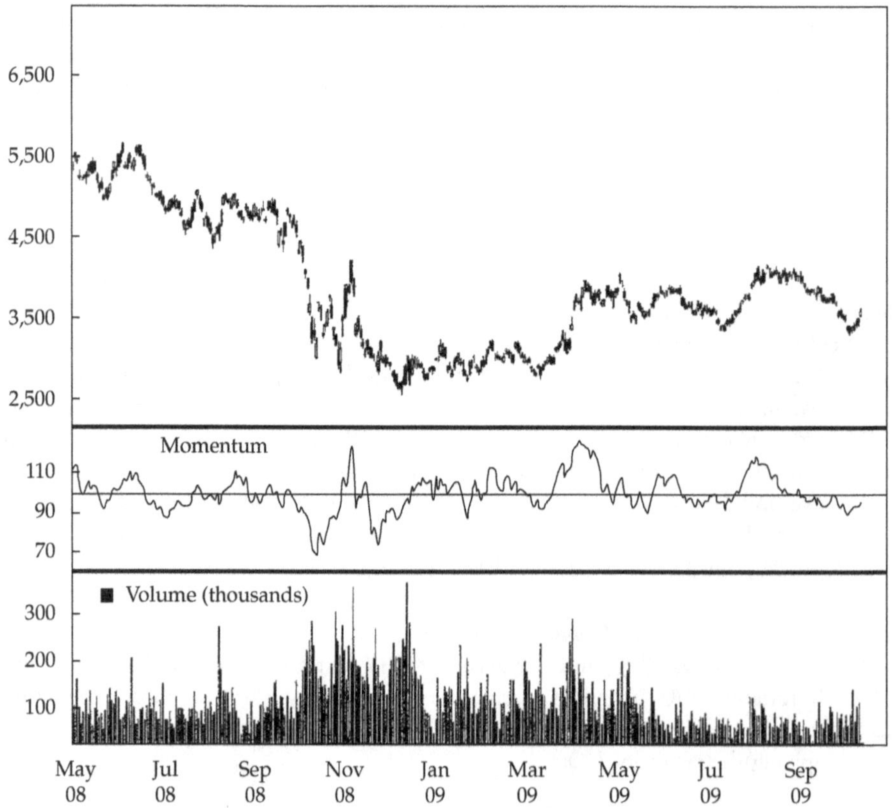

In Exhibit 12-25, the calculation method for the ROC oscillator for Toyota stock, traded on the Tokyo Stock Exchange, is for the oscillator to move around 100 and x is 12 days. Note that for this stock, the ROC oscillator tends to maintain a range between ¥85 and ¥115. So episodes when the oscillator moves outside this range are of particular interest to the technician. An extreme high means that the stock has posted its highest gain in any 12-day period at this point, and an extreme low reading means it has posted its greatest loss over any 12-day period. When investors bid up the price of a security too rapidly, the indication is that sentiment may be unduly bullish and the market may be overbought. Exhibit 12-25 shows that overbought levels of the ROC oscillator coincide with temporary highs in the stock price. So, those levels would have been signals to sell the stock. The other notable aspect of Exhibit 12-25 is the divergence when the share price hit a new low in December 2008 but the ROC oscillator did not. This divergence would have been a bullish signal and would have been interpreted to mean that, although the share price hit a new low, investor sentiment was actually higher than it had been previously. In itself, this information would not have been enough to warrant buying the shares because a downtrend in price was still in place, but it alerted the technician to the fact that the trend might end soon. The technician could then look for further indication of the trend's end and, with confirmation, might buy the stock.

3.4.2.2. Relative Strength Index

A **relative strength index** (RSI) is computed over a rolling time period.[6] It graphically compares a security's gains with its losses over the set period. The creator of the RSI, Welles Wilder, suggested a 14-day time period, and this period is generally the period used in most technical analysis software. The technician should understand that this variable can be changed and that the optimal time range should be determined by how the technician intends to use the RSI information. Factors that influence selection of the time period are similar to those that influence the selection of a time period for moving averages. Short time periods (such as 14 days) provide information about short-term price behavior. If 200 days is used, this short-term information will be smoothed out and, perhaps, will not be apparent at all.

RSI is a momentum oscillator and is not to be confused with the charting method called "relative strength analysis," in which the ratio of two security prices is plotted over time. The RSI provides information on whether or not an asset is overbought. The formula for the RSI is not intuitive and is best understood with an example. The formula is:

$$RSI = 100 - \frac{100}{1 + RS}$$

$$\text{where } RS = \frac{\sum(\text{Up changes for the period under consideration})}{\sum(|\text{Down changes for the period under consideration}|)}$$

Exhibit 12-26 shows closing prices for Ford Motor Company during the month of June 2009.

[6]This indicator is sometimes called the Wilder RSI.

EXHIBIT 12-26 Computation of RSI: Ford, June 2009

Date	Close	Up Changes	Down Changes
6/1/2009	6.13		
6/2/2009	6.41	0.28	
6/3/2009	6.18		−0.23
6/4/2009	6.36	0.18	
6/5/2009	6.36		
6/8/2009	6.38	0.02	
6/9/2009	6.26		−0.12
6/10/2009	6.19		−0.07
6/11/2009	5.98		−0.21
6/12/2009	6.11	0.13	
6/15/2009	5.93		−0.18
6/16/2009	5.67		−0.26
6/17/2009	5.71	0.04	
6/18/2009	5.68		−0.03
6/19/2009	5.72	0.04	
6/22/2009	5.38		−0.34
6/23/2009	5.53	0.15	
6/24/2009	5.63	0.10	
6/25/2009	5.68	0.05	
6/26/2009	5.61		−0.07
6/29/2009	5.78	0.17	
6/30/2009	6.07	0.29	
		1.45	−1.51

During this time, markets were still rebounding from the subprime crisis; automobile company stocks were unusually volatile and, to some speculators, presented interesting short-term trading opportunities. Suppose a trader decided to compute an RSI for the month of June. It would be a 22-day RSI with 21 price changes—11 up, 9 down, and 1 unchanged. To calculate the RSI, the trader would sum the 11 up changes, which sum to US\$1.45. The down changes total –US\$1.51; the absolute value drops the minus sign. The ratio of these two numbers is 0.96, so the RSI is

$$\text{RSI} = 100 - \frac{100}{1 + 0.96} = 100 - 51.02 = 48.98$$

The index construction forces the RSI to lie within 0 and 100. A value above 70 represents an overbought situation. Values below 30 suggest the asset is oversold. Again, as is the case with most technical tools, an analyst cannot simply learn the default settings and use them in every case. The 30–70 range is a good rule of thumb, but because the oscillator is a measure of volatility, less volatile stocks (such as utilities) may normally trade in a much narrower range. More volatile stocks (such as small-capitalization technology stocks) may trade in a wider range. The range also does not have to be symmetrical around 50. For example, in an uptrend, one might see a range of 40–80 but in downtrends, a range of 20–60.

The RSI measure often appears at the bottom or top of a price chart. Exhibit 12-27 shows a candlestick chart of Ford stock in 2009 with the corresponding RSI.

EXHIBIT 12-27 Candlestick Chart with RSI: Ford, January–August 2009 (price in U.S. dollars)

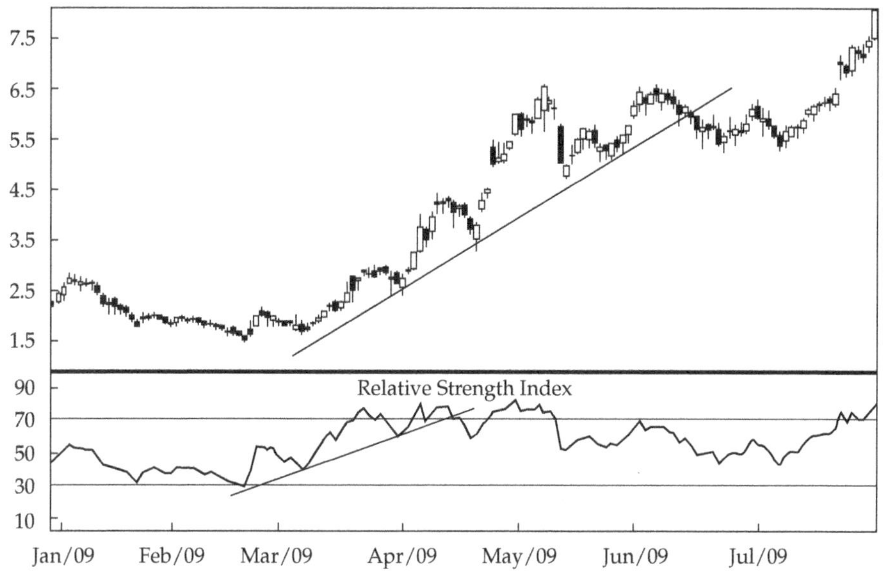

The candlestick chart of Ford stock prices in Exhibit 12-27 illustrates several aspects of the use of an RSI. For example, because the RSI oscillator was higher than 70 on 23 March so the stock was overbought at that time, a simple reading of the chart might have led to the conclusion that the trader should sell the stock. Doing so, however, would have caused the trader to miss a significant advance in the shares. A more careful technical analysis that took into account the trend would have indicated that the stock was in an uptrend, so RSI readings above 70 could be expected.

Because RSI is a price-based oscillator, the trader can also apply trend lines to analyze it. Note in Exhibit 12-27 that both the share price and the RSI oscillator were in uptrends from February until April but that the RSI uptrend was broken on 15 April, a potential warning that the uptrend in price might also break downward. In June, the share price broke its uptrend support line.

3.4.2.3. Stochastic Oscillator

The stochastic oscillator is based on the observation that in uptrends, prices tend to close at or near the high end of their recent range and in downtrends, they tend to close near the low end.

The logic behind these patterns is that if the shares of a stock are constantly being bid up during the day but then lose value by the close, continuation of the rally is doubtful. If sellers have enough supply to overwhelm buyers, the rally is suspect. If a stock rallies during the day and is able to hold on to some or most of those gains by the close, that sign is bullish.

The stochastic oscillator oscillates between 0 and 100 and has a default setting of a 14-day period, which, again, might be adjusted for the situation as we discussed for the RSI. The oscillator is composed of two lines, called %K and %D, that are calculated as follows:

$$\%\text{K} = 100\left(\frac{C - L14}{H14 - L14}\right)$$

where

C = latest closing price
$L14$ = lowest price in past 14 days
$H14$ = highest price in past 14 days

and

%D = average of the last three %K values calculated daily

Analysts should think about the %D in the same way they would a long-term moving-average line in conjunction with a short-term line. That is, %D, because it is the average of three %K values, is the slower moving, smoother line and is called the signal line. And %K is the faster moving line. The %K value means that the latest closing price (C) was in the %K percentile of the high–low range ($L14$ to $H14$).

The default oversold–overbought range for the stochastic oscillator is based on reading the signal line relative to readings of 20 and 80, but warnings about always using the default range for the RSI oscillator also apply in the case of the stochastic oscillator. In fact, noted technician Constance Brown has coined a term called the "stochastics default club" to refer to neophyte technicians who trade based solely on these defaults.[7] She has reported being able to develop successful trading strategies by using a time frame shorter than the 14-day default to calculate the stochastic oscillator. Apparently, enough traders are basing trades on the defaults to move the market for certain stocks. So, using shorter time frames than the default, she could trade ahead of the traders in the default stochastic club and generate a profit. Of course, other traders might be tempted to use an even shorter time frame, but there is a drawback to using a short time frame; namely, the shorter the time frame is, the more volatile the oscillator becomes and the more false signals it generates.

The stochastic oscillator should be used with other technical tools, such as trend analysis or pattern analysis. If both methods suggest the same conclusion, the trader has convergence (or confirmation), but if they give conflicting signals, the trader has divergence, which is a warning signal suggesting that further analysis is necessary.

The absolute level of the two lines should be considered in light of their normal range. Movements above this range indicate to a technician an overbought security and are considered bearish; movements below this range indicate an oversold security and are considered bullish. Crossovers of the two lines can also give trading signals the same way crossovers of two moving averages give signals. When the %K moves from below the %D line to above it, this move is considered a bullish short-term trading signal; conversely, when %K moves from

[7]Brown (1999).

above the %D line to below it, this pattern is considered bearish. In practice, a trader can use technical analysis software to adjust trading rules and optimize the calculation of the stochastic oscillator for a particular security and investment purpose (e.g., short-term trading or long-term investing).

The reason technicians use historical data to test their trading rules and find the optimal parameters for each security is that each security is different. The group of market participants actively trading differs from security to security. Just as each person has a different personality, so do groups of people. In effect, the groups of active market participants trading each security are imparting their personality on the trading activity for that security. As this group changes over time, the ideal parameters for a particular security may change.

Exhibit 12-28 provides a good example of how the stochastic oscillator can be used together with trend analysis. The exhibit provides the weekly price chart and stochastic oscillator for Petroleo Brasileiro ADRs, which are traded on the New York Stock Exchange, for June 2008 through June 2009. Note that during the downtrend on the left side of the chart the stochastic oscillator often moved below 20. Each time it reached 80, however, it provided a valid sell signal. When the downtrend ended in November 2008 and an uptrend began, the stochastic oscillator was regularly moving above 80 but each time the %D line moved above %K, a valid buy signal was given.

EXHIBIT 12-28 Weekly Price Chart and Stochastic Oscillator: Petroleo Brasileiro ADR, June 2008–July 2009 (price in U.S. dollars)

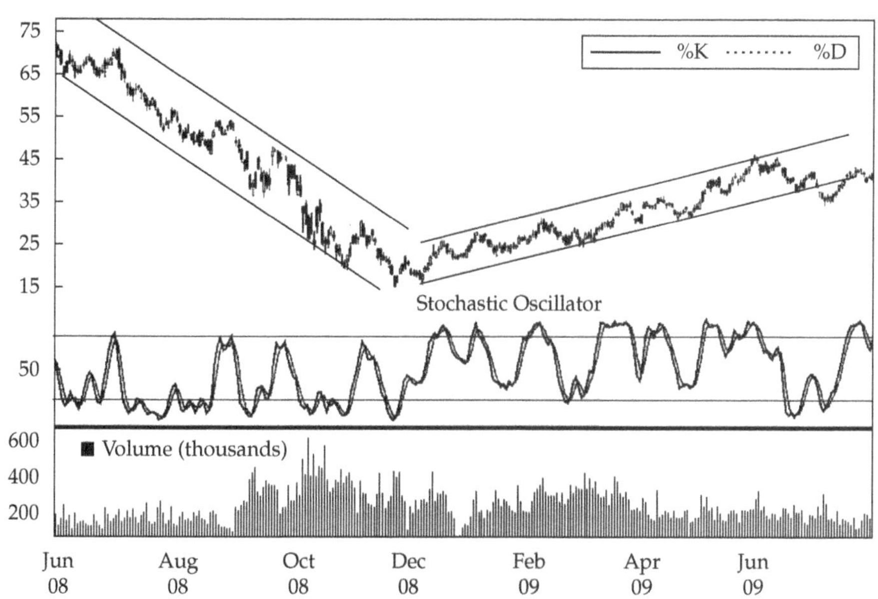

3.4.2.4. Moving-Average Convergence/Divergence Oscillator

The **moving-average convergence/divergence oscillator** is commonly referred to as MACD, which is pronounced Mack Dee. The MACD is the difference between a short-term and a long-term moving average of the security's price. The MACD is constructed by calculating two lines, the MACD line and the signal line:

- MACD line: difference between two exponentially smoothed moving averages, generally 12 and 26 days
- Signal line: exponentially smoothed average of MACD line, generally 9 days

The indicator oscillates around zero and has no upper or lower limit. Rather than using a set overbought–oversold range for MACD, the analyst compares the current level with the historical performance of the oscillator for a particular security to determine when a security is out of its normal sentiment range.

MACD is used in technical analysis in three ways. The first is to note crossovers of the MACD line and the signal line, as discussed for moving averages and the stochastic oscillator. Crossovers of the two lines may indicate a change in trend. The second is to look for times when the MACD is outside its normal range for a given security. The third is to use trend lines on the MACD itself. When the MACD is trending in the same direction as price, this pattern is convergence, and when the two are trending in opposite directions, the pattern is divergence.

Exhibit 12-29 shows a daily price chart of Exxon Mobil (at the top) with the MACD oscillator for March through October of 2005. Note the convergence in the bottoming of both the oscillator and price in May, which provided confirmation of a change in trend. This change was further confirmed by the MACD line crossing above the signal line. A bearish signal was given in September with the change in trend of both price and the oscillator and the crossover of the signal line by the MACD line. The fact that the MACD oscillator was moving up to a level that was unusually high for this stock would have been an early warning signal in September.

EXHIBIT 12-29 MACD and Daily Price Chart: Exxon Mobil, March–November 2005 (price in U.S. dollars)

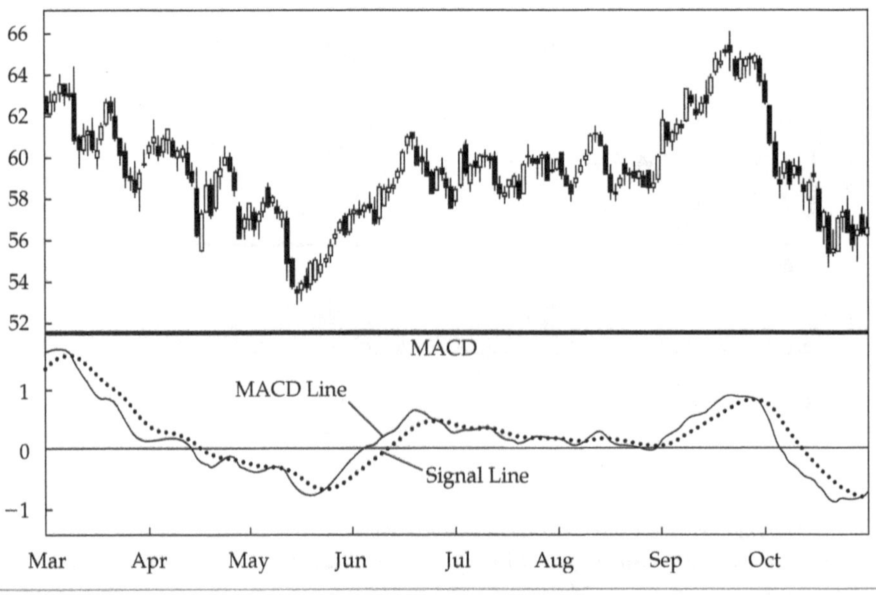

3.4.3. Sentiment Indicators

Sentiment indicators attempt to gauge investor activity for signs of increasing bullishness or bearishness. Sentiment indicators come in two forms—investor polls and calculated statistical indices.

3.4.3.1. Opinion Polls

A wide range of services conduct periodic polls of either individual investors or investment professionals to gauge their sentiment about the equity market. The most common of the polls are the Investors Intelligence Advisors Sentiment reports, Market Vane Bullish Consensus, Consensus Bullish Sentiment Index, and Daily Sentiment Index, all of which poll investment professionals, and reports of the American Association of Individual Investors (AAII), which polls individual investors. All but the AAII survey are subscription-based services. *Barron's* magazine publishes data from four of these surveys on a weekly basis.

By regularly polling, compiling these data over time, and presenting it graphically, these services provide technicians with an analyzable snapshot of investor sentiment over time. Technicians look at prior market activity and compare it with highs or lows in sentiment, as well as inflection points in sentiment, as a gauge when they are forecasting the future direction of the market.

The most widely used investor polls are all U.S.-based. One reason is that interpretation of the surveys is determined by comparing the survey results with market performance over time. To gauge a survey's usefulness in predicting major market turns, the survey must have been published over several cycles, and each of the surveys mentioned here, based on U.S. data, has been available for several decades.

3.4.3.2. Calculated Statistical Indices

The other category of sentiment indicators are indicators that are calculated from market data, such as security prices. The two most commonly used are derived from the options market; they are the put/call ratio and the volatility index. Additionally, many analysts look at margin debt and short interest.

The **put/call ratio** is the volume of put options traded divided by the volume of call options traded for a particular financial instrument. Investors who buy put options on a security are presumably bearish, and investors who buy call options are presumably bullish. The volume in call options is greater than the volume traded in put options over time, so the put/call ratio is normally below 1.0. The ratio is considered to be a contrarian indicator, meaning that higher values are considered bearish and lower values are considered bullish. But, its usefulness as a contrarian indicator is limited except at extreme low or high levels in relation to the historical trading level of the put/call ratio for a particular financial instrument. The actual value of the put/call ratio, and its normal range, differs for each security or market, so no standard definitions of overbought or oversold levels exist. At extreme lows where call option volume is significantly greater than put option volume, market sentiment is said to be so overly positive that a correction is likely. At extreme highs in the put/call ratio, market sentiment is said to be so extremely negative that an increase in price is likely.

The **CBOE Volatility Index** (VIX) is a measure of near-term market volatility calculated by the Chicago Board Options Exchange. Since 2003, it has been calculated from option prices on the stocks in the S&P 500. The VIX rises when market participants become fearful of an impending market decline. These participants then bid up the price of puts, and the result is an increase in the VIX level. Technicians use the VIX in conjunction with trend, pattern, or oscillator tools, and it is interpreted from a contrarian perspective. When other indicators suggest that the market is oversold and the VIX is at an extreme high, this combination is considered bullish. Exhibit 12-30 shows the VIX from March 2005 to December 2009.

EXHIBIT 12-30 VIX, March 2005–December 2009

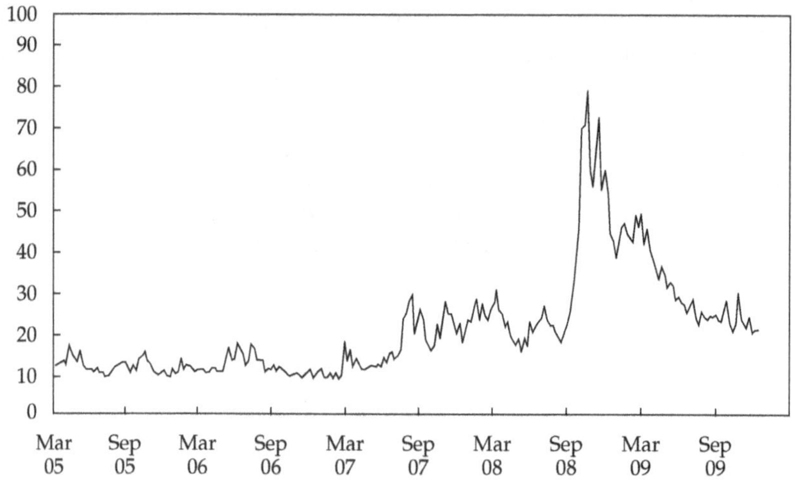

Margin debt is also often used as an indication of sentiment. As a group, investors have a history of buying near market tops and selling at the bottom. When the market is rising and indices reach new highs, investors are motivated to buy more equities in the hope of participating in the market rally. A margin account permits an investor to borrow part of the investment cost from the brokerage firm. This debt magnifies the gains or losses resulting from the investment.

Investor psychology plays an important role in the intuition behind margin debt as an indicator. When stock margin debt is increasing, investors are aggressively buying and stock prices will move higher because of increased demand. Eventually, the margin traders use all of their available credit, so their buying power (and, therefore, demand) decreases, which fuels a price decline. Falling prices may trigger margin calls and forced selling, thereby driving prices even lower.

Brokerage firms must report activity in their customers' margin accounts, so keeping track of borrowing behavior is relatively easy. Exhibit 12-31 provides a 10-year comparison of margin debt with the S&P 500. The correlation is striking: Rising margin debt is generally associated with a rising index level, and falling margin debt is associated with a falling index level. In fact, for the 113 months shown in Exhibit 12-31, the correlation coefficient between the levels of margin debt and the S&P 500 is 80.2 percent. When margin debt peaked in the summer of 2007, the market also topped out. Margin debt dropped sharply during the latter part of 2008 as the subprime crisis took the market down. Investors began to use borrowed funds again in the first half of 2009 when heavily discounted shares became increasingly attractive. Margin debt was still well below the average of the last decade, but the upturn would be viewed as a bullish sign by advocates of this indicator.

EXHIBIT 12-31 Margin Debt in U.S. Markets versus S&P 500, 2000–2009

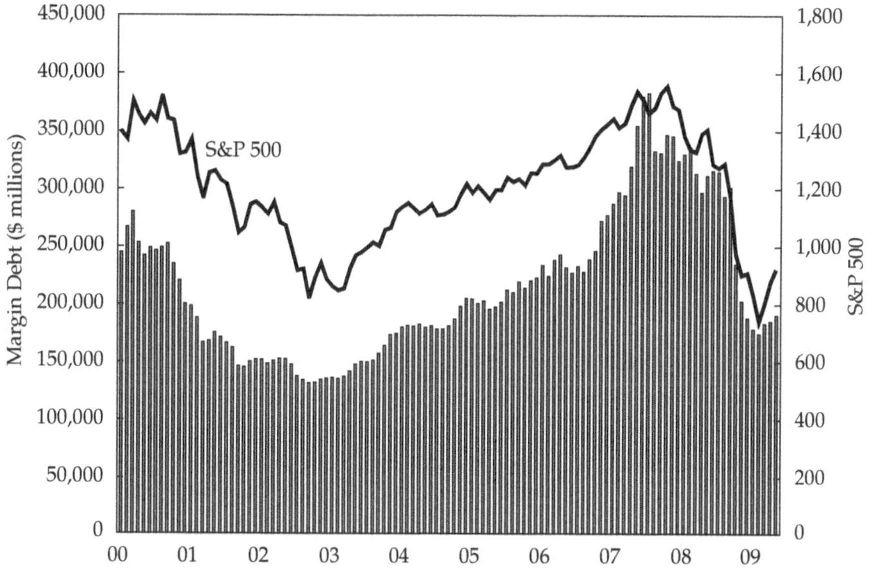

Source: New York Stock Exchange Fact Book.

Short interest is another commonly used sentiment indicator. Investors sell shares short when they believe the share prices will decline. Brokerage firms must report short-sale activity, and these statistics are aggregated and reported by the exchanges and the financial press on a monthly basis. The number of shares of a particular security that are currently sold short is called "short interest." The short interest ratio represents the number of days trading activity represented by short interest. To facilitate comparisons of large and small companies, common practice is to "normalize" this value by dividing short interest by average daily trading volume to get the short interest ratio:

$$\text{Short interest ratio} = \text{Short interest}/\text{Average daily trading volume}$$

EXAMPLE 12-3 Short Interest Ratio

At the end of September 2009, *Barron's* reported short interest of 10,936,467 shares in Goldman Sachs, with average daily trading volume of 9,086,174. At the same time, the short interest in TD Banknorth was 20,420,166 on average trading volume of 1,183,558 shares. Calculate the short interest ratio for both firms.

Solution: The short interest ratio for Goldman Sachs was 10,936,467 divided by 9,086,174, or 1.2 days. For TD Banknorth, the short interest ratio was 20,420,166 divided by 1,183,558, or 17.25 days.

There are differences of opinion about how to interpret short interest as an indicator. It is considered to show market sentiment and to be a contrarian indicator. Some people believe that if a large number of shares are sold short and the short interest ratio is high, the market should expect a falling price for the shares because of so much negative sentiment about them. A counterargument is that, although the short sellers are bearish on the security, the effect of their short sales has already been felt in the security price. The short sellers' next action will be to buy shares back to cover their short positions. When the short sellers cover their positions, those actions will provide a boost to the share price. Therefore, the short interest ratio constitutes future (and known) demand for the shares.

Regardless of the analyst's perspective, in Example 12-3, the TD Banknorth short interest ratio of approximately 17 is more noteworthy than the much lower figure for Goldman Sachs.

3.4.4. Flow-of-Funds Indicators

Technicians look at fund flows as a way to gauge the potential supply and demand for equities. Demand can come in the form of margin borrowing against current holdings or cash holdings by mutual funds and other groups that are normally large holders of equities, such as insurance companies and pension funds. The more cash these groups hold, the more bullish is the indication for equities. One caveat in looking at potential sources of demand is that, although these data indicate the potential buying power of various large investor groups, the data say nothing about the likelihood that the groups will buy.

On the supply side, technicians look at new or secondary issuance of stock because these activities put more securities into the market and increase supply.

3.4.4.1. Arms Index

A common flow of funds indicator is the **Arms Index**, also called the **TRIN** (for "short-term trading index").[8] This indicator is applied to a broad market (such as the S&P 500) to measure the relative extent to which money is moving into or out of rising and declining stocks. The index is a ratio of two ratios:

$$\text{Arms Index} = \frac{\text{Number of advancing issues/Number of declining issues}}{\text{Volume of advancing issues/Volume of declining issues}}$$

When this index is near 1.0, the market is in balance; that is, as much money is moving into rising stocks as into declining stocks. A value above 1.0 means that there is more volume in declining stocks; a value below 1.0 means that most trading activity is in rising stocks. Exhibit 12-32 shows the Arms Index for the S&P 500 on a daily basis for the first six months of 2009. The majority of the points lie above the 1.0 level, suggesting that the market continued to be in a selling mood. Note that the up spikes are associated with large price decreases in the index level and the down spikes reflect the opposite. The trendline shows a slightly negative slope, providing some slight encouragement for the bulls.

[8]This tool was first proposed by Richard W. Arms, Jr., a well-known technical analyst.

EXHIBIT 12-32 Arms Index for the S&P 500, January–July 2009

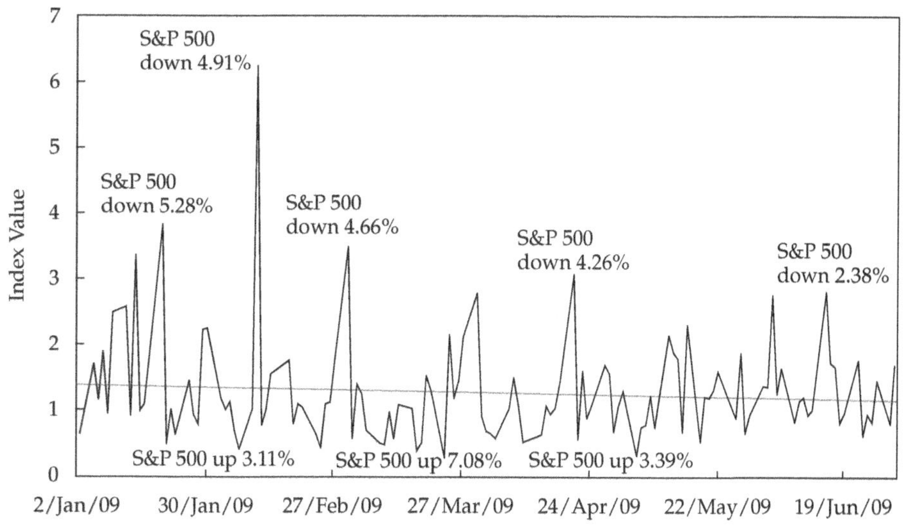

EXAMPLE 12-4 TRIN Indicator

Sarah Johannson, CFA, recently installed some investment software and is verifying the calculation of some of the statistics it produces. Her screen indicates a TRIN value of 1.02 for the NYSE and 1.80 for the Nasdaq market. These values seem to be unusually far apart to her, and she wonders whether they are both real-time statistics like the other market price data. To check whether they are real-time statistics, a few minutes later, she simultaneously captures the TRIN from her software display (slightly changed to 1.01 for the NYSE and 1.81 for Nasdaq) and on a separate monitor, she does a screen capture of NYSE and Nasdaq data, as follows:

		NYSE	Nasdaq
Number of issues	Advancing	850	937
	Declining	1,982	1,472
Volume	Advancing	76,921,200	156,178,475
	Declining	185,461,042	441,970,884

How does Johannson recalculate and interpret the TRIN value for the NYSE and Nasdaq?

Solution:
Johannson calculates the TRIN values for the NYSE and Nasdaq as follows:

$$\text{TRIN (NYSE)} = \frac{(850 \div 1{,}982)}{(76{,}921{,}200 \div 185{,}461{,}042)} = 1.03$$

$$\text{TRIN (Nasdaq)} = \frac{(937 \div 1{,}472)}{(156{,}178{,}475 \div 441{,}970{,}884)} = 1.80$$

Johannson concludes that her software is giving her current values and that the Nasdaq is having a much worse day than the NYSE.

3.4.4.2. Margin Debt
The previous section discussed the use of margin debt as an indicator of market sentiment. Margin debt is also widely used as a flow-of-funds indicator because margin loans may increase the purchases of stocks and declining margin balances may force the selling of stocks.

3.4.4.3. Mutual Fund Cash Position
Mutual funds hold a substantial proportion of all investable assets. Some analysts use the *percentage of mutual fund assets held in cash* as a predictor of market direction. It is called the "mutual fund cash position indicator." Mutual funds must hold some of their assets in cash in order to pay bills and send redemption checks to account holders. Cash arrives on a daily basis from customer deposits, interest earned, and dividends received. Cash also increases after a fund manager sells a position and holds the funds before reinvesting them. During a bull market, the manager wants to buy shares as quickly as possible to avoid having a cash "drag" hurt the fund's performance. If prices are trending lower, however, the manager may hold funds in cash to improve the fund's performance.

Exhibit 12-33 shows year-end mutual fund cash in the United States as a percentage of assets from 1984 through 2008. Over this period, the average cash percentage was 6.8 percent. An analyst's initial intuition might be that when cash is relatively low, fund managers are bullish and anticipate rising prices but when fund managers are bearish, they conserve cash to wait for lower prices. Advocates of this technical indicator argue exactly the opposite: When the mutual fund cash position is low, fund managers have already bought, and the effects of their purchases are already reflected in security prices. When the cash position is high, however, that money represents buying power that will move prices higher when the money is used to add positions to the portfolio. The mutual fund cash position is another example of a contrarian indicator.

Some analysts modify the value of the cash percentage to account for differences in the level of interest rates. Cash is not sitting in a desk drawer; it is on deposit somewhere earning interest. When interest rates are low, holding cash can be a substantial drag on the fund's performance if the broad market advances. When interest rates are high, holding cash is less costly.

EXHIBIT 12-33 Mutual Fund Cash Position, 1984–2008

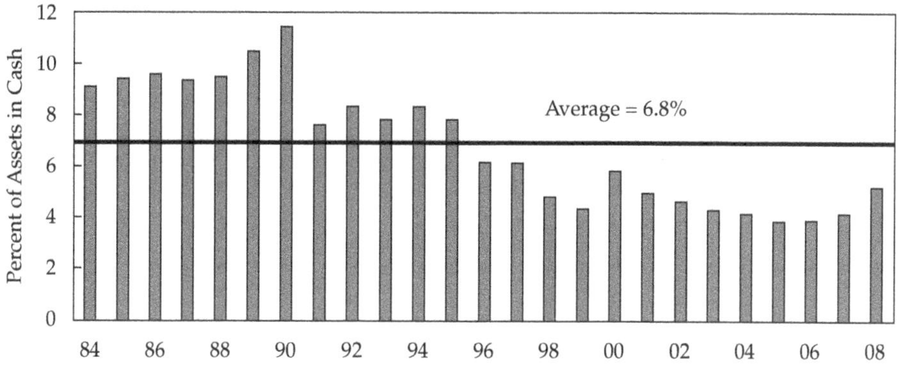

EXAMPLE 12-5 Market Indicators

At the request of a wealthy client, Erik Nielson is preparing a proprietary research report on the shares of a U.S. company. He has completed the part of the report dealing with fundamental analysis and wants to include a section on technical analysis. Nielson has gathered the following information:

Company Information:

- The 20-day moving average of the share price just rose through the 200-day moving average.
- RSI = 40.6.

Market Information:

- TRIN = 1.9.
- Mutual fund cash position = 7.0%

1. How should Nielson interpret each item of information?
2. Do these indicators, in the aggregate, lead Nielson to a buy, hold, or sell recommendation for the company's shares?

Solution to 1:

- Moving average: When a short-term moving average moves above a longer-term moving average, the movement is a golden cross and is a bullish signal.
- RSI: An RSI of 40.6 would be considered neutral. The RSI ranges between 0 and 100. Values greater than 70 are bearish; values below 30 are bullish.

- TRIN: A TRIN value above 1.0 means that there is more volume in declining stocks than in advancing stocks; therefore, a value of 1.9 is bearish.
- Mutual fund cash position: The 7.0 percent figure is near the long-term average, so it is a neutral signal.

Solution to 2: Of the four indicators, one is bullish, one is bearish, and two are neutral. Most analysts would view this result as "net neutral" and would recommend continuing to hold the stock. An alternative point of view might be that seeing a bullish indicator for the stock while the indicator for the overall market is bearish could be an argument for overweighting the stock.

3.4.4.4. New Equity Issuance

When a company's owners decide to take a company public and offer shares for sale, the owners want to put those shares on the market at a time when investors are eager to buy. That is, the owners want to offer the shares when they can sell them at a premium price. Premium prices occur near market tops. The new equity issuance indicator suggests that as the number of initial public offerings (IPOs) increases, the upward price trend may be about to turn down.

A supply-and-demand effect is also at work. Putting more shares on the market increases the aggregate supply of shares available for investors to purchase. The investment community has a finite quantity of cash to spend, so an increase in IPOs may be viewed as a bearish factor.

3.4.4.5. Secondary Offerings

Technicians also monitor secondary offerings to gauge potential changes in the supply of equities. Although secondary offerings do not increase the supply of shares, because existing shares are sold by insiders to the general public, they do increase the supply available for trading or the float. So, from a market perspective, secondary offerings of shares have the potential to change the supply-and-demand equation as much as IPOs do.

3.5. Cycles

Over the centuries, technicians have noted recurring cycles of various frequencies in the capital markets. The study of cycles in the markets is part of broader cycle studies that exist in numerous fields of study. Many observed cycles, such as one in U.S. equities tied to the cycle of U.S. presidential elections, have an obvious and rational justification. Other cycles do not. However, why cycles in fields seemingly unrelated to finance, such as astronomy or weather patterns, may influence the economy (and thus the capital markets) may have a logical explanation. For example, sunspots affect weather patterns on earth, which in turn affect agriculture and, therefore, capital markets because they are related to agriculture.

3.5.1. Kondratieff Wave

The longest of the widely recognized cycles was identified by Nikolai Kondratieff in the 1920s. Kondratieff was an economist in the Soviet Union who suggested that Western economies had a 54-year cycle. He traced cycles from the 1780s to the time he published this theory in the 1920s, and the economic depression of the 1930s was consistent with the cycle he identified. His theory was mainly tied to economic cycles and commodity prices, but cycles can also be seen in the prices of equities during the time of his work.

Kondratieff was executed in a Soviet purge in 1938, but his ideas have come into widespread acceptance, particularly since his works were translated into English in the 1980s. Two economists at the London School of Economics, E. H. Phelps Brown and Sheila Hopkins, identified a 50- to 52-year economic cycle in the United Kingdom. Together with Kondratieff, credit should be given to two Dutch economists, Jacob van Gelderen and Samuel de Wolff, who wrote about a 50- to 60-year economic cycle but published their work earlier, in 1913. Their work came to light only recently, however, so the long 54-year economic cycle is known as the **Kondratieff Wave** or K Wave.

3.5.2. 18-Year Cycle

The 18-year cycle is interesting because three 18-year cycles make up the longer 54-year Kondratieff Wave. The 18-year cycle is most often mentioned in connection with real estate prices, but it can also be found in equities and other markets.

3.5.3. Decennial Pattern

The decennial pattern is the pattern of average stock market returns (based on the DJIA) broken down on the basis of the last digit in the year. Years ending with a 0 have had the worst performance, and years ending with a 5 have been by far the best. The DJIA was up every year ending in a 5 from 1885 until 1995, but it declined 0.6 percent in 2005.

3.5.4. Presidential Cycle

This cycle in the United States connects the performance of the DJIA with presidential elections. In this theory, years are grouped into categories on the basis of whether they were election years or the first, second, or third year following an election. The third year is the year prior to the next election. The third year shows the best performance; in fact, the DJIA experienced a positive return in every pre-election year from 1943 through 2007. One explanation for this outcome is that with so many politicians up for re-election, they inject stimulus into the economy in an attempt to improve their chances to be re-elected.[9] Election years are also usually positive years for the stock market, but with less consistency. Post-election years and the so-called midterm year have the worst performance.

These long cycles are important to keep in mind when using other technical analysis tools. However, the long cycles described here and other theories about long cycles present a number of problems. The primary problem is the small sample size. Only 56 presidential elections have been held in the United States, and only 4 completed Kondratieff cycles have occurred in U.S. history. Another problem is that even with the small number of cycles, the data do not always fit the cycle theory, and when they do, that fit may not be obvious.

4. ELLIOTT WAVE THEORY

In a theory proposed by R. N. Elliott in 1938, the market moves in regular, repeated waves or cycles. He identified and categorized these waves and wrote in detail about aspects of market cycles. Elliott was an accountant by training, but in 1929, after he contracted a progressive intestinal illness at age 58 while working in Latin America, he was forced to retire. Then, he turned his attention to a detailed study of equity prices in the United States.

[9] In U.S. presidential election years, the vice presidency, all 435 House of Representatives seats, and 33 of the 100 Senate seats are also up for election.

A decade later, in 1938, he published his findings in a book titled *The Wave Principle.* In developing the concept that the market moves in waves, Elliott relied heavily on Charles Dow's early work. Elliott described how the market moved in a pattern of five waves moving up in a bull market in the following pattern: 1 = up, 2 = down, 3 = up, 4 = down, and 5 = up. He called this wave the "impulse wave." The impulse wave was followed by a corrective wave with three components: a = down, b = up, and c = down.

When the market is a bear market, as defined in Dow Theory—that is, with both of Dow's major indices in bear markets—the downward movements are impulse waves and are broken into five waves with upward corrections broken into three subwaves.

Elliott also noted that each wave could be broken down into smaller and smaller subwaves.

The longest of the waves is called the "grand supercycle" and takes place over centuries. Elliott traced grand supercycles back to the founding of the United States, and his successors have continued his work. Each grand supercycle can be broken down into subcycles until ending with the "subminuette," which unfolds over several minutes. The major cycles are:

- Grand supercycle
- Supercycle
- Cycle
- Primary
- Intermediate
- Minor
- Minute
- Minuette
- Subminuette

An important aspect of Elliott's work is that he discovered that market waves follow patterns that are ratios of the numbers in the **Fibonacci sequence**. Leonardo Fibonacci was an eleventh-century Italian mathematician who explained this sequence in his book *Liber Abaci,* but the sequence was known to mathematicians as far back as 200 B.C.E. in India. The Fibonacci sequence starts with the numbers 0, 1, 1, and then each subsequent number in the sequence is the sum of the two preceding numbers:

$$0, 1, 1, 2, 3, 5, 8, 13, 21, 34 \ldots$$

Elliott was more interested in the ratios of the numbers in the sequence because he found that the ratio of the size of subsequent waves was generally a Fibonacci ratio. The ratios of one Fibonacci number to the next that Elliott considered most important are the following:

$$1/2 = 0.50,\ 2/3 = 0.6667,\ 3/5 = 0.6,\ 5/8 = 0.625,\ 8/13 = 0.6154$$

He also noticed that the ratio of a Fibonacci sequence number to its preceding number is important:

$$2/1 = 2,\ 3/2 = 1.5,\ 5/3 = 1.6667,\ 8/5 = 1.600,\ 8/13 = 1.6250$$

These ratios converge around 1.618. In mathematics, 1.618 is called the "golden ratio," and it can be found throughout nature—in astronomy, biology, botany, and many other fields.

It is also widely used in art and architecture. The ancient Egyptians built the pyramids on the basis of this ratio, and the ancient Greeks used it widely.

As noted, Elliott numbered the impulse waves 1–5 and the corrective waves, a, b, and c. Exhibit 12-34 depicts the impulse and corrective waves in a bull market.

EXHIBIT 12-34 Impulse Waves and Corrective Waves

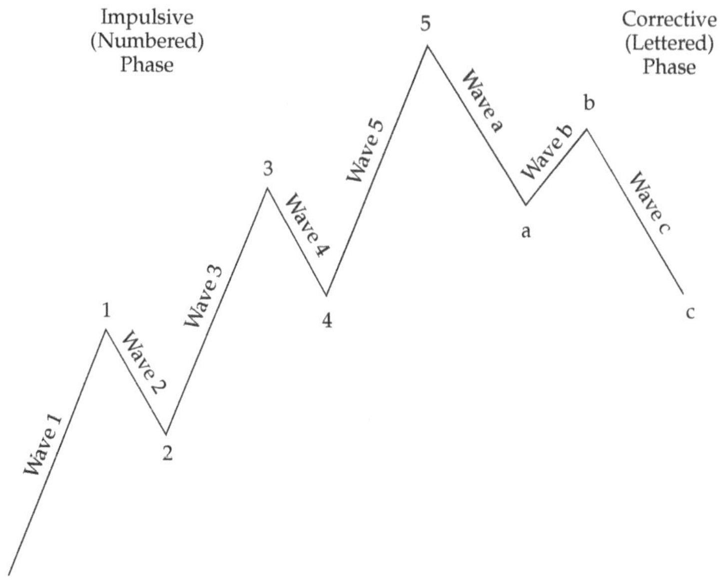

Elliott described the characteristics of each wave. Note the following, as shown in Exhibit 12-34:

- Wave 1 starts as a basing pattern and displays an increase in price, volume, and breadth.[10] Wave 1 consists of five smaller waves.
- Wave 2 moves down, retracing much of the gain in Wave 1 but not all of it. Common percentage retracements are Fibonacci ratios, such as 50 percent or 62 percent. Wave 2 never erases all of the gains from Wave 1. Wave 2 consists of three smaller waves.
- Wave 3 moves above the high of the first wave and has strong breadth, volume, and price movement. Most of the price movement in an uptrend typically occurs in Wave 3. Wave 3 consists of five smaller waves. Wave 3 often moves prices 1.68 times higher than the length of Wave 1, which is a Fibonacci ratio.
- Wave 4 is, again, a correction, and the ratio of the change in price during this wave to the price change during the third wave is also generally a Fibonacci ratio. Wave 4 commonly reverses 38 percent of the gain in Wave 3. Wave 5 is also an up wave. Generally, the price movement in Wave 5 is not as great as that in Wave 3. The exception to the rule is that

[10]Breadth is defined as the ratio of the number of advancing securities in an index or traded on a given stock market to the number of declining issues.

Wave 5 may become extended, as when euphoria overtakes the market. Wave 5 consists of five smaller waves.

After Wave 5 is completed, the market traces out a series of three corrective waves, labeled a, b, and c in Exhibit 12-34.

- Wave a is a down wave in a bull market; Wave a itself breaks down into three waves.
- Wave b is an upward movement and breaks down into five waves. Wave b is a false rally and is often called a "bull trap."
- Wave c is the final corrective wave. In a bull market, it does not move below the start of the prior Wave 1 pattern. Wave c breaks down into three subwaves.

This description of the waves applies to bull markets; in bear markets, the impulse waves are labeled A through E and the corrective waves are labeled 1, 2, and 3. Waves in the direction of the trend consist of five subwaves, and counterwaves consist of three subwaves.

In practice, a good deal of time is required to become proficient with **Elliott Wave Theory**. Wave counts may not become evident at first, and Elliotticians often have to renumber their wave counts on the basis of changes in market trends. This theory is widely used, however, and the patterns Elliott described can still be observed today.

As a technician begins to make initial judgments on wave counts, the next step is to draw lines representing Fibonacci ratios on the charts. These lines alert the technician to the levels at which trends may change in the future and can be used in conjunction with other technical tools for forecasting. Positive price movements generally take prices up by some Fibonacci ratio of prior highs (e.g., 1.5 or 1.62), and price declines generally reverse prices by a Fibonacci ratio (e.g., 0.50 or 0.667). Elliott Wave Theory is used in practice with Dow Theory, trend analysis, pattern analysis, and oscillator analysis to provide a sense of the general trend in the market. As Elliott's nine cycles imply, Elliott Wave Theory can be applied in both very short term trading as well as in very long term economic analysis, as is the case with most tools used in technical analysis.

5. INTERMARKET ANALYSIS

Intermarket analysis is a field within technical analysis that combines analysis of major categories of securities—namely, equities, bonds, currencies, and commodities—to identify market trends and possible inflections in a trend. Intermarket analysis also looks at industry subsectors, such as the nine sectors the S&P 500 is divided into, and the relationships among the major stock markets of countries with the largest economies, such as the New York, London, and Tokyo stock exchanges.

Intermarket analysis relies heavily on the field of economic analysis for its theoretical underpinning. The field was pioneered by John Murphy with his 1991 book *Intermarket Technical Analysis*. Murphy noted that all markets are interrelated and that these relationships are strengthening with the globalization of the world economy.[11]

[11] Murphy (1991).

Stock prices are affected by bond prices. High bond prices are a positive for stock prices since this means low interest rates. Lower interest rates benefit companies with lower borrowing costs and lead to higher equity valuations in the calculation of intrinsic value using discounted cash flow analysis in fundamental analysis. Thus rising bond prices are a positive for stock prices, and declining bond prices are a bearish indicator.

Bond prices impact commodity prices. Bond prices move inversely to interest rates. Interest rates move in proportion to expectations to future prices of commodities or inflation. So declining bond prices are a signal of possible rising commodity prices.

Currencies impact commodity prices. Most commodity trading is denominated in US dollars and so prices are commonly quoted in US dollars. As a result, a strong dollar results in lower commodity prices and vice versa.

In intermarket analysis, technicians often look for inflection points in one market as a warning sign to start looking for a change in trend in a related market. To identify these intermarket relationships, a commonly used tool is relative strength analysis, which charts the price of one security divided by the price of another.

Exhibit 12-35 shows the relative price of 10-year U.S. Treasury bonds compared with the S&P 500. The rise in T-bond price relative to the S&P 500 can be clearly seen. The inflection point in this chart occurs in March 2009. This point would signal that the time had come to move investments from bonds to stocks.

EXHIBIT 12-35 Relative Strength of 10-Year T-Bonds versus S&P 500, September 2008–July 2009

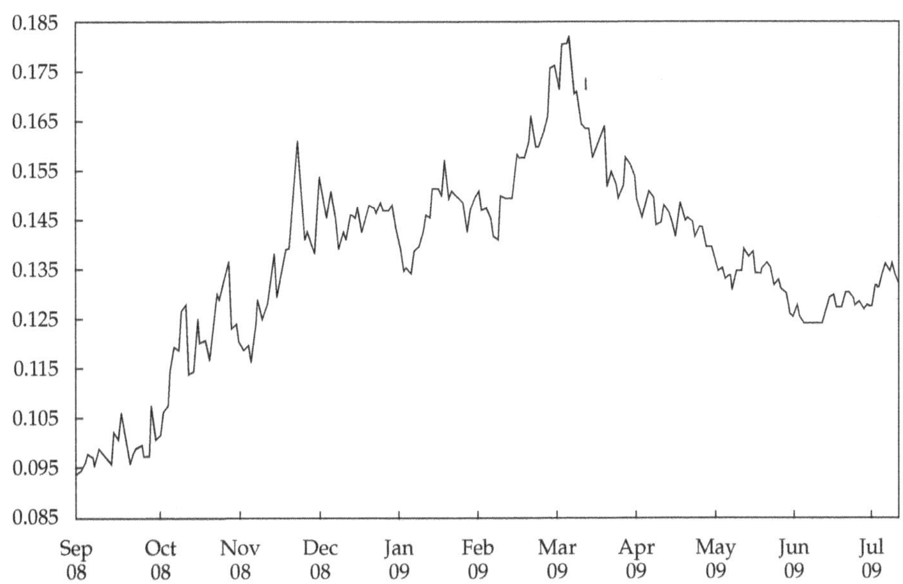

Exhibit 12-36 is a relative strength chart depicting the ratio between the S&P 500 and commodity prices. It shows a clear top and reversal of trend in December 2008. This inflection point shows U.S. stocks weakening relative to commodities and would indicate that allocating funds away from the U.S. stocks and into commodities might be appropriate.

EXHIBIT 12-36 S&P 500 Index versus Commodity Prices, November 2007–November 2009

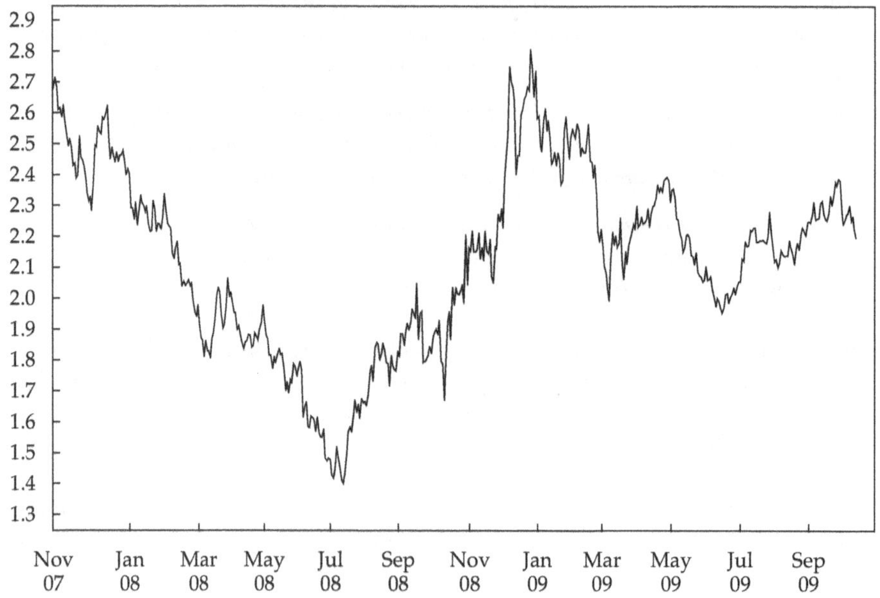

In addition to the preceding comparisons, once an asset category has been identified, relative strength analysis can be used to identify the strongest performing securities in a sector. For example, if commodities look promising, an investor can analyze each of the major commodities relative to a broad commodity index in order to find the strongest commodity.

Intermarket analysis can also be used to identify sectors of the equity market to invest in—often in connection with technical observations of the business cycle at any time. The equities of certain industry sectors tend to perform best at the beginning of an economic cycle. These sectors include utilities, financials, consumer nondurables, and transportation stocks. As an economic recovery gets under way, retailers, manufacturers, health care, and consumer durables tend to outperform. Lagging sectors include those tied to commodity prices, such as energy and basic industrial commodities, and also technology stocks.

Observations based on intermarket analysis can also help in allocating funds across national markets. Certain countries' economies are closely tied to commodities—for example, Australia, Canada, and South Africa. As economies evolve, these relationships change. So, the relationships must be monitored closely. For example, the Chinese equity markets have become much more advanced since 2000, the Chinese economy is much more industrialized than in the past, and its dependence on exports is currently strong.

6. SUMMARY

- Technical analysis is a form of security analysis that uses price and volume market data, often graphically displayed.

- Technical analysis can be used for any freely traded security in the global market and is used on a wide range of financial instruments, such as equities, bonds, commodity futures, and currency futures.
- Technical analysis is the study of market trends or patterns and relies on recognition of patterns that have worked in the past in an attempt to predict future security prices. Technicians believe that market trends and patterns repeat themselves and are somewhat predictable because human behavior tends to repeat itself and is somewhat predictable.
- Another tenet of technical analysis is that the market brings together the collective wisdom of multiple participants, weights it according to the size of the trades they make, and allows analysts to understand this collective sentiment. Technical analysis relies on knowledgeable market participants putting this knowledge to work in the market and thereby influencing prices and volume.
- Technical analysis and fundamental analysis are equally useful and valid, but they approach the market in different ways. Technical analysis focuses solely on analyzing markets and the trading of financial instruments, whereas fundamental analysis is a much wider ranging field encompassing financial and economic analysis as well as analysis of societal and political trends.
- Technical analysis relies primarily on information gathered from market participants that is expressed through the interaction of price and volume. Fundamental analysis relies on information that is external to the market (e.g., economic data, company financial information) in an attempt to evaluate a security's value relative to its current price.
- The usefulness of technical analysis is diminished by any constraints on the security being freely traded, by large outside manipulation of the market, and in illiquid markets.
- Charts provide information about past price behavior and provide a basis for inferences about likely future price behavior. Various types of charts can be useful in studying the markets: line charts, bar charts, candlestick charts, and point and figure charts.
- Relative strength analysis is based on the ratio of the prices of a security to a benchmark and is used to compare the performance of one asset with the performance of another asset.
- Many technicians consider volume information to be very important and watch for the confirmation in volume of a price trend or the divergence of volume from a price trend.
- The concept of trend is perhaps the most important aspect of technical analysis. An uptrend is defined as a security making higher highs and higher lows. To draw an uptrend line, a technician draws a line connecting the lows of the price chart. A downtrend is defined as a security making lower highs and lower lows. To draw a downtrend line, a technician draws a line connecting the highs of the price chart.
- Support is defined as a low price range in which the price stops declining because of buying activity. It is the opposite of resistance, which is a price range in which price stops rising because of selling activity.
- Chart patterns are formations appearing in price charts that create some type of recognizable shape.
- Reversal patterns signal the end of a trend. Common reversal patterns are the head and shoulders, the inverse head and shoulders, double tops and bottoms, and triple tops and bottoms.
- Continuation patterns indicate that a market trend in place prior to the pattern formation will continue once the pattern is completed. Common continuation patterns are triangles, rectangles, flags, and pennants.
- Price-based indicators incorporate information contained in market prices. Common price-based indicators are the moving average and Bollinger Bands.

- Momentum oscillator indicators are constructed from price data, but they are calculated so that they fluctuate either between a high and low, typically 0 and 100, or around 0 or 100. Some examples are momentum (or rate of change) oscillators, the RSI, stochastic measures, and MACD.
- Sentiment indicators attempt to gauge investor activity for signs of increasing bullishness or bearishness. Sentiment indicators come in two forms—investor polls and calculated statistical indices. Opinion polls to gauge investors' sentiment toward the equity market are conducted by a variety of services. Commonly used calculated statistical indices are the put/call ratio, the VIX, margin debt, and the short interest ratio.
- Flow-of-funds indicators help technicians gauge potential changes in supply and demand for securities. Some commonly used indicators are the ARMS Index (also called the TRIN), margin debt (also a sentiment indicator), mutual fund cash positions, new equity issuance, and secondary equity offerings.
- Many technicians use various observed cycles to predict future movements in security prices; these cycles include Kondratieff waves, decennial patterns, and the U.S. presidential cycle.
- Elliott Wave Theory is an approach to market forecasting that assumes that markets form repetitive wave patterns, which are themselves composed of smaller and smaller subwaves. The relationships among wave heights are frequently Fibonacci ratios.
- Intermarket analysis is based on the principle that all markets are interrelated and influence each other. This approach involves the use of relative strength analysis for different groups of securities (e.g., stocks versus bonds, sectors in an economy, and securities from different countries) to make allocation decisions.

PROBLEMS

1. Technical analysis relies most importantly on:

   A. Price and volume data.
   B. Accurate financial statements.
   C. Fundamental analysis to confirm conclusions.

2. Which of the following is *not* an assumption of technical analysis?

   A. Security markets are efficient.
   B. The security under analysis is freely traded.
   C. Market trends and patterns tend to repeat themselves.

3. Drawbacks of technical analysis include which of the following?

   A. It identifies changes in trends only after the fact.
   B. Deviations from intrinsic value can persist for long periods.
   C. It usually requires detailed knowledge of the financial instrument under analysis.

4. Why is technical analysis especially useful in the analysis of commodities and currencies?

   A. Government regulators are more likely to intervene in these markets.
   B. These types of securities display clearer trends than equities and bonds do.
   C. Valuation models cannot be used to determine fundamental intrinsic value for these securities.

5. A daily bar chart provides:

   A. A logarithmically scaled horizontal axis.
   B. A horizontal axis that represents changes in price.
   C. High and low prices during the day and the day's opening and closing prices.

6. A candlestick chart is similar to a bar chart *except* that the candlestick chart:

   A. Represents upward movements in price with X's.
   B. Also graphically shows the range of the period's highs and lows.
   C. Has a body that is light or dark depending on whether the security closed higher or lower than its open.

7. In analyzing a price chart, high or increasing volume *most likely* indicates which of the following?

   A. Predicts a reversal in the price trend.
   B. Predicts that a trendless period will follow.
   C. Confirms a rising or declining trend in prices.

8. In constructing a chart, using a logarithmic scale on the vertical axis is likely to be *most useful* for which of the following applications?

   A. The price of gold for the past 100 years.
   B. The share price of a company over the past month.
   C. Yields on 10-year U.S. Treasuries for the past five years.

9. A downtrend line is constructed by drawing a line connecting:

   A. The lows of the price chart.
   B. The highs of the price chart.
   C. The highest high to the lowest low of the price chart.

10. The following exhibit depicts GreatWall Information Industry Co., Ltd., ordinary shares, traded on the Shenzhen Stock Exchange, for late 2008 through late 2009 in renminbi (RMB).

CANDLESTICK CHART GreatWall Information Industry Co., Ltd. Price Data, November 2008–September 2009 (price measured in RMB × 100)

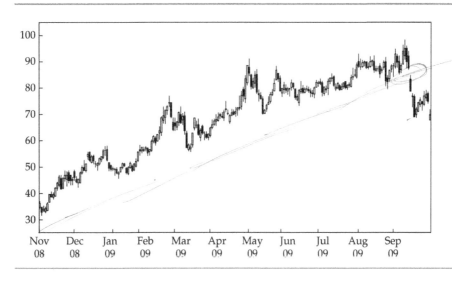

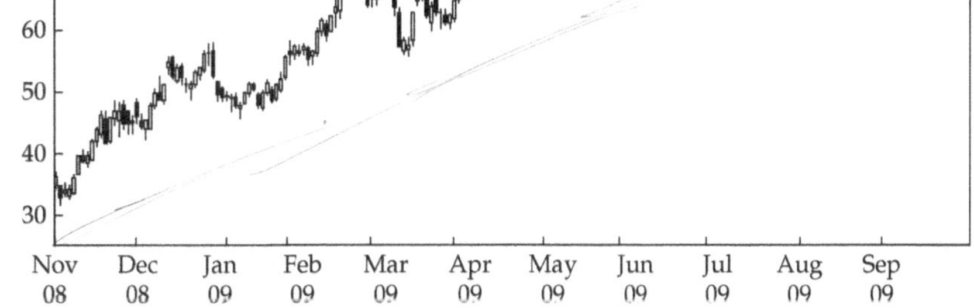

Based on this chart, the uptrend was *most likely* broken at a level nearest to:

A. 7 RMB.
B. 8.5 RMB.
C. 10 RMB.

11. The "change in polarity" principle states which of the following?

A. Once an uptrend is broken, it becomes a downtrend.
B. Once a resistance level is breached, it becomes a support level.
C. The short-term moving average has crossed over the longer-term moving average.

12. The following exhibit depicts Barclays ordinary shares, traded on the London Stock Exchange, for 2009 in British pence.

CANDLESTICK CHART Barclays PLC Price Data, January 2009–January 2010 (price measured in British pence)

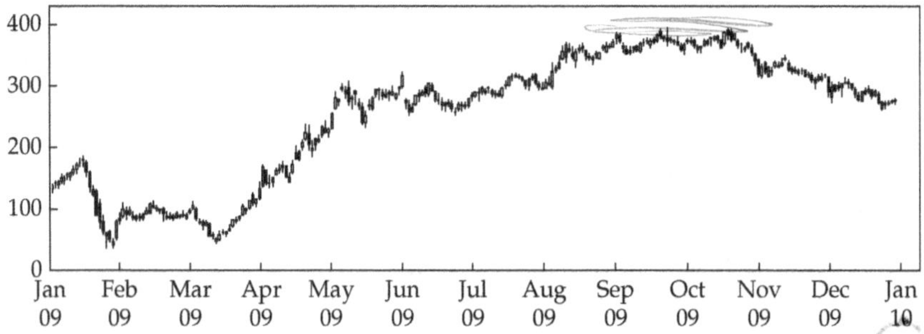

Based on this chart, Barclays appears to show resistance at a level nearest to:

A. 50p.
B. 275p.
C. 390p.

13. The following exhibit depicts Archer Daniels Midland Company common shares, traded on the New York Stock Exchange, for 1996 to 2001 in U.S. dollars.

CANDLESTICK CHART Archer Daniels Midland Company, February 1996–February 2001

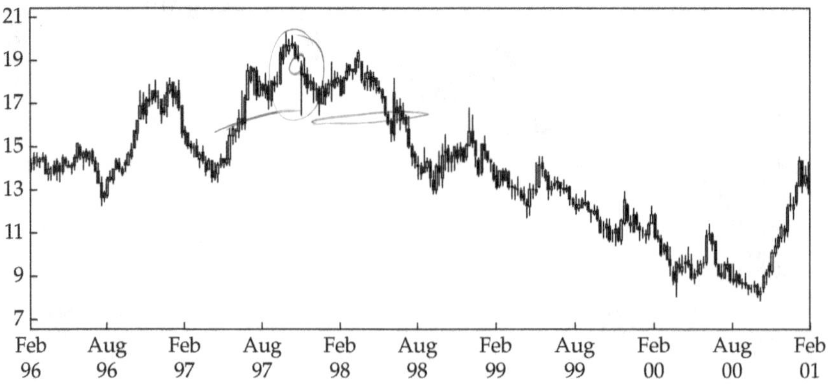

This chart illustrates *most* clearly which type of pattern?

A. Triangle.
B. Triple top.
C. Head and shoulders.

14. In an inverted head and shoulders pattern, if the neckline is at €100, the shoulders are at €90, and the head is at €75, the price target is *closest* to which of the following?

A. €50.
B. €110.
C. €125.

100 + (100 - 75)

15. Which flow-of-funds indicator is considered bearish for equities?

A. A large increase in the number of IPOs.
B. Higher-than-average cash balances in mutual funds.
C. An upturn in margin debt but one that is still below the long-term average.

16. A TRIN with a value of less than 1.0 indicates:

A. The market is in balance.
B. There is more volume in rising shares.
C. There is more volume in declining shares.

17. Bollinger Bands are constructed by plotting:

A. A MACD line and a signal line.
B. A moving-average line with an uptrend line above and downtrend line below.
C. A moving-average line with upper and lower lines that are at a set number of standard deviations apart.

18. Which of the following is *not* a momentum oscillator?

A. MACD.
B. Stochastic oscillator.
C. Bollinger Bands.

19. Which of the following is a continuation pattern?

A. Triangle.
B. Triple top.
C. Head and shoulders.

20. Which of the following is a reversal pattern?

A. Pennant.
B. Rectangle.
C. Double bottom.

21. Which of the following is generally true of the head and shoulders pattern?

A. Volume is important in interpreting the data.
B. The neckline, once breached, becomes a support level.
C. Head and shoulders patterns are generally followed by an uptrend in the security's price.

22. Nikolai Kondratieff concluded in the 1920s that since the 1780s, Western economies have generally followed a cycle of how many years?

    A. 18.
    B. 54.
    C. 76.

23. Based on the decennial pattern of cycles, how would the return of the Dow Jones Industrial Average (DJIA) in the year 2015 compare with the return in 2020?

    A. The return would be better.
    B. The return would be worse.
    C. The answer cannot be determined because the theory does not apply to both of those years.

24. According to the U.S. presidential cycle theory, the DJIA has the best performance during which year?

    A. The presidential election year itself.
    B. The first year following a presidential election.
    C. The third year following a presidential election.

25. What is a major problem with long-term cycle theories?

    A. The sample size is small.
    B. The data are usually hard to observe.
    C. They occur over such a long period that they are difficult to discern.

26. In 1938, R. N. Elliott proposed a theory that equity markets move:

    A. In stochastic waves.
    B. In cycles following Fibonacci ratios.
    C. In waves dependent on other securities.

27. All of the following are names of Elliott cycles *except*:

    A. Presidential.
    B. Supercycle.
    C. Grand supercycle.

28. To identify intermarket relationships, technicians commonly use:

    A. Stochastic oscillators.
    B. Fibonacci ratios.
    C. Relative strength analysis.

GLOSSARY

10-year moving average price/earnings A price-to-earnings ratio in which the numerator (in a U.S. context) is defined as the real S&P 500 price index and the denominator as the moving average of the preceding 10 years of real reported earnings on the S&P 500.

Abnormal returns The amount by which a security's actual return differs from its expected return, given the security's risk and the market's return.

Accelerated book build An offering of securities by an investment bank acting as principal that is accomplished in only one or two days.

Active investment An approach to investing in which the investor seeks to outperform a given benchmark.

Active return The return on a portfolio minus the return on the portfolio's benchmark.

Allocationally efficient Said of a market, a financial system, or an economy that promotes the allocation of resources to their highest value uses.

All-or-nothing order An order that includes the instruction to trade only if the trade fills the entire quantity (size) specified.

Alternative trading system Trading venues that function like exchanges but that do not exercise regulatory authority over their subscribers, except with respect to the conduct of the subscribers' trading in their trading systems.

American depository receipt A U.S. dollar-denominated security that trades like a common share on U.S. exchanges.

American depository share The underlying shares on which American depository receipts are based. They trade in the issuing company's domestic market.

American-style contract An option that can be exercised at any time until its expiration date.

Arbitrage A risk-free operation that earns an expected positive net profit but requires no net investment of money.

Arbitrage pricing theory A theoretical model that proposes a linear relationship between expected return and risk.

Arbitrageur A trader who engages in arbitrage (see *arbitrage*).

Arithmetic or mean return The average return on an investment over time.

Arms index (or **TRIN**) A flow-of-funds indicator applied to a broad stock market index to measure the relative extent to which money is moving into or out of rising and declining stocks.

Ask (offer) The price at which a dealer or trader is willing to sell an asset, typically qualified by a maximum quantity (ask size).

Ask size The maximum quantity of an asset that pertains to a specific ask price from a trader. For example, if the ask for a share issue is $30 for a size of 1,000 shares, the trader is offering to sell at $30 up to 1,000 shares.

Asset allocation The process of determining how investment funds should be distributed among asset classes.

Asset-based valuation model Valuation based on estimates of the market value of a company's assets.

Asset class A group of assets that have similar characteristics, attributes, and risk/return relationships.

Bar chart A price chart with four bits of data for each time interval—the high, low, opening, and closing prices. A vertical line connects the high and low. A cross-hatch left indicates the opening price and a cross-hatch right indicates the close.

Basket of listed depository receipts An exchange-traded fund (ETF) that represents a portfolio of depository receipts.

Behavioral finance A field of finance that examines the psychological variables that affect and often distort the investment decision making of investors, analysts, and portfolio managers.

Behind the market Said of prices specified in orders that are worse than the best current price; e.g., for a limit buy order, a limit price below the best bid.

Best bid The highest bid in the market.

Best efforts offering An offering of a security using an investment bank in which the investment bank, as agent for the issuer, promises to use its best efforts to sell the offering but does not guarantee that a specific amount will be sold.

Best offer The lowest offer (ask price) in the market.

Beta A measure of systematic risk that is based on the covariance of an asset's or portfolio's return with the return of the overall market.

Bid price The price at which a dealer or trader is willing to buy an asset, typically qualified by a maximum quantity.

Bid size The maximum quantity of an asset that pertains to a specific bid price from a trader.

Block broker A broker (agent) that provides brokerage services for large-size trades.

Blue chip companies Widely held large market capitalization companies that are considered financially sound and are leaders in their respective industry or local stock market.

Bollinger Bands A price-based technical analysis indicator consisting of a moving average plus a higher line representing the moving average plus a set number of standard deviations from average price (for the same number of periods as used to calculate the moving average) and a lower line that is a moving average minus the same number of standard deviations.

Book building Investment bankers' process of compiling a "book" or list of indications of interest to buy part of an offering.

Book value (or **carrying value**) The net amount shown for an asset or liability on the balance sheet; book value may also refer to the company's excess of total assets over total liabilities.

Bottom up With reference to investment selection processes, an approach that involves selection from all securities within a specified investment universe, i.e., without prior narrowing of the universe on the basis of macroeconomic or overall market considerations.

Broker An agent of a trader in executing trades.

Broker-dealer A financial intermediary (often a company) that may function as a principal (dealer) or as an agent (broker) depending on the type of trade.

Brokered market A market in which brokers arrange trades among their clients.

Buyout fund A fund that buys all the shares of a public company so that, in effect, the company becomes private.

Buy side firm An investment management company or other investor that uses the services of brokers or dealers (i.e., the client of the sell-side firms).

Callable (or redeemable) common shares Shares that give the issuing company the option (or right), but not the obligation, to buy back the shares from investors at a call price that is specified when the shares are originally issued.

Call market A market in which trades occur only at a particular time and place (i.e., when the market is called).

Call money rate The interest rate that buyers pay for their margin loan.

Call option An option that gives the holder the right to buy an underlying asset from another party at a fixed price over a specific period of time.

Candlestick chart A price chart with four bits of data for each time interval. A candle indicates the opening and closing price for the interval. The body of the candle is shaded if the opening price was higher than the closing price, and the body is clear if the opening price was lower than the closing price. Vertical lines known as wicks or shadows extend from the top and bottom of the candle to indicate the high and the low prices for the interval.

Capital allocation line A graph line that describes the combinations of expected return and standard deviation of return available to an investor from combining the optimal portfolio of risky assets with the risk-free asset.

Capital asset pricing model An equation describing the expected return on any asset (or portfolio) as a linear function of its beta.

Capital market expectations An investor's expectations concerning the risk and return prospects of asset classes.

Capital market line Financial markets that trade securities of longer duration, such as bonds and equities.

CBOE Volatility Index A measure of near-term market volatility as conveyed by S&P 500 stock index option prices.

Change in polarity principle A tenet of technical analysis that once a support level is breached, it becomes a resistance level. The same holds true for resistance levels; once breached, they become support levels.

Clearinghouse An entity associated with a futures market that acts as middleman between the contracting parties and guarantees to each party the performance of the other.

Clearing instructions Instructions that indicate how to arrange the final settlement ("clearing") of a trade

Closed-end fund A mutual fund in which no new investment money is accepted. New investors invest by buying existing shares, and investors in the fund liquidate by selling their shares to other investors.

Cobb-Douglas production function (Cobb-Douglas model) A production function (model for economic output) based on factors of labor and capital that exhibits constant returns to scale.

Commodity swap A swap in which the underlying is a commodity such as oil, gold, or an agricultural product.

Common shares A type of security that represents an ownership interest in a company.

Company analysis Analysis of an individual company.

Competitive strategy A company's plans for responding to the threats and opportunities presented by the external environment.

Complete market Informally, markets in which the variety of distinct securities traded is so broad that any desired payoff in a future state-of-the-world is achievable.

Constant returns to scale A characteristic of a production function such that a given percentage increase in capital stock and labor input results in an equal percentage increase in output.

Constituent securities With respect to an index, the individual securities within an index.

Continuation pattern A type of pattern used in technical analysis to predict the resumption of a market trend that was in place prior to the formation of a pattern.

Continuous trading market A market in which trades can be arranged and executed any time the market is open.

Convergence In technical analysis, a term that describes the case when an indicator moves in the same manner as the security being analyzed.

Convertible preference shares A type of equity security that entitles shareholders to convert their shares into a specified number of common shares.

Correlation A number between −1 and +1 that measures the co-movement (linear association) between two random variables.

Correlation coefficient A number between −1 and +1 that measures the consistency or tendency for two investments to act in a similar way. It is used to determine the effect on portfolio risk when two assets are combined.

Counterparty risk The risk that the other party to a contract will fail to honor the terms of the contract.

Covariance A measure of the co-movement (linear association) between two random variables.

Crossing network Trading systems that match buyers and sellers who are willing to trade at prices obtained from other markets.

Cumulative preference shares Preference shares for which any dividends that are not paid accrue and must be paid in full before dividends on common shares can be paid.

Cumulative voting Voting that allows shareholders to direct their total voting rights to specific candidates, as opposed to having to allocate their voting rights evenly among all candidates.

Currency The notes and coins held by individuals and businesses.

Currency swap A swap in which each party makes interest payments to the other in different currencies.

Cyclical company A company whose profits are strongly correlated with the strength of the overall economy.

Dark pool Alternative trading systems that do not display the orders that their clients send to them.

Data mining (or **data snooping**) The practice of determining a model by extensive searching through a dataset for statistically significant patterns.

Day order An order that is good for the day on which it is submitted. If it has not been filled by the close of business, the order expires unfilled.

Dead cross A technical analysis, a term that describes a situation where a short-term moving average crosses from above a longer-term moving average to below it; this movement is considered bearish.

Dealer A financial intermediary who acts as a principal in trades.

Defensive (or **stable**) **company** A company whose revenues and profits are least affected by fluctuations in the overall economic activity.

Defined benefit A pension plan that specifies the plan sponsor's obligations in terms of the benefit to plan participants.

Defined contribution A pension plan that specifies the sponsor's obligations in terms of contributions to the pension fund rather than benefits to plan participants.

Depository institution Commercial banks, savings and loan banks, credit unions, and similar institutions that raise funds from depositors and other investors and lend it to borrowers.

Depository receipt A security that trades like an ordinary share on a local exchange and represents an economic interest in a foreign company.

Derivative pricing rule A pricing rule used by crossing networks in which a price is taken (derived) from the price that is current in the asset's primary market.

Discriminatory pricing rule A pricing rule used in continuous markets in which the limit price of the order or quote that first arrived determines the trade price.

Display size The size of an order displayed to public view.

Divergence In technical analysis, a term that describes the case when an indicator moves differently from the security being analyzed.

Diversification ratio The ratio of the standard deviation of an equally weighted portfolio to the standard deviation of a randomly selected security.

Dividend discount model A present value model that estimates the intrinsic value of an equity share based on the present value of its expected future dividends.

Divisor A number (denominator) used to determine the value of a price return index. It is initially chosen at the inception of an index and subsequently adjusted by the index provider, as necessary, to avoid changes in the index value that are unrelated to changes in the prices of its constituent securities.

Double bottom In technical analysis, a reversal pattern that is formed when the price reaches a low, rebounds, and then sells off back to the first low level; used to predict a change from a downtrend to an uptrend.

Double top In technical analysis, a reversal pattern that is formed when an uptrend reverses twice at roughly the same high price level; used to predict a change from an uptrend to a downtrend.

Earnings surprise The portion of a company's earnings that is unanticipated by investors and, according to the efficient market hypothesis, merits a price adjustment.

Economic profit A company's total revenue minus its total cost.

Efficient market See *informationally efficient market.*

Elliott wave theory A technical analysis theory that claims that the market follows regular, repeated waves or cycles.

Enterprise value A measure of a company's total market value from which the value of cash and short-term investments have been subtracted.

Equal weighting An index weighting method in which an equal weight is assigned to each constituent security at inception.

Equity *q* The ratio of a company's equity market capitalization divided by net worth measured at replacement cost.

Equity risk premium The expected return on equities minus the risk-free rate; the premium that investors demand for investing in equities.

Equity swap A swap in which the rate is the return on a stock or stock index.

European-style contract An option that can only be exercised on its expiration date.

Exchange Places where traders can meet to arrange their trades.

Execution instructions Instructions that indicate how to fill an order.

Exercise The process of using an option to buy or sell the underlying.

Expected return The return an investor anticipates earning in the future.

Experience curve A curve that shows the direct cost per unit of good or service produced or delivered as a typically declining function of cumulative output.

Fed model An equity valuation model that relates the earnings yield on the S&P 500 to the yield to maturity on 10-year U.S. Treasury bonds.

Fibonacci sequence A sequence of numbers starting with 0 and 1, and then each subsequent number in the sequence is the sum of the two preceding numbers. In Elliott Wave Theory, it is believed that market waves follow patterns that are the ratios of the numbers in the Fibonacci sequence.

Financial leverage The extent to which a company can effect, through the use of debt, a proportional change in the return on common equity that is greater than a given proportional change in operating income; also, short for the financial leverage ratio.

Flag A technical analysis continuation pattern formed by parallel trendlines, typically over a short period.

Float-adjusted market-capitalization weighting An index weighting method in which the weight assigned to each constituent security is determined by adjusting its market capitalization for its market float.

Foreign exchange gains (or **losses**) Gains (or losses) that occur when the exchange rate changes between the investor's currency and the currency that foreign securities are denominated in.

Forward contract An agreement between two parties in which one party, the buyer, agrees to buy from the other party, the seller, an underlying asset at a later date for a price established at the start of the contract.

Free-cash-flow-to-equity models Valuation model based on discounting expected future free cash flow to equity.

Free float The number of shares that are readily and freely tradable in the secondary market.

Fundamental analysis The examination of publicly available information and the formulation of forecasts to estimate the intrinsic value of assets.

Fundamental (or **intrinsic**) **value** The underlying or true value of an asset based on an analysis of its qualitative and quantitative characteristics.

Fundamental weighting An index weighting method in which the weight assigned to each constituent security is based on its underlying company's size. It attempts to address the disadvantages of market-capitalization weighting by using measures that are independent of the constituent security's price.

Futures contract A variation of a forward contract that has essentially the same basic definition but with some additional features, such as a clearinghouse guarantee against credit losses, a daily settlement of gains and losses, and an organized electronic or floor trading facility.

Geometric mean return A measure of returns that assumes the investment amount is not reset at the beginning of each year and accounts for the compounding of returns.

Global depository receipt A depository receipt that is issued outside of the company's home country and outside of the United States.

Global minimum-variance portfolio The portfolio on the minimum-variance frontier with the smallest variance of return.

Global registered share A common share that is traded on different stock exchanges around the world in different currencies.

Golden cross A technical analysis term that describes a situation where a short-term moving average crosses from below a longer-term moving average to above it; this movement is considered bullish.

Good-on-close An execution instruction specifying that an order can only be filled at the close of trading.

Good-on-open An execution instruction specifying that an order can only be filled at the opening of trading.

Good-till-cancelled An order specifying that it is valid until the entity placing the order has cancelled it (or, commonly, until some specified amount of time such as 60 days has elapsed, whichever comes sooner).

Gross return The return earned by an asset manager prior to deductions for management expenses, custodial fees, taxes, or any other expenses related to the management and administration of an investment.

Growth cyclical A term sometimes used to describe companies that are growing rapidly on a long-term basis but that still experience above-average fluctuation in their revenues and profits over the course of a business cycle.

Head and shoulders pattern In technical analysis, a reversal pattern that is formed in three parts: a left shoulder, head, and right shoulder; used to predict a change from an uptrend to a downtrend.

Hedge funds Private investment vehicles that typically use leverage, derivatives, and long and short investment strategies.

Herding Clustered trading that may or may not be based on information.

Hidden order An order that is exposed not to the public but only to the brokers or exchanges that receive it.

Historical return The return an investor actually earned in the past.

H-model A variant of the two-stage dividend discount model in which growth begins at a high rate and declines linearly throughout the supernormal growth period until it reaches a normal growth rate that holds in perpetuity.

Holding period return The return that an investor earns during a specified holding period; a synonym for total return.

Homogeneity of expectations The assumption that all investors have the same economic expectations and thus have the same expectations of prices, cash flows, and other investment characteristics.

Iceberg order An order in which the display size is less than the order's full size.

Immediate or cancel (fill or kill) orders An order that is valid only upon receipt by the broker or exchange. If such an order cannot be filled in part or in whole upon receipt, it cancels immediately.

Income trust A type of equity ownership vehicle established as a trust issuing ownership shares known as units.

Indifference curve The graph of risk–return combinations that an investor would be willing to accept to maintain a given level of utility.

Industry A group of companies offering similar products and/or services.

Industry analysis The analysis of a specific branch of manufacturing, service, or trade.

Informationally efficient market (efficient market) A market in which asset prices reflect new information quickly and rationally.

Information cascade The transmission of information from those participants who act first and whose decisions influence the decisions of others (see also *herding*).

Information-motivated trader Traders who trade to profit from information that they believe allows them to predict future prices.

Initial margin The amount that must be deposited in a clearinghouse account when entering into a futures contract.

Initial margin requirement The margin requirement on the first day of a transaction as well as on any day in which additional margin funds must be deposited.

Initial public offering (IPO) The first issuance of common shares to the public by a formerly private corporation.

Interest rate swap A swap in which the underlying is an interest rate. Can be viewed as a currency swap in which both currencies are the same and can be created as a combination of currency swaps.

Intermarket analysis A field within technical analysis that combines analysis of major categories of securities—namely, equities, bonds, currencies, and commodities—to identify market trends and possible inflections in a trend.

Internal rate of return The discount rate that makes net present value equal 0; the discount rate that makes the present value of an investment's costs (outflows) equal to the present value of the investment's benefits (inflows).

Intrinsic value See *fundamental value.*

Investment banks Financial intermediaries that provide advice to their mostly corporate clients and help them arrange transactions such as initial and seasoned securities offerings.

Investment policy statement A written planning document that describes a client's investment objectives and risk tolerance over a relevant time horizon, along with constraints that apply to the client's portfolio.

January effect (also **turn-of-the-year effect**) Calendar anomaly that stock market returns in January are significantly higher compared to the rest of the months of the year, with most of the abnormal returns reported during the first five trading days in January.

Justified P/E The price-to-earnings ratio that is fair, warranted, or justified on the basis of forecasted fundamentals.

Kondratieff wave A 54-year-long economic cycle postulated by Nikolai Kondratieff.

Kurtosis The statistical measure that indicates the peakedness of a distribution.

Law of one price The condition in a financial market in which two equivalent financial instruments or combinations of financial instruments can sell for only one price. Equivalent to the principle that no arbitrage opportunities are possible.

Leverage In the context of corporate finance, leverage refers to the use of fixed costs within a company's cost structure. Fixed costs that are operating costs (such as depreciation or rent) create operating leverage. Fixed costs that are financial costs (such as interest expense) create financial leverage.

Leveraged buyout A transaction whereby the target company management team converts the target to a privately held company by using heavy borrowing to finance the purchase of the target company's outstanding shares.

Life-cycle stage The stage of the life cycle: embryonic, growth, shakeout, mature, declining.

Limit order Instructions to a broker or exchange to obtain the best price immediately available when filling an order, but in no event accept a price higher than a specified (limit) price when buying or accept a price lower than a specified (limit) price when selling.

Limit order book The book or list of limit orders to buy and sell that pertains to a security.

Linear scale A scale in which equal distances correspond to equal absolute amounts.

Line chart In technical analysis, a plot of price data, typically closing prices, with a line connecting the points.

Liquidity The ability to purchase or sell an asset quickly and easily at a price close to fair market value. The ability to meet short-term obligations using assets that are the most readily converted into cash.

Liquid market Said of a market in which traders can buy or sell with low total transaction costs when they want to trade.

Load fund A mutual fund in which, in addition to the annual fee, a percentage fee is charged to invest in the fund and/or for redemptions from the fund.

Logarithmic scale A scale in which equal distances represent equal proportional changes in the underlying quantity.

Long position A position in an asset or contract in which one owns the asset or has an exercisable right under the contract.

M^2 A measure of what a portfolio would have returned if it had taken on the same total risk as the market index.

Maintenance margin The minimum amount that is required by a futures clearinghouse to maintain a margin account and to protect against default. Participants whose margin balances drop below the required maintenance margin must replenish their accounts.

Maintenance margin requirement The margin requirement on any day other than the first day of a transaction.

Management buyout An event in which a group of investors consisting primarily of the company's existing management purchase all of its outstanding shares and take the company private.

Margin call A notice to deposit additional cash or securities in a margin account.

Margin loan Money borrowed from a broker to purchase securities.

Market A means of bringing buyers and sellers together to exchange goods and services.

Marketable limit order A buy limit order in which the limit price is placed above the best offer, or a sell limit order in which the limit price is placed below the best bid. Such orders generally will partially or completely fill right away.

Market anomaly Change in the price or return of a security that cannot directly be linked to current relevant information known in the market or to the release of new information into the market.

Market bid–ask spread The difference between the best bid and the best offer.

Market-capitalization weighting An index weighting method in which the weight assigned to each constituent security is determined by dividing its market capitalization by the total market capitalization (sum of the market capitalization) of all securities in the index.

Market float The number of shares that are available to the investing public.

Market model A regression equation that specifies a linear relationship between the return on a security (or portfolio) and the return on a broad market index.

Market order Instructions to a broker or exchange to obtain the best price immediately available when filling an order.

Market value The price at which an asset or security can currently be bought or sold in an open market.

Markowitz efficient frontier The graph of the set of portfolios offering the maximum expected return for their level of risk (standard deviation of return).

Minimum variance portfolio The portfolio with the minimum variance for each given level of expected return.

Modern portfolio theory The analysis of rational portfolio choices based on the efficient use of risk.

Momentum oscillator A graphical representation of market sentiment that is constructed from price data and calculated so that it oscillates either between a high and a low or around some number.

Money-weighted return The internal rate of return on a portfolio, taking account of all cash flows.

Moving average The average of the closing price of a security over a specified number of periods. With each new period, the average is recalculated.

Moving-average convergence/divergence oscillator A momentum oscillator that is constructed based on the difference between short-term and long-term moving averages of a security's price.

Multifactor model A model that explains a variable in terms of the values of a set of factors.

Multimarket index An index comprised of indices from different countries, designed to represent multiple security markets.

Multiplier models (or **market multiple models**) Valuation models based on share price multiples or enterprise value multiples.

Mutual fund A professionally managed investment pool in which investors in the fund typically each have a pro-rata claim on the income and value of the fund.

Net return A measure of what the investment has earned for the investor after deducting all managerial and administrative expenses.

No-load fund A mutual fund in which there is no fee for investing in the fund or for redeeming fund shares, although there is an annual fee based on a percentage of the fund's net asset value.

Noncumulative preference shares Preference shares for which dividends that are not paid in the current or subsequent periods are forfeited permanently (instead of being accrued and paid at a later date).

Noncyclical company A company whose performance is largely independent of the business cycle.

Nonparticipating preference shares Preference shares that do not entitle shareholders to share in the profits of the company. Instead, shareholders are only entitled to receive a fixed dividend payment and the par value of the shares in the event of liquidation.

Nonsystematic risk Unique risk that is local or limited to a particular asset or industry that need not affect assets outside of that asset class.

Normal distribution A continuous, symmetric probability distribution that is completely described by its mean and its variance.

Open-end fund A mutual fund that accepts new investment money and issues additional shares at a value equal to the net asset value of the fund at the time of investment.

Operationally efficient Said of a market, a financial system, or an economy that has relatively low transaction costs.

Option contract A financial instrument that gives one party the right, but not the obligation, to buy or sell an underlying asset from or to another party at a fixed price over a specific period of time. Also referred to as contingent claims.

Order A specification of what instrument to trade, how much to trade, and whether to buy or sell.

Order-driven market A market (generally an auction market) that uses rules to arrange trades based on the orders that traders submit; in their pure form, such markets do not make use of dealers.

Order precedence hierarchy With respect to the execution of orders to trade, a set of rules that determines which orders execute before other orders.

Overbought A market condition market sentiment that is thought to be unsustainably bullish.

Oversold A market condition market sentiment that is thought to be unsustainably bearish.

Participating preference shares Preference shares that entitle shareholders to receive the standard preferred dividend plus the opportunity to receive an additional dividend if the company's profits exceed a prespecified level.

Passive investment A buy-and-hold approach in which an investor does not make portfolio changes based on short-term expectations of changing market or security performance.

Passive portfolios Portfolios that replicate and track market indices, which are passively constructed on the basis of market prices and market capitalizations.

Peer group A group of companies engaged in similar business activities whose economics and valuation are influenced by closely related factors.

Pennant A technical analysis continuation pattern formed by trendlines that converge to form a triangle, typically over a short period.

Performance evaluation The measurement and assessment of the outcomes of investment management decisions.

Point and figure chart A technical analysis chart that is constructed with columns of X's alternating with columns of O's such that the horizontal axis represents only the number of changes in price without reference to time or volume.

Portfolio planning The process of creating a plan for building a portfolio that is expected to satisfy a client's investment objectives.

Position The quantity of an asset that an entity owns or owes.

Preference shares A type of equity interest that ranks above common shares with respect to the payment of dividends and the distribution of the company's net assets upon liquidation. They have characteristics of both debt and equity securities.

Preferred stock A form of equity (generally nonvoting) that has priority over common stock in the receipt of dividends and on the issuer's assets in the event of a company's liquidation.

Present value models (or **discounted cash flow models**) Valuation models that estimate the intrinsic value of a security as the present value of the future benefits expected to be received from the security.

Price multiple A ratio that compares the share price with some sort of monetary flow or value to allow evaluation of the relative worth of a company's stock.

Price priority The principle that the highest priced buy orders and the lowest priced sell orders execute first.

Price return Measures *only* the price appreciation or percentage change in price of the securities in an index or portfolio.

Price return index (or **price index**) An index that reflects *only* the price appreciation or percentage change in price of the constituent securities.

Price weighting An index weighting method in which the weight assigned to each constituent security is determined by dividing its price by the sum of all the prices of the constituent securities.

Primary capital market (primary market) The market where securities are first sold and the issuers receive the proceeds.

Principal business activity The business activity from which a company derives a majority of its revenues and/or earnings.

Private equity securities Securities that are not listed on public exchanges and have no active secondary market. They are issued primarily to institutional investors via nonpublic offerings, such as private placements.

Private investment in public equity An investment in the equity of a publicly traded firm that is made at a discount to the market value of the firm's shares.

Private placement When corporations sell securities directly to a small group of qualified investors, usually with the assistance of an investment bank.

Putable common shares Common shares that give investors the option (or right) to sell their shares (i.e., "put" them) back to the issuing company at a price that is specified when the shares are originally issued.

Put/call ratio A technical analysis indicator that evaluates market sentiment based upon the volume of put options traded divided by the volume of call options traded for a particular financial instrument.

Put option An option that gives the holder the right to sell an underlying asset to another party at a fixed price over a specific period of time.

Quote-driven market A market in which dealers acting as principals facilitate trading.

Random walk A time series in which the value of the series in one period is the value of the series in the previous period plus an unpredictable random error.

Rebalancing Adjusting the weights of the constituent securities in an index.

Rebalancing policy The set of rules that guide the process of restoring a portfolio's asset class weights to those specified in the strategic asset allocation.

Relative strength analysis A comparison of the performance of one asset with the performance of another asset or a benchmark based on changes in the ratio of the securities' respective prices over time.

Relative strength index A technical analysis momentum oscillator that compares a security's gains with its losses over a set period.

Resistance In technical analysis, a price range in which selling activity is sufficient to stop the rise in the price of a security.

Retracement In technical analysis, a reversal in the movement of a security's price such that it is counter to the prevailing longer-term price trend.

Return-generating model A model that can provide an estimate of the expected return of a security given certain parameters and estimates of the values of the independent variables in the model.

Return on equity A profitability ratio calculated as net income divided by average shareholders' equity.

Reversal pattern A type of pattern used in technical analysis to predict the end of a trend and a change in direction of the security's price.

Risk averse The assumption that an investor will choose the least risky alternative.

Risk aversion The degree of an investor's inability and unwillingness to take risk.

Risk budgeting The establishment of objectives for individuals, groups, or divisions of an organization that takes into account the allocation of an acceptable level of risk.

Risk neutral Said of an investor who does not care about risk, so higher return investments are more desirable even if they come with higher risk.

Risk premium The expected return on an investment minus the risk-free rate.

Risk tolerance The amount of risk an investor is willing and able to bear to achieve an investment goal.

Seasoned offering An offering in which an issuer sells additional units of a previously issued security.

Seasoned security A security that an issuer has already issued.

Secondary market The market where securities are traded among investors.

Secondary precedence rules Rules that determine how to rank orders placed at the same time.

Sector A group of related industries.

Sector indices Indices that represent and track different economic sectors—such as consumer goods, energy, finance, health care, and technology—on either a national, regional, or global basis.

Security characteristic line A plot of the excess return of a security on the excess return of the market.

Security market index A portfolio of securities representing a given security market, market segment, or asset class.

Security market line The graph of the capital asset pricing model.

Security selection Skill in selecting individual securities within an asset class.

Self-investment limits With respect to investment limitations applying to pension plans, restrictions on the percentage of assets that can be invested in securities issued by the pension plan sponsor.

Sell-side firm A broker or dealer that sells securities to and provides independent investment research and recommendations to investment management companies.

Semistrong-form efficient market hypothesis The belief that security prices reflect all publicly known and available information.

Separately managed account An investment portfolio managed exclusively for the benefit of an individual or institution.

Sharpe ratio The average return in excess of the risk-free rate divided by the standard deviation of return; a measure of the average excess return earned per unit of standard deviation of return.

Shelf registration A registration of an offering well in advance of the offering; the issuer may not sell all shares registered in a single transaction.

Short position A position in an asset or contract in which one has sold an asset one does not own, or in which a right under a contract can be exercised against oneself.

Short selling A transaction in which borrowed securities are sold with the intention to repurchase them at a lower price at a later date and return them to the lender.

Skewness A quantitative measure of skew (lack of symmetry); a synonym of skew.

Solow residual A measure of the growth in total factor productivity that is based on an economic growth model developed by economist Robert M. Solow.

Special purpose vehicle (or **special purpose entity**) A nonoperating entity created to carry out a specified purpose, such as leasing assets or securitizing receivables; can be a corporation, partnership, trust, limited liability, or partnership formed to facilitate a specific type of business activity.

Sponsored depository receipt A type of depository receipt in which the foreign company whose shares are held by the depository has a direct involvement in the issuance of the receipts.

Standard deviation The positive square root of variance.

Standing limit order A limit order at a price below market and which therefore is waiting to trade.

Statutory voting A common method of voting where each share represents one vote.

Stop order (or **stop-loss order**) An order in which a trader has specified a stop price condition.

Strategic analysis Analysis of the competitive environment with an emphasis on the implications of the environment for corporate strategy.

Strategic asset allocation The set of exposures to IPS-permissible asset classes that is expected to achieve the client's long-term objectives given the client's investment constraints.

Strategic groups Groups sharing distinct business models or catering to specific market segments in an industry.

Strong-form efficient market hypothesis The belief that security prices reflect all public and private information.

Support In technical analysis, a price range in which buying activity is sufficient to stop the decline in the price of a security.

Swap contract An agreement between two parties to exchange a series of future cash flows.

Systematic risk Risk that affects the entire market or economy; it cannot be avoided and is inherent in the overall market. Systematic risk is also known as nondiversifiable or market risk.

Tactical asset allocation The decision to deliberately deviate from the strategic asset allocation in an attempt to add value based on forecasts of the near-term relative performance of asset classes.

Technical analysis A form of security analysis that uses price and volume data, which is often graphically displayed, in decision making.

Technical indicator Any measure based on price, market sentiment, or funds flow that can be used to predict changes in price.

Terminal stock value (or **terminal value**) The expected value of a share at the end of the investment horizon—in effect, the expected selling price.

Tobin's *q* An asset-based valuation measure that is equal to the ratio of the market value of debt and equity to the replacement cost of total assets.

Top down With reference to investment selection processes, an approach that starts with macro selection (i.e., identifying attractive geographic segments and/or industry segments) and then addresses selection of the most attractive investments within those segments.

Total factor productivity A variable that accounts for that part of Y not directly accounted for by the levels of the production factors (K and L).

Total return Measures the price appreciation, or percentage change in price of the securities in an index or portfolio, plus any income received over the period.

Total return index An index that reflects the price appreciation or percentage change in price of the constituent securities plus any income received since inception.

Tracking risk (tracking error) The standard deviation of the differences between a portfolio's returns and its benchmark's returns; a synonym of active risk.

Trend A long-term pattern of movement in a particular direction.

Treynor ratio A measure of risk-adjusted performance that relates a portfolio's excess returns to the portfolio's beta.

Triangle pattern In technical analysis, a continuation chart pattern that forms as the range between high and low prices narrows, visually forming a triangle.

Triple bottom In technical analysis, a reversal pattern that is formed when the price forms three troughs at roughly the same price level; used to predict a change from a downtrend to an uptrend.

Triple top In technical analysis, a reversal pattern that is formed when the price forms three peaks at roughly the same price level; used to predict a change from an uptrend to a downtrend.

Turn-of-the-year effect See *January effect.*

Two-fund separation theorem The theory that all investors regardless of taste, risk preferences, and initial wealth will hold a combination of two portfolios or funds: a risk-free asset and an optimal portfolio of risky assets.

Underwritten offering An offering in which the (lead) investment bank guarantees the sale of the issue at an offering price that it negotiates with the issuer.

Unsponsored depository receipt A type of depository receipt in which the foreign company whose shares are held by the depository has no involvement in the issuance of the receipts.

Validity instructions Instructions that indicate when the order may be filled.

Value at risk (VAR) A money measure of the minimum value of losses expected during a specified time period at a given level of probability.

Variance The expected value (the probability-weighted average) of squared deviations from a random variable's expected value.

Variation margin payment Additional margin that must be deposited in an amount sufficient to bring the balance up to the initial margin requirement.

Venture capital Investments that provide "seed" or start-up capital, early-stage financing, or mezzanine financing to companies that are in the early stages of development and require additional capital for expansion.

Venture capital fund A fund for private equity investors that provides financing for development-stage companies.

Volatility As used in option pricing, the standard deviation of the continuously compounded returns on the underlying asset.

Vote by proxy A mechanism that allows a designated party—such as another shareholder, a shareholder representative, or management—to vote on the shareholder's behalf.

Weak-form efficient market hypothesis The belief that security prices fully reflect all past market data, which refers to all historical price and volume trading information.

Yardeni model An equity valuation model, more complex than the Fed model, that incorporates the expected growth rate in earnings.

REFERENCES

2009 Ibbotson Stocks, Bonds, Bills, and Inflation (SBBI) Classic Yearbook. 2009. Chicago, IL: Morningstar.

Acharya, Shanta, and Elroy Dimson. 2007. *Endowment Asset Management: Investment Strategies in Oxford and Cambridge*. New York: Oxford University Press.

Akerlof, George A., and Robert J. Shiller. 2009. *Animal Spirits: How Human Psychology Drives the Economy, and Why It Matters for Global Capitalism*. Princeton, NJ: Princeton University Press.

Alexander, John C., Delbert Goff, and Pamela P. Peterson. 1989. "Profitability of a Trading Strategy Based on Unexpected Earnings." *Financial Analysts Journal,* Vol. 45, No. 4: 65–71.

Arnott, Robert D. 2004. "The Meaning of a Slender Risk Premium." *Financial Analysts Journal,* Vol. 60, No. 2: 6–8.

Arnott, Robert D., and Peter L. Bernstein. 2002. "What Risk Premium is 'Normal'?" *Financial Analysts Journal,* Vol. 58, No. 2: 64–85.

Asness, Clifford S. 2003. "Fight the Fed Model." *Journal of Portfolio Management,* Vol. 30, No. 1: 11–24.

Avery, Christopher, and Peter Zemsky. 1998. "Multi-Dimensional Uncertainty and Herding in Financial Markets." *American Economic Review,* Vol. 88, No. 4: 724–748.

Bailey, Elizabeth, Meg Wirth, and David Zapol. 2005. "Venture Capital and Global Health." *Financing Global Health Ventures,* Discussion Paper (September 2005). www.commonscapital.com/downloads/Venture_Capital_and_Global_Health.pdf.

Bary, Andrew. 2008. "Does Extreme Stress Signal an Economic Snapback?" *Barron's* (24 November 2008): online.barrons.com/article/SB122732177515750213.html.

Basu, S. 1977. "Investment Performance of Common Stocks in Relation to Their Price-Earnings Ratios: A Test of the Efficient Market Hypothesis." *Journal of Finance,* Vol. 32, No. 3: 663–682.

Bessembinder, Hendrik, and Kalok Chan. 1998. "Market Efficiency and the Returns to Technical Analysis." *Financial Management,* Vol. 27, No. 2: 5–17.

Bikhchandani, Sushil, David Hirshleifer, and Ivo Welch. 1992. "A Theory of Fads, Fashion, Custom, and Cultural Change as Informational Cascades." *Journal of Political Economy,* Vol. 100, No. 5: 992–1026.

Block, S. 1999. "A Study of Financial Analysts: Practice and Theory." *Financial Analysts Journal,* Vol. 55, No. 4: 86–95.

Bodie, Zvi, Alex Kane, and Alan Marcus. 2007. *Essentials of Investments,* 6th Edition. New York: McGraw-Hill Irwin.

Bogle, John C. 2008. "Black Monday and Black Swans." *Financial Analysts Journal,* Vol. 64, No. 2: 30–40.

Boubakri, Narjess, Jean-Claude Cosset, and Anis Samet. 2008. "The Choice of ADRs." Finance International Meeting AFFI – EUROFIDAI, December 2007. http://ssrn.com/abstract=1006839.

Boujelbene Abbes, Mouna, Younes Boujelbene, and Abdelfettah Bouri. 2009. "Overconfidence Bias: Explanation of Market Anomalies French Market Case." *Journal of Applied Economic Sciences,* Vol. 4, No. 1: 12–25.

Brainard, William C., and James Tobin. 1968. "Pitfalls in Financial Model Building." *American Economic Review,* Vol. 58, No. 2: 99–122.

Brav, Alon, and Paul A. Gompers. 1997. "Myth or Reality? The Long-Run Underperformance of Initial Public Offerings: Evidence from Venture and Nonventure Capital-Backed Companies." *Journal of Finance,* Vol. 52, No. 5: 1791–1821.

Brav, Alon, Christopher Geczy, and Paul A. Gompers. 1995. "The Long-Run Underperformance of Seasoned Equity Offerings Revisited." Working paper, Harvard University.

Brealey, Richard. 1983. "Can Professional Investors Beat the Market?" *An Introduction to Risk and Return from Common Stocks*, 2nd edition. Cambridge, MA: MIT Press.

Bris, Arturo, William N. Goetzmann, and Ning Zhu. 2009. "Efficiency and the Bear: Short Sales and Markets around the World." *Journal of Finance*, Vol. 62, No. 3: 1029–1079.

Brown, Constance. 1999. *Technical Analysis for the Trading Professional*. New York: McGraw-Hill.

Brown, Laurence D. 1997. "Earning Surprise Research: Synthesis and Perspectives." *Financial Analysts Journal*, Vol. 53, No. 2: 13–19.

Calverley, John P., Alan M. Meder, Brian D. Singer, and Renato Staub. 2007. "Capital Market Expectations." *Managing Investment Portfolios; A Dynamic Process*, 3rd edition. Hoboken, NJ: John Wiley & Sons.

Campbell, John Y., and Robert J. Shiller. 1998. "Valuation Ratios and the Long-Run Stock Market Outlook." *Journal of Portfolio Management*, Vol. 24, No. 2: 11–26.

Campbell, John Y., and Robert J. Shiller. 2005. "Valuation Ratios and the Long-Run Stock Market Outlook: An Update." *Behavioral Finance II*. R. Thaler, ed. New York: Russell Sage Foundation.

Capaul, Carlo, Ian Rowley, and William Sharpe. 1993. "International Value and Growth Stock Returns." *Financial Analysts Journal*, Vol. 49: 27–36.

Carhart, Mark. 1997. "On Persistence in Mutual Fund Performance." *Journal of Finance*, Vol. 52, No. 1: 57–82.

Cavaglia, Stefano, Jeffrey Diermeier, Vadim Moroz, and Sonia De Zordo. 2004. "Investing in Global Equities." *Journal of Portfolio Management*, Vol. 30, No. 3: 88–94.

Chen, Kong-Jun, and Xiao-Ming Li. 2006. "Is Technical Analysis Useful for Stock Traders in China? Evidence from the SZSE Component A-Share Index." *Pacific Economic Review*, Vol. 11, No. 4: 477–488.

Chordia, Tarun, Richard Roll, and Avanidhar Subrahmanyam. 2005. "Evidence on the Speed of Convergence to Market Efficiency." *Journal of Financial Economics*, Vol. 76, No. 2: 271–292.

Cobb, C. W., and Paul H. Douglas. 1928. "A Theory of Production." *American Economic Review*, Vol. 18 (Supplement): 139–165.

Darrough, Masako N., and Thomas Russell. 2002. "A Positive Model of Earnings Forecasts: Top Down versus Bottom Up." *Journal of Business*, Vol. 75, No. 1: 127–152.

DeBondt, Werner, and Richard Thaler. 1985. "Does the Stock Market Overreact?" *Journal of Finance*, Vol. 40, No. 3: 793–808.

Dimson, Elroy, and Carolina Minio-Kozerski. 1999. "Closed-End Funds: A Survey." *Financial Markets, Institutions & Instruments*, Vol. 8, No. 2: 1–41.

Dimson, Elroy, Paul Marsh, and Mike Staunton. 2009. *Credit Suisse Global Investment Returns Sourcebook 2009*. Zurich, Switzerland: Credit Suisse Research Institute.

Dreman, D. 1977. *Psychology of the Stock Market*. New York: AMACOM.

Duffie, Darrell, Nicholae Garleanu, and Lasse Heje Pederson. 2002. "Securities Lending, Shorting and Pricing." *Journal of Financial Economics*, Vol. 66, Issue 2–3: 307–339.

Fama, Eugene. 1970. "Efficient Capital Markets: A Review of Theory and Empirical Work." *Journal of Finance*, Vol. 25, No. 2: 383–417.

Fama, Eugene. 1976. *Foundations of Finance*. New York: Basic Books.

Fama, Eugene. 1998. "Market Efficiency, Long-Term Returns, and Behavioral Finance." *Journal of Financial Economics*, Vol. 50, No. 3: 283–306.

Fama, Eugene, and Kenneth French. 1988. "Dividend Yields and Expected Stock Returns." *Journal of Financial Economics*, Vol. 22, No. 1: 3–25.

Fama, Eugene, and Kenneth French. 1992. "The Cross-Section of Expected Stock Returns." *Journal of Finance*, Vol. 47, No. 2: 427–466.

Fama, Eugene, and Kenneth French. 1995. "Size and Book-to-Market Factors in Earnings and Returns." *Journal of Finance*, Vol. 50, No. 1: 131–155.

Fama, Eugene, and Kenneth French. 1998. "Value versus Growth: The International Evidence." *Journal of Finance*, Vol. 53: 1975–1999.

Fama, Eugene, and Kenneth French. 2008. "Dissecting Anomalies." *Journal of Finance,* Vol. 63, No. 4: 1653–1678.

Fama, Eugene, and G. William Schwert. 1977. "Asset Returns and Inflation." *Journal of Financial Economics,* Vol. 5, No. 2: 115–146.

Fifield, Suzanne, David Power, and C. Donald Sinclair. 2005. "An Analysis of Trading Strategies in Eleven European Stock Markets." *European Journal of Finance,* Vol. 11, No. 6: 531–548.

Fisher, Irving. 1930. *The Theory of Interest: As Determined by Impatience to Spend Income and Opportunity to Invest It.* New York: Macmillan.

Fuller, Russell J., and Chi-Cheng Hsia. 1984. "A Simplified Common Stock Valuation Model." *Financial Analysts Journal,* Vol. 40, No. 5: 49–56.

Gan, Christopher, Minsoo Lee, Au Yong Hue Hwa, and Jun Zhang. 2005. "Revisiting Share Market Efficiency: Evidence from the New Zealand, Australia, U.S. and Japan Stock Indices." *American Journal of Applied Sciences,* Vol. 2, No. 5: 996–1002.

Gastineau, Gary L. 2002. *Exchange-Traded Funds Manual.* Hoboken, NJ: John Wiley & Sons.

Grable, John E., and Soo-Hyun Joo. 2004. "Environmental and Biopsychosocial Factors Associated with Financial Risk Tolerance." *Financial Counseling and Planning,* Vol. 15, No. 1: 73–82.

Graham, Benajmin, and David L. Dodd. 1934. *Securities Analysis.* New York: McGraw-Hill.

Grossman, Sanford J., and Joseph E. Stiglitz. 1980. "On the Impossibility of Informationally Efficient Markets." *American Economic Review,* Vol. 70, No. 3: 393–408.

Harris, Larry. 2003. *Trading and Exchanges: Market Microstructure for Practitioners.* New York: Oxford University Press.

Henry, Peter Blair, and Anusha Chari. 2007. "Risk Sharing and Asset Prices: Evidence from a Natural Experiment." Working Paper; Center on Democracy, Development, and the Rule of Law.

Hill, Charles, and Gareth Jones. 2008. "External Analysis: The Identification of Opportunities and Threats." *Strategic Management: An Integrated Approach.* Boston, MA: Houghton Mifflin.

Hirshleifer, David. 2001. "Investor Psychology and Asset Pricing." *Journal of Finance,* Vol. 56, No. 4: 1533–1597.

Hirshleifer, David, and Siew Hong Teoh, 2009. "Thought and Behavior Contagion in Capital Markets." *Handbook of Financial Markets: Dynamics and Evolution.* Klaus Reiner Schenk-Hoppe and Thorstein Hens, editors. Amsterdam and London: North Holland.

Ibbotson, Roger G., and Rex A. Sinquefield. 1989. *Stocks, Bonds, Bills, and Inflation: Historical Returns (1926–1987).* Chicago: Dow-Jones Irwin.

Ibbotson, Roger G., Jeffrey J. Diermeier, and Laurence B. Siegel. 1984. "The Demand for Capital Market Returns: A New Equilibrium Theory." *Financial Analysts Journal,* Vol. 40, No. 1: 22–33.

Investment Company Institute. 2007. "A Guide to Exchange-Traded Funds." www.ici.org/investor_ed/brochures/bro_etf).

Investment Company Institute. 2009a. "Trends in Mutual Fund Investing, December 2008" (20 March).

Investment Company Institute. 2009b. "Worldwide Mutual Fund Assets and Flows, Third Quarter 2008" (5 May).

Jacobs, Bruce I., and Kenneth N. Levy. 1988. "Calendar Anomalies: Abnormal Returns at Calendar Turning Points." *Financial Analysts Journal,* Vol. 44, No. 6: 28–39.

Jaffe, Jeffrey. 1974. "Special Information and Insider Trading." *Journal of Business,* Vol. 47, No. 3: 410–428.

Jegadeesh, Narayan, and Sheridan Titman. 2001. "Profitability of Momentum Strategies: An Evaluation of Alternative Explanations." *Journal of Finance,* Vol. 56: 699–720.

Johnson, Timothy C. 2002. "Rational Momentum Effects." *Journal of Finance,* Vol. 57 No. 2: 585–608.

Jones, Charles M., and Owen A. Lamont. 2002. "Short-Sale Constraints and Stock Returns." *Journal of Financial Economics,* Vol. 66, Nos. 2–3: 207–239.

Jones, Charles P., Richard J. Rendleman, and Henry. A. Latané. 1984. "Stock Returns and SUEs during the 1970s." *Journal of Portfolio Management,* Vol. 10: 18–22.

Kim, Donchoi, and Myungsun Kim. 2003. "A Multifactor Explanation of Post-Earnings Announcement Drift." *Journal of Financial and Quantitative Analysis,* Vol. 38, No. 2: 383–398.

Kim, Dongcheol. 2006. "On the Information Uncertainty Risk and the January Effect." *Journal of Business*, Vol. 79, No. 4: 2127–2162.

Kritzman, Mark. 1999. "Toward Defining an Asset Class." *Journal of Alternative Investments*, Vol. 2, No. 1: 79–82.

Lee, Charles M. C., Andrei Sheifer, and Richard H. Thaler. 1990. "Anomalies: Closed-End Mutual Funds." *Journal of Economic Perspectives*, Vol. 4, No. 4: 153–164.

Lintner, John. 1965a. "Security Prices, Risk, and Maximal Gains from Diversification." *Journal of Finance*, Vol. 20, No. 4: 587–615.

Lintner, John. 1965b. "The Valuation of Risk Assets and the Selection of Risky Investments in Stock Portfolios and Capital Budgets." *Review of Economics and Statistics*, Vol. 47, No.1: 13–37.

Maginn, John L., and Donald L. Tuttle. 1983. "The Portfolio Management Process and Its Dynamics." *Managing Investment Portfolios: A Dynamic Process*. Boston: Warren, Gorham & Lamont.

Malkiel, Burton G. 1995. "Returns from Investing in Equity Mutual Funds 1971 to 1991." *Journal of Finance*, Vol. 50: 549–572.

Mamudi, Sam. 2009. "More Investors Ditch Market-Beating Attempts, Embrace Index Funds." *FiLife* (in partnership with the *Wall Street Journal*; 27 February). www.filife.com/stories/more-investors-ditch-market-beating-attempts-embrace-index-funds.

Markowitz, Harry. 1952. "Portfolio Selection." *Journal of Finance*, Vol. 7, No. 1: 77–91.

McGahan, Anita M., and Michael E. Porter. 1997. "How Much Does Industry Matter, Really?" *Strategic Management Journal*, Vol. 18, No. S1: 15–30.

McWilliams, J. 1966. "Prices, Earnings and P-E Ratios." *Financial Analysts Journal*, Vol. 22, No. 3: 137.

Mehra, Rajnish. 2003. "The Equity Premium: Why Is It a Puzzle?" *Financial Analysts Journal*, Vol. 59, No. 1: 54–69.

Mehra, Rajnish, and Edward C. Prescott. 1985. "The Equity Risk Premium: A Puzzle." *Journal of Monetary Economics*, Vol. 15, No. 2: 145–162.

Miller, P., and E. Widmann. 1966. "Price Performance Outlook for High & Low P/E Stocks." *1966 Stock & Bond Issue, Commercial & Financial Chronicle:* 26–28.

Mobarek, Asma, A. Sabur Mollah, and Rafiqul Bhuyan. 2008. "Market Efficiency in Emerging Stock Market." *Journal of Emerging Market Finance*, Vol. 7, No. 1: 17–41.

Mossin, Jan. 1966. "Equilibrium in a Capital Asset Market." *Econometrica*, Vol. 34, No. 4: 768–783.

Murphy, John J. 1991. *Intermarket Technical Analysis: Trading Strategies for the Global Stock, Bond, Commodity, and Currency Markets*. New York: John Wiley & Sons.

Nicholson, S. 1968. "Price Ratios in Relation to Investment Results." *Financial Analysts Journal*, Vol. 24, No. 1: 105–109.

O'Shaughnessy, J. 2005. *What Works on Wall Street*. New York: McGraw-Hill.

Palkar, Darshana, and Stephen E. Wilcox. 2009. "Adjusted Earnings Yields and Real Rates of Return." *Financial Analysts Journal*, Vol. 65, No. 5: 66–79.

Pontiff, Jeffrey. 1995. "Closed-End Fund Premia and Returns: Implications for Financial Market Equilibrium." *Journal of Financial Economics*, Vol. 37: 341–370.

Pontiff, Jeffrey. 1996. "Costly Arbitrage: Evidence from Closed-End Funds." *Quarterly Journal of Economics*, Vol. 111, No. 4: 1135–1151.

Porter, Michael E. 2008. "The Five Competitive Forces That Shape Strategy." *Harvard Business Review*, Vol. 86, No. 1: 78–93.

Preston, R. 2009. "China's Foreign Reserves Top $2tn." *BBC News*, 15 July 2009.

Raja, M., J. Clement Sudhahar, and M. Selvam. 2009. "Testing the Semi-Strong Form Efficiency of Indian Stock Market with Respect to Information Content of Stock Split Announcement—A Study of IT Industry." *International Research Journal of Finance and Economics*, Vol. 25: 7–20.

Roll, Richard. 1977. "A Critique of the Asset Pricing Theory's Tests, Part I: On Past and Potential Testability of the Theory." *Journal of Financial Economics*, Vol. 4, No. 2: 129–176.

Roll, Richard. 1983. "On Computing Mean Returns and the Small Firm Premium." *Journal of Financial Economics*, Vol. 12: 371–386.

Ross, Stephen A. 1976. "The Arbitrage Theory of Capital Asset Pricing." *Journal of Economic Theory*, Vol. 13, No. 3: 341–360.

Rozeff, Michael S., and Mir A. Zaman. 1988. "Market Efficiency and Insider Trading: New Evidence." *Journal of Business*, Vol. 61: 25–44.

Schoenfeld, Steven A. 2004. *Active Index Investing*. Hoboken, NJ: John Wiley & Sons.

Schwert, G. William. 2003. "Anomalies and Market Efficiency." *Handbook of the Economics of Finance*. George M. Constantinides, M. Harris, and Rene Stulz, editors. Amsterdam: Elsevier Science, B.V.

Scott, James, Margaret Stumpp, and Peter Xu. 2003. "Overconfidence Bias in International Stock Prices." *Journal of Portfolio Management*, Vol. 29, No. 2: 80–89.

Sharpe, W., G. Alexander, and J. Bailey. 1999. *Investments*. Upper Saddle River, NJ: Prentice-Hall.

Sharpe, William. 1964. "Capital Asset Prices: A Theory of Market Equilibrium under Conditions of Risk." *Journal of Finance*, Vol. 19, No. 3: 425–442.

Sharpe, William, Peng Chen, Jerald Pinto, and Dennis McLeavey. 2007. "Asset Allocation." *Managing Investment Portfolios: A Dynamic Process*, 3rd edition. Hoboken, NJ: John Wiley & Sons.

Siegel, Jeremy J. 1992. "The Equity Premium: Stock and Bond Returns Since 1802." *Financial Analysts Journal*, Vol. 48, No. 1: 28–38.

Siegel, Jeremy J. 2005. "Perspectives on the Equity Risk Premium." *Financial Analysts Journal*, Vol. 61, No. 6: 61–73.

Sihler, William. 2004. *Introduction to Hedge Funds*. UVA-F-1529. Charlottesville, VA: Darden Business Publishing.

Singletary, Michelle. 2001. "Cautionary Tale of an Enron Employee Who Went for Broke." Seattlepi .com (10 December). www.seattlepi.com/money/49894_singletary10.shtml.

Smithers, Andrew, and Stephen Wright. 2000. *Valuing Wall Street*. New York: McGraw-Hill.

Solow, Robert. 1957. "Technical Change and the Aggregate Production Function." *The Review of Economics and Statistics*, Vol. 39: 312–320.

Stimes, Peter C. 2008. *Equity Valuation, Risk, and Investment: A Practitioner's Roadmap*. Hoboken, NJ: John Wiley & Sons.

Strömberg, Per. 2008. "The New Demography of Private Equity." The Global Economic Impact of Private Equity Report 2008, *World Economic Forum*.

Taleb, Nassim N. 2007. *The Black Swan: The Impact of the Highly Improbable*. New York: Random House.

Tobin, James. 1969. "A General Equilibrium Approach to Monetary Theory." *Journal of Money Credit and Banking*, Vol. 1, No. 1: 15–29.

Treynor, Jack L. 1961. *Market Value, Time, and Risk*. Unpublished manuscript.

Treynor, Jack L. 1962. *Toward a Theory of Market Value of Risky Assets*. Unpublished manuscript.

Tversky, Amos, and Daniel Kahneman. 1981. "The Framing of Decisions and the Psychology of Choice." *Science*, Vol. 211, No. 30: 453–458.

Waring, M. Barton, and Laurence B. Siegel. 2003. "The Dimensions of Active Management." *Journal of Portfolio Management*, Vol. 29, No. 3: 35–51.

Waring, M. Barton, Duane Whitney, John Pirone, and Charles Castille. 2000. "Optimizing Manager Structure and Budgeting Manager Risk." *Journal of Portfolio Management*, Vol. 26, No. 3: 90–104.

Wilcox, Stephen E. 2007. "The Adjusted Earnings Yield." *Financial Analysts Journal*, Vol. 63, No. 5: 54–68.

Xin, Z., and S. Rabinovitch. 2009. "China Central Bank Taps on Brakes as Money Supply Surges." *Reuters*, 15 July 2009.

Yardeni, Edward E. 2000. "How to Value Earnings Growth." *Topical Study #49* (Deutsche Banc Alex Brown).

Yardeni, Edward E. 2002. "Stock Valuation Models," Prudential Financial Research, *Topical Study #56* (August 8).

Yau, Jot, Thomas Schneeweis, Thomas Robinson, and Lisa Weiss. 2007. "Alternative Investments Portfolio Management." *Managing Investment Portfolios: A Dynamic Process*. Hoboken, NJ: John Wiley & Sons.

Zarowin, P. 1989. "Does the Stock Market Overreact to Corporate Earnings Information?" *Journal of Finance,* Vol. 44: 1385–1399.

Zheng, Jinghai, Angan Hu, and Arne Bigsten. 2009. "Potential Output in a Rapidly Developing Economy: The Case of China and a Comparison with the United States and the European Union." *Federal Reserve Bank of St. Louis Review,* Vol. 91, No. 4: 317–348.

Zheng, Jinghai, Arne Bigsten, and Anagang Hu. 2006. "Can China's Growth be Sustained? A Productivity Perspective." *Working Papers in Economics 236,* Göteborg University, Department of Economics.

ABOUT THE AUTHORS

Howard J. Atkinson, CFA, has 23 years of investment management industry experience. He joined BetaPro Management Inc., an affiliate of Horizons ETFs, as executive vice president in October 2006. Prior to joining BetaPro, Mr. Atkinson was responsible for the exchange-traded products business at Barclays Global Investors Canada Limited and has held positions with a national investment dealer as well as major mutual fund companies. He is a past president of the Toronto CFA Society board of directors and is a member of the S&P/TSX Canada Index Advisory Panel. In addition, he recently achieved the ICD.D designation from the Institute of Corporate Directors.

Mr. Atkinson is the author of four books, including *The New Investment Frontier III: A Guide to Exchange Traded Funds for Canadians* (Insomniac Press, 2005) and *Les fonds négociés en bourse: Un outil de placement novateur pour l'investisseur avisé* (Transcontinental, 2003). He has been a contributing writer and frequent analyst referenced in many major Canadian newspapers, including the *Globe & Mail*, *National Post*, *Toronto Star*, *Vancouver Sun*, and *Ottawa Citizen*. In February 2010 he was recognized by ACTIF, Quebec's premier financial education cooperative, as the Top Educator for his efforts to foster financial literacy among Canadians.

Alistair Byrne, CFA, is a principal in the investment practice at Investit. He works with asset managers and other financial services firms on investment process and product development projects and market research. He has particular expertise in pension fund investment and defined contribution pension schemes. Dr. Byrne's investment management experience includes over 10 years at AEGON Asset Management UK, where he was investment strategist and head of equity research. He has also held academic positions at the University of Edinburgh and Strathclyde business schools, and has run his own financial services consultancy. Dr. Byrne has a PhD in finance from the University of Strathclyde in Glasgow. His research has been published in a number of academic and professional journals, including the *Financial Analysts Journal*. He is a visiting fellow at the Pensions Institute at Cass Business School in London.

W. Sean Cleary, CFA, is the BMO Professor of Finance and Director of the Master of Management in Finance, Queen's School of Business, Queen's University. Dr. Cleary holds a PhD in finance from the University of Toronto, as well as an MBA. He is Chair of Awards for the Toronto CFA Society and is the former president of the Atlantic Canada CFA Society. He is a co-author of *Introduction to Corporate Finance*, and is the Canadian author of the first three editions of the textbook *Investments: Analysis and Management*, by W. S. Cleary and C. P. Jones.

Dr. Cleary has published numerous research articles in various journals, including the *Journal of Finance*, the *Journal of Financial and Quantitative Analysis*, the *Journal of Banking and Finance*, and the *Journal of Financial Research*, and his publications have been cited over 600 times. He regularly serves as a reviewer for many of the top finance journals. Dr. Cleary frequently appears in the media on television, on the radio, and in the newspapers.

Robert M. Conroy, CFA, is the J. Harvie Wilkinson Jr. Professor of Business Administration at the Darden School of Business, University of Virginia. A professor in the finance area, Dr. Conroy has published numerous articles and is the author of many cases on valuation and capital markets. He has taught at the International University of Japan, Helsinki School of Economics, and IESE in Barcelona. At Darden he has served as the Associate Dean for Degree Programs and Director of the Tayloe Murphy Institute, and has served on the MBA committee at the Stockholm School of Economics. Before coming to Darden in 1988, Dr. Conroy taught at the University of North Carolina and Duke University. He received an MBA in finance from the University of Connecticut and a DBA in finance from Indiana University. He has been a CFA charterholder since 1996.

Patrick W. Dorsey, CFA, is director of Equity Research for Morningstar, a leading provider of independent investment research. He is responsible for the overall direction of Morningstar's equity research, as well as for communicating Morningstar's ideas to the media and clients. Mr. Dorsey joined Morningstar in 1998 as a senior equity analyst covering the telecommunications equipment and computer hardware industries, and became head of Morningstar's equity research team in 2001. He played an integral part in the development of Morningstar's economic moat ratings and the methodology behind Morningstar's framework for competitive analysis. Mr. Dorsey is also the author of *The Five Rules for Successful Stock Investing* and *The Little Book That Builds Wealth*, both published by John Wiley & Sons.

Mr. Dorsey holds a master's degree in political science from Northwestern University and a bachelor's degree in government from Wesleyan University. He appears regularly on the Fox Business Network, writes a monthly column on investing for *Money* magazine, and has been quoted in publications such as the *Wall Street Journal*, *Fortune*, the *New York Times*, and *BusinessWeek*.

Pamela Peterson Drake, CFA, is the J. Gray Ferguson Professor of Finance and Department Head, Department of Finance and Business Law in the College of Business at James Madison University. She received a BS in accountancy from Miami University and a PhD in finance from the University of North Carolina at Chapel Hill. Professor Drake previously taught at Florida State University and Florida Atlantic University. She has published numerous articles in academic journals, and is the author or co-author of several books. Professor Drake teaches courses in financial analysis, business finance, and quantitative finance. Her expertise is in financial analysis and valuation.

Anthony M. Fiore, CFA, is a vice president at Silvercrest Asset Management Group LLC, and a research analyst for the firm's equity portfolios. Prior to Silvercrest, Mr. Fiore was a senior equity analyst at Standard & Poor's, where he covered the machinery, industrial conglomerates, and diversified commercial services industries. Previously, Mr. Fiore was a generalist equity analyst and portfolio manager at State Street Global Advisors in the firm's Global Fundamental Strategies group. He received a BS in business administration from the University of Vermont with a concentration in finance.

Ryan C. Fuhrmann, CFA, is president and founder of Fuhrmann Capital LLC, an Indiana-based investment management firm. Mr. Fuhrmann received his BBA degree in finance from the University of Wisconsin–Madison in 1996 and an MBA degree from the University of Texas at Austin in 2002. He settled on a pursuit of investing after taking a class entitled "Security Analysis" while in Madison and began his investment career at Northern Trust Corporation in Chicago shortly thereafter. Since that time he has focused on analyzing equity securities and active portfolio management from a value-investing perspective. Mr. Fuhrmann has been a CFA charterholder since 2000, is a past board member of the CFA Society of Dallas, and is a current member of the CFA Society of Indianapolis. He is also an adviser to Butler University's student-managed investment fund and is involved with the Eiteljorg Museum of American Indian and Western Art in a treasury capacity.

Larry Harris holds the Fred V. Keenan Chair in Finance at the University of Southern California Marshall School of Business. His research, teaching, and consulting address regulatory and practitioner issues in trading and in investment management. He has written extensively about trading rules, transaction costs, and market regulations. His introduction to the economics of trading, *Trading and Exchanges: Market Microstructure for Practitioners*, is widely regarded as a must read for entrants into the securities industry.

Dr. Harris served as chief economist of the U.S. Securities and Exchange Commission from July 2002 through June 2004. He currently serves on the boards of Interactive Brokers, Inc.; the Clipper Fund, Inc.; and the CFA Society of Los Angeles, and as the research coordinator of the Institute for Quantitative Research in Finance (the Q-Group). Dr. Harris is a former associate editor of the *Journal of Finance*, the *Review of Financial Studies*, and the *Journal of Financial and Quantitative Analysis*, and a former practitioner at UNX, Inc., an electronic pure agency institutional equity broker, and at Madison Tyler, LLC, as a broker-dealer engaged in electronic proprietary trading in various markets. He received his PhD in economics from the University of Chicago in 1982.

Paul D. Kaplan, CFA, is quantitative research director at Morningstar Europe in London. He is responsible for the quantitative methodologies behind Morningstar's fund analysis, indexes, adviser tools, and other services. Dr. Kaplan conducts research on investment style analysis, performance and risk measurement, asset allocation, retirement income planning, portfolio construction, index methodologies, and alternative investments. He led the development of quantitative methodologies behind many of Morningstar's services, including the Morningstar family of indexes. Many of Dr. Kaplan's research papers have been published in professional books and publications. He received the 2008 Graham and Dodd Award and was a Graham and Dodd Award of Excellence winner in 2000.

Before joining Morningstar in 1999, Dr. Kaplan was a vice president of Ibbotson Associates and served as the firm's chief economist and director of research (Morningstar acquired Ibbotson in March 2006). Prior to that, he served on the economics faculty of Northwestern University, where he taught international finance and statistics. Dr. Kaplan holds a bachelor's degree in mathematics, economics, and computer science from New York University and a master's degree and doctorate in economics from Northwestern University.

Dorothy C. Kelly, CFA, has worked in financial services for more than two decades in areas such as operations, equity research, business development, and training and assessments. She has worked for a variety of domestic and multinational organizations, including brokerage, venture capital, and asset management firms; educational institutions; and CFA Institute. As principal of Deucalion, LLC, she has produced customized research, educational materials, training, and assessments in the areas of investments, ethics, leadership, and strategy for business leaders, finance professionals, and MBA students. Her work has been published by CFA Institute and Darden Business Publishing. An active member of CFA Institute, Ms. Kelly has served in a variety of capacities and areas, including CFA examination development, CFA grading, the development of ethics case studies for the CFA curriculum, moderating an ethics forum for the CFA curriculum, and providing live ethics training on behalf of CFA Institute. A graduate of Johns Hopkins University, Ms. Kelly has studied in both Madrid and Paris. She holds an MBA degree from the Colgate Darden Graduate School of Business at the University of Virginia.

Asjeet S. Lamba, CFA, is an associate professor with the Department of Finance at the University of Melbourne, Australia. He has an MBA in finance from the University of

Michigan and a PhD in finance from the University of Washington. His main teaching and research interests are in investments, corporate finance, and international finance. His research has been published in several leading academic journals and he regularly presents his ongoing research at academic and professional conferences. Dr. Lamba actively serves various professional organizations, including CFA Institute, where he is involved with reviewing the candidate curriculum as well as serving on the Disciplinary Review Committee.

Michael G. McMillan, CFA, is Director, Ethics and Professional Standards in the Education Division of CFA Institute. Dr. McMillan joined CFA Institute in 2008 after more than a decade as a professor of accounting and finance at Johns Hopkins University's Carey School of Business and George Washington University's School of Business. Prior to pursuing a career in academia, he was a securities analyst and portfolio manager in the San Francisco Bay area. He has a doctorate in accounting and finance from George Washington University, an MBA from Stanford University, and a BA from the University of Pennsylvania. He is a member of the CFA Society of Washington, D.C., and the East African Society of Investment Professionals.

John J. Nagorniak, CFA, is an independent director of the Columbia Nations mutual funds. He is a graduate of Princeton University and received an MS degree from the Sloan School at the Massachusetts Institute of Technology. He served as Chairman of Franklin Portfolio Associates for over 24 years and was CEO from 1982 to 2000. Prior to Franklin, Mr. Nagorniak was senior vice president and chief investment officer at State Street Bank and Trust Company. Prior to that he was director of Investment Management Technology for the John Hancock Mutual Life Insurance Company.

Mr. Nagorniak is past president of the Investment Technology Association and has been on the council of that organization and the council of the Quantitative Discussion Group. He is also a past president of the Boston Security Analysts Society and past chair and trustee of the Research Foundation of CFA Institute. He received his CFA charter in 1980. Mr. Nagorniak has pursued many charitable endeavors, including serving as volunteer head of Princeton University's annual fund-raising efforts. He is currently a director of the Massachusetts Institute of Technology Investment Company and a member of the MIT Supplemental 401(k) Oversight Committee.

Ian Rossa O'Reilly, CFA, has 40 years' experience analyzing publicly traded equities and stock market strategy, including 25 years as managing director of Institutional Equity Research at Canadian Imperial Bank of Commerce. He has been a CFA charterholder since 1977 and is a past board member and chairman of CFA Institute. He has also been a member of the Accounting Standards Board of the Canadian Institute of Chartered Accountants and is a past president of the Toronto CFA Society. Mr. O'Reilly holds an MA in mathematics and economics from Trinity College, University of Dublin, Ireland, and is a fellow of the Canadian Securities Institute.

Jerald E. Pinto, CFA, is Director, Curriculum Projects, in the Education Division at CFA Institute. Before coming to CFA Institute in 2002, he consulted to corporations, foundations, and partnerships in investment planning, portfolio analysis, valuation, and quantitative analysis. He worked in the investment and banking industries in New York City from the late 1970s on, and taught finance at New York University's Stern School of Business. He is a co-author of *Quantitative Investment Analysis* and *Equity Asset Valuation*, and was a co-editor and co-author of chapters of the third edition of *Managing Investment Portfolios: A Dynamic Process*, all published by John Wiley & Sons. He holds an MBA from Baruch College and a PhD in finance from the Stern School, and is a member of CFA Virginia.

Wendy L. Pirie, CFA, is Director, Curriculum Projects, in the Education Division at CFA Institute. Prior to joining CFA Institute in 2008, she taught for over 20 years at a broad range of institutions: large public universities; small, private, religiously affiliated colleges; and a military academy. She primarily taught finance courses but also taught accounting, taxation, business law, marketing, and statistics courses. Dr. Pirie's work has been published in the *Journal of Financial Research*, *Journal of Economics and Finance*, *Educational Innovation in Economics and Business*, and *Managerial Finance*. She holds a PhD in accounting and finance from Queen's University at Kingston, Ontario, and MBAs from the Universities of Toronto and Calgary. She is a member of CFA Institute, New York Society of Security Analysts, and CFA Society of Chicago.

Barry M. Sine, CMT, CFA, is the Director of Research of CapStone Investments, a boutique investment bank headquartered in San Diego, California. He utilizes fundamental, quantitative, economic, and technical tools to identify promising investment opportunities. He has frequently been a top-ranked analyst in the *Wall Street Journal*'s "Best on the Street" analyst rankings. Sine has also held positions with JPMorgan, Prudential Securities, and Oppenheimer. He is a director of the New York Society of Security Analysts and a past director of the Market Technicians Association. He founded and was the first director of the CMT Institute, which administers the Chartered Market Technician (CMT) designation for technical analysis. Sine holds an MBA in finance and international business from New York University's Stern School of Business and a BA in finance and economics from Fairleigh Dickinson University.

Vijay Singal, CFA, is the J. Gray Ferguson Professor of Finance at the Pamplin College of Business, Virginia Tech. He is an accomplished teacher and researcher with numerous articles in top finance journals on a wide variety of topics, including mergers, corporate governance, pricing and market power, executive compensation, index changes, short selling, currency risk management, and market efficiency. He is the author of *Beyond the Random Walk*, which has been reissued in paperback by Oxford University Press. His research has been cited in the *Wall Street Journal*, the *New York Times*, the *Washington Post*, and the *Chicago Tribune*, among others. He was the department head of finance from 2003 to 2009.

Prior to entering academia, Dr. Singal worked for 10 years at the Oil and Natural Gas Corporation in India, holding various positions, finally as a joint director of finance. Some of his responsibilities included negotiating major contracts with shipyards in Norway, Singapore, France, and Japan; negotiating and managing foreign currency loans; and optimizing insurance coverage for major assets of the company. Singal graduated from the Indian Institute of Technology, Kanpur, with a bachelor's degree in chemical engineering and from the Indian Institute of Management, Calcutta, with an MBA in finance. He holds a PhD in finance from the University of Michigan.

Frank E. Smudde, CFA, is an equity fund manager with All Pensions Group Asset Management (APG) in the Netherlands. Prior to joining the predecessor company to APG in 2001, he worked in equity research at FDA in Amsterdam. Mr. Smudde received his MSc degree in business economics from Rijksuniversiteit Groningen in 1995, and has held the CFA charter since 2002.

Peter C. Stimes, CFA, is retired vice president and principal of Flaherty & Crumrine Inc. (F&C), an investment advisory firm in Pasadena, California. He served at various times in the capacities of portfolio manager, head of quantitative research and securities analysis, and chief financial officer of the closed-end funds managed by F&C. Mr. Stimes obtained his education at the University of Chicago, receiving his BA degree in 1977 and an MBA in 1980. He has been a CFA charterholder since 1984.

During his career, Mr. Stimes has produced or co-written various papers and analyses for presentation to CFA Institute, the Internal Revenue Service, the Joint Committee of Taxation of the U.S. Congress, and both state and federal utility regulatory authorities. He is also the author of *Equity Valuation, Risk, and Investment: A Practitioner's Roadmap* (John Wiley & Sons).

Robert A. Strong, CFA, is University Foundation Professor of Investment Education at the University of Maine. He has been visiting professor of finance at Harvard University, where he was Deputy Director of the Summer Economics Program from 1997 to 1999. The University of Maine Alumni Association selected him as the 2005 Distinguished Maine Professor, and the Carnegie Foundation named him the 2007 Maine Professor of the Year. Dr. Strong received a bachelor's degree in engineering from the United States Military Academy at West Point, an MS in business administration from Boston University, and a PhD in finance from Penn State. He is the author of three textbooks on portfolio management, investments, and derivatives. Dr. Strong is past president of the Maine CFA Society and serves on four investment committees and two corporate boards.

Gerhard Van de Venter, CFA, is Deputy Head of the School of Finance and Economics at the University of Technology, Sydney, Australia. He was previously Director, Curriculum Projects, in the Education Division at CFA Institute. He began his career in South Africa as a financial analyst in the agricultural sector and later as a dealer on the Bond Exchange, trading in fixed-income securities. Dr. Van de Venter's academic career spans over a decade during which he has taught finance and investments and has published a number of papers on financial planning. He holds a PhD in finance from the University of Technology, Sydney, and is a member of CFA Institute and the New York Society of Security Analysts.

Stephen E. Wilcox, CFA, is a professor of finance at Minnesota State University, Mankato (MSU). Dr. Wilcox earned a BS degree from MSU in 1979, an MBA from Indiana University in 1981, and a PhD from the University of Nebraska in 1991. He earned the professional designation of Chartered Financial Analyst (CFA) in 1992. Dr. Wilcox is a former chair of the Department of Finance and was a major contributor toward the creation of the Maverick Fund, a student-managed investment fund, at MSU. Most of his research deals with valuation issues in the equity and derivative markets. Dr. Wilcox has participated in CFA exam grading and served in various capacities as a consultant for CFA Institute. He has also served as a consultant for tax-sheltered annuity plans and as an expert witness in the valuation of privately held companies.

ABOUT THE CFA PROGRAM

The Chartered Financial Analyst® designation (CFA®) is a globally recognized standard of excellence for measuring the competence and integrity of investment professionals. To earn the CFA charter, candidates must successfully pass through the CFA Program, a global graduate-level self-study program that combines a broad curriculum with professional conduct requirements as preparation for a wide range of investment specialties.

Anchored by a practice-based curriculum, the CFA Program is focused on the knowledge identified by professionals as essential to the investment decision-making process. This body of knowledge maintains current relevance through a regular, extensive survey of practicing CFA charterholders across the globe. The curriculum covers 10 general topic areas, ranging from equity and fixed-income analysis to portfolio management to corporate finance, all with a heavy emphasis on the application of ethics in professional practice. Known for its rigor and breadth, the CFA Program curriculum highlights principles common to every market so that professionals who earn the CFA designation have a thoroughly global investment perspective and a profound understanding of the global marketplace.

www.cfainstitute.org

INDEX

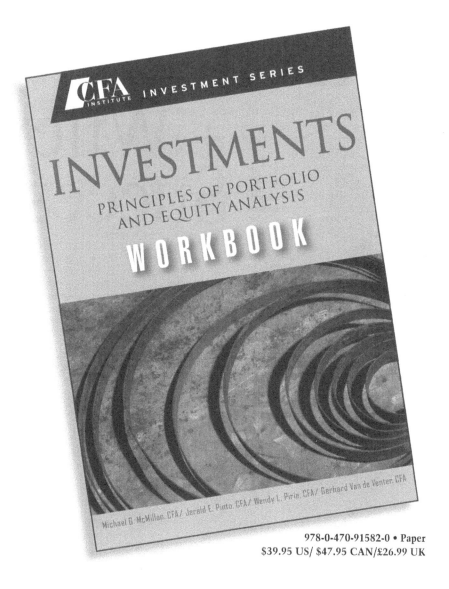

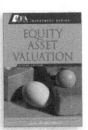